The Epic of America

THE EPIC OF AMERICA

An Introduction to Rafael Landívar
and the *Rusticatio Mexicana*

Andrew Laird

Duckworth

First published in 2006 by
Gerald Duckworth & Co. Ltd.
90-93 Cowcross Street, London EC1M 6BF
Tel: 020 7490 7300
Fax: 020 7490 0080
inquiries@duckworth-publishers.co.uk
www.ducknet.co.uk

A catalogue record for this book is available
from the British Library

ISBN 0 7156 3281 7
EAN 9780715632819

Typeset by Ray Davies
Printed and bound in Great Britain by
MPG Limited, Bodmin, Cornwall

Contents

Contents

Acknowledgements

The Institute for Research in the Humanities at the University of Wisconsin-Madison awarded me a Solmsen Fellowship in 2003-4 which made the pursuit and completion of this and other projects possible within a year. The British Academy 44th International Congress of Americanists Fund supported a visit to Mexico City in 2003, giving me a further occasion to benefit from the hospitality of the Instituto de Investigaciones Filológicas (IIFL) at the National Autonomous University of Mexico (UNAM). I am very grateful to those institutions and to many individuals associated with them, including Mauricio Beuchot, Birute Ciplijauskaité, John B. Dillon, Luis Villar, and Martha Patricia Irigoyen Troconis, Coordinator of the Centro de Estudios Clásicos in the IIFL.

Donald Russell kindly suggested a number of improvements to my English translation of the *Funebris Declamatio* in this volume. The personal debt I have to Arnold Kerson for helping to orient me in his field of expertise easily matches my considerable debt to his important publications. Veronika Coroleu Oberparleiter, Bruce Gibson, Sabine MacCormack, and Simon Swain have also lent their support to this project in various ways.

The Middle American Research Institute of Tulane University, New Orleans, Louisiana, USA very generously permitted the inclusion in the second part of this book of the work by Graydon W. Regenos from Volume 1, Number 5 of the Institute's Philological and Documentary Studies (1948): 'Rafael Landívar's *Rusticatio Mexicana* [Mexican country scenes]. The Latin Text, with an introduction and an English prose translation'. Marcela Alejandra Suárez of the University of Buenos Aires allowed me to make use of her transcription of the record of Landívar's death from Bologna for this book, and I also wish to thank the editors of *Grazer Beiträge Supplementband* 9 (Salzburg-Horn, 2005) for permission to incorporate in Chapter 3 some paragraphs from an article I published in that volume (pp. 144-53): 'Allegories of colonialism in Rafael Landívar's *Rusticatio Mexicana*'.

A.L.

The Ausonians will keep the language of their fathers and their customs. Their name will be the same as it is now. The Trojans will be joined with them in body only, and then be submerged. I will add further customs and rites of worship, and I will make them all Latins with one tongue.

Virgil, *Aeneid* 12.834-7

As you are in possession of a sharp mind, cast off old ideas and embrace new ones. Use your judgment to unlock the manifest secrets of nature. Apply all the powers of your intellect to the search, and through this rewarding work uncover the treasures that belong to you.

Rafael Landívar, *The Cross of Tepic* 108-12

PART I

ESSAY STUDIES

Prologue

Landívar, Latin and Colonialism

The coining of the term 'Latin America' some time in the middle of the nineteenth century had nothing to do with Latin. The name may have originated in France, when the French had designs for the economic and political development of Central and South America. The expression *América Latina* gained currency later at around 1898, after the Cuban War of Independence had inclined Spanish Americans to lay claim to origins that pertained to Europe more generally, than to Spain in particular. The idea of a *Latin* America was soon invoked again, in opposition to the Anglo-Saxon America of the United States, which became the next military power to threaten the former Spanish colonies. But Latin American identity was not conferred on all the inhabitants of these new nations and republics. It was supposed to exclude the large indigenous populations, the numerous descendants of African slaves and other groups, and it also obscured the Jewish and Arabic presence in Hispanic culture.[1]

The term 'Latin literature' has also involved exclusions (though of far less consequence than the chauvinistic naming of an entire continent). That term is commonly, if cliquishly, taken to mean only Roman literature. Until very recently, works of Latin poetry and prose – no matter how engaging or accomplished, no matter how important the issues they raise – were of little interest to classicists, if those works had been produced after antiquity. Even now, as Latin of the early modern period (roughly 1500-1800) is becoming the object of more systematic study, certain connoisseurish preferences or prejudices have endured. For example, some texts, simply because they were penned by major *vernacular* authors, persist in overshadowing others which in their time were far more influential. The Latin writing of Italy, France, and England always commands more attention than comparable material from other parts of Europe, including Ireland and Iberia. And remarkably for this day and age, authors from outside Europe continue to be ignored.

Rafael Landívar (1731-93) was one of the most outstanding poets from the Americas to write in Latin. In the fifteen books of the *Rusticatio Mexicana*, his most ambitious work, Landívar described the lakes, volcanoes, and wildlife of Mexico and of his native Guatemala, as well as the livelihoods and recreations of people in the Mesoamerican region. This panorama of nature, culture, and production is elevated both by its presentation in hexameter verse and by the use of numerous allusions and illustrations from Greek and Roman literature. Although several eight-eenth-century poets sought to emulate Virgil's *Georgics*, the *Rusticatio Mexicana* is exceptional because it offers a unique perspective on a crucial transitional period in the history of New Spain. Through this work, Landívar indicates the central place of labour in colonial society, demon-strates the value of indigenous knowledge and tradition, and gives some consideration to the historical significance of the Spanish conquest of Mexico. His poem is also unusual because it accommodates the aesthetics of the sublime and reflects more general trends in Enlightenment thought. In addition, elegiac and pastoral modes convey the exiled author's nostal-gia for his American homeland: Rafael Landívar was expelled from the Spanish territories in 1767, so that his didactic epic was completed and published in Italy.

There have been four translations of the *Rusticatio Mexicana* into Spanish, including two in verse, and one English version by Graydon Regenos which is reproduced in Part II of this volume. Few, if any, European works in Latin from the 1700s have prompted so many vernacu-lar renderings. On the other hand, Landívar's impressive prose oration and his two surviving short poems are little read because they have not been easily available. These texts, never before published together with the *Rusticatio Mexicana*, are here translated into English for the first time.

Landívar and his exiled compatriots wrote mainly in Latin because they had inherited, and continued to develop, a tradition of humanism in Mexico that stretched back more than two centuries to the time of the Spanish conquest. Early on, that tradition had responded to the indige-nous languages and cultures, and absorbed new forms of knowledge in order to enhance the scholarship and learning transplanted from Renais-sance Europe. And later, towards the end of the colonial period, Latin arguably provided Landívar and some other writers a means of demon-strating their Mexican (as opposed to Spanish) identity – in a way that the language of Spain could not. The abundance and diversity of Mexican discourses in Latin, the interaction of Latin with Spanish and also with languages like Nahuatl, and the changing role of Latin in the isthmus all involve ideological questions which cannot be divorced from issues of linguistic and literary history.

Landívar's work is introduced, presented and analysed here in order to highlight paradigmatically the appeal and the historical importance of Latin writing from Spanish America *in general*. For this reason, the first of the essay studies in Part I gives an account of the classical tradition in New Spain from the defeat of the Aztecs in 1521 to the time of the Bourbon Reforms in the mid-eighteenth century. Such an account, in only a few pages, of 250 years of cultural development and its broader historical context can only be selective and partial. But that overview should suffice to show that the phenomenon of Mexican humanism offers many lines of enquiry for interdisciplinary research in the future. The existence of this field is not just of consequence for the history of scholarship: it challenges prevalent pictures of European literary and intellectual history as much as it dispels some widespread misconceptions about Hispanic American culture.

The second essay assembles from primary sources what little is known about Rafael Landívar's life, education, and the circumstances of his expulsion and exile. His shorter works are examined for the first time in terms of their immediate background as well as in relation to their literary models. The third chapter then offers a new presentation of the reception, themes and form of the *Rusticatio Mexicana*. While this account is certainly meant to be accessible, it also seeks to constitute a significant advance on previous treatments of the poem. Close reading of certain passages will be combined with due emphasis on Landívar's classical, Renaissance and Enlightenment sources. The coverage cannot be comprehensive, but the narrower focus of this discussion, after the narratival approach of the first two chapters, should demonstrate that the enigmatic content of the *Rusticatio Mexicana* rewards close and careful reading: each book of the poem could generate a range of historical interpretations as well as substantial literary commentary.

The detailed 'Notes on the Essay Studies' supply the further information and bibliography that might be required for a broader orientation in the classical tradition and intellectual history of colonial Mexico. Additional material can be found in the notes on the texts and translations and in the further commentary accompanying Landívar's own Notes to the *Rusticatio Mexicana*. The Indices and Bibliography are, again, more than usually extensive for this relatively small volume – in the hope that it can serve as a useful point of departure for any readers inclined to pursue their own explorations of a sorely neglected avenue of Latin studies.

However, this book and the texts it introduces are bound to meet with indifference from classicists who deem such material irrelevant to the business of interpreting or promoting the literary, historical and other legacies of Greece and Rome. Their assumption partly has its basis in the consistent omission of Latin America from histories of the classical tradition. Yet anyone who examines the presence of classical culture in colonial Mexico may end up reinterpreting various aspects of Roman (and sometimes Greek) literature and history. The study of humanism always engenders further, deeper knowledge of the ancient texts which humanists themselves studied or imitated – and this will be borne out by some of what is to follow. And with regard to *promoting* the legacy of classical antiquity, neo-Latin writing frequently highlights the centrality of classical learning for a number of disciplines. Besides, once the multivalent connections between the Greco-Roman tradition and the ethnically complex Hispanic American heritage are better understood, classical studies may have a new part to play in today's curricula, which are naturally bound to reflect the cultural diversity of society at large.

Where the field of Latin American studies is concerned, the colonial era, once regarded as a stagnant, uneventful epoch intervening between the conquest and the separation from Spain, has become the focus of far more concentrated attention. Forms of postcolonial theory, developed in Mexico, the United States and elsewhere, have led to an increasingly widespread view that historical enquiry into the colonial period itself cannot be pursued without reference to its contemporary consequences. Those consequences, the 'colonial legacies', are part and parcel of the extensive prejudice, injustice, and physical hardship actually and presently experienced by many peoples and ethnic groups all over Latin America today. The privileged few who address the history and literature of the region therefore carry an obligation to speak for the victims of despotism and exploitation, past and present, who are in no position to speak for themselves.[2]

This moral or political imperative has accompanied a marked proliferation of theoretical discussion in the current study of colonial history and literature – though a disinclination to fanfare new methodologies does not, of course, have to imply opposition or indifference to the moral issues.[3] But two general approaches or principles now prevalent in the study of colonialism are worth addressing here, simply because anyone holding to them may feel less than enthusiastic about the material assembled in this volume. The first principle is, wherever possible, to extend and modify the canon of texts and sources in order to admit testimonies that represent underprivileged groups (or 'subaltern subjects') as part of the process of cultural de-colonisation. The Latin writings by indigenous Mexicans described in Chapter 1 may be considered acceptable examples of such testimonies. The second principle is to interpret the literary output of historically privileged authors in the light of the inequitable colonial situation – because that colonial situation, which prompted their artistic productions, is seen to be ongoing. This second approach rather precludes engaging with literary works from a literary perspective: to do so, it is maintained, amounts to collusion with the coloniser, and complicity in the oppressive circumstances that brought those literary works into being.

It goes without saying that neither of those principles – as they have just been summarised at any rate – are original to colonial or postcolonial theory. Issues of canon-formation and tensions between the political and the aesthetic have fuelled debate in criticism ever since the days of Plato. But given the exigencies imposed by an all too recent history, it is not difficult to see why it might be productive and worthwhile to apply such strategies to the study of sources from a colonial epoch in particular. Thus one may question the desirability of promoting an author like Landívar, who belonged to one of the higher echelons of New Spanish society, and whose literary works – a Ciceronian declamation, a Horatian ode, a

Baroque sonnet, and a didactic epic – would have been accessible only to a lettered elite. At the very least, according to the second of the two approaches outlined above, works of this kind should be subjected to political rather than literary criticism, and assessed as direct products of the colonial situation and its injustices.

Reference will certainly be made to the successive historical phases which very palpably determined the course of Mexican humanism, but the sustained application of political or ethnohistorical criticism to particular works is not so easy to accomplish. There is a real possibility that the same things end up being said about one text as about another: that the text is ethnocentric, that it affirms *criollo* i.e. *Spanish* American (as opposed to indigenous or *mestizo*) identity, that it is a representation or reflection of the colonising subject. And however much our assessments in these terms aspire to be veridical, opinions can never lay claim to the status of demonstrations. For example, a recently expressed view that the *Rustica-tio Mexicana* is 'a treatment of an imposing and portentous nature and of political events that have to be controlled' is not easy to reconcile with my own less theorised view that Landívar himself addresses some injustices of the colonial situation, and neither view can ultimately be proven.[4] (It is of course possible to adopt either one of those positions and still be acutely aware of 'colonial legacies' and of the ever-present material and ideological ramifications of those legacies.)

Latin authors like Rafael Landívar are in many ways exceptional – and consideration of them may well pose more problems for the politically alert historian than consideration of the vernacular authors who belonged to the dominant groups in New Spanish society. For one thing, the predicament of exile Landívar shared with other Jesuits (who also wrote in Latin) would automatically incline his readers, in the past just as much as in the present, to interrogate the colonial hierarchy, and Landívar's position within it – irrespective of whether the author did so himself. And emphasis should be laid on the fact that the *Rusticatio Mexicana* sought to champion Mexico, its population, and its culture, in the wake of European polemics against the Spanish American regions, their inhabitants, and their mental and physical capacities. Here again, readers will find themselves engaging with historical issues that have a contemporary resonance. The cheerful indifference shown by present-day scholars to Latin America and to the legacy of its humanism is not very far removed from the bigotry and prejudice shown towards the Americas and their peoples, which Landívar and his compatriots encountered in Europe in the 1760s.

These vexed questions are not meant to be resolved here, and anyone perusing this preface might wonder how things could have got so complicated. None of the issues raised so far have given much impression of what Landívar is actually like to read. Whilst his manner of expression is flawlessly classical, the contents of all his works exhibit a tension, which Octavio Paz has identified as a feature common to all modern American

7

literature: 'a conflict between ... cosmopolitan and nativist tendencies, between Europeanism and Americanism'.[5] Since Paz made this observation with regard to nineteenth and twentieth-century writing, its relevance to a Neoclassical author of the 1700s might be questioned – comparisons with figures like Jorge Luis Borges, Carlos Fuentes, and Gabriel García Márquez would seem too anachronistic to be of any use for characterising the nature of Landívar's achievement.

But such comparisons turn out to be rather illuminating: in a funeral address he delivers for a Guatemalan archbishop, Landívar involves the gods of pagan antiquity; and in the same speech he curiously recalls the Roman legend of a woman who breastfed her mother to save her from a sentence of death by starvation. And in an instructive verse treatise which was committed to the scientific principles of the Enlightenment and supported by learned footnotes, Landívar explains how beavers drive wrongdoers out of their communities; he describes how a normally peaceful mountain stream responds angrily to loud noises by turning into a raging torrent; and he informs his reader of a small bird with a gigantic beak which can cure an ailing heart with the touch of its tongue. These mythological, dreamlike or fantastic elements, some apparently derived from folk traditions, intrude almost unnoticed into what is predominantly serious or factual discourse. In this respect at least, Rafael Landívar anticipated the modern, quintessentially Latin American genre of magic realism.

1

The Circles of Time:
Classical culture in colonial Mexico

(i) The early impact of Greece and Rome on the New World

When Hernán Cortés reached Yucatán in 1519, he discovered that a Spaniard, named Jerónimo de Aguilar, was already living on an island off the coast. The chronicler Bernal Díaz described the conquistadors' first impression of the castaway, who had been enslaved by the Mayas:

> When he arrived, several soldiers asked. 'Where is the Spaniard?' For they could not distinguish him from an Indian. His hair was cut like a native's and he had on one old sandal with the other tied to his belt. He wore a ragged cloak, and a worse loincloth. Tied up in a bundle in his cloak was a Book of Hours, old and worn.[1]

This curious figure, who was originally a clergyman from Écija in Andalusia, is frequently credited with being the first person to convey the Latin language to Mexico in 1511, after he had been shipwrecked on a voyage from Darién to Panama.[2] As Aguilar was in holy orders, he would have been obliged to recite each day the hymns and prayers contained in the battered breviary that he kept as his most treasured possession. Aguilar's singular bad luck had meant that Latin was very possibly the first European language to be sounded out loud in Mexico, a decade before the death of Montezuma and the fall of the Aztec city of Tenochtitlán in 1521.

As well as being the language of the Catholic church, and of legal and monarchical authority, Latin was the normal medium for education and all kinds of intellectual pursuits in Renaissance Europe.[3] But Latin also retained its powerful identity as the language of ancient Rome – an identity it continued to retain even after it passed across the Atlantic. The classical tradition in general had an early role, on the ground, in shaping the first direct perceptions of the Americas.[4] A fascination with Greek and Roman antiquity even prompted the conquistadors to re-enact scenarios from ancient history books: Cortés, for example, notoriously likened himself to Alexander the Great, Julius Caesar, and other figures.[5] Roman imperialism in particular provided a kind of model for the Spaniards (though this model was not uncontested); and from the 1500s onwards, the achievements of the Incas and Mayas were compared to those of ancient Mediterranean peoples, and in one or two cases even attributed to the Carthaginians.[6]

The impact of Greece and Rome on the New World is most often considered in terms of the varied and conflicting European discourses about the Americas. Prominent among them are exchanges which constituted what is now known as the 'Controversy of the Indies'. This battle of books and speeches, conducted in Latin and Spanish, came to a head in Valladolid in Spain in 1550-1. The Aristotelian humanist Juan Ginés de Sepúlveda appealed to Aristotle's notion of the 'natural slave' to argue that the barbarian Indians should be subjected by the Spaniards; Bartolomé de las Casas, a Dominican who had spent much of his life in Cuba and Central America, held that all humans were equally rational, and, challenging the application of the term 'barbarian' to the Indians, he insisted that war and slavery should not be imposed upon them.[7] The debate did not just draw upon classical philosophy: the acceptability of the Roman empire as a historical precedent also played an important part in the arguments of both sides.[8]

Ethnographers like Peter Martyr, Bernardino de Sahagún, and Gonzalo Fernández de Oviedo informed such debates by sometimes applying classical paradigms to the cultures they described.[9] This process could also be reversed: reports about the indigenous pagans from the new Spanish territories were occasionally used to shed light on practices in pre-Christian Greece and Rome.[10] But far more frequently, it was recognition of the classical past in the 'discovery' of America which found expression in European literature and poetry. The *Araucana,* a Castilian epic begun in 1569 by the Spanish poet Alonso de Ercilla, ennobled the vanquished Araucanians of Chile by comparing them to the heroes of Greek and Roman history and myth.[11] From the sixteenth to the eighteenth centuries, a number of European poems in Latin about Columbus appeared which were closely modelled on Virgil: Fracastaro's didactic epic *Syphilis* and Stella's *Columbeid* are the earliest and best known examples.[12]

However, there is little awareness of how rapidly – and how deeply – classical culture took root in the New World itself, and there is still less awareness of the classical humanistic tradition that emerged from *within* Spanish America. Much of its intellectual and literary output was in Latin. The vigorous production of Latin writing began in the early 1500s and it continued through the colonial period, at least until late in the eighteenth century – and in some quarters it carried on even after that. This body of Latin writing, still mostly accessible only in early printed books or in manuscripts, represents a vast and complex cultural legacy. Some of the texts that make up this extensive corpus were written by authors who were indigenous or who were *mestizos* ('of mixed race'); nearly all of these texts accommodate perceptions and experiences that are specifically 'American' – and classical illustrations are often used to convey those perceptions and experiences.

In order to sketch out the more immediate context for the work of Rafael Landívar, the following sections of this chapter will focus more specifically on Mexico (or New Spain) where much of Landívar's education and intellectual formation occurred; his native Guatemala was an adjacent territory. It should be noted nonetheless that classical learning and humanism have also been prominent in other parts of Spanish America.[13]

(ii) 'Indian' Latinists in the 1500s

If study of the classical tradition is combined with the cultural history of colonial Mexico, an immense body of work in Latin is laid open: not only school texts, commentaries, and grammars, but also original works of poetry, letters, dialogues, and treatises on subjects ranging from indigenous languages to political philosophy and Platonism. The impact of the Italian Renaissance was as great on Mexico as it was on Spain, if not greater.[14] Books, ideas, and even individual scholars from Italy and other countries soon followed the conquistadors to the New World.[15] And the European learning that was brought to Mexico, was conveyed in Latin. Inevitably the Latin language adopted new expressions and fresh meanings as a result of its transplantation: 'the American words incorporated by [Mexican] writers, whether indigenous or Spanish, endow neo-Latin with a new tone, though they still seem alien ... this was the way by which neo-Latin in New Spain secured, in some of its best moments, attributes that were absolutely American.'[16]

Latin soon ceased to be a possession exclusive to the Europeans. Cortés himself realised that in order to legitimise possession of this new territory, Spain was obliged to evangelise its inhabitants. The Franciscan missionaries, who were themselves struggling to learn Nahuatl (the tongue of the Mexica or 'Aztecs') and other languages, saw that indigenous recruits were needed to act as interpreters, and no doubt – after the brutality of the conquest – they were also needed as cultural intermediaries to help convert the Indians to Christianity. Two colleges were set up early on for this purpose: San José de los Naturales in 1527, and Santa Cruz de Tlatelolco in 1536. There were other initiatives to educate the Indians and improve their circumstances: the Spanish humanist Vasco de Quiroga founded two *hospital-pueblos,* in Michoacán and in Mexico City. Quiroga apparently intended these communities to follow the blueprint of the ideal society portrayed in Thomas More's *Utopia* (1518) – and their ordinances were established less than two years after More's death in 1535.[17]

While the College of San José functioned to teach liturgical Latin, music, and art to children of the indigenous elite, the curriculum in the College of Santa Cruz de Tlatelolco was more ambitious: pupils drawn from the indigenous nobility of various regions of Mexico were selected to learn not only Latin but also rhetoric, philosophy, medicine, and theology. This institution, founded long before a number of Oxford and Cambridge colleges, could claim to be the first university in America. The languages of instruction were Nahuatl and Latin.[18] Spanish was omitted, not because

11

the pupils were unfamiliar with it, but in order to fulfil the aims of their education: to establish an order of indigenous clergy who could convey church doctrine and other knowledge in their own language.

Initial progress was slow but within two or three years the Indians were able to read and write in Latin: Fray Toribio de Benavente remarked that 'there are many among them who are proficient in grammar, who can compose lengthy, well researched speeches and verses in hexameters and pentameters'.[19] Not everyone believed such proficiency could be possible. Another Franciscan, Juan de Torquemada is one of the chroniclers to record this revealing anecdote:

> A priest who did not know a word of Latin had (like many others) an unfavourable view of the Indians and could not believe that they knew Christian doctrine, nor even the *Pater noster* ['Our Father'], although several Spaniards assured him that they did. The priest, still unconvinced, wanted to test out his lack of conviction on some Indian or other, and it was his fortune to bump into one of the students without realising he was a Latinist. He asked him if he knew the *Pater noster* and the Indian replied that he did. He told him to say it: the Indian recited it well. Not content with that the priest ordered him to say the Creed. After he recited it nicely, the cleric challenged a word the Indian had said: *natus ex Maria Virgine* ['born of the Virgin Mary'] and retorted that it should be *nato ex Maria Virgine* ['to/with one born of the Virgin Mary']. As the Indian insisted on saying *natus* and the clergyman on saying *nato*, the Indian student needed to prove his point by resorting to grammar, as he was right to corrrect the priest in this way, and he asked him (speaking in Latin): *Reverende Pater, Nato, cuius casus est?* ['Reverend Father, '*Nato*' – what case is it?']. As the clergyman did not know even this much, nor how to reply, he had to go on his way, ashamed and confused.[20]

And predictably enough, there were those, who though they recognised that the Indians *could* acquire such learning, did not believe that they *should* do so. The rapidity with which indigenous Mexicans came to master Latin could be seen as evidence of their demonic nature: Jerónimo López, a Castilian official, in a letter to the king of Spain, reported a priest's description of one of the Franciscan colleges, presumably Santa Cruz, as 'hell' and its students as 'disciples of Satan.'[21] But this fear was probably a cloak for a more substantial concern – that the possession of European knowledge might enable those who held it to question or challenge the authority of their Spanish rulers.[22]

Instruction of the Indians was not to continue in the same fashion. The introduction of the first printing press in Mexico in 1539 and the formal establishment of the Royal and Pontifical University in 1553 as a new centre of learning reflected a transition in the culture of New Spain, and the interests of Europeans took over from those of the indigenous population.[23] Yet the legacy of the Indian colleges had a key role in determining the evolution of humanism and the classical tradition in New Spain over the course of the next two centuries. The Indians produced grammars, dictionaries, and sermons in indigenous languages; they translated works of classical Latin (Pseudo-Cato, Aesop's *Fables*) as well as Christian texts into Nahuatl. There are at least three Indian Latinists whose writings survive: Antonio Valeriano, a Latin orator; Pablo Nazareo, who translated from Latin into Nahuatl the cycle of lessons for the church year and numerous sermons; and Juan Badiano who rendered an Indian inventory of medicinal herbs into Latin (the Nahuatl original by Martín de la Cruz is now lost) as the *Libellus de medicinalibus indorum herbis* (1552): one of the many copies made of this text is in the library of Windsor Castle. The almost insufferably humble tone of Badiano's prologue illustrates his facility with Latin, while it also raises questions about the ways in which the indigenous scholars were seen, or saw themselves.[24] The specific entries in the book itself, which consist of recipes or prescriptions for a variety of conditions, constantly combine Latin and words in Nahuatl so that the resulting language has been characterised as '*mestizo*' in itself:

> Putrescentibus auribus radix maçayelli, herbae xoxouhquipahtli semen, aliquot tlaquilin folia cum salis mica in aqua calfacta instillata commodant plurimum. Et sub auriculis duarum arbuscularum frondes tritae illinantur. Arbusculae vocantur toloua et tlapahtl. Lapides pretiosi cetlahuitl, tlahcalhuatzin, eztetl, xoxohouhqui chalchihuitl cum arboris tlatlanquaye frondibus tritis in calfacta aqua attriti instillatique conclusas aures adaperiunt.

> For mouldering ears, the root of *macayelli*, the seed of the *xoxouhquipahtli* herb, some leaves of *tlaquilin;* all infused in warm water with a pinch of salt can be very helpful. The leaves of two plants may be ground and applied under the ears. The plants are called *toloua* and *tlapahtl*. The precious stones *cetlahuitl, tlahcalhuatzin, eztetl, xoxohouhqui chalchihuitl*, ground and infused in warm water, with the crushed leaves of the *tlatlanquaye* tree, open blocked ears.

> Badiano, *Libellus de medicinalibus*
> *indorum herbis*, folio 14 v.

The Mexican names are given for plants which have no European equivalents. But such New World knowledge of nature and its benefits is not only conveyed, but also legitimised by its expression in Latin. In this respect the Indian Badiano's *Libellus* represents an early – and significant – precedent for the *Rusticatio Mexicana,* which was written by a Spanish American two centuries later. Other precursors, both cited by Landívar, were José de Acosta (1540-1600) and Francisco Hernández (1517-87), the 'Pliny of New Spain', a Spanish physician and botanist.[25] Hernández's natural history in Latin was allegedly informed by the pictorial inventories of plants and animals made by Nezahualcoyotl, the 'philosopher king' of Texcoco.[26] Some Latin dialogues by Francisco Cervantes de Salazar constitute a further, more literary, model for the *Rusticatio Mexicana* from this early period: as well as portraying Mexico City, its environs, and the

University, the dialogues also describe such things as native fruits, trees, and customs of the Indians.[27]

The importance placed on the conversion of the indigenous nations in the sixteenth century meant that Mexican humanism developed a specific character. It did not simply lay emphasis on studying classical texts: it was a 'human humanism, vital, alive that gave pride of place to consideration of the human individual'.[28] Although the majority of Latin books were religious in nature, the Royal and Pontifical University of Mexico was modelled on the University of Salamanca in Spain. There were a number of important Mexican Spanish humanists including Fray Juan de Zumárraga and Fray Alonso de la Veracruz, the first professor of philosophy at the University. Alonso de la Veracruz's most important work, *De dominio infidelium et iusto bello* ('On the government of non-Christians and just war') defends the rights of the Indians, and seems to have been influenced by the work of his mentor, Francisco de Vitoria.[29]

The boundaries of classical learning were radically expanded after the Jesuits arrived in Mexico in 1572 and founded a network of colleges. Their curriculum, known as the *Ratio studiorum*, ensured that pupils became adept at Latin poetry and prose through imitation of a wide variety of classical authors. Padre Vincenzo Lanuchi from the College of Rome, one of the first Jesuit scholars in Mexico, aimed to organise programmes of study in grammar, poetics, and rhetoric. He had the ambitious aim of publishing excerpts from a wide selection of Christian and pagan authors including Cicero, Virgil, Ovid, Martial, Gregory of Nazianzus, Ambrose, and Jerome, along with some humanists including Lorenzo Valla and Juan Luis Vives.[30]

At this point it is worth inserting a *caveat* – even into an account of the progress of classical learning as cursory as the one offered here: the history of scholarship can never be disengaged from the heavier history of power struggle and of economic and political change. The appearance of the Jesuits in New Spain in the wake of the Counter-Reformation was not all good. In the words of an authoritative modern historian, it led to 'the century of the Conquest [being] concluded with heresy-hunting and Baroque scholasticism dominating Mexican high culture.'[31] 'Baroque scholasticism' may not be the kindest designation for the Mexican literature of this period, but certainly it has to be conceded that the achievements to be adumbrated below were largely – though not entirely – the work of a privileged ecclesiastical elite.[32]

(iii) Baroque Latin literature in the 1600s

New Spanish society stabilised over the course of the seventeenth century, and numerous books – again principally on poetry, grammar, and rhetoric – continued to be published. A leading figure at this time was Bernardino de Llanos (1560-1669), a native of Ocaña near Toledo in Spain. His first book, *Illustrium autorum collectanea* ('Anthology of eminent authors'), which was published in 1604, incorporated excerpts from rhetorical texts and treatises on poetics by Spanish and Italian humanists. A second book, *Solutae orationis fragmenta* ('Fragments of prose discourse'), now lost, was printed in the same year and incorporated selections of Cicero, Caesar, Sallust, Quintus Curtius, Aesop (in Valla's Latin translation), and Livy. But Llanos' 1605 anthology is of greater literary historical interest: *Poeticarum institutionum liber, variis ethnicorum, christianorumque exemplis illustratus* ('Book of poetic education, illustrated by various examples from pagan and Christian writers'). The first part advanced a definition of poetic practice, proposing a theory of the genres supported by a wide range of classical sources: Virgil, Catullus, Claudian, Silius Italicus, Ovid, Seneca, Terence, Horace, Tibullus, Propertius, and Martial. The second part contained a comparable selection of Christian poets; the third presented the poems that Llanos' own students wrote as school exercises. Llanos himself authored verse in a markedly Virgilian style.

Latin poetry had already been composed in Mexico in the 1500s – the *Dicolon Icasticon* of Cristóbal de Cabrera was printed in 1540 – and much more was produced in the seventeenth century.[33] Horace's *Ars Poetica*, which went through more than fifteen printings in New Spain, disseminated Aristotelian poetic theory: Horace's treatise and the Italian humanist commentaries on it exerted an enormous influence.[34] But, as in Europe, it was Virgil who provided the fundamental model and enduring inspiration for Latin poetry in colonial Mexico. In addition to the poems in the 1605 anthology, a single manuscript preserves a number of further works by Llanos and other authors, some anonymous, which take the form of extended 'eclogues' and verse dialogues.

From the mid-1600s, three Latin poets stand out in particular: Juan de Valencia, William Lamport, and Mateo de Castroverde. Valencia, a Mercedarian friar based in the convent of Atlixco in Puebla, wrote a *Theressiad* in 350 elegiac couplets, in honour of Saint Teresa of Avila. The poem which was sent to Spain for publication is now lost. However a handful of verses were quoted by a contemporary chronicler of the Mercedarian Order, Juan de Pareja.[35] The only complete couplet to survive runs as follows:

> Signa te signa temere me tangis et angis
> Roma tibi subito motibus ibit amor

> Sign yourself with your signs, at random you touch me and torment me:
> Rome is for you suddenly in commotion; [your] love will advance.
> Juan de Valencia, *Theressiad*

This reference to Saint Teresa's miraculous stigmata is not easy to read, punctuate, or translate. That is because each of these two verses is a palindrome: the individual letters of each line when read from right to left have precisely the same sequence as they do when they are read from left to right. The two other isolated verses Pareja preserved have the same property: the whole composition could thus have been read palindromically, from end to end. If Juan de Valencia did indeed complete this poem, its length would have made it a remarkable achievement, virtually unique in all of Latin literature.[36]

William Lamport, who was born in Wexford, Ireland in 1615, is less famous as a Latin poet than as a brigand, playboy, and adventurer who supposedly proclaimed himself king of Mexico.[37] Educated by Irish and Spanish Jesuits, he arrived in New Spain in 1640 as an agent of the Duke of Olivares, a chief minister to Philip IV. However, in 1642 Lamport was arrested and charged by the Inquisition of conspiring against Spain to liberate the Indians and African slaves, of associating with Indian sorcerers and studying astrology, and of plotting to establish himself as monarch of an independent Mexico. After being jailed for nine years, Lamport escaped briefly in December 1650 and flyposted the walls of Mexico City with denunciations of the Inquisition. He was promptly recaptured and imprisoned for another nine years before being burnt at the stake in 1659. It was during his incarceration that this Irishman wrote, in Latin, 918 psalms, a number of hymns, and some compelling devotional poems. These works still remain unedited, but William Lamport's imitation and adaptation of Horatian metres give ample proof of his expertise in classical prosody.[38]

Far less is known about Mateo de Castroverde (1595-1644), a Jesuit missionary, who at around 1645 composed in Latin a *Panegyric of the Conception of Mary celebrated in America*.[39] The Panegyric has not survived in entirety but seventy lines are incorporated into a predominantly Spanish composition: *El triunfo parténico* ('The Triumph of the Virgin') by Carlos de Sigüenza y Góngora. Sigüenza y Góngora (1645-1700), whose maternal relative was the influential Spanish poet Luis de Góngora y Argote, was a major force in Mexican intellectual history – as a *belle-lettriste* and polymath.[40] In 1683, Sigüenza y Góngora published *El triunfo parténico*, a compilation of more than 500 other works, which he had presented to the University of Mexico for a competition to honour the Immaculate Conception. The following lines of Castroverde's *Panegyric*, canonised by Sigüenza y Góngora, were to be echoed by later New Spanish Latin poets, including Villerías y Roelas (see pp. 20-1 below), and Landívar:[41]

> Mexicus interea toto celeberrima mundo
> ingeniis, opibusque vigens, cui summa potestas
> cum summa pietate manet, cupit ultima amoris
> edere signa sui.

Meanwhile Mexico most renowned in all the world for her talents, flourish-

ing in her wealth, for whom utmost power abides with utmost piety, desires
to show forth the latest signs of her love.

Castroverde, *Panegyric*

Sensuous and paradoxical diction endows Castroverde's subsequent hexameters with a distinctive quality, as they go on to describe an unsettling,
apocalyptic *fiesta* in honour of the Virgin.

In the later part of the seventeenth century, the Virgin Mary became
even more prominent in Mexican literature: it was at this time that
testimonies of the miraculous appearance of the Virgin of Guadalupe – the
event reputedly occurred in 1531 – began to abound. There have been
various accounts of the apparition: historians of the tradition give priority
to what is often regarded as the 'Urtext' for the miracle, the *Nican
mopohua* ('Here it is recounted') published in Nahuatl by Laso de la Vega,
vicar of Guadalupe in 1649.[42] Luis Becerra Tanco, a close friend of
Sigüenza y Góngora, translated the Nahuatl version, doctoring it in places
in the interests of supposed historical accuracy.

The story is well known. In December 1531, an Indian named Juan
Diego was walking at dawn past the hill in Tepeyac, to the north of Mexico
City, to attend mass. He caught sight of a colourful rainbow and heard the
sound of beautiful singing. As he turned towards the sound, the Virgin
Mary appeared and spoke to him, declaring that she was the mother of
God, and that a temple should be established on the hill from where she
might help him and all those devoted to her. She enjoined him to give a
faithful account of this to the bishop. The bishop at first did not believe
him and sought a sign. The Indian returned and unfastened his cloak, in
which the Virgin had instructed him to gather flowers from the hill. The
bishop then saw the image of the Virgin on the cloak and ordered a church
to be built in the place she appeared – the very site where the indigenous
inhabitants had once worshiped Tonantzin, an expiatory goddess whose
name means 'our mother' in Nahuatl.[43]

Sigüenza y Góngora, whose best known work, the *Primavera indiana*
(1668) was about the Virgin of Guadalupe, published the *Glorias de
Querétaro* (1680) to mark the completion of the temple of Nuestra Señora
de Guadalupe in the provincial capital of Querétaro. These poems are just
two examples of the extensive Guadalupan literature in Spanish.[44] The
first known work in Latin to honour the Virgin of Guadalupe was published
in 1669 by José López de Abilés: the *Poeticum viridarium* ('Poetic pleasure
garden') in 210 elegiac couplets. It was in a book which was produced under
the direction of Becerra Tanco and contained verses, including anagrams
and acrostics, by Tanco himself and another author, Miguel Sanchez.[45]

A further Guadalupan poem in Latin, by Bernardo Ceinos de Riofrío,
came out in 1680. This represents a more significant landmark in the
development of Mexican humanist literature than many critics have
realised.[46] As indicated by its full title – 'A Virgilian centonic monument of

the miraculous apparition of the Virgin Mary', this work is a *cento*, a medley of 365 verses, all hexameters or hemistichs recycled from Virgil, conjoined to narrate the miracle of Tepeyac. Although Riofrío follows Becerra Tanco's account of the miracle, his poetic version is difficult to follow. The Guadalupan theme tends to be most successfully conveyed when the contours of Virgil's discourse are followed *more* closely rather than when the original verses are broken up. For example, the speech of Aeneas to his mother, Venus, from *Aeneid* 1.327-34 (*'O quam te memorem Virgo ...?*) usefully furnishes Juan Diego with words to address his own divine Mother in verses 201-8 of the *cento*.

The primary meaning of the word *cento* in Latin is 'patchwork cloth or cloak' – as Riofrío states in his prose preface to his poem. The *cento* is thus an appropriate literary vehicle for his subject, given both the role of Juan Diego's cloak in the story and the significance of the Virgin herself as 'cloak of protection' for the people of Mexico. But the importance of Riofrío's *Centonicum virgilianum monimentum* for literary history was its aspiration to epic narrative. It pointed a way forward for the Latin poets of the next century who were to compose on a far more ambitious scale. Even when they do not treat the Guadalupan myth as a central subject, all of those poets, including Landívar, would incorporate the legend into their works.

The Virgin of Guadalupe is more than a generic hallmark responsible for the gestation of original Latin epic in New Spain: she was later to become a symbol of Mexican nationhood.[47] An affirmation of pride, at least in Spanish American humanistic achievement, can be found in the poem written to introduce Riofrío's Guadalupan *cento* by Bartolomé Rosales. Rosales' panegyrical epyllion was entitled *Aulica musarum synodus crisis apollinea in laudem authoris* ('The Aulic Synod of Muses and the Judgment of Apollo in praise of the Author'). It opens with Mercury's arrival at the abode of the Muses. Mercury informs Apollo that the ghost of Virgil appeared to him in a dream. We then hear Virgil explain that he has been resurrected in America:

> Nunc iterum toto celebrandus in orbe poeta
> pulchrior exurgo, faciesque reficta refulget.
> Nunc et in orbe novo resonat romana Thalia
> quae redimita rosis Indis caput extulit undis.
> O vos Pyerides vobis nova gloria surgit:
> nunc meus in *Rosea* vultus *Imagine* maior
> noscitur, auctus honos eludet tempora vivax.

Now I rise again, more beautiful still, as a poet to be celebrated all over the world and my features, refashioned, shine once more. Now Roman Thalia sounds again in the New World as she raises her head from the waters, garlanded with Indian roses. O you Pierides, your new glory is rising, now

my countenance is greater in the image of the roses and my honour, enhanced and alive, makes mockery of time ...

Rosales, *Aulica musarum synodus* 108-14

Mercury then tells Apollo that a *cold river* has quenched for good the
flames that threatened the survival of the *Aeneid,* which Virgil had
wanted to burn. 'Cold river' *(frigidus rivus)* is the meaning of *Riofrío* in
Spanish. Thus, according to Mercury, the centonist Riofrío has saved
Virgil's work (and the art of pagan antiquity) from the flames by enabling
the tide of Latin verse to flow all the way from Helicon to Mexico – an idea
echoed in later European Latin poetry.[48] In this short narrative sketch,
Bartolomé Rosales sought to promote not only the work of Bernardo
Ceinos de Riofrío, but also by implication the entire tradition of classical
learning that was flourishing in New Spain.

Any review of that tradition in the late seventeenth century must take
into the consideration the achievement of Sor Juana Inés de la Cruz,
(1648-95) the poet and feminist *avant la lettre.* She is now a celebrated icon
of Spanish colonial literature – and she also has a cameo in Landívar's
Rusticatio Mexicana.[49] Sor Juana is best known for her Castilian plays and
poems, notably the highly ornate *Primero sueño* which takes Baroque
'gongorism' to new levels. However the extent of her Latin writing has
been largely unrecognised. Latin verses are worked into some of her
villancicos – endeavours in an early Renaissance Spanish verse form with
a refrain. The different levels of Latin intrusion into these compositions
have been distinguished typologically as quotation, parody, collage, ma-
caronic verse, etc., but Sor Juana's best Latin verses are embedded in her
Neptuno alegórico. The poem was composed on the occasion of the entry
into Mexico City by the Count of Paredes, the Marqués of Laguna, as the
new Viceroy: a pun on *laguna* ('lake') explains the involvement of the
aquatic deity Neptune. Sor Juana's other Spanish compositions also show
the influence of a number of classical Latin authors, particularly Virgil,
Horace, Ovid, Martial, and Ausonius. It is worth emphasising that there
was a complicated traffic between Latin and Spanish literature in Mexico,
just as in Spain: mannerist writing in Castilian was conspicuously Lat-
inised, while the new Latin literature that was produced sometimes
reflected the contemporary stylistic and aesthetic trends like *culteranismo*
and *conceptismo* that competed in vernacular writing.[50]

(iv) The Golden Age of Mexican Latin in the 1700s

The eighteenth century saw several significant advances in Latin literature, philosophy, and other forms of learning. The time is widely regarded
as the period in which humanist achievement in New Spain reached its
peak. Francisco Xavier Alegre, José Rafael Campoy, Francisco Xavier
Clavigero, and Diego José Abad, who were leading Jesuit scholars from the

later 1700s, merit at least as much recognition for their accomplishments as their now better known contemporary, Rafael Landívar. The reputation of this epoch as a floruit of Latin writing rests in no small part on some outstanding works that were mostly published in Italy, after the Jesuits were expelled from Mexico in 1767. But even before that, the Latin literature produced in New Spain had begun to show a preoccupation with Mexican or American cultural identity – a preoccupation which was to become increasingly pronounced.

The beginning of the eighteenth century marked a transition in literary taste and practice from Baroque Mannerism to Neoclassicism, as artificiality of style, allusiveness, and difficult conceits were supplanted by less ornate and more lucid forms of expression. This transition is best exemplified by José Antonio de Villerías y Roelas (1695-1728). Although Villerías was a secular layman, he had benefited from a Jesuit education, having mastered Latin and Greek before going on to study jurisprudence at the University of Mexico from 1714-24.[51] The poverty Villerías experienced and his failure to find an appropriate position, either as an academic or as a lawyer, in itself gives an indication of why so many Mexican writers from the colonial period were in religious orders. Difficulty in securing a place in the political or administrative hierarchy was common for *criollos* (the name now routinely given to people of European origin born in the New World), unless they had patronage or wealth of their own.[52]

In his short life, Villerías wrote in Latin, Greek, and Spanish. His works include a rendering of the Vulgate *Song of Songs* into Latin verse, *Victor* (a heroic poem of 300 hexameters), translations from Greek of various epigrams and of the ancient grammarian Corinthius' treatise on Greek dialects; as well as twelve original Greek epigrams. In Latin he also composed original epigrams, hymns, short poems, epithalamia, and a couple of prose works – a *Farrago* in two chapters, and a long pathological text addressed to a physician called Jacobo Stevenson. Only Villerías' Spanish texts went to press in his lifetime: the *Máscara*, a burlesque poem which describes a triumphal University procession, the *Llanto de las estrellas* ('Lament of the stars') detailing the funeral rites of Luis I, and the *Escudo triunfante del Carmelo* – a versified rendering of a devotional work by Gabriel Cerrada, a Carmelite friar. From a modern critical and historical perspective however, Villerías y Roelas' masterpiece was undoubtedly the *Guadalupe,* a Latin epic narrative in four books, a total of 1,755 hexameters.

The epic is concerned with the special destiny of New Spain as a dominion of the Virgin Mary. This is a full blown poetic account of the Guadalupan myth, but its conception and structure take after the *Aeneid*: Juan Diego and Bishop Zumárraga are the mortal protagonists; the divine agents include Pluto, as god of the Underworld, and the Aztec goddess Tonantzin who conspire to oppose Mary's divine plan for the future of Mexico.[53] The aversion that these pagan deities have to the Spaniards (whom they plan to expel from the New World) recalls Juno's antipathy to the Trojans, and her resistance to the future ordained for Italy in Virgil's *Aeneid*. And, as is also the case with the *Aeneid*, the narrative of the *Guadalupe* offers both predictions and flashbacks which call attention to a larger historical panorama that extends beyond the story directly presented. Thus the opening book rehearses the European conquest and evangelisation of the Aztecs (1.63-112); in the second book the god Atlas, now exiled from Europe and dwelling in a secret part of the lake of Mexico, prophesies the Virgin's future role in Mexico (2.62-100, 222-59), and an *ekphrasis* of the murals in Atlas' grotto provides a resumé of the indigenous history of the isthmus (2.101-221).[54]

The *Guadalupe* is a triumph of patriotic syncretism: Cortés is praised at the same time as the courage of his indigenous adversaries is affirmed. For Osorio Romero who edited this text, Villerías' language is striking for its incorporation of Nahuatl words into the Latin hexameter.[55] One example is Pluto's proud enumeration of his minions in the angry soliloquy which (echoing Neptune's words from *Aeneid* 1.132-5) sets the story of the poem into motion:

> Namque habeo indociles Otomites, more ferarum
> sub Jove degentes, et terrae gramine pastos;
> Guastecos graveis, cultos sermone Tarascos,
> atque Matalzincas et pictos corpora Mecos,
> quos ego: Sed melius juvat hoc mox dicere factis.

'I have at my disposal the indocile Otomi, who subsist under heaven like beasts and live on the grass of the ground; the grave Guastecos, the Tarascans of refined speech; and the Matlalzincas and the Chichimecs with their tattooed bodies, whom I ... But it is better to speak this soon – with actions.'

Villerías y Roelas, *Guadalupe* 1.126-30

Villerías' poem was never published in his lifetime. However, it may have been known to his contemporary, the bibliographer Juan José de Eguiara y Eguren who ranks Villerías among writers 'of consummate poetic skill'.[56] And in a survey of Guadalupan literature published in 1782, Francisco Xavier Clavigero, who was born three years after Villerías' death in 1728, claims to have seen a manuscript copy of his poem.[57] Thus the possibility that Villerías y Roelas had an influence on the later heroic poets of Clavigero's generation (including Landívar and Alegre) cannot be ruled out.[58]

Expression of a growing national pride was not confined to poetry and Guadalupan literature. Eguiara y Eguren's monumental *Bibliotheca Mexicana* is more than a bibliography: it represents both a demonstration and a dynamic assertion of Mexican intellectual achievement in several spheres of knowledge. Though never completed, it was designed to provide a comprehensive catalogue, entirely in Latin prose, of every Mexican author from the conquest up to 1755 (when the first volume was published). Arranged in alphabetical order of authors' first names, the *Bibliotheca Mexicana* was preceded by a series of *anteloquia,* prologic excursuses, by Eguiara himself on the archaeology of pre-Hispanic cultures. Only those prologues and entries from A-C went into print before Eguiara died in 1763. His conception of the *Bibliotheca* had been motivated by one particular European polemic about the paucity of culture and learning in the New World. This was a Latin letter published in 1735 by a Spaniard, Manuel Martí, who was Dean of Alicante. Martí offered a bleak picture of cultural and intellectual life in Spanish America to a pupil named Antonio Carillo, who had thought about continuing his studies in Mexico:

> Quo te vertes apud indos, in tam vasta litterarum solitudine? Quem adibis, non dicam magistrum, cuius praeceptis instituaris, sed auditorem? Non dicam aliquid scientem, sed scire cupientem? Dicam enucleatius a litteris non abhorrentem? Ecquosnam evolves codices? Equas lustrabis bibliotecas? Haec enim omnia tam frustra quaeres, quam qui tondet asinum vel mulcet hircum. Eugepae! Abice has nugas atque eo iter converte, ubi et animum excolere queas et honestum vitae subsidium tibi parare et novos honores capessere.[59]

> Where will you turn in the Indies, a vast wilderness when it comes to literature? Whom will you go to? – I won't say 'which teacher will instruct you?', but whom will you find even to listen to you? I won't say 'will you find anyone who knows anything?', but will you even find anyone who *wants* to know anything? In a nutshell: will you find anyone who doesn't recoil from the study of literature? What documents will you unroll? What libraries will you consult? You'll search for all these things with as much success as someone who tries to shave an ass or milk a he-goat. Oh very good! Forget such nonsense – and put yourself on a path where you'll be able to cultivate your mind, make a decent living for yourself, and acquire new prestige.
>
> Martí, *Epistulae* 7.16

Martí's letter is quoted at length in the first prologue of the *Bibliotheca Mexicana*; much more of Eguiara's prefatory material consititutes a fascinating and informed response to his prejudiced remarks. Others responded to this provocation: it was the subject of a rebuttal in an inaugural lecture delivered in Latin at Mexico University by Juan Gregorio de Campos y Martínez in 1745, and published in the same year.[60]

A better known response to Martí's ludicrous charges is the *Aprilis Dialogus* by Vicente López.[61] López, himself a native of Córdoba in Spain, was also the author of some Guadalupan hymns and other poems in Latin. His 'April Dialogue' was written as part of the prefatory material to herald the *Bibliotheca Mexicana*. It presents a conversation between a Spaniard, a Belgian, and an Italian, conducted under a shady plane tree in a villa outside Mexico City. Leonardo Bruni Aretino and other writers of Latin dialogue in Renaissance Italy had been prone to adopt such *loci amoeni* or 'pleasant places' as venues in their dialogues, although the detail of the plane tree ultimately goes back to Plato's *Phaedrus*.[62] López's interlocutors in the *Aprilis Dialogus* specifically address – among other topics – access to books in America, the benefits of chocolate for intellectual inspiration, Eguiara y Eguren's enterprise, and the painting of the Virgin of Guadalupe.[63] The setting in April may allude to the month in which the first volume of the *Bibliotheca Mexicana* was published.[64] But Antony Higgins may also be right to suggest that this setting in springtime is meant to glorify Mexico: 'as a place in which humanist scholarship is being re-elevated to the state of vitality it enjoyed in Europe during the fifteenth and sixteenth centuries ... the intellectual culture of New Spain is projected as a scene in which standards of erudition and eloquence similar to those set in motion by humanism in Western Europe are being attained'.[65]

However, in the later 1700s, Mexico was far from a *locus amoenus* in social and economic terms. The period was certainly no 'golden age' of political history, and the negative impact of events on New Spain's literary culture was the very least of its catastrophes.[66] Between 1759 and 1788, Carlos III of Spain began the reorganisation of the Spanish Empire, known as the 'Bourbon Reforms'. The objective of the ensuing legislation was to extend royal authority in New Spain, by reducing the region's autonomy whilst radically increasing fiscal revenue. The *Visitador General* in the 1760s, José de Gálvez, further alienated the role of the *criollo* elite from the administration, and the power of peninsular Spaniards in the high court and local government was thoroughly consolidated.

In order to restrain the social influence of the Catholic church, the Crown promoted royal patronage and sought to diminish the standing of the clergy: the consequent secularisation of parishes was disruptive and it particularly angered local populations. But perhaps the gravest policy of all was the expulsion of the Jesuits from all the Spanish territories in 1767. As a modern historian has commented, 'This decree was motivated in part by the notable successes the Jesuits had achieved all over the Spanish empire as well as their total obedience to the papacy. The decision would bring severe consequences, however, because of the opposition it provoked in New Spain's society.'[67]

In the climate of such increasingly overt social and political engineering from a geographically remote imperial power, it is hardly surprising that Spanish Americans had begun to see themselves as less European. The more revolutionary currents of post-Enlightenment thinking would also play a great part in Mexican intellectual history – and they are reflected in Jesuit writings of the time. Culturally as well as economically, the *criollos* began to perceive their interests as being more closely linked to those of the Indians and other groups. This may have been another factor that had led to the more or less self-conscious fashioning of an independent body of 'New World' knowledge to reflect a new level of intellectual autonomy.[68]

The Bourbon Reforms, more than anything else, determined the fortune of New Spanish humanism in the 1700s. The expulsion of the Jesuits – who by this time were the main torchbearers of classical learning – meant that Latin literary production in Mexico itself was all but extinguished. However, were it not for this expulsion, many Latin texts by Hispanic American authors in Europe would probably not have come into being. Nearly 700 members of the Society of Jesus were forced to leave New Spain in June 1767: Rafael Landívar was one of them. Most of these men eventually settled in Italy, but they suffered considerable hardship, and by 1773 more than 300 had died.

The conceit of forced migration to Hesperia has a ring familiar to readers of Virgil. But the Jesuits were bringing with them new Latin poetry and other writing on classical themes *from* the New World *back* to Europe at a point when Latin writing, even in Italy, had long gone into decline.[69] Landívar and his peers wrote about their homeland because they were in exile, and they expressed themselves in Latin in order to demonstrate to new European readers the universal, transtemporal value of Mexican learning. There is some irony in the fact that the repression of the Jesuits caused the final flowering of Mexican humanism: a number of outstanding works in Latin, Spanish, and Italian were written by Jesuit refugees in Europe, especially in Italy, in the 1770s and 1780s.[70]

Of those works, the *Rusticatio Mexicana* has enjoyed unique recognition – no doubt because in dealing with the country life of Mexico and Guatemala it is the only sustained Latin poem in New Spanish literature on an American theme. Landívar's life and work will be addressed in the next two chapters: here it remains to outline the fortunes and achievements of some of his contemporaries – most of whom he knew personally. Their thought and writing – particularly their accommodation of Enlightenment philosophy, science and natural history – also have a bearing on Landívar's work and on the context in which it was produced. Moreover, as noted above, they are important intellectual figures in their own right.

Padre José Rafael Campoy (1723-77) was an influential teacher who inclined the Jesuits of his generation to embrace Enlightenment ideas. From 1737-41 he studied philosophy in the Colegio de San Ildefonso in Mexico City (where Diego José Abad was one of his colleagues) and then entered the Jesuit novitiate at Tepotzotlán. In the 1740s, Campoy developed an enthusiasm for Aristotle and Cicero. He eventually entered the Colegio Máximo de San Pedro y San Pablo, by this time the central educational institution in New Spain. There Campoy met Alegre, Clavigero, Castro, Dávila and others who were to become prominent scholars, as well as Landívar himself. 'No one could write an encomium of any of these men' wrote a contemporary biographer of José Rafael Campoy, 'without frequently mentioning Campoy's name.'[71] Campoy had undertaken a commentary and Spanish translation of Pliny's *Natural History* which was lost when the decree of expulsion took him by surprise in Veracruz. In exile, he lived in Ferrara and Bologna and continued his researches on Pliny. Although none of Campoy's writings survive, he mastered several disciplines and he made a radical contribution to the reform and expansion of the Jesuits' teaching in New Spain. Under Campoy's direction, their curriculum came to accommodate mathematics, Greek, modern languages, and, most significantly, the ideas of modern thinkers such as Descartes, Bacon (whose *De Scientarum dignitate atque incremento* was translated into Spanish by Castro), Gassendi, Locke, and Newton.[72]

The endeavours of Francisco Xavier Clavigero (1731-87) were in a similar spirit: according to Juan Luis Maneiro, he was the first to present a taught course, in Latin, which provided systematic coverage of contemporary philosophy – first in Morelia in 1763, and the following year in Guadalajara.[73] But his influence was to extend far beyond Jesuit circles. Among the works Clavigero continued to produce in exile was an extensive *Ancient History of Mexico* (1780), originally published in Italian. The *History* was in part a counterblast to an astonishingly polemical book in French, entitled *Recherches philosophiques sur les Américains* (1768), by a Dutch cleric named Cornelius de Pauw. De Pauw, commending the achievements of Newton, Leibniz, Descartes, Locke, and others, held that no book worth reading had ever come out of America. He characterised the indigenous Americans 'as a race of men who have all the faults of a child, as a degenerate species of humanity, cowardly, impotent, without physical force or vigour, and without elevation of spirit'. The calendars and magnificent buildings of the Aztecs could be explained away as the fabrication of cynical, unscrupulous Spaniards. De Pauw partly rested his arguments on the thesis of a French naturalist, George-Louis Leclerc Buffon who had argued that America was an immature continent in geological terms: consequently all forms of life (including human beings) which inhabited it were deficient, and weaker than those in Europe.[74]

It is not impossible that such an attack on American nature prompted Landívar's *Rusticatio Mexicana,* much as the *Bibliotheca Mexicana* of Eguiara had been incited some years before by Martí's defamation of American culture.[75] Certainly De Pauw's absorption of Buffonish reasoning explains why Clavigero's *History* is prefaced with a natural historical description of Mexico. Clavigero went on to distinguish the civilised Peruvians and Mexicans from other American peoples – and affirmed from his own experience that the Indians were capable of learning all the sciences. He observes (as Cicero did for Latin) that although classical Nahuatl has no equivalents for Greek philosophical categories of matter, substance, and accidents, the language can accommodate the full meaning of the Bible as well as advanced mathematical calculations (*Disertación* 6.6-7).[76] Clavigero had himself produced a grammar of the 'Mexican language'.[77] Addressing the charge that the Mexicans no longer possessed the calibre of their ancestors prior to the conquest, the Jesuit historian responded with a pointed analogy:

It cannot be doubted that present day Mexicans are not at all like their ancient forbears, just as the modern Greeks are not like those who lived in the times of Plato and Pericles (Clavigero, *History* 1.17).[78]

Greece was then under the rule of the Ottoman Turks: in comparing the indigenous Americans to the Greeks, Clavigero is also aligning imperialist Spaniards with the Turks. That comparison alone was probably enough to prevent his history from being published in Spanish, until after Mexico secured independence from Spain in 1821.[79] Clavigero was praised for his defense of American culture in an accomplished poem of 110 Latin hexameters (probably composed by Maneiro).[80]

Enlightenment thought and the need to respond to a different kind of European polemic also help to characterise the achievement of another major Jesuit author from New Spain: Diego José Abad. Abad, who was born in Michoacán in 1727 and died in Bologna in 1780, wrote a substantial didactic epic in 43 short books, the *De Deo, Deoque Homine Carmina Heroica* ('Heroic Verses on God, and on God as Man'). This impressive poem reflects its author's wide-ranging interests in philosophy, science, and letters.[81] Abad absorbed Greek, Roman, and Renaissance sources, as well as later literature in Spanish and in Latin – Melchior De Polignac's *Anti-Lucretius: De Deo et Natura* is recalled in his poem's title and evoked throughout the work itself.[82] But although Abad celebrated the scientific advances of the Enlightenment in his *De Deo*, he condemned any progressive ideas which might constitute a threat to Catholic doctrine.[83]

The *De Deo* contains a number of references to Mexico which point to its author's attachment to his native country.[84] The pseudonym – *Labbe Selenopolitanus* – under which Abad published the 1773 and 1775 editions of the poem is also very telling in this respect. That assumed name was explained by the poet's friend and biographer, Manuel Fabri:

> *Labbeumque, se, paullo immutato nomine, et Selenopolitanum, seu Urbis Lunae [id est enim patria lingua Mexicus sonat, ut plerique credunt] Civem appellavit.*[85]

> He called himself *Labbe* by changing his own name slightly, and *Selenopolitanus*, or 'Citizen of the City of the Moon' – that is what 'Mexico' means in the language of his fatherland, as most people believe.
> Fabri, *Specimen vitae auctoris*

The adoption of a hellenised version of a Nahuatl name is a powerful way of describing oneself as a Mexican; at the same time *Labbe Selenopolitanus* eschews any Spanish constituents: *L'abbé*, the French for 'abbot', is the meaning of *Abad* in Spanish.

Abad used the same *nom de plume* for his other surviving work in Latin: the *Dissertatio ludicro-seria* (1778) – a witty but trenchant response to an allegation made by Giambattista Roberti that 'only Italians could write

Latin properly.'[86] 'Just as some Italians were annoyed that Spaniards dared to speak to them about music', explains Miguel Batllori, 'others took offence that they considered themselves just as accomplished Latinists as the natives of Italy'.[87] The belief was that the Spanish Baroque, along with the influence of 'decadent' classical authors from Spain, like Lucan, Seneca, Martial, and even Quintilian had led to a spread of bad taste. Clementino Vannetti, another Italian who had been conspicuous in this anti-Spanish campaign, did however recant – and this recantation seems to have been prompted by his own recognition of Abad's talents. Vannetti admitted Abad as a member of the exclusive Accademia Rovoretana in Trento, and fulsomely praised the Mexican's poetic achievement in a letter to the poet: 'it can be said not that you have been graced by the Muses, but that the Muses have been graced by you.'[88]

José Mariano Iturriaga and Andrés Diego de la Fuente were other Latin poets exiled to Italy. Iturriaga is credited with authoring a Latin hexameter narrative about Salvatierra, a Milanese Jesuit, and his courageous mission in the late 1600s to the inhospitable territory of California.[89] Fuente wrote an ekphrastic Guadalupan epic in three books published in Faenza in 1773.[90] However, the most proficient literary scholar and poet of this generation was Francisco Xavier Alegre, whom Landívar himself characterised as 'learned in the art of Apollo.'[91]

Alegre, who also settled in Bologna, was born in Veracruz in 1729. After studying at the University of Mexico, he joined the Company of Jesus at Tepotzotlán and mastered Latin, Greek, Hebrew and Italian before becoming Professor of Literature at the Colegio Máximo de San Pedro y San Pablo. He also learnt French and English, and taught in Cuba and Yucatán, returning to Mexico City in 1765. Alegre's output prior to his exile two years later included his lost *Lyrics and Georgics in Praise of Blessed Mary of Guadalupe* and another Latin work: a translation of the Homeric *Batrachomyomachia*.[92] His history of the Jesuit movement in New Spain was completed after his expulsion from Mexico, along with his literary works which will be discussed here for their bearing on Landívar. After Alegre died in 1788, his extensive studies of ethics on theological principles, the *Institutiones Theologicae*, were published in seven volumes in Venice between 1789 and 1791. That magisterial work shows its author's commitment to progressive Enlightenment social and political thought: Alegre upheld popular sovereignty and rejected slavery out of hand.[93]

Very probably Alegre had begun in Mexico his annotated Spanish translation, or rather elaboration, of Boileau's *L'Art poétique* which was finished in Bologna, in 1776.[94] The *Arte poética de Mr. Boileau* offers a form of comparative criticism as it seeks to integrate Spanish literature with the traditions of classical antiquity and with other vernacular literatures. Although its basic approach is grounded in Horace and Aristotle, a number of references to the notion of the 'sublime' may well have been absorbed directly from Longinus' *On the Sublime* (as well as from Boileau's treatise and his French translation of Longinus).[95] These principles seem to have influenced Landívar: a similar kind of literary cosmopolitanism, along with an application of Longinian sublimity, can be discerned in the *Rusticatio Mexicana* which was completed only a few years later.

Alegre also published a Latin verse rendering of Homer's *Iliad* in Forlì in 1773. Italian humanists such as Andreas Divus and Angelo Poliziano ('Politian') had produced such translations of Homer in the Renaissance, but Alegre's accomplishment can still command respect even if it is of little benefit to modern readers. The *Alexandriad*, Alegre's original Latin epic in four books about the capture of Tyre by Alexander the Great – possibly written as a school exercise – was eventually printed together with his *Iliad* translation.[96] The poem's historical sources include Quintus Curtius, Josephus, and Diodorus Siculus. Although his epic diction is decisively Virgilian, Alegre's use of decorative conceit unites his early poem more obviously to the *culteranismo* of the Spanish Baroque than to the apparently Neoclassical style of Abad and Landívar. The *Alexandriad* can also be read as an historical allegory: there are some grounds for believing Alexander may be a prototype for Cortés, as the 'Carthaginian' city of Tyre might be aligned with Tenochtitlán.[97] At any rate, directly after Alexander's slaughter of the Tyrian leader Ninus, a river symbolically connects these locations, enabling the epic to close with an explicitly Mexican theme:

> Hactenus Aemathios Vatem memorasse triumphos
> Sit satis, arboream recubat dum lentus ad umbram,
> Qua per Mexiceos liquidus perlabitur agros
> Anthius, ac placidis foecundat jugera limphis,
> Et Guadalupaei surgunt felicia templi
> Culmina, pinnatoque minantur in aethera clivo.
> Fors olim tua, Diva parens, graviore cothurno
> Signa canam, laudesque tuas procul ultima Thule
> Audiet, ac positis numen venerabitur aris.

May it be enough for the Poet to have commemorated the Emathian triumphs to this extent, while he reclines peacefully under the shade of a tree where the liquid Anthius flows through the fields of Mexico, and makes the hills fertile with its peaceful waters and where the turrets of the Guadalupan temple rise and push into heaven on a winged ascent. Perhaps one day, Divine Progenitor, I will sing of your signs in a more serious style, and distant Thule will hear your praises, and put up altars to venerate your godly power.

Alegre, *Alexandriad* 4.578-86

This appeal to the Virgin of Guadalupe simultaneously echoes *Eclogue* 10.70-4 and the end of *Georgics* 4, as well as other verses by Virgil, Politian, and Sannazaro.[98] Alegre addresses the matter of his general debt to Virgil in a Latin letter to an 'Antonius'. This text serves as a preface to the *Alexandriad*, and it effectively constitutes another treatise on poetics:[99]

> Fatemur inquam nimiam quandam, ac verbo dicam, puerilem Virgilio adhaesionem toto in opusculo relucere. Quis tamen hanc eandem in omnibus illis non videat, qui aliqua cum laude post decimum tertium saeculum scripserunt? Etenim Francisci Petrarchae Africa; Pontani Hesperides, Darchii Canes Venatorii, Fracastorii Siphylis, Vidae Poema de morte Christi, Jacobi Sannazarii Virginis Puerperium, Rapini Horti, aliorumque Scriptorum opera plurima Virgilium undequaque redolent. Quid? Virgilius ipse totus quotus est, nonne, ut Lilius Giraldus ajebat, ex optimorum imitatione evasit?

> We certainly admit that there is an excessive, or to be honest, childlike dependence on Virgil throughout this little work. Who though would not see the same in all those who have, with some distinction, written since the thirteenth century? For Francesco Petrarch's *Africa,* Pontano's *Hesperides,* Darcio's *Hunting Dogs,* Fracastoro's *Syphilis*, Vida's Poem on the death of Christ, Iacopo Sannazaro's *Virgin Birth*, Rapin's *Gardens* and very many works by other writers smack of Virgil on every side. So? Is it not the case that Virgil himself, for all that he is, has, as Lilio Giraldi said, come out from imitation of the best?

> Alegre, *Antonio suo*

Narrative epic is Alegre's main concern, in an essay which refers to a wide range of other classical authors and vernacular poets including Camoens, Tasso and Milton. But this excerpt shows that Alegre is seeking to inscribe his own work in a tradition of canonical humanist poetry, much of which is didactic. And it also indicates the range of the Latin poetry that was available to Alegre and his peers in Italy, if not in Mexico: most of the authors listed in the excerpt given here are echoed, quite unmistakably, in the *Rusticatio Mexicana*.[100] Here – as in his *Arte poética* – Alegre might be pointing to some views that his friend and contemporary, Landívar held as well.

In fact, the exiled Hispanic Jesuits in Italy formed a very close-knit community. The Jesuit historian Decorme records that Landívar occupied the same house as Alegre, Clavigero, and Dávila in Bologna: it can be surmised that exchanges of ideas between these individuals would have been routine.[101] Knowledge of the texts and ideas that circulated among these individuals and their predecessors affords the best means of understanding Rafael Landívar's particular achievement. His work is very much a product of the complex, multicultural tradition of humanism that has been sketched out in the preceding pages.

The expulsion of the Jesuits in 1767 severely ruptured the continuity of the classical tradition all over Spanish America, but it did not put an end to it. It is true that through the 1800s, there was a decline of classical culture in the seminaries: some actually preferred the Latin of Christian authors like Aquinas, Bonaventure, and even Fulgentius to the classical styles of Cicero, Sallust and Tacitus.[102] Nonetheless, Spanish translations of ancient Greco-Roman authors began to proliferate at this time, and Mexican works in Latin and Spanish were collected and catalogued by bibliographers including José Mariano Beristáin de Souza, José María Lafragua, and a Chilean, José Toribio Medina. The historian Joaquín García Icazbalceta (1825-94) was another important editor and translator of a number of humanist texts. In the past century, poets, translators and scholars contributed in a variety of ways to the study of Latin writing in New Spain.[103] Their endeavours have enabled modern philology and literary criticism to join forces with the Mexican tradition of humanism which, though it has diminished, has never disappeared.[104]

2

Devotion and Exile:
Rafael Landívar and his earlier compositions

(i) A life in Guatemala, Mexico and Italy

In the early 1700s, Pedro Landívar y Caballero, a young nobleman from Navarra in Spain, came to Guatemala 'with no more capital than a sword'.[1] Settling in the prosperous city of Santiago de los Caballeros (now Antigua), he eventually managed to secure an annual income of ten thousand pesos a year from a government gunpowder monopoly, and married a *criolla* from El Panchoy, Doña Juana Xaviera Ruiz de Bustamante. The birth of their son Rafael on 27 October 1731 was recorded in the baptismal records of the parish church of San Sebastián.[2] Pedro Landívar had two brothers in Spain who were in religious orders: it is likely that he came to want more for his talented son than a future in explosives.

Very little information about Rafael Landívar's life is available. The known details are mostly derived from data in public records and Jesuit catalogues.[3] There is, however, a brief biography. This is one of an unpublished series of lives of Jesuits exiled to Italy, by Padre Félix Sebastián (1737-1815), a Spanish missionary who also settled in Bologna.[4] While Sebastián provides a couple of anecdotes and some revealing insights on Landívar's character, his narrative often reads like a hagiography which seeks to emphasise the exemplary piety of its subject. The account is quite unlike the detailed and substantial intellectual biographies – in Latin – of Campoy, Castro, Clavigero, Abad, Alegre, and others, by Juan Luis Maneiro and Manuel Fabri. Unfortunately those more thorough chroniclers did not devote a specific study to Rafael Landívar, even though Maneiro, who returned to Mexico in 1799, did take with him an autograph copy of Sebastián's work.[5]

Schooling for the elite in the Spanish colonies almost inevitably consisted of a Jesuit education: the young Landívar attended the College of San Francisco de Borja, probably from the age of seven.[6] He became a Bachelor of Philosophy on 16 February 1746: rhetoric, and very possibly, astronomy and geography, would have been on his curriculum as well.[7] He graduated to the University of San Carlos in Guatemala to read theology and received a Master of Arts degree. In 1749, the year of his father's death, Landívar went to Mexico; he entered the Jesuit novitiate at the renowned seminary of Tepotzotlán in February of 1750.[8] There, according to Félix Sebastián, 'he made great advances in the humanities, advances which later brought so much honour to him as he was an eloquent rhetorician and a very lucid poet.'[9] He proceeded in 1753 to the Colegio Máximo de San Pedro y San Pablo where he was formally examined in philosophy and theology – to great acclaim. This led to Landívar's appointment at the Colegio del Spírito Santo in Puebla as a *maestro de Sintaxis*, before he was recalled to the Colegio Máximo to teach rhetoric: it is likely that here he would have worked alongside Campoy, Alegre, and other influential figures. In 1755, at the age of 24, Rafael Landívar was ordained, and celebrated his first mass in the church of Tepotzotlán.[10]

After thus spending eleven years in Mexico, Landívar returned to Guatemala as Professor of Grammar and Instructor in Rhetoric at San Borja. In 1764 he became Prefect of the Congregation in the College. The following year he made a solemn vocational vow – to commit himself to educating the young.[11] The circumstances in which this obligation was to be fulfilled could not have been foreseen. Landívar had already become Rector of his Jesuit seminary when the arrest and expulsion of the Jesuits was enforced on 26 June 1767, the feast of the Sacred Heart. Something of the draconian quality of Carlos III's decree is betrayed by the monarch's own words:

> Moved by very grave causes ... and other urgent, just, and necessary reasons, which I reserve in my royal mind ... I have ordered that the Jesuits be expelled from all my dominions of Spain, the Indies, and Philippine Islands, and other adjacent regions, priests as well as coadjutors or lay-brothers, who may have made the first profession, and the novices, who may wish to follow them; and that all the properties of the Society in my dominions be taken ....[12]

The Jesuits and those loyal to them were surrounded by troops and deported without warning, and without the chance to contact friends and relatives outside the Society. The consequences were catastrophic: altogether 5,000 Jesuits were driven out of Spain and its empire; Don Rafael de Zelis recorded the names and particulars of the 678 (including himself) who were exiled from Mexico and Guatemala. In New Spain and the Captaincy of Guatemala, 39 colleges and eight missions were vacated. The departure of the twelve members of the Society from Guatemala alone deprived between 300 and 400 children of an education.[13] And worse still, the perilous journey of the refugees left a trail of corpses: by August 1768, 102 members of the Society had perished.

Félix Sebastián outlines the consequences of these events for Landívar:

> Placed entirely in the hands of Divine Providence, he left his college, country, relatives, and all that he held most precious in life and was forced to take the hazardous journey to the Fort of San Felipe on the dangerous coast of the Gulf of Honduras. Once there he embarked for Havana, from that place to Cádiz, from there to Cartagena in the east, and then to Corsica, where he

was stranded in the port of Ajaccio. Here he remained for six months, and marooned once again by the French invaders of the island, he secured a passage to the Italian mainland.[14]

Some have left more detailed firsthand accounts of the harrowing transatlantic journey. López de Priego described in a letter to his sister, a nun in Puebla, the destitution of his Mexican comrades in Corsica: Landívar was among them. 'Of our members who had already arrived there', writes López de Priego, 'some were living under stairways, some in kitchens, others in stables.'[15]

Landívar joined the large community of Spanish Jesuits in Bologna, where he became the director of a Jesuit centre of study, which became known as 'La Sapiencia'; from 1770 he occupied a house with Clavigero, Alegre, and Dávila. Sebastián describes Landívar's 'acute sorrow at the Brief of Suppression of his beloved Mother, the Company of Jesus' – this refers to the papal brief of Clement XIV, issued on 16 August 1773 at the instigation of the Spanish ambassador, José Moniño.[16] Landívar's natural mother died alone in Guatemala in the same month two years before; his only sister, Doña Rita Josefa, had died as a widow when he was already bound for Italy. No less painful would have been the news – within the same month again – that an earthquake had devastated Santiago de los Caballeros on 29 July 1773.[17] After the dissolution of the Society in Bologna, Landívar's means of subsistence diminished still further, and he was obliged to reclaim his mother's inheritance. This led to a troublesome lawsuit which was only resolved some years after his own death.[18] A need for money might have been one of Landívar's motivations for composing the *Rusticatio Mexicana*.

The first ten-book edition of the poem was published in Modena in 1781. This may have been a strategic decision, because Modena was the city with which Gerolamo Tiraboschi, a Jesuit savant, had long been associated.[19] Tiraboschi had been one of the many Italian scholars to criticise the *seicentismo* of Spanish writers. That Italian term for seventeenth-century stylistic mannerism has connotations comparable to those of 'euphuism' in English. Tiraboschi also maintained, along with Roberti, Bettinelli and others, that Spaniards could not write Latin as correctly and elegantly as Italians.[20] Landívar's poem gave the lie to this – and its refinement of style came to be extolled by Tiraboschi himself. The definitive edition of the poem in fifteen books, with an appendix, came out in Bologna the following year.[21]

Landívar succumbed to an unidentifiable illness in the spring of 1793: the archive of his parish of Santa Maria delle Muratelle records that he was unable to assist in celebrating mass at its patronal festival of the Annunciation on the 25 March. He jovially diagnosed the complaint to his friends: morir, y presto! The record of the deceased in his parish states that he died on 27 September at 1 pm.[22] The last sentence of Sebastián's account is as follows:

His Corpse was buried in the Parish Church of Santa Maria delle Muratelle, of whose Parishioners he was at that time Rector; and his memory remained impressed on all who knew him, as they loved him for his goodness, they revered him for his holiness, and esteemed him for his kindness, tokens by which they said he could be recognised as a worthy Jesuit.[23]

Very possibly Landívar did not set much store by his literary activity. Félix Sebastián certainly does not present a biography of a poet or author, but rather a portrait of a devoted clergyman: 'his life can be summed up in two words: Prayer and Study'.[24] Landívar's writing is treated only in a brief paragraph:

> To entertain himself somewhat, he wrote, in Latin verse, for which he had a great facility, one Work, which he gave to the Press with the title *Rusticatio Mexicana, seu rariora quaedam ex agris Mexicanis decerpta* [*Life in the Mexican Countryside, or some scattered things gathered from the fields of Mexico*]. A work which has been much appreciated by the Scholars of Italy, whose Critics have bestowed praise on it, of which the said work is deserving, as it is unique in its class [*línea*]. This pursuit occupied him only for a short while, since he took it up to occupy his mind, as he always devoted his attention to his real concerns: Holy Scripture, Theology, and Asceticism.[25]

If Landívar did indeed put so little time into his writing, his achievement is all the more impressive. The *Rusticatio Mexicana* suffices to display its author's breadth of ability by incorporating a variety of subjects and poetic styles that others would be hard pressed to harmonise within a single work. Three earlier literary pieces penned by Rafael Landívar also survive: a 'Funeral Declamation' in Latin prose that was published in Mexico, and a Latin ode and Spanish sonnet that were printed in Italy. These shorter works have received barely any critical discussion, but they reward careful reading. As well as informing our assessment of the author of *Rusticatio Mexicana* by giving a fuller impression of his circumstances, training, and abilities, the compositions certainly command appreciation for their own merits.

(ii) Pagan scripture and a Christian funeral

For many readers today, the prospect of a lengthy oration – especially the eulogy of a bishop who died in Guatemala nearly three centuries ago – is unlikely to be enticing. But this address contains more than a few surprises. 'In the speech', Joaquín Antonio Peñalosa has remarked, 'there is not one single quotation of Holy Scripture or of the ecclesiastical writers – quotations that were required in church oratory of the time'.[26] Instead, Landívar adroitly deploys ideas and modes of expression from classical Greek and Latin sources to enhance the emotional effect of his words: we are powerfully reminded that this kind of panegyric has its origins in Roman antiquity.[27] Before commenting on the Declamation itself, it is necessary to say something about the more immediate background to this text.

There are few sources of information about Francisco José de Figueredo y Victoria, the second Archbishop of Guatemala, to whom the Declamation is devoted.[28] Figueredo was born in the Nuevo Reyno de Granada, now Colombia, no later than 1685, as he was over eighty years old when he died. In 1740, he became bishop of Popayán, an important city in the New Kingdom of Granada during the colonial period. He was made Archbishop of Guatemala in 1751, arriving there two years afterwards. In spite of his advanced age and frail health (he was blind at the end of his life), he conducted episcopal visits of his vast diocese: a primacy which would have extended southwards from Chiapas, to León in Nicaragua, covering the present territories of Belize and El Salvador. Figueredo was fond of the Jesuits and he was an active benefactor of their College in Guatemala. Before his death on 24 June in 1765, he asked to be buried in the church of the College. A few more details of the Archbishop's character and of the support he gave to the Jesuits can be gleaned from Landívar's Declamation: Figueredo's exemplary conduct, humility, and capacity to provide comfort and consolation (*Declamatio* 1, 2); his study of Grammar in his early youth at the Jesuit College of Popayán which led to his fondness for the Society (4); his work for its benefit in Popayán (3); his immediate attention to those in need and his allocation of funds to the College of Guatemala to ensure its survival after his translation there (7, 9); his donation of a cupola and of other costly items for the temple (10); and his defence of the Society from opponents and detractors (11).

The Dean of the Cathedral of Guatemala granted permission for Figueredo's funeral to be held in the church of the Jesuit College of Saint Luke instead of the Cathedral, and he decreed that the Jesuits would be responsible for preaching at the occasion. Landívar tells us (5) that Figueredo wanted to be buried in his black Jesuit cassock, but the Dean stipulated that his archepiscopal decorations should be worn as well so that 'the humble soutane will be exalted by pontifical dress'.[29] The lavish funeral was attended by both the diocesan and Jesuit chapters, the staff of the Royal University, other clergy, monks, and members of the local population. The Vigil was held at 4 pm on 7 August 1765, when Landívar delivered his oration in Latin. On the following day, at 9 am, a mass was celebrated at which Padre José Ignacio Vallejo preached in Spanish. The details of these arrangements were recorded in a small volume published in Puebla de los Angeles (now Puebla, Mexico) by decree of the Vice Provincial of the Society of Jesus in New Spain, Padre Pedro Reales. The date of publication for this book of 39 leaves – amounting to 73 printed pages – is given as 26 February 1766.

It is in this publication that Landívar's funeral declamation was first preserved. The long title of this short book will here be abbreviated to *El llanto de los ojos* ('The Weeping of the Eyes').[30] The title goes on to herald

Father Francisco Xavier Molina's account of the funeral, but no indication is given there of the other two discourses the book contains: Landívar's oration and Vallejo's Spanish sermon.[31] In his elaborate description of the funerary honours accorded to Figueredo, Molina mentions the Latin oration without naming Landívar:

> [When] the solemn Vigil ended with the final lesson which the Priest intoned, a Jesuit made an eloquent declamation in the Latin language.[32]

But Landívar's name *is* given in the extended title of his actual speech.[33] However its omission from the title page of *El llanto de los ojos* helps to explain why this prose oration has been so rarely read.[34]

The Declamation can still be admired as a literary endeavour, even in translation. It met an obligation – deeply felt by the Guatemalan Jesuits – to honour their defender and patron. Latin funeral orations were a common form of commemoration in New Spain:[35] Landívar explicitly says his aim is to ensure 'that the cause of our great grief may not ... lie hidden from posterity in all future ages' (2). The speech was meant to be appreciated long after the occasion of its twenty minute recital at the Vigil, and the period of just over six weeks between Figueredo's death and the funeral would have allowed good time for this address to be prepared – and it may well have been further refined for publication.

The Declamation has a traditional rhetorical structure: a formal preface or *exordium* (1) is followed by the elaboration of the reasons for the Society's grief. These constitute the main body (*narratio*) of the speech – which is carried forward by four major classical *exempla* or analogies (4-11). The text concludes with a forceful *peroratio* (12) incorporating a series of *apostrophes* or direct addresses – to Figueredo himself; to the Society of Jesus; to Libitina the Roman goddess of death; and finally, again, to the Society deprived of her son. That conceit – of Figueredo's relation to the Society as akin to the relation between a child and its parent – pervades the whole speech. The theme is introduced early on when Landívar says the Society has lost its 'best *son*' (2). The comparison is then complicated: Figueredo has also fulfilled the duties of the 'best of *parents*' (3). But the idea of Figueredo as child is what predominates, so that the Society, embodied by the audience of the oration, can be figured as a bereaved mother: *Societas* is a feminine noun in Latin.[36]

Two sustained classical *exempla* are determined by this general theme. The story of a mother killing herself after her son has been executed (6) is an illustration of *maternal* love to answer the questions Landívar has just posed to his audience at the end of the previous section: 'Should the Society not then recognise a man like this as a son? Should she not grieve at his most bitter passing? And will she not shed continuous tears?' (5). The next major illustration from ancient Rome involves *filial* love and piety. Landívar rehearses the famous story of a daughter who secretly breast-feeds her mother to save her from dying of enforced starvation (8).[37] The connection of this narrative to the argument of the speech is engineered by a kind of multiple correspondence. Landívar's avowal that 'Figueredo deserves to have a monument consecrated to him in the hearts [of the Jesuits] for ever, as *Pietas* did long ago' (7) leads directly into the opening of his second story: 'Antiquity ensured that an ancient temple was built to Piety' (8). Aggravated by poverty and starvation, the Society of Jesus in Guatemala was 'on the very point of perishing' just as the condemned mother in Rome was 'wasting away with hunger'. The fact that Figueredo relieved the Society 'at his own expense' parallels the ingenuity and generosity of the daughter's action in sustaining her mother. Figueredo has 'well earned eternal commemoration' while the Roman daughter is 'surely worthy of immortality'.

We also discover Figueredo had drawn his own inspiration for his acts of filial piety from quite a different realm of classical learning altogether: Plato's saying that 'each man ought to realise that everything he possesses belongs to those who brought him forth and brought him up'(9).[38] The Declamation also involves a network of less developed conceits – notably the outpouring of grief is visualised as a flood (1); the flood is conjoined with imagery of war and physical disease (2), eventually becoming a torrent which breaks its banks (12).

Overall, the language is markedly classical; its style *resembles* Cicero more than it echoes him, although diction and devices from the *Catiline Orations* – a common model in this period – are echoed in places.[39] Landívar's speech exhibits the thorough absorption of a Latin idiom which, for the orator and his peers, was very much alive. The choice of appropriate words and expressions suggests genuine fluency rather than a laborious attempt to stitch together an array of phrases of ancient provenance. However, the two occasions on which classical authors are explicitly cited indicate that a conscious creative method is at work in the use of sources. The first is Figueredo's quotation of Plato (9), mentioned earlier. Landívar does not specify the source of that quotation, which comes from Plato's *Laws*:

> Next after these gods [of Olympus, of the State and of the Underworld] the intelligent man will offer worship to the daemons, and after them, to the heroes (*herôsi*). Following these are private shrines customarily dedicated to ancestral gods; and after those, the honours to living parents. To them, righteous law requires that *the debtor should pay back his first and greatest debt, the longest standing of all obligations, and he should consider that everything he has acquired and possesses belongs to those who brought him forth and brought him up*, so that he ought to be disposed to serve them to the utmost of his ability ....
>
> Plato, *Laws* 717b-c

The words Figueredo liked to quote are in italics – but the *whole* of this passage must have been known to Landívar because Plato's advocation of reverence to heroes and ancestral gods seems to influence the direction the speech takes next. The Declamation proceeds to lay stress on the importance of celebrating the Archbishop's memory (10), and describes Figueredo's tomb as a place where 'reverent homage' (*prosequi reverentia*) can be paid to him. Thus Plato's recommendation that heroes and ancestors should be glorified, though not actually quoted by Landívar, still underlies what he goes on to say – and the sentiment will be amplified by consideration of the honours bestowed on military heroes in ancient Rome.

This point leads into the second explicit citation (at 11) of an antique author: the fourth-century AD Christian poet Aurelius Prudentius:

Ijs, Prudentio teste, summam Roma reverentiam praestabat, eos laudibus efferebat, eosdem divinis non nunquam honoribus cumulabat.

As Prudentius attests, Rome bestowed the highest reverence on these heroes, sounded out their praises, and on many occasions heaped divine honours upon them.

Landívar, *Declamation* 11

Prudentius is then quoted, though not precisely. The first word italicised below marks an indisputable deviation from his original phrasing, and the next two words in italics indicate variant readings which are also significant:

> Et tot templa Deum (*inquit*) quot in *urbe* sepulchra
> Heroum numerare licet: quos fabula Manes
> Nobilitat, noster populus *veneratur*, adorat.

'There are as many temples of Gods', *he says*, 'that one may count as there are heroes' tombs in the *city*. Our people *venerates*, adores the dead who are glorified by legendary fame.'

Landívar, *Declamation* 11

Here are the verses of Prudentius' poem as they appear in modern editions of the text:

> Et tot templa deum *Romae* quot in *orbe* sepulcra
> Heroum numerare licet, quos fabula Manes
> Nobilitat, noster populus *veneratus*, adorat.[40]

There are as many temples of gods *in Rome* that one may count as there are heroes' tombs in the *world*. Our *reverential* people adore the dead, who are glorified by legendary fame.

Prudentius, *Against the Oration
of Symmachus* 1.190-2

Viewed together, these differences are critical, given the purpose and context of the original verses. Prudentius' poem was a forceful retort to a tract written by a proponent of paganism, Quintus Aurelius Symmachus in the 380s AD.[41] As prefect of Rome, Symmachus had argued that the Altar of Victory should be restored to the senate-house.[42] But Prudentius, who was a Christian, vigorously opposed this, and his opposition extended to the whole apparatus of paganism – and the veneration of heroes and ancestors to boot. The invective tone of his polemic makes that very clear indeed, as it leads up to the lines Landívar manipulated:

> This rumour or mistake [that it was the god Mars and not a nobleman who had raped Rhea Silvia] inclined our Italian ancestors to celebrate the rites of Mars on the field of Romulus, to inscribe on the Capitol (which was founded on the rocks of the Palatine) the names of their 'forefather' Jupiter and of the Greek goddess Pallas, to summon Juno from her seat in Carthage: these gods were related to Mars. This misapprehension also caused their leaders to fetch the nude figure of Venus from Mount Eryx, to carry the Phrygian mother of the gods from Mount Ida in Phrygia, and to import the Bacchic orgies from leafy Naxos. The majesty of earth-born divinities thus had one single residence [in Rome]: *there are as many temples of the gods in Rome that one may count as there are heroes' tombs in the world. Our reverential people adore the dead, who are glorified by legendary fame.*
>
> Prudentius, *Against the Oration of Symmachus* 1.180-92

Landívar completely reverses the late antique poet's original message and he positively encourages his audience to *revere* the memory of Figueredo. It is conceivable that Landívar simply reproduced the verses as he encountered them in an anthology. But in the case of an author like Prudentius, the substitution of *inquit* for *Romae* at least, is not so likely. Prudentius and other early Christian Latin writers had been commonly read since the Middle Ages and were prescribed to indigenous students of Latin in Mexico in the 1500s.[43] Prudentius' vehement opposition to idolatry would have found a new significance in the Indian colleges. The fact that Prudentius himself was a patriotic Roman who came from Spain, may have further enhanced his importance for New Spanish humanists.[44]

There are two indications that Landívar himself tampered with his source here. The first is circumstantial: Landívar exhibited knowledge of the original context of his previous classical citation from Plato (and copies of the *Laws* were rarer than texts of Prudentius). The second indication is internal: *inquit* ('he [Prudentius] says') is a definite modification of the original text. The word *inquit* is fitted into the hexameter verse, but that intrusion of 'he says' of course signals that what we are hearing cannot possibly be what Prudentius actually wrote. Such customisations of a passage to meet the needs of an occasion are not uncommon in humanist writing: this is a rhetorical declamation with social and religious objectives – not an academic treatise that needs to display scholarly precision.

Landívar is able to indulge an enthusiasm for the culture of pre-Christian Rome which Prudentius would not have shared. In this funeral address – a formal part of a Christian vigil – Landívar refers to Libitina (the Roman goddess associated with death) on three occasions (2 and 12), quotes from the Twelve Tables (11), and makes a pagan exclamation (5) *me hercle*: 'By Hercules!' He even compares Figueredo to Phoebus Apollo (9). Ancient pagan funeral practices are also commended, and the rites of the indigenous Guatemalans are described as well (3). That sole reference to aboriginal Americans in the Declamation is brief but, in a speech of this kind, it amounts to a meaningful recognition. It anticipates the kind of benign ethnographic observation to be found in the *Rusticatio Mexicana* – a work which relates Mesoamerican culture to European traditions of knowledge in a variety of ways.

While the Spanish sermon of Vallejo preached on the occasion of the funeral itself would have been comprehensible to a range of social groups in the congregation, Landívar's Latin oration would have been designed more exclusively for an ecclesiastical audience. The content of this address therefore had to complement that of the traditional sermon rather than reduplicate it. Landívar's elegant deployment of his learning and his capacity to endow the classical past with a palpable presence make the *Declamatio Funebris* a humanist *tour de force*.

(iii) Poetic monuments in miniature

José Ignacio Vallejo (or 'Ballejo'), who had preached at Figueredo's funeral as Superior at the Seminary of San Borja, also settled in Bologna.[45] There he wrote a life of Saint Joseph, and a study of Saint Joachim and Saint Anne, the parents of the Virgin Mary.[46] In 1779, Vallejo's *Vida de la Madre de Dios y siempre Virgen María* ('The Life of the Mother of God and ever Virgin Mary') was printed in Cesena. Rafael Landívar composed a Latin ode and a Castilian sonnet in honour of this biography of the Virgin. Both poems were presented on page 9 of Vallejo's published book.

The Latin ode establishes a delicate parallel between Vallejo and God himself. God, in his role as *workman* (*Opifex Deus* 13) offers Mary as a Virgin and Mother free from original sin (2-3), while Vallejo has produced a work (*opus* 22, 26) that cannot be sullied or defiled (24-8). The concision of the poem and its alcaic metre point to the model of Horace's *Odes*. But Landívar's composition does not follow the structure or central theme of any particular Horatian ode, and might well draw more direct inspiration from a later source.[47] However, at the end of his ode, Landívar assures Vallejo that his biography will secure his reputation for posterity:

tuumque, Joseph, illustre nomen
marmore perpetuabit Orbis.

2. Rafael Landívar and his earlier compositions

And the World will perpetuate in marble your own illustrious name, Joseph.

Landívar, *Ode* 27-8.

That may well be a glancing reference to Horace's poetic characterisation of his own achievement:

Exegi monumentum aere perennius
regalique situ pyramidum altius,
quod non imber edax, non Aquilo impotens
possit diruere aut innumerabilis
annorum series et fuga temporum.

I have constructed a monument more enduring than bronze, higher than the regal setting of the pyramids, which neither the corroding rain nor the impotent North Wind can ever destroy, nor the countless series of years, nor the flight of time.

Horace, *Odes* 3.30.1-5

This apparently tenuous echo of Horace might be confirmed by consideration of Landívar's accompanying sonnet.

The sonnet is the sole example of any writing by Rafael Landívar in Spanish. The superlative praise it bestows on Vallejo exemplifies the literary mannerism that was still prevalent at this time. The poem opens by asserting that the biographer's portrait of Mary is superior to anything that the fabled Greek painters Apelles and Protogenes could have achieved. Although such *ut pictura poesis* comparisons – derived from Horace, *Ars Poetica* 361 – were very common, this application of the topos here may specifically allude to the divine image of the Virgin on Juan Diego's cloak in Villerías' epic *Guadalupe*. That image was described as superior to 'anything impressive once accomplished by Zeuxis with his brush, or Protogenes of Rhodes or Coan Apelles' (4.101-2: *Quicquid peniculo quondam admirabile Zeuxis,/Protogenesque dedit Rhodius, vel Cous Apelles*).[48]

Landívar describes Vallejo's *pluma* ('feather', 'quill') as following the flight of the Eagle of Saint John of the Apocalypse – John appeared to portray the Virgin Mary in the biblical book of Revelation. Vallejo's brush is so dextrous that it has been able to infuse the image of Mary with a life and soul. Landívar's Latin ode had also referred to Vallejo's 'brush' (*penicillo* 23), which adumbrated Mary's virtues, as Clio, the Muse of history, infused fire into the biographer's own soul. Both poems give Vallejo's Christian name in its Hebrew form, *Joseph,* in order to highlight its connection with Saint Joseph, the spouse of the Virgin.

There is an ode of Horace in which the poet's hope for literary immortality is conveyed by his imagined metamorphosis into a bird – with feathers growing from his shoulders (*nascunturque leves ... umerosque plumae* Horace, *Odes* 2.20.11-12). However, a well-known sonnet by the peninsular Spanish poet Luis de Góngora (1561-1627) provides a more

41

obvious model for Landívar's conceit of the *pluma*.[49] Góngora's sonnet, entitled *Para la cuarta parte de la 'Pontifical' del Doctor Babia*, was also written to celebrate a pious biographical endeavour – the lives of three popes completed by Luis Babia, chaplain of the Royal Chapel of Granada. In the sestet, a quill pen is also raised to celestial heights, and transformed:

> Pluma, pues, que claveros celestiales
> eterniza en los bronces de su historia,
> llave es ya de los tiempos, y no pluma.

The quill, then, that renders heavenly keys eternal in the bronzes of its history, is now the key to times past, and not a quill.

Góngora, Soneto 26.9-11

This may recall the indestructible records of the Fates in Ovid's *Metamorphoses*, but Góngora's metaphor of the 'bronzes of history', in which the keys of heaven are forged, more obviously evokes Horace, *Odes* 3.30: the composition subtly echoed in Landívar's own Latin ode.[50] Thus Góngora and Horace are conjoined to provide a further, more recondite connection between Landívar's two poems. That conjunction of influences is of considerable interest. Horace's prescriptions on poetry were the essence of Neoclassicism.[51] Góngora, on the other hand, embodied the excesses of Baroque *seicentismo* so deplored by Tiraboschi and his fellow Hispanophobes: the particular verses evoked by Landívar are a celebrated example of that very tendency.[52] But it is worth noting that Alegre, though he was generally critical of Góngora, compared another of his sonnets – favourably and pointedly – to an ode by Horace.[53] Landívar's juxtaposition of the two poets becomes more significant in the light of this contemporary parallel.

That inclination to publish a Gongorine sonnet along with a Horatian ode should prompt pause for thought. Landívar is usually regarded as a Neoclassical author, but literary historical classifications should never be applied too rigidly – and European protocols of period and style are not always best applied to non-European writers. The review of the *Rusticatio Mexicana* to follow will underline the pluralistic quality of Landívar's poetics – a pluralism that is quite exceptional for eighteenth-century literature. But even if they are taken alone, the earlier writings surveyed in this chapter give ample proof of Rafael Landívar's ingenuity and technical accomplishment.

The Recollection of Arcadia: Conception and design in the *Rusticatio Mexicana*

(i) Reception of the poem

Prior to a *coup d'état* orchestrated by the United States' Central Intelligence Agency in 1954, Guatemala had enjoyed an exceptional decade of democracy and reform.[1] During those 'Ten Years of Spring', Rafael Landívar's contribution to his nation's literary heritage was officially recognised. Jorge Luis Arriola Ligorría, ambassador and champion of the 1944 revolution, located the poet's remains in Santa Maria delle Muratelle, and arranged their return from Bologna to Antigua. The year 1950, declared an *Año Landivariano* in honour of this event, saw the publication of a facsimile of the 1782 edition of the *Rusticatio Mexicana* in Guatemala and the foundation of a periodical dedicated to the study of Landívar.[2]

The *Rusticatio Mexicana* could have done little to establish its exiled author's reputation in his own lifetime, but Alexander von Humboldt referred to the poem in his *Political Essay on the Kingdom of New Spain*, printed in London in 1811 – less than twenty years after Landívar's death. Humboldt remarked that the eruption of the volcano of Jorullo in Michoacán was 'sung in hexameter verses by the Jesuit father Rafael Landívar'.[3] And in 1806, Juan María Maury had quoted a passage from the *Rusticatio Mexicana* in a note to his short narrative poem, *La agresión británica*, which was published in Madrid.[4] The Spanish literary historian, Marcelino Menéndez y Pelayo, claimed that his childhood reading of Maury's poem had aroused his 'immense curiosity to acquire and read' the *Rusticatio Mexicana*.[5] The work fully lived up to Menéndez y Pelayo's expectations. In his *Antología de poetas hispanoamericanos*, Spain's most eminent critic praised Rafael Landívar at length:

> He is one of the most excellent poets to be encountered in the domain of modern writing in Latin. We shall not hesitate to recognise in Father Landívar the astonishing qualities of a poet, who, in my judgement, failed only by not writing in the vernacular, so as to steal the palm from all the American poets in that category ... Not even in Rapin and Vanière do we find such fresh and ingenious inspiration, so great a richness of descriptive imagination, and so great a variety of forms and poetic resources ... The *Rusticatio* should not be considered as a poem that is restricted to agricultural themes like the four divine books of Virgil's *Georgics* ...it embraces

much more, by providing a complete picture of nature and country life in Northern America: a rich and extensive assembly of physical peculiarities and social customs that are not known in Europe.[6]

There are indications that the Bologna edition of Landívar's poem had been circulating in Mexico by the early 1800s, though it was probably Menéndez y Pelayo's influential commendation that more or less directly led to a number of excerpts from the *Rusticatio Mexicana* being translated into Spanish verse towards the end of the nineteenth century.[7] The first complete renderings were both produced in Mexico in 1924: a prose version in a bilingual edition by Ignacio Loureda and Federico Escobedo's popular verse translation entitled *Geórgicas Mexicanas* – the 'Mexican *Georgics*'.[8]

Rafael Landívar is still regarded as an important poet in Guatemala, and a university has been named after him, even though the subject of his principal work was *Mexican* country life. The playfully rococo subtitle of the 1781 edition also lays emphasis on this: 'Some rather scattered things gathered from the fields of Mexico and arranged into ten books by Rafael Landívar'.[9] The poet explained in his prefaces to both editions of the *Rusticatio Mexicana* that he had chosen his title because the poem was mostly about Mexico. 'But it is also', he added, 'because I realise that all of New Spain is commonly called by the name of 'Mexico' in Europe, with no account taken of the different kingdoms.'[10] In fact the poem will refer to various parts of America: the third book is entirely devoted to Guatemala; and Landívar's verse dedication is addressed to his birthplace, the former Guatemalan capital, Santiago de los Caballeros. Those dedicatory verses, which convey the poet's nostalgia for his city (envisaged as a phoenix rising from the ruins of the 1773 earthquake) have been translated from Latin into the indigenous American languages of Quiché, Cakchiquel, and even Quechua, as well as into French, German, and Italian.[11]

A sense of pan-Hispanic cultural pride, which goes beyond any particular national enthusiasm, helps to account for the attention given to the *Rusticatio Mexicana* in the Spanish-speaking world.[12] Indeed the mistaken assumption that Landívar originally wrote the work in Spanish is not at all uncommon. The poem has certainly received far more critical acclaim than any other Latin text composed in the colonial period, and no assessment of the *Rusticatio Mexicana* can disregard its author's origins or the territories that are its subject. As a consequence, attempts to establish the work's merit on purely artistic grounds are bound to beg the question of whether a disinterested critical verdict is conceivable in a case like this. A major purpose, perhaps *the* major purpose, of the *Rusticatio Mexicana* was to impress upon European readers the wonder, beauty, and wealth of its author's American homeland. Even today the poem's literary value is to some extent bound up with its success in achieving that end.

(ii) Ancient and early modern influences

Shortly after Landívar begins his poem, he asserts that his themes are new and unprecedented. This assertion is made in an invocation to Apollo which could not be more classical in style:[13]

> Tu, qui concentus plectro moderaris eburno,
> Et sacras cantare doces modulamina Musas,
> Tu mihi vera quidem, sed certe rara canenti
> Dexter ades, gratumque melos largire vocatus.

You who play with an ivory plectrum and teach the holy Muses to sing in rhythmic measures, you are at my right hand side as I have called you to bestow on me a sweet melody, as I sing of things which are in fact true but indeed strange.

Rusticatio Mexicana 1.28-31

This novel subject matter – the geography, wildlife, traditions, and forms of production in the American countryside – will be enhanced by the poet's elegant display of humanist classical learning and Enlightenment scientific knowledge. The *Rusticatio Mexicana* draws from an astonishingly wide range of Greek and Roman authors including Homer, Hesiod, Lucretius, Horace, Ovid, Lucan, Pliny, and Apuleius; from prominent Renaissance humanists like Petrarch, Fracastoro, and Thomas More; and from later Latin writers as diverse as Melchior de Polignac and Athanasius Kircher. In his annotations to the poem Landívar also makes reference to Spanish vernacular poets, to natural historians of Europe and the New World, and to a number of other Jesuit scholars – some of whom were his compatriots or contemporaries.

The *Georgics* of Virgil provide the most obvious model for the idea of the *Rusticatio*. Virgil's classic accomplishment was at once a didactic poem about country life, a celebration of the land of Italy, and an ideological and ethical vision for Rome. Landívar's endeavour is comparably didactic: it imparts natural historical knowledge and techniques of cultivation and manufacture. And it is also driven by a moral commitment – to scientific investigation in tandem with Christian piety – which is tactfully conveyed throughout. But in place of Italy, Landívar commends the region of 'septentrional' America to the Italian readers of his own time.

Other features of the *Rusticatio Mexicana* were suggested by the *Georgics*. Like Virgil, Landívar devotes each individual book to a specific topic, and like Virgil, he is also prompted by those practical subjects to consider some broader concerns: urban life, war, miraculous events, and natural disasters. For Landívar, as for Virgil, mythology intrudes into the realm of lived experience: classical deities are invoked, and figures like Phoebus, Vulcan, and Bacchus personify aspects of the phenomenal world.[14] Landívar's presentation of the society of beavers in Book 6 of the *Rusticatio*

Mexicana exhibits an obvious debt to the description of the social life of bees in *Georgics* 4.149-250. Last but not least, Virgil provided Landívar with a poetic language, metre, and form. Federico Escobedo praised Landívar's imitation of Virgil's hexameters in the prologue to his 1924 translation: 'the imitation ... is not servile, but free and unencumbered.'[15] The *Rusticatio Mexicana* actually absorbs many more words and phrases from Virgil's *Aeneid* than it does from the *Georgics*.[16]

The Guatemalan critic José Mata Gavidia firmly dismissed what he called the 'the Virgilian myth': the view, prompted by Menéndez y Pelayo's assessment, that Landívar was an 'American Virgil'. For Mata Gavidia, who took into account the respective contexts in which Virgil and Landívar worked, such a comparison was far from apt:

> Virgil in the *Georgics* is the poet of the ideal of what the Roman citizen *ought to be* as he returns to farming; Landívar is the poet of the American countryside as it is. Virgil in the *Georgics* seeks to bring the Romans to a life in the country that is already lost, as he wants to incline them to the glorious agricultural past. Landívar does not sing of what ought to be, but of the excellences of the present of Northern America, and its countryside, which is superior to the marvels of the old world. Virgil writes his work in the midst of comfort and his patrons' generosity; Landívar creates a work born of the bitterness of an exile.[17]

These observations check the temptation to compare Landívar directly with Virgil, but they do not in any way diminish the importance of the *Georgics* for the *Rusticatio Mexicana*. An impression of their influence can be modified, however, by consideration of some related Latin texts which would have affected the way a poet like Landívar read and regarded the *Georgics*.

Four Roman prose works on agriculture survive from antiquity: Cato the Censor's utilitarian but chaotic treatise *De agri cultura*, dating from the 160s BC; the *Res Rusticae* ('Country Matters'), an engaging dialogue composed in 37 BC by the polymath Marcus Terentius Varro; the twelve books of Columella's *Res Rustica,* produced in the 60s AD; and fourteen books by a sixth-century writer, Palladius Rutilius Taurus Aemilianus. These ancient agricultural authorities, who became known in the Renaissance as the '*scriptores rei rusticae*', were first published together in Venice in 1472, and that collection went through several reprintings. Cato and Varro were also independently anthologised in New Spain. Varro, praised in antiquity by Quintilian as the 'most erudite Roman of all', was especially venerated in the middle ages and the Renaissance: Petrarch hailed him as the third great luminary of Rome, after Cicero and Virgil.[18] Unexciting as these studies of farming from Roman antiquity may seem today, the classical idealisation of rustic life fascinated early modern readers and inspired a strong tradition of humanist Latin poetry on aspects of agriculture and country living.

3. Conception and design in the Rusticatio Mexicana

A seminal text in that tradition was the *Rusticus* ('The Countryman'), published in Florence during the 1480s by Angelo Ambrogini Poliziano, or 'Politian', the most renowned scholar of the Medici circle. The *Rusticus* was one of his *Silvae,* a series of Latin hexameter poems on literary subjects. Politian's work was evidently known in Mexico from the later 1500s: the *Silvae* in particular were widely read in European countries including Spain, and their popularity continued well into the eighteenth century.[19] Politian made a collation of the 1472 *editio princeps* of the *scriptores rei rusticae* from a codex in the library of San Marco in Florence – and Cato, Varro, and Columella supplemented Virgil and Hesiod as the key sources for his *Rusticus.*[20] As the *Rusticus* described and praised the life and activities of the countryman through the different seasons of the year in only 569 verses, the text was more morally didactic than technically instructive. Some scientific observation is communicated, but Politian's achievement really consists in his poetic virtuosity and knowledge of ancient literature about rustic life.

The portrait of the countryman in the *Rusticus* is an important model for the *Rusticatio Mexicana* in some more detailed respects. First, the *Rusticus* synthesised the prescriptions of Virgil's didactic poetry with the 'bucolic' or 'pastoral' modes of his *Eclogues*: the shepherd Tityrus (who represents Virgil) passes Politian a pipe and asks him to renew the 'Ascraean song' – the archaic verse of the Greek didactic poet Hesiod.[21] Landívar likewise blends didactic with pastoral (along with elements of epic) in his own composition: numerous phrases from Virgil's *Eclogues* are recalled, and some of those allusions are developed and sustained.[22] Secondly, Politian set a precedent for Landívar by accommodating a cosmopolitan range of sources in prose and verse which went far beyond Virgil, Hesiod, and the Roman *scriptores rei rusticae*: Lucretius, Pliny, Claudian, Julius Pollux, and Politian's own Italian poetry are among the influences involved.[23] And rather in the way Virgil originally professed to apply Hesiod's *Works and Days* to a new Roman scenario by composing the *Georgics* in the first place, Politian grafted the classical accounts of farming onto an idealised vision of the Tuscan countryside.[24] Landívar goes further still by transplanting ancient rustic lore to an exposition of country life in the New World.

Other humanist poets of the Italian Renaissance whose didactic works would have been known to Landívar include Giovanni Pontano and Marco Girolamo Vida.[25] However, two later neo-Latin poems, both published in Paris by French Jesuits and both read in New Spain in the 1700s, were very important for the *Rusticatio Mexicana*: René Rapin's four book poem on gardens, *Hortorum Libri IV* (1665), and Jacques Vanière's *Praedium Rusticum* ('The Country Estate'), which first appeared in 1707.[26] Though it followed Virgil's *Georgics* in form and structure, Rapin's *Horti* took into account the gardening fashions in his own time, as well as earlier developments in France in the mid-1500s. An idea of the sublime seems to have informed the close of Rapin's third book on the decorative use of water, where 'great sheets of water, and canals like rivers' are associated with a 'majesty' – which turns out to be the *majestas* of the Louis XIV himself.[27] Landívar too associates waterfalls with his own *criollo* appropriation of sublimity (discussed below at pp. 62-4).

Rapin's work is less redolent of the weightier Roman *scriptores* than the sixteen books of Vanière's *Praedium Rusticum* – although Vanière ranged far beyond his sources (which included Charles Estienne's earlier *Praedium Rusticum*, a Latin prose treatise on gardening produced in the later 1500s).[28] In the course of composing his verse *Praedium*, Vanière gradually came to eschew mythological illustrations and anecdotes. The tone of his poem is more solemnly didactic than that of the *Rusticatio Mexicana*, but alone of Landívar's literary influences Vanière has the special distinction – denied even to Virgil – of being openly acknowledged as a model. The epigraph on the frontispiece of the 1782 edition of the *Rusticatio Mexicana* was taken from the first book of the *Praedium Rusticum* and a second tribute is paid to Jacques Vanière in the actual text of Landívar's poem:[29]

> Quis tamen has memoret, postquam Vanierius omnes
> Providus implevit pretioso munere chortes,
> Aoniamque tulit, Phoebo plaudente, coronam?

> Who may tell of these [hens], now that provident Vanière has filled every poultry-yard with the generous gift of his song and carried away an Aonian crown, to Phoebus' applause?
>
> *Rusticatio Mexicana* 13.23-5

Landívar's apparently unprepossessing title, which can be translated awkwardly as 'Mexican Country Living', is supposed to signal both a debt to the earlier writers who addressed rustic subjects and an aspiration to contribute to a potent and vital current of early modern literature. Even if this brief survey of prototypes for the *Rusticatio Mexicana* can only give a limited impression of their presence in the poem, the complex genealogy of Landívar's project should at least be clear: it involves much more than the imitation of Virgil's *Georgics*. It is worth emphasising again that Landívar also draws from sources in modern vernacular languages as well as in Latin. The influence of those scientific sources is first made evident in the prose preface which complements the literary tone of the initial verse dedication. The expression of the *Rusticatio Mexicana* lies somewhere between the divergent styles of these two short prefatory texts, which will now be considered in turn.

(iii) Dedication to Guatemala City

At the beginning of this short composition, the poet visualises Guatemala from afar: 'how I enjoy rehearsing your delights in my *mind*' (*Quam juvat,*

Alma, animo pervolvere dotes 3); 'Now I *seem* to see your leafy mountains' (*Jam mihi frondosos videor discernere montes* 5). Landívar is recollecting features of his native territory that provide him with 'sweet relief in dire circumstances' (*inque arctis rebus dulce levamen* 14).[30] Such expressions in elegiac couplets recall the way Ovid envisaged Rome in his exile poetry.[31] An Ovidian resonance is especially conspicuous when Landívar snaps out of his reverie:

> Sed fallor: placidam, Ah versant ludibria mentem,
> Illuduntque animo somnia vana meo.

But I am deceived: my tranquil mind is shaken by the taunts of empty dreams that play with my heart.

Urbi Guatimalae 15-16

These lines themselves play a trick on readers familiar with the Roman poet. Anyone who detects this reminiscence might expect Landívar to turn (as Ovid would at this point) to the hardships of his exile. But Landívar does not mention his absence from his city. Instead he is concerned with the disappearance of the city itself, which is now 'a heap of stones', with no houses, no temples, no streets full of people. An earthquake destroyed Santiago de los Caballeros in 1773: a brief but harrowing account of the event is given later in *Rusticatio Mexicana* 3.47-60. Here in the dedication, the disaster is likened to everything being 'struck by the winged fires of Jove' (*Jovis alatis ignibus icta forent* 22). The comparison is appropriate enough, and probably rather more so than Ovid's use of similar words in *Tristia* 1.3.11 (*qui Jovis ignibus ictus*) to convey how he was *emotionally* affected by the decree which relegated him to Tomis from Rome.

Landívar's next verse takes another unexpected turn: 'But why do I grieve at this?' Expectations of a reference to exile are frustrated again. The poet's answer to his own question could not be more uplifting: 'Rising from the tomb are high buildings, lofty temples are soaring into the sky' (*Surgunt ... sepulcro* 24). This suggests Christian resurrection, and other religious intimations are latent:

> Jamque optata venit civibus alma quies.

Now comes the bountiful peace the citizens longed for.

Urbi Guatimalae 26

The theological import of the famous words *Jam redit et Virgo* ('Now returns the Virgin'), from Virgil, *Eclogue* 4.6 might be in play – that pagan coinage acquired a Christian significance because Virgil's fourth 'Messianic' Eclogue was long thought to have predicted the birth of Christ. The word *alma* ('bountiful') which has associations with maternity, was earlier used of Guatemala in verse 3. The poet's 'dear Parent, sweet Guatemala'

(1) is, like Mary, a 'parent coming back to life' (*rediviva Parens* 29), and, in the phrase 'a manifest triumph *born* from sudden death' (*clarum subita partum de morte triumphum* 31), the word *partum* connotes childbirth.

The theme of maternity was prominent in Landívar's funeral declamation for Archbishop Figueredo, and the Virgin Mary was the subject of his short poems. But further associations are made here between the city of Guatemala and the Virgin Mary. The Assumption of the Virgin, which commemorates the passage of Mary's body and soul to heaven – one of the most important feast days in the Roman Catholic calendar – falls on 15 August. The hopeful significance of the Assumption, only two weeks after the 1773 earthquake on 29 July, would not have been lost on survivors of the catastrophe. Two years before, Landívar's own mother had died during the octave of that feast, on 18 August 1771 – something which could well be relevant to this composition. There is a more delicate connection to the Virgin in these lines of the *Urbi Guatimalae*. A description of newly built temples rising up to the sky and an image of springs swelling into a river had also been conjoined in Alegre's verses to the Virgin of Guadalupe at the end of his *Alexandriad*:

> Anthius, ac placidis foecundat jugera limphis,
> Et Guadalupaei surgunt felicia templi
> Culmina, pinnatoque minantur in aethera clivo.

And [the river] Anthius makes the hills fertile with its peaceful waters, and the turrets of the Guadalupan temple rise and push into heaven on a winged ascent.

Alegre, *Alexandriad* 4.581-3

Landívar would have known these verses about the construction of the temple to the Virgin in Mexico.[32] Possibly they prompted him to hail the city of Guatemala as a 'spring and source of life' (*vitae fons, et origo* 2), and a connection between the Virgin and running water is made much more fully in Book 12, on *Fontes* ('Springs'). There, a description of the healing powers of the salt springs near the shrine of the Virgin of Guadalupe is followed by an account of their role in the Virgin's miraculous apparition (12.12-56).

A number of thematic elements in the *Urbi Guatimalae* recur in the *Rusticatio Mexicana* – Landívar's implicit references to his exile are among them. This opening poem is thus endowed with a programmatic significance. The resurrection of his city as 'Mother' is a 'manifest triumph' (*clarum ... triumphum* 31), born out of sudden death which the poet seeks to celebrate on his lyre (*plectrum ... Accipe* 33-4). That is echoed in the *Appendix* by the celebration of Christ's resurrection, before God as 'Father':

3. Conception and design in the Rusticatio Mexicana

Tu sola Omnipotens summi Sapientia *Patris*,
Provida quae toto terrarum ludis in orbe
Cuncta regens uno mundi confinia nutu,
Dextra fave, dum *plectra* manu percussa trementi
Certa tui celebrant *clari* monimenta *triumphi*.

You alone, Omnipotent Wisdom of the supreme *Father*, who are providently at play in all the lands of the earth, ruling over all the confines of the world with a single nod, be gracious, as my *plectrum*, struck by my trembling right hand celebrates the unfailing memorial of your *manifest triumph*.

Appendix 16-20

In this and other ways the supplementary beginning of the work is linked to the account of the Cross of Tepic in Mexico at the end.[33]

The term 'Appendix' belies the importance of that final section, as it brings the whole composition to a formal close and also recalls the dedication which first heralded it. Taken together, the dedication and *Appendix* nicely epitomise the spatial and topical range of the entire poem: the city of Guatemala offers a contrast to the rural location of Tepic, which has no large or impressive buildings (*App.* 33-43). Other features shared by these opening and closing texts characterise other aspects of the *Rusticatio Mexicana*: a strong devotional element (*App.* 11-20); reference to the poet's own sorrows – and to song as a remedy for them (*Urb. Guat.* 33-4, *App.* 101); and the benign hopes expressed for his addressees – the poet who promised the inhabitants of Guatemala City a peaceful future (*Urb. Guat.* 23-34) later urges a youth to cast aside past ideas in favour of 'new' Enlightenment thought (*App.* 94-112).

Finally, the curious action of beginning a study of the countryside with the mention of a *city* has a very significant precedent: Tityrus' enthusiastic description of Rome to Meliboeus, in the first of Virgil's *Eclogues*. Indeed an observation on the *Rusticatio Mexicana* by Antony Higgins – that it was 'presented as the fruit of a humanist labour to be offered in the service of a city envisaged as the capital of a state' – could just as well apply to that encomium of Rome in Virgil's pastoral poem.[34] Even so, Mexico City generally looms large in the poetry of New Spain. In particular, it was the subject of *La Grandeza Mexicana* (1604), a celebrated vernacular panegyric in eight 'chapters' by Bernardo de Balbuena.[35] It is no accident that the history of the *Urbs Mexicus* (1.32) is the very first topic to be addressed in the first book of the *Rusticatio Mexicana*.

(iv) The defences in the Preface

The scholarly tone of Landívar's prose preface stands in contrast to the more personal expression of his poetic dedication. The poet first explains his use of the word *Mexicana* in the title (see (i) earlier in this chapter) before laying stress on the veridical quality of his work. What he will

51

relate, he says, he has either seen himself, or ascertained on the authority of reliable eyewitnesses. This assertion is strikingly similar to one that can be found in the preface to another book on the natural history of Chile, by another Spanish American Jesuit, Juan Ignacio Molina:

> I have seen and observed constantly the things that I state. Not content with my own judgment, I have consulted impartial writers, worthy of respect for their knowledge, who have been [to America], and they endorse all my observations.[36]

Molina's *Saggio sulla storia naturale del Chili* came out in Bologna in 1782 – the very same city and year in which the second, extended version of the *Rusticatio Mexicana* was published. Molina's preface was a pointed response to the criticisms of America by Europeans, including De Pauw, who had never travelled there – and his essay was effectively a *defence* of Chile and the Americas. Landívar is more tactful, just as he was in giving his reason for his choice of title: he merely hinted at European ignorance of New Spain. Nonetheless, his appeal to the value of eyewitness accounts indicates that he, like Molina, saw autoptic testimony as the best response to the anti-American polemics of Buffon, De Pauw, and others.[37]

Next Landívar expresses two caveats. The first is an admission that he could have said more about mines. Mining did have an important role in the economy and society of colonial Mexico and had also come to be a common subject of neo-Latin didactic poetry, but still this remark is odd.[38] Few would expect a detailed treatment of the industry in a poem about *rusticatio* – i.e. country living or husbandry. The account of gold and silver mining in Book 7 and the subsequent book, on processing the metals, appear to provide adequate coverage. Landívar's second caveat is no less curious:

> Lector benevole, te monitum velim, more me poetico locuturum, quotiescumque inanium Antiquitatis numinum mentio inciderit.

> Kind Reader, I would like you to be advised that I will be talking in a poetic way every time mention is made of the meaningless divine powers of Antiquity.
>
> *Monitum*

As Greek and Roman deities had adorned Christian humanist poetry since the 1300s, such a proviso seems rather unnecessary. One possible reason for this declaration could be that Landívar is seeking to mark the divergence of his own poetic practice from the more literal style of his predecessor, the Jesuit didactic poet, Jacques Vanière.[39]

The last part of the *Monitum* is concerned with the way in which the poem's content is to be expressed. The writer emphasises that he has above all striven for clarity in his ambitious attempt to convey difficult material in Latin verse, and that he has reworked or 'recalled to the anvil' his coverage of subjects that are more widely known. The image of the anvil and Landívar's characterisation of his procedure here ('making several changes, adding some things, removing others') reflect precisely the methods of composition recommended by Horace:

> Quintilio si quid recitares, 'corrige, sodes,
> hoc', aiebat, 'et hoc'. melius te posse negares
> bis terque expertum frustra, delere iubebat
> et male tornatos incudi reddere versus.

> If you were to read anything out to Quintilius, he would say 'Correct this, if you don't mind – and this.' Should you say you could do no better after making two or three vain attempts, he would ask you to destroy them and take your badly turned verses back to the anvil.
>
> Horace, *Ars Poetica* 438-41

Horace also attacks 'ambitious ornament', ambiguous phrasing, and obscurity a few lines later (*Ars* 447-9). Landívar is aligning his own poetic principles with those advanced in the *Ars Poetica* – that text had come to be a talisman as much as a manual of Neoclassical poetics. The *Monitum* closes with two elegiac couplets quoted from a 'Golmarius Marsiglianus' which lament the difficulty of conveying topics in a metre that might resist the subject matter.[40]

The general principles of the *Monitum* are reflected in Landívar's poem; and its academic tone is echoed in the poet's own annotations to the text. Those notes can explain references by adding further details of nomenclature and topography, they can affirm the writer has seen the things he describes, or else they cite – often at length – respectable authorities to substantiate certain observations: the *Dictionnaire raisonné universel d'histoire naturelle* published in 1768-9 by Jacques-Christophe Valmont de Bomare is a favoured source.[41] Occasionally, the notes justify or explain Landívar's Latin usage – again this seems to be in order to anticipate and avert possible criticism – and they clearly display the writer's close knowledge of the language.[42] Through those annotations, which originally appeared as footnotes below the pages of the actual text in the 1782 printing, the author probably sought to regulate, to some degree at least, the responses of readers to his poem.

(v) Epic structure and scientific form

The strategies Landívar used to win over his readers in Italy evidently succeeded: the second edition of the poem appeared only one year after the first. A coda to the 1781 text indicates that the poet had anyway planned to extend the original length of the *Rusticatio Mexicana* for the second edition, from ten books to fifteen.[43] The *Appendix* of 112 verses was also added. The sequence of topics of the books in that definitive second edition is curious at first sight: Mexican lakes, volcanoes, Guatemalan waterfalls, cochineal and purple, indigo, beavers, silver and gold mines, processing of silver and gold, sugar, horses and cattle, flocks and herds, springs, birds, wild animals, and games.

All that can be discerned from such a list are certain clusterings: features of physical geography in Books 1-3; processes of production and manufacture in 4-9 with the exception of 6 (though the beavers treated in that book are industrious creatures); animals in 10-14 (with the exception of 12 which is about springs) and a description of local sports and games in 15. The system of organisation can be explained by a comparison of these contents with those of the first edition of the poem:

First edition: Modena 1781	*Second edition: Bologna 1782*	
	Dedicatory verses to Guatemala City	
Monitum: Preface (4 paragraphs)	*Monitum*: Preface (5 paragraphs)	
	Librorum Index: Titles of books	
	Argumenta: Summary of poem	
	Errata	
Book 1: Mexican Lakes	Book 1: Mexican Lakes	[*Lacus Mexicani*]
Book 2: Jorullo (volcanoes)	Book 2: Jorullo (volcanoes)	[*Xorulus*]
Book 3: Guatemalan Waterfalls	Book 3: Guatemalan Waterfalls	[*Cataractae Guatimalenses*]
Book 4: Cochineal and Purple	Book 4: Cochineal and Purple	[*Coccum, et purpura*]
	Book 5: Indigo	[*Indicum*]
Book 5: Beavers	Book 6: Beavers	[*Fibri*]
Book 6: Silver and gold mines	Book 7: Silver and gold mines	[*Fodinae argenti atque auri*]
Book 7: Silver & gold refining	Book 8: Silver & gold refining	[*Argenti, atque auri opificium*]
	Book 9: Sugar	[*Saccharum*]
	Book 10: Horses/Cattle	[*Armenta*]
	Book 11: Herds/Flocks	[*Greges*]
	Book 12: Springs	[*Fontes*]
Book 8: Birds	Book 13: Birds	[*Aves*]
Book 9: Wild animals	Book 14: Wild animals	[*Ferae*]
Book 10: Games	Book 15: Games	[*Ludi*]
	Appendix: The Cross of Tepic	[*Crux Tepicensis*]

The first edition roughly followed a tripartite scheme (Landscape – Production – Zoology/Ethnography), which was loosened by the addition of extra books for the second edition. It may be relevant that other full length poems in Latin by Landívar's Mexican contemporaries set little store by traditional conventions of length and arrangement: Abad's *De Deo* was also composed in instalments, and Alegre's *Alexandriad* breaks from standard classical practice by treating its martial subject in only four short books.

In any case, the *Rusticatio Mexicana* should certainly not be regarded as a farraginous assemblage. The poet specifically indicates the order of his narrative (*RM* 1.7-17; 7.1-5; *App.* 1-10), as if he is taking his addressee on a virtual excursion. The text is supposed to be read in a linear way, in the sequence in which it is presented, like a lecture course in which elements of information are presented, neither chronologically nor according to their actual importance, but so that they can be best enjoyed and comprehended by those listening. The first few books soon establish some crucial points of reference. They provide a basic mapping of Mexico and Guatemala, with details of flora, fauna, history, and culture. The important tales of the two cities of Mexico (1.32-6) and Guatemala (3.11-60) are told early on (with some formulaic parallels between them); the city of Oaxaca is described as well (4.12-15).

At least one thematic device in the poem works to give the impression of an overarching structure. *Katabases* or journeys to the world of the dead mark the midpoint of the stories of Homer's *Odyssey* and Virgil's *Aeneid*. The third of the six books of Lucretius' didactic poem *De rerum natura* ('On the Nature of Things') is also concerned with death and the mortality of the soul. Landívar pays homage to these distinguished precedents by inserting a journey to the Underworld in a central book of his own poem. The introduction to the account of gold and silver mining is as follows:

> Nunc coelum linquo, nunc terrae lapsus ad ima
> Aggredior cantu, Plutonis regna, fodinas;
> Regna refulgenti semper radiata metallo,
> Et quae divitiis complerunt prodiga mundum.
>   Tu, qui pennatis telluris viscera plantis
> Saepe subis, clara munitus lampade dextram
> Advenias, monstresque viam, lumenque ministres
> Obsecro ...

Now I leave the light of heaven, now descending to the lower parts of the earth with my song, I come upon the realms of Pluto, the mines, realms ever gleaming with shining metal, and which abundantly supply the world with wealth.

   You, as you often go down to the bowels of the earth on winged feet, I beg you to come equipped with a clear torch, to show the way and provide a light...

Rusticatio Mexicana 7.6-13

Virgil's invocation of the gods of the underworld in *Aeneid* 6.264-7 appears to be echoed in these lines, and the darkness of the mine will enable Landívar to recall further poetic devices from the sixth book of the *Aeneid*. His account of mining correspondingly constituted the *sixth* book of the original 1781 edition of the *Rusticatio Mexicana*. The figure of the torch-bearer addressed in the passage quoted above also sustains this evocation of the classical Underworld. By his winged feet, the figure is recognisable as Mercury, who functioned as the mediator between the dead and the living; appropriately enough, the god also supervised the circulation of goods and commodities.[44] But Landívar's plea to the torch-bearer most obviously recalls the invocation of Epicurus from the proem of Lucretius' book on death:

> E tenebris tantis tam clarum extollere lumen
> Qui primus potuisti inlustrans commoda vitae,
> Te sequor, O Graiae gentis decus, inque tuis nunc
> Ficta pedum pono pressis vestigia signis

You, who out of such great darkness first managed to raise so great a light, illuminating the benefits of life, I follow you, O glory of the Greek race, and I now firmly plant my own steps along the trail you laid down.

Lucretius, *De rerum natura* 3.1-4

This metaphor of illumination is quite appropriate for Landívar, given that the Epicurean scientific principles advanced in the *De rerum natura* had such importance for the Enlightenment. And that particular Lucretian evocation is especially appropriate to headline a book about the excavation of precious metals, since Lucretius had emphatically declared in the very same proem (*De rerum natura* 3.12-13), that Epicurus' words were *golden* (*aurea dicta, aurea*). The close of Landívar's *katabasis* on mining also sustains his own application of Lucretius' mock-heroic mode, by listing the crimes of those who occupy a new version of Tartarus: the wayward occupants of this subterranean realm are all very much alive (7.302-19).[45]

A basic structural feature is also discernible in the individual books of the *Rusticatio*. The books are informally divided into smaller blocks of verse of uneven length, mostly consisting of between 10 and 25 hexameters. In the 1782 text, a paragraph indentation marks the beginning of each such segment. Later editors, including Regenos (in this volume), set apart these groupings of verses, as if they were stanzas. This is justified because Landívar himself conceived of these groupings in a lengthy analytic breakdown of the whole poem.[46] An impression of this can be given by an excerpt from the first part of the *Argumentum* for Book 14:

> *Facta propositione, & invocatione, a v. 1. ad 8. sylva describitur, a 9. ad 14.*
> *Bobis jubati* (Cibolo) *descriptio, ejusque furoris, a 15. ad 35. eum venandi ratio, a 36. ad 50.*

> Propositio and invocatio pronounced, from verse 1 to 8. A wood is described, from 9 to 14.
> Description of the maned ox (*bison*), and of its fierce temper, from 15 to 35. Method of hunting it, from 36 to 50.

Vernacular equivalents (in Spanish, Italian, or Mesoamerican languages) of some Latin words are the only data in the *Argumenta* which are not always supplied in the poem. As they are of thus little benefit to English readers, the *Argumenta* have not been included in this volume.

However, the technical terms – *propositio* and *invocatio* – which are employed in Landívar's analytic resumés, to anatomise the opening verses of each book, offer a very important general insight. A *propositio* was the term for the statement of what was to be covered or proven in a lecture or treatise; the *invocatio,* to a god, muse, or tutelary deity, is a common feature of poetic literature.[47] The beginning of every book in the *Rusticatio* thus initiates a dialectic between two kinds of writing: the intellectual discourse of science and natural history on the one hand, and the artistic and more subjective discourse of poetry on the other. This paradigm for the individual books reflects the way the work as a whole fluctuates between the sober protocols of the introductory *Monitum* and the more emotional tone of the dedicatory elegiacs to Guatemala City.

The opening of Book 4 nicely illustrates the complexities of interaction between the knowledge conveyed and the art which conveys it. First, the *propositio*:

> Postquam Neptuni vitreos invisimus agros,
> Regnaque Vulcani tremulis armata favillis,
> Visere fert animus roseum cum Murice Coccum,
> Ac totum fixis oculis lustrare laborem.

Now we have seen Neptune's crystal fields and the realms of Vulcan armed with restless embers, my spirit moves me to view the rosy cochineal and murex, and to fix the gaze of my eyes on their toil.

Rusticatio Mexicana 4.1-4

The language referring to the volcanos and waterfalls of the preceding books is conspicuously elevated. The expression *fert animus* ('my spirit moves me') echoes the first verse of Ovid's *Metamorphoses*.[48] Conversely, the subsequent *invocatio* to the goddess Minerva, though it includes a reference to the myth of Arachne, soon turns to some rather technical questions:

> Tu, quae puniceo, Tritonia Virgo, colore
> Intextos auro Regum perfundis amictus,
> Et Lydam laetaris acu vicisse puellam;
> Dic mihi, quae dederit regio tibi provida fucos
> Atque orbem Cocco, tyrioque impleverit Ostro;
> Quis legat haec campis, quae mittant semina terrae,
> Et quo nascantur regalia germina cultu.

You, Tritonian Maiden, who perfuse with a purple hue the garments of kings interwoven with gold, and who delight in having defeated the Lydian girl at the needle, tell me what region provided your dyes and filled the world with

cochineal and Tyrian purple, tell me who gathers them in the fields, what
lands put forth the seeds, and by what process these regal shoots may grow.
Rusticatio Mexicana 4.5-11

The *propositiones* and *invocationes* are subject to as much fluctuation as
the material they preface. The literary allusion to Arachne's downfall in
this invocation (the Lydian maiden lost a weaving contest with Minerva,
who turned her into a spider) will bear on the technical content of Book 4.[49]
It is emphasised later (4.94-123) that the vengeful spider, actually referred
to as *Arachne* (4.116), poses the most constant, lethal threat to the
precious cochineal beetles.

The two features of the *Rusticatio Mexicana* that have been highlighted
here – its oscillation between technical and poetic modes and the subdivi-
sion of its constituent books into small segments – are designed to secure
and maintain the reader's attention as the poem adheres to its educational
agenda. The fluctuation between the two modes provides ornament and
variety, whilst the segmentation of the text achieves a cinematic effect,
allowing the same subjects to be treated from different perspectives – from
distant historical or spatial vantage points, as well as in 'close-up'. The
segmentation also allows the poet to abandon a topic briefly, and then
return to it: adversative words (*sed, tamen, interea*) often mark the beginning of such smaller units of the poem.

Although Landívar offers many compelling vignettes, there are no
stories comparable to the mythological digressions in Roman didactic
poetry – such as the Aristaeus epyllion in Virgil's *Georgics* or the An-
dromeda interlude in Manilius' *Astronomica*.[50] However, a sustained
narrative is used in the second book of the *Rusticatio Mexicana* to convey
the effect of a volcanic eruption.[51] An unknown old man appears in the
region of Jorullo to prophesy its destruction. Some of his words echo Virgil:
'I see rocks of fire, horrid rocks of fire, rolling across the fields' (*RM* 2.76).[52]
The seer's white beard and coarse clothing bring to mind the image of an
Old Testament prophet: he is later compared to Jonah (2.92-3), who was
also unknown in Nineveh.[53] The stranger's prediction is couched in classical language (2.71-7). At the same time, this very use of calendrical
knowledge recalls the methods of divination practised in Mesoamerica
before the Spanish conquest. So it is appropriate that the *indigenous*
countrymen (*indigenae*) pay heed to the stranger's words, which are
spread through neighbouring towns and cities by the winged figure of
Rumour. But none of this impresses the *criollo* landowner (*colonus*). In his
own speech, which is based on Ascanius' reproach to the Trojan women in
Aeneid 5.670-3, he rebukes the natives for their 'feminine' cowardice in
seeking to leave behind their ancestral homes and gods (2.104-11). The
landowner's oration has barely finished when the earth is heard to groan
and the fearful catastrophe begins (2.114-27). A priest makes the third and
final speech (2.151-6), urging the people to obey heaven's will and avoid

imminent death by taking flight.[54] The narrator's factual account of the eruption that follows (2.184-94) is supported by the empirical observations in Landívar's notes to this passage.

This miniature epic is principally modelled on Virgil's account of the fall of Troy, although other classical sources – notably Lucretius, Lucan, and Pliny – heighten its impact.[55] The speaking personages are there to offer a succession of human perspectives on the natural catastrophe: Landívar artfully does not give them names or flesh out their identities. The dramatic narrative is subordinated to the argument of the second book – and it is telling that readers never seem to feel the absence of speaking characters in the other books of the poem. The combination of pace and variety removes the need for elaborate digressions or dramatic interludes in the *Rusticatio Mexicana*.

(vi) Exile and the poet's voice

Landívar's poetic persona is a construction of elegant simplicity, inconspicuous enough to facilitate engagement with some very technical topics. The narrator is sometimes explicitly located in Italy (2.301, *App.* 100), sometimes implicitly (e.g. 1.32, 12.277-82, 14.17). On other occasions he situates himself in an American location: for example in Book 13, he seems to be directly encountering the birds he describes. Occasionally, the poet seems to place his addressee in the settings he conjures up, and the use of the second-person singular is particularly dense in some books, e.g. 7 and 14. As well as securing, again, a rich variety of approaches to the subjects addressed, these rhetorical modifications make the voice of the poet more enigmatic and harder to fathom. In this regard, it is worth considering the extent to which innovative use of the first person had long been a characteristic of vernacular Spanish poetry and prose.

Rafael Landívar is often regarded as a writer of exile poetry. This could be because awareness of his historical position – as a victim of colonial oppression – has affected the assessment of his literary achievement. The Spanish word for an 'exile', *destierro,* literally means 'one who is torn from the land': a word which has all the more poignancy when applied to the writer of a poem *about* land. Nonetheless, it is important to realise that the issue of exile is never very directly addressed in the *Rusticatio Mexicana*.[56] Landívar does not write autobiographically, and he certainly does not indulge in the mannered self-fashioning that is so characteristic of Ovid's plangent poems from the Black Sea. Instead he refers in more general terms to his 'grief' or *cura,* and always counterbalances such references by immediately turning to the more heartening consideration of his poetic enterprise – implying that it is the solution to his predicament. (1.18-27, 12.277-89, *App.* 94-101). This bears out a common observation about the condition of exile: 'habits of life, expression, or activity in the new environment inevitably occur against the memory of these things in another environment ... both the new and the old environments are vivid, actual, occurring contrapuntally'.[57]

The latter part of Book 2 of the *Rusticatio Mexicana* provides an example of this 'contrapuntal' interaction. Having recounted the disastrous effects of volcanic eruptions on the valley of Jorullo, the poet describes how – as he was composing verses by the river Reno in an attempt to distract himself from his preoccupations (2.300-1) – he witnessed the city of Bologna being overturned by an earthquake. The ensuing chaos and panic offer a parallel to the aftermath of the calamity in Mexico described earlier. Landívar seeks to explain the new Italian catastrophe in poetic terms: Mount Vesuvius is characterised as 'begrudging' Bologna's stability, after having laid Naples to waste so many times. This aetiology is then underlined by a more scientific argument. Vesuvius, we are told, directs his fire, personified by Vulcan, to follow a vein of sulphur through a series of subterranean passages until it reaches a cavern beneath Bologna. The combustible gases compressed there are then ignited. The theory resembles some Greco-Roman accounts of volcanic activity, which had been synthesised by early modern scholars, including the seventeenth-century German Jesuit polymath Athanasius Kircher – an enormously influential thinker in New Spain.[58]

However, Landívar substantiates his theory by appealing to a precedent witnessed in Mexico: the volcanic mountain of Colima became dormant only to send a stream of fire underground which prompted Jorullo to erupt seventy miles away. Book 2 ends with a prayer to the Virgin Mary, petitioning her to provide help and comfort to the people of Bologna. Landívar's use of 'we' and 'our' (2.312, 341) in relation to the Italian city has been overlooked: here the poet clearly signals his involvement with the fortunes of his adopted home.[59] This could not stand in stronger contrast to the way Ovid distanced himself from Tomis and sometimes caricatured its inhabitants.[60] Landívar's experience of a calamity in the New World has informed his intellectual understanding of a natural disaster in Europe, as well as deepening the sense of compassion that would be engendered by such a catastrophe: the earthquake in Guatemala had occurred only eight years before the seismic activity which shook Bologna in 1781.

Exile poetry can be determined by literary convention as well as by individual experience: 'exile, far from rendering the writer impotent ... allows the purest functioning of the writer as a writer.'[61] In the case of Ovid, this functioning was largely accomplished by the poet's formulation and reformulation of personal responses to his predicament. Landívar, on the other hand, seeks to write rather more directly and referentially about the processes and phenomena which he is no longer able to witness or perceive. This quality of the *Rusticatio Mexicana* can be aligned with the paradox of poetic representation itself – which has been understood since antiquity as an attempt to render present what is absent. For Rafael

Landívar, exile has far more importance as a creative mechanism than it does as a subject or theme.

(vii) Functions of the sublime

It was noted in Chapter 1 that Landívar's Mexican contemporaries Francisco Xavier Alegre and Agustín Pablo de Castro were familiar with the ancient Greek rhetorical theorist known as 'Longinus'. Longinus' account of genius ventured to explain why 'divine' writers abandon precision of detail to seek excellence: nature (*physis*) itself implants in our minds 'an irresistible desire for what is great and, in relation to ourselves, supernatural (*daimoniôterou*)'. Longinus continued:

> The universe therefore is not wide enough for the range of human speculation and intellect. Our thoughts often travel beyond the boundaries of our surroundings. If anyone wants to know what we were born for, let him look round at life and contemplate the splendour, the grandeur, and beauty in which it everywhere abounds. It is a natural inclination that leads us to admire not the little streams, however pellucid and however useful, but the Nile, the Danube, the Rhine, and above all the Ocean. Nor do we feel so much awe before the little flame we kindle, because it keeps its light clear and pure, as before the fires of heaven, though they are often obscured. We do not think our flame more worthy of admiration than the craters of Etna, whose eruptions bring up rocks and whole hills out of the depths, and sometimes pour forth rivers of the earth-born, spontaneous fire.[62]

These remarks are not in complete harmony with the message of the *Rusticatio Mexicana*, but there are some obvious affinities. The travel of thoughts – from one location to another – is a fundamental element of the poem. Whilst bathetic descriptions of small creatures, humble livelihoods, or local topography show Landívar's capacity to see the world in a grain of sand, the accounts of lakes, volcanoes, and waterfalls in the first three books of the poem present majestic and sometimes terrifying geographical features. The poet strives to excite wonder in his readers at unusual, extraordinary phenomena – even when, as he declares at the end of the *Monitum*, it is a challenge to convey them in poetic language.

Longinus' treatise not only illuminates Landívar's poetic activity; it may have done much to inspire it. For Longinus, sublimity was both a condition for, and an index of, greatness in poetry or prose which enabled a writer or speaker to stun or transport his audience. *On the Sublime* is principally devoted to an exposition of the *sources* of sublimity. The two most important sources are both endowed by nature: great thoughts and noble emotion. Longinus then identifies the effective use of rhetorical figures, of diction, and of arrangement as the three technical sources. Although the idea of sublimity has its origin in earlier Greek and Roman rhetorical theory, it is without a precise parallel in classical thought:

Longinian sublimity extends beyond oratory to provide a criterion of quality for literature more generally, and considerable emphasis is placed on the importance of individual talent.

During the eighteenth century the sublime gathered a new momentum and new meanings, quite disengaged from Longinus' original formulation. The enlarged category of the sublime helped poets and other literary authors to articulate the sense of wonder engendered by awe-inspiring scenes and natural phenomena, which were too unruly or irregular to conform to the order and unity that constituted the classical idea of beauty.[63] And in the wake of Edmund Burke's *Enquiry into the Origin of our Ideas on the Sublime and the Beautiful* (1757) and Kant's *Critique of Judgment* (1790), the sublime facilitated the individual's disinterested contemplation of both art and nature.[64] It thus helped to bring about a transition from conformity to poetic norms (the hallmark of Neoclassicism) to a more individually oriented aesthetic (which characterises Romanticism). The ideological bearing of such later cultural and intellectual developments of the sublime on the literature of colonial New Spain in general, and on the work of Landívar in particular, has been explored in depth by Antony Higgins.[65]

Nonetheless, Alegre and Landívar were still bound by something closer to the ancient formulation of sublimity, whether or not that was mediated to them by their reading of Boileau's 1672 translation of Longinus.[66] These Jesuits would have thus regarded the sublime as an adjunct to Neoclassical Horatian poetic theory, and not as something that destabilised it. At the same time, other influences would have been in play. First, Landívar would have aligned Longinus' natural sources of sublimity with *ingenio*, the Baroque concept of authorial talent and wit – derived from the Latin *ingenium*, which Horace himself contrasted with a poet's training and technique.[67] Secondly, Rafael Landívar is bound to have been alert to the *theological* significance of the sublime, as it was indicated, on more than one occasion, by Longinus – who though a writer of pagan antiquity apparently quoted from the book of Genesis (*On the Sublime* 9.9) and also declared that 'sublimity raises us towards the spiritual greatness of god' (*On the Sublime* 35). In his *Appendix*, Landívar fuses the apprehension of the sublime with religious revelation. This is highlighted by the simile he uses to convey the effect of seeing the natural formation of a cross outside the village of Tepic. With its artful word order, the simile aspires to the sublimity of the phenomenon it seeks to illustrate:

> Ceu quondam celso sublata cacumine montis
> Arbore laeta viret, lucoque obscura nigranti
> Tot tibi densa cruces offert, quot robora, sylva.

Just as a forest, exalted on a lofty mountain peak, joyfully green with trees

yet darkened by its black grove, presents you with crosses, as many as there
are tree trunks in its dense foliage.

Appendix 53-5

The juxtaposition of *celso* ('lofty') with *sublata* ('exalted') reinforces the
suggestion that these two words have a reflexive, metapoetic significance.
Rafael Landívar's own experience of the natural world must have affected
his response to Longinus' account of sublimity. Very probably he connected
physical nature quite directly with the 'natural' sources of sublimity. This
is not unwarranted by a reading of Longinus' text: cognates of the same
Greek word, *physis,* are used for both conceptions, and illustrations from
the natural world are frequently employed to characterise successful
effects in classical poetry and oratory.

Landívar is as much concerned with the awe that nature can inspire as
he is with any practical purposes it may serve. His explanation for the
appearance of a rainbow over the waterfall at San Pedro Mártir ends with
Phoebus' admiration of its effect: *ostentat varios, Phoebo mirante, colores*
(3.267). This is followed by an account of the water's progress out of a
cavern and over a steep precipice on its course to the Pacific Ocean. Every
year at winter the 'noble' youth of Guatemala hurry to wonder at the sight
(3.278-80).[68] The intensity of the contemplation of the scene by the young
men is given considerable emphasis:

> Concava suspenso perlustrent lumine saxa.
> Omnia mirantur, montemque, amnemque, specusque.
> Ore tamen presso nutus, et signa sequuntur,
> Sive salutatum pubes exoptet amicum,
> Seu velit ad tectum prono jam Sole reverti.

They scan the vaulted chamber by the light of a hanging lantern. They
admire everything: the mountain, the river, the cavern. But they suppress
their voices and follow only nods and gestures, if a young man should desire
to greet a friend or to return home at sunset.

Rusticatio Mexicana 3.283-7

Here the apprehension of natural wonder renders spoken language unnecessary, even undesirable. The idea of silence leads associatively to the
peroration that closes the book. The poet urges the peoples of Egypt to
'keep silent' about their green fields enriched by the Nile (3.288-9) and he
also insists that the ancient world in general should keep silent about its
seven wonders (3.290-1): the Guatemalan valley is what provides the
ultimate *locus amoenus.*

The preference Landívar expresses here for his native country over the
region of the Nile is significant. On two previous occasions in Book 3, he
used illustrations from Egypt to convey the splendour of the natural
features he was describing: the man-made pyramids of the pharaohs could

not match the grandeur of the natural cavern (3.165-70); and the fearful noise of the adjacent cataract – which also makes conversation both impossible and impious (cf. 3.285 above) – was compared to the Egyptian river (3.192-208). These alignments of Guatemala with ancient Egypt have further ramifications, but the key point here is that it was Longinus himself who had claimed that 'natural inclination' led to admiration of the Nile.[69] Landívar boldly asserts the greater sublimity of the Guatemalan scenery and its supremacy over the wonders of the Old World – and possibly he is also hinting at the American landscape's capacity to generate poetry as well as birdsong (293-5).[70] In this way, the end of Book 3 closes the triptych of books in the *Rusticatio Mexicana* which are devoted to grand natural features connoting the sublime.[71]

(viii) Literary history, Sor Juana Inés de la Cruz and Cornelius Gallus

An important passage from the first book affirms that the contemplation of nature in the New World, with its silence and tranquillity, can directly lead to poetic expression:

> Discurrunt placidi per amoena silentia ripae,
> Queis cordi tranquilla quies, quos cura fatigat,
> Et quos facundae juvat indulgere Minervae.
> Tunc capti tacita rigui dulcedine ruris
> Littora concentu replent quandoque Poetae.

They move placidly over the silent and delightful retreats of the lakeside and find tranquil peace of mind. As they are exhausted by care, they find pleasure in giving play to eloquent Minerva. Then captivated by the soundless sweetness of this well-watered countryside they fill the shores with melody, ever as Poets.

Rusticatio Mexicana 1.273-7

These lines herald a pantheon of writers from New Spain, in a scenario somewhat reminiscent of the *bella scuola* of ancient classical poets in the fourth canto of Dante's *Inferno*. However, Roman authors like Virgil and Propertius might have offered a more direct model with their elevated surveys of Latin love poetry in hexameter or elegiac verse.[72] In his prose preface to the *Rusticatio Mexicana*, Landívar had declared 'there will be no place for fiction [*fictio*], if you except that which brings on the poets singing by the Mexican lake'. This licence allows past and present authors to appear more or less in alternation and it enables the author's contemporaries to be shown in Mexico singing poetry which they more probably completed under the duress of exile (*cura*).

This panorama was probably designed to convey something of the richness and diversity of the literature of New Spain to European readers.

3. Conception and design in the Rusticatio Mexicana

Landívar's annotations to 1.278-89 make this obvious because they presuppose that readers will not be familiar with the writers he mentions. Their works in Latin and in the vernacular range from devotional poetry to epic, lyric, and comic drama. But in the main text of Book 1, five of the seven poets listed have their achievements characterised in some detail. We are told that one of them, Diego José Abad, was 'fired by the holy gadfly as he sang *sublime* praises to the Lord in verse' (1.281-2). The choice of the word 'sublime' as a commendation is unlikely to be accidental. Some years before the *Rusticatio Mexicana* was first published, Clementino Vannetti, secretary of the Italian Accademia Rovoretana had praised Abad's *De Deo* (1773) for being written in such a form 'that the *sublimity* of the images and the profundity of the ideas, correspond marvellously to the divinity of the argument.'[73]

Landívar's survey culminates in a fanciful depiction of Sor Juana Inés de la Cruz, who has long been regarded as Mexico's greatest literary figure.[74] Landívar says her melodic verses immobilised the tide of the lake, stopped birds in mid-flight, and moved rocks (1.289-92). These are very conventional figures of the 'pathetic fallacy', Ruskin's term for crediting nature with human feeling – a device which abounds in the *Rusticatio Mexicana*.[75] But the particular figures employed here were also very conventionally applied in classical literature to the mythological poet Orpheus and, in Virgil, to the Roman poet Cornelius Gallus, who is credited with the invention of Latin love elegy.[76] An association between Sor Juana and Gallus is delicately sustained in the following verses:

> Ne vero Musas livor torqueret amarus,
> Ipsa Aganippaeas jussa est augere Sorores.
> Non sic argutis florentia prata Caystri
> Insonuere modis, niveus cum littore Cycnus
> Alterno moriens miscet suspiria cantu.

And so that bitter envy should not torment the Muses, Sor Juana herself was bidden to increase the number of the Sisters of Aganippe. Not even the flowery meadows of Cayster sounded with such music, when, along its bank, the snow-white Swan blended his dying sighs with song.

Rusticatio Mexicana 1.293-7

The first sentence here (293-4) plays on the epithet attached to Sor Juana herself: 'Tenth Muse'.[77] In his song of Silenus (*Eclogue* 6), Virgil had Gallus being welcomed by the Muses. Landívar underlines that affinity between Sor Juana and Gallus by his using the epithet *Aganippaeas* (294) for the Muses: Aganippe was the goddess of their Aonian spring and daughter of the river Permessus – where (in *Eclogue* 6.64-6) the Muses receive Gallus. Aganippe is also associated with Gallus in Virgil's tenth *Eclogue* (10.9-12).

The second sentence in the passage quoted above (295-7) affirms that

Sor Juana's singing excels the swan song of Cycnus. Virgil's version of the myth of Cycnus (*Aeneid* 10.189-93) connected him with *poetry*: mourning for his beloved Phaethon, Cycnus 'sang and solaced his sad love with the Muse' under the shade of Phaethon's grieving sisters who had been turned into poplar trees. Cycnus then turned into a swan and left the earth, following the stars with his voice.[78] That story also turns out to be linked to Gallus by Virgil: Silenus, the rustic Arcadian of *Eclogue* 6, sings of the metamorphosis of Phaethon's sisters into trees (*Ecl.* 6.62-3) immediately before he turns to Gallus' warm reception by the Muses (*Ecl.* 6.64-6) – to which Landívar has already alluded.[79] Cycnus' transformation into a bird also bears on Sor Juana, who was known to her contemporaries as the 'Phoenix of Mexico'.

There is some historical basis for such an association between Sor Juana Inés de la Cruz and Cornelius Gallus. Landívar would have known the tradition that Virgil's fourth *Georgic* substituted an account of Orpheus for a eulogy of his friend Gallus, who was compelled to commit suicide after his pride led him to offend the Emperor Augustus.[80] The events which occurred in the latter part of Sor Juana's life are comparable in some respects. The most scholarly woman in Spanish America was actually tricked into writing her intellectual manifesto of 1691, the *Respuesta a Sor Filotea de la Cruz* ('Reply to Sor Filotea').[81] It turned out that the tract which provoked Sor Juana's defiant rebuttal had not been penned, as she had believed, by a fellow nun – but by the Bishop of Puebla himself, Manuel Fernández de Santa Cruz.[82] The unintended offence caused by Sor Juana led to her being forced to write a statement of self-condemnation in blood. She was also compelled to stop writing, and to surrender her musical and scientific instruments as well as her library, which reputedly contained 4,000 volumes. After two years of penance, ministering to nuns afflicted by a fatal epidemic, Sor Juana died in 1695. As may have been the case with the learned Cornelius Gallus, it was an excess of confidence in the face of a despotic authority which brought the erudite Mexican poetess to a kind of martyrdom.

Sor Juana's most conspicuous feature in Landívar's imaginative portrayal is her capacity to interfere with the natural world. This is all the more striking given that his poem has the natural world as its subject. As the preceding section of this chapter sought to show, various parts of the *Rusticatio Mexicana* suggest that the sublimity of nature can have an impact on poetry. But in this scene in Book 1, that pattern is uniquely reversed. The greatness of Sor Juana's individual talent can act on land, water, and wildlife – exemplified by the waves, rocks, and birds that are in thrall to her enchanting song. That reversal has been seen as an affirmation of the *criollos'* actual power over their own environment.[83] But it might simply be a straightforward expression of the poet's admiration for Sor Juana: in a note to this passage, Landívar informs the reader that

66

she was 'rightly to be counted among the Muses' on account of her 'very graceful poetry' (*elegantissima carmina*).[84]

At a time when the enthusiasm for the elaborate poetry of the seventeenth century had steadily declined in Spain and New Spain alike, Landívar's celebration of its figurehead is exceptional. Sor Juana was far from conspicuous in the Mexican humanist literature of the later 1700s: she is never mentioned by Abad or Alegre. Indeed Alegre's critical tastes are strongly Neoclassical (though he does recognise Góngora's achievement) – and in the first lecture he gave in Mexico, the *Prolusio grammatica de syntaxi* (1751), Alegre urged his students to communicate in plain, direct language.[85] Moreover, the decadence of Spanish *seicentismo* was even more despised in Italy where Landívar was writing.[86]

In fact the *Rusticatio Mexicana* is generally seen as standing in stark opposition to the *conceptismo* and *culteranismo* of Baroque poetics. The very opening lines of the poem have lent a good deal of weight to this prevalent view:[87]

> Obtegat arcanis alius sua sensa figuris,
> Abstrusas quarum nemo penetrare latebras
> Ausit, et ingrato mentem torquere labore;
> Tum sensum brutis aptet, gratasque loquelas;
> Impleat et campos armis, et funere terras,
> Omniaque armato debellet milite regna.

Let another conceal his thoughts in arcane figures, whose obscure hidden meanings no one would dare to penetrate, and torment his mind with unrewarding labour. Let him then give sense and pleasant utterances to brutes; and let him fill the fields with arms and the lands with death, let him make war on every kingdom with armed soldiers.

Rusticatio Mexicana 1.1-6

The first of these exhortations does indeed look like a round repudiation of obscure Baroque poetry. However, as is often the case with Landívar, things are more complicated than they first appear. What the lines suggest about the place of the *Rusticatio Mexicana* in literary history actually challenge the standard view of Landívar as a straightforwardly Neoclassical poet.

Landívar's insistence on leaving 'arcane figures' and 'abstruse meanings' to others recalls the rhetorical device of *recusatio* in classical love elegy – whereby a poet expresses his reluctance to address more serious subjects. But these very lines themselves become obscure and enigmatic. What does Landívar mean here by '[giving] sense and pleasant utterances to brutes' (4)? The 'brutes' could literally be dumb animals – or warriors to whom other previous epic poets have ascribed motives and eloquent speeches. The fact that the expression 'in the manner of brutes' (*brutorum more*) is used at the very end of the work (*App.* 106) provides a clue. There

67

the expression is used to characterise a lazy person who has no interest in science.

The next exhortation in this opening passage 'let him fill the plains with arms' may contain a very recondite echo of the beginning of a Renaissance Latin epic: Petrarch's *Africa*.[88] Petrarch had used a similar phrase to refer to another poet in turn – Lucan – in order to compare Lucan's war poem with his own:

> Ille autem Emathiam Romanis ossibus implet.
> Ipse ego non nostri referam modo temporis acta.

> That poet [Lucan] fills Emathia with Roman bones. I myself [Petrarch] will not just recount things done in our own time.
>
> Petrarch, *Africa* 1.52

The line in which Landívar subtly echoes Petrarch is as follows:

> Impleat et campos armis, et funere terras.

> Let him fill the fields with arms and the lands with death.
>
> *Rusticatio Mexicana* 1.5

Something else is achieved by the pairing of the words *campos* ('fields') and *terras* ('lands'). The same pairing occurs again two verses later, when Landívar characterises his own endeavour:

> Me juvat omnino, *terrae* natalis amore,
> Usque virescentes patrios invisere *campos*

> Out of love for my native *land*, I enjoy most of all visiting the ever green *fields* of my country ...
>
> *Rusticatio Mexicana* 1.7-8

The parallel is clear enough: between the poet's *own* beloved land and fields, and those lands and fields subjected to those 'armed soldiers who conquer every kingdom'. Landívar is right to claim that he avoids celebrating war, though he does mention it on occasions. But his suggestion that he also avoids conveying hidden meanings is demonstrably false. These opening verses themselves display a capacity for allegorical or figurative expression which will be shown in many of the books to follow.

(ix) Allegories of ethnicity, conquest and colonialism

The existence of allegory in the *Rusticatio Mexicana* is effectively proven by the account of the beavers in Book 6.[89] It was remarked earlier that this account is modelled poetically on Virgil's presentation of the bees in

Georgics 4.149-250. Landívar's beavers, who are anthropomorphised as peaceful and virtuous lovers of freedom (6.39-54), govern themselves on principles which are even more pronouncedly utopian than those of Virgil's bees:

> Ut vero finem tectis posuere superbis,
> Privatae studio vitae nudata caterva
> Tota sodalitio rursus se prompta resignat.

When [the beavers] have finished building their impressive homes, the whole group discards its inclination for a private existence and readily commits itself once again to a community life.

Rusticatio Mexicana 6.195-7

As well the utopian writing of the sixteenth century, later books like Tomasso Campanella's *City of the Sun* and Bacon's *New Atlantis* had currency in Mexico.[90] Arnold Kerson has also pointed out some ways in which the ideas of eighteenth-century Enlightenment thinkers like Rousseau, Voltaire, Montesquieu, Morelly, and the Abbé de Mably might have influenced Landívar's description of the beavers.[91] But the beavers' rotation of labour (6.190-4) and their patterns of domestic organisation (6.224-37) have a particular resemblance to the practices adopted by the citizens of Thomas More's *Utopia*.[92] Remarkably, the beavers' mud-daubed dwellings (6.174-6) with their front and back entrances, one on the water (6.133-5), are like the houses which More described in the second book of his fictional dialogue:

> Nulla domus est quae non ut ostium in plateam ita posticum in hortum habeat. Quin bifores quoque facili tractu manus apertiles ac dein sua sponte coeuntes quemvis intromittunt; ita nihil usquam privati est. Nam domos ipsas uno quoque decennio sorte commutant ... aedes initio humiles ac veluti casas et tuguria fuisse, e quolibet ligno temere factas, parietes luto obductos. Culmina in aciem fastigiata stramentis operuerant. At nunc omnis domus visenda forma tabulatorum trium ...

> Every house has a front door to the street and a back door to the garden. The double doors, which open easily with a push of the hand and close again automatically, let anyone come in – so there is nothing private anywhere. Every ten years they exchange the houses themselves by lot ... [Originally] the first houses were low, like cabins or peasant huts, built slapdash out of any sort of lumber, with mudplastered walls. The roofs rising up to a central point, were thatched with straw. But now their houses are all three storeys high and handsomely constructed ...[93]

More, *Utopia* Book 2

The *Utopia* had begun to circulate in Mexico in the 1530s, when the Spanish humanist Vasco de Quiroga was already attempting to apply principles ostensibly derived from More, Plato, and Lucian, in the communities he established for the Indians near Mexico City and in Michoacán.[94] While Quiroga saw Catholic teaching as axiomatic, he also believed the Indians were morally superior to the Spaniards and that the peoples could live together without the Indians acquiring Spanish vices. The beavers of the *Rusticatio Mexicana* could then be aligned to the Indians – whom Quiroga had idealised and whom he had compared to the Christian apostles in their simplicity and humility.[95] Landívar uses the word *natio* for the community of beavers (6.231) – and later in a note to 15.336 he uses the same word – *nationes* – to designate the status of the Nayarits, Tarahumaras and other peoples from northern Mexico. But the beavers' social organisation might also represent the Jesuit ideal of people inhabiting a world independent of earthly states and monarchies.[96] The emphasis on community life among the beavers can be viewed, for instance, in the light of Landívar's constant invocation of the concept of the Jesuit Society (*Societas*) in his funeral oration for Figueredo. In the end, the significance of the allegory of the beavers is impossible to establish – it is complex and perhaps deliberately open-ended.

Another allegorical sketch towards the end of Book 13 may yield a firmer interpretation. This is how an endearing description of a parrot begins:

> Sed jam desertis humanae vocis imago
> Saepius in sylvis resonat, meque ipsa vocavit.
> Quas ego dum reputo voces, et lumina circum
> Volvo, garrit honos nemoris resupinus in alno
> Psittacus.

But now the image of a human voice quite often resounds in the deserted woods and has itself called me. While I reflect on these sounds and turn my eyes around, the pride of the forest, a parrot, chatters, relaxing in an alder tree.

Rusticatio Mexicana 13.293-7

The description abruptly takes a grim turn:

> Cum vero garrit, plauditque sibi ipsa volucris,
> Arripit incautam, plumasque et viscera vellit
> Praepetibus pennis, armatusque unguibus ales.
> Subter enim frondes habitu formosa superbo
> Alituum Regina ferox, et gloria sylvae
> Regnat avis, pedibus, rostroque insignis adunco.
> Illa nigro totum corpus fucata colore,
> Intextis variat plumis candentibus alas,
> Quas pandit volitans bis senas lata per ulnas,
> Et curvis digitos, ac longis unguibus armat.
> Incolit obscuro nigrantes robore lucos
> Sepositosque agros, avibus praedaque frequentes.
> Ut tamen hostili ventrem saturare rapina

3. Conception and design in the Rusticatio Mexicana

Ardet avis, castrisque suis optata propinquat
Praeda, nemus subito linquit Jovis armiger atrum.

As this winged creature chatters and applauds itself, a bird armed with swift wings and claws snatches it up unawares and tears out its feathers and bowels.

For under the leaves, fine in her proud attire, the fierce Queen of winged things reigns, also the glory of the wood, a bird renowned for her feet and hooked beak. Her whole body is coloured in black and her wings, which, when she stretches them in flight are twelve cubits wide, are interspersed with gleaming white feathers, and she arms her toes with long curved talons. She inhabits groves which are black with dark oak, and distant fields thick with birds and prey. And when she burns to glut her stomach with inimical plundering and the desired prey approaches her camp, the armbearer of Jupiter suddenly leaves her black grove.

Rusticatio Mexicana 13.304-18

Aspects of this encounter recall a well known classical fable which originated in archaic Greece: the story of the hawk and the nightingale recounted in Hesiod's *Works and Days*.[97] There, the hawk, having seized the nightingale in his sharp talons and carried her into the air, adds insult to injury by informing his victim that even though she is a singer, she is subject to his wishes. The moral and purpose of the story has been much debated, but Hesiod begins by addressing the tale to kings, who, he says, already know it. All that throws interesting light on a brief note Landívar appends to 13.313, the verse which describes the eagle's talons:

Inter plures Aquilas, quae Americam incolunt, praestantiorem elegi, Aquilam regiam vulgo dictam.

Among several eagles which inhabit America, I have chosen the more conspicuous one, the eagle commonly called 'royal'.

An Iberian bird of prey known as the 'Imperial eagle' functioned as a regal emblem in Spain.[98] That apparently routine observation endows the surprising and gruesome killing of the parrot with further significance. A parallel between parrots and the indigenous human inhabitants of the New World – both vulnerable to the violence of European invaders – was drawn in a famous Latin poem of the Renaissance: Girolamo Fracastoro's poem *Syphilis,* published in Italy in 1530.[99] Thus the tension in this passage between the eagle as 'glory of the wood' (*gloria sylvae*) and the indigenous Mexican parrot which was also 'pride of the forest' (*honos nemoris*), symbolises a violence which involves more than different species of bird. A clue to this is the curious metaphor characterising the parrot as the 'visual image of a *human* voice' (*humanae vocis imago*).

One consideration might appear to threaten the interpretation of this passage as a historical allegory. The eagle had also been revered a potent symbol among the indigenous Mexicans: the sighting of an eagle perched on a nopal cactus devouring a serpent was the famous omen which led to the foundation of Tenochtitlán. However, any awkward ambiguity here is dispelled by the introduction of another bird which eats snakes – the *cenchris*, or hawk:

> Sin vero pedibus serpentem sustulit uncis,
> Unguibus, et rostro discerpit corda furentis,
> Dum rabiem vita ponat, fugiatque sub umbras.

If with his clawed feet he has carried off a serpent, with his talons and beak he plucks out the heart of the raging creature, until it lays aside its rage along with its life and flees down to the shades.

Rusticatio Mexicana 13.353-5

The hawk kills its victim in Aztec style by ripping out its victim's heart – and the diction of this account poignantly recalls Aeneas' ruthless despatching of Turnus in the closing verse of Virgil's *Aeneid*.

Another more general significance may be attached to the poet's account of one of the last stages involved in the processing of gold:

> His ita continuo vulgi sudore peractis,
> Argentum tractum, tractumque examinat aurum
> Praepositus curis Hispano ab Principe missus.
> Hic parvos globulos lamnam glomerabit in unam,
> Indeque mordaci convulsum forcipe frustum
> (Quod sibi pro digna curae mercede reservat)
> Igne probat, quantumque rapax absconderit auri
> Argentum proprio commixti pondere, noscit.

When the crowd of workers have finished their long sweated labour, an official sent by the Spanish king weighs up the extracted silver and gold. He will roll the small lumps into one piece, and then, after using his sharp pincers to prise off a little chunk (which he keeps for himself as a well deserved reward for his trouble), he tests it in the fire and ascertains how much gold the greedy silver has hidden away, mixed with its own weight.

Rusticatio Mexicana 8.268-75

How do we interpret this portrait of the Spanish prefect? There is obviously some irony about his inspection being described as 'trouble' (*cura*) – as this vignette directly follows an account of the really arduous work done by the young men at the furnaces. The metaphor in which the 'greedy silver' has hidden the gold away is not exactly reassuring in this context. It seems to predicate this official's behaviour as corrupt – the implication might even be that this corruption is a general attribute of officials from peninsular Spain.

The issue of Spanish hegemony is first raised very early in the poem, when mention is made of the *Hispani* who aggressively imposed their rule on Mexico in a passage which echoes the proems of two Latin epics: Virgil's *Aeneid* and Villerías y Roelas' *Guadalupe*.[100] Landívar does not present the Spanish conquest as anything other than as a transfer of power, and there is no attempt to whitewash it as an opportunity to spread the Christian faith:

> Urbs erat occiduis procul hinc notissima terris
> Mexicus, ampla, frequensque, viris, opibusque superba,
> Indigenis quondam multos dominata per annos:
> Nunc vero Hispani, populis, Mavorte subactis,
> Sceptra tenent, summaque urbem ditione gubernant.

There was a city far from here in the western lands, Mexico, very famous, large, and populous, distinguished for its men and resources. It was once ruled for many years by its indigenous inhabitants, but now the Spanish hold the sceptres, having conquered the people in war, and they govern the city with their supreme authority.

Rusticatio Mexicana 1.32-6

The subsequent account of the later invasion and settlement of Guatemala City (3.24-6) is very similar in tone. If anything, it makes such interference on the part of the Spaniards look even less legitimate. The ensuing natural disasters (3.27-8, 3.47-60) that occur shortly after the Spaniards' incursions might even represent a kind of nemesis for their usurpation of Guatemala.

Throughout the *Rusticatio Mexicana,* and in his annotations to the poem, Landívar exclusively reserves the term *Hispanus* for Iberian Spaniards. Apart from *colonus* ('settler'), there was no Latin word at his disposal for *criollo*, the once derogatory term now commonly used by historians to specify American-born Spaniards in the colonial period. Instead the adjective *Mexicanus* is routinely used for both Spanish Americans (like Landívar himself) and indigenous Americans.[101] There are more specific regional designations: in the poet's notes *Michoacanensis* and *Veracrucensis* are applied respectively to Diego José Abad, who was born in Michoacán, and to Francisco Xavier Alegre, who came from Veracruz.[102] Forms of the Latin for 'Indian', *Indus* (as well as *indigenus*) are also used of indigenous Americans: *Indus* is tellingly applied to Juan Diego, for instance, in Landívar's account of the miracles associated with the Virgin of Guadalupe (12.38-56). But Landívar very frequently refers to indigenous Mexicans and Guatemalans simply as 'people', 'boys', 'youths', or 'men', according to context. In short, his usage always discriminates between European and American Spaniards, but it does not consistently seek to distinguish between Spanish and indigenous Americans.

But in the end, few of the apparent instances of political and historical allegory in the *Rusticatio Mexicana* can be interpreted decisively. This is not necessarily because Landívar meant to be evasive in his approach to questions which involve the interests of different social or ethnic groups.[103] It is more probably due to the fact that texts from a colonial epoch are very prone to generate diverse or contradictory readings. The various indigenous American peoples, *mestizos*, *criollos*, Spaniards, and other Europeans would all have had different stories to tell, and different morals to draw, about their respective histories and about matters of ethnic identity.

(x) Afterword

Those who attempt to provide even the most straightforward description of the *Rusticatio Mexicana* are faced with several challenges. Its poet acknowledges customary oppositions between art and science, only to follow the didactic tradition by fusing 'objective' discourses like zoology and ethnography with the subjectivity of personal response and recollection. Oppositions and differences between Europe and America may have led to the conception and creation of Landívar's work, but the resulting text does not belong exclusively to either continent. The spatial and temporal position of the speaker of the poem is maintained in a state of flux throughout: sometimes he addresses his reader from the actual locations he describes; at others his observations are framed as vivid reminiscences conjured up from exile in Italy.

Though very much a product of the Enlightenment, the *Rusticatio Mexicana* ultimately resists periodisation: its conceits and allegorical modes evoke the Baroque; its diction is classical; and its construction of an individual poetic voice through an enthusiasm for nature prefigures sentiments that were to be expressed in later Romantic poetry. The poetics of the sublime conjoin with reflections of a theological nature to point to a unique conception of transcendence. Future literary assessments of the text will also need to take cognisance of the potential influence of Castilian and Spanish American *vernacular* literature and poetics on Landívar: Bernardo de Balbuena's *La Grandeza Mexicana* is just one important antecedent, of which only the briefest notice has been given here. The scientific and geographical content of the *Rusticatio* could be considered for its bearing on actual phenomena and environments, as well as for its relation to other early modern authorities. Landívar's poem also provides some exceptional insight on the cultural and intellectual history of New Spain and Guatemala in the 1700s. Its implications for contemporary understanding of colonial society and its tensions – briefly indicated in the Preface to this volume – have only begun to be explored.

A sense of all these potential points of departure has made me nervous about the extent to which the present chapter has been preoccupied by literary matters and by Landívar's use of classical sources. It is difficult for anyone with an interest in Latin studies to see beyond the edifice of *Quellenforschung* (now renovated by theories of intertextuality) which still stands at the heart of the discipline. Even the most progressive Latinists may be startled to discover that the only monograph in English on the *Rusticatio Mexicana* – Antony Higgins' *Constructing the Criollo Archive* (2000) – refers to Virgil's *Georgics* on only two occasions. That apparent negligence is salutary for classicists, who are prone to regard early modern Latin texts merely as forms of homage to Cicero, Virgil and other ancient authors. In the colleges and seminaries of eighteenth-century Mexico, Landívar and his peers wrote in Latin with the same facility as they wrote in Spanish. The circumstances which prompted them to continue to use Latin – as they taught and worked in a wider society which they readily acknowledged to be multicultural and multilingual – raise a number of questions. Those historical questions must be more pressing than the business of establishing precisely which ancient sources informed the Latin diction of these writers.

Much more remains to be said about Landívar – and indeed about Mexican humanist literature as a whole – than could possibly be conveyed in these preliminary chapters. Landívar's works possess many virtues, but ultimately their most appealing characteristic (which applies to the Funeral Declamation and to the short Marian poems, as much as to the *Rusticatio Mexicana*) is the considered optimism that underlies them. Such optimism is the more remarkable given the difficult circumstances in which all of these texts were produced. It is only to be hoped that the achievement of Rafael Landívar and of other Latin authors from Latin America will be more widely recognised, as English-speaking scholars come to realise that the United States was far from the first American nation to accommodate and transform the European classical tradition – or indeed to take up any other form of literate learning.[104] Histories of humanism need to incorporate the rich classical culture in Spanish America, just as the boundaries existing for the humanities today need to be redefined, in order to admit the abiding centrality of Latin writing in the early modern age.

Notes

Prologue: Landívar, Latin and Colonialism

1. Pym (2000), 191 (citing Gallego Morell (1990), 52): ' "Latin" America was thus an identity defined by negation, being both duplicitously non-colonial and impeccably non-Anglo-Saxon.' Habinek (1998), 31, discusses the circumstances of the original nomenclature, with further bibliography at 176.

2. The essays in Bolaños and Verdesio (2002) make important advances and constitute, with Gustavo Verdesio's lucid opening chapter, a good introduction to the theoretical issues confronting colonial Latin American studies. The work of Walter Mignolo (1993, 1995) among others, has been very influential in the USA. The interdisciplinary journal *Chicomóztoc* – established in Mexico in 1988 – is devoted to the role of *descolonización* in the humanities (cf. Téllez 2003).

3. Knight (2002), xvii is salutary: 'Some of the supposedly "new" cultural history involves a semantic repackaging of older ideas and topics. "Subalterns" for example, were once called workers and peasants ... So I think I write "subaltern history" [in this book] just as I write prose, though I do not make an issue of it.'

4. Bolaños (2002), 40: here epitomising Higgins (2002).

5. Paz (2001), 60.

1. The Circles of Time: Classical culture in colonial Mexico

1. Bernal Díaz del Castillo 1.29, ed. Ramírez Cabañas (1944), 130.

2. Méndez Plancarte (1944), 6-7; Osorio Romero (1991a), 7; Herrera Zapién (2000), 3-4; Téllez (2003), 97 attach significance to this episode. The essays in Gray and Fiering (2000) address a variety of important issues raised by the interactions between European and American languages in the western hemisphere during the colonial period.

3. Waquet (2001) is a stimulating, though very partial and negative, account of the role of Latin in early modern Europe.

4. E.g. Greenblatt (1991), (1993); Grafton, Shelford and Siraisi (1992); Todorov (1984). Leonard (1992) is a seminal survey of the literature read by the conquistadors. Gruzinski (2002) considers some of the larger implications of European Renaissance culture on Latin America.

5. Macc. Armstrong (1953); Bosworth (2000); and Lupher (2003), 9-13 etc. Identification of Alexander with Cortés is implicit in Alegre's eighteenth-century Latin *Alexandriad* (pp. 28-9 in this volume).

6. The *mestizo* historian, the Inca Garcilaso de la Vega (1539-1616) compared the Incas to the Romans: MacCormack (1998). The Croatian Dominican Vinko Paletin argued in the 1550s that the Mayan inscriptions at Chichen Itza were in Punic and that the Carthaginians had once possessed the Indies. Thus the Roman Empire had proper title to these Punic territories, which, via the Papacy, could pass to the Spaniards: Lupher (2003), 167-86. This can be compared to the later claim of a Spanish Dominican, Gregorio García in the early 1600s: the natives of America were descended from the lost tribes of Israel. But García's insistence that the Carthaginians had constructed the Incan and Mayan monuments was meant to suggest that Spaniards and natives had common ancestors. See Brading (1991), 195-200, 382; García (1980) (= 1607).

7. Las Casas (1967), Sepúlveda (1951).

8. Lupher (2003), 43-188.

9. Eatough (1998), (1999a) on Martyr; Sahagún (1981), León Portilla (2002) on Sahagún; more generally, Lupher (2003) and Mason (1994).

10. Juan Luis De La Cerda's commentary on Virgil occasionally shows how the conquest of America could bear on the routine exegesis of ancient texts. See Laird (2002), 190-1. In a Spanish translation of the *Georgics* (1596), the Galician Juan de Guzmán, supposedly resident in the New World, offered a *silva de varia lección* of indigenous American words by way of comment on 48 verses of Virgil: Morreale (2002).

11. On Ercilla, see Quint (1993), 131-210, Kallendorf (2003), and Lupher (2003), 298-316.

12. For Fracastoro, see edition of Eatough (1984) as well as Eatough (1999b) and Haskell (1999); Hofmann (1994) treats a number of Latin epics about Columbus including Gambara, Stella, and Carrara.

13. See e.g. MacCormack (1991), (1998) on colonial Peru; Rivas Sacconi (1993) on later humanism in Colombia; Miranda Cancela (2003) on the later classical tradition in Cuba.

14. Taylor and Coroleu (1999) illustrates the range of peninsular Spanish humanism; Rubio (1934).

15. See Micheli (1976-1977) on Italian interactions with New Spain; Peconi (1978) on Italian books and presses, Torre Villar (1973) on Belgian books in Mexico; Leonard (1992), Millares Carlo (1986), Griffin (1991) and Osorio Romero (1980) all address the circulation of European titles.

16. Osorio Romero (1991a), 8.

17. Accounts of Vasco de Quiroga's project include Zavala (1955) and Gómez (2001). Acuña (1988) is a text of *De debellandis indis,* a work attributed to Quiroga.

18. Téllez (2003) describes a trilingual vocabulary of Spanish, Latin and Nahuatl from the early 1500s, modelled on the Spanish humanist Nebrija's renowned Spanish-Latin dictionary: Téllez notes that the indigenous copyist appears to be better versed in Latin than Spanish.

19. *Historia de los indios de la Nueva España,* trat. 3, ch. 12, §389 quoted in Osorio Romero (1990), xxvi = Motolinía (2001), 243. (Fray Toribio is known as 'Motolinía', a kind of nickname given to him by the Indians.) Compare an account by the chronicler Bernardino de Sahagún who himself taught at Santa Cruz de Tlatelolco: Sahagún (1981): book 10, ch. 27. Abbott (1987) explores traditions of rhetoric and oratory in pre-Hispanic Aztec culture.

20. Juan de Torquemada (d. 1629), *Monarquía indiana* 5.43 quoted in Osorio Romero (1990), xxvii. The same story is attested by Gerónimo de Mendieta, *Historia ecclesiastica indiana* book 4, ch. 15, and by Motolinía (2001), 243.

21. Jerónimo López's letter is quoted in Osorio Romero (1990), xxxix.

22. Jerónimo López himself evidently had political anxieties: Lupher (2003), 229-34.

23. Griffin (1991) is a history of the Cromberger Press in Seville and Mexico in the 1500s. As Brading (1991), 299 notes, the University of Mexico eventually came to compete with the best in Europe at the time: Irigoyen Troconis (2003) assembles some important essays on the university culture of New Spain.

24. Herrera Zapién (2000), 33-4 discusses this passage from the *Libellus.* The transcription can be found in Cruz (1991), 12: the excerpt quoted next follows there at 26.

25. For Acosta, see Landívar's Notes 2 and 3 to *RM* 1.145 and 1.190 respectively (pp. 262-3 below), and Acosta (2003). It was Landívar's contemporary, the historian Clavigero (or 'Clavijero') who first called Hernández, 'el Plinio de la Nueva España': Clavigero (2003), 14. See Landívar, Note 5 to *Rusticatio Mexicana* 1.220 on the *centzontlus* bird (p. 264 below), and Hernández (2003), 5-51.

26. Editions of Francisco Hernández's *Rerum medicarum Novae Hispaniae thesaurus seu plantarum animalium mineralium mexicanorum historia* include a printing in Rome, in 1649. For Clavigero's account of Hernández and Nezahualcoyotl, see Brading (1991), 458 and Clavigero (2003), 160 and *passim*; the importance of natural history for Clavigero is further discussed on p. 26 below.

27. Francisco Cervantes de Salazar, who had a chair in rhetoric, was one of the first professors at the University of Mexico. A speech he delivered in Latin for the inauguration of a plan of studies for the University established his reputation. In 1554 he published some Latin dialogues by the Spanish humanist, Luis Vives, along with some of his own in the same volume: León Portilla (2001) is a facsimile edition of part of the 1554 volume, with a Spanish translation by García Icazbalceta.

28. Méndez Plancarte (1994), xi: 'un humanismo humano, vital, vivo e integral, que eleva al primer plano la consideración de la persona humana.'

29. Heredia Correa (2000a); Redmond and Beuchot (1987).

30. Herrera Zapién (2000), 66; Osorio Romero (1980), 107 gives bibliographical details. Mack (2005) assesses the place of Vives' *De ratione dicendi* (1533) in the history of Renaissance rhetoric.

31. Knight (2002), 51.

32. Difficulties and ethical problems involved in reading historical and literary texts from the colonial period are discussed in Bolaños and Verdesio (2002).

33. The *Dicolon Icasticon* is given in full in Herrera Zapién (2000), 29-30.

34. Méndez Plancarte (1937) is a full study of Horace in the Mexican classical tradition; Herrera Zapién (1991) is another treatment.

35. See Pareja (1883), 96-8, cited in Osorio Romero (1990b), 28-9 and Herrera Zapién (2000), 80-1.

36. Pareja quotes the opening line of Valencia's poem (*Asseret e Roma nisi lis in amore Teresa*) and another isolated verse (*e, Roma sit era rogo, cogor aretis amore*). Such compositions are more properly known as *versus retrogradi*: Sarolli (1971), part 2, sv. 2 (b). They find their origins not in antiquity but in medieval poetry: actual medieval examples of *versus retrogradi* tend to be no longer than 40 lines. Newton (1973) is an edition of the epanaleptic elegiacs of Laurence of Amalfi; Enzinger (1998) is a miscellaneous collection of Latin palindromes on the internet.

37. Troncarelli (2001) is an account of Lamport's colourful life.

38. A selection of these works is edited in G. Méndez Plancarte (1948).

39. Zambrano (1965), 107-13 gives some biographical details.

40. Leonard (1929) is still a good account of Sigüenza y Góngora; Beltrán (1975) summarises the Mexican savant's achievements in mathematics, astronomy and natural history; Mayer (2000-2) is a comprehensive survey. The influence of the Spaniard Luis de Góngora y Argote on Landívar's sonnet is discussed in this volume on pp. 41-2.

41. An echo of the description of Carthage in Virgil, *Aeneid* 1.12-14 is also at work in Landívar, *Rusticatio Mexicana* 1.32-3: *Urbs erat ... notissima .../Mexicus,*

Notes on the Essay Studies

ampla, frequensque, viris, opibusque, superba ('Mexico was a renowned city, large and popular, distinguished for its men and resources') as it is in Villerías y Roelas' characterisation of Mexico before the conquest in the proem to his *Guadalupe* epic. Landívar's stichometric correspondence with Villerías' verses (*Rusticatio Mexicana* 1.32-3; *Guadalupe* 1.32-3) draws further attention to the community between these verses of Virgil and Castroverde. Other historical associations between Mexico and Carthaginians, are given in n. 6 above.

42. Brading (2001) and Poole (1995) are useful introductions to the extensive literature on the *Nican mopohua*.

43. This unsettled the missionary-ethnogapher Bernadino de Sahagún. The appendix to his *Historia* (*c.* 1576) is in Sahagún (1981) 3, 352. See also pp. 79-80 n. 53 below on Tonantzin.

44. Peñalosa (1987) is an anthology of seventeenth-century texts; Peñalosa's other volumes assemble literature from subsequent centuries: *siglo XVIII* (1988); *XIX* (1985); *XX* (1984). Francisco Cabrera recently published a new Latin epyllion on the theme: *Laus Guadalupensis: Latino carmine expressa* (Cuernavaca, 1990): for Cabrera's contemporary Latin poetry, see p. 82 n. 104 below.

45. These works are edited in Peñalosa (1987). López de Abilés is discussed in Osorio Romero (1991b), 128-32.

46. Osorio Romero (1991b), 134 refers to the cento as a 'Horatian monster' and cites the negative verdict of the later eighteenth-century critic, José Ignacio Bartolache. Laird (forthcoming) assesses Riofrío's endeavour more positively.

47. Knight (2002), 185. Brading (2001) is a full account of the importance of the Virgin of Guadalupe for Mexico's political history.

48. The opening of the *De mentis potu* (1689) published in Naples by Tommaso Strozzi has Apollo and the Muses flee from the Turkish barbarians – to a new Parnassus in Mexico. See further Haskell (2003), 87, and p. 80 n. 54 below on Atlas.

49. *Rusticatio Mexicana* 1.289-97: see Landívar's Notes on this passage and pp. 64-7 above. The authoritative edition of Sor Juana is by Alfonso Méndez Plancarte (1994) in four volumes; the critical account of her achievement in Paz (1988) has been enormously influential.

50. *Conceptismo*, which is best represented by Francisco de Quevedo, involved puns and a kind of wit (comparable to the 'conceits' of English Metaphysical poetry). The poetic principles of *conceptismo* were promoted in a celebrated 1642 treatise, *Agudeza y arte de ingenio* ('Sharpness and the art of talent') by the Spanish Jesuit, Baltasar Gracián. *Conceptismo* is often conceived as being in virtual opposition to *culteranismo* – originally a pejorative term for the intensive use of erudite classical language and allusion in the tradition of Luis de Góngora. However, conceit and wit, like classical allusion, are generally widespread in European poetry of the seventeenth century. For definitions of these Spanish terms: Ward (1978), 128-9 and 143-4; Preminger (1965), 175-6 (sv. 'cultism'); and Leonard (1983), 31. Leonard's study is a comprehensive account of the role and context of the 'Baroque' in seventeenth-century Mexico.

51. Giard (1995).

52. Israel (1975) and Knight (2002), 279-83 provide accounts of the earlier background.

53. Tepeyac, where the Virgin appeared, was the site of Tonantzin's worship. In *Guadalupe* 1.147-8, Tonantzin is the daughter of Pluto: *nataque quam patria lingua dixere Tonanthin, /nostra, quod (infandum!) Mater sonat ore latino* ('his daughter whom in their native tongue they called Tonantzin which – unspeakably! – means "our Mother" in the Latin language'). Speakers of Nahuatl still refer today to the Virgin Mary as 'Tonantzin'. Sigüenza y Góngora's *Primavera indiana* octave 24 had already aligned Pluto with the evil forces of indigenous religion and, significantly, presented Tepeyac as the original domain of *Pluto*, rather than Tonantzin.

54. Atlas' translation to the Lake of Mexico in Villerías plays on an association between Atlas and Gabriel (the angel who in Guadalupan iconography bears the Virgin on his shoulders). The association was already made by López de Abilés, in the *Poeticum viridarium* 152: *Coeli fortis Atlas iste mihi Gabriel* ('Heaven's strong Atlas is my Gabriel').

55. Osorio Romero (1991a), 38. Osorio Romero (1991b) provides not only a commented edition and Spanish translation of the *Guadalupe* at 259-375 but also a full study of Villerías himself and the literary precedents to his poem.

56. '*politissimis multis, Sariñana, Rinconio, Cardenas, Villeria, Zamora aliisque permultis, omnibus numeris in re poetica absolutissimis*': Eguiara y Eguren in *Anteloquia* 18 of the *Bibliotheca Mexicana*, ed. Millares Carlo (1996), 183.

57. Clavigero in his *Breve Ragguaglio della Prodigiosa e Rinomata Immagine della Madonna de Guadalupe del Messico* (1782), published in Cesena, Italy, mentions Villerías and Andrés Diego de la Fuente (pp. 20-1, 27 above) as two Latin epic poets who treated the theme of the Virgin of Guadalupe. Clavigero wrote: 'We have further seen a long Latin poem in manuscript by Giuseppe Villerías, a Mexican poet': Osorio Romero (1991b), 201.

58. In addition to the curious stichometric correspondence between Villerías' *Guadalupe* and the *Rusticatio Mexicana* observed in n. 41 above, a possible echo of Villerías in Landívar's Castilian sonnet is identified in this volume at p. 261 (n. 10).

59. Manuel Martí, *Epistularum libri duodecim* (Amsterdam, 1735), vol. 2, book 7, letter 16, quoted in Millares Carlo (1996), 56-7.

60. Brading (2001), 131, 154-5, 235 details further responses offered in Spanish to Martí's remarks: by José de Mercado in 1744, the influential preacher Ita y Parra (1743), the Franciscan José Torrubia in 1744, and the nineteenth-century bibliographer José Mariano Beristáin de Souza in 1816. Torrubia noted that Martí had merely echoed the earlier Spanish bibliographer Nicolás Antonio who affirmed in 1663 that 'in the Indies all is traded save books'.

61. A Latin text is in Vargas Alquicira (1987).

62. Compare the opening of the second book of Bruni, *Ad Petrum Paulum Histrum Dialogus* composed in the early 1400s: Garin (1952), 76. A plane tree is in Plato, *Phaedrus* 230b-c.

63. Haskell (2003) examines a poem on chocolate, the *De mentis potu, sive De cocolatis opificio*, by the Neapolitan Jesuit Tommaso Strozzi: n. 48 above.

64. The viceregal *imprimatur* for the *Bibliotheca Mexicana*, dated 28 April 1755, precedes the original text of the first volume.

65. Higgins (2000), 34.

66. Knight (2002), 202-331 relates these events, which eventually led to insurgency and Mexican independence.

67. Guedea (2000), 280.

68. This '*criollo* archive' of knowledge is explored thoroughly in Higgins (2000). It was Immanuel Kant himself who gave currency to the term 'Enlightenment' (*Aufklärung*), with his influential definition first published in a Berlin newspaper in 1784, entitled *Was ist Aufklärung?*: Kant (1963), 3.

69. The mathematician and scientist Jean Le Rond d'Alembert (1717-83) abandoned Latin for French in his famous *Encyclopédie*. Waquet (2001) is a wide-ranging though partial account of the tensions between Latin and the vernacular in Europe from the fifteenth century onwards.

70. Batllori (1966). Deck (1976), 96-9 is a short bibliography of Jesuit works published in Italy at this time. For material in Italian archives, on or by exiled Mexicans, see Guzmán (1964) and Revelli (1926). Torre Villar (1980) is an essential handbook for sources in European collections.

71. Maneiro (1988), 276-95 is a Spanish translation of Juan Luis Maneiro's life of Campoy in his three-volume work, *De vitis aliquot mexicanorum* (Bologna, 1791-2).

72. Navarro (1983), 111-33 and Beuchot (1998), 138-76 survey philosophy in eighteenth-century Mexico.

73. Maneiro (1988), 452-4.

74. Roger (1970).

75. Browning (1985), 30 argues the poem was prompted by these factors and points out in a note that Landívar and Clavigero (whose *Historia Antigua* vigorously defended Mexico against such criticisms) occupied the same house in Bologna with twelve other Jesuits: see also the works cited in n. 101 below.

76. Clavigero (2003), 769-75.

77. Clavigero's 'rules of the Mexican language' are in Clavigero (1974), and translated into English in Clavigero (1973).

78. Clavigero (2003), 65.

79. Brading (1991), 454.

80. For Osorio Romero's Latin text and Spanish translation of the poem (preceded by a prose letter), see Maneiro (1988), 56-65.

81. Beuchot (1998), 153-6 decribes Abad's philosophical interests.

82. De Polignac's popular *Anti-Lucretius* was published in 1742, but written in the 1600s.

83. *De Deo, Carmen* 19 celebrates scientific achievement, but other parts of the work (e.g. the attack on Epicurus' successors in 42) chastise contemporary *philosophi*: Kerson (1988); Leeber (1965).

84. Passages in the *De Deo* mentioning or alluding to Mexico include: 1.62 (*gens ignota diu*), 3.16 (*Orizabaeus ... mons*), 9.119, 15.12-25 (description of climate), and 18.184; 23.109 (Christ's Nativity introduces the Mexican passion flower); 42.613-29 (the Virgin of Guadalupe); 42.608-9 (Montezuma and the last Inca). See further Laird (2004a).

85. Manuel Fabri, *Specimen Vitae Auctoris* in Fernández Valenzuela (1974), 84. A relevant Latin annotation to an edition of Abad's *Dissertatio* is given in Kerson (1991), 364.

86. Kerson (1991), 364 in the introduction to his text and translation of the *Dissertatio*. Heredia Correa (2000b) also offers a text, Spanish translation and notes.

87. Batllori (1966), 35 is quoted in Kerson (1991), 357 n. 2. See also Deck (1976), 32-5.

88. Vannetti's *Epistula ad Abadium* quoted in Fabri's Latin biography, *Specimen Vitae Auctoris*, in Fernández Valenzuela (1974), 86. Vannetti's five books of letters, *Epistularum libri,* were published in Padua in 1795.

89. The poem is conventionally titled the *Californias*: Castro Pallares (1979) is a text and Spanish translation. On Salvatierra and on the Jesuit missions to California, see Venegas (1929) and Crosby (1994) respectively.

90. Fuente (1971) is a facsimile of the *Guadalupana B. Mariae Virginis Imago, quae Mexici colitur, carmine descripta* originally printed in Faenza, Italy in 1773.

91. Landívar, *Rusticatio Mexicana* 1.285.

92. Bush Malabehar (2002) is an edition of Alegre's *Batrachomyomachia*.

93. Alegre, *Institutionum Theologicarum Libri XVIII*, vol. 3, 289-90 (lib. VI, *propositio* 11, no. 32).

94. In his 'translation' Alegre generally substitutes Spanish authors for French; he eliminates Boileau's fourth book, but provides extensive commentary in his notes to the text: see further Kerson (1981) and Deck (1976). The text is included, along with other unpublished writings by Alegre, in García Icazbalceta (1889), an edition of 150 copies.

95. In his Latin biography of Agustín Pablo de Castro (another Mexican Jesuit scholar who went to Italy), Juan Luis Maneiro records that he read Longinus, Hermogenes, Lucian and other rhetoricians 'very avidly' with the intention of translating them into Spanish: Maneiro (1988), 511. The role of Longinian sublimity in the *Rusticatio Mexicana* is examined on pp. 61-4 of this volume.

96. In a prose preface to the *Alexandriad*, Alegre says he composed the poem twenty years before its publication. Buelna Serrano (1994) has a text of the poem.

97. This case is made in Laird (2003).

98. Notably *Aeneid* 1.441-8 describing the construction of the temple to Juno in Carthage: Laird (2003), 171-2 and above, n. 41. The passage of Alegre's *Alexandriad* quoted here has some resemblance to Politian's *Ambra* 590-625: a text is in Bausi (1996) and in Fantazzi (2004).

99. Pimentel Álvarez (1990), 1-10 contains a modern Latin text (and Spanish translation) of the letter on the *Alexandriad*. Kaimowitz (1990) is an English translation of the 1776 edition, with introduction. The proper Latin title of Giovanni Darcio's 1543 poem is *Venusini canes* ('Dogs of Venosa'); Girolamo Vida's *Christias* was first published in 1535; Iacopo Sannazaro's *De partu Virginis* dates back to 1526. Alegre's views have much in common with the theories of imitation espoused by Petrarch and later Italian humanists: McLaughlin (1995) is an illuminating study of *imitatio* in the Renaissance.

100. For the literature available to the Mexican Jesuits in Italy, see Deck (1976), 31-45; Landívar's absorption of Petrarch, Fracastoro, Vanière and others is indicated in Chapter 3 of this volume. Battista Spagnoli (known as 'Mantovano'), Sannazaro and Vida, and the late antique poet Juvencus, were anthologised in Pedro de Salas' *Thesaurus Poetarum*, which was published in Mexico City in 1641: cf. Osorio Romero (1980), and n. 15 above.

101. Decorme (1941) vol. I, 456; Ronan (1977), 94.

102. As Herrera Zapién (2000) notes at 210-11, clerics like José Ramón Arzac who deemed the style of Fulgentius preferable to that of Cicero were clearly confusing content with form.

103. The achievements of Gabriel Méndez Plancarte (1905-49), Agustín Millares Carlo (1893-1980), and, more recently, Ignacio Osorio Romero (1941-91) merit particular mention.

104. Twentieth-century Latin poets in Mexico include Federico Escobedo, translator of Landívar; Thomas Twaites Varmington (who was born in Coventry, England in 1870, and died in Mexico City in 1959); and Francisco José Cabrera (born 1918) whose epyllia or short epic '*cantos*' include *Mexicus-Tenochtitlan, Angelopolis, Quauhnahuac, Laus Guadalupensis* (n. 44 above), and *Quetzalcóatl CMXCIX–MCMXCIX*. The former three poems – each on a Mexican city – are now available in Cabrera (2004). Beuchot (2001), 33-5 has a short biography of Cabrera.

2. Devotion and Exile: Rafael Landívar's life and earlier compositions

1. Villacorta (1931), 6.

2. The actual text of the entry is given in Chamorro (1987), 9. Landívar's date of birth is also given in the Catalogue of the members of the Jesuit order expelled from Mexico in 1767, compiled by Don Rafael de Zelis (who was himself among them) in Cuevas (1944), 231-93.

3. Villacorta (1931) combines archival information with a reconstruction of social historical background; cf. Scheifler (1950a) and the more colourful if sometimes unreliable account in Mata Gavidia (1950), 9-19. Zambrano and Gutiérrez Casillas (1977), 31-2 is a reliable chronology with bibliographical sources. Chamorro (1987), xiv cites the following (which I have not been able to consult): Batres Jáuregui (1957), Carboni (1951), and a sequence of articles from 21-27 October 1931 in the Guatemalan newspaper *El Imparcial,* including an account of Landívar's ancestry (22 October), his life in Bologna (26 October), a text of his will (24 October).

4. The part of Sebastián's *Memorias de los Padres, y Hermanos de la Compañia de Jesús de la Provincia de Nueva España* devoted to Landívar (vol. 2, 247-55) was printed in Pérez Alonso (1950).

5. Pérez Alonso (1950), 24-5. Zambrano and Gutiérrez Casillas (1977), 98-9 and Osorio Romero in Maneiro (1988), 7-25 give further details of Maneiro's life.

6. Sebastián §2 in Pérez Alonso (1950), 25; a confusion in Villacorta (1931), 41 between Colegio San Lucas and the Colegio San Francisco de Borja is corrected in Scheifler (1950a), 33. San Borja was named after Francis Borgia, the Third General of the Society of Jesus in the sixteenth century. Borgia directed the order to teach the laity, and thus secured its footing in the courts of France, Spain and Portugal.

7. Lanning (1956), 161 notes that botany and astronomy were popular in Guatemala, even before they became a formal part of the curriculum at the University of San Carlos in 1793. Cultivation of these particular sciences had also been a characteristic of the pre-Hispanic Mayan civilisation.

8. Zelis' 1786 *Catálogo,* reproduced in Cuevas (1944), 262-3.

9. §5 in Pérez Alonso (1950), 26.

10. Villacorta (1931), 58.

11. Scheifler (1950a), 36 n. 19 notes a translation of the Latin autograph of the vow.

12. Moses (1919), 104-6 gives the full text in English.

13. The estimate is in Scheifler (1950a), 37: Scheifler n. 25 quotes the Rector of the University of Guatemala speaking a decade later in 1778: 'the absence of the professors at the College is felt each day'.

14. §14 in Pérez Alonso (1950), 29. Ferrer Benimeli (1994) explains the historical and political complexities which led to the movement of the Jesuits from Corsica to Italy.

15. 'Carta de un Religioso de los extintos jesuitas a una Hermana suya' in Cuevas (1944), 19-80.

16. Cross and Livingstone (1997), 498 on 'Dominus ac Redemptor'.

17. The effects of this are described in Landívar's dedicatory verses to the city which precede the *Rusticatio Mexicana* and in 3.47-60.

18. Scheifler (1950a), 37; Chamorro (1987), xxxiii.

19. Bertoni (1937), Batllori (1966).

20. See Scheifler (1950b), and pp. 26-7 n. 81 above.

21. A facsimile of this edition is in Mata Gavidia (1950).

22. Landívar's death notice, written by Caietano Tomba, parish priest of Santa Maria delle Muratelle, is given below, pp. 283-4.

23. Sebastián §21: Pérez Alonso (1950).

24. Sebastián §16: '*La vida, que entabló en su austero retiro está dicha en dos palabras: Orar, y Estudiar*': Pérez Alonso (1950), 29.

25. Sebastián §17 in Pérez Alonso (1950), 30: this testimony's reliance on the authority of others' verdicts on the *RM* (and its laborious transcription of the poem's title) could suggest that Sebastián did not feel equipped to assess Landívar's literary competence for himself. Possibly if Sebastián himself set little store by Latin verse, he assumed the same of Landívar. Landívar's modesty, frequently evident from the rest of his account, might have given rise to such an assumption.

26. Peñalosa (1998), 273.

27. MacCormack (1975) is a detailed treatment of Latin prose panegyric in late antiquity, including an account of its origins in the *Laudatio funebris* of the Roman Republic at 146-8.

28. Juarros (1936), 209, cited in Accomazzi (1961), 20-1 n. 2 bis.

29. Peñalosa (1998), 272.

30. The full title on the first page of the volume consists of 22 centre-justified lines divided as follows: 'EL LLANTO/ DE LOS OJOS DE LOS JESUITAS/ DE GUATHEMALA/ EN LA MUERTE DE SU LUZ,/ EL ILLMO. Sr. DOCTOR/ D. FRANCISCO JOSEPH/ DE FIGUEREDO, Y VICTORIA,/ Obispo, primero de Popayan, y despues Arzobispo/ Dignissimo de Guathemala./ Quien bajo la alegoria de una Antorcha Luciente sobre el/ Candelero en su vida, se llora apagada en su muerte./ *POR EL P. FRANCISCO XAVIER MOLINA*,/ *de la Compañía de Jesus*,/ Describiendo los Funerales obsequios, que como â su Benefactor/ Insignissimo le hizo, y celebró en su Templo/ EL COLEGIO DE LA COMPAÑIA DE JESUS./ Quien para monumento perpetuo de su gratitud los saca â luz publica,/ DEDICA, Y CONSAGRA/ AL MUY ILUSTRE VENERABLE Sr./ DEAN, Y CABILDO/ SEDEVACANTE DE LA SANTA IGLESIA METROPOLITANA/ DE GUATHE-MALA./ CON LICENCIA/ En el Colegio Real de San Ignacio de la Puebla de los Angeles/ Año de 1766.'

31. Molina's text is printed on folios 9-21 (reverse); Landívar's Declamation occupies fol. 22 recto – 28 recto; Vallejo 30 recto – 38 recto. Copies of the volume can be found in the Biblioteca Palafoxiana in Puebla, Mexico, and the Bancroft Library in Berkeley, California: BANCxF1207.E8.v.3:7. A self-standing impression of Landívar's text is in an untitled anthology of funeral speeches compiled by the bibliographer José María Lafragua (1813-75), in the Fondo Reservado of the National Library of Mexico: BNM Libros raros y curiosos 1358 LAF.

32. 'Cerrada con la última lección, que cantó el Preste la solemne Vigilia, declamó con eloquencia en idioma latina un Jesuita', quoted in Accomazzi (1961), 15. The page of Molina's account from which this comes follows Landívar's speech apparently at random in Lafragua's anthology (n. 31 above).

33. See the title text of the Declamation below at p. 97 – equivalent to folio 22 (recto) of *El llanto de los ojos*.

34. Peñalosa (1998), 267-8 complains that scholars have continued to cite the speech erroneously as a self-standing work of Landívar (proving either they have not read it or that they have read it in Lafragua's compilation) whilst others disregard it altogether. The misattributions in Mata Gavidia (1950), 18, and

Zambrano and Gutiérrez Casillas (1977), 32 are rooted in Beristáin de Souza (1980-1 = 1816-21) and Sommervogel (1893), vol. 4, 1457 [both key bibliographical resources for the study of Mexican humanism]. However the edition of Accomazzi (1961) was not known to Peñalosa, whose own Spanish translation and edition of the Latin text was produced in 1998.

35. Latin oratory continued in New Spain for well over a century after the Jesuit expulsions. Osorio Romero (1976) which reviews Cicero's influence in the *aulas,* in the Royal and Pontifical University and in Jesuit Colleges, treats funeral orations (151-64) – with a bibliography (165-216) of printed editions of 86 separate Latin speeches. These were composed between 1603 and 1895. Landívar's Declamation in *El llanto de los ojos* is numbered 54 (at 199).

36. Figueredo himself 'called the Society his Mother' (4): *Ab illaque die Ignatium Parentem nominare, Societatem Matrem vocitare.*

37. Landívar's diction indicates that he draws closely on the two Roman sources for this story, Valerius Maximus and Pliny: see n. 13 to my translation on p. 260 below. However, the possibility of Landívar encountering the episode in an anthology or later sourcebook cannot be excluded. It suits the design of the speech to follow the version of the story in which a girl saves the life of her mother (and not of her father as in other traditions).

38. Landívar does not specify the dialogue. The quotation is actually from Plato, *Laws* 717b.

39. Compare e.g. Cicero, *Catiline* 2.1 (*abiit, excessit, evasit, erupit*) and Landívar, *Decl.* 4 (*extendit, audaxit, cumulavit*); *Catiline* 1.5, 4.11 and Landívar, *Decl.* 6 (*Quae cum ita sint*); *Catiline* 4.1 (*deos immortales!*) and Landívar, *Decl.* 7 (*Deum immortalem!*). Other resemblances include: *Decl.* 2 (*absit verba invidia*) and Livy 9.19 (*absit iniuria verbo*); *Decl.* 12 (*infixus animo haeret dolor*) and Virgil, *Aeneid* 4.4 (*harent infixi pectore*). Osorio Romero (1976), 163-4 quotes the *exordia* of two Latin orations delivered in Mexico within the same year (one by Vicente Antonio de los Ríos in 1761, and the other by Ildefonso López de Aguado in 1762) to show how closely they are modelled on the *exordium* of Cicero's first oration against Catiline (*Catiline* 1.1).

40. This is quoted from the edition of Lavarenne (1948), 143 which converges with the text in Bergman (1926). Lavarenne's apparatus records *urbe* in some key seventh- to ninth-century manuscripts: *urbs* and *orbis* were often associated, and frequently confused by copyists. However, the argument here is primarily concerned with Landívar's substitution of *inquit* for Prudentius' *Romae.*

41. Symmachus, *Relatio* 3. The text is in Barrow (1973).

42. Matthews (1996) has bibliography on the controversy.

43. Osorio Romero (1980), 64 and (1990).

44. Spanish and New Spanish Jesuits exiled in Italy found themselves having to defend the quality of Hispano-Roman authors. See pp. 26-7 above.

45. According to Zambrano and Gutiérrez Casillas (1977), (16), 614 (sv. 'P. Vallejo, José'), Vallejo was born in Jalostotitlán in the Mexican diocese of Guadalajara in 1718. After joining the Jesuits in 1741, he studied humanities at the renowned Jesuit seminary of Tepotzotlán in 1745 (as did Landívar ten years later) and theology in Mexico City. Ordained by 1751, he taught grammar in the College of Chiapas before becoming professor of philosophy at the Colegio de Guatemala in 1755, where he remained until 1767, having become prefect of the Congregation (1761) and teacher of theology there (1767) as well as Superior of the Seminary of San Borja (1764). Vallejo was in Spain before joining the Jesuits in Italy. He died in Bologna in 1785 and was buried in the church of Santa Maria della Purità.

Part I: Essay Studies

46. *Vida del Señor San Joseph* (Cesena, 1774); *Vida de San Joaquín y Santa Ana* (Cesena, 1774).

47. Horace had many imitators in New Spain: Méndez Plancarte (1937). Piastra (1994) surveys Renaissance Latin Marian poetry in Italy. The Virgin of Guadalupe prompted an abundance of such poetry in Mexico: see p. 79 nn. 44-5 above.

48. For Villerías' *Guadalupe*, see Chapter 1 (iii) above. The text was known to Landívar's compatriot – and housemate – in Italy, Francisco Xavier Clavigero: pp. 81-2 nn. 75 and 101 above.

49. The poem is numbered 26 in Ciplijauskaité (1985), 83-4. I am extremely grateful to Biruté Ciplijauskaité for drawing this sonnet of Góngora to my attention: its evocation by Landívar could have implications for the poetic programme of the *Rusticatio Mexicana*: see pp. 64-8 above.

50. Ovid, *Metamorphoses* 15.810: Jupiter tells Venus she may herself inspect 'the events [recorded on] tablets of bronze and solid iron' (*ex aere et solido rerum tabularia ferro*).

51. The *ut pictura poesis* principle (*Ars Poetica* 361) functions metapoetically in Landívar's sonnet and ode: that Horatian coinage is cited by Alegre in his *Arte poética de Mr. Boileau* to support the assertion that the sublime should be clear and unaffected: Alegre in García Icazbalceta (1889), 28; cf. Higgins (2002), 128.

52. La *'Pontifical' del Doctor Babia* had been singled out for praise by Baltasar Gracián in his 1642 manifesto for Baroque poetics, *Agudeza y arte de ingenio* 'Sharpness and the art of inventiveness': Ciplijauskaité (1985), 83-4.

53. Alegre in his *Arte poética de Mr. Boileau* concedes that Góngora sometimes shows 'a sublimity of talent (*una sublimidad de ingenio*) equal, if not superior to the Greeks and Romans' and compares Góngora, *Sonnet* 17 (*Oh, claro honor de líquido elemento*) with Horace, *Odes* 3.13 (*O fons Bandusiae, splendidior vitro*): García Icazbalceta (1889), 23.

3. The Recollection of Arcadia: Conception and design in the *Rusticatio Mexicana*

1. The *coup* led to the longest civil war in Latin American history: Handy (1996).

2. Ordoñez Mazariegos (2003), 103. The facsimile is in Mata Gavidia (1950); the periodical *Estudios Landivarianos* was published through the 1950s.

3. Humboldt (1811), 211 cited in Nemes (1971), 299. The second book of the *Rusticatio Mexicana* (*RM*) treats volcanic and seismic activity.

4. Maury (1806), 32 quotes *RM* 7.163-5, 169-70 (on the use of gunpowder in mining) to gloss his own verse *Miro, peñascos estallar deshechos*: 'I gaze, as rocks are blown apart'. Born in Málaga in 1772, the Neoclassical vernacular poet Juan María Maury y Benítez was exiled to France in 1814.

5. Menéndez y Pelayo (1958), clxvi.

6. Menéndez y Pelayo (1958), clxv-clxix.

7. Gómez Álvarez and Téllez Guerrero (1997) list a copy in the library of Antonio Bergosa y Jordán, who was Bishop of Oaxaca from 1802 to 1817.

8. Loureda (1924), Escobedo (1969). Valdés (1965) and Chamorro (1987) are more recent translations. Couttolenc Cortés (1973), a study of Escobedo, offers a useful account of classical and literary culture in the late nineteenth and early twentieth centuries in Mexico at 23-49.

9. Unless otherwise specified, this chapter refers to the longer Bologna (1782) edition of 15 books. The full titles of the two original editions are as follows: *Rusticatio Mexicana, seu rariora quaedam ex agris mexicanis decerpta atque in* *libros decem distributa a Raphaele Landivar, Mutinae 1781*; and *Rusticatio Mexicana, editio altera auctior et emendatior, Bononiae 1782*.

10. Leaving aside the anti-American and anti-Hispanic intellectual currents with which Clavigero and Abad were concerned, Landívar's comment may be in response to the ignorance routinely encountered by Spanish Americans in Italy. López de Priego, reports that the first Jesuits to arrive from the Americas were regarded by the Italians as a 'different species': his barber asked if the sun was the same colour in the Indies; others jibed that 'over there' no one knew the nominative case: Cuevas (1944), 56-7.

11. Mata Gavidia (1950), 103; Suárez (2003), 86.

12. Henríquez Ureña (1945), Chamorro (1987), and Suárez (2004), studies by scholars from the Dominican Republic, Costa Rica, and Argentina respectively, show that interest in the *RM* is by no means confined to Guatemala and Mexico.

13. Landívar's diction here could be connected to a number of classical Latin sources including Propertius, *Elegies* 2.1.9 (*sive lyrae carmen digitis percussit eburnis*), 3.2.9 (*Apolline dextro*); Ovid, *Fasti* 1.6 (*en tibi devoto numine dexter ades*); Statius, *Silvae* 5.5.31 (*eburno pollice*); *Aetna* 4 (*dexter venias*).

14. On intertextuality and Landívar's use of classical mythology see Suárez (2004).

15. Escobedo (1969), xviii.

16. See further Gil Alonso (1947), 117-22. Fracastoro's *Syphilis* is another neo-Latin poem modelled on Virgil's *Georgics* which echoes the *Aeneid*: see now Hardie (2004), as well as Eatough (1984) and Eatough (1999b).

17. Mata Gavidia (1950), 29. Landívar's poetic reflections on exile are discussed here on pp. 59-61: the amount of critical attention given to those reflections outweighs the relatively moderate emphasis given to them in Landívar's actual text.

18. Quintilian, *Institutio* 10.1.95: *vir Romanorum eruditissimus* (cf. Plutarch, *Romulus* 12.3); Petrarch, *Trionfo della Fama* 3.38: *il terzo gran lume di Roma* (cf. Petrarch, *Familiares* 24.6.). These commendations of Varro, as well as his work, would have been known in New Spain: Millares Carlo (1986); Osorio Romero (1980).

19. Laird (2004b), 27; Coroleu (1999), (2001) on Politian's influence in Spain.

20. Fantazzi (2004), xiv.

21. Fantazzi (2004), xiv; Politian, *Rusticus* 5-6.

22. Gil Alonso (1947), 117-24 and throughout.

23. Politian's own *Stanze per la giostra* is echoed in his *Rusticus*: Bausi (1996) provides a detailed inventory of sources for the *Silvae*.

24. See Mynors (1990), 125 on Virgil, *Georgics* 2.176.

25. Pontano, *De Hortis Hesperidum* ('On the Gardens of the Hesperides') a poem about growing oranges, and Vida, *De Bombycum Cura et Usu* ('On Keeping Silkworms'). Vida may have been a model for the account of cochineal beetles in *RM* 4.28-205. Both are listed in Kerson (1990), 150 (along with the *Rusticus*, *Horti*, and *Praedium Rusticum*) as significant precedents for the *RM*, and a less well known work by Girolamo Lagomarsini, *De Origine Fontium* ('On the Source of Springs') which was first recited in Rome in 1726: cf. *RM* 3 on springs. Compare the inventory of modern Latin poetry given by Landívar's friend Alegre, quoted at p. 29 above.

26. Haskell (2003), 17-60 provides excellent coverage of both these poems; Osorio Romero (1980), 81 refers to their reception in Mexico. Both Rapin and Vanière make mention of the Americas in their compositions.

27. See the text of Rapin in McDonald (1932), 162.

28. See further Haskell (2003), 38.

29. The epigraph is from Vanière, *Praedium Rusticum* 1.21-2: *Secreti tacita capior dulcedine ruris: / Quod spectare juvat, placuit deducere versu.* ('I am captivated by the silent loveliness of the remote countryside. As it is a joy to behold, so has it been a pleasure to render in verse.'). Valdés (1965), 24 identifies two possible echoes of Vanière by Landívar: (i) four verses from *Praedium Rusticum* 1 (beginning *Composito glomerare gradu* on horse-taming) in *RM* 10.71-5; (ii) some verses from *Praedium Rusticum* 12 (beginning *Colla rigent hirsuta jubis/Dira rubent*) in *RM* 15.47-58. Verses are not numbered in any of the editions of the *Praedium Rusticum.*

30. Compare *artis in rebus* from Ovid, *Epistulae ex Ponto* 3.2.25-6: *arctus* is an alternative form of the adjective *artus.*

31. Compare e.g. Ovid, *Tristia* 4.2.57, *haec ego summotus qua possum mente videbo* (the poet imagines himself witnessing a Triumph in Rome); *Epistulae ex Ponto* 2.8.19-21: *hunc ego cum spectem, videor mihi cernere Romam;/fallor ...* .

32. See Landívar's Notes on the *Rusticatio Mexicana*, sv. Book 1, n. 9 (on *RM* 1.285) at p. 265. Alegre's *Alexandriad* was first published in Forlì in 1773, some years before the first edition of the *RM*, as it had been composed by Alegre prior to his exile. A manuscript version of the *Alexandriad* is also preserved in Mexico.

33. The end of Landívar's *Appendix* (106) also recalls the proem of *RM* 1.1-6: see pp. 67-8 above.

34. Higgins (2000), 120-1. Virgil *Ecl.* 1.19: *Urbem quam dicunt Romam, Meliboee* ('The city they call Rome, Meliboeus').

35. Although *La Grandeza Mexicana* ('The Greatness of Mexico') is in Spanish, it shows the evident influence of classical sources, notably Virgil, Ovid and Lucan. Balbuena (2001) is a modern edition. A full account of the cultural importance of cities in Spanish and colonial Spanish American culture is provided by Kagan (2000); Rama (1996) has been a very influential and adventurous interpretation of the subject.

36. Translated and quoted in Browning (1985), 13.

37. Browning (1985); Chapter 1, pp. 25-6 above.

38. Brading (1971). For Jesuit poetry on mining see Haskell (2003) and Mariano (forthcoming) on the *Brasilienses Aurifodinae* ('The Gold Mines of Brazil'), a Latin didactic poem of 1,823 verses composed by Basílio da Gama in the 1760s.

39. Vanière had made explicit his decision to refrain from employing themes from classical myth: Haskell (2003), 38-60. The incorporation of classical myth into humanist poetry had been much debated in the Italian Renaissance and preoccupied Petrarch, Boccaccio, Salutati and Pontano among others. Spagnoli ('Mantovano') adorned his biblical poems with pagan deities, forcefully defending this practice in his *Apologeticon*, first published in 1488: a text is in Marrone (2000). The debate acquired fresh momentum in Mexico during the 1500s, where polytheism was seen to pose a practical threat to Christian teaching: Gruzinski (2002), 91-106; Lupher (2003), 229-34, and 273-88 on 'pagan survivals'.

40. I have not been able to locate this poet: possibly Golmarius Marsiglianus has been invented to bamboozle readers, and the elegiac verses are really Landívar's own.

41. Jacques-Christophe Valmont de Bomare (whom Landívar refers to as 'Bomare'), a mineralogist and natural historian, was not an original thinker, but an extraordinarily successful writer and lecturer: Burke (1976).

42. See the following Notes by Landívar: Book 3, Notes 3 and 4; Book 4, Notes 3 and 5; Book 8, Note 2.

43. Before the word *Finis*, the 1781 Modena edition has these words: *Quae huic complendo carmini desiderari possunt, alias fortasse dabimus, vita comite* ('The things possibly required for this poem to be finished, we shall perhaps provide another time, if life is kind.')

44. Mercury escorts souls to the Underworld in Virgil, *Aeneid* 4.242-4; cf. Horace, *Odes* 1.10.16-20. Ovid, *Fasti* 5.681-90 presents the Roman god as patron of cheating merchants, a role which is also appropriate here (*RM* 7.287-319). Hardie (1986), 278 discusses the attributes of Mercury, with useful bibliography.

45. *RM* 7.302-19 can be compared to *Aeneid* 6.608-28. Kerson (1990) distinguishes the 'mock-heroic' mode from the 'miniature epic' form in the *RM*, examining the sketches of cochineal worms in Book 4 as an example of the former, and the account of the volcanic and seismic activity in Book 2 for the latter. Even neo-Latin poets opposed to Lucretius' Epicureanism were prone to imitate his parodic or mock-heroic style: see Yasmin Haskell's discussion of Tomasso Ceva and other Jesuit didactic poets in Hardie (forthcoming). In the same volume Eric Baker assesses Lucretius' bearing on Kant and the European Enlightenment. For another possible echo of Lucretius' proem to his third book, see n. 68 below.

46. The *Argumenta Totius Carminis* come after the *Monitum* and the general table of contents in the Bologna edition: (1782), viii-xxviii.

47. Chamorro (1987), xxxviii-xxxix tabulates the sequence of divinities invoked at the beginning of each book of the *RM* and notes: 'the poet opens the performance of his song by invoking the propitious assistance of the leader of the Muses [Apollo], and culminates it with a command for silence from the Delphic bard, as he invokes the 'Almighty Wisdom of the Supreme God' [*Appendix* 16] to help him herald the brilliant triumph of the Cross.'

48. Ovid, *Metamorphoses* 1.1; Lucan, *Pharsalia* 1.67.

49. The canonical version of the story of Arachne is in Ovid, *Met.* 6.1-145: Feeney (1991), 190-4 discusses the metaliterary implications of the Ovidian episode. Kerson (1990), 160 considers the mock-heroic qualities of the inimical spider. Valdés (1965), 116 proposes a connection between *Lydam ... puellam* in RM 4.7 and the figure in Acts of the Apostles 16:14 ('one who heard us was a woman named Lydia ... a seller of purple goods, who was a worshipper of God'), but it is not clear what the significance of such a connection would be.

50. Virgil, *Georgics* 4.315-558; Manilius, *Astronomica* 5.538-630. The preface by Vanière apologising for the inclusion of mythological metamorphoses in the earlier books of his *Praedium Rusticum* may have influenced Landívar's practice: p. 88 n. 39 above.

51. This occurred in September 1759, in Jorullo.

52. Virgil, *Aeneid* 6.86-7 (the Sibyl's grim prediction to Aeneas): *Bella, horrida bella/et Thybrim multo spumantem sanguine cerno* ('I see wars, horrific wars, and the Tiber foaming with streams of blood').

53. Jonah 3:3-8.

54. Higgins (2000), 149: 'This demonstration of ecclesiastical practicality identifies the cleric as the incarnation of the more pragmatic form of priestly agency developed by the Jesuits, particularly in their interventions in overseas contexts.'

55. Kerson (1990), 151-7 helpfully examines this 'mock epic' narrative in relation to passages in Lucretius and Virgil. George (1998) refers to Edward George's own unpublished teaching text on the classical sources in relation to *RM* 2 for use in the contemporary classroom.

56. Higgins (2000), 113: 'The small body of criticism written about Landívar's poem prior to the last twenty years tends to reconstruct the work as the exile's expression of nostalgia for his homeland.' Exile is also a theme in some more recent discussions cited by Higgins at 253 n. 11: Chamorro (1987), xxxii, xxxviii, and Osorio Romero (1989).

57. Compare Said (2000), 186. Ellen Finkelpearl drew my attention to this essay and to other discussions of exile. Cheney (2002), 15 notes that the application of 'career criticism' to literary texts has given further prominence to 'the idea of travel, the metaphor of journey, and in particular the writer in motion.' Claassen (1999) considers various presentations of exile by Greek and Roman authors.

58. Sigurdsson (1999) is a history of theories about volcanoes from classical times. Kircher – best known for his studies of Egypt, the Orient, Lull's logic, and magnetism – published his *Mundus Subterraneus* in 1664, having visited Vesuvius and Etna in 1638. Osorio Romero (1993) assembles the correspondence between Kircher and some New Spanish scholars between 1655 and 1677. A handwritten inscription in an edition of the *Mundus Subterraneus* in the Biblioteca Palafoxiana in Puebla, indicating the book was acquired in 1761, proves Kircher's volcanology enjoyed currency in New Spain more immediately prior to the expulsion of the Jesuits. The sixteenth-century account of American volcanoes in Acosta (2003) must have been known to Landívar, whose Notes draw from other parts of Acosta's work: see my comments on Landívar's Note 3 to *RM* 1 at p. 263 below.

59. Contrast the use of *nobis* ('for us') at 13.17. In Book 13 the poet constantly positions himself in the American location he describes – although 13.357-8 hint at his relocation. It is tempting to read the account of the healing powers of an unnamed bird in 13.375-80 as a veiled reference to the author's predicament of exile: by drinking the same water the creature's tongue has touched the sick man can relieve a 'broken heart' (*dirum fracto pellit de pectore morbum*). See also p. 64 above and n. 70 below.

60. E.g. *Epistulae ex Ponto* 4.13. Habinek (1998), 198-69 and (2002), 59 propose that Ovid performs as a 'colonising subject' in his exile poetry, 'do[ing] the work of empire': Davis (2002) offers powerful criticism of this position.

61. Hardie (2002a), 296. Claassen (1999) analyses literary devices pertaining to exile in Cicero, Ovid, Boethius, and Dio Chrysostom.

62. *On the Sublime* 35.3-36.1 (tr. D.A. Russell): Russell and Winterbottom (1972), 494. Laird (2006) contains discussion and bibliography on Longinus and his influence. The Longinian passage quoted here is evidently echoed in Kant's *Critique of Judgment* §28 (= Kant (1987), 120): 'Consider bold, overhanging, and as it were, threatening rocks, thunderclouds piling up in the sky and moving about accompanied by lightning and thunderclaps, volcanoes with all their destructive power, hurricanes with all the devastation they leave behind, the boundless ocean heaved up, the high waterfall of a mighty river, and so on. Compared to the might of any of these our ability to resist becomes an insignificant trifle.' Kant's *Critique* was published in 1790 – not long after the *Rusticatio Mexicana*.

63. Ashfield and Bolla (1996); Monk (1960).

64. Burke (1987); Kant (1987), book 2, 'The Analytic of the Sublime'. The remarks from Kant's *Critique of Judgment,* quoted above in n. 62, had they not been published a decade later, might have been regarded as a prescription for the *RM* – as a poem which gives prominence to thunderstorms, volcanoes, earthquakes, rock formations, and to human vulnerability in face of nature's power. Landívar's conception of sublimity is *not* the same as Kant's, but the pervasiveness of Longinus' influence on all kinds of writers in this period is very evident.

65. Higgins (2000), (2002).

66. On Boileau and Longinus, see Brody (1958). Early Latin translations of Longinus include those by Domenico Pizzimenti *De Grandi Orationis Genere* (first printed Naples, 1566), Pietro Pagani, *De Sublimi Dicendi Genere* (Venice, 1572 reprinted with Pizzimenti in Venice, 1644), Gabrielle dalla Pietra, *De Grandi sive Svblimi genere orationis* (Geneva, 1612, with reprintings 1638-63); Da Falgano produced a manuscript Italian translation, *Della altezza del dire* in 1575: Weinberg (1950) gives bibliographical details. However I have discovered nothing to indicate these versions of Longinus were available in New Spain. If Alegre, Landívar or Agustín Pablo de Castro read Longinus in Mexico (p. 82 n. 95 above), it would have been in Greek: Robortello's *editio princeps* (Padova, 1554), the Aldine text of Paulus Minutius (Venice 1555), or possibly Franciscus Portus (Geneva, 1569).

67. Horace *Ars Poetica* 408-52. Higgins (2002), 126 notes that 'as the discourse of *gongorismo* became more dominant, [late seventeenth-century] Spanish American thought would accord greater importance to the concept of *ingenio*, according a stronger role of agency to the author'.

68. The site is best visited in winter: Landívar explained earlier (3.133-4) that in summer it is plagued with flies, gnats, and poisonous spiders. The word *nobilis* might convey the *sensibility* of the young men (cf. Longinus 9.1-2 for association of sublimity with innate greatness) as opposed to their social status. But Higgins (2000), 164 holds that the sublimity of this scene is appropriated by Landívar 'as a symbol of *criollo* patrimony' – although there is nothing to suggest that the youths are not indigenous.

A possible articulation of sublimity in Seneca, *Quaestiones naturales* 5.15.1-3 offers a striking parallel to Landívar's vignette. Seneca relates that men sent by Philip II of Macedon to explore an abandoned mine found vast reservoirs of water held in the generous embrace of the earth: a sight which prompted a sensation of *horror* for those who beheld it but of *voluptas* for Seneca as he read of it. Likewise, Landívar conjoins fear and pleasure in the earlier part of this description: the words *horreret, terret, horrendum* and *terrere* are employed in *RM* 3.239-54 of a place which also captivates birds with its 'sweetness' (*RM* 3.236)! Jim Porter sees the influence of the Lucretius 3.28-9 on this passage of Seneca: *His ibi me rebus quaedam divina voluptas/ percipit atque horror* ('At these things a kind of divine pleasure and a horror take hold of me'). Although Bailey (1947) iii, 992 interprets Lucretius' expression in terms of Roman religious emotion, compare Kant's claim (n. 62 above) that the apprehension of nature's might is 'all the more attractive the more fearful it is, provided we are in a safe place' with *RM* 2.10-11!

69. In Landívar's dedicatory poem, the old city of Guatemala was compared to the Egyptian phoenix, as his expression *Phariae volucri* ('the bird of Pharos') indicates: *Pharius* was a common transferred epithet for 'Egyptian' in imperial Roman poetry. (The phoenix is connected with Egypt in Herodotus, *Histories* 2.73 and Tacitus, *Annals* 6.28.) For Sigüenza y Góngora's associations between Mesoamerica and Egypt which drew from the *Oedipus Aegyptiacus* (1652-4) of his contemporary Athanasius Kircher, see Brading (2001), 115, and my comments on Landívar's Note on *RM* 10.115, pp. 272-3 below. Kant in his *Critique of Judgment* §28 (Kant (1987), 108) considers the the Egyptian pyramids in relation to 'aesthetic comprehension', but not the Nile: for Longinus' remark about the Nile, see n. 71 below.

70. Landívar's possible allegorisation of the healing power of poetry as a bird in 13.375-80 may be relevant: n. 59 above.

71. Compare Russell (1964), xlvi: 'L[onginus]'s remarks in 35 about man's natural inclination to admire the grander works of nature – Nile, Danube, Rhine, Ocean, Etna – nourished the notion that there were certain topics in themselves sublime.' As well as Kant's *Critique of Judgment* (1790) §28 quoted in n. 62 above, Ann Radcliffe's contemporaneous novels exemplify this: *A Sicilian Romance* (1790); *The Romance of the Forest* (1792); *The Mysteries of Udolpho* (1794).

72. Virgil, *Eclogues* 6.61-86, 10.1-15; Propertius, *Elegies* 2.34.61-94; cf. Ovid, *Amores* 1.15.

73. *Etenim videbantur non solum tersa, plena, poetica; sed etiam eiusmodi, ut Imaginum sublimitate, gravitate sententiarum, Argumenti Divinitatem mirifice subsequerentur.* Vannetti, *Epistula ad Abadium* in Manuel Fabri, *Specimen vitae auctoris,* in Fernández Valenzuela (1974), 86. Compare p. 27 above on Vannetti.

74. Menéndez y Pelayo (1958): 'For our purposes, Mexican poetry of the seventeenth century can be reduced to one name which is worth many: that of Sor Juana Inés de la Cruz.'

75. Ruskin's discussion of the pathetic fallacy is in ch. 12 of *Modern Painters* (1856), but such forms of personification go back to Homer. An impressive instance is *RM* 12.290-316, where the fallacy operates in both the tenor *and* the vehicle of a sustained simile: the spring of Ixtlán, which recoils in apparent fright from anyone who seeks to examine it, is compared to the 'sensitive plant' (which modestly folds its leaves when suddenly touched). Landívar's Notes 9 and 10 to Book 12 (p. 276 below) indicate he accepts the evidence for both phenomena.

76. Ovid, *Tristia* 4.10.53 confirms Gallus as creator of the genre: Courtney (1996) has further information and bibliography.

77. The first volume of Sor Juana's collected works published in Madrid in 1689 was entitled *Inundación castálida de la única poetisa, musa décima* ('Castalian inundation of the unique poetess, the tenth muse'). The expression 'Tenth Muse' originates in a Greek epigram in praise of Sappho: Palatine Anthology 9.506. In antiquity this epigram was attributed to Plato.

78. Cycnus is *not* associated with poetry on the occasions he appears in Ovid *Metamorphoses.* Harrison (1991), 121 is an important note on *Aeneid* 10.191: *maestum Musa solatur amorem* 'he solaced his sad love with the Muse'. Harrison (i) compares a similar phrase Virgil uses of Orpheus (*Georgics* 4.464), who has long been identified with Gallus by Virgil's readers and (ii) notes 'the use [in *Aen.* 10.191-2] of the themes of singing in the shade and songs of unhappy love irresistibly recalls both the style and content of the *Eclogues'.* The network of intertexts here in *RM* 1.289-97 underlines that association, but the notion of poetry as consolation for sorrow is also crucial to Landívar's poem: see the discussion of exile at pp. 59-61 above.

79. These allusions to *Eclogue* 6 could suggest Silenus is here playfully adopted as a *porte-parole* by Landívar: Virgil characterises Silenus as a didactic poet who sings to his students, the shepherds, of nature and of surprising phenomena.

80. Suetonius, *On Grammarians* 16 and *Life of Augustus* 66.2; the comments of the Servian corpus on Virgil, *Eclogue* 10, and *Georgics* 4, would have been known to Landívar as they had enjoyed a wide circulation since the Middle Ages. Raaflaub and Samons (1990), 423 is a good recent treatment of Gallus' condemnation and suicide.

81. The *Respuesta* is in vol. 4 of the *Obras Completas* of Sor Juana: Méndez Plancarte (1994). Sayers Peden (1997) is an excellent anthology of Sor Juana's work which includes a Spanish text and facing English translation of the *Respuesta.*

82. Leonard (1983), 173-92 recounts these events.

83. Higgins (2000), 142: 'amid the favourable surroundings of the lake and its shores, the poets, in turn, are held to have enhanced its pastoral order and harmony with their measured verse... Landívar canonizes [Sor Juana's] unique talent by again placing Mexican cultural production within the framework of classical humanism'.

84. Landívar's Note (13) on Sor Juana is the most commendatory of those on Mexican authors in this part of the work.

85. On this lecture by Alegre and its pedagogical implications, see Van der Poel (1990). Deck (1976), 23 notes that the clarity advocated in the *Prolusio* was 'in accord with the Rules for Preachers and with the Constitutions of the Jesuit Order'.

86. See pp. 27, 33 and 42 above.

87. Compare e.g. Nemes (1971), 303; Higgins (2000), 130-1.

88. In his letter on the *Alexandriad*, Alegre, Landívar's Mexican contemporary in Italy, refers to Petrarch's *Africa*. The relevant passage was quoted above, p. 29.

89. The term 'allegory' is taken broadly here – simply to denote one meaning being conveyed by another: see my discussion in Boys-Stones (2003), 151-75.

90. José Rafael Campoy, who taught at the Colegio Máximo, would have exposed Landívar to these and other modern thinkers such as Descartes, Locke and Newton; see p. 24ff. above, and Navarro (1983), 111-33.

91. Kerson (1976); cf. Higgins (2000).

92. More's *Utopia* ed. Logan, Adams, Miller (1995), 112.

93. Logan, Adams, Miller (1995), 119-20.

94. Zavala (1965) assembles Silvio Zavala's essays on More and Vasco de Quiroga in Spanish, French and English. Further works are cited in n. 17 on p. 77 above.

95. *Colección de Documentos Inéditos del Archivo de Indias*, Madrid 1864-89, xiii, 420, quoted in Zavala (1965). The famous *Apologética Historia* of Las Casas was an attempt to ennoble the Indians; in Landívar's time, Clavigero's *Ancient History of Mexico* (book 1, ch. 17) suggested that the Mexicans were less avaricious than the Spanish: Clavigero (2003), 64. In a modern history of the Aztecs – a people who lived on waterways – Vaillant (1965), 122-34 emphasises their strong community spirit and notes at 34 that 'personal fortunes were non-existent'.

96. Compare Higgins (2000), 183.

97. Hesiod, *Works and Days* 202-12 discussed by West (1978), 204-5 and Daly (1961); compare the story attributed to Aesop and the later Latin fable: numbered 4 and 567 in Perry (1952), 322, 612.

98. See my comment on Landívar's Note (5) on 13.313, p. 278 below.

99. Fracastoro, *Syphilis* 3.151-99. Eatough (1984), 182 notes on this passage: 'The violence which is here inflicted on those lovely innocent creatures mirrors the violence that was to be inflicted on the Indians. It is an irony that the Indians in Columbus' procession at Seville carried parrots in cages. Parrots were involved in that first fateful exchange of gifts between Indians and Spaniards at which Columbus noted the natives' potentiality for "service".'

100. This passage echoes *Aeneid* 1.12-14 and *Guadalupe* 1.16-40, including 1.33-4: *Dives opum, dives pictai vestis, et auro/ Dives* ('[Mexico] rich in resources, in coloured cloth, rich in gold'.) The stichometric correspondence between *RM* 1.32-3 and *Guadalupe* 1.32-3 was noted above, p. 79 n. 41. The fact that Landívar and Villerías are both recalling Mateo de Castroverde's Latin panegyric adds to the complex layering of allusion in this passage. On Castroverde's surviving verses, see pp. 16-17 above.

101. The *criollo* writers Zapata and Alarcón are each classed as *Mexicanus* in Landívar's Notes 10 and 12 to Book 1; as are the indigenous *voladores*: see Landívar's Note 2 on 15.236.

102. See Landívar's Notes 7, 8, 9 and 11 to Book 1.

103. Landívar's indisposition to question the employment of African workers on sugar plantations has elicited conflicting readings: Mata Gavidia (1950), 69 regards the poet as compassionate, partly on the basis that Landívar requested in his will that his mother's slaves should be freed; Haskell (2003), 315-16 does not. However, Alegre argued against slavery in his *Institutiones Theologicae*: Deck (1976), 22-3. The Mexican poets exhibit far more humanity in this regard than Jesuits from other nations, who still depended on slave labour: the *Brasilienses Aurifodinae*, composed in 1762-4 by the Brazilian Basílio da Gama is unquestionably complacent about slavery (p. 88 n. 38 above). The endeavours of the Peruvian Juan Pablo Viscardo y Guzmán (1748-98) at least show that the Jesuits could play a politically progressive role with regard to Spanish American independence: Batllori (1953) and Viscardo y Guzmán (2002).

104. Leonard (1983), 157-71 offers a salutary comparison between the respective reading habits in the colonies of New England and New Spain, in a lively account of the American book trade in 1683.

PART II

TEXTS AND TRANSLATIONS

Prefatory note

Detailed discussion of textual issues is rarely necessary for works which have been in print *ab initio*, but the following points and caveats may be useful:

The *Funebris Declamatio* was originally published in F. Molina, *El llanto de los ojos* (Puebla de los Angeles, 1766) and next appeared in an untitled, undated anthology of funeral speeches compiled by José María Lafragua in the nineteenth century. Editions of the Declamation itself were later published by Gervasio Accomazzi (Guatemala, 1961), and by Joaquín Antonio Peñalosa (Mexico, 1998). Accomazzi's text was not known to Peñalosa, whose transcription contains some errors and omissions. Unlike Accomazzi's version, the text in this volume follows the orthography of the 1766 printing (e.g. *consilijs* for *consiliis*), with the exception of a few irregularities which I have sought to correct. On these occasions, the original readings are given below the Latin text. The twelve paragraph-like sections of the speech have been numbered for convenient reference.

Landívar's ode and sonnet were published in Vallejo's *Vida de la Madre de Dios* (Cesena, 1779). Peñalosa (1998) has an edition of these poems.

The text of Landívar's Latin annotations to the *Rusticatio Mexicana* in this volume is taken directly from the 1782 printing, and again, the original form and spelling have been preserved. The same applies to the poet's quotations in Spanish, French and Italian. My English translations of these items, as with the Declamation and the poems, are intended to be literal rather than literary.

Graydon Regenos' text of the *Rusticatio Mexicana* was based on the second Bologna edition. That 1782 printing, promisingly billed as an *editio emendatior,* is in fact riddled with typographical errors. Below an absurdly short list of only six errata (two of which direct the reader to the wrong verses), Landívar wrote:

Si quae sunt alia, ipse corriges.
If there are other errors, you may correct them yourself.

95

There is little reason to believe the poet was really cavalier about such matters – and still less if the competent production of the *Funebris Declamatio* in Mexico some years before is anything to go by. Landívar's remark rather suggests that he had given up on the bungling Bolognese compositors of the Typographia Sancti Thomae Aquinatis. Even the line numbering of the 1782 edition, in multiples of 5, is often defective. For example, what is strictly verse 381 of Book 11 is numbered '380', so that there are reckoned to be 448 verses in the book rather than the actual 449; similarly, verse 61 of Book 15 is mislabelled '60', so that there appear to 335 verses in the book instead of 336.

Twentieth-century editors of the *Rusticatio Mexicana* have not really confronted this problem: Octaviano Valdés simply followed the erroneous system of the original and Ignacio Loureda did not apply any numbering to the verses of his text. Regenos, who gives numerical references below each grouping of verses (on these groupings see pp. 56-8 above), remedies the two inconsistencies I have just specified. However, where in Book 3 of the 1782 edition, a group of verses numbered 131-6 in fact constitutes only four verses, Regenos follows suit: his paragraph of four verses is thus labelled 'll. 131-6'. For better or worse, the flawed stichometry of the poem seems to have become a convention.

Regenos takes account of Landívar's errata, and he makes further, uncontroversial corrections of his own, although one or two new errors have crept in (e.g. *folatia* for *solatia* in the penultimate line (33) of the opening elegy, *Urbi Guatimalae*.) There are a few comparable slips in the translation (e.g. 'Iris' instead of 'Isis' in the rendering of *Isiaci* at 3.200), and other points one might query: at 13.312 the wingspan of the eagle perhaps should be given as twelve cubits rather than six (*bis senas lata per ulnas*). The style of the English rendering often has a vintage feel: 'social diseases' now appears a rather outmoded expression for syphilis (*gallica pestis* 12.211).

Nonetheless, taken as a whole, Regenos' translation is highly readable and his text of the *Rusticatio Mexicana* represents a significant improvement on its source. Without them, this introduction to Rafael Landívar would have been a forlorn document. Graydon Regenos' endeavour certainly deserves more diffusion than it has had to date, and it also merits recognition for being the first attempt to present a major work of American Hispano-Latin literature to an English readership.

Bibliographical details for the earliest printed editions of the *Funebris Declamatio*, the Marian poems, and the *Rusticatio Mexicana* are given above on p. 84 nn. 30-4; p. 40; and p. 86 n. 9, respectively.

FUNEBRIS
DECLAMATIO
PRO JUSTIS
A SOCIETATE JESU
EXSOLVENDIS
IN AMPLISSIMI JUXTA, AC VENERANDI
PONTIFICIS FUNERE
ILL^{MI}. SCILICET,
D.D.D. FRANCISCI
JOSEPHI DE FIGUEREDO,
ET VICTORIA,
POPAIANENSIS PRIMUM EPISCOPI,
DEINDE
ARCHIEPISCOPI GUATHIMALENSIS
DIGNISSIMI,
A P. RAPHAELE LANDIVAR
Societatis Jesu.

1. ADSUM, AUDITORES AMPLISSImi, non illius scrutator consilij, quod vitae placuit Auctori, ut Illustrissimus D.D.D. FRANCISCUS JOSEPHUS DE FIGUEREDO ET VICTORIA, lachrymabili sane, acerboque funere raperetur: adsum incredibilis pietatis admirator: adsum acerbissimi doloris meritum, atque extremum Societatis universae luctum vobis omnibus nunciaturus. Quid enim acerbius unquam eventurum putatis, quàm uno ictu Principem benignissimum, Societatis delicium obijsse? In tanta enim rerum vicissitudine, ac temporum perturbatione, hoc se Societas recreabat, ac solabatur uno: in illum intuens, suarum, quas dolet, calamitatum memoriam abjiciebat: atque ipsius undique benignitate suffulta in spem animum pene labentem erigebat. Ah! quoties ille irrumpentibus conviciorum turbis Societatem obrutam roboravit! Aut poenarum alluvione prope demersam eripuit! Ea, qua semper floruit, animi lenitate, sereno vultu, ac demissis in terram oculis, terrena respuere, inhiare coelestia, in unoque omnium Moderatore Deo spem salutis constituere, nostros homines hortabatur: felici adeò orationis exitu, ut non lachrymas modò proprià tabescentium calamitate comprimeret; verùm & corda densissimis antè obducta tenebris hilararet. Quis enim usquam esse posset, aut ita humanitatis expers, quin tanto amoris argumento conniveret; aut tam barbaris assuetus moribus, qui suae in nos benevolentiae obsisteret hortatrici? Maximè cùm eorum omnium suo ipse praeluceret exemplo. Nihil est enim in dignitatis apice commendandum, quod coeteris non praetulerit: nihil in pietatis tramite adeò abjectum, quod tumidus umquam fastidierit: nihil demùm arduum, sublimiusve, quod maxima in Deum caritate non perfecerit aliquando. Cùm de Ecclesiasticae honore dignitatis ageretur, pompam ducebat: quid illustrius? Cùm sibi redderetur, vestes utique despectissimas, pannoso similis, induebat: quid demissius? Cùm invi-

97

dorum calumnijs impeteretur, tamquam meritas luiturus poenas reticebat: quid mansuetius? Cùm debitis alumnorum officijs pro dignitate exciperetur insigni beneficium gratiâ rependebat, compensabat: quid aut isto gratius, aut illo justius? Sed cùm haec, atque id generis alia nimia, prolixaque satis oratione indigeant, uno omnia complexurus verbo, ne multus sim, asseram confidenter, sic FIGUEREDO praefuisse, ut nemo possit attentiùs obedire; sic dictis audivisse, ut nemo queat magnificentius imperare. Quae quidem in adversis fortitudinem, in laboribus constantiam, in convitijs demissionem, inque omnibus omnia nostros homines admonebant.

2. Nunc autem, Auditores amplissimi, carissimo orbata Patrono, omnique solatio destituta Societas singultibus modum praescribet? Suspiria cohibebit? A lachrymis unquam temperabit? Quin etiam dies noctesque fletibus junget, ac tanti Principis memoriam suis luctibus perennabit? Dolor namque, qui, vocis aditu intercluso, cordis intima corrodebat, praeruptis iam praecordiorum ergastulis erumpit. Oculis lachrymarum undae minitantur, vocem suspiria intercludunt, ac denique, praeteriti memor ipsam cordis Regiam obruit dolor, ac suffocat. Non modò quod solito Societatem praesidio unius funere Libitina privaverit; sed praecipuè quod audenti falce dignum immortalitate Principem subsecuerit. Utinam & mortem pro viro tanto oppetere nobis contigisset. Libenter quisque, non secus quàm ad laurum evocatus, supremum gratulabundus diem obijsset. Atque ut tanti causa doloris nec vestrum aliquem fugiat, neque omnium saeclorum posteritatem futuram latere possit, animadvertite, quaeso, viri ornatissimi, in amplissimi demortui Principis casu Societatem (absit verbo invidia) Filium optimum perdidisse. Quod dum perficio, nostri causam doloris obortis fortasse lachrymis cognoscetis.

3. Nec me quidem praetervolat, Auditores, quàm abundè Pontifex Illustrissimus optimi Parentis munia in Societatem expleverit. Novi equidem, quantum ille pro Societatis salute, cùm Guathimalae, tùm etiam Popayani desudaverit: quantum, utrobique honoris ipsi cumulaverit: quantum denique illius prae suo decus procuraverit: adeo ut magni illius Ludovici Delphini aemulus nunquam sibi altiùs videretur extolli, quàm cùm laudibus Societatem filiam affici conspiciebat. Verùm haec missa facio; tum quòd vestrum neminem latere arbitror, tum praecipue, quod filij nomen gratius ipsi (siquis est sensus in morte) videatur. Cùm enim intento animo aureum illud Antiquitatis oraculum secum ipse meditabundus evolveret, *Nihil est tam honorificum liberis, quàm debitum honorem parentibus offerre*, honoris satis, ac gloriae providisse existimabat, si apud omnes nostrae filius Societatis audiret. Hinc & matris honore Societatem afficiebat, & filij se cognomento delectabat. Cujus in funere debuerat illa, fateor, aut Graecorum, Romanorumque legibus tumulum ex lilijs construere, aut saltem, Indorum more, castissimis manibus apparatu candido parentare. Sed cùm haec quàm longissimè â nostrum omnium dolore abhorreant, & tecta, & parietes, & vestibula, & urbis etiam compita, atratis modó squalere vestibus optaremus. Hujusce autem acerbissimi doloris meritum vestrismet objecturus oculis, Auditores, paucis, quae ipsi saepius observastis, exponam.

4. Vix enim, aut ne vix quidèm, adolescentiam iniverat FIGUEREDO, cùm ad graviora conversus prima Grammatices rudimenta edocendus in nostris aedibus admittitur Popayani. Praeclara indoles, modestia, ingeniumque pueri experrectum mirum est, quantam sibi benevolentiam conciliaverint; eorum in primis, qui suam maturiùs demissionem mirabantur. Ille, ut erat beneficij memor, amorem amore rependebat, eos praecipuè amplexans benevolentiae signis, â quibus literarum praeceptiones ediscebat. Hinc sensim, ut solet, et sine sensu effervere amor, novas in dies vires assumere, tantoque ardore flagrare ut ex illo tempore Societatem filiali coleret reverentia: quin, aut temporum injuriae, aut invidorum garrulitas, aut (quod caput est) ipse honoris, ac dignitatis apex suam in nos benevolentiam corruperint. Quam enim â puero in Societatem concepit, eandem prorsus mira animi constantia extendit, adauxit, cumulavit. Verùm cùm haec aliaque innumera exigua sibi viderentur, satis suo facturus studio inventum amor planè maximum cogitavit. Petijt enixé, obtinuitque ab R. admodum Societatis universae Praeposito Generali, ut inter ejusdem alumnos Societatis, annuente Sanctissimo, morti proximus cooptaretur. Rescriptum accipit, veneratur. Ab illaque die Ignatium Parentem nominare, Societatem Matrem vocitare, eaque animi demissione Praepositos nostros audire, ut omnibus profectò admirationi esset Ecclesiae Principem sacris redimitum infulis, eas ultrò amori, suaeque in Societatem benevolentiae maluisse posthabere.

5. Quid, si illud commemorem, cùm nostratum indumentum ferale voluit amiculum? Quid, cùm non alibi, quàm in nostris aedibus suum jussit corpus tumulandum? Quid, cùm supremum obiturus diem, quae olim vota obtulerat, innovavit? Filium profecto Societatis optimum! Dignum me herclè, quem Societas tota clarissimo Verdunensi Episcopo Carolo de Lorena conferret. Hic nostram amplexurus vitam sese ultrò dignitatibus abdicavit: ille ab hostium jaculis incolumem Societatem servaturus retinuit. Hic delicijs, opibusque abjectis perpetuam coluit paupertatem: thesauros ille, ut nostros homines egenos aleret, reservavit. Hic communem evasurus hostem in Societatem confugit: ille ita se totum dederat Societati ut tamen pro ejusdem salute in arenam posset dimicaturus prodire. Quoties enim viperinis Societatem morsibus dilaniantes increpavit! Quoties detrahentes reprehendit? Quoties denique ab innumeris, quibus impetebatur, hostibus illaesam, catafractamque servavit? Hunccine autem, Auditores amplissimi, Societas filium non agnoscet? Acerbissimum ejusdem casum non doleat? Lachrymisque assiduis non tabescet?

Funebris Declamatio

6. Lictores olim flagitiosum juvenem sententia Judicis obtruncaverant, eoque loci suffixum caput exposuerant unde brevi posset supplicium evulgari. Res pro voto cessit: patrati sceleris fama vulgatur, supplicium innotescit atque eo usque per urbem totam divagatur, ut miserae praecordia matris rigido pugione confoderet. Vix enim emortui comperit lanienam filij, cùm furenti similis in publicum dolore acta prodivit. Filij caput spectat, lachrymatur, coelum gemitibus, suspirijs, querimonijs implet. Quid verò tunc? Flagitiorum memoria acerbitatem imminuet? Dolorem sedabit? Aut saltem materna viscera debito sceleribus cruciatu consolabitur? Ah minime gentium. Domum quippe reversa mater tanto dolore correpta est, ut ejus magnitudine praefocata, eo ipso die, propria morte filium scelestissimum parentaverit. Tantùm scilicet parentum pietas dominatur in corde. Quae cum ita sint, Auditores, quis nobis jure succenseat, quòd Illustrissimum FIGUEREDO, Caritatis specimen, demissionis ideam, omnis probitatis exemplar, ac Societatem praeterea filiali prosequentem amore deploremus? Materna quidem certe Societatis viscera ferali ejusdem memoria adeo commoventur, ut dolorem suum omni sint posteritati aequatura. Quid verò, si ejus in nos beneficientiae memoriam refricemus? Nulla profecto gratia tanta erit, quae suis erga nos meritis vel ex parte quidem aequare possit. Quamobrem curae nobis semper erit, ne quae praestari[i] â nobis gratia possit, â vobis ullo unquam tempore desideretur, exigatur.

7. Repetite memoria, viri ornatissimi, pristinas hujusce Guathimalensis Collegij aerumnas, publicasque nostrorum omnium calamitates: quas ille nisi minuisset, relevasset, pepulisset:[ii] Deum immortalem! Quid in tanta temporum injuria de nobis actum arbitramini? Quae domestica incommoda nostros homines agitarent? Quae fames viscera miserorum atque intestina corroderet? Quae Cruces vitam utique aerumnosam affigerent? Precario sane victitarent, atque stipem ostiatim nostri homines quaesivissent nè (Deo ita disponente) proprijs FIGUEREDO sumptibus nostram omnium egestatem sublevasset. Meminerat enim verò parentum egestatibus subvenire filiorum esse muneris, nostramque vicem ita doluit, ut ab hocce Collegio egestatem exulare modis omnibus studuerit: suo satis munere numquam fecisse arbitratus, donec & presentem amandaret inopiam, & commodiùs in posterum rationes nostras constitueret. Sibi quippe jam dudum persuasum habuerat, non alio in nostras regiones appulisse consilio, quàm ut nostratibus jam jam pereuntibus subveniret. *Huc ego*, ajebat, *huc ego divino plané consilio appuli ut Societatis inopiam meis sumptibus sublevarem.* Multis itaque impensis nummis, & inopiam avertit, & solatium adhibuit, & ab imminente prorsus excidio liberum Collegium hocce Guathimalense firmavit. Dignus propterea, cui, ut Pietati olim, aeternum in pectore monumentum consecretur.

i *nequae praestarè*
ii *pepulisset:::*

100

8. Sacrum Pietati fanum Antiquitás ibi erigendum curavit, ubi digna profecto immortalitatis filia morte matrem turpissima liberavit. Sceleris, nescio cujus particeps mater, atque iccirco capitis condemnata, Triumviro donatur in carcere strangulanda. Carceris autem Praefectus spectaculum horrens feminam custodit, atque inedia pedetentim conficiendam decernit. Nec tamen ita clanculum custodivit, ut ejus consilium filiam posset speculantem latere. Haec, ut unicè matrem diligebat, â Praefecto effusis precibus exoravit, ut sibi matrem quotidie invissere solatij causa liceret. Singulis diebus eam Praefectus, nequid cibi, aut potus inferret, excutiebat. Hic illa angustijs urgeri, angi, acerbissimè afflictari. Quid enim, consilij in tanto constituta discrimine caperet? Inedia matrem tabescere pateretur? At quî ferre poterat filialis amor? Aliquam exspiranti alimoniam inferret? At illud vetitum â Praefecto cognoscebat. Quò igitur sese vertere posset, ignorabat, neque ullum ad solatium aditum aperiebat. Verùm quid unquam amor intentatum reliquit? Aliquot matrem diebus (auscultate facinus ab hominum memoria clarissimum, omnique saeculorum admiratione dignum) aliquot matrem diebus uberum suorum lacte filia comperta est sustentasse. Quis unquam, Auditores amplissimi, quis tale vel maximo praeditus ingenio cogitaret? Certior de re tota Senatus factus, ac tanta in matrem pietate commotus, vitam matri, matrem filiae dedit, perpetuam utrique alimoniam assignavit, ipsum verò locum extructo Pietati templo consecravit. Nunc vero Auditores? Quis tam erit insipiens, qui clarissimum hocce pietatis exemplum non miretur, aut tam omnis expers humanitatis, qui sempiterna dignum memoria non judicet? Judicet ita sane. Oculos tamen in eum conjicite, qui nostram promeruit memoriam sempiternam.

9. Compertum quidem est vobis, viri ornatissimi, vestrumque neminem latere censeo, quanta Collegium hocce Societatis Guathimalense paucis abhinc annis laborarit inopia. Eo quippe egestatis pervenerat, ut inediae posset omnibus condemnatum videri. Angustior enim, quàm urbis postulat amplitudo, paucis quotidie alendis deficiebat annona: nihil parco utique, eique humili, indumento supererat: pro sacris peragendis, vix, aut ne vix quidem, aere alieno gravata praedia sufficiebant: adeo ut de hujusce excidio Collegij tot aerumnis, angustijsque vexati non nunquam primores nostratum cogitaverint, suaviùs illius ducentes[iii] excidiùm, quàm in urbis medio homines inopia tabescentes conspicere. Affulsit tamen orbi dies, clariorque post tot nubila Phoebus illuxit. Deus quippe, quae sua est in homines miseratio, â Meridie ad Septentrionem, â Peruvio ad novam nostram Hispaniam, Popayano Guathimalam usque, insignem pietate filium attulit Societati. Vix enim nostram comperit egestatem, cùm tabescentium inedia misertus, se totum ad eorundem solatium, levamen convertit; nihil cogitans aliud, quàm de ipsorum inopia sublevanda. Hinc modo nobis annonam emittebat modo quibus egentibus subveniret, pe-

---

iii *duducentes.* Accomazzi *deducentes*

cunias ministrabat: ea tamen munificentia, ac largitate, ut gravissimum Platonis oraculum sibi omnino accipiendum judicaret: *Putare*, ajebat ille, *putare quisque debet, omnia quae possidet, eorum esse, qui genuerunt, & educarunt*.

10. Sed in primis munificum se ac liberalem in nostro augendo templo, exornandoque FIGUEREDO exhibuit. Quapropter templi tholum recens Guathimalam appulsus[iv] construxit: argenteum Eucharistiae Solium confecit: pensiles ex argento lichnucos condonavit: aliaque innumera, quibus recensendis tempus non suppetit, regali plane beneficentia impertivit. Hisce omnibus, Auditores, quis sanae mentis in dubium unquam revocabit, Illustrissimum Guathimalensem Archiepiscopum optimi munia filij in Societatem explevisse? Quid enim est, aut esse potest quod in ipso unquam desiderare possitis? Societatem ad mortem usque medullitus adamasse? Adamavit. Incolumem eandem ab hostibus custodisse? Custodivit. Nostratum vota emisisse? Emisit. Collegium hocce ab excidio liberasse, ejusdem inopiae pro re nata subvenisse? Liberavit, subvênit. Utinam & nos pro tanto in Societatem amore, beneficentia, largitate, dignis ejusdem memoriam laudibus afficere valeamus. Sed cùm beneficiorum amplitudini nulla profecto gratia neque ex parte quidem possit aequare, hocce ut minimùm Mausoleum extet suae in nos benevolentiae monumentum, nostri amoris indicium atque obsequentis animi argumentum sempiternum: ubi & ejus cineres quiescant, & eos continenter prosequi reverentia possimus.

11. Quod si vestrum aliquis lege XII tabularum sancitum meminerit, nequis mortuorum corpora in urbe unquam sepelienda tentaret, meminerit etiam, honorem huncce heroum corporibus eandem ultrò sanctionem contulisse. Hinc & corpora Romae tumulari, & statuas consecrari, & carminibus quandoque eorum gesta celebrari, qui pro aris, & focis strenuè dimicantes obijssent: ut optimà de religione, ac patria meriti nunquam secum famam, nomenque sepelirent; quin etiam illustriùs ad omnium saeculorum memoriam retinerent. Ijs, Prudentio teste, summam Roma reverentiam praestabat, eos laudibus efferebat, eosdem divinis non nunquam honoribus cumulabat.

> *Et tot templa Deum (inquit) quot in urbe sepulchra*
> *Heroum numerare licet: quos fabula Manes*
> *Nobilitat, noster populus veneratur, adorat.*

Quis autem, si gesta gestis conferamus, erit cum Illustrissimo FIGUEREDO comparandus? Cujus in Societatem merita si nos silentio immemores beneficiorum tegeremus, vos, viri ornatissimi, vos, patres religiosissimi, vos, amantés patriae cives, in urbe, in foro, in compitis

iv *apulsus*

vulgaretis. Toties enim pro Societate dimicavit, quoties improborum laces-
sitos convitijs sua nos auctoritate defendit: totque incolumis reportavit
trophaea, quot nobis infestissimas linguas objurgatione compescuit: adèo
ut tali nos ductante Heroe omnes una exterriti hostes aufugerent.

12. Praeterquamquod ita è vivis extollitur FIGUEREDO, ut nostram
nunquam memoriam aufugiat: ita sepelitur, ut aeternum corda incolat
redivivus. Ut ea possit verba meritò[v] usurpare Societas, quae olim
Valeriam conjugem decorarunt: *Exteris*, ajebat, *exteris obijsse conjugem
meum, non diffiteor,*[vi] *mihi autem vivit: & ita vivit, ut ejus memoria*[vii]
spiritum hactenus duxisse tribuerim. Vivis profecto, Prìnceps Illustris-
sime; vivis: & ita vivis, ut vitae isti tuae nulla unquam allatura sit finem
aetas. Quem enim â te spiritum hausit Societas, huncce tibi memor
beneficiorum restituit: ut semel a Libitina laniatus nostris in cordibus
regnaturus in aevum reviviscas. Utere igitur lubens nova hacce lucis
usura, ut tuo ibi fruentes aspectu & hilares te clarissimam Societatis
progeniem praedicemus & Parentem veneremur, & spiritum ducere unà
tecum aliquando possimus. Nisi enim nova hac utere luce, Deum immortalem! Quot nobis calamitates impenderent! Quo moerore vexaremur!
Quantasque Guathimalense Collegium aerumnas, ac vulnera pateretur!
Compressus namque ad hoc temporis moestitiae torrens, praeruptis fortasse pontibus, omnium corda vastaturus erumperet. Quae dum vixeris,
comprimentur: dum amore nos foveris, stringentur: dumque tuo nobis
gaudere aspectu licuerit, hocce ut minimùm solatio adhibito,
respirabimus. Fruere igitur, Societas alma, tanti Principis benignitate,
munificentia, praesidio: fruere ac laetare aspectus suavitate: fruere:[viii]
Verùm quid loquor? O fugaces hominum spes! O citò praetereuntia gaudia!
Evanuit velut umbra, in momento avolavit, quem spirantem adhuc amor
crediderat; luctuoso funere correptus est FIGUEREDO. Siccine separas
amara mors? Siccine subsecas illustre caput? Siccine dignum immortalitate Principem arripis? Debueras clarissimo Principi reverentiam exhibere: debueras nobis potius vitam adimere, quàm sobolem Societati
carissimam obtruncares: debueras:[ix] sed quid unquam foederis nesciae
obstitit Libitinae? Quandoquidem eodem omnes censere jure, eademque
gaudet mensura dimetiri. Miseret me tui, Societas alma, neque ullum, quo
te in spem erigam, aditum invenio: quippe qui te dolore transfixam intro-
spicio, ejus in nos benignitatis memoriam repetentem. Reminisceris profecto amoris magnitudinem, quo te ad mortem usque prosequutus est
FIGUEREDO: reminisceris laborum antiquorum, quibus quotidie nos
olim afflictabat inopia: reminisceris etiam munificentiae, ac largitatis,

v *metitò*
vi *difiteor*
vii *memoriae*
viii *fruere:::*
ix *debueras:::*

quibus jam diu munita undique conservaris: & tanta subitò ablata progenie (satiùs dixerim Parente) ita tuo infixus animo haeret dolor, ut ne ad tempus quidem aliqua leniri posse consolatione videatur. Verumtamen id tibi solatio esse debet, Principem è vivis sublatum, omnibus jam amandatis laboribus, inter Coelites relatum imperare. Videre iamque mihi videor, eò usque Principem FIGUEREDO conscendisse gloriae, ut nitidis redimitus infulis coelesti Pontificum caetui adscribatur. Inde, sua te (nunc maximè) benignitate protegente, & tuam pro tempore egestatem sublevabit, & solatium adhibebit, & suo utique munitam praesidio incolumem in aevum conservabit. Quî enim fieri posset, ut tui memoriam in patria regnans aboleret, qui nulli parcens sudori ad mortem te ardentissimè adamavit? Solare igitur, alma Parens, & abstersis continuò lachrymis, quem terrarum incolam observasti, eundem, confectis iam mortalis vitae stipendijs, coelestem civem in patria regnantem venerare, cum ibi, ut credimus, *requiescat in pace.*

AD MAJOREM DEI GLORIAM.

FUNERAL
DECLAMATION
FOR THE DUE RITES
TO BE CELEBRATED
BY THE SOCIETY OF JESUS
ON THE DECEASE
OF THE NOBLE REVEREND PRIEST,
MOST RENOWNED
DOCTOR MONSIGNOR FRANCIS
JOSEPH DE FIGUEREDO
Y VICTORIA,
FORMERLY BISHOP OF POPAYÁN,[1]
THEN
MOST WORTHY
ARCHBISHOP OF GUATEMALA
BY PADRE RAFAEL LANDÍVAR,
Society of Jesus.

1. I am not here before this honourable audience to assess the plan – which pleased the Author of Life – for the most illustrious Doctor of Divinity Master FRANCISCO JOSÉ DE FIGUEREDO Y VICTORIA, to be snatched away by a lamentable and bitter death. I am here as an admirer of his astonishing piety. I am here to declare to all of you the justified and extreme grief of the whole Society. For what do you think could be harder to bear than for the kindest of Principals, the joy of the Society, to die in one stroke? For in such momentous turns of events and times of disruption, the Society found relief and consolation in him alone. By looking to him, the Society put aside any memory of the misfortunes for which it grieves; supported by his kindness in all circumstances, it raised its faltering spirits to hope. Ah! How often did he give strength to the Society when she was worn down by the crowds of insults bursting in upon her! Or how often did he rescue her from the flood of woes in which she had almost submerged! With that gentleness of spirit in which he always excelled, with a peaceful countenance and with his eyes lowered to the ground, he urged our people to reject earthly things, to yearn for what was of heaven, and to set our hope of salvation in the one God, Judge of all. The outcome of his speeches was so happy that not only did it check the tears of those who were languishing in their own misfortune, it also succeeded in lightening up hearts that had beforehand been shrouded in deepest darkness.

Who could there be anywhere who could be so bereft of human feeling as to be blind to such great proof of affection, or so acclimatised to barbarous ways as to resist the teaching implied in his kindness to us? Especially since this man himself illuminated all these things with his own example. For there is nothing commendable, in the height of dignity, in which he did not excel others; there was nothing in the path of piety so lowly, that he scornfully avoided it. Finally there was nothing so arduous or exalted that he did not accomplish at some point, with the very great love for God that he had. When it was a matter of showing respect for the Church's standing, he used to lead the procession: what could be more glorious? But when it came to his own due, he used to wear the most unsightly clothes, like a ragged beggar: what could be more humble? When he was set upon by the slanders of the envious, he was silent – as though on the point of paying a penalty he deserved: what could be more meek? When he was welcomed by pupils with the display of respect due to his rank, he returned their kindness with remarkable grace, and matched it: what indeed could be more gracious than that, or more righteous? But since all these and other things of a similar sort need a long and very prolix speech, I will encompass all this in one word so as not to go on too long: I will affirm proudly that FIGUEREDO held his authority in such a way that no one could obey more attentively than he, and he received others' commands in such a way that no one could be a more impressive commander. These were then the things that encouraged our members to be brave in adversity, to be determined in our toils, to be humble in the face of insults – and to have all of these qualities in all our circumstances.

2. So I ask this honourable audience, will the Society, bereft of her dearest protector and deprived of all consolation, impose a limit on grieving? Will she suppress her sighs? Will she ever refrain from tears? Or will she rather join days and nights together with weeping and perpetuate the memory of her great Principal in mourning? For grief, finding access to words shut off, gnawed away at the inner recesses of our hearts and has now broken through the prison of our hearts and burst forth. Torrents of tears threaten our eyes, sobs choke our voice and now the painful memory of the past smothers and suffocates the very palace of the heart. By the demise of this man alone, the Goddess of Death has not just deprived our Society of its customary protector: with her bold scythe she has actually cut down a Principal worthy of immortality.[2] If only we could be allowed to face death in the place of so great a man! Willingly each and everyone would gladly face his last day just as if he had been called to victory. And so that the cause of such great grief may not escape each of you nor lie hidden from posterity in future centuries, eminent members, I urge you to bear in mind that in the death of its honoured Principal the Society (may there be no resentment of this expression!)[3] has lost the best of its sons. As I make this case, you will perhaps recognise the cause of our grief by the tears that spring from my eyes.

3. Neither does it escape me, members of the audience, how generously this illustrious priest fulfilled the duties of the best of parents for the benefit of the Society. I know for certain how hard he laboured for the security of the Society in Guatemala, and in Popayán too; how much prestige he built up for it in each of those cities; and indeed how hard he sought to secure its reputation rather than his own: to the point that – in emulation of the great Dauphin Louis[4] – he would never see himself being more highly extolled than when he saw praise conferred on the Society, as though it were his own daughter. I make this point to pass over it; partly because I think none of you is unaware of this, but more importantly because (if in death there is any awareness of these things) the name of son would seem far more welcome to him. For when he pondered meditatively with deliberate concentration on that golden oracle of antiquity: *Nothing brings as much honour on children as showing the honour owed to their parents,* he used to think that he would obtain sufficient honour and glory if he could be called, by everyone, the 'son' of our Society.[5] In this way he attached the honour of a mother to the Society and he took pleasure in the name of son. For his funeral, I avow that the Society should have followed the customs of the Greeks or Romans by constructing a burial mound out of lilies,[6] or at least it should have followed the custom of the Indians by honouring the deceased with the purest hands and white clothing. But since these practices are not at all in keeping with the grief we all feel, we have preferred our roofs, walls, chambers, and even the crossways of the city to be darkened with blackened sheets of cloth. In order to present the propriety of this bitter grief to your own eyes, members of the audience, I will set out in a few words things you yourselves often observed.

4. Hardly having reached adolescence, or even before then, FIGUEREDO, already inclined to weightier studies, was admitted to our house at Popayán to be taught the basic elements of Grammar. It is wonderful what good will the boy's outstanding talent, modesty and newly aroused mind secured for him – especially among those who previously admired his humble disposition. But he, mindful as he was of kindness, repaid love with love, embracing with special signs of good will those from whom he learnt the precepts of literature. From then on, gradually and imperceptibly his enthusiasm grew, as is often the case, and acquired new strength day by day, until it burned with so much ardour that from this time he revered the Society with filial devotion. The perils of the times, the gossip of the envious, and – what is more to the point – his own high level of honour and worth did nothing to damage his good will towards us. That good will to the Society he conceived from boyhood; and with a truly admirable constancy of mind he extended, increased, and multiplied it.[7] But since this and many other things seemed of little note to him, his love planned to put into effect a truly grand design which his devotion had conceived. He strenuously sought, and obtained, from the most reverend General Superior of the Society, admission as a member of the same Society whenever he would be close to death, with the assent of His

Holiness. He received the reply and held it in veneration. From that day he began to name Saint Ignatius[8] as his Father, to call the Society his Mother, and to heed our superiors with such humility of heart that it certainly amazed everyone that a Principal of the Church, crowned with a holy mitre, preferred to hold these honours in second place to his love and benevolence for the Society.

5. What if I recall that he wanted our distinctive cassock to be his funeral cloak? Or that he asked for his body to be buried in our church and nowhere else? That facing the last day of his life, he renewed the vows that he had made long ago? Surely this was an excellent son of our Society! He deserves, by Hercules,[9] to be compared in the eyes of the whole Society to the celebrated Bishop of Verdun, Charles of Lorraine.[10] For he was one who on the point of embracing our way of life, renounced all his privileges of his own free will, as Figueredo was set to keep our Society safe from the darts of its enemies. Charles of Lorraine after casting aside luxuries and wealth, lived in longstanding poverty, whilst Figueredo kept back his goods to sustain our needier members. Charles of Lorraine took refuge in the Society to escape from the enemy they had in common; Figueredo had entirely devoted himself to the Society so that he could show himself in the arena to fight for the safety of the same. How many times did he shout down those who were seeking to tear apart the Society with their viperous jaws? How often did he denounce her detractors? And how often did he keep her unscathed, and clad in armour against the countless enemies who accosted her? Honourable hearers, will the Society not then recognise a man like this as a son? Should she not grieve at his most bitter passing? And will she not dissolve in floods of tears?

6. In days of old, the lictors, on a judge's sentence, had beheaded a young criminal and put his head up on display in that very place from where news of the punishment could be quickly publicised. Things went according to plan. News of the crime committed became public, the punishment became well known and spread right through the whole city, and pierced through the bowels of the poor mother of the man with a hard sword. She had scarcely discovered the butchery of her son, when driven by grief she appeared in public like a woman gone mad. She sees her son's head, she weeps, and fills heaven with her groans, sighs and laments. What does this mean? Will awareness of his misdeeds lessen her agony? Will it calm her grief? Will the pain of a mother's wounds be soothed to any degree by the fact that this execution was merited by the crimes? No way in the world. And in fact after her return home, she was seized by a grief so great that, overcome by its magnitude, she made the solemn sacrifice of her own death on the same day to honour her villainous son. Such is the power parental love has over the heart. As this is so,[11] who would there be who would be right to censure all of us here because we mourn the illustrious

108

FIGUEREDO, who was a model of Charity, the image of humility, the exemplar of goodness, and who, besides all that, bestowed on our Society the love of a son? Our Society's maternal heart is so moved by the memory of his death that it will match its grief to that of all time to come. And what if we do lay open again our recollection of his kindness to us? Surely no thanks will ever be so great that it could possibly equal what his kindness towards us merits, not even in part. So it will always be our responsibility to ensure that the gratitude which can be rendered by us should never be missed or needed by you at any time.

7. Recall to your memory, illustrious men, the hardships this College of Guatemala endured in earlier years, and the public misfortunes of all our members. If he had not reduced, alleviated or eliminated those hardships and misfortunes – God almighty![12] – what do you think would have become of us in such adverse times? What internal distresses would plague our people? What famine would eat away at the bowels and entrails of such poor men? What crosses would weigh on a life already grievous enough? Clearly our people would have to subsist by begging, and to seek a living door to door, if (by God's providence) FIGUEREDO had not relieved the needs of all of us at his own expense. He was truly mindful of the fact that it is the duty of children to help their parents in need, and he was so aggrieved at our plight that he sought in every way he could to drive poverty from this College's doors: he did not ever think he had done enough out of his own generosity, until he had both dispelled our current lack of means and arranged for our provision in the future. He had in fact long held this persuasion: that the only reason he landed in our territory was to help our people when they were on the very point of perishing. 'Here', he used to say, 'have I landed under divine direction, that I should relieve the poverty of the Society at my own expense'. And so by spending great sums of money, he managed both to ward off poverty and to bring comfort, as well as to fortify this free College of Guatemala when it was under the imminent threat of destruction. For all that, he deserves to have a monument consecrated to him in our hearts for ever, as Piety did long ago.

8. Antiquity indeed ensured that a sacred temple was built to Piety, on the site where a daughter, surely worthy of immortality, rescued her mother from a very shameful death.[13] The mother, party to some crime and condemned to die on account of it, was consigned to gaol by the Triumvir to be strangled. But the governor of the gaol, revolted by the prospect of that spectacle, kept the woman under guard and decreed that she should be finished off gradually, by starvation. But he did not keep her under such close guard that his plan could go unnoticed by her watchful daughter. She, as she loved her mother dearly, implored the governor with profuse prayers to be allowed to visit her mother every day in order to comfort her.

Each day the governor searched her, to prevent her bringing in any food or drink. At this point anxiety weighed on her, tortured her, and distressed her severely. What plan could she adopt in the face of such an urgent situation? Should she allow her mother to waste away with hunger? But how could a daughter's love endure this? Could she bring in anything to nourish the dying woman? But she knew this was forbidden by the Governor. She did not know where to turn and she could not see the way to any comfort. But in the end what has love ever left untried? After several days – hear now of a deed very famous in human history and meriting the admiration of every age – after several days, it was discovered that the daughter had been sustaining her mother with the milk of her own breasts. I ask my honourable audience: who ever would have thought of such a thing, however ingenious? The senate was moved by such great piety to a mother, after it was informed about the whole matter. It granted life to the mother and the mother to her daughter, assigning a lifelong pension to each of them, and it consecrated the site of the gaol itself by building a temple to Pietas. And now, my hearers, who will be so foolish as not to wonder at this brilliant example of piety or who will be so devoid of human feeling that he would not judge it worthy of eternal commemoration? Let him indeed so judge it. But all of you, cast your eyes on this man who has well earned eternal commemoration from us.

9. It is well known to you, eminent men, and I do not think it escapes any one of you, under how much deprivation this Guatemalan College of the Society laboured only a few years ago. It had reached such a level of poverty that it could indeed be regarded by everyone as condemned to die of starvation. The food supply was too meagre for the demands of a city of this size and there was not enough even to feed a few people each day: nor was there anything left in the way of clothing, no matter how scant and wretched. As for the rites of worship, our heavily mortgaged property was sufficient only for them to be conducted with difficulty, and sometimes not even at all. Our superiors were so troubled by the scale of hardship and suffering of the College that on more than one occasion they thought about closing it down: bringing the College to an end seemed less unattractive than the prospect of its members wasting away with hunger in the middle of the city. But then day gave light to the world and Phoebus shone forth all the more splendidly after all those clouds.[14] God, whose property is to show pity to mankind, brought to our Society – from the equator to the north, from Peru to our part of New Spain, from Popayán all the way to Guatemala – God brought a son renowned for his piety. As soon as he was aware of our dire poverty, taking pity on those who were starving, he devoted himself entirely to their comfort and relief, and thought of nothing other than the alleviation of their dire need. From then on, he was sending out provisions to us at one moment, at another he was providing funds to minister to those in want. He did this with such generosity and largesse that he decided to take upon himself the full burden of Plato's oracle: 'Each man ought to realise' he used to say, 'that everything he possesses belongs to those who brought him forth and brought him up'.[15]

10. But the main way in which FIGUEREDO proved himself lavishly generous was in the extension and decoration of our temple. On this account, having just arrived in Guatemala, he built a cupola for the church; he produced a silver ciborium for the Eucharist; he donated hanging candelabras also made of silver, and he bestowed with truly royal generosity countless other things which there is no time to survey here. Given all these things, who of sound mind in this audience will call into doubt the fact that the most Illustrious Archbishop of Guatemala fulfilled his obligations to the Society as one of her finest sons? What is there, or what can there be that you could find lacking in him? That he should have deeply loved the Society through and through right up to his death? He deeply loved her. That he should have protected and kept the same Society safe from her enemies? He did so. That he should have made public our vows and wishes? He made them public. That he should have freed this College from the threat of destruction and helped it in need as if it were his own? He freed the College and came to its help. If only we too were capable of lavishing on his memory the praises he deserves, in return for the great love, kindness and generosity he showed to the Society! But since there is certainly no gesture of thanks, not even in part, to match the enormous extent of his kindnesses, may this small tomb stand as a monument of his goodness to us, as evidence of our love, and as an eternal proof of the humble gratitude in our hearts. It is a place where his ashes may rest and where we can continue to pay reverent homage to them.

11. If any of you recalls the sanction in the law of the Twelve Tables,[16] that no one should ever attempt to bury the dead inside the city, he should also remember that the same sanction, even so, conferred this very honour on the bodies of heroes. Hence bodies were buried in Rome itself, statues were consecrated, and on occasions the achievements of those who died strenuously fighting for their altars and hearths were celebrated in song. This was so that those who had been well-deserving with regard to religion and country should not have their fame and reputation buried along with themselves, but keep that reputation with increased splendour for the memory of all ages to come. As Prudentius attests, Rome bestowed the highest reverence on these heroes, sounded out their praises, and on many occasions heaped divine honours upon them:

'There are as many temples of Gods' he says, 'that one may count as there are heroes' tombs in the city. Our people venerates, adores the dead who are glorified by legendary fame.'[17]

Who then, if we were to compare one set of achievements with another, will there be to compare with the illustrious FIGUEREDO? If I were to forget his kindnesses and cover up with silence all the services he did for the Society, it would be you, eminent men, most reverend fathers, citizens and lovers of your country, who would broadcast them in the city, in the square, and at the crossroads. He campaigned for the Society every time he used his authority to defend us when we were set upon by the slanders of our shameless opponents; the trophies he brought back unscathed were as many as the tongues so hostile to us that were silenced by his rebuke. Our leader was a hero of such a kind that all our enemies at once fled away in terror.

12. Quite apart from the fact that FIGUEREDO leaves the world of the living in such a way that he will never escape our memory, he is buried in a way that he may come to live for ever in our hearts, so that the Society might rightly appropriate for herself the words which once did credit to the Empress Valeria: 'I do not disavow that my husband has died on foreign ground; but to me he yet lives, so much so does he live that I would grant that he has been drawing breath even up to now by my memory of him.'[18] You do indeed live, Illustrious Principal, you live, and so much so do you live that no age may come to bring an end to this life of yours. The very breath which it drew from you, the Society has restored to you, mindful of your kindnesses, so that after being cut down once by the Goddess of Death you may live again to rule in our hearts for ever. Therefore be happy to take advantage of this new light, so that we can then rejoice in the sight of you, joyfully proclaim you as our Society's most splendid son, venerate you as a parent, and find ourselves able to draw breath alongside you at any time. But if you do not put this new light of yours to use – God almighty! – how many calamities would befall us! With what sadness would we be afflicted! What great tribulations and injuries would the College of Guatemala have to endure! For a torrent of misery, which has been contained up now, would perhaps break the bridges, and burst out to devastate the hearts of everyone. This will be contained while you live; while you cherish us with your love, it will be restrained, and while we are allowed to rejoice in the sight of you, we shall have at least this comfort and we shall live. So rejoice, provident Society, in the kindness, generosity, and support of your great Principal! Rejoice and take pleasure in the sweet sight of him. Rejoice – but what am I saying? O the elusive hopes of men! O joys that pass so quickly! He has vanished like a shadow, he has flown away in a moment, he whom our love had trusted was still alive. FIGUEREDO has been taken from us by the death we mourn. Bitter death, is this how you part us? Is this how you cut down a glorious head? Is this how you snatch away a Principal who deserves immortality? To our most illustrious Principal you should have shown respect. You should have taken away *our* life, rather than that of our

Society's dearest child. You should have done that. But what has ever stood in the way of the Death Goddess, ignorant as she is of any accord? She delights in judging everyone on the same principle, and measuring all by the same rule. I pity you, provident Society, and I cannot find any way of inspiring you with hope: since I myself see how you are pierced through with grief, as you go over your memory of his kindness to us. You surely recall the extent of his love, which FIGUEREDO lavished on you right up to his death: you remember the labours of times past, with which, in that period, our poverty afflicted us every day. And you also remember the lavish generosity, thanks to which you have been secure for a long time. Now you are deprived of so great a child – I should rather say 'Parent'– grief is lodged so firmly in your heart that it does not look as if it can be eased for a moment.[19] But even so, it must be of some consolation to you that our Principal, now all his work is done, has been lifted up from those who are living and brought back to rule among those in heaven. Already I seem to see our Principal FIGUEREDO has ascended to a high realm of glory, where he has been crowned with a gleaming mitre and numbered in the celestial throng of Pontiffs. From there he can now very powerfully protect you with his kindness, ease your poverty as the need arises, offer comfort, and keep you all the more safely fortified under his guard for all time. For how could it be that, reigning in his own country of heaven, he should lose the memory of you, he who loved you most ardently until his death, sparing no toil? Be comforted then, provident Mother, wipe away your tears, and venerate the man whom you knew as a dweller on earth, now that the service of his mortal life is done, as a citizen of heaven reigning in his own country, for there, as we believe, he *rests in peace.*

TO THE GREATER GLORY OF GOD.[20]

The Marian Poems

A Horatian ode and a Castilian sonnet (1779)

In honorem B. Virginis Mariae atque operis commendationem
Raphael Landivar Guatimalensis canebat

ODE

[1]
En, ut Mariam, aequo Pater ordine,
Primi Parentis crimine liberam,
et Virginem Matremque, diu
censuerit decorare foetu,

[2]
Ut Virgo nobis ediderit Deum;   5
et pectus atris icta doloribus,
per vulnera ensesque, et probrosa,
astiterit generosa Nato.

[3]
Benigna formabat populos fide,
mores docebat Christiades pia;   10
evecta donec Coelum abivit
Angelico celebranda cantu.

[4]
Hanc Angelis Reginam Opifex Deus,
hanc Inferis idem Dominam dedit,
nobisque clementer redemptis   15
egregiam pietate Matrem.

[5]
Hujusce, Joseph, maxima munera,
vitaeque tempus, sacraque munia,
solerti adumbras penicillo,
ignem animo insinuante Clio.   20

[6]
Non turpat atris fabula sordibus
insigne opus, commentaque inania
foedare non audent, pudendus
nec potuit contemnere fastus.

[7]
Sub astra Musae laudibus efferant   25
modisque commendent Marianum opus;
tuumque, Joseph, illustre nomen
marmore perpetuabit Orbis.

114

In honour of the Blessed Virgin Mary and in commendation of this work, Rafael Landívar of Guatemala sang as follows[1]

ODE

[1] See how[2] the Father with just ordinance had long deemed to honour Mary, free from the sin of our first ancestor, and at once a Virgin and Mother, with his offspring,

[2] how the Virgin brought forth God for us; her breast was smitten with grim suffering inflicted by wounds and swords, and in shame she nobly[3] positioned herself at the side of her Son.

[3] In her kindness she gave the peoples a formation in faith, she piously taught Christian ways;[4] until borne up to Heaven she departed, praised by Angelic song.

[4] God the Creator gave her to the Angels as Queen, he too gave her to the Underworld as Mistress, and to us, mercifully redeemed, as a Mother outstanding in devotion.

[5] It is Her, Joseph, her great gifts, the sequence of her life, and of her sacred offices that you portray with your skilful brush, as Clio[5] infuses her fire into your soul.

[6] Common talk does not smear with dark grime your glorious creation, and empty fictions do not presume to sully it, nor could shameful pride dismiss it.

[7] May the Muses with their praises raise up to the stars[6] and commend with their measures your Marian work; and the World will perpetuate in marble[7] your own illustrious name, Joseph.

Castilian sonnet

El mismo en alabanza del autor

SONETO

Ni el esmero de Apeles aplaudido,
ni el acaso o portento celebrado
de Protógenes, habrían formado
retrato de María más cumplido.

El Águila de Patmos has seguido
en tu vuelo, Joseph, vuelo encumbrado;
por sabio con tu pluma has dado
a la Copia el color que le es debido.

Sus virtudes, sus dones, su belleza,
sus dolores, sus gozos e hidalguía,
el blanco fueron de su gran proeza.

Mas absorta de amor su fantasía,
el pincel gobernó con tal destreza,
que dio el alma a la imagen de María.

The same in praise of the author

SONNET[8]

Neither the care of renowned Apelles, nor the fortune or famed genius of Protogenes would have formed a more complete portrait of Mary.[9] You followed the Eagle of Patmos in your flight,[10] Joseph,[11] a lofty flight; as a sage with your feather quill[12] you have given to the Copy the colour it deserves.

Her virtues, her gifts, her beauty, her sufferings, her joys and nobility were the target of your quill's great enterprise. But its imagination permeated with love governed the paintbrush with such dexterity that it gave its soul to the image of Mary.

116

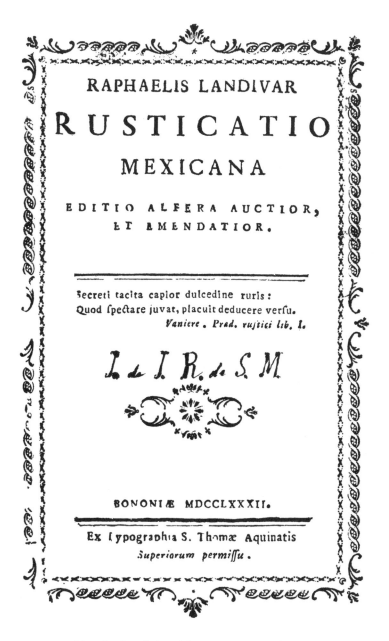

RAPHAELIS LANDIVAR

RUSTICATIO

MEXICANA

EDITIO ALTERA AUCTIOR,
ET AMENDATIOR.

Secreti tacita capior dulcedine ruris:
Quod fpectare juvat, placuit deducere verfu.
Vaniere . Prad. rufiici lib. I.

L de J. R. de S. M.

BONONIÆ MDCCLXXXII.

Ex Typographia S. Thomæ Aquinatis
Superiorum permiffu .

Facsimile of the title page, 1782 edition

RUSTICATIO MEXICANA

The Latin text and an English prose translation
by Graydon W. Regenos

URBI GUATIMALAE
Raphael Landivar

Salve, cara Parens, dulcis Guatimala, salve,
    Delicium vitæ: fons, et origo meæ:
Quam juvat, Alma, tuas animo pervolvere dotes,
    Temperiem, fontes, compita, templa, lares.
Jam mihi frondosos videor discernere montes,
    Ac jugi virides munere veris agros.
Sæpius in mentem subeunt labentia circum
    Flumina, et umbrosis littora tecta comis:
Tum vario cultu penetralia compta domorum,
    Plurimaque Idaliis picta vireta rosis.
Quid vero, aurato repeto si splendida luxu
    Serica, vel Tyrio vellera tincta mari?
Hæc mihi semper erunt patrii nutrimen amoris,
    Inque arctis rebus dulce levamen erunt.
Sed fallor: placidam, Ah! versant ludibria mentem,
    Illuduntque animo somnia vana meo!
Nam quæ arces, magnique caput spectabile regni
    Urbs fuerat nuper, nunc lapidum cumulus.
Non ædes, non templa manent, non compita genti,
    Nec qua tuta petat culmina montis habet.
Omnia præcipiti volvuntur lapsa ruina,
    Ceu Jovis alatis ignibus icta forent.
Quid tamen hæc doleo? Surgunt jam celsa sepulcro
    Limina, se tollunt ardua templa polo.
Flumine jam fontes undant, jam compita turba,
    Jamque optata venit civibus alma quies.
Scilicet, ut Phariæ volucri, felicior urbi
    E proprio rursus pulvere vita redit.
Gaude igitur, rediviva Parens, Urbs inclyta regni.
    Excidioque novo libera vive diu:
Et clarum subitâ partum de morte triumphum
    Laudibus ipse tuum promptus in astra feram.
Interea raucum, luctus folatia, plectrum
    Accipe; sisque loco muneris ipsa mihi.

Urbi Guatimalae

TO THE CITY OF GUATEMALA

Rafael Landívar

Hail, dear mother-city, fair Guatemala, hail—joy of my life, its fountain and its source. How it pleases me, gracious city, to reflect upon your blessings—your temperate climate, your fountains, streets, temples, and houses. Now, methinks, I see your wooded mountains and your verdant fields graced with perennial spring. Again and again there steals into my mind the thought of your winding rivers and of their banks covered with shady leaves, then of your elegantly adorned homes and of your gardens brightly colored with roses sacred to Venus. But why do I mention your silks gleaming with a golden richness, or your fleeces dyed in Tyrian purple? These things will always foster in me a love for my native land, and they will be a sweet relief in my adversities. Yet I am deceived. My tranquil mind, alas! is mocked, and idle dreams disappoint my heart. For the city which had recently stood as a citadel and the illustrious capital of a mighty kingdom is now a heap of stones. No houses remain, no temples, no streets for the people; nor is there a mountain peak wherein they may seek refuge. All things have come tumbling down as if struck by Jupiter's winged firebrands. But why do I mourn? Even now great buildings are rising up from the tomb, and lofty temples are soaring into the sky. Fountains are now filling their streams, streets are now crowded with people; and the delightful tranquillity for which the people longed is now at hand. Indeed, a more fortunate life is coming back again to the city out of its own dust, just as it did to the Phoenix, the Egyptian bird. Rejoice, therefore, in your return to life, O mother, glorious city of the realm, and live long, free from further ruin; and I shall promptly extol to heaven your illustrious triumph over sudden death. Receive, meanwhile, my harsh strains, a consolation for my grief, and be, for your part, my source of satisfaction.

MONITUM

Rusticationis Mexicanæ huic carmini præfixi titulum, tum quod fere omnia in eo congesta ad agros Mexicanos spectent, tum etiam quod de Mexici nomine totam Novam Hispaniam vulgo in Europa appellari sentiam, nulla diversorum regnorum ratione habita.

In hoc autem opusculo nullus erit fictioni locus, eam si excipias, quæ ad lacum Mexicanum canentes Poetas inducit. Quae vidi refero, quæque mihi testes oculati, cæteroquin veracissimi, retulere. Præterea curæ mihi fuit oculatorum testium auctoritate subscripta, quæ rariora sunt, confirmare.

Ad fodinas quod attinet, plura in hoc carmine desiderari fateor. Neque enim mihi proposui exactissimam ejus laboris notitiam exhibere; quippe qui magnæ molis volumen exigeret; sed præcipua dumtaxat, scituque digniora.

Denique ut inoffenso pede carmen hocce percurras, Lector benevole, te monitum velim, more me poetico locuturum, quotiescumque inanium Antiquitatis numinum mentio inciderit. Sancte equidem scio, ac religiose profiteor, hujusmodi commentitiis numinibus sensum nullum ineffe, nedum vim, ac potestatem.

Vereor tamen, ne dum ista percurreris, aliqua interdum subobscura offendas. In argumento quippe adeo difficili omnia latino versu ita exprimere, ut vel rerum ignaris sub aspectum cadant, arduum quidem est; ne dicam impossibile. Nihilominus claritati, qua potui diligentia, ut providerem, plurimum in iis, quæ nunc primum in lucem prodeunt, adlaboravi: vulgata vero ad incudem revocavi; in quibus plura mutavi, non nulla addidı, aliqua substraxi. Sed verendum est adhuc, ne incassum desudaverim, neque eorum satis desiderio fecerim, qui in rebus etiam suapte natura difficillimis nullum vellent laborem impendere. Solatio tamen mihi erit, quod hac super re Golmarius Marsiglianus cecinit:

Heu! quam difficile est voces reperire, modosque
Addere, cum novitas integra rebus inest.
Sæpe mihi deerunt (jam nunc præsentio) voces:
Sæpe repugnabit vocibus ipse modus.

Monitum

AUTHOR'S PREFACE

I have entitled this poem *Rusticatio Mexicana*, not only because nearly everything contained in it relates to the fields of Mexico, but also because I realize that it is customary in Europe to call the whole of New Spain, Mexico, without taking into account the different countries.

Now in this little work there will be no place for fiction, with the exception of the story which represents the bards as singing along the shore of the Mexican lake. I relate those things which I have seen and those that have been told to me by eyewitnesses, entirely trustworthy, however. Besides, I have been careful to confirm the more unusual things written on the authority of eyewitnesses.

I confess that more is to be desired in this poem on the subject of mines, for I have not proposed to display a very exact knowledge of this industry since that would require a very large volume, but I give only the important facts and those things worth knowing.

Finally, in order that you, my gentle reader, may read this poem inoffensively, I would have you know that I am going to speak in the manner of a poet whenever mention is made of the false deities of the ancients. I solemnly realize and devoutly confess that such fictitious deities have no understanding, much less any power and might.

I fear, moreover, that while you read these pages you will sometimes find certain passages obscure for, in a subject so difficult, to express everything in Latin verse in such a manner that it will be clear to those unacquainted with the subject matter is indeed difficult, if not impossible. Nevertheless, I have endeavored with as much diligence as possible to provide clarity, especially in those matters which now for the first time are being brought to light. The things of common knowledge, on the other hand, I have returned to the anvil.[1] In these I have made several changes. I have inserted certain things and removed others. But still I must fear lest I have persevered in vain and failed to satisfy the desire of those who would not wish to devote their time to things which, by their very nature, are very difficult. But I shall find comfort in the verses which Golmario Marsigliano wrote on this theme: "Alas! how difficult it is to find words, and to fit those words to the meter when the subject is wholly new. Often words will fail me (even now I foresee it), often the meter itself will rebel against the words."

---

1. *I. e.*, to revise, retouch [G.W.R.].

123

I

Obtegat arcanis alius sua sensa figuris,
Abstrusas quarum nemo penetrare latebras
Ausit, et ingrato mentem torquere labore;
Tum sensum brutis aptet, gratasque loquelas;
Impleat et campos armis, et funere terras,
Omniaque armato debellet milite regna.

[*ll. 1-6*]

Me juvat omnino, terrae natalis amore,
Usque virescentes patrios invisere campos,
Mexiceosque lacus, et amoenos Chloridis hortos
Undique collectis sociis percurrere cymba:¹
Tum juga Xoruli visam, Vulcania regna;
Et vitreos celso latices de colle ruentes;
Coccineumque dein, Tyriumque, Indumque,
    venenum:
Oppida mox Fibri telis, ferroque fodinas
Aggrediar; luteisque astringam sacchara formis:
Hinc fusum regione pecus, fontesque sequutus
Et volucres, et lustra canam, ludosque docebo.

[*ll. 7-17*]

Debueram, fateor, maesto praecordia peplo
Induere, et lacrymis oculos suffundere amaris:
Nam flores dum prata dabunt, dum sydera lucem,
Usque animum, pectusque meum dolor altus habebit.
Sed tantum cogor celare in corde dolorem,
Corde licet cauto rapiat suspiria luctus.
Quid tristes ergo gemitus de pectore ducam?
Ardua praecipitis conscendam culmina Pindi,
Musarumque Ducem supplex in vota vocabo;
Ambit enim quandoque dolens solatia pectus.

[*ll. 18-27*]

Tu, qui concentus plectro moderaris eburno,
Et sacras cantare doces modulamina Musas,
Tu mihi vera quidem, sed certe rara canenti
Dexter ades, gratumque melos largire vocatus.

[*ll. 28-31*]

Urbs erat occiduis procul hinc notissima terris
Mexicus, ampla, frequensque, viris, opibusque,
    superba,
Indigenis quondam multos dominata per annos:
Nunc vero Hispani, populis, Mavorte subactis,
Sceptra tenent, summaque urbem ditione gubernant.
Plures hanc vitreo circumdant fonte lacunae,

Let another conceal his thoughts in obscure figures whose hidden meaning no one would venture to interpret or worry his mind with the thankless task. Let another bestow reason and pleasant discourse upon dumb animals, let him cover the fields with armies, the earth with death, and let him vanquish entire nations by armed force.

But I, through love for my native land, enjoy most of all to visit the ever verdant fields of my country and, accompanied by friends assembled from everywhere, to go by boat across the lakes of Mexico, and to pass along the lovely gardens of Flora.¹ I shall then behold the ridges of Jorullo, Vulcan's domain, and the clear waters that rush down the steep slopes; after that I shall give attention to cochineal, to purple dye and indigo. Thereupon, I shall advance with spear into the cities of the beaver, and with a pick I shall descend into the mines; and I shall condense sugar in earthen molds. When I have tended the herds and flocks which are scattered over the countryside and have visited the springs, I shall then sing of the birds and beasts, and describe the sports of the people.

I ought, I confess, to have put on the garb of mourning and to have shed bitter tears, for as long as flowers grow in the meadow and stars give forth their light, my heart and soul will be filled with deep sorrow. But I am obliged to hide this grief in my heart, though the distress force sighs from my guarded breast. But why should I utter mournful groans? I shall climb the steep ascent of Pindus and call suppliantly upon the leader of the Muses, for he always comforts my heart whenever it is sad.

You that play on the ivory lyre and teach the sacred Muses to sing in rythmic measure, be propitious to me as I sing of themes true yet strange, and grant me sweet melody as I invoke you.

Far from here, in the western world, was a well-known city called Mexico, large and populous, distinguished for its men and rich in resources. It was ruled for many years by the natives of the country, but now the Spanish hold sway, having conquered the people in war; and they rule the city with supreme authority. Many crystal lakes surround this city attracting

Quae blando parvas allectant gurgite puppes.
Non tamen has omnes mens est celebrare canendo:
Nam quae sepositae prospectant longius urbem,
Flumine nec tanto turgent, quod fama frequentet,
Nec nitidos squamma pisces, florumque natantes
Areolas, Anatumque vadis examina pascunt.
At quae purpureos Phoebi remeantis ab umbris
Infringit radios, et quae declinat ad Austrum
(Apta quibus flexus donat commercia rivus)
Fluctibus exundant, spumosaque littora pulsant:
Deliciae populi, et florentis gratia ruris.

[*ll. 32-48*]

Has prope frondosis consurgunt oppida ripis,
Quae nomen geminae, famamque dedere paludi:
Hoc Chalcum, Texcucum illud longaeva vetustas
Dixerat, atque ambo patria de voce vocarat.
Tunc alias aliis recto discrimine limphas
Praetulit, et vario prudens celebravit honore.
Nam licet angustis geminae loca tuta carinis
Exhibeant, serventque altis pro moenibus urbem,
Allicit at vero cives argentea Chalcis,
Quod laetas segetes, quod puris pascat in undis
Arboreis intexta comis peramoena vireta:
Gloria prima lacus, et culti dedecus agri.

[*ll. 49-60*]

Hic dulces vasto latices exaggerat alveo:
Namque per obscuros tranquilla fluenta canales
Colligit, et tenues etiam sine nomine rivos,
Puraque gramineis undantia flumina campis.
Non rapidum Boream, non illuc Aeolus Austrum
Mittit, nec saevis Eurus, Zephyrusque procellis
Ardua luctantes sese in certamina poscunt.
Murmure sed posito, ventisque in claustra fugatis,
Incubuit puris tranquilla malacia limphis.

[*ll. 61-69*]

Sed tanto quamvis exuberet aequore Chalcis,
Fons tamen in mediis manat pellucidus undis,
Quem neque flaventi permiscet littus arena,
Arva nec infecto deturpant proxima limo:
Sed clarus, sed purus aquis, sed vitreus humor,
Vel minimos possis ut qui labuntur ad ima,
Lustrare obtutu facili, et numerare lapillos.
Hic vero tanta saliens e gurgite rivus
Eructat gelidam vi, ut summas impete coeco
Scandat aquas, magnosque dein se extendat in orbes.
Ceu quondam grajus bibulis Alphaeus in oris,
Obscuro postquam rapidus se condidit antro,
Labitur impatiens gressu properante per umbras

to their gentle waves small craft. But it is not my intention to celebrate them all in song, for those which are remote, lying some distance from the city, are not large enough to attract attention. Their waters supply neither bright scaly fish, nor floating flower gardens, nor flocks of ducks. But the lake which reflects the purple rays of Phoebus as he returns from the darkness, and the one which lies toward the south (a winding stream affords a convenient means of communication between them) send high their surging billows and beat against their foaming shores, the delight of the people and the glory of the green countryside.

Along the grassy shores of these lakes arise towns which have given to each body of water its illustrious name. The people long ago in their own vernacular had given them the names, Chalco and Texcoco. Then the discerning person, observing proper distinctions, preferred the one or the other and variously extolled its praises. For although both provide safe harbors for small vessels and protect the city in place of high walls, yet the citizens are attracted by silvery Chalco because there grow upon its pure waters joyous crops and a lovely turf, interspersed with thick-leafed trees, the chief glory of the lake and the shame of the cultivated field.

This lake fills its vast bed with fresh waters, gathering them quietly through underground channels and from tiny unnamed streams and clear rivers which flow across the grassy plains. Neither the swift north wind nor the south wind does Aeolus send there, nor do the competing east and west winds challenge one another to fierce combat with their violent tempest, but since the winds have been driven into their cells and their roaring hushed, a peaceful calm has settled over the clear waters.

But although the Chalco has such an overabundance of water, nevertheless in the midst of its waves arises a clear spring which does not mingle with the yellow sands of the shore, nor is sullied by mud from the neighboring farm lands. But its waters are so crystal clear and pure that you can readily see at a glance and even count the pebbles as they fall to the bottom. Indeed this spring, as it bounds from the abyss, thrusts forth its cool stream with such violence that it reaches the surface of the lake by a force unseen and then expands in large circles. Just as at one time the Greek river, Alphaeus, as it was flowing along its moist banks, quickly hid itself in a dark cave and glided with impatient haste

Immensum subter pelagus, fluctusque sonantes,
Sicanios donec liceat contingere fines,
Ore, Arethusa, tuo revomens argenteus amnem:
Haud secus occultos sequitur fons ille meatus,
Optatas donec fugiens pertingat ad auras.

[*ll. 70-87*]

Unde tamen jugis ducatur fontis origo,
Quove reluctantes consurgant impete lymphae,
Incertum. Quis enim certis se noscere signis
Dicat, conclusum secretis aera fossis
In varias cogi brumali frigore guttas
Acturas exinde leves per gramina limphas,
Et largos etiam praerupto e pumice rivos.
Ni potius nigras subiens maris unda cavernas
Inde per angustas quaerat spiracula rimas,
Dum sale sub terris posito, pravoque sapore
Irruat in campos humor, fontesque, lacusque
Impleat, et grata recreet dulcedine plantas.
Aut certa irrigui ducant exordia fontes
Montibus ex altis, pluvia, glacieque gravatis.
Haec mens, haec animis potior sententia constat,
Queis natura parens miranda arcana reclusit,
Arduaque ostendit fontis primordia nostri.
Nam quamvis clivos campus sejungat ab undis,
Et nulli aprico consurgant gramine colles,
Alta tamen gemini tollunt fastigia montes
Proxima syderibus, clademque minantia coelo,
Plurima quae glacies Borea concreta nivali
Usque tegit, multasque rigens se tollit in ulnas.
Haec sensim ventis, Phoebique ardore soluta
Ima petit montis penetrans illapsa latebras,
Guttarum donec rapido velut agmine facto
Erumpat, vincatque undas fugitiva palustres.

[*ll. 88-114*]

Additur huic aliud, quo non praestantius ullum,
Prodigium, insigne, insuetum, cui nomen in aevum.
Ardua crux niveo, solidoque e marmore secta
Artificis dextra, ferrique rigore polita
Tollitur irrigui fontis submissa profundo
Fixa solo, terraeque simul sic mordicus haerens,
Ut nullo possit nisu, nulla arte revelli.
Quis vero sit casus, quaeve laboris origo,
Aeternis clausere umbris monumenta vetusta.
Castalium posthac sileat Cirrhaeus Apollo,
Et Lybicas Ammon contemnat Jupiter undas,
Vel quos clara dedit latices Arethusa pudicos:

through the darkness beneath the boundless sea and resounding billows until it could reach the land of Sicily and cast forth its silvery stream through your mouth, O Arethusa, so this spring follows a secret course until in its flight it succeeds in reaching the air.

But it is uncertain where the perennial spring has its source or by what force its surging waters arise. For who would say that he has definite proof that air confined in underground chambers is condensed by wintry cold into manifold drops which will send forth waters trickling through the grass as well as abundant streams from clefts in the rocks? Might it not rather be true that the water of the sea flows back into dark caverns and from them seeks to find an outlet through narrow crevices until it forces its way into the fields and fills the fountains and lakes and refreshes all plant life with its delightful freshness, having left its saltiness and brackish taste beneath the surface of the earth? Or, it may be that the gushing springs really arise out of the high mountains heavily laden with rain and ice. This belief, this theory, is preferred by those to whom mother nature has revealed her wondrous secrets and shown the inaccessible source of our spring for, although a plain separates the higher ground from the lake and no hills emerge from its sunny pastures, there are, however, two mountains which lift their towering crests skyward menacing heaven with ruin. They are always covered with ice frozen to a depth of many feet by the north wind's cold blasts. This ice, when slowly melted by the winds and the warmth of Phoebus, begins to run down the mountainside, penetrating hidden recesses as it glides along until, having marshaled, as it were, a swift column of drops, it bursts forth in a rapid stream overflowing the waters of the lake.

In addition to this, there is another unsurpassed phenomenon. It is extraordinary, unprecedented, and of undying fame. A high cross, cut out of solid marble by the sculptor's hand, white as snow and polished with tempered steel, arises from the depths of a flowing spring, so firmly and securely set in the earth that it can be removed by no effort or device. Indeed, ancient chronicles have hidden in everlasting darkness the occasion for this work or its origin. Let Cirrhaean Apollo hereafter keep silent concerning his Castalia, and let Jupiter Ammon hold in disdain his Lybian waves or the pure waters of celebrated Arethusa. Let all the water

Juaeque suos sileant fluvialia numina fontes,
Solaque Mexiceum commendet fama fluentum,
Nobile Christiadum fecit cui tessera nomen.
[*ll. 115-129*]

Nunc agite, et quoniam concedunt astra quietum
Aequor, et angustas allectant caerula puppes,
Ocyus exiguam subducam margine cymbam,
Dotales pulchrae visurus Chloridis hortos,
Quos Indi patrio dicunt sermone *Chinampas.*
Tu tamen interea, Zephyri pulcherrima conjux,
Quae pictis ornata rosis dominaris in arvis,
Dic mihi, quis flores levibus commiserit undis,
Et mare culturae tumidum subjecerit agri,
Munere quando tuo rident pomaria gemmis.
[*ll. 130-139*]

Mexicei primum media statuere palude
Urbem, aliquot tandem magni post lustra futuram
Imperii sedem. Tanto tamen ardua fastu
Templa Deum, Regumque arces, turresque, domosque
Constituit, tantumque brevi gens inclyta crevit,
Ut Regi,[2] cui tota diu subjecta tributum
Solverat, ingentes curarum immitteret aestus;
Scilicet augeri gentemque, urbemque dolebat.
Quare aliud miseram gravius, nec viribus aequum
Vectigal jussit crudelis pendere gentem;
Ducere odoratos submissis fluctibus hortos
Frugibus insignes, cultosque virentibus herbis.
Quod si jussa viri fieri tunc posse negarent,
Excidio mulctare urbem, populumque parabat.
Ingemuere omnes, gemituque augusta replebant
Templa Deum: sparsis bacchatur turba capillis.
Omnia sed prudens vincit solertia gentis.
[*ll. 140-156*]

Ingenio freti cives, animique vigore
Accingunt se operi, tectisque, undisque relictis,
Nigrantes penetrant sylvas, atque avia cursu,
Quaerere textilibus frondosa arbusta genistis.
Cuique suum partitur opus, sua munera cuique:
Pars lento vellit faciles e vimine ramos,
Pars onerat cymbas, pars remis ducit onustas:
Fervet opus, durosque juvat perferre labores.
At postquam sylvae magnum congessit acervum,
Cunctaque consilio maturo turba paravit,
Concurrit, texitque leves e fronde tapetas
Oblongae storeae similes; quos moenia propter
Expandit, textosque salo committit aperto,

deities be silent concerning their fountains, and let fair fame extol only the Mexican waters to which the symbol of Christianity has given an illustrious name.

And now that the stars afford a tranquil sea and the blue waters invite small boats, I shall hastily draw my little skiff down from the bank to visit the elegant gardens of lovely Flora, which the Indians call in their native language *Chinampus.* And you, meanwhile, O beautiful wife of Zephyr, as arrayed in many-colored roses you reign over the fields, tell me who intrusted flowers to the capricious waves and subjected the swelling sea to agriculture, for thanks to you the orchards smile with buds.

At the outset the Mexicans established in the middle of a marsh a city to become finally after many years the seat of a mighty empire. But with such pride this illustrious people erected majestic temples to the gods, and palaces for their kings, and castles and homes, and they grew so rapidly that the king,[2] to whom they had long been subject and to whom they had paid tribute, was beset with grave misgivings. He was, of course, pained to see this people and city growing. He therefore ruthlessly bade these unfortunate people pay another kind of tribute, more burdensome and beyond their means. They must bring to him over the calm waters sweet-scented gardens rich in fruits and covered with green vegetation. And if the men should declare that these demands could not then be met, he was ready to exterminate both the city and the people. They all groaned and filled the sacred temples of the gods with their lamentations. With dishevelled hair the crowds ran about wildly. Yet all things were overcome by the ready ingenuity of the people.

Relying on their wit and alertness of mind, the citizens set themselves to the task, and leaving behind their homes and the waters they go deep into the dark forest and into places far away in search of thick-leafed groves of broom trees for mats. Each one is assigned his task, each one his special duties. Some quickly tear the branches from the pliant stem, some load the boats, while others move the cargo along with their oars. They briskly carry on the work, and cheerfully perform these difficult tasks. Now when the workmen have piled high the branches and prepared everything with due deliberation, they come together and weave from these boughs light carpets which resemble long mats. They spread them out near the city walls,

127

Callibus hinc atque hinc multis super alta relictis.
Ne tamen infensi spargant conamina venti,
Aut mare surripiat pronum fugientibus undis,
Cauta trabes fundo nodoso ex robore figit,
Vimineasque ligat storeas ad tigna rudenti.

[*ll. 157-174*]

Haec ubi felici norunt confecta labore
Mexicei, proras certatim ad littora vertunt,
Mox agros repetunt hilares, fusique per arva
Effodiunt campis pingues ad semina glebas.
Non ita sollicitae carpunt per florea rura
Nectar apes densae, magnis alvearia silvis
Cum nova conficiunt, replentque examina melle.
Tum lembos onerant collecto cespite pubes,
Et vaga multiplici convolvunt aequora remo.
Ast ubi distentos undis venere tapetas,
Quisque superfundunt lectas sine vomere glebas,
Udaque frugiferae committunt semina terrae.
Hic jacit in campos granum Cereale natantes,
Hic olerum gaudet laetum diffundere semen.
Nec desunt, queis, veris honos, Regina vireti
Culta rubet, Veneri quondam sacrata profanae.[3]
Ut vero mediis vernantem fluctibus agrum
Conspexit, concors festivo turba tumultu
Exultat, remisque movens per caerula nantem
Ardua crudeli persolvit dona tyranno.
Ast alios undis hortos sibi cauta reservat,
Qui Florae gemmis addant Cerealia dona,
Et quos assidue subigens diuturna propago
Incorrupta sui servet monumenta laboris.

[*ll. 175-198*]

Sin autem praedo cultu nudaverit hortum,
Turbidus aut ventus maturis frugibus obsit,
Errantem limphis alio traducit agellum,
Saevaque versutus declinat damna colonus.
Hinc totidem genti ridentia floribus arva,
Quot nantes placide videas super alta tapetas.

[*ll. 199-204*]

Has agri fluitantis opes, hunc aemula cultum
Proxima ripa dolet, seseque virentibus Ulmis,
Et Cerasis, faetaque Pyro, Maloque rubenti,
Et Lauro, et Pinu, Cedroque, et Quercubus altis,
Vereque certatim distinguit prata perenni.

[*ll. 205-209*]

and they place them when woven on the open waters, leaving many paths here and there over the deep. But in order that angry winds not cast hither and thither the results of their labor or the receding sea carry them away with its swiftly moving waters, they take precautions by fastening the wicker mats by rope to posts of knotty oak driven into the bottom of the lake.

When the Mexicans find that their work has met with success, they turn their prows eagerly toward the shore. They then return to the gay fields, and scattering themselves out over the plowed land dig up rich soil for the seeds. Not so busily do throngs of bees throughout the blossoming countryside gather nectar when in the great forest they are building new hives and supplying their swarms with honey. Next the men load their boats with the soil which they have collected and they beat the restless waters with many a stroke of the oar. And when they have come to the carpets extending out over the waters, they spread over them the dirt which has been gathered and consign the moist seeds to the fertile soil. One man scatters grains of wheat over the floating fields, another finds pleasure in sowing fertile vegetable seeds, and there are not wanting those for whom the flower once sacred to pagan Venus blushes, the glory of spring, the lovely queen of the garden.[3] And when the people see the green field in the midst of the billows, all are exceedingly happy and, pushing with their oars the floating field across the blue waters, they render the exacting gift to the cruel tyrant. But with foresight they reserve for themselves other gardens on the lake in order to add the gifts of Ceres to the blossoms of Flora, and by cultivating them assiduously, preserve them as an undying memorial of their labor.

But if a thief should strip the well-tilled garden, or a violent storm damage the ripened harvest, the ingenious husbandman moves his little floating field over the waters to another place and avoids these grievous losses. So the people have as many fields smiling with flowers as there are mats seen floating quietly over the waters.

The adjoining shore is envious of this wealth and splendor of the floating land and tries to rival it by adorning itself with green elms, cherry, fruitful pear, ruddy apple, laurel, pine, cedar, and stately oaks, and gracing its meadows with perennial spring.

Lacus Mexicani

Quin etiam luco volucres tot condit opaco,
Ut blando percussa sonet modulamine sylva.
Hinc pennata cohors vario distincta colore
Gaudet iter liquidum pictis abscindere pennis
Gutture festivos lusus per inane canoro
Effingens, dulcesque ciens per littora cantus.
Dulce canit Passer,⁴ roseis quem fusa capillis
Crista tegit, plumaeque fluunt per colla rubentes.
Ludit et insignis raro discrimine vocum
Alituum Princeps, quo non vocalior alter,
Centzontlus,⁵ prisco volucris non cognitus orbi,
Qui voces hominum⁶ simulat, volucrumque, canumque,
Et modulos etiam sociantis carmina plectro.
Nunc canit ad numerum, nunc Milvum fingit edacem,
Nunc simulat felem, litui nunc signa canori
Reddit, festivusque latrat, lugetque, pipitque.
Inclusus cavea gaudet volitare canendo,
Jungereque insomnes modulis noctesque, diesque.
Non ita compositis deflet Philomela querelis
Moesta scelus, densis nemorum cum tecta sub umbris
Populeas tremulis sylvas concentibus implet,
Lusibus ut ripas hilarat Centzontlus amoenis.

[ll. 210-231]

Hoc melos, has undas, haec littora grata frequentat
Nobilis exiguis pubes devecta phasellis,
Vere novo, croceis cum nantes floribus agri
Luxuriant, pictisque rosis ver prata coronat:
Quisque levem gemino conscendit remige puppim
Demulcens animum suavis modulamine plectri;
Cui procul obscuris respondet vocibus Echo,
Sylvaque dulcisono cantu percussa remugit.
Tunc celeres ducunt dubia in certamina cymbas,
Pronaque remorum⁶ᵃ contorquent caerula plausu,
Dum viridi puppim signet victoria lauro.
Mox circum areolas victi, victorque natantes
Obliquos penetrant calles, sinuosaque circum
Littora discurrunt, actis per florea lembis.
Ceu quondam Theseus Creta generosus in alta
Elusit coecos labyrinthi pervigil orbes
Ancipiti lustrans fallacia limina flexu:
Haud secus incertos vestigat remige calles
Nutantes peragrans hortos urbana juventus.

[ll. 232-250]

Moreover, it hides so many birds in its shady wood that the re-echoing forest resounds with soft melody. There the winged companies bedecked in many colors joyously make their way on bright-colored wings through the clear sky, filling the air with music and causing the shore to ring with their sweet songs. Sweetly sings the sparrow⁴ bedecked with a wide rose-colored crest, his neck draped with reddish down. There also frolics the *centzontlus*,⁵ prince of birds, noted for the remarkable range of his songs and surpassed by no others in the quality of his voice, a bird unknown to the Old World. It simulates the voice of men,⁶ of birds, and of dogs, and even strains of music sung to the accompaniment of the lyre. At one time he sings in rhythm, now he imitates a rapacious kite, again he mocks a cat, or repeats the call of a blaring bugle; he merrily barks, he frets, he chirps. When confined to a cage he amuses himself by flitting about and singing and continues his melodies day and night without sleeping. Not with such soft plaintive strains does sad Philomela lament her misfortune while concealed beneath the deep shadows of the woodland she fills the poplars with her tremulous notes, as the *centzontlus* enlivens the shores with his charming mockery.

Such is the music, such are the waters, and such the lovely shores to which in early spring the gallant young men come in their little boats at the time when yellow flowers are blooming in profusion on the floating fields and spring crowns the meadows with bright roses. Each one embarks on a light double-oared skiff, lightening his spirits with gentle strains of music, to which in the distance Echo indistinctly replies; and the forest, struck by the sweet melodies, resounds. Then they draw up their swift boats for hard-fought contests and churn the soft waters with the beating of the oars⁶ᵃ until victory decks a vessel with the green laurel. Then both losers and winner alike cut oblique paths around the floating gardens and travel along the winding shores, pushing their boats through the flowers. As once upon a time in proud Crete noble Theseus skillfully escaped from the secret windings of the labyrinth, groping his way along the bewildering turns of the treacherous maze, so these young men of the city trace with the oar uncertain pathways across the swaying gardens.

Sunt etiam interdum, curvo quos prendere pisces
Aere juvat, prensosque vagas deducere ad oras,
Dum procul a tergo ripaque, hortisque relictis,
Effusum penetrant cymbis, ac remige pontum.
Hinc caute dapibus tectum fallacibus hamum,
Quem tereti ducit lino fatalis arundo,
Piscibus objiciunt, jussique silentia servant.
Continuo circum glomerat se copia nantum;
Nec tamen infensos ullus contingere pastus
Audet; sed rursus tendit declivis in ima.
Mox repetit cursum; gelidis mox labitur undis:
Itque, reditque viam, donec pellectus odore
Dente venenatas avidus depascitur escas.
Nec mora: deprensum calamo piscator ad auras
Extollit, tota socium plaudente corona.
Ille cavam moriens tremulis quatit artubus alnum,
Dum calamis alios rursus de more paratis
Turba capit. Tanto nutat sub pondere cymba.
Exultant animis illi, praedaque potiti
Occiduas redeunt omnes ad tecta sub umbras.

[*ll. 251-270*]

Ast ubi vesanus cessavit vere tumultus,
Inque urbem numerosa vadis se turba recepit,
Discurrunt placidi per amoena silentia ripae,
Queis cordi tranquilla quies, quos cura fatigat,
Et quos facundae juvat indulgere Minervae.
Tunc capti tacita rigui dulcedine ruris
Littora concentu replent quandoque Poetae.
Hic pius aethereo flagrans Carnerus[7] amore
Terribiles Christi plagas, ludibria, mortem,
Opprobriumque crucis numeris deflevit amaris.
Hic clarus sacro succensus Abadius[8] oestro
Occinuit Domino sublimes carmine laudes.
Haec quoque terrifico strepuerunt littora cantu,
Pelaei cum fata viri, cum ferrea bella
Doctus Apollinea cantaret Alegrius[9] arte.
Quin sua littoreis signarunt nomina truncis
Zapata,[10] et Reyna,[11] et socco celebratus Alareo,[12]
Tristia lenirent dulci cum taedia plectro.
Ut tamen occinuit modulis Joanna[13] canoris,
Constitit unda fluens, ruptoque repente volatu
Aere suspensae longum siluere volucres,
Visaque dulcisono concentu saxa moveri.
Ne vero Musas livor torqueret amarus,
Ipsa Aganippaeas jussa est augere Sorores.
Non sic argutis florentia prata Caystri

There are also at times those whose delight is to catch fish on a hook and to bring their catch back to the winding shore, having gone in skiffs into the open waters far out from the shore and the gardens. Having then carefully wrapped deceptive bait about a hook, fastened to a thin line which hangs from the deadly pole, they cast it to the fish and observe a strict silence. At once a school of fish assembles, yet none dares touch the dangerous food, and they go down again toward the bottom. Soon they turn back, again they are gliding through the chilly waters. They go away, and return again until, attracted by the scent, they feed greedily upon the deadly bait. At once the fisherman hooks and raises a fish into the air with his pole, while all the company applauds. The fish in dying shakes the light vessel with his trembling body, while the men again arrange their tackle in proper order and catch others. The boat sways beneath the load. The men are in high spirits and all return to their homes with their catch as the shades of evening draw near.

But when the mad rush of spring is over, and large crowds of people have returned across the water to the city, they stroll peacefully along the delightfully quiet shore, those who are wearied with care and who desire undisturbed rest, and those who are devotees of eloquent Minerva. Then the bards, captivated by the restful loveliness of the country along the lake, sometimes fill the shores with melody. Here devout Carnero,[7] on fire with divine love, bewailed in mournful numbers the terrible stripes of Christ, His mockery, death, and ignominy on the cross. Here illustrious Abad,[8] fired with holy zeal, sang glorious praises to the Lord. These shores resounded with songs of terror, too, when Alegre,[9] skilled in Apollo's art, sang of the fate of Peleus' gallant son and of cruel wars. Moreover, Zapata[10] and Reyna[11] and the celebrated comic poet, Alarcón,[12] engraved their names on the trees along the shore when to the accompaniment of the lyre they lightened wearisome cares. Moreover, when Joanna[13] sang her melodious songs, the water stopped flowing, and birds suddenly interrupted their flight and for a long time held themselves suspended silently in the air, and rocks were seen to move as a result of the sweet-sounding melody. And lest bitter envy irritate the Muses, she was ordained herself to increase the number of the sisters of Aganippe. Not with such sweet strains did the flower-covered meadows of the Caystros resound when

Insonuere modis, niveus cum littore Cycnus
Alterno moriens miscet suspiria cantu.
[*ll. 271-297*]

Sed jam praecipiti labuntur flumina cursu,
Totaque per longum stagni fugit unda canalem,
Qui piger irrorat campos, qui intersecat urbem,
Qui varios sequitur sinuoso fonte meatus,
Abruptis donec spumanti vortice ripis
Volvitur in salsam praeceps per saxa lacunam,
Jordano similis, proprias cum perderet undas
Dulces, mixtus aquis foetentibus Asphaltitae.
Nam puris quamvis Texcuci rura fluentis
Exsudent, dulcique palus se nutriat unda,
Unda tamen salso, mordacique incubat alveo,
Qui latices vitiat ripasque ingratus acerbat.
Hinc macies herbis, virgultisque horrida tabes:
Non ibi fas terrae geniales ducere fructus,
Nec licet armentis jucundum carpere gramen:
Urit enim patulos pestis saevissima campos.
Aequora quin etiam salso foedata sapore
Flumineos propriis pisces a fluctibus arcent.
Quod siquem dulcis pertaesum Chalcidis ardor
Coecus agat salsam nando penetrare paludem,
Pestiferas ut tangit aquas, letho occidit atro.
[*ll. 298-318*]

Subdola praeterea fallit maris unda phasellos:[14]
Vix etenim pelago consurgens Phoebus eoo
Palantes coelo stellas, noctemque fugavit,
Caerula cum placidos ostentant mitia fluctus.
Ast ubi Sol tenues contraxit corpora in umbras,
Ac medium cursu flagrans trajecit Olympum,
Colligit Auster atrox rabiem, magnoque tumultu
Aequora commiscet, spumasque ad littora volvit.
Nunc praeceps levibus sub cymbis unda dehiscit,
Nunc violenta redit, seseque ad sydera tollit.
Parvula cymba gemit repetito verbere laesa,
Et nautae valido Superos clamore fatigant:
Ac nisi sollicitus clavum Palinurus ad oras
Dirigat, exiguam demergent fata profundo.
[*ll. 319-332*]

Sed tamen infidis extat sua gratia limphis.
Nam cum Chalcensem deglutiat ore canalem,
Et lacus innumeros absorbeat undique fontes,
Ingressos alveo latices concludit avaro,
Nec guttam permittit aquae fugere inde per arva,
Quin tantis repletus aquis, lacus ipse redundet.
Ceu mare, cum medias terras interluit undis,

along its bank the snow-white swan interrupted his dying sighs with song.

And now the rivers glide along with swift course, and all the water of the lake escapes through a long canal which gently moistens the fields, intersects the city, and follows many winding paths until, bursting over the banks in a whirlpool of foaming waters, it rolls swiftly over the rocks into a salty lake, like the Jordan when it lost its own freshness by mingling with the bitter waters of the Dead Sea. For although the fields of Texcoco yield streams of fresh water, and the lake is fed with these fresh streams, yet the water settles in the salty and brackish bed which taints it and renders the banks unpleasant. For this reason the grass is blighted, and the shrubbery suffers terrible ruin. There the earth can not bring forth a plentiful harvest, nor the herds browse on tender grass, for a deadly pestilence devastates the open fields. Moreover, the lake, contaminated by saltiness, keeps the river fish from its waters. And if anyone, having wearied of fresh Chalco, should be driven by blind desire to swim out into the brackish lake, he succumbs to a dreadful death as soon as he touches these baleful waters.

The treacherous waves of this body of water also endanger light boats,[14] for scarcely has Phoebus arisen from the eastern sea and routed the roving stars of the sky, and driven away the night, when the dark blue waters gently reveal their quiet waves. But when the sun has shortened shadows and crossed the middle of Olympus in its blazing course, the violent south wind summons its fury and with a mighty onrush churns the sea and rolls the foaming billows toward the shore. Now a swiftly rolling wave breaks beneath the light skiff, now it reappears with violence and lifts itself toward the stars. The little vessel, buffeted by the continuous lashing, groans and the sailors importune the powers above with loud cries; and unless a skillful Palinurus directs the helm toward shore, the fates will send the little boat down to the bottom.

But still these treacherous waters have a distinctive charm, for although the lake swallows the Chalco canal and takes in countless springs from every side, it keeps within its ravenous shores the waters which have entered it, permitting not a drop to escape through the fields, for though replenished with such large quantities of water, the lake itself does not overflow its banks. It is like the sea which washes the

131

Concitaque oceani patulo bibit aequora rictu,
Quin terrae insidientur aquae, quin flumen ab oris
Exeat, aut aliis ineat commercia pontis.[15]

[*ll. 333-342*]

Nil tamen antiquus spectavit gratius orbis
Insidiis, quas turba gregi parat Inda volanti.
Principio fluvialis Anas, pars prima paludis,
Aethereas persaepe plagas, fluctusque secabat
Mexiceos, nec tela virum, fraudesve timebat.
Quin etiam lacuum ripis errare sueta
Saepius indigenas audens ludebat inermes.
Sed tandem audacem gentis solertia vicit.
Crescit enim densis ventosa cucurbita sylvis,
Supremisque haeret truncorum pendula ramis
Congrua Neptuno, Bacchoque futura lagena.
Has inter solers majores deligit Indus,
Et vacuas mittit vitreas innare per undas,
Major ubi alituum collecta est turba natantum.
Horret Anas primum, tantisque exterrita monstris
Littora flebilibus fugiens clamoribus implet.
Ast ubi nulla vident dispendia ferre vagantes,
Linquit corda pavor, redeuntque ad stagna volucres.
Illae Anates innant circum, non amplius ullam
Exterrent, reduces nec turbant mole volantes.
Tunc Indus capiti vacuam versutus adaptans
Assimilem prorsus reliquis errantibus alto,
Membra procellosis, collo tenus, abdit in undis,
Inceditque solo, nusquam prope littus amoenum
Profundo; incautum (quod secta cucurbita rimis
Ostendit) donec sensim penetraverit agmen.
Tunc alias nantum atque alias discrimine nullo
Surripit occultus dextra, pedibusque prehensas
Subjectis mergit limphis; et praecoce letho,
Quin fraudem obscuram praesentiat ulla volantum,
Contorta velox animam cervice revellit.
Scilicet incultae tanta est industria genti!

[*ll. 343-374*]

FINIS LIBRI PRIMI

surrounding regions with its waves and drinks the restless waters of the ocean with wide-open jaws without imperiling the land, overflowing the banks, or having any communication with other seas.[15]

Nothing, however, has the Old World observed with greater interest than the snares which the Indians set for wild fowl. In early times the duck, native of the streams and the chief inhabitant of the lake, frequently soared through the regions of the sky and cut paths through the waters of Mexico without fear of the weapons of men or of their cunning. In fact they would often wander along the shores of the lakes and brazenly mock the unarmed natives. But finally the ingenuity of the race triumphed over this presumptuous bird. Now in the deep forests grow large hollow gourds which dangle from the highest branches of the trees, suitable for serving as flasks for Neptune or for Bacchus. The crafty Indian selects from them the larger ones and lets them float over the glassy waters where the flocks of birds gather and swim about in large numbers. At first the ducks shrink away in fear and, alarmed at such strange objects, fly away and fill the shores with plaintive cries. But when they see the gourds harmlessly floating about, fear leaves their hearts and they return to the water. The gourds then float past the ducks and no longer frighten nor trouble any of them. Then the wily Indian, having fitted on his head a gourd exactly like those floating on the water, conceals himself up to his neck in the storm-tossed waves and walks on the bottom, which, along the lovely shore, is nowhere very deep, until he has slowly made his way into the unsuspecting flock seen by him through slits cut in the gourd. Then, without being seen, one after another he seizes indiscriminantly by the feet, and thrusts them down beneath the surface; and before any of the birds becomes aware of the sly trick, he quickly twists their necks, bringing them to an untimely death. Such is the ingenuity of this uncivilized race.

Xorulus

II

XORULUS

Nunc quoque Xoruli[1] Vulcania regna canendo
Persequar, et nigras montis penetrabo cavernas,
Qui mala tot populis, clademque minatus acerbam
Divite florentes populavit germine campos,
Flammarumque globos, et ruptis saxa caminis
Impatiens vomuit, gelida formidine gentes
Concutiens, postrema orbis quasi fata pararet.

[*ll. 1-7*]

Nam quamvis animum delectent floribus horti,
Claraque fertilibus labentia flumina pratis;
Sunt tamen interdum, vigili quos horrida visu
Aspectare juvat longe, et reputare tuendo.

[*ll. 8-11*]

Tu, Pomona ferax, montis perpessa furorem,
Et levibus tetri Vulcani exusta favillis,
Dicito, quas campis usit Xorulus aristas;
Quas nigro densas spoliavit robore sylvas;
Quisve furens armis bellum commisit Olympo,
Horrida nocturnis praebens spectacula flammis;
Omnia quippe gravem referunt ambusta ruinam.

[*ll. 12-18*]

Vallis erat veteri Xoruli nomine dicta
Undique diffusos late porrecta per agros
Melligenis cannis, armentisque apta ferendis;
Plurima cui pingues humectant flumina campos,
Ac multo taciti distinguunt subere luci.
Haec partim cannis ascripserat arva colonus,
Mollia quae centum dives findebat aratris;
Innumeris partim gregibus tribuebat alendis.
Roscida nectareo implentur cellaria melle,
Canaque fictilibus conflantur sacchara formis.
Lanigeras nullum pecudes capiebat ovile;
Sed sylvis passim, campisque errabat apertis
Turpe pecus, vigilum turba comitante Molossum,
Quam pastor circum baculo sylvestris agebat.
His armenta boum, leviumque colonus equorum
Junxit, qui ridens carpebant aequore gramen,
Aut luco placidi captabant frigus opacum.

[*ll. 19-35*]

Ne tamen agricolam subeant fastidia campi,
Provida chortales auxit fortuna volucres,
Quae mites fessum recreent, animique vigorem

JORULLO

And now I shall proceed to sing of Jorullo,[1] Vulcan's realm, and I shall enter the dark caverns of the mountain which threatens so many people with evil and dire misfortune, which has devastated the fields that abound in rich harvests, and with ungovernable fury has belched forth balls of fire and rocks from its bursting furnaces as if it were planning the world's final doom, arousing in the people cold chills of fear.

For although the gardens with their flowers, and the clear streams that glide through the fertile meadows delight the soul, yet there are those who at times are pleased to watch and study with keen eye scenes of horror, observing them from a distance.

Will you, O fertile Pomona, who have endured the fury of the mountain and have been scorched by dread Vulcan's flying sparks, tell what harvests of grain Jorullo has burned in the fields, what thick forests of black oak it has despoiled, or with what weapons it began to wage a violent war against Olympus, revealing through its flames scenes of horror in the night, for the general conflagration bespeaks heavy damage.

There was a valley, called in early times Jorullo, which extended in all directions far over the wide countryside and was suited to the cultivation of sugar cane and to cattle raising. Many a river waters its fertile plains and many a quiet grove of cork adorns it. A portion of this land the wealthy farmer had set apart for cane and turned over with a hundred plows; a part he devoted to the feeding of his vast herds. The storehouses were freshly filled with delicious honey, and white sugar was condensed in earthenware molds. No folds confined the thick-fleeced flocks, but far and wide through the woods and open fields the shaggy herd ranged, tended by a pack of watch dogs which the rustic shepherd guided with his staff. To these the husbandman added herds of cattle and swift horses which grazed upon the lush grass of the plain or peacefully enjoyed the shady coolness of the grove.

But lest the farmer become weary of the field, good fortune had increased his barnyard fowl to refresh him, when tired, by their mild and gentle

Ingenio reparent blando, pressumque malignis
Curis perfundant tacita dulcedine pectus.
Hinc Anatum numerosa cohors, hinc garrulus Anser,
Et Gallina suae custos fidissima prolis.
Vastam complebant chortem; quos pone sequentes
Assiduo teneri pipiebant murmure pulli.
Hos inter pictus, volucris Junonia, Pavo
Tempora sydereo graditur diademate cinctus,
Gemmata gaudens nunc terram verrere cauda,
Nunc sursum pictae stellata volumina tollens
Ferre gradum tumidus vano splendore colorum,
Et lente varios sese versare per orbes.
Quin etiam celeres, Cythereia turba, columbae
Aethera per liquidum celsa de turre ruebant
Alternos formare globos, rapidoque volatu
In gyrum duci, pennisque obducere Solem.
Cum vero e campis consueta ad tecta redirent,
Atria vasta domus, ceu nubes densa, tegebant,
Quaeque sibi, pullisque dapes lectura tenellis,
Mollia qui lautae fierent obsonia mensae.

[*ll. 36-58*]

Eminet haec inter clari domus alta coloni
Antiqua constructa manu, cultuque superba,
Prae foribus magna famulorum adstante caterva.
Hanc prope surgebant parvi penetralia templi,
Quod pietas olim multo lustraverat auro,
Assiduoque frequens populus sacravit honore.

[*ll. 59-64*]

His fallax opibus gnavum fortuna colonum
Auxerat, et grata tranquillum pace bearat,
Cum subito senior, genti non cognitus ante,
Lutea quem vestis, crudusque tegebat amictus,
Cana spectandus barba, venerandus et ore,
Sistitur, et moestis miscens suspiria verbis,
Tempus erit, dixit, quo non crudelius ullum,
Septenos postquam Phoebe compleverit orbes,
Autumnusque nigras aequarit lucibus umbras;
Cum Vulcanus edax isthaec impune per arva
Saeva furet, vallisque cadet consumpta favillis.
Ignea per campos volvi saxa, horrida saxa,
Et longo mersum Xorulum funere cerno.
Dixit: et agricolas trepidos, ac multa parantes
Quaerere longaevus gressu properante reliquit.

[*ll. 65-79*]

Haec vero miseri pavido dum corde volutant
Indigenae, servantque imis infixa medullis,
Extemplo pennata volans per rura, per urbes
Turbida fama ruit tantae praenuncia cladis:

nature, to reinvigorate his mind, and to flood his heart with sweet restfulness when overwhelmed by worries and troubles. Here a large flock of ducks, there the garrulous goose, and the hen, a most faithful attendant of her brood, filled the spacious yard. They are followed by their little ones, chirping constantly. Among them struts Juno's bird, the brightly colored peacock, with a starry diadem around his temples, now merrily sweeping the ground with his bejewelled tail, and now stepping about with swollen pride in the brilliance of his gaudy colors, and turning slowly around in circles. There was, besides, the company of birds dear to Venus, fleet-winged doves that would descend through the air from a high tower to form one flock after another and circle around in swift flight, darkening the sun with their wings. When, however, they returned from the fields to their lodging places, they would cover the large yard like a thick cloud to find food for themselves and their tender squabs, soon to become a dainty dish for the elegant table.

In the center of all these stands the stately house of the renowned countryman, built long ago in a magnificent style. A large number of servants stand before the door. Nearby stood a little sanctuary which the devout had once richly adorned with gold, and which throngs of people continuously honored with worship.

Fickle fortune had brought this prosperity to the industrious farmer and had blessed his tranquil life with a satisfying peace when suddenly there appeared an elderly man, hitherto a stranger to the people, clad in cheap and coarse attire, having a remarkable white beard and possessing a venerable appearance. Interspersing his sad remarks with sighs he said: "A time is coming, and none has ever been worse, after Phoebe will have completed seven revolutions and autumn's dreary nights are equal to the days, when ravenous Vulcan will rage with impunity through these cruel lands, and the valley will lie consumed in ashes. Molten rocks I see rolling through the fields, rocks of horror, and Jorullo sunk in lasting ruin." Thus spoke the aged man, and with hasty steps he left the farmers startled and eager to ask him many questions.

Now while the distressed inhabitants were pondering these words in their troubled hearts and keeping them firmly fixed in their minds, at once the alarming report went flying through the fields and cities warning of the great disaster:

Scilicet excidium Xorulo instare tremendum;
Nec laetas illic segetes, armenta, domosque,
Nec glebas homines doctos versare futuros:
Omnia quin potius flammis peritura propinquis.
Continuo turbati omnes, ac lethifer horror
Ossa quatit, gelidoque rigent in corpore venae.
Tunc subito properare domo, simul arva tumultu
Deserere, et sylvas ardent habitare remotas.
Qualis ubi Jonas Ninive praesagus in ampla
Ultricem Regi cecinit, populoque ruinam;
Tunc trepidare omnes, magnusque ululatus ad auras
Pallidaque ancipiti tenuari membra timore:
Haud secus agricolum venturi conscia casus
Turba timet, magnaque omnes formidine pallent.

[*ll. 80-97*]

Nuncius interea domini perstrinxerat aures
Rumor, et in vulgus volitans infausta ferebat,
Attonitis subito cladis terrore futurae
Agricolis armenta boum, pecudesque relinqui.
Advolat ille citus, violentisque ocyor Euris
Accurrens valli, pavidis sic voce profatur:
Quae vos, o miseri, quae vos dementia cepit,
Ignoti vanis tantum concedere dictis,
Ut gazas, et rura patrum, patriosque penates,
Et quidquid vobis majorum cura paravit,
Omnia praecipites cursu mittatis inerti?
Hic vigor, haec virtus animi, pectusque virile?
Ah! pudeat trepidare viros, pudeatque trementes
Femineo fugisse metu flaventia culta.
His mulcebat herus nutantia pectora verbis,
Ignotique viri spernenda oracla monebat.

[*ll. 98-113*]

Jamque pavor sensim lassos dimiserat artus,
Cum subito mugire solum, raucoque fragore
Horrendum procul auditae resonare cavernae.
Aequora quin etiam tranquillo assueta labori
Nocte, dieque tonant sonitu concussa tremendo.
Ut solet interdum nubes densata vapore
Fervidus aequoreis quam Titan extulit undis,
Purpureas vibrare faces, atque ignibus uri,
Terrificumque ciens coelo tenebrosa fragorem
Aethera permiscet, campos, montesque tumultu:
Non aliter pinguis nigrantia viscera vallis

that terrible destruction was threatening Jorullo, that there would be no abundant crops, nor herds, nor homes, neither would there be men skilled in tilling the soil, but everything was destined rather to perish in the approaching flames. Straightway everyone was in a state of excitement. Mortal fear shook their frames, and their veins hardened within their cold bodies. Then sudden anxiety prompted them to hasten from their homes, at the same time to abandon their farms, and to find shelter in far distant forests. Just as when the prophet Jonah warned the king and his people in mighty Nineveh of the vengeance that would come upon them, all trembled with fear, the air was filled with their loud lamentations, and their pale bodies grew lean with anxiety, in the same manner many farmers, aware of the calamity that was to befall them, were frightened, and all grew pale from intense fear.

Meanwhile the rumor which was bruited about had reached the ears of the overlord, and, flying everywhere, it was bearing the unhappy tidings that the farmers, panic-stricken because of the impending disaster, were abandoning their herds and flocks. Swiftly he ran into the valley with a speed greater than that of the rushing east wind and thus addressed the frightened people: "What madness, ye wretched people, oh! what madness has taken possession of you to be putting so much trust in the idle words of a stranger, to forsake everything in cowardly flight—your treasures, the estates of your fathers, your ancestral homes, everything provided you through the diligence of your forefathers? Is this courage; is this strength of character and fortitude? Ah, shame on you, men, frightened and quaking with womanly fear, for having fled from the golden harvests!" With these words the master calmed their faltering hearts and urged them to disregard the stranger's prophecies.

And now fear had slowly left their weary bodies when suddenly the earth began to roar, and in the distance they could hear the dreadful rumbling of the caverns. Moreover, the plain, accustomed to peaceful activities, thundered day and night, blasted by the dreadful noise. As a black cloud, filled with the moisture which the hot sun has drawn from the waters of the sea, sometimes hurls bright-red flashes of lightning and is charred by the flames, and causing a terrific crash in the sky turns heavens, fields, and mountains into an uproar, thus the rich valley, thrown into great disorder, resounded on

Inferno passim resonant turbata boatu.
His rursus concussi animi, noctesque diesque
Horrida venturae reputant praesagia cladis.
[*ll. 114-127*]

Utque propinquavit Librae Sol aureus altae,
Extemplo vallis visa est trepidare profunda,
Et nemus, excelsaeque domus, templumque moveri,
Parvaque terribili nutare mapalia motu.
Sub pedibus qua terra patet quassata vacillat,
Nec titubante gradu potis est consistere planta:
Genua labant, penitusque fugit vestigia tellus.
Tunc stridere trabes tecti, penetralia scindi,
In praeceps volvi trepido magalia casu.
Quin etiam solido constructum marmore templum
Attolli visum sursum tellure tumente.
Interea Solem nubes obduxerat atra,
Incubat et tristi suspecta malacia coelo,
Infandamque viris portendunt omnia cladem.
[*ll. 128-141*]

Attonitis primum torpebant verba palato,
Luminaque obtutu terror defixerat uno.
Sed tremulas magno voces agitante dolore,
Dant gemitum, maestisque omnes clamoribus auras
Complent, et caros humectant fletibus agros.
Pars lacrymans fatum incusat, pars poplite flexo
Imbelles tendit supplex ad sydera palmas,
Parsque onerat Superum sacris altaria votis.
Quos tremula affatur pavidos sic voce Sacerdos:
Quid juvat ignavos longo indulgere dolori,
Et caput interea tanto objectare periclo?
Maturare fugam, campisque excedere praestat.
Oh! fugiamus, ait, fugiamus funera: coelum
Permittit, suadetque fugam: fugiamus, amici:
Sic decet his monitos mortem vitare minantem.
Dixit: et ante alios per apricae devia vallis
Carpit iter, terramque celer vix signat eundo.
Caetera turba ducem pedibus sectatur anhelum,
Et rapido velox cursu jam cominus urget
Femineis vastos complens ululatibus agros.
Sic gazas, sic illa domos, sic arva relinquit.
Ceu quondam graecae tenebrosa volumina flammae
Dardanidae fugere citi, perque avia caros
Deseruere lares, patriamque, et Troia regna,
Labentis patriae transfixi corda dolore.
[*ll. 142-166*]

all sides with an infernal roar. The people were again shaken by these events and reflected day and night on the dreadful prophecy of impending disaster.

When the golden sun drew near to the high constellation of Libra, at once the deep valley was seen to tremble, the woods and lofty houses and the temple were shaken, and small huts were seen tottering from the terrific quake. Under foot, along the open ground, the earth was shaking and rocking, and as one's feet were unsteady, it was impossible to stand, for the knees would collapse and the earth utterly elude the foot. Then the timbers of the roof began to creak, living quarters were torn to pieces, little huts quickly tumbled down. Even the temple, built of solid marble, seemed to be lifted by the surging earth. In the meantime a black cloud hid the sun, ominous calm settled over the sullen sky, and everything betokened unspeakable disaster for the people.

At first they were dazed, their words clung to the roof of their mouths, and their eyes remained riveted in one fixed gaze. When, however, great anguish drove to utterance their faltering tongues, they groaned and filled all the air with mournful cries, and they wet the beloved fields with their tears. Some were tearfully complaining of their fate, others on bended knee suppliantly stretched their defenseless hands toward heaven, while others loaded the altars of the supernal powers with sacred offerings. With trembling voice the priest thus spoke to these frightened people: "What does it profit you, like cowards, to indulge in prolonged grief and meanwhile expose your lives to such peril? It is better to speed our flight and to escape from this land. Oh! let us flee," he said, "let us flee from death. Heaven grants it and urges us to escape; let us flee, my friends. Warned by these signs it thus behooves us to avoid the threat of death." He spoke, and before all the others he crossed the sunny valley barely touching the ground as he swiftly sped along. The rest of the people followed their excited leader and soon pressed close behind him in the swift race, filling the whole countryside with unmanly cries of woe. Thus they left behind their wealth, homes and fields, as once upon a time the Dardanians swiftly fled before the black wreaths of fire started by the Greeks and over the byways left behind their beloved homes and land and the kingdom of Troy, grief-stricken over the fall of their country.

Xorulus

Jamque procul miseris Xoruli abscesserat arvis
Extremum gaudens populus vitasse periclum,
Cum nova turbatis Vulcanus monstra minatur.
Tempus erat, quo clara suos Latonia currus
Aethereas emensa plagas declivis agebat;
Quin tamen interea roseos Aurora jugales
Annueret rapido segnis submittere plaustro,
Cum subito tellus horrendo rupta fragore
Evomit Aetnaeas furibunda ad sydera flammas,
Ingentesque globos cinerum, piceasque favillas,
Obscura densans totum caligine coelum.
Flammea saxa volant rutilis decocta caminis
Et crebro tellus casu tremefacta dehiscit.

[*ll. 167-179*]

His autem pubes rursus conterrita monstris
Longius ire parat, tutaque in sede locari,
Nullus ubi terrae convellat moenia motus,
Nec rutilis bacchans Vulcanus saeviat armis.
Namque flagrans intus rabidi vesania campi
Vicinas magnis urgebat motibus arces,
Totque furens taedas vasto vibrabat hiatu,
Ut magno celsas superarent impete nubes,
Purpureaque urbes implerent luce remotas.[2]
Quin etiam cineres liquidum per inane volantes
Disjunctos populos[3] passim pressere timore.
Tot vero interea flammatae fragmina rupis
Impatiens ructat monstris faecunda vorago,
Ut saxum saxis, ac rupes rupibus addens
Ingentem mediis montem[4] glomeraverit agris.

[*ll. 180-194*]

Una tamen cunctis non satis esset abyssus,
Quatuor hanc circum, sectis compagibus, ora
Ardenti Vulcanus edax torrente recludit,
Horrendum pecori, gentique auctura periclum:
Quae postquam lapidum densus praeclusit acervus,
Desuper et flavas ignis congessit arenas,
Indomitum tellus uno vomit ore furorem.
Non ita limphatus bacchatur Vesvius igne,
Parthenopem facibus terret cum proximus urbem;
Horrida nec tantis Siculos quatit Aetna ruinis,
Cum ferrum dura tractant incude Cyclopes,
Aut motu Enceladi Trinacria tota vacillat.

[*ll. 195-206*]

Decolor hinc tabes sylvas obduxerat atras,
Nigrantesque diu quercus, altaeque cupressus
Lurida tendebant exutae brachia fronde.

And now the people had left the ill-fated fields of Jorullo, happy to have escaped extreme danger, when Vulcan threatened the refugees with new terrors. It was the time when bright Diana, having crossed the wide expanses of the sky, was driving her chariot on its downward course, but lingering Aurora, meanwhile, was not yet consenting to have her rosy-hued steeds yoked to her swift car, when suddenly the earth burst open with a dreadful blast and furiously hurled to the stars flames like those of Etna along with huge masses of ash and burning pitch, blotting out the whole sky with a black cloud. Red-hot rocks, baked in fiery furnaces, were flying, and the earth, constantly slipping and trembling, was rent asunder.

Now the people, again alarmed by these ominous signs, made ready to move farther away and to establish themselves in a safe place where no disturbances of the earth would destroy their city nor a drunken Vulcan run amuck with his red-hot weapons. Indeed the convulsion which raged within the tempestuous earth was besetting neighboring cities with great earthquakes and violently hurling so many sparks from its vast mouth with such tremendous force that they rose above the clouds and filled cities far away with reddish glow.[2] And the ashes, flying through open space, brought fear to widely scattered peoples.[3] In the meantime, moreover, the monstrous abyss petulantly belched forth so many fragments of molten rock, heaping rock upon rock and boulder upon boulder, that it created a large mountain[4] in the midst of the fields.

But since one opening was not sufficient for all the eruption, ravenous Vulcan rent the structure of the earth and made four openings around this one with his stream of fire to increase the dreadful danger for man and beast. But when these became obstructed by a thick pile of rock, and the fire had deposited yellow sand on top, the earth gave vent to its ungovernable fury from a single opening. Not with such a fit of madness is Vesuvius inflamed when it terrorizes the neighboring city of Naples with its brand of fire; nor with ruin such as this does dreadful Etna shake Sicily while the Cyclops are forging weapons on their hard anvils, or the entire island is shaken by restless Enceladus.

From this a withering blight had enveloped the dark forests; the shady oaks and tall cypresses stretched forth their faded branches,

137

Gramina marcescunt pratis, et mellea dona
Nectareum combusta solo fudere liquorem.
Igne pecus pavidum, fortisque ad aratra juvencus
Occidit, aut lethum fugit per aperta viarum.
Insuper egregii sedes antiqua coloni
Prona cadit, magnamque trahit labefacta ruinam.
Templaque jam pridem cultu decorata superbo
Impete lapsa ruunt, casuque per aequora circum
Contremuit tellus, montesque dedere fragorem.
Undique mors instat, pavor undique, et undique
     terror.

[*ll. 207-219*]

Permeat hic etiam lucos, et lustra ferarum
Turbatas cogens densis excedere regnis.
Quaeque fugit sylvas, obscuroque antra recessu,
Ac veteris prorsus jam nunc oblita furoris
Oppida, ceu saltus olim, cicurata frequentat.
Sic Leo, sic atrox Ursus, sic prava Lycisca,[5]
Sic praeceps animi, ac mitescere nescia Tigris,
Et quicquid latebris lucus concludit opacis,
Praesidium quaerunt hominum per tecta gemendo.
Ceu cum postremus mundi post tempora finis
Concutiet terrore feras; hominesque trementes
Motibus insolitis, flammisque vorantibus orbem
Tuta in speluncis atris habitacula quaerent,
Inque vicem vacuas errabunt bruta per urbes:
Haud secus exterret vallem Vulcania pestis.

[*ll. 220-234*]

Ast ubi compositus tenuavit Mulciber ignes,
Terraque paulatim motu lassata quievit,
En nova Xoruli vertex portenta minatur
Disjunctis latura metum, mortemque propinquis.
Plurima pastorum sedato turba timore
In patrios maerens sensim remeaverat agros,
Dispersumque pecus campis revehebat apertis,
Ardua cum montis velat fastigia nubes
Horrida, sulphureo, nigroque coacta vapore.
Exiguo primum scintillat lumine nimbus,
Arrectas ullus sonitus quin verberet aures.
Sed vires fulgor paulatim nactus eundo
Horrendum extemplo tonitrum cum fulmine misit,
Concussique gravi fremuerunt murmure colles.
Ingeminat nubes ictus, et fulgura passim
Purpureis accensa rogis per nubila densa,
Perque agros lucent; totidem mittuntur ab alto
Ardentes longum, coelo reboante, sagittae,

bereft of foliage. Grass withered in the meadows, and stores of honey were burned and spilled their sweet fluid on the ground. The frightened herd and the strong ox at the plow perished in the fire or escaped death over the open roads. Moreover, the old homestead of a prominent farmer fell in ruins and brought destruction in its fall. And temples, handsomely adorned long ago, violently collapsed and fell, the surrounding earth was shaken by the fall, and the mountains roared. Death stalked everywhere, panic was everywhere, and terror was everywhere.

This consternation pervaded the forests too and the haunts of wild animals, forcing them in their distraction to leave their secluded realms. All fled from the woods and the dark recesses of the caves, and becoming utterly forgetful of their former ferocity and now tame, they crowded into the towns as once they haunted the forests. Thus the lion, thus the fierce bear, the mischievous prairie dog,[5] and the tiger, impetuous and wild, and every animal that lurks in the shady depths of the forest howled about the houses seeking the protection of men. Just as, finally, the end of time will fill wild beasts with terror, and the people, trembling with fright at the unusual tremors and at the world-devouring flames, will seek haven in dark caves, and beasts in turn will roam through the desolate cities, in like manner the ruin wrought by Vulcan threw the valley into a state of fear.

But when Vulcan had relaxed and calmed the conflagrations, and the earth, exhausted by the agitation, had gradually come to rest, behold the crest of Jorullo threatened further evils destined to bring anxiety to far distant peoples and death to those near at hand. Most of the shepherds had put aside their fear and had slowly returned in sadness to their paternal lands, bringing back again the flocks that were scattered over the open fields, when a dreadful cloud charged with black sulphurous fumes veiled the mountain's lofty summit. At first the cloud gave forth a feeble light, though not a single sound reached the listening ear. But it gradually increased in brightness as it moved along and suddenly burst out into a flash of lightning and gave forth a terrific clap of thunder. The hills shook and reverberated with a heavy rumbling sound. Flashes of lightning continued, and their brightness, intensified on all sides by blazing fires, illuminated the heavy clouds and the fields; such were the many thunderbolts that fell, burning a long

Elisaeque cadunt sonitu per jugera flammae;
Nec potis est ullus taedas numerare trifulcas.
Tam crebris udus late micat ignibus aether!
Tot nigrans torquet lethalia spicula nimbus!
Scinditur in partes jaculata e nubibus Ornus,
Praecipitesque cadunt ingenti murmure Cedri.
Hinc subita innumerae mulctantur morte bidentes,
Et montana pavens tremulo fulgore juvencus
Ire parat, spargitque amplis pecuaria sylvis.
Haec nova Xoruli grassatur valle quotannis,
Omnia quae tristi replet vicinia luctu,
Pernicies infausta gregi, pecorisque magistris.
Sic rabie bacchans semper Xorulus iniqua
Aut flammis campos replet, aut ferit oppida telis.
[*ll. 235-266*]

Quin etiam gelidas montis vesania limphas
Confundit, nimioque urget violenta calore.
Vitreus amnis erat clivo delapsus ab alto
Aspera diffugiens levibus per saxa fluentis,
Cultaque ductilibus perfundens aequora rivis.
Hic gelido teneras spargebat flumine plantas,
Arentesque greges magno recreabat in aestu.
At postquam tetras abrupit flamma cavernas,
Terraque montanis arsit Xorulia taedis,
Igneus undantem descendit fervor in amnem,
Fluminaque ante gelu pecori jucunda petulco
In calidas abeunt fumanti gurgite limphas.
Nec praeceps quisquam pedibus tranaverit amnem,
Amissa quin pelle luat temerarius ausum.
Ut tamen ad medium properat Sol igneus orbem,
Unda prius fervens aestum tepefacta remittit.
Ut solet in Libycis Cyrenes limpidus agris
Fons undantis aquae media fervescere nocte,
Et contra rutilo Solis fervore rigere:[6]
Haud secus ardentes amnis Xorulius undas
Praepes agit, Phoebique dein ardore tepescit.
[*ll. 267-287*]

Accedunt nec parva tamen solatia tantis
Excidiis; sua nam campis sua gratia major.
Vallis enim primum nimio ferventior aestu,
Replevit postquam Xorulus cuncta ruinis,
Graminaque infensus maculavit caede cruenta,
Nec Libico enervat languentia membra calore,
Frigore nec Scytico torpent ad munia palmae;
Aere sed gaudent populus, pecudesque benigno.
Sic laetos quamquam spoliavit germine campos,

trail of fire through the resounding sky, and the flames that came thundering down in bits over the fields; nor could anyone number the three-pronged bolts. Such were the countless fires flashing across the moist skies! Such were the deadly shafts discharged by the black cloud! A mountain ash, struck by a bolt from the clouds, was split to pieces, and cedars fell with a mighty crash. Countless flocks were suddenly killed, and the young bull, shaking with fear at the flashes of light, set out for the mountains and dispersed his herd through the great forests. This new disaster, filling all the neighborhood with untold sorrow, rages each year in the valley of Jorullo, bringing misfortune to the herds and to their keepers. Thus Jorullo with untoward violence ever fills the fields with flames or strikes the towns with its darts.

Moreover, the raging of the mountain also agitates the cool waters and makes them boil from the excessive heat. There was a sparkling stream which flowed down a steep slope, spreading out over the rough rocks and watering the farm lands with its lively flow. It sprayed the tender plants with its cool waters and refreshed the thirsty flocks in the hot season. But now that the fire has burst open the black caverns and the flames from the mountain have kindled the country of Jorullo, the burning heat descends upon the stream, and the waters, which by their coolness had hitherto satisfied the frisky herd, turned into hot steaming whirlpools. And no one may plunge into the stream and swim across it without paying for his rashness with the loss of his skin. When, however, the blazing sun is hastening toward the middle of its course, the water, previously hot, gives up its heat and becomes cool. As in the land of Libya Cyrene's clear fountain of running water is wont to become hot in the middle of night, yet to freeze under the beating rays of the sun,[6] so also the stream of Jorullo is a swiftly moving body of hot water, but later becomes cool in the hot sunshine.

Yet, even so, there is no slight consolation in the face of these disasters, for the fields take on a greater glory. Indeed the valley which before was too hot, now that Jorullo has filled every place with ruin and angrily stained the meadows with bloodshed, does not wilt faint bodies with the heat of Libya, nor does Scythian cold make hands too numb for work, but men and beasts alike rejoice in a mild climate. Although the fertile fields were thus despoiled of plant life,

Terraque per lustrum nullis fuit apta serendis
Fructibus; at vero ex illo tot tempore foetus,
Antiquum ut vincant praesentia commoda damnum.

[*ll 288-299*]

His ego dum modulis conabar fallere curas
Ad vaga per campos properantis flumina Reni,
Extemplo stridere trabes, reboare cavatae
Ima domus, nutare solum, tectumque moveri;
Et quae firma diu multos stetit una per annos,
Ex imo verti nunc visa Bononia fundo.
Corda pavent, gelidosque quatit tremor horridus artus.
Excessere omnes domibus, consistere contra
Nec possunt, tota passim discurritur urbe.
Actus enim rabida livoris tabe Vesevus,
Postquam Parthenopem toties concusserat urbem,
Ac flavas toties consumpsit saevus aristas,
Nostras stare arces, turresque, urbemque dolebat.
Hinc sensim tenues per subterranea regna
Vestigans aditus, inferna callidus arte,
Sulphureae tandem pressit vestigia venae,
Felsineam donec licuit penetrare cavernam.
Contigit ut vero convexum Mulciber antrum,
Continuo nitrum, sulphurque, atrumque bitumen
Subjectis ussit facibus; Vulcanus habenis
Immissis saevit, crassisque vaporibus antri
Aera densatum violento ardore relaxat.
Protinus in gyrum laxatus volvitur aer
Hinc atque hinc: quaerit qua tellus secta dehiscat
Irrequietus amans angusto carcere solvi.
Mox contracta furens ingenti murmure rumpit
Vincula, concutiens superam conamine molem,
Aethereum donec fusus contingat inane,
Et liber, praecepsque ruat per prata, per undas.
Non secus atque olim (si fas est credere dictis)
Infensus populis, flammisque Colima⁷ superbus
Sub densa varios fodit tellure meatus,
Arva quoad subter Xorulia, sulphura taedis
Accendit, motuque agros quassavit acerbo.
Inde vomens, ruptis vallis compagibus, ignem,
Extinxit veteres simulata pace caminos,
Xoruli ut vasta penitus fornace reclusa
Per nova versutus ructaret culmina flammas.
Quis vero infernus cum rumor fertur ad aures,
Aut fremit horribili tellus conterrita motu,

and for many years the land was rendered unsuitable for agriculture, yet since that time production has been so great that the new advantages offset the former losses.

While I was attempting to beguile my worries with these verses near the roaming waters of the Reno which hurry across the plains, suddenly the beams of the house began to creak, its foundations resounded, the earth shook, and the house tottered; and Bologna which had stood unshaken and intact for many years now seemed to be turning over from its very foundations. People's hearts were filled with dismay, and cold chills shook their limbs. All fled from their houses, nor could they withstand the dangers, but ran to and fro throughout the entire city. For, indeed, Vesuvius, driven by a violent and consuming envy, now that it had harassed the city of Naples so many times, and violently wasted the yellow harvests so many times, disliked to see the castles and the towers of our city standing. Therefore, slowly searching small passageways through the regions under the ground, for it was skilled in this diabolical business, it finally followed a vein of sulphur until it succeeded in penetrating the caves of Bologna. And when Vulcan reached the vaulted chambers, straightway he put his torches to the niter, sulphur, and black pitch, and set them afire. As he raged without restraint, his intense heat released the gases in the cave compressed by the heavy fumes. Forthwith the free gas whirled round and round in every direction seeking a place where the earth was split open, restlessly intent on freeing itself from the narrow prison. Presently with a loud explosion it madly burst its tight bonds, shaking mightily the earth above and making its escape, it reached the open air and rushed along freely over the meadows and across the waters. Just as once (if one may trust the story) Colima,⁷ angry at the people and with an air of defiance, burrowed several passageways through the solid ground until it set on fire the sulphur which lay beneath the fields of Jorullo and shook the country with a violent movement. Then emitting a stream of fire through the dislocations of the valley, it ceased its former eruptions, feigning peace, that, when the wide crater of Jorullo was entirely blocked, it might slyly send forth its flames through new openings. But who, when the report of subterranean sounds comes to his ears

Ingenti subito mentem formidine pressus
Non pariter nobis (terris avertite nostris,
O Superi, monstrum) Xorulia fata timebit?

[*ll. 300-342*]

Sed paveant alii, paveant, Jesseia Virgo,
Qui tua perversis maculant praeconia linguis,
Et queis, grata olim, forsan tua munera sordent.
Quid vero paveat praeclara Bononia cladem,
Cum tua perpetuis cumulans altaria donis
Promeritos demissa tibi persolvat honores,
Et dignas memori referat de pectore grates?
Quare age, Virgo Parens, populo succurre vocata,
Auxilioque urbem facilis solare gementem:
Et dum clarus equis lustrabit Phoebus Olympum;
Altaque praecipites fugient in caerula fontes,
Munus inoblita famosa Bononia mente
Extremas mundi semper celebrabit ad oras.

[*ll. 343-355*]

FINIS LIBRI SECUNDI

or when the earth rumbles and shakes violently, will not suddenly suffer great mental anguish, and like me (avert, ye gods, the omen from our lands) fear the fate of Jorullo?

But let others quake with fear, yes, quake with fear, O Virgin Mother of Jesus, who defile your name with their wicked tongues, and to whom your gifts, once pleasing, perhaps seem base. But why should fair Bologna fear disaster, since in ever loading your altars with offerings she humbly renders you due honor and with an unforgetting heart returns suitable thanks? Therefore, Virgin Mother, come help your people who call upon you, and graciously comfort the sorrowing city with your assistance; and so long as bright Phoebus drives his horses across Olympus, and streams make haste to flow into the blue waters of the sea, far-famed Bologna will not forget to make known your favors to the uttermost parts of the world.

III

CATARACTAE GUATIMALENSES

Sat monti, et flammis, nocuis sat carmine nimbis,
Excidioque datum. Repetam nunc flumina cantu,
Flumina per duras saltu spumantia cautes,
Grata verecundae captant ubi frigora Nymphae.
[ll. 1-4]

Naiadum formosa cohors, Dryadesque puellae,
Lactea quae vitreis perfusae corpora limphis
Et nemus, et fluvium, vallemque habitatis opacam,
Dicite, quis praeceps adigat per inane fluentum,
Aptaritque lares vobis sub rupibus altis,
Si rupes, Nymphae, si vere flumen habetis.
[ll. 5-10]

Urbs infausta fuit, suavi Guatimala coelo,
Dives aquis, populoque frequens, ac frugibus uber.
Hancce solo primum fundaverat Indus amoeno
Montis inaccessi positam radicibus urbem
Arboribus densam crebris, ac floribus agri
Incultis certe, sed qui viridantia montis
Semper odorato pingebant terga colore.
Quin etiam felix duro sine vomere tellus
Maturos hortis fundebat prodiga fructus.
Quos inter celsi montis radice sub ima
Cautibus e vivis manat fons vitreus unda,
Fortis ubi epotis aestum pulsare juventus
Gaudet aquis, dulcique rigat pomaria rore.
Hanc urbem, hos agros olim gens Inda colebat.
Ut vero Hispani regnum ditione tenere,
Juraque devictae coeperunt dicere genti,
Extemplo alluvies montanis fluctibus aucta
Templa Deum, gentisque lares absorpsit, et urbem.[1]
[ll. 11-28]

Tunc alio Hispanis visum transferre colonis
Reliquias urbis, mediaque in valle locare,
Quam circum norant celsis pro moenibus apte
Surgere sydereos elato culmine montes
Frondibus insignes, undisque, ac vere perenni.
Hic, procul indigenis antiqua sede relictis,
Hispani posuere novi fundamina regni,
Ingentemque urbem vasta in convalle locarunt
Callibus instructam rectis, multoque patentem
Circuitu; quam nulla unquam contagia diri
Vexabant morbi; nimio nec Cynthius aestu,

THE WATERFALLS OF GUATEMALA

Enough attention has been given in my poem to the mountain and its fires, enough to baleful clouds and devastation. The subject of my song shall now turn to rivers, rivers whose foaming waters bound over the hard crags where modest nymphs enjoy the refreshing coolness.

O lovely band of naiads and nymphs of the wood who bathe your fair bodies in the sparkling waters and dwell in forest, stream, and shady dell, tell me who causes the stream to plunge through empty space, providing you a home beneath the steep rocks, if actually you inhabit the rocks and streams.

There was an ill-fated city, Guatemala, lying beneath fair skies, abundantly provided with water, populous, and rich in the fruit of the field. This city had first been established by the Indians at the foot of an impenetrable mountain, in a beautiful country thickly wooded and covered with flowers of the field, though wild, yet ever fragrant and painting the green ridges of the mountain with bright colors. Moreover, the fertile soil in their gardens, even without aid of the hard plowshare, yielded an abundance of ripe fruits. In the midst of these appeared at the very foot of a high mountain a clear spring which flowed from the natural rock, where their strong sons gladly relieved the summer heat by drinking of its waters and irrigated their orchards with its refreshing stream. This city, these fields an Indian tribe once inhabited. But when the Spaniards began to hold sway and to dispense justice over the vanquished tribe, at once a flood, fed by mountain torrents, swept away the temples of the gods, the homes of the people, and their city.[1]

Then it seemed good to the Spanish settlers to move the remnants of their city to another site and to rebuild it in the middle of a valley around which they noticed mountains conveniently lifting their lofty summits into the heavens to serve as high walls, remarkable for forests and water and perennial springtime. Here the Spaniards, having left the native people behind in their former location, established a new seat for their kingdom, and in this wide valley they founded a large city, provided with straight streets and spreading over a wide area. This city was never ravaged by dreadful dis-

142

Cataractae Guatimalenses

Nec gelido populum Boreas horrore fatigat.
Templa laboratis accisa e rupe columnis
Ardua, Panchaeo semper fragrantia thure,
Undique fulgebant auro lustrata corusco.
Limina tum pulchro passim decorata nitore,
Luxuriesque agri, ac rorantes gramina fontes
Aeternum dederant urbi nomenque, decusque.

[*Il. 29-46*]

Urbs tamen infelix, quam sors suprema manebat,
Ingenti demum terrae concussa tremore[2]
Tota labat, nulloque ruunt discrimine tecta.
Templa, domusque cadunt, saxisque obstructa rotatis
Nulla per antiquos restabat semita calles.
Interea nubes, coelum quae umbrosa tegebat,
Lugentique diem, Solemque amoverat urbe,
Effusos subito praeceps se volvit in imbres,
Foedavitque omnes undanti flumine gazas
Infectas limo, terraque, undaque sepultas.
Tollitur inde virum clamor, maestusque ululatus
Femineus, totumque replent suspiria coelum.
Et patres natum, et nati doluere parentes
Suppositos terrae, vulsamque a sedibus urbem.

[*Il. 47-60*]

Hujus in aspectu, qua Phoebus vergit in Austrum,
Arduus exsurgens sublimi vertice clivus
Aethereas lustrare plagas, ac tangere visus
Astra supercilio, bellumque indicere coelo.
Ampla solo figit patulo fundamina moles,
Flectitur et vastos adeo diffusa per arcus,
Ut per bis denas leucas volvatur in orbem.
Mox arctat massam, sensimque arctata volumen
Hoc magis imminuit, quo udas petit altior auras,
Aligeras donec fastu ventosa superbo
Vincat aves cono, densata et nubila vincat.
Qualis ubi aerio nimbos abrumpit Olympus
Vertice, et aethereos ausus conscendere tractus
Astra petit, Phoebemque amens, Phoebumque
minatur:
Haud aliter pulchri frondosa cacumina montis
Nubibus abruptis crista, se in sydera tollunt.

[*Il. 61-76*]

At vero paucis, gelidum qua respicit axem,
Undat aquis clivus: multo tamen amne profusus
Usque fluit, pelago saevit qua turbidus Auster,
Humectatque vagis Australia terga fluentis:
Quem circum densa montem tegit arbore lucus
Incomptus ramis, tenebrisque obductus opacis,

eases, neither were its people distressed by excessive heat or by the north wind's icy blasts. Lofty temples on pillars made of quarried stone and ever redolent with Arabian incense appeared on every side, gorgeously adorned with bright gold. The many homes, handsomely built, the fertility of the land, and the springs which poured over the meadows had soon given eternal fame and glory to the city.

But the unfortunate city, awaiting its final doom, was at last shaken by a mighty earthquake[2] and completely destroyed. Its buildings tumbled down everywhere. Temples and houses fell, and no pathway remained through the streets, blocked, as they were, by the rolling stones. Meanwhile a thick cloud, darkening the sky and depriving the sad city of daylight, suddenly resolved itself into a torrential downpour and ruined all their treasured possessions, covering them with mud and burying them under the earth and the flood. Then arose the shouting of men and cries of distress from the women, and their lamentations filled all the air. Fathers grieved for their sons who were buried underneath the earth, and sons grieved for their fathers, and they all grieved for their city that had been torn from its foundations.

Within sight of this, in a region where Phoebus turns southward, towers a high mountain whose uplifted summit seems to pierce the heavens and touch the stars with its brow, and to be declaring war upon heaven. Its great mass rests upon a foundation extending over a wide area and sends out such great buttresses that it is twenty leagues in circumference. Then it becomes smaller and still smaller, the higher it reaches into the misty air, until its windswept peak proudly rises above the winged creatures and higher than the thick clouds. As Olympus bursts through the clouds with its windy crest and, daring to mount the regions of heavens, reaches to the stars and wantonly threatens the moon and the sun, so the wooded crest of this beautiful mountain bursts through the clouds and rises toward the stars.

Now the side which faces the icy north has few streams, but on the other side where the turbulent south winds rage over the ocean, copious streams flow continuously and water the southern slopes along their winding courses. This mountain is completely covered with a dense forest having closely interwoven branches, and is enveloped in deep darkness which the

Quas genus aligerum modulis oblectat acutis,
Praesertim teneram foveat si femina prolem.
Ast loca radici populus vicina profundae
Excolit, et duro tractat versata ligone,
Nunc fruges teneras, Cereris nunc semina sulcis
Spargens, nunc ramos figens ex arbore demptos.
Hinc etiam vario distinguit gramina flore
Cum violis calthas, cum nardis lilia miscens,
Quae montem gemmis propria statione decorant.
Sola venenatis florum Regina rubetis
Usque rubescentes foetus cum lucibus aequat.
Florida perpetuo distinguens munere prata.
Turba tamen solers Australia terga frequentat,
Maturos citius lectura ex arbore fructus,
Fervida quod pingui tellus uligine laeta
Largius edat opes nigra spectabilis umbra.
Sic Pepones, sic Pruna manu, Citrosque, Nucesque
Innumerosque alios foetus plebs Inda legebat
Fertilis assiduis terrae proventibus uber.

[*ll. 77-101*]

Insuper in magnos se mons abscindit hiatus
A summo passim porrectos culmine ad imam
Radicem; sed quos foliis virgulta tenellis
Undique distinguunt, annosa et robora densant,
Exuto donec demissa per aequora fastu
Planet iter, purisque riget sata laeta fluentis.

[*ll. 102-107*]

His prudens opibus rarum natura jugavit
Portentum, celsum decorat quo prodiga clivum.
Occiduas siquidem properat cum Phoebus ad undas,
Obvia quotidie medium praecingere montis
Gaudet inaccessi candenti ex vellere nubes.
Lenta gradu primum madido procedit ab Austro
Parrhasium simulans cursu petere ardua plaustrum:
Sed facili magnum flexu sinuata per arcum
Eoum certat gressu contingere Solem,
Circumdatque diu nigrantes Ilice lucos
Albenti zona, montemque per ilia cingit.
Ut vero longum septem conversa trioni
Circumiit, texitque levi velamine terga,
Algenti rursus nubes obvertitur ursae,
Inceditque gravi tenuis per culmina gressu,
Excelsos donec sinuoso syrmate clivos
Verrat, et aethereas levior se tollat in auras.

[*ll. 108-124*]

Saepe etiam duplici zona praecingere visa
Candida sublimem variantia nubila montem.
Mox commota duplex venti spiramine zona

feathered race makes merry with shrill notes, especially when the mother is fledging her tender brood. But the people till the land near the foot of the mountain and prepare it with the stout hoe, now to arrange in furrows the young plants, now to sow seeds of grain, or to set out slips cut from a tree. Then, too, they adorn their meadows with various kinds of flowers, mixing marigolds with violets, and lilies with nard, which in their individual places beautify the mountain with their blossoms. Alone among its prickly thorns the queen of flowers blooms all day long embellishing the blossoming meadows with everlasting glory. Moreover, these intelligent people crowd the southern slopes to pick ripe fruit from the trees, for the warm earth, rich and moist, and noted for its deep shade, produces an abundance of fruit. Thus it was that the Indians used to gather melons, plums, and citrus fruits along with nuts and countless other crops, richly supplying themselves with the continuous produce of the fertile land.

On top, the mountain splits apart on every side into large ravines which extend from the summit to the base, but are overgrown everywhere with young shrubs and thickly covered with aged oaks until, having lost its steepness, it forms a level road across the low descending plains and waters the joyous crops with its fresh streams.

In addition to these gifts, nature has wisely presented an amazing phenomenon by which she lavishly adorns the lofty mountain. Every day as the sun is hastening toward the western sea, a white fleecy cloud appears and encircles the middle of the impenetrable mountain. Slowly at first it proceeds from the rainy south, as if on its laborious journey to the great bear, but, gently turning, it forms a great arch and tries to reach the east, for a long time forming a white band around the black forests and enveloping the heart of the mountain. When, however, it has surrounded the northern slopes of the mountain for a considerable time, covering them with a thin mantle, the light cloud again heads toward the cold bear and majestically treads the peaks until it sweeps its trailing robes across their summits and rises more lightly still into the ethereal air.

Often too, white clouds are seen to shift and form a double band around this high mountain. Finally, the two bands are cleared away by the wind, the one toward the west, the other in the

Haec petit occiduum, Solem petit illa recentem,
Et propriam quaerit pulsa in contraria metam,
Amplaque frondosi montis per terga feruntur.
[*ll. 125-130*]

Hujus in Australi pagus radice jacebat
Martyris augusto Petri de nomine dictus,
Ardenti sub sole situs, nimioque calore,
Et culice, et musca, nocuaque infestus Arachne:
Sed quem prodigiis mirum natura replevit.
[*ll. 131-136*]

Propter enim pagum longo se scindit hiatu
Et rimam tellus aperit rescissa profundam,
Qua saliens amnis scopulis illiditur altis,
Ac praerupta cavas effingunt saxa cavernas.
Haec autem sapiens latebris natura recondit;
Nec potis est ullus miros penetrare recessus,
Ni scalis lapsus vallem ducatur ad imam.
Ast ubi planta solum patuli compressit hiatus,
Consistit subita stupefactus imagine rerum
Obtutuque animus perstat suspensus in uno.
Namque statim, dextram fluvii labentis ad oram,
Objectat se oculis ingens sub rupe cavata
Porticus aequa jugo, multasque extensa per ulnas,[3]
Naturae constructa manu, saxoque rigenti
Sculpta olim. Tenues fastigia lata per auras
Diffugiunt muros nullis innixa columnis;
Sed scopulo nodata rudi compagibus arctis
Pendula tecta volant bis dena ab moenibus ulna.
Quin etiam tecti liquidum per inane profusi
Aerio pendent durati e fornice coni,
Pensilis in terram coni mucrone reverso.
Non nullos autem pendenti e rupe revulsos
Horrendo, fama est, sonitu traxisse ruinam.
Inde gravis cunctis lustrum spectantibus horror.
Praeterea rupes partes diffusa per omnes
Aspera vestibuli pervadit strata cavati
Mobilibus saxis, parvisque aspersa lapillis.
Omnia caute rigent, murique, et strata, tholusque.
Non ita bis seni famosa palatia Reges
Construxere olim, fastus monumenta superbi,
Ad laetas Nili faecunda uligine ripas,
Cum sibi praeclarum duodeno pignore nomen
Perpetuare ardent, famamque extendere in aevum;
Ut miram dives decorat natura cavernam.
[*ll.137-170*]

Rupis in adversa, fluviique in parte sinistra
Tollitur undosas collis faecundus ad oras,
Plurima quem crispa myrteta virentia fronde

direction of the rising sun; and thus driven in opposite directions they strive to reach their respective goals as they traverse the ridges of the wooded mountain.

At the southern base of this mountain is a district, devoutly named in honor of Peter Martyr, which lies beneath a warm tropical sun and is infested with mosquitoes, flies, and poisonous spiders, yet it is an extraordinary place which nature has filled with wonders.

Near this spot the earth gapes apart, and the breach reveals a deep gorge in which a stream dashes against the high rocks as it rushes along, and the steep cliffs form vast caverns. But nature has wisely covered these marvellous recesses with darkness; nor can anyone enter them unless he descends by ladder to the bottom of the valley. But when his feet have reached the floor of the spacious chasm, he stands amazed at the unexpected sight, and his eyes remain fixed in one gaze. For at once his eyes encounter on the right bank of the stream underneath the hollow rocks an immense arcade resembling a yoke and extending for many cubits.[3] It was constructed long ago by the hand of nature and carved out of the solid rock. The wide ceiling, unsupported by pillars, extends from the walls into the thin air, yet it is securely fastened to the rocky ledges and hangs twenty cubits above the walls. Moreover, throughout the open spaces of the vast chamber, solid cones hang from the vaulted ceiling with their sharp ends pointing toward the ground. It is said, however, that some of these, having broken loose from the overhanging rocks, have fallen with a terrific noise. For this reason all who behold this sight are filled with grave misgivings. And as sharp rocks are scattered everywhere, the floor of the vaulted chamber is filled with loose fragments and bestrewn with small stones. Everything is bristling with jagged rock—the walls, the floor, and the ceiling. In no such way did the twelve kings, beside the fertile banks of the Nile's rich waters, once build their famous palaces, monuments of their exalted pride, yearning to perpetuate their illustrious names with a dozen memorials and to extend their glory forever, as has bountiful nature adorned this marvelous cave.

On the side opposite the cliff and to the left of the buffeted banks of the stream, a green hill rises. It is adorned with many green curly-leafed myrtles and covered with a thick grove

Exornant, densusque tegit frondentibus ulmis
Lucus, et alituum recreat pennata sonoris
Turba modis, vario corpus distincta colore.
Pica⁴ tamen forma, multisque coloribus aucta
Unguibus e trunco pendens inversa recurvis
Rauca sonat, crocitatque rudi per culmina voce.
Est tamen adverso multo spectabilis antro,
Dum virides quercus, ac frondes inter opacas
Contorquet caudam, sinuatque volumina plumae
Caeruleis aspersa notis, croceoque veneno,
Totaque purpureo mirum fucata nitore.
Roscida ceu quondam pluvio Thaumantias arcu
Nubila depingit, varioque colorat amictu
Tellurem pulchro gaudens circumdare gyro,
Quoque magis terrae fumantis nubila densat
Halitus, hoc formosa polo nitet amplius Iris:
Haud aliter pictis pennis spectanda volucris
Umbrosum nitido variat nemus omne colore.

[*ll. 171-191*]

Haec inter, lustrum dextra, collemque sinistra,
Volvitur in praeceps undanti flumine rivus,
Inque imam vallem scopulo descendit ab alto:
At tanto fluvius cumulo se volvit aquarum,
Ut rauco vallis resonet concussa fragore,
Ingentique nemus strepitu, lustrumque reclament.
Vox aures refugit, nec fas est verba profari,
Ni levibus placeat voces committere ventis.
Qualis in Isiaci pingui tellure Canopi
Arva per, et cautes undantia flumina Nili
Excurrunt, saltuque agitur cataracta rapaci,
Horrisono quatiens montes, auresque tumultu:
Haud secus horrendo sonitu spelunca resultat,
Cum crebra fluvius cautes diverberat unda.
Tum lapsus patulum circum se fundit in aequor
Vortice spumosum torto, cunctisque timendum,
Quod rotet in gyrum nantes, tumuletque sub undas.

[*ll. 192-208*]

Inde fluit praepes vallis per opaca profundae,
Abducitque graves violento flumine truncos
Saxa repentino fodiens declivia lapsu.
Vix etenim saltu vallem demissus ad imam
Se diro noscit conclusum carcere, et altae
Praecinctum rupis duris complexibus amnis,
Cum crudas subito conatur rumpere cautes,
Ingentemque fodit viva inter saxa canalem.
Scinditur in partes rupes fluvioque perenni
Concavat umbrosas aeterna nocte cavernas,
Solis inaccessas radiis, muscoque virentes,

of spreading elms. Many kinds of bright-plumaged birds enliven these woods with their sweet song. The magpie,⁴ for instance, graced with many beautiful colors, makes a raucous sound and fills the hilltops with its hoarse cries as it hangs upside down from a limb, holding on by its claws. It is a very beautiful sight to behold when across from the cave it waves its tail among the thick leaves of the green oaks and ruffles its feathers dotted with spots of deep blue and yellow and wondrously tinted all over with bright purple. As Iris, dripping with dew, sometimes paints the clouds with her rainbow and mantles the earth with many colors, joyfully spanning the sky with a beautiful arch, and the more the vapor from the misty earth condenses into clouds, the more does lovely Iris shine in the sky, so this bird, esteemed for its brilliant plumage, brightens all the shady woodland with its colors.

Between the two, the cave on the right, and the hill on the left, a surging stream rolls swiftly along, descending from a high precipice into a deep valley below. Now this stream carries such a volume of water that the valley shakes and resounds with a thundering noise. The sound of the voice escapes the ear, nor is speech permitted, unless one wishes to address himself to the thin air. As in the fertile land of Canopus where Iris is worshiped, the surging waters of the Nile overrun the fields and the rocks, and a cataract plunges swiftly down, shaking the mountains and deafening the ears with its thundering roar, so the cave reverberates with a fearful sound as the stream lashes the rocks with its continuous flood of water. Then, having fallen, it spreads out in swirling eddies over a vast foam-covered area, an object of fear to everyone, for it engulfs those who swim in it and buries them beneath its waves.

Then it flows swiftly on through the dark ravine, carrying away heavy logs with its strong current and hollowing the rocky slope by its steep descent. Scarcely, indeed, has the bounding stream reached the bottom of the gorge and become aware of cruel confinement and the restraints of the hard walls of rock, when suddenly it attempts to break through the hard barrier and burrows a large channel through the solid rock. The rock is broken apart and the continuous stream forms caverns, darkened by everlasting night, untouched by the rays of the sun

Quas nec pes hominum tetigit, nec vafra Lycisca
Desertas audet timida contingere planta.
Has inter rapidus celeri pede labitur amnis
Adversis passim perrumpens flumina saxis,
Extremas donec cautis delapsus ad oras
Praecipites iterum demens agat impete fontes.

[*ll. 209-225*]

Namque pavimenti perrumpit saxa barathrum
Vorticibus flexis, gelidaque undante tremendum,
Tartara cui subter, Plutonis regna, propinquant,
Et foveam tenebris circum nigrantibus umbrant.
At fossa ingentem facile diffusa per orbem
Undique pro muris scopulis praecingitur altis,
Quos montana olim saltu graviore peresos
In vasis teretem disjunxit limpha figuram,
Multaque frondosis ramis virgulta recondunt
E laceris saxi costis exorta rotundi:
Quae pictae quandoque, loci dulcedine captae,
Arguto volucres hilarant certamine cantus.
Imminet huic barathro rupes, altissima rupes,
Et quam lapsuram profunda horreret abyssus.
Hinc violentus aquis rursus labentibus amnis
Mittitur in fossam praeceps, summaque ruit vi.
Tunc latices fluvius tumulo delapsus ab alto
Distrahit in minimas venti spiramine guttas
Inque levem totus casu dissolvitur imbrem.
Undique limpha volat, ceu nubes cana, per auras.
Plena tamen gelida, terret quae subter, abyssus
Perstrepit horrendum, circum spumante barathro,
Undaque curvatas ripas corrodit avara
Absorbens torto disjunctas gurgite cautes.
Ceu mare, cum validi permiscent aequora venti,
Nunc undas tumidum faciles jaculatur in astra,
Ut coelum credas jamjam contingere pontum;
Nunc fundum retegit, dissectis fluctibus, imum
Tartareas ardens sonitu terrere cavernas:
Tunc rabido cautes coedit, murosque furore,
Absorbetque cavas sinuoso vortice pinus:
Non aliter vallo saxi praecincta cavati
Unda ferit crudas, deglutitque anxia rupes.

[*ll. 226-258*]

Incolit hunc amnem proles Thaumantis in arcu,
Quem lapsu fingit celeri quandoque sonorum
Flumen inaurato percussum lumine Solis.
Scilicet ut Phoebus cursu petit aureus aequor
Hesperium, fessosque regit temone jugales,

and green with moss. These desolate caverns have never been touched by the foot of man, nor does the cunning coyote have the courage to step inside. Through their center the stream flows swiftly on, forcing its waters through the rocks that oppose it on every side, until it finally reaches the edge of the cliff and again madly and violently hurls its waters over the precipice.

Through the rocky floor a tremendous chasm is opened up, filled with swirling eddies and cold surging waters close to Tartarus below, Pluto's realm, which overshadows the chasm on every side with intense darkness. But the pit quickly widens into a large circle and is surrounded on all sides by high walls of rock which long ago the mountain stream wore away with its falling waters and shaped into a smooth bowl. These walls are hidden by many thick bushes growing out of the ragged edge of the hollowed rock which colorful birds, charmed by the loveliness of the place, often make merry by their sweet rivalry in song. Overhanging this pit is a rock, a very high rock, such that if it were to fall it would shake the very depths of the abyss. From it the impetuous stream of surging waters again rushes headlong into the abyss, falling with the greatest force. Thereupon, the waters, having descended over the high precipice, are broken apart by the force of the wind into very small drops which, in falling, are entirely converted into light mist. On every side water is flying through the air like a white cloud. Moreover, the abyss, filled with the chilly waters, brings terror to the regions below and the foam-covered pit produces a dreadful roar. Its waves greedily eat away the curving banks and devour the rocks torn loose by the whirlpools. Just as the sea, when its surface is agitated by violent winds, now quickly lifts its swelling waves toward the stars until you would think the sea to be on the point of touching the sky, and then parts its waves and lays bare the ocean's floor, eager to bring terror to the caves of Tartarus with the loud sound, and then with ungovernable fury breaks down cliffs and walls and swallows up boats in its swirling eddies, so the surging waters confined within the wall of the rocky depression strike the rough rocks and greedily swallow them up.

Iris, the daughter of Thaumas, visits this stream in her bow which the roaring river creates in its rapid fall when struck by the golden light of the sun. For indeed, when fair Phoebus is drawing near the Hesperian sea and

Tunc demissa polo Junonis Nympha sereno
Insidet effusis placide Thaumantias undis
Objectatque amnem radiis, ut luce refracta
Ostentet varios, Phoebo mirante, colores.
[*ll. 259-267*]

Ut vero Nymphae pictos excussit amictus,
Arrositque altam repetito verbere fossam
Amnis, agit latices scopuli per terga recisi,
Et patulum gressu barathrum pernice relinquit.
At corrosus aquis, exsecta rupe, canalis
Tartareis adeo pronus demittitur umbris,
Ut nullum fluvii murmur circumsonet aures;
Sed tacitus fundo, praepesque adlabitur imo,
Pacifici donec pelagi revolutus ad oras
Flumina mordaci confundat dulcia limphae.
[*ll. 268-277*]

Nobilis huc properat Guatimala tota quotannis
Tempore quo rigidis torpent Aquilonibus artus,
Brumaque immiti tabescunt gramina campi.
Pensilibus scalis ad saxea tecta relati
Ponte domant fluvium, donec sub rupe recepti
Concava suspenso perlustrent lumine saxa.
Omnia mirantur, montemque, amnemque, specusque.
Ore tamen presso nutus, et signa sequuntur,
Sive salutatum pubes exoptet amicum,
Seu velit ad tectum prono jam Sole reverti.
[*ll. 278-287*]

Arva Paraetoniae sileant viridantia gentes,
Ubere quae dives foecundat flumine Nilus:
Et septem sileat veterum miracula mundus
Garrula queis laudum solvit praeconia fama.
Omnia convallis superat portenta decore,
Rara verecundis praebet quae umbracula Nymphis
Semper odorifero fragrantia germine montis,
Et suavi semper volucrum resonantia cantu.
[*ll. 288-295*]
FINIS LIBRI TERTII

guiding his weary steeds along, then it is that Iris, Juno's nymph, dispatched from the calm sky, quietly settles over the falls and exposes the mist to the rays of the sun in order that, by refracting the light, she may display the various colors, while Phoebus looks on in wonder.

When the stream has put aside the nymph's many-colored mantle, and by constant lashing has worn away the deep abyss, it forces its waters over the top of the steep rock and swiftly abandons the spacious chasm. Moreover, the river bed, hewn out of the rock and eaten away by the stream, descends so abruptly to the shades of Tartarus that not a sound of its flow strikes the ear, but silently and swiftly it passes to the lowest depths until it returns to the shore of the Pacific and mingles its fresh waters with the salty water of the sea.

All Guatemala hastens to this place every year at the time when the stiff north winds benumb the body and the grass is withered in the fields by winter's cold. Letting themselves down on hanging ladders to the stone roof, they cross the river by bridge, and then gaining access to the rocky cavern, they hang up a light and examine the vaulted chamber. They marvel at everything—the mountain, the river, and the cavern. With a hushed silence they communicate only by signs and nods if a man should wish to greet a friend or desire to return home at sunset.

Let the peoples of Egypt keep silent about their green fields enriched by the fertile waters of the bountiful Nile, and let the ancient world keep silent concerning its idly-heralded seven wonders. This valley surpasses in beauty all wonders, affording unparalleled shade for the modest nymphs ever scented with fragrant mountain flowers, and always reverberating with the sweet songs of birds.

IV

COCCUM, ET PURPURA

Postquam Neptuni vitreos invisimus agros,
Regnaque Vulcani tremulis armata favillis,
Visere fert animus roseum cum Murice Coccum,
Ac totum fixis oculis lustrare laborem.

[*ll. 1-4*]

Tu, quae puniceo, Tritonia Virgo, colore
Intextos auro Regum perfundis amictus,
Et Lydam laetaris acu vicisse puellam;
Dic mihi, quae dederit regio tibi provida fucos,
Atque orbem Cocco, tyrioque impleverit Ostro;
Quis legat haec campis, quae mittant semina terrae,
Et quo nascantur regalia germina cultu.

[*ll. 5-11*]

Floret in Hesperio multo spectabilis orbe
Urbs populosa viris, domibusque ornata decoris,
Mercibus insignis, templisque augusta superbis,
Vallis Oaxacae[1] fecit cui nobile nomen.
Undique florentem circumdant aequore campi
Immenso, pinguique satis, ac divite gleba;
Frigus ubi ardenti commiscuit aura calori,
Temperieque levat pecudesque, hominesque benigna.
Perpetuis lucent distincti floribus agri,
Et vestita ferax foliis vernantibus arbos
Altera maturis curvatur prodiga pomis,
Altera dum teneros fructus tibi cauta reservat.
Hinc salices videas se crista efferre comanti
In coelum, pinguique adeo turgescere ventre,
Ut magno circum gyro ducatur in orbem
Ac multas arbor sinuetur crassa per ulnas.[2]

[*ll. 12-27*]

Hos inter dives gemmat Nopalis in arvis
Edita sex ulnas terra, suffultaque trunco
Imbelli, quem nulla comis frons mobilis ornat,
Ardentem pecudi Phoebum neque submovet umbra.
Carnosas vero Nopalis vivida frondes[3]
Induit intextas duro subtemine fibrae,
Munitasque rubis canis, ac pelle virenti
Obductas, ovum referunt quae saepe figura.
At frondes quamvis fortis compago coarctet,
Interiora tamen replet circumfluus humor
Coccineis quondam pascendis vermibus aptus.
Nec tamen hoc videas folium pubescere ramis;
Sed frondes frondis natas mirabere limbo,
Altera ut alterius culmen radice coronet.

COCHINEAL AND PURPLE

Now that we have visited Neptune's crystal
fields and Vulcan's fiery realms, I am disposed
to give my attention to rose-colored coccus and
murex and to study carefully their processing.

Do you, O Tritonia, maiden goddess, who steep
with purple the royal robes interwoven with
gold and delight in having excelled the Lydian
maiden in needlework, tell me what region provided you with dyes and supplied the world with
coccus and with Tyrian purple, who gathers
these in the fields, what lands furnish the
seeds, and by what cultivation the royal plants
are produced.

There flourishes in the western world a very
important city, having a large population and
adorned with beautiful houses. It is famous for
its commerce and distinguished by its majestic
temples. The valley of Oaxaca[1] has given to
it an illustrious name. This prosperous city is
surrounded on all sides by vast plains of very
rich soil where the winds bring a mixture of
cool and hot temperatures and refresh both
men and beasts with a temperate climate. The
fields are ever brightly arrayed with flowers,
and the fruit trees are clothed in verdant foliage,
one generously bending under the weight of
ripened fruit, another holding back its tender
fruit for you. Then you may see willows lifting their leafy crests high into the sky, with
trunks so thick that they cover a wide area and
have a circumference of many cubits.[2]

Among these trees the rich nopal grows in the
fields, rising six cubits above the ground and
supported by a feeble trunk with not a single
twig of waving leaves to adorn it or to provide
shade to protect the herd from the blazing
rays of the sun. On the live stalk, however,
appear fleshy branches,[3] interwoven with hard
strands of fiber, protected by white prickles and
covered with green skin. These often have the
shape of an egg. Although the branches are
solidly constructed, the interior is succulent
and provides at the proper time nourishment
for cochineal insects. You will not see leaves
growing on the branches, but you will be amazed
to see branches growing on the end of branches,
one crowning the head of another with its roots.

149

Quin et luteolis vestitur floribus arbor
E folio exortis patulo, lumboque sub ipso;
Quos subit armatus densata cuspide fructus
Deformem celso tollens in vertice florem.
[*ll. 28-45*]

Hanc vero campis optes si figere plantam,
Planta tibi nullos adducet parca labores.
Arripe deciduas vernanti ex arbore frondes,
Arreptasque manu latum mox projice in agrum,
Et frondes jactae, laetis seu miseris arvis,
Seu crudas inter sitienti pondere cautes,
Ocyus educent totidem cum foenore partus.
[*ll. 46-52*]

Haec domus antiqua, haec augusta palatia vermis
Coccinei, tenerum gaudet qui haurire liquorem
Arboris, et longam foliis educere prolem.
Nascitur haec ramis prisca de stirpe parentum,
Moribus ingenuis, niveoque ornata colore,
Civiles exosa neces, exosa tumultus,
Et contenta suis Nopalis frondibus udae
Praelia nulla movet, nulli succensa minatur,
Nec petulans hostes pubes invadit inermes.
[*ll. 53-61*]

Cauta genus totum sexus partitur in ambos,
Queis propriis natura dedit se prodere signis.
Hinc marium dorsum rubro suffusa colore
Parvula stilla notat, membris candore relicto
Femineis; vestitque ambos tenuissima pellis,
Quam si dura tibi manibus tractare libido,
Protinus effuso rorantem sanguine cernes.
[*ll. 62-68*]

Hunc autem forma simulat porcellio vermem;
Sed caput hic condit, crurisque, et calcis egenus
Reptat inexpertus rigidae per brachia plantae.
Ast adeo lente serpentia membra movebit,
Ut folio intentum, tractoque e fronde liquori
Ignava corpus credas reparare quiete.
[*ll. 69-74*]

Ut vero insectum rubrum bibat arbore succum,
Ac proprio cives possit ditare cruore,
Vere novo, cum Phoebus adest, cum bruma recessit,
Cum laeti rident redivivo gramine campi,
Algentesque calor Titanis temperat auras,
Educit clausos velatis cannabe cistis
Quos laribus vermes industria cauta reservat.

Moreover, the tree is covered with yellowish flowers which grow out of the very fringe of the flat branches and under which a prickly fruit grows, holding the shriveled flower on its outer end.

Now if you should desire to plant this thrifty tree in the fields, it will involve no trouble. Break off branches from a green tree and scatter them over the wide field, and it makes no difference whether you plant them on good soil or among hard dry rocks, for they will quickly produce as many or even more young plants.

This is the old habitat, this the stately palace of the cochineal insect which joyously feeds upon the tree's sweet juice and brings forth its numerous young on the branches. This insect, having been born on these trees, has a long ancestry. Its body is white as snow. It is gifted with a gentle nature, abhoring murder among its fellows, abhoring civil disorder; and contented with the succulent nopal branches, it creates no strife; it does not in anger indulge in threats, nor does it wantonly attack a defenseless foe.

Nature wisely divides this entire species into the two sexes and has permitted the identity of sex to be revealed by special signs. Accordingly, a tiny dot of red marks the bodies of the males, while those of the females remain white. A very delicate skin covers both, and if you should willfully take one into your hands, immediately you will observe drops of blood oozing out.

Now this insect is shaped like the wood louse, but its head is concealed, and as it has no legs and feet, it crawls awkwardly along over the plant's stiff branches. Indeed, so slowly will it move its creeping body along that you will think it is clinging to the leaf, intent on drawing out the juice and nourishing its body in idle repose.

Now in order that the cochineal insect may drink the ruddy juice of the tree and be able to enrich the people with its own blood, in early spring, when the sun is bright and winter is past, when the glad fields are smiling with fresh grass, and the heat of the sun tempers the chilly air, then these insects, having been safely kept in the house, are brought out in baskets covered with hemp. Then the farmer spreads

Mox varios trunci foliis disseminat altis
Tenuia gossipio relegens corpuscula blando,
Femineumque pecus maribus permiscet opimis.
Continuo lentae Nopali mordicus haerens
Ingentique vorans dulces conamine frondes
Nocte, dieque bibit pubes argentea succos.
Hic maribus pigris fragilis se femina miscet,
Demissisque ovis immensa examina truncis
Educat, et niveis extendit civibus urbem.
Haec foliis reptat, patrumque exempla secuta
Vernantes habitat ramos, ac provida rostris
Vestigat, sugitque liquentia mella juventus.

[*ll.* 75-93]

Quis tamen innocuam crudeli crederet hoste
Invadi, fatisque feris concedere gentem?
Vix tamen arrectis pubes albescere ramis
Coepit, cum subito vastis plebs turbida campis
Consurgit, foliisque acies inimica propinquans
Infestis pubem telis oppugnat inermem.
Implicat insectum crudelis aranea filo,
Ventreque disrupto fumantia viscera sugit;
Improba vel raptat rostro gallina tenaci;
Ni prius adrepens trunci per brachia vermis
Exterus insontis pubis corpuscula rodat.
Quin etiam trucibus legio numerosa volantum
Arripit insectum rostris, raptique per aethram
Infanda sublimis agit de morte triumphum.
Ut solet interdum rabie lupus actus ovile
Expugnare rapax, agnisque indicere bellum:
Tunc teneros matrum raptos complexibus agnos
Dilaniat saevus, rabidusque per arva cruento
Devorat imbelles, reliquis balantibus, ore.

[*ll.* 94-112]

Quare opus est nullis sordescere foecibus agrum
Putrida quae insectis nocuis alimenta ministrant;
Atque herbas omnes Nopalem vellere circum,
Tigna veneniferis laqueis ne sumat Arachne.
Inde juvat magnam pueros impendere curam,
Qui pravas vigilent volucres arcere flagello,
Et quos armatos audax gallina pavescat.
Si vero exili subrepat aranea planta
Nocte sub obscura, vermesque cruenta trucidet,
Pelle loco subito, cassesque, et funera pelle,
Ne foliis serpat putris contagio mortis.

[*ll.* 113-123]

them out in various places on the tall branches of the trees, gathering up the frail little bodies with soft cotton, the females along with the fat males. At once these silvery creatures cling tenaciously to the nopal, greedily feeding upon the sweet boughs and drinking the juice all through the day and night. Here the frail females, having united with the indolent males, lay their eggs and produce in the trees large swarms, thus adding little snow-white citizens to the population of their city. The little ones crawl along the branches and in imitation of their parents, dwell upon the green boughs, diligently searching after and sucking the delicious juices.

But who would believe that this innocent family is attacked by a fierce enemy and succumbs to a bitter fate? Yet scarcely are they beginning to whiten the tall branches when suddenly a turbulent mob rises up in the wide fields, approaches the branches in a fierce line of battle, and attacks these young defenseless creatures with deadly weapons. The cruel spider winds her web around the insect, and having torn apart its belly, sucks out the reeking entrails; or a villainous chicken snatches them up in her greedy mouth, unless a worm intrudes, and crawling along the branches of the tree, devours the tiny bodies of these innocent creatures. Vast numbers of birds snatch up these insects in their fierce beaks, and carrying them high up into the air, triumphantly inflict unspeakable death. Thus a greedy wolf, driven by madness, assails a sheepfold and wages war upon the lambs. Having snatched the young lambs from their mothers' sides, he savagely tears them to pieces, and raging through the fields with bloody mouth he devours the defenseless creatures amidst the bleating of the rest.

It is necessary, therefore, that the ground be free of filth which provides food for deadly insects, and all the weeds around the nopals should be pulled out so the spider will have no support on which to fasten her deadly snares. Then too it is advantageous for the boys to exert great care to chase away the harmful birds with sticks, and thus armed, strike terror into the bold hen. But if in the darkness of night a spider should creep up stealthily, and mercilessly slaughter the insects, drive her out of the place at once, break up the web, and stop the carnage, lest the scourge of death spread over the branches.

Nec satis est Coccum tetro defendere ab hoste,
Ni simul a rigido ventorum flamine serves,
Coccineamque sagax subducas frigore gentem.
Frigus enim, pluviaeque graves, ventique minaces
Horrida jucundae portendunt fata juventae,
Purpureoque feri perfundunt arva cruore.
Hinc plantas debes clivo fixisse sub alto,
Qui gelidum vasta Boream compage refraenet,
Et frigus tenera turba propellat acerbum.
Si tamen algenti pubes statione prematur,
Ligna para, magnisque focis praecinge rigentem,
Ignibus ut crebris letho tepefacta resistat.
Turbidus at campis cum latis irruit imber,
Grandinis aut pecori minitatur verbera nimbus,
Desuper injectis vermes absconde tapetis;
Ut latis velat storeis gens Inda quotannis.
Gens siquidem solers tignis hinc inde locatis,
Quae patulas celso Nopales vertice vincant,
E densis amplum storeis velamen adaptat,
Quod modo fune super ducit, modo fune reducit.
[*ll. 124-143*]

His tutatus obit virides porcellio ramos,
Mensibus ac binis succo nutrita recenti
Longaevos referunt sobolis jam membra parentes,
Humoremque altis quem pubes frondibus hausit,
In rubrum gracili transformat ventre liquorem.
Qualis ubi Assyrio celebris subtemine Bombyx
Frondosum cupidus Mori depastus honorem
Majores gaudet procera mole referre,
Quasque habiles carpit festino tempore frondes
Ventre coquit tenui, coctasque in serica vertit:
Haud secus e succo niveus Nopalis alumnus
Perficit exili regalem ventre colorem.
Mox, ubi turba levis majores induit artus,
Coccineoque vorax opplevit corpora succo,
Vernantes aliquot vellit radice colonus
Ramos, albenti natorum examine plenos,
Et trabibus calidae suspendit dextra culinae;
Aut conclusa cavis, obductisque agmina cistis
A rigido Boreae tutatur flamine venti,
Inque novae prolis servat gens cauta parentes.
[*ll. 144-163*]

Tum reliquos campis plantae super alta relictos
Gossipio munita manus legit impigra vermes
Praecipiti miseros mactandos postea letho.

And it is not enough to keep the members of the cochineal family from a ruthless enemy unless at the same time you shield them from hard gusts of wind and carefully remove them from the cold. For cold, heavy rains, and threatening winds betoken horrible death for the gay young insects, and the raging elements cause the ground to become drenched with purple blood. So you must plant your trees along the side of a large hill, that its ponderous mass may ward off the mighty force of the icy north wind and keep bitter cold from the tender multitude. If, on the other hand, the insects are located in a cold place, bring logs and surround them with large bonfires when they are cold, so that, warmed by the numerous fires, they may be saved from death. And when a rainstorm is sweeping across the wide fields, or hail threatens to strike the colony, protect them with coverings as do the Indians, who throw wide mats over them every year. These clever people, having erected on this side and that timbers which exceed the height of the spreading nopals, fasten to these a large awning made of thick matting which they draw back and forth overhead by means of a rope.

Thus protected, the cochineal insects overrun the green branches, and the young ones, having fed on the fresh juice for two months, now have bodies as large as those of their aged parents, and the juice which they have drawn from the tall branches turns into a red fluid in their tiny stomachs. Just as the silk-worm, celebrated for its Tyrian thread, after greedily feasting on the glorious leaves of the mulberry, is happy to have a long body like those of its elders, and just as it digests and turns into silk within its little stomach the soft leaves on which it greedily feeds, so the white nursling of the nopal produces in its tiny stomach the royal color. Then when the little creatures have developed large bodies and have greedily gorged themselves with purple juice, the farmer breaks off a few green branches swarming with the white young insects and hangs them from the rafters of his warm kitchen, or the people carefully protect them from the hard north winds by confining them in large covered baskets and keep them to become the parents of a new crop.

Then, provided with cotton, they quickly gather the remainder of the insects which remain on top of the trees in the fields, that the poor creatures may then be swiftly put to death.

Coccum, et Purpura

Agmina quippe Indus distendit lecta tapetis,
Innocuumque gregem calido rigat improbus amne,
Dum totum saevo videat succumbere fato.
Ni placeat niveos flammis extinguere cives
Immeritos, auri caeco exitialis amore.
Tunc ingens valido fornax accenditur igne,
Tota quoad magno rutilet flammata calore:
Fornacem pubes, semotis ignibus, intrat,
Tostaque purpuream vitam fornace relinquit.
Aut Indus certe diffundit chortibus amplis
Sole sub ardenti, torretque examina Sole.
Ceu quondam Bombyx fatis cessurus iniquis
Nunc rutilis Phoebi telis substernitur alti,
Nunc atris jacitur conclusus vimine flammis,
Vitaque lethiferas moriens vanescit in auras.
[*ll. 164-181*]

His ubi suppliciis mactavit barbara gentem
Coccineam, traxitque cavis plebs Inda caminis,
In rubrum mansuetus abit porcellio Coccum
Puniceum condens nivea sub pelle colorem;
Quo Galli, et Batavi, Venetusque, Hispanus, et Anglus,
Et Russi, et Belgae, totusque intingitur orbis.
[*ll. 182-187*]

Ne tamen haec lucri quemquam deludat imago,
Noverit hoc Indis coelum servasse colonis.
Saepe etenim cives quaestus ingentis amore
Coccineos aliqui magno conamine gnatos
Frondibus aspersos avidi excepere colendos.
Ipse tamen dulces pastus porcellio frondes,
Aut magnam passus ventorum murmure cladem,
Aut propriam renuens foliis educere prolem,
Elusit domini misero tentamina casu
Desidia gazas consumens pravus inerti.
Indica gens autem duros edocta labores
Perferre, algentes nec mollis pallet ad imbres,
Nec rubram metuit quassantem lampada Phoebum.
Hinc omnes tolerat casus tranquilla verendos,
Et Lunam, et Solem, pluviamque, et frigus, et aestum,
Invigilatque diu Cocco noctesque diesque,
Vermibus infestos abigens candentibus hostes.
Improba cura quidem, sed tanto debita lucro.
[*ll. 188-205*]

Nunc agite, et quando coeptis Parnassia turba
Dextra favet, pontumque aperit Thetis alma serenum,
Aspera purpureum cogam per littora sucum,
Quem doluit periisse semel cum Murice Sarra;
At micat occiduo jam dudum pulchrior orbe.[4]
[*ll. 206-210*]

The Indians spread them on mats and cruelly dip them in hot water until they are sure that the innocent creatures have met their dreadful doom. Or it may please them, in their blind lust for filthy lucre, to kill these guiltless white creatures with fire. In that case a large oven is heated with coals until it is red-hot from the intense heat. The fire is then removed, and the insects are thrown into the oven, in which, having been baked, they leave behind their purple remains. Or the Indian sometimes spreads them out on a wide patio under the hot sun and bakes them. Thus the silk-worms, awaiting their dire fate, sometimes are spread out under the bright rays of the noon-day sun, and sometimes are placed in baskets and cast into the consuming flames, and their life passes away in the deadly air.

When the Indian has cruelly slain the cochineal family by these methods and has taken them out of the ovens, the soft insect is now changed into a red grain and hides beneath its white skin a scarlet dye used by the people of France, Holland, Italy, Spain, England, Russia, Belgium, and the entire world.

But that this vision of wealth not deceive anyone, let him realize that heaven has reserved this industry for the Indian farmers, for often certain avaricious citizens, eager to enrich themselves, have taken great pains to cultivate the young cochineal insects which lie scattered over the branches. But while the insects fed on the sweet leaves, they either suffered heavy loss from the howling winds or, refusing to produce their young on the leaves, mocked the efforts of their master, causing him distressing losses and maliciously wasting his wealth by their indolence and sloth. The Indian people, on the other hand, taught to endure hardships, are not easily daunted by the cold rains, nor do they dread Phoebus when he brandishes his bright red lamp. Thus unperturbed, they bear all things that might be feared—the moon and sun, the rains, and cold and heat; and day and night they keep a long vigil over their white cochineal insects, warding off dangerous enemies. It is a troublesome task, to be sure, yet required for such great returns.

And now, since the Muses favor my efforts and gentle Thetis unveils the peaceful sea, along the rocky shore I shall collect purple juice, the loss of which, together with murex, Thetis once mourned, but which now shines more beautifully in the Western World.[4]

153

Abditur extremis Americae pagus in oris
Magnus, et aequoreis non multum dissitus undis,
Cui dedit Australi fluvius commercia ponto,
Immensoque leves pelago committere cymbas.
Usque calet pagus ferventi torridus aura:
Fontibus at dives, semperque virentibus agris
Et Solem placida lucorum temperat umbra,
Et turbae pomis teneris refrigerat aestum.
Hunc Indi pagum veteres dixere Nicoyam,
Purpura sed famam dedit, ac memorabile nomen.
[*ll. 211-220*]

Horret enim curvo spumantis littore ponti
Perpetuum dorsum, rupisque immobilis ordo
Ventorum furiis, altisque obnoxius undis.
Mordicus his limax scopulis affixus adhaeret,
Mole quidem parvus, sed claro insignis ab Ostro,
Mobile cui tegmen subtilis concha ministrat,
Egregiosque lares, cunasque, et triste sepulchrum.
Hoc Indus pelagi cupidus per saxea quaerit
Littora, et inventum saxo Conchyle revellit,
Asservatque diu cyathis turgentibus unda,
Reptantis donec turbae glomeretur acervus.
[*ll. 221-231*]

Tu, prius abruptis vellas quam cautibus Ostrum,
Suspice, num Phoebe lumen reparata resumat,
Exactosque dies primo lucentis ab ortu.
Purpureo siquidem replet Conchylia fuco
Ardua cum crescens extollit cornua Luna.[5]
Si vero defessa suos contraxerit ignes,
Tardaque cornigero sensim fulgore senescat,
Desine spumosam reptare per aspera concham,
Ni velis ingratum frustra tolerare laborem.
[*ll. 232-240*]

Nec latet haec Indam prudens industria gentem:
Quaerit enim pubes aspris Conchylia ripis
Immemor omnino donantis munera Phoebes.
Non tamen insipiens cyathis educit ab altis,
Elicietve cavo pretiosum Murice succum,
Ni prius attento perlustret lumine coelum.
Ast ubi Luna novis orbis fastigia bigis
Irradiat, pubes brevibus munita lapillis
Extrahit e cyatho conchas, frangitque sub ictu.[6]
Cauta tamen dextra quaerit; prompteque recludit
Purpureum tumido conclusum ventre colorem.
Mox detecta super ducto Conchylia filo,
Murice gossipium rutilo, vel serica tingit,
Littora cui numquam similem Sarrana dedissent.
Fulgenti, vivoque micant fucata liquore

Hidden away in a remote part of America is a large province not very far from the sea. It is joined to the sea on the south by a river which permits small craft to sail out into the high seas. This province is always hot and parched by hot winds, yet rich in springs and in fields which are always green. Quiet shady groves relieve the effect of the sun's heat, and mellow fruits refresh the people. The early Indians called this place Nicoya, but its purple has brought fame and a memorable name.

Along the curving shore of the foaming sea stands a continuous cliff with its rocks unmoved by the fury of the winds or the buffeting of high waves. Clinging tenaciously to these rocks is a shell-fish, small in size, it is true, but famous for its brilliant purple. Its thin shell affords a movable cloak, an excellent home, a cradle, and a cheerless tomb. The Indian eagerly searches for it among the rocks of the seashore, and having found one, he pulls it from the rock and keeps it for a long time in a vessel of water until he has collected a large number of the crawling creatures.

Before taking a shell-fish from the jagged cliffs, observe whether a new moon is again appearing and consider how many days have passed since the return of its light, for the moon, when it is increasing and lifting high its horns, fills the shell-fish with its purple fluid.[5] If, however, the moon is waning and lessening its light, and the brightness of its horns is gradually fading away, let the foam-covered snail continue to crawl over the sharp rocks, unless you wish to waste your time on a useless task.

This industry is not unknown to the clever Indian tribe, for these people hunt for shellfish along the rocky coast wholly unmindful of the gifts of the munificent moon. Yet they are not so foolish as to take them out of the deep vessels or to extract the precious juice from the shell without first scanning the heavens with a keen eye. And when the moon-goddess, riding in her new chariot, is illuminating the vault of heaven, the people, having provided themselves with small stones, remove the shells from the container and burst them open.[6] Then deftly searching with their fingers they quickly take out the purple dye concealed in the swollen stomachs. Soon they are drawing a thread through the extracted juice and dyeing cotton or silk with purple such as the shores of Tyre

Coccum, et Purpura

Serica, quem nunquam vastat longaeva vestustas,
Acribus aut mersum limphis lixivia delent.
Quin etiam gelida vestis purgata frequenti
Clara nitet, gaudetque omnem deludere nisum
Mordicus aeternum servans immota colorem.
[ll. 241-260]

Quis tamen haec, Musae, primus Conchylia legit,
Et lanam rutilo docuit medicare veneno?
Fertur in horrenti Sarrani littore ponti
Divitias raptasse maris, Conchyle, molossus,
Atque avidum fuco rictum foedasse cruento.
Anxia tota domus percussum vulnere ducens
Ora vigil, rostrumque manu rimatur anheli
Puniceam stringentis adhuc frendente rapinam
Morsu; conaturque undis purgare cruorem.
Sed dum labra canis rorantia Murice tergit,
Murice tota manus, vitreusque intingitur amnis,
Purpureisque aspersa notis spectabile signum
Candida lina ferunt; licuit dum forte retentam
Dente venenato pretiosam vellere praedam,
Ingentemque oculis longum lustrare nitorem.
[ll. 261-275]

FINIS LIBRI QUARTI

never produced. Silks dyed in this bright and sparkling liquid are never effaced by the passing of time nor destroyed when immersed in a strong solution of lye. Indeed, a garment, though washed many times in cold water, keeps its luster and continues to hold fast its color, resisting every effort to fade it.

But who, O Muses, was the first to gather these shell-fish and to show how to dye wool in the scarlet fluid? The story is told that on the stony shore of the Tyrian Sea a dog snatched up a mollusk, a treasure of the sea, and stained his gluttonous jaws with its scarlet juice. Anxiously the whole household, believing him hurt, carefully examined the mouth and lips of the animal, panting and still clutching the bright-red prey between his gnashing teeth, and they tried to wash out the blood with a stream of water. Now as they were cleaning the dog's lips, wet with the drops of scarlet juice, their entire hands were covered with purple, the water which had been clear was stained, and the white linens bespattered with purple bore conspicuous marks. Finally it chanced that they were able to bring out the precious prize which had been held between the stained teeth of the dog and to examine closely its exquisite luster.

V

INDICUM

Nunc, ubi coccineum collectum frondibus altis,
Sidoniumque dedi sublatum rupe venenum,
Indica prima sequor,¹ ruptis quae vomere terris
Occiduae praebet patiens industria gentis.
[*ll. 1-4*]

Tu, Dea nata Jovis, patrique accepta propago,
Quam coelum delectat acu simulare serenum
Sydera lucenti fingens radiantia filo,
En tibi caeruleos perfectos arte colores,
Queis famosa manu clarum superabis Olympum.
Ne tamen ipse tuos evertam nescius agros,
Dextra fave, praesensque meum moderare laborem.
[*ll. 5-11*]

Principio tractus coeli fervore praeustos,
Phoebus ubi vires frangit sudore liquatas,
Delige, virgultis culto jam rure serendis.
Nam lectos si forte agros horrore nivali
Obsideat frigus, vexetve infesta pruina,
Nec calamis unquam segetum laetabere natis,
Arida nec magnos reparabunt jugera sumptus.
Tum vigil incultae glebae perpende vigorem;
Quod versata ferat semen, quod dura recuset,
Quoque tibi lucro facienda impendia possit
Reddere. Quae videas nigris compacta medullis
Aequora, crede mihi, turgescunt ubere gleba,
Nec meliora satis praestat natura ferendis.
Quod si densus humum delectam lucus obumbret,
Aut crebris immixta rubis virgulta replerint,
Ocyus immitis sylvam prosterne bipenni,
Cumque rubis aspris frondosa arbusta revelle;
Quae siccata vehat plaustris operosa juventus,
Ac multos aggesta domi conservet in annos.
[*ll. 12-30*]

Nec satis haec campos aptabit cura recisos,
Ni reliquum flammis lignorum vulgus adurat
Accensoque furens per gyrum Mulciber igne
In cinerem frondes dispersas aequore vertat.
Scilicet Aetnaeo tellus tepefacta calore
Mollis hiat, gremioque sales studiosa recondit,
Pinguibus ut deinceps frondescat dives avenis.
[*ll. 31-37*]

INDIGO

Now that I have told of cochineal juice gath‑
ered from the high branches and of Tyrian dy‑
taken from the rocks, I shall now turn to the ex‑
cellent indigos¹ which the western people pro‑
duce with patient toil when the earth has been
broken with the plow.

Do you, O goddess, daughter of Jupiter,
child dear to her father, whose delight it is t
embroider a likeness of the clear sky, represent
ing the bright constellations with gleaming
threads, behold the colors of the sky, perfected
by art, by which you will excel bright Olympu
in the glory of your handicraft. But lest in
ignorance I ruin your fields, be propitious an‑
favorably guide my work.

In the first place, select as ground for plant
ing indigo a tract of land already under culti‑
vation in a hot climate where the sun saps you
strength. For if wintry cold should happen t‑
beset the land which you select, or a killing
frost devastate it, you will never have the joy
of seeing a new crop, nor will your barren acre
repay you for your heavy expenses. Conside‑
carefully, then, the quality of the soil when un
cultivated, what seed it will receive when plowed
what it will refuse if it is hard, and what profit
can accrue to you after the necessary expenses
The level fields which you see composed of thick
black loam, believe me, swell with a rich soil
nor does nature provide any better for the
growing crops. But if a thick grove cast
shadow over the ground which you have selected
or a mixture of bushes and brambles cover it
mercilessly fell the trees at once and pull out the
thick bushes along with the thorny brambles
and when the wood is dry, let industrious boy‑
carry it away in wagons and pile it up at home
to be saved for many years to come.

And even this effort to clear the lands wil
not suffice unless the men set fire to the remain‑
ing brush and let Vulcan rage all around and
reduce to ashes the branches scattered over the
ground. Indeed, the soft earth, heated by the
fire, gapes open and eagerly buries the mineral
substances in its bosom so that later it may rich
ly produce luxuriant stalks of indigo.

Ut vero clades, semotis ignibus, agri
Cessavit retroque pedem Vulcanus in antrum
Arripuit siculam, submittunt dura juvenci
Colla jugo dociles, crebro qui vomere nigras
Proscindunt glebas, et campi tecta recludunt
Viscera collectis nuper foecunda salinis:
Iugera ni potius placeat versare ligone,
Tota quoad glebis aequarit dextra solutis.
Tunc opus est campos turba tractare frequenti,
Auget quae longo sumptus operosa labore.
Hunc tamen obliquo crebro praeponit aratro
Antiquumque tenax servat dementia morem.
Hinc multam videas effusam gramine plebem
Et rastris versare agros, et jugera dextra
Aequare, et sulcos validis aptare lacertis.

[*ll. 38-52*]

Haec ubi, praeruptis agri compagibus, aptat
Aequora seminibus credendis illico terrae,
Agricolum minimum (mordax quod forte Sinapi
Credideris) semen dispergit turba per arvum:
Ut solet auratam Cererem per rura colonus
Fundere venturae pellectus imagine messis.
Post, ubi foecundo telluris semen in alvo
Intumuit, rupitque ferax praecordia matris,
Innumeris totus vestitur campus aristis,
Prataque virgultis rident obducta tenellis.
Sed quamvis tanto florentia jugera cultu
Luxurient, tellusque comanti pullulet umbra,
Ne praeceps gratere tibi: via quippe colonum
Longa manet. Nam quae primum de semine pubet
Herba, adeo modicum concludit ventre venenum,
Ut raro quaestus impendia facta rependant.
Hinc sinit aurato curvari semine culmos,
Et curva deinceps praecidit falce juventus,
Lugentemque studet purgari funere campum,
Venturam messem longum expectare coacta.
Tunc senis tollunt segetes caput altius ulnis[2]
Frondibus explicitis, parvumque imitantibus ovum,
Caeruleum queis larga super natura colorem,
Atque infra viridem mixtum flavente reliquit,
Floribus intextis subrubro ardentibus igne.
Ridet ager, facilesque Notus, si spiret, avenas
Undantes, tumidi ceu ponti caerula, versat
Hac illac jactans densata volumina flabris.

[*ll. 53-80*]

And when the fire has ceased its devastation of the field and Vulcan has retired into his Sicilian cave, the docile oxen, having submitted their calloused necks to the yoke, cleave the black soil with many a furrow, breaking open the bosom of the earth recently enriched by the supply of minerals. The people may prefer, however, to work the ground with a spade until it is well tilled and smooth. In that case a vast multitude of workers is needed in the fields; and since they work long hours, this increases the expenses. But even so, they frequently prefer this outmoded practice to the use of the slanting plow, and they foolishly cling to it. Hence you will see many people scattered over the landscape working in the fields with hoes, leveling the ground by hand, and making furrows by strength of arm.

As soon as the farmers have broken the ground, and the soil is ready to receive the seed, they sow the tiny grains (you might take them for pungent mustard seed), just as a planter, allured by the prospect of the coming harvest, casts the seeds of golden grain over his fields. And when the seed has swollen in the fertile bosom of mother earth and burst forth in abundance from her womb, all the field is clothed with countless shoots and becomes a meadow, gayly covered with young plants. But although your productive land, through intensive cultivation, is flourishing, and the ground is deeply shaded by leaves, be not too fast to congratulate yourself, for a long road lies ahead for the farmer. Indeed the stalk that first rises from the seed holds within itself such a modicum of juice that the profits received seldom equal the expenses incurred. For this reason the boys allow the tops to bend beneath the weight of the golden seed and then cut them with a sickle, and though eager to have the sorry field recover from its ruined condition, they are forced to wait a long time for the coming harvest. At that time the stalks stand over six cubits high[2] and have spreading leaves which resemble the shape of a small egg, on the top of which nature has lavishly left a bluish tinge, and underneath green mixed with yellow. Among these are clusters of pink flowers. The field is gay, and when the south wind blows, it whirls the light waving blades about as it does the blue waters of the swelling sea, tossing them around in crowded circles this way and that with its gentle breezes.

157

Continuo forti pubes armata securi
Herbosam invadit segetem, pravoque labore
Culta diu laetó populatur germine rura.
Non tamen imprudens omnes succidit aristas,
Nec totos una spoliabit messibus agros:
Quin solers potius campis non amplius herbae
Arripiet, quam quod socium densata caterva
Caeruleum de fronde trahens studiosa venenum
Exsecti fruticis vitreo suffocat in amne.
Villicus hinc binas mulas messoribus addit,
Quas deinceps tumidis supponat quisque maniplis
Pondere praefixo gravibus, ventremque ligatis,
Inque domos etiam medio sub Sole vehendis.
Scilicet ingratis operis constricta morari
Non, nisi cum coeli Titan petit arduus alta,
Limina nota redux messorum turba revisit.
[*ll. 81-96*]

Interea plebes communi sede relicta,
Quae pridem dominus solerti mente paravit,
Stagna situ purgat studiosis provida curis.
Nam simul atque herbis aptantur rura serendis,
Colle sub acclivi, vitreus qua profluit amnis,
Sumptibus haud parvis tollit tria stagna colonus,
Mole quidem varia, sed quae firmissima vallo
Postea congestis obsistunt omnia limphis.
Grandius extrema collis radice recumbens
In superas effert labrum sublimius auras,
Et reliquis adeo muro supereminet alto,
Ut tinctos exinde bibant subjecta liquores.
Hujus sub vasta protendit mole politos
Inferius muros, labroque minore recessum
Non ita diffusum praebet labentibus undis.
Subjacet huic minimum, subnixumque aggere firmo
Excipit hospitio purgatos amne colores.
Stagna micant intus sudore, atque arte polita,
Omnia quae solers opifex laevavit ad unguem,
Ne color exsecti latebris se condat hiatus.
[*ll. 97-116*]

Haec ubi turba levis, collis per terga recepto
Flumine, stagna parat, sordesque attenta relegat,
Continuo sectis majoris labra maniplis
Opprimit, atque sinum pretioso pondere replet.
Ne tamen herba dein immissis adnatet undis,
Aut fugitiva lacu frigentia balnea vitet,
Oblongis transversa premit plebs cauta tumentem
Arboribus, cogitque inflatum ponere fastum.
Vitrea tum longo deducta fluenta canali

At once the men, having provided themselve
with stout sickles, fall upon the well-tilled field
of grass and pitilessly strip them of their luxuri
ant growth. Yet they are not so foolish as to cu
off all the stalks, nor will they rob at one tim
the entire fields of their harvests, but rathe
will they be careful not to take any more plant
from the fields than the company of workmen
who diligently extract the purple juice from th
leaves can steep in the sparkling waters. Th
manager than gives to each harvester two mules
On these, large and cumbersome bundles ar
firmly fastened to be carried home about midday
Hence the harvesters, required to remain a
their tiresome jobs, do not return to their home
until the ascending sun reaches the zenith o
the sky.

In the meantime, the others, having left thei
barracks, thoroughly clean the vats already pro
vided by the diligent manager, for as soon a
the fields are being prepared for sowing th
indigo, he installs at no small expense thre
vats at the foot of a hill where a clear stream
flows. Now these vats are of different sizes, bu
they all securely retain within their walls th
accumulated waters. The largest, located jus
at the foot of the hill, rises higher into the ai
than the others, and its walls stand so mucl
higher than those of the others below that the
drink the colored liquors from it. Below thi
large one stands another with polished side
and, because of its smaller dimensions, not pro
viding so much room for the waters that flo
into it. At its base lies the smallest vat, sup
ported by a strong embankment and ready t
welcome the dye when purified in the water. Th
three vats glisten inside, having been diligentl
and painstakingly scoured, for the skilled work
man has polished them to perfection to preven
the color from penetrating dark crevices.

When the busy workmen have installed thes
vats on a stream descending from the brow of a
hill and thoroughly cleaned them, at once the
thrust the bundles of cut indigo over the edg
of the largest container and fill it with th
precious burden. Now to prevent the herb from
floating when the water has been let in, or from
shunning the cold bath by escape, the men hold
it down as it rises by throwing across oblong
timbers, and they cause it to put aside its swollen pride. Then a stream of clean water is al-

Prompta super fundit, donec virgulta trabali
Pondere pressa tegat, prorsusque obduxerit amnis,
Inque diem patiens linquit submersa futuram.
Postera lux vero cum terris clara refulsit,
Ac flavos eduxit equos Sol aureus Alto,
Attento Custos animo vestigat inertem
Limpham; num priscum conservet clara nitorem;
An potius viridi referat virgulta colore.
Ut tamen unda viret, fucoque imbuta recenti
Expressos herbae traxit de cortice succos,
Ocyus ille amnem, labri siphone recluso,
Praecipitare jubet, stagnique virente liquore
Subjecti ventrem juxta replere supinum,
Tinctaque continuo misceri flumina motu.

[*ll. 117-139*]

Propter enim surgit fluvio revolubilis orbis,
Qui mersum labro circum rotat impete tignum
Armatum patulis utraque ex parte batillis.
Haec, simul atque unda replet viridante juventus
Inferius stagnum, rivo de colle reducto
Pensilis aerato prompte rota volvitur axe,
Inque orbem tignum convolvens mobile, stagni
Flumina tincta recens fundo permiscet ab imo;
Dum crebro jactata salem faex exuat ictu,
Pondereque acta suo praeceps petat ipsa profundum.
Principio totum spumis exuberat aequor
Caeruleis, magnisque tumens liquor undique bullis
Imminet audaci ripas transcendere saltu.
Sed sensim, spuma tenues abeunte per auras,
Coelesti fucata labris jacet unda veneno,
Praecipitesque ruunt alto de flumine faeces
Herbarum, liquidum simulantes corpore coenum.
Inde coloratum fulgenti vase liquorem[3]
Dextra rapit, raptumque statim densare perita
Nititur; ac vasis, digito explorante, profunda
Saepius attrectans, coeat num limus in unum
Vestigat, granumque abdat sub fonte coactum.
Si nondum fundo coenosa residat amurca,
Ulterius tignis opifex agitare rotatis
Stagna jubet, rursusque vigil tentamen aquali
Ingeminat, dum grana cado densata profundo
Sidant. Tunc motu prorsus consistere jusso,
Tincta tacent, longumque lacu stipata quiescunt
Caerula. Mox rimam sensim reserare magister

lowed to enter through a long canal and quickly fill the vat, until the blades, held down by the weight of the timbers, are covered and completely concealed by the water. They are then allowed to remain submerged until the following day. On the next day, when the golden sun has brought forth from the deep his guilded chariot and the light of day has begun to cast its bright beams across the earth, the man in charge carefully examines the still water to see whether it is as clear as before or whether it is taking on the green color of the plants. And when the water is turning green and becoming saturated with the fresh color drawn from the juices of the bark, the attendant quickly opens a siphon projecting over the edge of the vat and allows the greenish fluid to run out and fill the one lying just below; and he orders the colored water to be stirred continuously.

For this purpose there stands nearby a water wheel which forces a wooden shaft equipped on either side with wide paddles to rotate over the edge of the vat. As soon as the boys have filled the lower container with the green liquid, the hillside stream causes this wheel, mounted on a brass axle, to rotate gently, and as it turns round and round, the shaft vigorously beats the colored waters from the very bottom of the vat until a scum is precipitated by the repeated beating and quickly sinks to the bottom by its own weight. At first the whole surface is covered with blue foam, and the fluid, swelling up on every side in large bubbles, threatens to spill over the sides in a wild leap. Gradually, however, while the foam disappears into thin air, the blue-stained waters remain in the container, and the sediment from the plants, like mud, sinks below the surface of the waters. Then an experienced hand, catching in a shining vessel[3] a sample of the colored fluid, attempts at once to settle it and by rubbing his fingers over the bottom ascertains whether sediment is collecting and hiding its granules in condensed form beneath the water. If the muddy sediment is not yet settling on the bottom, the manager orders his men to continue agitating the waters with the revolving paddles and then carefully makes a re-examination with the pan until the particles are condensed and resting on the bottom. Then he orders the beating to be stopped completely, and the blue substance remains at rest for a long time under the water. Later the manager orders his men slowly to open up a crack extending along the entire length of the

(Quae labrum a summo porrecta abscindit ad imum,
Quamque vigil creta pubes obstruxerat ante)
Imperat: et subito vinclis, ac carcere liber,
Qua data porta ruit, praecepsque adlabitur amnis.
Post alia atque alia duratae parte revulsa
Argillae, obstrusum recludit dextra meatum,
Undantique sinit limphas decedere labro,
Caeruleum dum pone lutum contendat abire.

[*ll. 140-176*]

Tunc creta rursus pubes obturat hiatum,
Inque lacus minimi gremium capulatur amurca
Fictilibus collecta cadis; ubi flumine rursus
Purgatur reliquo, fundoque coacta residit.
Ipse coloratum credas subsidere coenum
Sordibus imbutum glaucis, ac fonte liquatum:
Hoc tamen ampla luto gazas Guatimala cogit
Ingentes, totusque auget commercia mundus.

[*ll. 177-184*]

His ubi coenosas fruticis plebecula faeces
Exsiccat solers, denso subtemine saccos
In conum textos tignis suspendit ab altis,
Unde fluat liquidum, puro stagnante colore.
Mox extracta sinu minimi limosa labelli
Ilicet in saccos massa haec transfunditur arctos;
Quae suspensa diu quaerens per densa meatus
Exiles, ima guttatim parte liquorem
Expellit, ceramque refert compacta tepentem.

[*ll. 185-193*]

Hinc tabulata super facilem plebs sedula massam
Expandit, Phoeboque objectans saepe rubenti
Infestum prorsus consumit Sole madorem.
Humida massa leves, alvo fumante, vapores
Evomit, et tenuis consurgit fumus in auras.
Nec mora: duratam radiis, Zephyroque frequenti
Comminuit vulgus, massamque in grana reducit,
Indica vulgato patriae de nomine dicta.[4]

[*ll. 194-201*]

Quid vero, densis veniant si nubibus imbres,
Indica dum radiis indurat caerula Phoebus?
Flumina tunc glauco currunt imbuta veneno,
Granaque per campos fugiunt liquefacta patentes.
Quare opus est, Soli suppostam obsidere massam
Excubiis, quae tecta Jovis subjecta procellis
Explorent vigiles, pluviaque instante sodales
Admoneant, massamque citi sub tecta reponant.

[*ll. 202-209*]

vat from top to bottom and which had previously
been carefully sealed with clay, and the water,
suddenly freed from captivity and imprisonment, rushes through the opening made for it
and flows swiftly away. Then as one portion
after another of the hard clay is removed, the
passageway which had been blocked is opened
and the surging waters are allowed to escape
from the vat until the blue sediment is about
to follow.

Then the men again seal the gap with clay,
and the sediment is gathered up in earthenware
vessels and poured into the smallest container
where it is again washed in water from the rest
of the stream and, having condensed, settles to
the bottom. You would believe that colored
earth, permeated with bluish gray and soaked
with water, was settling. But noble Guatemala
derives great riches from this mud, and the
commerce of the entire world is increased.

When the experienced men have thus drained
off the plant's muddy sediment, with stout cords
they suspend from high beams cone-shaped bags
from which the liquid may flow, but leave behind the pure dye. Then the muddy substance
is taken from the smallest vat and poured directly into the narrow bags. Having been allowed
to hang for a long time, it searches out little
passageways through the thick cloth, forces the
water out of the bottom drop by drop, and when
thick, resembles soft wax.

Then the busy workmen spread the soft substance out on a platform where, by repeated ex-
posure to the rays of the sun, it becomes free
of all harmful moisture. The damp substance,
steaming at the center, discharges a light vapor
which ascends into the air. When the substance
has become hardened by the rays of the sun and
the wind, the workmen reduce it to grains commonly called indigo after the name of their
country.[4]

But what is to be done if heavy clouds of rain
should come while Phoebus is hardening the
indigo with his rays? In such a case the rivers
are stained with blue, and the grains, having
melted, escape through the open fields. It is
necessary, therefore, that alert watchmen guard
the substance while it is exposed to the sunlight
in order to discover what houses are threatened
by Jupiter's storms and, whenever it is about
to rain, to warn their comrades and quickly place
the substance under cover.

Interea labrum putrefactis vulgus onustum
Exonerat calamis, magnumque attollit acervum
Exsucci fruticis, Vulcani alimenta futurum;
Pullulat unde ferox armata proboscide musca
Ausa manus hominum, pecudumque invadere tergum,
Purpureumque fero flumen deducere rostro.
Hinc persaepe manus rorantes sanguine cernes,
Cruraque per gyrum violentis saucia plagis.
Quin etiam levibus deducta per aera pennis
Occupat audacter penetralia celsa domorum,
Invaditque dapes tetris advecta popinis
Deturpans mensas epulis admixta paratis.
Omnia peste gemunt, moerent hominesque, pecusque.
Non secus atque olim luco delapsa nigranti
Invasere Phryges subito Stymphalia monstra,
Ac praedata dapes foedarunt omnia turpi
Proluvie, tristique implerunt pectora luctu.
Ut tamen immitem possit solertia pestem
Flectere, et ingratos vitare proboscidis ictus,
Tegmine turba manus, et laevi crura papyro
Praemunit; ramosque tholis suspendit ab altis
Glutine perfusos lento, quos densa volantum
Ore petat legio, pedibusque infausta ligatis
Promeritas subeat crudeli funere poenas.

[*ll. 210-233*]

FINIS LIBRI QUINTI

In the meantime the workmen remove the decayed stalks from the vat and pile high the pulp to serve as fuel for Vulcan. In this there breeds a fly provided with a fierce proboscis which dares to assail the hands of men and the backs of animals, bringing forth a stream of purple blood with its cruel bite. Hence you will often see hands dripping with blood and limbs irritated all around by the sharp stings. Moreover, as it swiftly wings its way through the air, it dares to pervade the privacy of the home, and coming into dirty inns, it devours the food and pollutes the table by entangling itself in the food that has been served. All creatures, both men and beasts, are grieved and distressed because of this pest. In the same way the Stymphalian monsters once upon a time flew out of a dark forest, made a sudden attack upon the Phrygians, plundered their food, and befouled everything with unseemly filth. They filled the hearts of the people with bitter anguish. In order, however, that the people may be able to shun this merciless pest and to avoid the painful wounds inflicted by its proboscis, they ingeniously protect their hands with gloves and their legs with sheets of paper, and they hang from the high ceilings branches smeared with a sticky substance to which swarms of flies are attracted, and in which, becoming hopelessly entangled, they deservedly pay the bitter penalty of death.

VI

FIBRI

Quid moror astutos telis invadere Fibros[1]
Ac varios animo gentis versare labores,
Ingeniumque sagax, atque altis oppida muris,
Delicias nemorum, ripaeque undantis honorem.
[*ll. 1-4*]

Tu Dictynna potens, gravidis assueta pharetris
Per nemus, et campum Fibros agitare fugaces,
Dic mihi, quae fuerit cautae solertia gentis,
Quis labor, et vires, quae dotes, raraque membra:
Et quos ad fluvium Fibros confixero telis,
Hosce tibi sacras mactabo pronus ad aras.
[*ll. 5-10*]

Occulit in sylvis ingens America vetustis,
Qua Nova-frigentes-Hispania vergit ad Ursas,
Agmina densa feris sylvarum tecta recessu:
Quas inter cautum, praestantique indole Fibrum[2]
Sortitum magnas turpi sub corpore dotes.
Huic ternas vegetum corpus non longius ulnas
Flexibiles duplici circumdant ordine crines:
Subter enim dura rorantes pelle capillos
Exilis latitat non major pollice villus,
Villus ab augusto decoratus vertice Regum,
Mollia quod blando superet prope serica tactu.
Ille caput quadrum, parvosque attollit ocellos,
Exiguamque aurem, quae ferme clauditur orbe,
Et rictum longis mordacem dentibus armat,
Robora queis cinctus sylvis annosa recidit,
Ac diris palmas compressus morsibus urget.
Tum natura manus digitis instruxit aduncis,
Unguibus et digitos munivit provida curvis,
Plurima quos vigiles adhibent ad munia Fibri.
Ast alio donat deformes munere calces:
Nam teretes fortis digitos membrana revincit,
Ut magnos quadrupes temnat fluviosque, lacusque.
Hinc etiam miranda tibi rarissima cauda
Undique multiplici squama vestita rigenti,
Atque oleo, aut crassa semper pinguedine fusa,
(Quam cautus loculis tectis sub ventre recondit,
Et cui Castoreum dixit de voce Machaon).
Obsistat nocuo prolixa ut cauda madori.
[*ll. 11-38*]

Sed turpes quamvis, insuetosque induat artus,
Attamen ingenuos sortitur bellua mores.
Hinc, nec dente ferox proprios in praelia poscit

BEAVERS

Shall I not now rush with spear upon the clever beavers[1] and watch their various activities, consider their keenness of mind, and study their high-walled towns, the delight of the woods and the glory of the river bank?

Do you, O mighty Dictyna[1a] who, with a full quiver, are wont to hunt the fleet-footed beavers through forest and field, tell me what skill belongs to this wary animal, what work it performs, what strength it has, what talents and extraordinary body, and I shall humbly sacrifice to you on your sacred altar all the beavers along the stream which I transfix with the arrow.

The great continent of America, where New Spain extends toward the cold north, hides in its primeval forests crowded herds of wild animals that lurk in the recesses of the forest. Among these is the beaver[2] a wary and intelligent animal, possessing great gifts beneath a shaggy exterior. Its lively body, not over three cubits long, is covered with a double layer of soft fur. On the tough skin underneath the wet hair lies concealed a fine fur no longer than the length of the thumb, fur which has had the distinction of gracing the exalted heads of kings, for it is almost softer to the touch than silk. The animal has a square head, small eyes, and tiny ears almost round, and jaws provided with long sharp teeth with which it gnaws down aged oaks or, when captured, fiercely bites the hands. Besides, nature has provided its paws with hooked toes and wisely supplied the toes with claws which the diligent beavers use for many purposes. And their irregularly shaped feet have been given another function, for a stout membrane binds together their slender toes that they may have no fear of large rivers and lakes. They also have a very strange and unusual kind of tail, thickly covered all over with hard scales and, that this broad tail may resist the evil effects of dampness, it is always bathed in oil or a thick fatty substance carefully concealed in a secret pocket under the belly to which Machaon[3] gave the name *castoreum* after the name of the beaver.

But although this animal possesses an awkward and peculiar body, yet it has inherited noble traits. Consequently, it does not fiercely challenge to battle with its teeth those enemies

Invida quos rabies in se commoverat, hostes,
Nec nimia fragilis pellecta cupidine rerum
Insomnes dubio nutrit sub pectore curas.
Non ira, aut odio, ventrisque furore movetur,
Non rabie ultrici, non curis angitur ullis:
Ac nisi libertas pretioso tangat honore,
Nulla Fibrum poterit curae prosternere moles.
Ast si ferratis captivum dextra catenis
Vinciat, aut cavea servet violenta retentum,
Protinus ingenti transfixus corda dolore
Angitur, et querulis caveam clamoribus implet:
Nec prius a tanto cessabit bellua fletu,
Quam notos repeat praerupto carcere lucos.

[*ll. 39-54*]

Hunc etiam placuisse Fibris mirabere morem,
Quod vigil ingenium, solersque industria ripis
Hospitium populo, fluviisque repagula condat,
Ingentemque urbem tranquilla pace gubernet.
Vix etenim Phoebus, rapto in sublimia curru,
Lampade succendit fulgenti Sydera Cancri,
Cum subito pecudes, sylvarum pube coacta,
Conveniunt, urbisque parant attollere molem,
Perfugium sociis, et propugnacula bello.
Explorant saltus, fluviosque, et amoena paludis
Littora, ubi tacitae frondescant arbore ripae.
Area tranquilli non raro ad fluminis undas
Deligitur; gaudetque amnes habitare juventus.
Ne tamen alluvies aedes inopina revellat,
Concutiat socios, urbemque a culmine vertat,
Ante domos ripis ponat quam callida turba,
Objicit e truncis densata repagula rivis,
Illuviem ut froenent, aequataque flumina ducant.

[*ll. 55-72*]

Incipit umbrosum pubes corrodere truncum
Vertice sublimen, ripisque, undisque propinquum,
Qui queat adversum lapsus contingere littus.
Corruit annosum, secta radice salictum,
Oppositasque super considens fluminis oras
Adnectit ripam, ceu pons aptatus, utramque.
Littora cuncta sonant, magnoque excita fragore
Saepe cavis Echo resonat vocalis in antris.
At Fiber impavidus salicem tellure revulsam
Conscendit, tensique recidit brachia trunci.
Ut solet interdum teneris bellator ab annis
Fundere tela gravi sonitu raptata per auras:

whom the passion of greed has incited against it, nor is it attracted by an inordinate desire for food, nor does it cherish within a restless heart the disquieting cares of a weakling. Not by anger, hate or ravenous appetite is it affected, nor is it tormented by a desire for revenge, or by any cares; and unless it be robbed of the precious gift of freedom, no amount of trouble can reduce it to prostration. But if it be imprisoned and bound by iron chains, or forced to stay inside a cage, at once its heart is sore distressed, and it frets and fills the cage with its plaintive cries, nor will it put an end to its bitter laments until it has broken from its prison and returned to its familiar haunts in the forest.

You will marvel, too, at the habit which the beavers have been pleased to follow by reason of their alert disposition and industrious nature, to establish along the river banks living quarters for their people, to construct dams across the streams, and to rule their great city with uninterrupted peace. Scarcely indeed does Phoebus, as he mounts the sky in his car, brighten the constellation of Cancer[4] with his flaming torch, when all of a sudden colonies of beavers, having assembled their members from the woods, come together and prepare to build their city, a refuge for their fellows and a defense against war. They search the woods, the streams, and the lovely lakes whose quiet shores are lined with trees. A spot is usually chosen near the waters of a gently flowing river; and the young ones enjoy their habitation along the streams. But that a sudden flood not tear away their houses, frighten their comrades, and overturn the city, these astute creatures erect thick barriers of tree trunks across the streams to bridle the force of the flood and cause an even flow before building their houses along the banks.

The workers begin to gnaw at the trunk of a tall shady tree which stands beside the bank of a stream and which, upon falling, can extend to the other side. Cut off near the root an aged willow falls, and lodging against the opposite bank of the river, connects both sides as if a bridge had been constructed. The banks reverberate throughout, and resounding Echo, awakened by the loud noise, repeats the sounds in her deep caverns. But the beaver, unafraid, climbs upon the overturned willow and lops off the branches of the long trunk. As a man who has been a warrior from early youth is wont sometimes to hurl darts that speed through the air

Turba repentino jaculi stridore pavescit;
Ille tamen saevos fertur generosus in hostes:
Haud secus impavido labentis murmure corde
Excipit, et pubes urget nemorosa laborem.

[*ll. 73-88*]

Impigra mox ripas se fundit turba per omnes:
Quisque suas explet partes, sua munera quisque.
Pars findunt teretes frondoso littore truncos,
Pars lentos caedit viridanti ex ilice ramos,
Et pars argillae cumulos humentis acervat.
Fervet opus, Sylvamque cohors operosa fatigat.
Ut vero prudens operi jam cuncta paravit,
Omnia traducit fluvii torrentis ad oras:
Hic ramos, hic dente sudes mordace prehensas,
Hic vehit argillam sinuatae syrmate caudae;
Caetera quae pubes vectat festina sub undas,
Pontis ubi molem ripae stupuere saligni,
Cunctaque sudanti populo studiosa ministrat.
Ad salicem denso glomerantur in agmine fabri
Objectare vagis meditata repagula rivis.
Intrat inaccessas pubes animosa sub undas,
Qua ripas nectit tensum super alta salictum,
Et subtus manibus fundum cavat illa fluenti,
Ungue quoad rigido fossam confecerit altam.
Caetera tum pubes longa super arbore sidens
Robora subjectis immergit pinguia limphis,
Dum mersum fossor, directa cuspide, tignum
Includit foveae, circumque adstringit arenam.
Tigna solo sidunt, feriunt sed vertice pontem,
Pondere qui molem fluvii defendit ab ira.
Ut primam fixere trabem sub ponte juventus,
Unguibus ulterius fodiunt, et caetera figunt
Tigna solo, flumen donec premat ordine recto
Truncorum series, totamque intersecet undam.
Fixa dein teneris adnectunt robora ramis,
Argillaque opplent objectae molis hiatus.
Mox aliam atque aliam praecisa ex abiete firmant
Arboream seriem, ramis, ac glutine vinctam,
Nullam quae pressi guttam sinit ire fluenti.

[*ll. 89-122*]

Praeterea moles raram sortita figuram,
Adversis qua firma trabes objecerat undis,

with a heavy sound, and the crowd is startled by the sudden twang of the weapon, and he valiantly rushes upon his cruel foe, in like manner these inhabitants of the forest, undaunted by the crashing sound of falling timber, ply their work.

Then the busy throng spreads out all along the banks, each one playing his own role, each one discharging his own duties. Some split the round trunks which lie along the green bank, others cut off stout branches from a green oak, and still others form piles of moist clay. The work is carried on with dispatch, and the forest is overrun by this busy army. When they have at last carefully prepared everything for the construction, they bring it all to the edge of the swiftly moving stream. One carries branches, another brings poles tightly clutched in his mouth, while a third carries clay in the hollow of his curved tail. The rest of the workers hastily bring these supplies underneath the waves at the place where, to the amazement of the banks, the willow bridge has been constructed, and they diligently supply the toilers with everything. The laborers gather in a close line near the willow to throw a barrier against the vagrant waters. The spirited animals go beneath the inaccessible waves where the willow extends over the deep waters and connects the banks, and with their feet hollow out the river bottom below until they have dug a deep trench with their hard claws. Then the others, sitting overhead on the long tree, sink heavy oak stakes into the waters below, while an excavator places them in the trench in an upright position and packs sand around them. The stakes rest on the bottom, but their upper ends touch the bridge, which by its own weight protects the structure from the violence of the stream. When these young workers have fixed the first pole under the bridge, with their claws they dig a hole farther on and set the rest of the stakes in the ground until a straight row of them leans against the river and intersects the entire stream. Then they connect these oak stakes with small branches and seal the cracks of the dam with clay. After that, they make secure the row of stakes by binding them together one after another with branches and resin extracted from the fir tree, which allows not a drop of backwater to leak through.

The dike, moreover, having an extraordinary appearance on the side where its strong timbers have been thrown up against the opposing waters,

Dejectu facili declivis conditur amne.
Qua vero rapidum tignis detrudit ab altis
Torrentem, moles elata fronte superbit.
Hinc patula videas denas radice per ulnas
Extendi, ternasque superbo vertice molem.
Mox super argillam, ramosque, et robora claustri
Aptatos aperit pubes operosa meatus,
Quos minuente premit, crescentique explicat amne,
Abluat ut ripas aequali flumine rivus.
Ac veluti pelagi cum gens praedives in undis
Cautibus e ruptis altam prope littora molem
Objectat ponto, lembisque exponit asylum :
Ille minax crebro molem diverberat aestu,
Nec tamen adversam potis est abrumpere meram :
Haud aliter Fibri spumantia flumina fraenant.
Si quando laceret contexta repagula limpha,
Diruat aut pravus venator calce frequenti,
Ingestis acies ramis eversa resarcit.

[*ll. 123-142*]

His ubi turba citum compressit sedula flumen,
Magnificam genti, munitamque extruit urbem,
Littus ubi plenum fraenatas exhibet undas.
Protinus in parvas legio divisa cohortes
Argillam ripis, ramosque, et fragmina rupis
Colligit, et raro condit penetralia cultu
Ipsa super vitrei stagnantia littora rivi,
Eluat ut semper tranquillo moenia lapsu.
Haec manus ovatam laribus dat gnava figuram,
Illa domos gaudet muris habitare rotundis;
Utraque firma tamen tecti fundamina ponit
Argilla, et saxis, truncisque innexa recisis
Et quae ventorum ludant immota furorem.
Hinc ulnis binis pingues mirabere muros,
Ac multos tectum ripa firmare per annos.

[*ll. 143-157*]

Nobilis in varios sedes distincta penates,
Infernas, superasque simul complectitur aedes,
Aptaque solerti praebet penetralia turbae.
Horrea praeterea tuta intra septa domorum
Exhibet ; at semper populi secreta cubili.
Haec binae decorant insueta palatia portae,
Altera, quae fluvii compressas respicit undas,
Altera, quae lucos offert adversa silentes.
Ampla tamen fluvio semper convertit hiatum
Sedula quam muris concinnat turba, fenestra.

conceals itself in the water along a gentle incline. But on the side where it thrusts the swift current away from its high timbers, it rises proudly upward. You will therefore see the construction extending at the bottom ten cubits in width, and three cubits at the top. Then the busy toilers open up convenient passageways across the dike of clay and branches and beams, which they close when the stream is low, but open when it is rising, in order that the banks be washed by an even flow. And just as when a wealthy people extends a high mole of broken rocks from the shore to the waves of the open sea to serve as a breakwater and harbor for small craft, and the sea threateningly lashes the barrier with frequent swells, yet cannot break away the obstruction, so the beavers curb the foaming rivers. If ever the water should break through the interwoven barrier or an unscrupulous hunter kick it down, an army of beavers repairs the damage by the insertion of branches.

When the industrious workers have thus curbed the swift river, they build for their people a city, magnificent and strongly fortified, where the banks hold in check a full stream. Dividing themselves at once into small units they collect clay, branches, and pieces of rock from the banks, and with extraordinary care erect their quarters at the very edge of the sluggish stream that it may always bathe the walls with its gently lapping waters. This one diligently builds an oval house, that one prefers to live in a house with round walls, yet both make the foundations of their houses strong by interweaving them with clay and rocks and short sticks to mock the violence of the winds and to stand unshaken. You will therefore be astonished to see walls two cubits thick, and houses that stand on the bank for many years.

The excellent house, divided into several apartments, offers accommodations both above and below, and affords suitable quarters for the ingenious members. It provides, moreover, safe storerooms within its walls, yet always separate from the living quarters. Two entrances embellish these extraordinary mansions, the one overlooking the waters of the dam, the other, on the opposite side, facing the silent woods. A large window which the busy workers insert in the walls is also open on the side of the river.

Desuper hanc molem fornix curvatus obumbrat
Textilibus ramis, udaque adstrictus arena,
Quem neque praecipites dissolvunt fluctibus imbres,
Nec rapido saevae versant Aquilone procellae.
[*ll. 158-171*]

Quin etiam pubes grati studiosa nitoris
Perpolit agresti tectorum moenia luxu.
Quare udo manibus limo per rura coacto
Conficit experti mixtum durabile plantis,
Irroratque domum cauda, duratque, politque.
Ut solet interdum penetralia celsa potentum
Obturare opifex, murosque, et tecta polire,
Turpibus obsistant auratae ut sordibus aedes,
Ocyus aut labes laevi de fornice pellant:
Haud aliter Fibri, nitido gens inclyta cultu,
Flumineis quaerunt laribus, servantque nitorem.
Inde locum gnavi propria intra moenia lectum
Obducunt, ramisque apte frondentibus ornant.
Gaudet enim luco pubes assueta virenti
Lucorum speciem juxta intra tecta locare.
Non ita formoso magnatum tecta decore
Resplendent, muri quamtumvis serica gestent,
Argentumque, aurumque una laquearia velent.
[*ll. 172-189*]

Si quando tantis operis vexata juventus
Viribus effetis succumbat fracta labori,
Provida tunc sociis occurrunt agmina fessis,
Ac totum subito pondus deponere jussis
Indulgent placida vires renovare quiete.
[*ll. 190-194*]

Ut vero finem tectis posuere superbis,
Privatae studio vitae nudata caterva
Tota sodalitio rursus se prompta resignat.
Praenoscit luces, mensesque experta futuros,
Horrida queis campos devastat frigore bruma,
Albescunt frondes, glacieque aspersa rigenti
Saepe gelu torpent praerupto flumina cursu.
Arida tunc abies, umbraque exuta comanti
Nulla requirenti demittit pascua Fibro.
Hinc ne tota ruat misero respublica casu
Impigra dumosos perlustrant agmina saltus
Pabula mature rigidis lectura pruinis.
Quisque suum sectatur iter; fusique per arva,
Ocyus ut virides populentur frondibus agros,

This structure is arched on top with a network of branches held together by moist earth which is not softened by torrential downpours, nor overturned by the savage blasts of the fierce north wind.

These creatures, moreover, being also lovers of the beautiful, finish the walls of their houses in rustic splendor. To accomplish this they gather in their paws moist earth from the fields, and having skillfully kneaded it into a durable consistency, they daub it on the walls with their tails, allow it to harden, and then polish it. As an artisan is often wont to redecorate the stately mansions of the rich and to make smooth the walls and ceilings that the gilded halls may be free from uncleanliness or the smooth archways more readily repel dust, so the beavers, a class of animals noted for their refined manners, seek to keep their river homes tidy. They carefully select a place in their own homes which they appropriately decorate with green branches, for these animals, accustomed to the greenness of the woods, like to arrange the interior of their living quarters according to the way of the woods. Not with such lovely splendor shine the mansions of the great though their walls be draped with silk and their fretted ceilings be embossed with silver and gold.

If ever the young workers, wearied by such arduous toil, should become exhausted and break down beneath the strain, at once the wise company runs to the assistance of its comrades, bids them give up the entire work immediately, and allows them to recuperate their strength with undisturbed rest.

Now when they have finished their magnificent houses, they all give up their desire for a private existence and immediately resign themselves again to community life. They know from experience the days and the months when icy winter lays waste the fields with cold, when foliage is white with frost, and when the rivers are constantly covered with ice and move along sluggishly in the freezing cold. Then the fir tree, dry and bereft of shady leaves, sends down no nourishment to satisfy the beaver's needs. In order, therefore, that the entire colony not perish with a dreadful fate, the dauntless animals search at the proper season throughout the thickly covered woodlands to find food for winter. Each one pursues his own way, and, to pillage more quickly the green fields of leaves,

Fibri

Diversi diversa petunt, qua lucus odorus,
Ruraque sollicitos allectant frondea truncis.
Hic teneros vellit florenti ex ilice ramos,
Hic truncos avidus vernanti cortice nudat,
Exuviasque omnes nemoris sub tecta reponunt.
Turba dein complet dapibus de robore sectis
Horrea vasta domus socio fabricata labore,
Ordineque arboreas epulas insomnis acervat,
Aptius ut socii lucorum frusta resumant.
Qualis ubi albenti succidit rure colonus
Immensam segetem, tectumque opplevit avarus,
Atque alias aliis imponens cautus aristas
Rite locat tectis numerosum messis acervum :
Haud secus optata replet cum bellua fronde
Horrea, concisos disponit in ordine ramos.

[ll. 195-223]

His tandem magno populi sudore peractis,
Quaeque cohors proprios habitat tranquilla penates.
Quatuor haec cives, senos domus illa recludit,
Bisque simul denos tectum quandoque tenebit.
Utque annos pubes revereretur prona seniles,
Infirmis superas linquit senioribus aedes,
Infernasque sibi tribuit moderata juventus.
Natio tunc placidae cedit nemorosa quieti,
Pabula depascit communi credita tecto,
Et prolem gaudent similem generare parentes.
Nulla domos unquam praeceps discordia miscet,
Nulla movet pravas contentio turbida lites;
Nec foedis unquam spoliantur tecta rapinis,
Sed cives alma tranquilli pace fruuntur.

[ll. 224-237]

Quod si quando domus solers granaria latro
Impetat alterius, messisque expilet acervum
Aut turpare lares immundis sordibus ausit,
(Quippe aliqui peccent, ingens ubi turba, necesse est)
Pellitur ille domo, perditque urbemque, domumque
Compulsus nemorum rigidos habitare recessus.

[ll. 238-243]

Interea populus fluviali sede relictus
Alternis corpus vento recreabit, et amne.
Nunc siquidem patulis effundit membra fenestris,
Jucundasque capit, Zephyris halantibus, auras,
Nunc gelidas fluvii postica immergit in undas

they spread out over the countryside, some going in one direction, others in another, where the scented groves and the fields attract the eager throngs by their thick trees. This one tears off young branches from a thrifty oak, another eagerly strips green bark from the trunk, while all carry the spoils of the forest inside their houses. Then they fill the large storerooms of their houses built in the common enterprise with the food gleaned from the trees, and without stopping for sleep they pile the pieces of wood in rows that their companions may more conveniently get them. As a farmer, when he has harvested a large crop from his land and has eagerly filled his house, carefully piles the ears one on top of the other, properly storing his bountiful harvest in bins, so the beaver, when he has filled his storerooms with delicious branches, arranges them in an orderly manner.

When at last these duties have been performed with great effort on the part of the beavers, each division peacefully occupies its own quarters. One house accommodates four members, another six, sometimes a house will hold twenty at one time. Since the young are disposed to respect old age, they courteously leave the upper apartments to the old and infirm, and take the lower rooms for themselves. Then this tribe of the forest resigns itself to peaceful rest, eating the food placed in the common storeroom and rejoicing in the reproduction of its own kind. No violent dissention ever disturbs their homes, no bitter strife leads to vexatious quarrels, nor are their homes ever looted by infamous burglary, but the citizens calmly enjoy peace and prosperity.

But if sometime a sly thief should assail the storerooms of another's home and steal a large amount of provisions, or should make bold to defile the home with uncleanliness, for some are sure to commit crime where there are so many, he is driven from the house, and forfeits city and home, being forced to inhabit the rough recesses of the forest.

In the meantime, those left in their river home will refresh their bodies alternately in the open air and in the stream. For now, while the zephyrs gently blow, they spread themselves out in the open windows and catch the delightful breezes, again they lower the rear of their bodies into the cold waters of the stream, holding on

Membra cohors, ulnasque fenestrae in limine ponit.
Sic ignava diu pubes operosa laborem
Praeteritum sarcit, limphisque refrigerat artus.

[*ll. 244-251*]

Quaelibet at legio proprios educere foetus,
Progenieque nova certat protendere gentem.
Foemina constanti semper jucunda marito
Post quatuor lunas, cum terris bruma recessit,
In lucem mittit partus enixa gemellos,
Ni ternos conjux generet foecunda parenti.
Educat illa genus laribus subducta benignis,
Progenies donec matrem jam pone sequatur,
Eliciatque suo teneras e limine plantas.
Tunc sociata nova genitrix suavissima prole
Sedula vernantes, legio ceu caetera, lucos
Advolat, et crustas truncorum pascitur udas.
Impiger at genitor, simul ac vernantia flore
Prata novo rident, tectis se surripit altis,
Crudelisque domi sobolem cum matre relinquit.
Nec repetit caros gens errabunda penates
Ni Libram solito Titan fervore revisat.

[*ll. 252-268*]

Saepe etiam placidis fluvii de finibus acti
Apricos habitant campos, sylvisque pererrant,
Quos socii exilio damnant ob crimina cives.
Aut quos compellunt venantes, urbe relicta,
Et ripa, et caris pavidos excedere tectis,
Palantesque diu lucos habitare silentes.
Haec ubi turba subit, tantum aversata periclum,
Nec fluvios deinceps froenat, nec limina condit,
Sed contenta vadis habitat dispersa cavernas,
Stagna queis solers addit torpentia pubes.
Semper enim foveam rivi labentis ad oras
Effodiunt Fibri, blando qui flumine limen
Irroret, propriaque fluat gravitate sub antrum.
Hic Fiber undanti corpus refrigerat amne,
Et vitam degit nigris extorris in umbris.

[*ll. 269-283*]

Dum tamen egregiam placidus Fiber incolit urbem,
Aut antro latitat patriis expulsus ab oris,
Exciti saevi variis de finibus hostes
Moenia perturbant, miscentque timore recessus.

to the window sill with their forelegs. Thus the industrious animals, remaining idle for a long time, make amends for their past toil and refresh their bodies in the waters.

Now each community endeavors to bring forth its own kind and to perpetuate the race with young offspring. The female, ever attractive to her faithful mate, after four months have passed and winter has receded from the land, brings forth into the light of day twin offspring, unless, being especially prolific, she bear a set of triplets for her mate. In the privacy of her cheerful hearth she raises her family until finally the young ones follow along behind their mother lifting their soft feet over the threshold. Then the gentle mother, accompanied by her young, rushes eagerly into the green forest like the rest and feeds on the succulent bark of the trees. The vigorous father, on the other hand, as soon as the green meadows smile with spring flowers, steals away from his magnificent home, heartlessly leaving the mother and children behind. And the wanderers do not return to their dear homesteads until the sun with its customary warmth visits again the constellation of Libra.[5]

Often too, those members of the community who on account of their crimes have been condemned to exile by their comrades, having been driven from the peaceful riverside, dwell in the open fields and wander about through the forests. Or there are those which, when they have left their city and the bank, are forced by hunters to withdraw in fear from their beloved homes and to dwell for a long time as wanderers in the silent woods. When any, having escaped from grave danger, undergo such an experience, they do not then bridle the rivers and establish homes, but content with water live apart in holes into which they skillfully introduce quiet pools of water. For the beavers always dig a hole along the banks of a stream so that the gently flowing waters will reach the edge and fall inside by their own weight. Here the beaver refreshes his body in the waves of the stream and lives an exile's life in the darkness of his den.

But while the peaceful beaver is residing in a splendid city or hiding in a cave, a refugee from his ancestral shores, fierce animals come forth from various quarters, throw the city into an uproar, and fill the homes with fear. Thus the

Fibri

Sic Vulpes, sic Marta ferox, Carcajus, et Ursus,
Plebs armata minis, caecoque agitata furore
Imbellis valido laniabunt viscera morsu.

[*ll. 284-290*]

Acrius at nullus Fibrorum castra fatigat,
Quam violentus homo, telis metuendus et astu.
Hinc pecus in sylvis arrectis auribus astat;
Et simul ac cupidas hostilis fertur ad aures
Rumor, qui fluvio forsan demersus in alto
Membra lavat socius, cauda diverberat amnem,
Insuetoque urbis sonitu penetralia replet.
Angitur imbellis trepido respublica signo,
Et magno miscens sublimia tecta tumultu
Turba ruit pavitans foribus festina superbis,
Tuta petit cursu, pedibusque ignava salutem
Quaerit, et impendens vitat versuta periclum.
Nam quamvis subito moveatur prompta fragore,
Vafra tamen technis hostem deludit acerbum.
Callida rimatur, qua ferreus hostis in urbem
Tendat; num sylvas penetret, num flumina tranet:
Retia si norit lucorum tensa latebris,
Arripit illa fugam fluviali concita porta,
Ac submersa vado vitrei petit ima fluenti,
Evaditque necem celeri gens cauta natatu.
Oppida si vero tranando territet hostis,
Protinus adversis excedunt agmina valvis,
Telaque diffugiunt obscuris abdita lucis.
Nec reduces flumen, tectumque amissa redibunt,
Ni prius e notis hostis decesserit oris.

[*ll. 291-315*]

Quare opus est rigida Fibros invadere bruma,
Cum nix algenti praetexit vellere campos
Fluminaque Alpina glacie concreta rigescunt:
Gens praecincta viris linquit nemorosa penates,
Et, qua duratum flumen recludit hiatus,
Quos dudum tacito venator foderat astu,
Volvitur in fluvium, tectisque adlabitur undis.
Venantum ripis patienter turba moratur,
Et fraudes gaudet pecoris tolerare sagacis.
Mox niveas amnis praepes dispersa per oras

wolf, thus the fierce marten, the carcajou, and the bear, beasts provided with menacing weapons and driven by ungovernable fury, will tear out the vitals of the peace-loving beaver with their powerful teeth.

But nothing plagues the camp of the beavers more keenly than cruel man, who must be feared because of his darts and on account of his trickery. For this reason they stand in the forests with ears erect, and as soon as a hint of an enemy reaches ther listening ears, a companion who perhaps is bathing in the deep waters of the river, lashes the water with his tail and fills the houses of the city with a strange sound. The peaceful community is worried by the alarm, and great confusion spreads through their magnificent halls. Frightened crowds rush like cowards through the high gates, seeking to save their lives by flight and relying on the swiftness of their feet to carry them to a place of safety. They escape the threatening danger by strategy, for no matter how suddenly they are aroused by the unexpected noise, they subtly deceive their fierce enemy by trickery. They skillfully watch to see from which direction the armed foe is approaching the city, whether he is coming through the forest, or swimming across the river. If they discover nets stretched in the recesses of the forest they swiftly speed their flight from the exit on the side of the stream, and diving under the water toward the bottom of the crystal waters, safely escape death by swimming. If, on the other hand, the enemy, swimming across the river, should bring terror to their city, they immediately make their departure from the exit on the opposite side and avoid his darts by hiding in the dark woods. And those that have escaped will not come back again to their river homes until the enemy has withdrawn from their familiar shores.

It is necessary, therefore, to attack the beavers in cold winter weather when snow has blanketed the fields with a white fleece, and the rivers are frozen solid by Alpine cold. These dwellers of the forest, surrounded by the males, leave their hearth, and where holes, secretly chopped out shortly before by the hunter, appear in the solidly frozen river, they roll off into the water and glide along underneath the roof of ice. The hunters wait patiently on the banks, gladly allowing the clever animals to be deceived. Then quickly scattering out along the

169

Occupat abscissos latitans sub fronde meatus:
Cum vero gelido discedunt aggere Fibri,
Perque cavum fessi tollunt capita alta foramen,
Obtruncat subito venator colla bipenni,
Aut manibus certe per mollia crura prehensam
Extrahit insignem concreto e gurgite praedam
Multa reluctantem, fatumque astumque gementem.
                                                    [*ll. 316-332*]

Territus at crebro venator frigore, et imbre
Munitos renuit cives invadere ferro
Retia contentus vafrae disponere genti.
Explorat prudens, qua degant agmina sylva,
Quos inhient pastus, quas undas illa frequentent:
Et queis adduci crustis, Fibrumque teneri
Comperit, hisce sagax venator retia tendit.
Advolat ille plagis mensae pellectus odore
Infelix, fraudem imprudens nec sentit iniquam:
Sed dum mella vorax exsecti corticis haurit,
Incidit in laqueos tectos sub fronde maligna,
Implexusque gemit luco sine fine sub alto,
Venator donec compressi colla bacillo
Comminuat, jugulumque ferus mucrone recidat.
Qualis ubi nurui demens aconita noverca
Praeparat in cyatho, cyathumque urbana propinat;
Illa dolum potat, tantique ignara pericli
Funus inexpletis deglutit faucibus atrum:
Non aliter falso decepti munere Fibri
Tranquillam mutant violento funere vitam.
                                                    [*ll. 333-352*]

Saepe tamen laqueis astutam fallere gentem
Venantes taedet, magnoque angore fugacem
Exspectare diu, sylvisque absumere luces.
Hinc juvat umbrosos canibus praecingere saltus
Versutosque procul cives invadere telis.
Ut siquidem pavidos fidi cinxere molossi,
Fulmineum subito jacitur magno impete plumbum,
Effunditque solo morientem vulnere Fibrum.
                                                    [*ll. 353-360*]

Castoreum primum quatuor medicina crumenis
Extrahit, aegrotis aptum latura juvamen;
Quod mox in tetrum deformat cana venenum
Omnia quae facile suevit mutare vetustas.
Membra dein pecoris pretioso vellere nudant

snow-covered banks of the stream and hiding under bushes, they man the openings. And when the weary beavers are withdrawing from their cold rampart and lifting high their heads through an opening, the hunter suddenly cuts their necks with his ax, or at least catches hold of their soft legs with his hands and drags his splendid booty out of the icy waters, while the animals struggle desperately, bemoaning the deadly trick.

But the hunter, frequently deterred by cold and rain, is disinclined to attack with sword these well-fortified citizens, being content to stretch nets for the crafty tribe. He painstakingly finds out in what forest they dwell, what foods they like, what streams they frequent, and cleverly baits his nets with those barks by which he knows the beaver to be attracted and held. The hapless animal, lured by the scent of food, heedlessly flies into the toils without suspecting foul play, and as he greedily extracts the sweet juices from the pieces of bark, he falls into the snares concealed under the treacherous leaves, and becoming entangled, cries unceasingly in the deep woods until the hunter beats the imprisoned animal over the neck with a club and savagely slashes his throat with a knife. As a deranged step-mother prepares a cup of poison for her son's wife and amiably offers her the cup to drink, and the latter, unaware of dire peril, takes the deceptive drink and drains the cup of black death with great relish, thus the beavers, deceived by the treacherous gifts, exchange their peaceful life for a violent death.

But hunters often grow tired of beguiling the crafty tribe with nets, of impatiently waiting so long for the timid creatures, and of spending their days in the forest. For this reason they choose to encircle the shaded groves with their hounds and from a distance rush upon these clever denizens of the forest with darts. And when the faithful dogs have surrounded the frightened animals, the lightning-like missile is suddenly shot with a mighty force and brings the beaver, wounded and dying to the ground.

First of all, castoreum is extracted for medicinal uses from four pouches, designed to bring prompt relief to the sick. This soon changes into a dark fluid through the process of aging, which quickly alters all things. Then the hunters strip the precious pelts from the bodies;

Fibri

Venantes, spoliisque ferae vaga turba potita
Nunc caput elatum cingit, decoratque galero,
Nunc caligas fessis subtiles cruribus aptat,
Nunc etiam toto pellit de corpore frigus.

[*ll. 361-369*]

FINIS LIBRI SEXTI

and these spoils, falling into the possession of the roaming throng, sometimes provide a covering and an adornment for their proud heads, sometimes they are made into fine boots for their weary limbs, and again they are used to ward off cold from the entire body.

VII

FODINAE ARGENTI ATQUE AURI

Jam mihi visa lacus fluitantia rura per undas;
Jam juga Xoruli ruptis flammata caminis;
Et salientis aquae magno cataracta fragore;
Jam Coccum legi, Tyriumque, Indumque nitorem;
Arduaque astutis posui penetralia Fibris:
Nunc coelum linquo, nunc terrae lapsus ad ima
Aggredior cantu, Plutonis regna, fodinas;
Regna refulgenti semper radiata metallo,
Et quae divitiis complerunt prodiga mundum.

[*ll. 1-9*]

Tu, qui pennatis telluris viscera plantis
Saepe subis, clara munitus lampade dextram
Advenias, monstresque viam, lumenque ministres,
Obsecro; dum caecos libeat lustrare recessus,
Argentumque, Aurumque, et subterranea regna.

[*ll. 10-14*]

Tollitur occidua telluris parte supina
Clivorum series, series longissima visu,
Radices totum patulas diffusa per orbem,
Et quae mole gravi prolixam subsecat oram.
Orta sub Australi terrae nascentis arena
Continuata jugis Scythicam decurrit ad Ursam
Innumeros glomerans sublimi vertice montes,
Nunc pulchros sylvis, rigidos nunc undique saxis,
Nunc etiam piceas efflantes ore favillas.
Hinc atque hinc vastae diffundunt aequora valles
Fontibus undantes, simul et fluvialibus undis,
Quas sequitur pleno Cerealis copia cornu.
Qualis odoratis pater Apenninus in arvis
Tollitur in coelum, tractusque intersecat omnes,
Aequora nunc dextra fundens, nunc ille sinistra,
Munificusque vagis ditat pomaria rivis:
Non secus immensos series montana per agros
Funditur, occiduasque plagas sinuata recidit.
His opulenta jugis omnes America fodinas
Occulit, educitque nitens operosa metallum.

[*ll. 15-34*]

Quae si magna tibi ferro terebrare cupido,
Ante latebrosi findas quam viscera montis,
Praestat inaccessas terrae discernere venas;
Quae ferat argentum, quae fulvo competat auro,
Et quae promittat gravidum pro munere plumbum.

THE MINING OF SILVER AND GOLD

I have now considered the lands that float over the waves of the lake, the ridges of Jorullo with flames shooting forth from fiery furnaces, the waterfalls leaping down with a great crashing sound, and the glory of cochineal, purple, and indigo; I have described the lofty abodes of the cunning beavers. Now I leave the upper air, now I descend into the depths of the earth and essay to sing of mines, Pluto's realm, a realm ever glittering with shining metal and abundantly supplying the world with riches.

You, who often on winged foot go down into the bowels of the earth holding in your hand a lighted torch, come and show me the way and provide a light, I beg, while I may be permitted to examine the dark recesses, the silver and gold, and the subterranean realms.

There rises in the western part of the country a chain of mountains, a chain that is seen stretching far into the distance, extending its wide roots out over the whole country and cutting the fertile land with its ponderous mass. Starting from the southern coast where the land rises out of the sea the range runs uninterruptedly toward the Scythian bear, containing countless mountains with towering peaks, sometimes covered with beautiful forests, sometimes beset on every side with jagged rocks, or again belching forth ashes black as pitch. On each side extend wide valleys of level land abounding in springs as well as streams and attended by the full horn of bountiful Ceres. As father Apennine rises heavenward in the scented fields and cuts asunder whole tracts of land, providing valleys now on the right and now on the left, and richly supplies the orchards with winding streams, so the mountain range stretches over a vast territory and cuts the regions of the west by its sinuous course. In these ridges bountiful America conceals all her mines and from them brings forth, after much effort, the shining metal.

Now if you have a strong desire to bore into the mountain with steel, it is better, before splitting apart the dark recesses, to distinguish between the inaccessible veins of the earth to see which produces silver, which resembles yellow gold, and which promises to yield heavy lead as

Quippe superficiem telluris vena supremam
Conscendit, gaudetque caput supponere dio.
Inde per occultos nigra caligine tractus
Scinditur in partes, diversaque brachia tendit,
Nunc recta effundens montis per viscera ramos,
Nunc demissa ruens centrum telluris ad imum.
Quin etiam late multas extensa per ulnas
Multiplici quandoque riget stipata sodali,
Diversis abdens thesauros improba crustis.
Hinc primum bibulae crusta sociatur arenae,
Dein alia plumbi, flavae tum tegmine terrae:
Mox recludit opes, quas aut fornace solutas
Excipias, aut quae nequeant par esse labori
Merces; thesauri donec tibi copia manet
Argento vivo e rupe elicienda tenaci.
Divitias persaepe suas dabit altera vena
Purior, et crustis nusquam comitata molestis;
Sed quae mordaci nunquam durissima ferro
Cedat, Vulcani tantum cessura furori.
Quod si laesa silex primum solvatur ad ictum,
Ocyus immensis undabunt oppida gazis.[1]

[*ll. 35-60*]

Ut tamen argenti venas novere periti,
Incipiunt montem duro perrumpere ferro,
Effodiuntque ingens repetitis ictibus antrum.
At quae principio clivo traxere cavato
Invenies passim latum neglecta per agrum.
Nam quamvis aliquae dederint opulenta fodinae
Saxa sub ingressum, reliquae dant paucula grana
Argenti, nunquam faciendis sumptibus aequa.
Divitias magnas tellus sub corde reservat,
Prodiga queis altum fodientes ilia ditat.
Hinc omnes ferro certant penetrare profunda,
Thesauros donec reddat cum foenore tellus.

[*ll. 61-72*]

Ut vero collis reserat labor ille latebras,
Altaque rescindit sudans operarius antra,
Caligant omnes horrendae noctis in umbris,
Nullaque per sectas apparet semita rimas:
Pes titubat trepidus, nec fas est tendere gressum,
Nedum consueto paulum indulgere labori.
Tunc opus accensis operam praecedere taedis,
Horrentesque prius facibus pulsare tenebras,
Quam labor assiduo findat praecordia vecti.
Volvitur in tectum piceo glomeramine fumus,

a reward. This is possible because the vein protrudes above the surface of the earth and is inclined to lift its head into the daylight. Then through regions concealed in deep darkness it splits apart and stretches forth its branches straight through the bowels of the mountain, sometimes descending toward the very center of the earth. Indeed, when it has extended over an area many cubits wide, it sometimes becomes solidly enveloped with many a neighboring substance and thus mischievously hides its treasures inside various incrustations. It is first associated with a layer of wet sand, then with another of lead, and again with a covering of yellow earth. Finally, it hides its riches, which may be obtained when melted in a furnace or, if that is too much trouble, purchased, until you have on hand a store of riches to be separated from the stubborn rock with quicksilver. Very often another vein, purer and in no way attended with troublesome incrustations, will yield its wealth, but which, because of its extreme hardness, will not yield to the sharp steel, but only to Vulcan's fury. If, however, the rock when struck breaks apart at the first blow, untold wealth will quickly flood the towns.[1]

Now when experts have discovered veins of silver, they begin to burst their way through the mountain with the hard steel, and with repeated blows excavate an enormous tunnel. That which they first extract from the tunneled mountainside you will find carelessly strewn over the open country, for although some mines have yielded valuable stones near the entrance, the rest yield paltry grains of silver not worth an outlay of expense. The earth keeps in its heart its vast wealth with which it lavishly enriches those who delve deeply into its bosom. Therefore all strive to penetrate with pick the innermost part of the earth until it gives up its treasures along with interest.

Now when such industry is unlocking the hidden recesses of the mountain, and the sweating workman is cutting out deep tunnels, all are enveloped in the frightful darkness of night, nor is a pathway to be seen through the narrow openings. The timorous foot hesitates and is not permitted to take a step, much less to continue as usual with the work even for a little while. It becomes necessary, then, to precede the work with lighted torches and to dispel the terrific darkness with lights before attempting to split apart the innermost recesses

Omnia qui nigra subito fuligine turpat:
Nigrescunt muri, tectumque, et strata cavernae,
Fossoresque brevi corpus nigrantur, et ora.
Quid vero non cogat opum vesana cupido?
Insistunt operi, facibusque hinc inde locatis
Nigrantes penetrant aditus, murosque fodinae
Ictibus abrumpunt crebris, impressa secuti
Antra per et rupes nitidae vestigia venae.

[*ll. 73-90*]

Ne vero collis, secta radice, ruina
Corruat infanda, tumuletque repente sub umbris
Fossores, pubes submisso robore tectum
Excipit, et cameras montis per opaca recurvat;
Ni rigeat locuples immoto pumice clivus:
Tunc satis est arcus tecto donasse figuram,
Ut vacet amotis operi gens dura periclis.

[*ll. 91-97*]

Rupibus abscissis, tenebrisque ab luce fugatis
Divitias persaepe jugo deturbat ab alto
Invida praecipitem mittens fortuna laborem.
Sed fidens animis terrae descendit ad ima
Et patiens plebes scalarum munere venam
Persequitur, retegat donec jucunda metallum.
Quod si iterum praeceps thesaurus volvitur orco,
Se praeceps iterum pubes demittit in orcum.
Hinc magnas aedes imitatur saepe fodina
Infernos complexa lares, complexa supernos,
Et vastis suffulta per intervalla columnis
Arte laboratis, ipsaque e rupe recisis,
Quas domino nunquam licuit contingere ferro,
Argento quamvis fulcrum praedives abundet.

[*ll. 98-111*]

Ast ubi congeriem thesauri turba retexit,
Consistit, magnamque fodit sub colle cavernam,
Immensisque vigil sustentat culmina fulcris,
Ne collapsa ruant, pereatque oppressa juventus.
Tunc operam prudens partitur cuique Magister:
Alter enim taedas dextra, lumenque ministrat,
Alter inaccessos proscindit cuspide muros,
Et legit e muris alter salientia frusta
Secernens pingues recto discrimine cautes.

[*ll. 112-120*]

of the mountain with repeated blows of the pick. Black wreaths of smoke roll upward to the ceiling, quickly covering everything with black soot. The walls become black, the ceiling, and the floor of the cavern, and in a short time the bodies and faces of the miners are black. But to what does an insane passion for wealth not drive men? They pursue their work with diligence. With torches placed here and there they penetrate the dark recesses and with repeated blows break away the walls of the mine, pursuing through crevices and rocks the outlines of the glistening vein.

But lest the mountain, when its roots are severed, collapse with unspeakable disaster and instantly bury the miners in the darkness, the men support the roof with oak pillars and arch the chambers throughout the dark recesses, unless the richly laden walls stand erect, having their rocks unmoved. In that case it is enough merely to give the roof the form of an arch so that the sturdy men may be able to work free from dangers.

When the rocks have been split apart and darkness has yielded to the light, envious fortune very often thrusts her riches downward from the summit of the mountain, making it necessary for the work to be carried on along a steep incline. But the patient men, relying on their courage, descend to the depths of the earth and with ladders continue to follow the vein until with joy they uncover the metal. And if again the treasures turn downward into the lower regions, down again into the lower regions the men descend. Hence the mine often resembles a large house having apartments above and below, and resting at intervals on massive columns artistically wrought and carved from the rock itself which the master of the mine may never touch with iron bar no matter how rich in silver the pillar may be.

Now when the crowd of workmen have discovered a rich deposit, they stop and excavate a large tunnel underneath the mountain, carefully supporting the roof with enormous pillars that it may not collapse and fall and crush the young miners to death. Then the experienced director assigns to each man his task. One, holding in his hand a torch, furnishes light, another breaks through the impenetrable walls with a pick, while still another gathers the pieces as they fly from the walls and selects with consummate skill the profitable stones.

Fossor opes primum, puero praebente lucernam,
Verberat, et multis lapidem quatit ictibus unum.
Saxa gemunt intus teli contusa rigore
Totaque terribili reboat spelunca tumultu.
Ceu quondam Siculi massam Cyclopes ahenam
Aetnaeis valido tractant conamine in antris,
Concutiuntque nigras magno stridore cavernas.

[*ll. 121-127*]

Quod si prava silex chalybi obdurata resistat,
Amne reluctantem vincit constantia gentis.
Lucifer algentem buccis turgentibus undam
Colligit; et fossor teretes dum more lacertos
Tollit, quas tenet ore puer jacit impete limphas,
Missile flumen aquae toties jaculatus ab ore,
Ille gravem quoties vectem suspendit ab ictu,
Saxa quoad tandem muro madefacta revellant.

[*ll. 128-135*]

His vexata silex rabidam se fundit in iram
Exitiumque viris, fatumque intentat acerbum.
Vix etenim frendens, rupta compage, dehiscit,
Cum tetrum quandoque vomit furibunda vaporem,
Qui vitam citius lethali vulnere rumpit.
Ut tamen e secto fossor cognoscit hiatu
Surgere densatum lento glomeramine fumum,
Corripit e muro corpus, properusque recedit
Mortiferae donec fossae vapor ora requirat.
Si vero immotus sistat, paulumve moretur,
Protinus infelix fato concedit iniquo.
Non secus atque olim limpha pollutus Avernus
Ore venenatam revomens ad sydera nubem
Infanda superas mactabat caede volantes,
Ni peterent aliud sinuato tramite coelum.

[*ll. 136-150*]

Sin autem rupes ausint non cedere rivis,
Tunc decet omnino, scalprum superare rebelles
Armatum chalybe, ac laevi mucrone coruscum;
Quod bini versant juvenes, urgentque laborem.
Hic etenim dextra lucentia spicula adaptat,
Hic quatit a tergo repetito vulnere caelum,
Et puer interea silicem rigat ore gementem.
Hisce altum terebrant dura sub rupe foramen,
Quod plus dimidio solertia pulvere complet
Sulphureo, reliquum sabulo impletura rigenti.
Mox ingesta premit, densatisque ictibus urget,
Dum cautes simulent, pulsuque astricta rigescant.
Ast pulvis semper pressa constrictus arena
Sulphuream pariter, longamque foramine caudam

At first, while a boy holds a lantern, the miner pounds the rich ore and strikes a single stone with repeated blows. The rocks groan within as they are crushed by the inexorable tool, and the whole mine re-echoes with a terrible din. Thus at times in Sicily the Cyclops with violent stroke hammer the lumps of brass in the caves of Etna and shake the dark caverns with a mighty din.

But if the obstinate rock stubbornly resist the steel, the persistent people overcome this resistence with water. The light-bearer draws cold water into his mouth until his cheeks are puffed out, and while the miner lifts as usual his sinewy arms, the boy forcibly squirts out the water which he holds in his mouth, ejecting a stream each time the workman lifts his heavy bar after a stroke, until at last they break away the water-soaked rocks from the wall.

The rock, abused in this way, flies into a violent rage and threatens the men with death and dire destruction, for scarcely is the main body of the rock broken and splitting apart with a grating sound, when it sometimes madly emits a deadly gas which cuts off life more swiftly than a mortal wound. Whenever the miner observes thick clouds of smoke rolling up from the crack which he has split open, he rushes away from the wall and hastily abandons the place until the fumes make their escape through the mouth of the deadly mine. If, however, the ill-starred man should stand motionless or tarry a while, he succumbs at once to a bitter fate. So it was that once Avernus with its contaminated water exhaled poisonous fumes into the sky from its mouth and brought unspeakable death to the birds above, except to those that sought by a circuitous route a different part of the sky.

Now if the rocks should fail to yield to the streams of water, it is then altogether necessary to overcome their obstinacy with a sharp and shiny steel chisel. Two young men operate it and carry on the work. The one adjusts the shining point, the other from behind shakes the vaulted chamber with repeated blows, while, in the meantime, a boy moistens the groaning rock with his mouth. Having thus chiseled a deep hole into the hard rock, they skillfully fill it more than half full with powdered sulphur, the rest with sharp sand. Then they press and pack this filler with repeated hammering until it is firmly compressed and hard as rock. Now the powder which is kept in a state of compression by the packed sand sends out a long fuse also

175

Demittit, rapidis arsuram postea flammis.
Huic fossor taeda confestim subjicit ignem,
Ac pernice fuga praesens vitare periclum
Praecipitat, vastas condens se pone columnas.
Tum montana silex ingenti explosa fragore
Emicat, et saltu diversa in frusta dehiscit.
[*ll. 151-170*]

Saepe etiam caelo montis durissima crusta
Obsistit, gaudetque omnem deludere nisum.
Ast infracta cohors taedis accingitur atris,
Lignorumque altum rupi supponit acervum,
Igne reluctantis crudum victura rigorem.
Nocte, dieque nigri collis penetralia fumant,
Aetneo donec cautes superata furore
Quod gremio celat, tradat submissa metallum.
[*ll. 171-178*]

Indubium vero vitae discrimen adiret,
Fumantem quisquis vellet penetrare fodinam.
Inde prius caute pubes lustrare recessus
Cogitur; an fumus penitus decesserit antris,
An potius pravo condat se callidus astu.
Nam solet interdum foveae petere arduus alta,
Immotusque diu subter convexa latere.
Cum vero praepes fossis immissa juventus
Imprudens clausum celeri movet aera gressu,
Paulatim fumus summa de caute revulsus
Omnia pervadit vastae penetralia fossae,
Suffocatque brevi compresso gutture plebem.
[*ll. 179-190*]

His mulctata jugi nigrantia viscera poenis
Argenti subito scopulos, aurique profundunt,
Quod sursum prompti demisso corpore gestant
Adnixi scalis vulgus, queis cura gerendi;
Grandibus aut potius taurino e tergore peris
Includunt, peramque jubent ad culmina tolli.
[*ll. 191-196*]

Nam simul ac sudor penetrat praecordia montis
Ulterius colles opus est terebrare cavatos,
Auris ut captis pulmo praelargus anhelet,
Ac taedas flatu pascat mutabilis aer,
Utque dein patulo demissus restis ab ore
Saxea montanis abducat frusta cavernis.
Hinc plebes recta terebrant a culmine collem,
Viscera perfodiunt, rectoque foramine tendunt,
Praecipuam donec contingant cuspide fossam,
Aera permutent antris, Solemque ministrent.

of sulphur which later will quickly ignite. To this the miner hastily brings his torch, and rushing back in great haste to avoid instant danger, he hides behind the enormous pillars. Then the rock of the mountain, exploding with a loud crashing sound, leaps forth and breaks apart into many pieces as it bounces along.

Often the crust of the mountain, being extremely hard, resists even the chisel and is pleased to mock every effort. But the undaunted workmen provide themselves with their smoky torches and pile a large amount of wood underneath the rock to overcome its stern resistence with fire. Day and night the innermost recesses of the black mountain send forth smoke until the rock, subdued by Etnean fury, submissively surrenders the metal concealed in its bosom.

Now if anyone should wish to enter the smoking mine, he would certainly risk his life. Hence the men must first carefully examine the innermost chambers to see whether every trace of smoke has disappeared from the caverns or whether out of malicious treachery it is slyly hiding. Sometimes, indeed, it is wont to rise to the top of the mine and hang motionless for a long time under the vaulted roof. But when a group of inexperienced lads rush into the mine and swiftly stir up the stale air as they move about, gradually the smoke descends from the top of the rock, pervades the whole interior of the vast cavern, and soon suffocates them.

When this harsh treatment has been inflicted on the dark recesses of the mountain, they suddenly yield rocks of silver and gold; and those whose business it is to carry these rocks promptly convey them from below on bended shoulders, climbing up the ladders, or rather, having put them in large cowhide bags hoist them to the top.

Now as soon as they have worked their way into the heart of the mountain, it is necessary for them to bore another opening into the mine that the lungs may freely inhale the fresh air, that a change of air keep the torches burning, and, furthermore, that a rope may be dropped from the large opening to draw out the pieces of rock from the excavation in the mountain. So the men drill straight into the mountain from the top, they dig through its innermost parts, and continue the boring straight down until with the point of their picks they reach

Desuper artifices barathri nigrantis ad ora
Constituunt vastas sylvestri rupe columnas,
Antlia queis magnis trabibus compacta locatur
Ingenti circum, tortoque inclusa rudenti
Armato passim vacuis e pelle cylindris.
Cumque gravis levibus versatur machina mulis
In gyrum ductis, velox temone rotato
Altera pera cavi fauces ascendit hiatus,
Altera dum sectae fertur subducta fodinae.
His pubes alto lapides e colle revulsos
Elicit ad superas, lignis stridentibus, auras.

[*ll. 197-217*]

Saepe tamen largi lacero de pumice rivi
Emanant, multisque replent spelaea fluentis,
Obvia quae grato obstant importuna labori.
Quin etiam sectas undanti fonte cavernas
Opplerunt quandoque amnes, quos tollere fossis
Antlia nulla satis situlo munita frequenti:
Hoc siquidem collis sudabat largius undis,
Quo mage limosos potabat machina fontes.
Tunc decet ingestis foveam concludere saxis,
Ni vesanus opes, vitamque absumere malis.

[*ll. 218-227*]

Est tamen interdum, magnae cui copia gazae,
Qui collem transversa ferit, per viscera largum
Effodiens aliud, scissa radice, foramen.
Radicem terebrat montis, Magneteque caecam
Demonstrante viam penetrat praecordia ferro,
Antra quoad gelida vectes undantia rumpant,
Excedantque suo compulsae pondere limphae,
Aequora perfundant rivis, antrumque relinquant.

[*ll. 228-235*]

Quod si rupta fluat non multo flumine rupes,
Cisternae similem limphis aptare recessum
Est opus; inque solo puteum reserare profundum,
Quo proprio nocui salientes impete rivi
Accurrant, fossaque omnes glomerentur in una,
Sub longi omnino, rectique foraminis ore.
Desuper interea situlis aptare rudentes
Est opus; ut versis acri sub verbere mulis,
Ima petat putei situlorum mobilis ordo;
Quos coelo deinceps stridenti mole reducat
Antlia, turgenti vomituros ventre fluenta.

[*ll. 236-246*]

the main excavation and let in fresh air and sunlight. Over the entrance to the black pit skilled workmen construct from the rough rock enormous pillars on which they erect a windlass mounted on large beams. This has large twisted ropes wrapped about it provided at intervals with hollow cylinders made of leather. And when the heavy machine is turned by nimble-footed mules driven around in a circle, the pole is rotated and one bag quickly rises to the top of the entrance as another is lowered into the mine. Thus with the creaking machines the men lift into the upper air the stones which they have torn out of the depths of the mountain.

Often, however, streams flow in profusion from the broken rock and fill the pit with great volumes of water which obstruct and grievously delay the pleasing work. In fact, streams have sometimes filled the mines with such a flood of water that no machine equipped with ever so many buckets could remove it, for the faster the machine would suck up the muddy waters, the more abundantly would the streams issue from the mountain. In such a case it is necessary to close the mine with piles of rock, unless in madness you choose to waste both life and fortune.

There is, however, at times a man who finds a great abundance of treasure by cutting across the mountain, splitting it open at the base and opening up another large excavation through its heart. He bores through the roots of the mountain, and guided along the dark way by a magnet, penetrates with his pick its innermost recesses until he bursts into caverns flooded with icy water, and the waters propelled by their own weight flow out, overrun the plain, and thus escape.

But if the cleft rock exudes only a small stream, it is necessary to provide for it a cistern-like pit by opening in the earth a deep hole into which the troublesome waters may trickle by the force of their own weight and all be brought together into one pool underneath the mouth of the long and upright shaft. Overhead it is necessary, in the meanwhile, to fasten buckets to the ropes, in order that, as the mules circle about under the sting of the whip, the moving chain of buckets may be lowered to the bottom of the pool and brought back again into the upper air on the creaking windlass to spew out the water from their distended bellies.

177

Si tamen huic renuat puteo succedere limpha,
Quod multis submissa ulnis tranquilla residat,
Altera torpentes attollat machina fontes
Interiora super speluncae strata reposta;
Quam pariter muli, subducti faucibus antri,
Instructam situlis ipso sub colle rotabunt,
Cisternamque brevi replebunt tempore rivis,
Antlia quos labris educet prima supernis.

[*ll. 247-254*]

In superum limphis eductis aera fundo,
Ignibus, et ferro fossor sub colle labori
Insistit, dorsoque ferunt ad montis hiatum
Omnia concisae vectores fragmina cautis.
Desuper assiduus, patuloque sub ore fodinae
Insomni portam custos statione tuetur,
Fidus ubi collis recipit fragmenta cavati,
Et multis large succurrit promptus egenis:
Nunc animis frustum lapidis purgantibus offert,
Nunc Divis, Verboque Patris, castaeque Parenti;
Donaque largitur vexat quos tristis egestas.
Caetera malleolis plebi scindenda resignat;
Quae saxum saxo secernit divite vanum,
Atque alio vectat madidis sub pondere mulis,
Eruat ut venis thesauros arte peritus.

[*ll. 255-269*]

Cum vero domino pensum solvere diurnum
Fossores, avidi rursus sibi quisque laborant,
Dilaniant rupes, ac terrae viscera findunt,
Ingentemque sibi cumulabunt cautis acervum.
Postibus advectum superis ad limina custos
Excipit, et fidus medium disjungit aperte,
Inque duas aequo resecat discrimine partes.
Ante omnes fossor partem sibi deligit unam,
Et custos aliam domino sub tecta reponit.

[*ll. 270-278*]

Interdum pueri (Vulpes quos improba plebes
Nominat) horrendi subeunt penetralia collis
Frustula lecturi caeco sub monte relicta,
Sed monstranda dein custodi ad limina fossae,
Omnia qui rursus partes secernit in aequas.
Provida ceu quondam pingues formica per agros
Incedit, cogitque relicti farris acervum;
Haud secus imbellis lustrat spelaea juventus.

[*ll. 279-286*]

If, however, the water, resting many cubits below, should refuse to flow into this pit, another machine, installed inside the mine across the roadway, hoists the sluggish waters. It, too, is equipped with buckets and is operated beneath the very mountain itself by mules introduced into the mine. In a short time they will fill the cistern with the water, which will in turn be drawn out through the opening above by the first windlass.

When the water has been brought from the bottom of the mine into the air above, the miner underneath applies himself to his work with pick and fire, and the carriers bear on their shoulders all the broken rock to the opening of the mountain. Just outside the entrance to the mine a trustworthy guard keeps constant watch. He faithfully receives the fragments chiseled from the mountain and is ready to give generous aid to many who are in need. Now he offers a bit of stone for the souls in purgatory, now to God, and to the Son of God, and to the Holy Mother; and he lavishes gifts upon those distressed by dire poverty. The remainder he hands over to the men to break with mallets. They separate the precious stone from the worthless and carry it to another place on mules sweating beneath the load in order that a man skilled in the art may extract the treasures from the veins.

Now when the miners have finished a day's work for their master, they then greedily work, each for himself. They tear to pieces the rocks, split apart the bowels of the earth, and heap high for themselves an enormous pile of stones. When this has been brought through the upper gateway, the guard at the entrance takes it and in the presence of all impartially divides and evenly separates it into two parts. In the presence of everyone the miner selects one part for himself, and the guard puts the other portion inside the house for the master.

At times boys, whom the waggish populace call foxes, descend into the frightful recesses of the mountain to gather up bits of rock left behind in the darkness, but these must be shown to the guard at the entrance to the mine, who again divides everything into equal shares. As the wise ant often marches through the fertile fields and collects a pile of grain which has been left behind, in the same manner do these young boys search through the mines.

Fodinae Argenti, atque Auri

Ast, si quod possunt, frustum sibi quisque reservat,
Lucifer, et pueri, fossorque, humerisque vehentes
Peras, absconditque sagax industria furtum,
Horrenti quamvis pellatur turba fodina,
Ni prius e toto detrudat corpore vestes,
Concessa tantum quae servat casta pudorem.
Hac tamen effossor celat sub veste lapillos;
Alter in effictis crudeli vulnere plagis;
Et rigidis alter praetexit frusta capillis.
Janitor at solers attento examinat ore,
Perlustratque diu velamen, vulnera, crines:
Quae reperit domino furtim sublata reservat;
Quae vero latuere, sibi fur jure recondit,
Quin domino deinceps poenis urgere latronem,
Aut raptata sibi liceat deposcere frusta.
[*ll. 287-301*]

Scilicet has semper fodiunt mercede cavernas
Impatiens tolerare jugum faex infima vulgi:
Quos inter multis, gravibusque obnoxia poenis
Improba gens latitat, plebique admixta laborat.
Turpibus addictum poenis ob crimina furem,
Crudelesque manus rorantes sanguine cernes,
Et qui perfectae ruperunt vincula vitae,
Gaudentes potius tetros habitare recessus,
Quam sacro submissa jugo supponere colla.
Est scelus in tuto, gestit sine vindice crimen,
Nec loca Praetor adit poena exercere nocentes,
Ni velit ingentem turbam, Martemque ciere,
Ac vitam saeva campis effundere pugna.
Haec circum tetras habitat scelerata fodinas,
Divitiasque parat congestis turba metallis;
Quae subito ad fossae nigrantia limina vendit,
Seu merces fuerint proprii condigna laboris,
Seu potius foedis nuper sublata rapinis.
[*ll. 302-319*]

FINIS LIBRI SEPTIMI

Now if they can, each one keeps a fragment for himself—the light-bearer, the boys, the miner, and those who carry the bags on their shoulders—and they conceal their theft by studied deception, although they may not leave the rocky mine until they have first removed all their clothes, save only the garment which protects their modesty. Yet even under this a miner hides stones, another conceals them in wounds which he wantonly inflicts, and yet another hides bits of stone in his coarse hair. But the watchman at the gate with a keen eye examines and closely scrutinizes the clothes, the wounds, and the hair. Whatever he finds that has been stolen he saves for the master, but whatever escapes his notice the thief properly hides away for himself, nor is the master permitted later to punish the thief or demand the return of the pieces stolen from him.

Naturally, the lowest dregs of society, unwilling to submit to the yoke, work these mines for hire, among whom vicious individuals, guilty of many serious offenses, escape detection and work mingling with the crowd. You will see a thief condemned to punishment for heinous crimes, and murderous hands dripping with blood, and those who have broken the bonds of a righteous life, preferring rather to inhabit the dreary recesses of the earth than to submit to the onerous yoke. Wickedness is shielded, crime goes unpunished, nor does a judge go to these places to prosecute the guilty unless he wishes to incite the vast mob to war and to pour out his life on the bloody field of battle. In the vicinity of the dreary mines these vicious characters live, and they get their wealth by collecting metals, which they immediately sell at the entrance to the dark mine, either as a worthy reward for their own efforts or as loot recently taken by infamous thievery.

VIII

ARGENTI, ATQUE AURI OPIFICIUM

Post sectas dudum magno sudore fodinas
Protinus advectas opulenta in praedia cautes
Comminuam, saxisque vigil conabor avaris
Eruere argenti pretiosum pondus et auri,
Ac totum partis orben complere talentis.

[*ll. 1-5*]

Tu, quae maerentes oculis, Fortuna, serenis
Aspicis, et velox gaudes succurrere lapsis,
Aspice terribili languentem membra labore,
Impensasque diu tanto conamine curas:
Promissas quondam gazas mihi fida reserva,
Rupeque contrita thesauros dextra revelle:
Et gemmas dum terra ferat, dum gramina campus,
Delubris suspensa tuis mea vota videbis.

[*ll. 6-13*]

Sunt procul a fossa florentes divite fundi
Chortibus insignes vastis, ac dulcibus undis,
Porticibusque amplis, cellisque, et grandibus aulis,
Acer ubi magnas fornaces ignis adurit,
Et pistrina gravis, firmataque machina ferro
Ossa terunt collis nitidis foecunda metallis.
Huc montana vehunt nervosi fragmina muli,
Aspera quae rursus magnis exscindere clavis
Protinus aggreditur plebes, rescissaque pulsu
Distrahit in parvos, saxo frendente, lapillos.

[*ll. 14-23*]

His vero scrupis iterumque iterumque terendis
Ardua consurgit ferratis machina pilis
Ponderis ingentis, lucentique aere coruscis,
Quam circum mulae cursu pernice volantes
Aut gravido motant labentia flumina casu.
Assidue impubes palis armata juventus
Subjiciunt pilis parte ex utraque metalla,
Ictibus ut crebris citius domet horrida saxa,
Atque asprum moles flectat versata rigorem,
Exilem donec reddat contritus arenam,
Et tenuis volitet secto de pumice pulvis.
Hunc capsae excipiunt pilarum pondera juxta
In longum positae, fortique ligamine moli
Fixae, quas operit caute tenuissima tela
Ex aere in filum ducto densata perite.

[*ll. 24-38*]

PROCESSING OF SILVER AND GOLD

Now that I have with much toil worked the mines, I shall forthwith crush the stones which have been carried to the rich estates and diligently try to bring forth precious quantities of silver and gold from the avaricious rocks and fill the whole world with the riches obtained.

You, O Fortune, who look with serene eyes upon the sorrowing, and are pleased to bring prompt relief to the wretched, behold my body weary with the tremendous task and regard the pains long spent on so great an endeavor. Faithfully reserve for me the wealth which once you promised and propitiously wrest from the crushed rock its treasures, and so long as the earth yields its precious stones, so long as grass grows in the fields, you will see my offerings hanging in your shrines.

Some distance from the mine are flourishing estates, known for their spacious grounds, fresh waters, wide colonnades, storehouses, and magnificent buildings. In these a lively fire heats large furnaces, and a heavy mill and an iron-supported machine grind the bones of the mountain filled with shining metals. To this place sturdy mules convey the rough ore from the mountain, and the men immediately set about to split it apart with heavy sledges and grind it, when thus broken, into fine pieces.

Now to crush these sharp pieces again and again, a large machine is set up equipped with heavy iron pounders and shining brass. This is kept in motion by mules flying briskly around, or by a heavy waterfall. Young boys standing on each side steadily shovel the ore under the pounders that the revolving machine may quickly break the sharp stones by its repeated blows and overcome their strong resistence. The process is continued until the stones have been crushed into fine sand, and light dust flies from the rock. This is caught in boxes placed alongside the massive pounders and securely fastened to the machine. A very thin gauze of finely woven bronze wire securely covers them.

Argenti, atque Auri Opificium

Improbus ille labor pueris discrimina vitae
Saepe tulit, miseros properata morte trucidans.
Pulvis enim patulis inclusum naribus altum
Pervadit cerebrum, pectusque adlabitur imum,
Ternaque vernantem vitam post lustra resolvit.
Quare opus est pretio pueros conducere magno,
Ausint ut tantum vitae discrimen adire.

[ll. 39-45]

Saxea si quando ferratas frustula plagas
Effugiant, pilisque rebelli mole resistant,
Haec pistrina domat replicatis orbibus acta,
Dum tenuata gravi sinuati pondere saxi
Se tollant flatu, tenuis quasi pulvis, ad auras.

[ll. 46-50]

Haec ubi trita diu volitant tenuissima vento,
Excipit aequato subito vasta area dorso,
Vulgus ubi attritis saxis effingit acervos,
Humectat limphis, madidoque ex pulvere coenum
Conficit, et plenis aspergit deinde salinis.
Postera lux terris ut Phoebi lampade fulsit,
Calce terit densa crassum salsugine limum,
Admiscetque sali praefixo tempore vulgus.

[ll. 51-58]

Tunc omnes limi languores arte peritus
Explorat morbis crebro torpentis acerbis;
Scilicet, an gelidis tabes cruciatibus aegrum
Urgeat, an potius pestis febrilis adurat.[1]
Hinc vivo argento salsum cratere resolvit
Limum; dein prudens missis examinat undis,
Undique vasa movens, acto in contraria limo.
Tum digito pressum subsidens vase metallum
Incipit algentis plumbi simulare colorem,
Et gelido limum morbo languere revelat.
Ast si lacte fluat, turbetque albedine limphas,
Aegrotum retegit magna tabescere febri.
Sed morbis praesens aptat medicina levamen.

[ll. 59-71]

Coenosum frigus vexet si forte metallum
Doctus Apollinea gelidum fovet arte Machaon.
Saxa cupri contrita diu sale condit acerbo
Iratis mixtum cocturus postea flammis,
Donec aquae infusum tabum, saniemque referre
Viderit, ac tetra foedare putredine fontes.
Tunc aegrum rutilo tendit sub Sole trementem,
Desuper aspergit cuprum, morbumque repellit.

[ll. 72-79]

This is hazardous work and frequently endangers the lives of the boys, cutting short their wretched existence by an untimely death. For the dust, having blocked the cavities of the nose, penetrates the top of the brain and passes down into the lower part of the chest, breaking off the thread of life in its bloom following the third lustrum. The boys must therefore be paid good wages for daring thus to risk their lives.

If at any time pieces of rock should escape the strokes of the iron and stubbornly resist the crushers, they are driven between the stones of a mill and bruised until they are reduced to fine particles under the weight of the heavy rock and rise up in a gust of wind like fine dust.

When these particles of pulverized rock have floated about in the air for a considerable time, they suddenly alight on the level surface of the spacious grounds where they are formed by the men into piles and moistened with water. From the moist powder mud is formed and then sprinkled with an abundance of salt. When the following day has lighted the earth with the lamp of Phoebus, the men treat the thick mud which they have saturated with salt, and at a definite time they add more salt.

Then an expert in the industry seeks to discover all the diseases of the mixture, for it often suffers grievous disorders, to find out whether the illness is causing the patient excruciating chills, or whether high fever is consuming it.[1] Hence he dissolves the salty mixture in a bowl of quicksilver. Then after adding water he carefully examines the vessel, moving it in every direction and shifting the mud from side to side. After that, if the metal, when pressed by the finger, settles in the vessel and begins to assume a cold leadlike appearance, it is evident that the mud is suffering with a cold. But if it should become milky and cause the water to turn white, this is an indication that the mud is ill and being consumed with high fever. For these diseases, however, medicine affords a prompt relief.

If a cold should happen to irritate the metallic mud, a physician skilled in Apollo's art administers warm relief. Crushed rocks of copper he lays for a long time in strong brine and afterwards heats the mixture over raging flames until he sees it giving up puss-like matter and rendering the water turbid in its decomposition. Then he spreads the trembling patient under the bright sun, sprinkles the copper upon it, and thus repels the disease.

181

Tardius aegroti migrat de corpore febris:
Nam simul atque aegrum cognovit chorte jacere,
Argentum-vivum dextra capit ille perita
Fortiter arctatum densatis pectine telis,
Ut binis valide compresso e tegmine palmis
Grandinis in morem discedat vividus imber
Carbaseos penetrans, scissa compage, meatus.
Hoc madefacta gravi perfundit rore metalla,
Argentoque lutum foecundat fossile vivo.
Mox sapiens medicus nocui non immemor aestus
Paeonia combusta levat praecordia calce.

[*ll. 80-90*]

Ocyus ingreditur planta calcare frequenti
Rursus turba lutum, permiscens coena medelis,
Continuatque dies pravum bis quinque laborem.
Ut solet interdum tumidis undantia botris
Stringere praela diu, pedibusque urgere racemos
Turba, quoad fluido roret vindemia Baccho:
Haud aliter pravo sudori assueta juventus
Chortibus in vastis crebro pede calcat acervos.
Ast ubi quisque lutum contrivit praepete planta,
Continuo in conum cumulum gens provida cogit,
Impositaque notat coni super alta papyro
Argenti vivi pondus, cuprique, salisque.

[*ll. 91-102*]

Cum vero mixti, revolutis lucibus, optat
Explorare gradum, viresque probare magister,
E cumulo raptum limum dissolvit aquali
Perfusum gelida. Dives descendit arena
In fundum subito, coeno super alta relicto;
Quod profundit humi, prono cratere, peritus,
Et cauta sabulum sidens examinat arte,
Vascula nunc dextrae inclinans, nunc ille sinistrae,
Argenti donec limbus retegatur ad oras
Jactati sabuli. Limbum mox pollice calcat,[2]
Observatque vigil, digito num fimbria pressa
Argento sudet vivo; num sicca receptum
Hauserit, et nulla roret tunc urceus unda.
Si nil sicca fluat, rursus perfundere vivum
Est opus argentum, et rursus calcare metalla.
Integrat haec eadem prudens tentamina rector,
Dum dives gravido desudet flumine. limbus.
Si tamen argento compressa lacinia vivo
Distillet prompte, cumulo nihil additur olli,
Sed cellis missus fontano tergitur amne.

[*ll. 103-122*]

Fever departs more slowly from the unhealthy substance. As soon as the doctor discovers illness on the grounds, he takes in his skilled hands quicksilver firmly packed in a closely woven net. As he presses this tightly between his two hands, the quicksilver breaks up, passes through the meshes of the net, and falls like a brisk shower of hail. With this heavy spray he treats the dampened mixture. Presently, being a wise physician, he recognizes the injurious malady and relieves the feverish breast with healing lime.

Quickly the workers begin again to tread the mud, trampling it again and again and mixing medicines into it, and for ten days they continue the tiresome work. As workers in the vineyard are often wont to fill the juicy presses with bursting grapes and press the fruit beneath their feet until the juice of Bacchus flows forth, so in the same manner young men, inured to weary toil, trample again and again the deposits on the spacious grounds. And when each one with agile step has finished kneading the mud, at once he wisely fashions his mound into the shape of a cone and indicates on a paper placed on top the amount of the mercury, copper, and salt.

Now when the director desires after a few days to grade and test the richness of the mixture, he takes a sample from a pile and dissolves it in a pan of water. The rich sand sinks at once to the bottom leaving a scum on top which is drained off onto the ground by skillfully tilting the pan. Then with painstaking care and deftness he examines the sandy sediment, shifting the vessel now to the right, and now to the left, until a band of silver is discovered on the edge of the agitated sand. He then presses[2] this band with his thumb and carefully observes whether the pressure causes any mercury to ooze out, or whether, being dry, it has entirely absorbed it and left the vessel free of moisture. If it is dry, mercury must be poured over the metal again, and it must be trampled again. The wise director repeats these same tests until the heavy fluid oozes from the rich border. Now if the edge, when pressed, readily emits drops of mercury, nothing is added to the deposit, but it is sent to a storeroom where it is washed in water from the spring.

Argenti, atque Auri Opificium

Est lacus in cellis sublimis quatuor ulnis
Undique praecinctus ferratis orbibus alvum,
Cuí medius residet turbo versatilis axe
Armatus multis infracto e robore palis,
Concita praecipiti versant quem flumina lapsu,
Quadrupes aut cursu circum pernice revolvit.
Huic tergendus aquis limi succedit acervus
Chortis in immensa toties calcatus arena.
Desuper effusis pendenti e fornice limphis,
Dum turbo celerem facilis sinuatur in orbem,
Immissus rapidis limus convolvitur undis.
Ut vero lentus motu desistit anhelo
Turbo, paulatim dives subsidere fundo
Nititur argentum, coenumque innare per amnem;
Quod juvenis, parvo cupae siphone recluso,
Fundit humi: fluvioque iterum conspersa recenti,
Inque orbem ductis palis cunctantia volvit
Coena cado, rursusque dein cratere relegat,
Dum fundo penitus purgata metalla residant.
[*ll. 123-141*]

Ne tamen albenti lateat faex sordida massa,
Roboreis ipsam rursus detergere mactris
Aggreditur pubes: vitreo quas fonte repletas
Nunc movet hac lente, nunc velox commovet illac,
Nunc faeci admixtas undanti projicit alveo
Limphas, quoad totum pulsarit dextra fluentum,
Puraque siccato sidant in vase metalla.
[*ll. 142-148*]

Conifer interea tigno suspenditur alto
E lino densus compacto stamine saccus,
Aptusque argentum tardare, hydrargyro abacto:
Hic tracto mactris aperit se saccus acervo,
Argentumque tenax retinet subtemine purum,
Et vivum gremio majori ex parte repellit,
Quod clausum pateris vulgus sub tecta reponit.
[*ll. 149-155*]

Demissis terrae celso de robore peris,
Argentum tandem gremio depromit avaro
Exultans tractare manu plebs ductile pondus,
Indeque colludens varias effingere formas.
Ceu quondam teneris puerorum coetus in annis
Cecropia gaudet festus colludere cera,
Et genio indulgens graciles formare figuras,
Nunc dextra vitulum fingens, nunc vascula formans,
Nunc parvam cistam, nunc alto culmine montem:
Haud secus argento facili plebs infima ludit.
Quisque tamen gravidas ingenti pondere lamnas
Conficit, aut tenera globulos de mole figurat.
[*ll.156-167*]

In this storeroom is a tank four cubits deep, girded all around with iron hoops, and in the center a spindle equipped with many paddles of bent wood rotates on an axis. This is turned by a swift waterfall or by a mule circling about at a lively pace. Into this is placed for cleansing a quantity of mud, trampled upon so many times in the large courtyard. When water has been introduced from an overhanging conduit and the turbine is whirling swiftly around, the mud, having been thrown in, is rolled around by the rapidly moving waters. But when the turbine has slowly come to rest, gradually the rich silver tends to settle to the bottom, while scum floats on the surface of the water. This a boy pours on the ground by opening a little siphon on the tank. Again he sprinkles with fresh water the mud left in the tank and whirls it around with the revolving paddles, and again he removes scum until the metal, completely purified, lies on the bottom.

Lest, however, some impurity lie concealed in the white substance, the men undertake once more to wash even this in wooden vessels. Having filled these containers with clean water, they now move them slowly in one direction and now swiftly in another, and now they cast from the vessel the waters filled with the impurities until all are driven out, and the pure metal remains in the dry container.

In the meantime there is suspended from a high beam a closely woven linen bag having the shape of a cone and made in such a way as to retain the silver but discharge the quicksilver. This bag is filled with the deposit taken from the basin, and because of its texture tenaciously holds the pure silver but discharges most of the mercury. The men place this in trays and store it away in the house.

When the men have taken the bags from the lofty beam and lowered them to the ground, at last they draw the silver out of the avaricious bosoms, glad to take into their hands the ductile substance and then to amuse themselves by modeling various objects. As a happy group of young children enjoys playing with wax and fashioning simple figures to suit the fancy, now molding in the hand a calf, now making a little vase or a small box, and now again a steep mountain, in like manner the simple folk play in the easily worked silver. Each one, indeed, makes heavy plates or forms little round balls from the soft substance.

Ut vero e globulis possint Hydrargiri abire
Reliquiae, suavis densata in crate locatur
Argenti moles, aerata casside tecta
Et supra pubes Vulcano effundit habenas.
Flexilis hinc flammae vesano massa furore
Argentum vivum subjectis ponit ahenis,
Argento puro, solidoque in crate relicto:
Praemia quae tandem reddit fortuna laboris.
[*ll. 16S-175*]

Flammatis etiam non nunquam turba fluentis
Thesauros sectis educit provida venis,
Arida quod rupes ingenti exusta calore
Saepius imminuat permixta calce talenta.
Hinc limum patula plebes ut chorte madentem
Calcat, et argento perfundit sedula vivo,
Protinus Assyrio latices immittit aheno,
Imponitque atro crepitantibus igne caminis.
Illa tumet subito, clademque minata lebeti
Aestuat, et labris flagrat spumantibus unda.
Tunc tritum pubes infundit prompta metallum,
Arentemque levat limphis ardentibus aestum;
Ut solet interdum versatus Apollinis arte
Febriles calidis ignes compescere thermis.
Pervigil interea limphas examinat arte
Consuetum geminans opifex tentamen aquali,
Qui fidus moli doceat nihil addere limo,
Aut ollam potius replere hydrargyro adaucto.
Cum vero coenum pateris posuisse talenta
Indicat expertus repetito examine crater,
Continuo sordes opifex depromit aheno,
Desuper interdum puero sedante fluentis
Iratam cyatho massam, cyathique furorem.
Divitias fundo lotas tunc cacabus alto
Occulit, et misso cautus sub fonte recondit.
Ast opifex longo cochleari armatus avarum
Invadit cyathum, sensimque evellere fundo
Curat opes, mactraeque simul, quae proxima, donat.
Reliquias limi vitreis tum tergit in undis,
Ac demum argentum flagranti casside purgat.
[*ll. 176-205*]

Si vero solvenda cava fornace metalla
Traxeris e fossis, fornaces construe binas,
Disjunctasque simul longo connecte canali.
Utque graves tulerint abscisso e colle rudentes
Pinguia saxa, terat repetitis machina plagis,
Grandiaque in parvos rescindat frusta lapillos,

Now that the remainder of the mercury may easily separate itself from the grains of silver, a quantity of the soft metal is placed on a closely woven screen and covered with a metal cap over which the men allow Vulcan to have free rein. Then the pliant substance, subjected to the raging violence of the flames, deposits the mercury in kettles placed below, while the silver is left on the screen, pure and solid, the reward which fortune finally renders them for their trouble.

Sometimes, too, the clever workers extract treasures from the severed veins with hot water, for when the dry ore is baked by intense heat it frequently loses its value by fusion with lime. For this reason, when the men have trampled the wet mixture on the spacious floor and carefully drenched it with quicksilver, they immediately place water in a copper boiler and heat it over a roaring fire. Suddenly the water rises, and as if to destroy the container, heaves and boils over the foaming brim. Then they immediately pour in the crushed ore and relieve it of its dryness by the boiling water, as a man skilled in the art of Apollo frequently reduces high fever by the application of hot baths. Meanwhile the specialist, following the usual procedure, tests the water in a pan in order that he may confidently tell his men whether to add nothing more to the soft mud, or to fill the kettle with quicksilver. Now when repeated examinations of the boiler indicate that the mud has deposited its riches on the bottom, immediately the man in charge removes the sediment from the boiler, while a boy, standing near, settles the angry substance in a vessel of water and calms its violence. Then the vessel conceals these elegant riches on its deep bottom underneath the water. But the artisan, provided with a long spoon, invades the avaricious vessel and slowly manages to bring this wealth up from the bottom and immediately places it in an adjoining trough. He then washes the rest of the mud in clear water and finally purifies the silver in a hot crucible.

But if you should extract from the mines metals which have to be smelted in furnaces, construct two separate furnaces and connect them with a long duct. When the heavy cables have brought up the rich ore through the opening in the mountain, let a machine crush it with repeated blows and break the large pieces into

Argenti, atque Auri Opificium

Quos plumbo socio calida in fornace recondas
Desuper aspersis argillae suavis arenis.
Tunc Vulcano omnes plebes immittit habenas,
Quin tamen ignitas effundat nescia prunas
Frusta super: tumidis sed flammae follibus actae
Pervadunt totum, mixto sudante, caminum.
Frustula clausa diu flammisque afflicta tremendis
Mollia solvuntur, rorantque ardentibus undis,
Quae longum penetrant, ceu quondam limpha,
    canalem,
Fornacemque petunt gressu pernice propinquam.
Concava descendit resolutum strata metallum
Torrida jam flammis, cinefactaque arbore tecta.
Follibus acta dein fornacem flamma pererrat,
Pabula cui pueri siccata fronde ministrant,
Dum sordes opifex flammato in fonte natantes
Inde trahit dexter, virgaque educit adunca.
[ll. 206-227]

Interea rutilo liquefacta metalla camino
Ardenti jactata foco cava littora fluctu
Concutiunt, bullitque furens argentea limpha.
Ceu mare, cum valido jactantur flumina vento,
Nunc valles undis aperit, nunc sydera pulsat,
Nunc quatit horrendo curvatas verbere ripas:
Haud aliter flammis argenteus aestuat humor.
Ast ubi colluvies calida fornace recedit,
Torrentique vorax Vulcanus decoquit igne
Argentum, extemplo fundo devolvitur imo
Tota superficies, fluctusque immota serenos
Ostentat: subito folles arcentur, et ignis,
Ac nigra vulgus lamnam fornace revellit.
[ll. 228-240]

Non ita sollicito pueros sudore fatigat
Progenies phoebi, Phoebique simillima proles,
Caeteraque exsuperans Aurum fulgore metalla,
Cui fortuna potens habitare palatia donat,
Augustoque thronum firmare in vertice Regum.
Prae reliquis Aurum mortalia pectora raptat,
Quod dominum citius ditet, parcatque labori.
Vix etenim moles aeratis horrida pilis,
Ac solido trivit pistrinum pondere saxa,
Cum vivum plebes argentum mittit arenis,
Admiscetque gravem sinuata mole per orbem.
Tunc opulenta fluit pretioso terra metallo,
Quod gaudens recipit gremio pistrina profundo.
Hinc tractum pubes immissis abluit undis,
Exprimit ablutum peris, et casside mundat.

small pebbles. Having mixed these with lead, bury them under a sprinkling of soft grains of clay. The men then let Vulcan have free rein, not by foolishly throwing live coals over the pieces of stone, but by allowing flames, stirred by a distended bellows, to pervade the whole chamber, while the mixture exudes drops of moisture. The bits of soft stone, engulfed by the fierce flames and subjected for a long time to extreme torture, melt and run in a molten stream which flows like water into the long duct and hurriedly makes its way into the neighboring furnace. The melted ore sinks to the rounded base of the furnace, already hot beneath the smoldering ashes. Then fanned into a flame with the bellows and fed dry logs by the boys, the fire pervades the furnace, while the director skillfully draws off with a hook the scum which floats on the molten stream.

In the meantime, the melted silver, agitated in the red-hot furnace by the heat of the blazing fire, shakes the round walls with its waves and boils furiously. As the sea, when its waters are agitated by a strong wind, now opens up its waters into valleys, now lashes the stars, and now shakes the curving shores with terrific blows, in like manner the molten silver seethes among the flames. But when the impurities have disappeared from the hot furnace, and ravishing Vulcan has boiled down the silver with his consuming fire, immediately the whole surface sinks to the very bottom, becoming still and calm. At once the bellows are put aside, the fire is removed, and the men take the sheet of silver out of the black furnace.

Gold, on the other hand, does not weary the boys with such distressing toil, gold, a child of Phoebus and similar to Phoebus, surpassing all other metals in splendor. Mighty fortune allows it to inhabit palaces and to be enthroned on the august head of kings. More than all other things gold captivates the heart of mortals, for it more quickly enriches its possessor and frees him from toil. Scarcely indeed has the machine, bristling with metal pounders, and the massive mill crushed the rocks until the men throw mercury over the dust and run it through the heavy rollers of the mill. The mill gladly receives into its deep bosom this rich stream of precious earth. The men then take it out and wash it in water, after which they squeeze it through bags and purify it in a crucible. Just

185

Qualis ubi armatus fertur mucrone maniplus,
Invaditque virum generoso sanguine natum,
Mox aditus circum sepit, septumque fatigat,
Ingeminatque audax ictus, mortemque minatur;
Ille nequit contra telis obsistere turbae,
Sed prudens tantum curat vitare periclum
Audaci subito submittens colla catervae:
Non aliter fulvum Phoebi de stirpe metallum
Crudeli cedit, prona cervice, latroni.
[*ll. 241-264*]

Non nunquam binis etiam de more paratis
Purgabit clarum pubes fornacibus aurum,
Augeat ut quaestum domino, sumptusque recidat.
[*ll. 265-267*]

His ita continuo vulgi sudore peractis,
Argentum tractum, tractumque examinat aurum
Praepositus curis Hispano ab Principe missus.
Hic parvos globulos lamnam glomerabit in unam,
Indeque mordaci convulsum forcipe frustum
(Quod sibi pro digna curae mercede reservat)
Igne probat, quantumque rapax absconderit auri
Argentum proprio commixti pondere, noscit.
Mox auri pretium pariter perpendit in igne,
Et quintam Sceptro partem de jure reponit.
Unde sigillata argentique, aurique metalla
Continuo dominus caute sub tecta recondit.
[*ll. 268-279*]

Si tamen ipse velis fugitivos cudere nummos,
Est opus argentum primum divellere ab auro
Albaque luteolis removere metalla metallis,
Arte viam ductante novam, flammisque ministris.
Nec tamen ipse tuas poteris secernere gazas:
Nulli quippe licet doctum exercere laborem
Servatum lectis augusto ab Rege ministris.
[*ll. 280-286*]

Grandibus haec lamnis argenti turba receptis
Accingunt operi. Pars frondes admovet igni,
Pars vitreas lamnis ampullas deligit aptas,
Et pars suppeditat flumen rodentis aquai.
Frustula mox lamnae Stygiis commixta fluentis
Excipit in vitreum tumefacta cucurbita ventrem,
Sedula cui prunas pubes supponit edaces,
Et magnis acuit succensum follibus ignem.
Intus aquae fervent, pretiosaque frustula rodunt,
Argentum donec, resoluta mole, liquescat,
Percurratque nitens spumanti flumine vitrum.

as when armed men while marching along attack a man of noble birth, immediately cut off every avenue of escape, and torment the besieged man, wantonly striking him again and again and threatening death, but he, unable to resist the weapons of the crowd, wisely tries to escape such danger by promptly submitting his neck to the insolent band, so it is that the golden metal, descended from Phoebus, yields with bended head to the merciless thief.

Sometimes, too, the men will refine the sparkling gold in double furnaces, arranged in proper manner, to increase the master's profits and reduce the cost.

When these operations have been completed through the persistent efforts of the men, an inspector, sent by the king of Spain, examines the extracted silver and gold. He rolls the small pellets into a single plate, and from this he snips off with his stout pincers a small piece which he keeps for himself as a fitting reward for his trouble. This he tests in the fire, and he determines how much gold the greedy silver has appropriated and concealed within its own mass. Then in the same manner he tests with fire the value of the gold and duly sets aside a fifth part for the crown. As soon as the pieces of gold and silver have been stamped, the overseer carefully hides them in a safe place.

But if you yourself should wish to coin money, a fleeting possession, you must first separate the silver from the gold, the white metal from the yellow, using new scientific methods and assisted by fire. Yet you will not be able to set your treasures apart for yourself, since no one is permitted to perform this exacting work except ministers chosen by his majesty, the king.

This staff, having received the large plates of silver, sets to work. Some bring wood for the fire, others select appropriate glass beakers for the plates, and still others provide acid. Soon the bulging glass receives into its belly pieces of metal along with Stygian water. Under this the busy men place live coals and make a hot fire with the help of a large bellows. The waters boil within and eat away the precious particles until the silver, breaking apart and going into solution, moves through the glistening glass in a foaming stream. Then an expert hand stretches

186

Provida tunc cupreum portendit dextra bacillum,
Immissaeque vitri scite per colla retorti
Ardentem virgae contingit cuspide massam.
Illico fervescens intus (mirabile visu!)
Massa ruit praeceps, aestusque repente quiescit.
Ima petit purum calidis sub fluctibus aurum,
Argentumque tenet flavo propiora metallo,
Desuper illuvie, ac limphis, cuproque relictis.
Ut vero vitrum semotis ignibus alget,
Disjunctas lamnas, secta compage, recludit,
Ac finem tanto ponit fortuna labori.

[*ll. 287-308*]

FINIS LIBRI OCTAVI

forth a copper rod, inserts it carefully into the neck of the glass retort, and touches the hot substance with the point. Thereupon—wonderful to behold!—the substance boiling furiously inside falls and suddenly ceases its boiling. Pure gold settles to the bottom under the hot liquid, and silver occupies a position next to the yellow metal, while scum, water, and copper remain on top. Now when the fire has been removed and the glass has cooled, the separate layers of different composition are revealed, and fortune brings to an end the wearisome task.

SACCHARUM

Secretas telluris opes, opulentaque terrae
Viscera vulgus amet. Luteis me dulcia formis
Cogere mella juvat: non quae Sicania campis
Carpit apes, truncisque cavis studiosa recondit;
Sed quae Mexiceus praelis expressa colonus
Atque recepta cadis igni condensat ahenis,
Fictilibusque trahit candentia sacchara conis.
[*ll. 1-7*]

Tu, puer, incurvi solers monstrator aratri,
Rustica qui validos formas ad munia tauros,
Adsis, O! ruptisque agris, glebisque subactis,
Semina nectareae sulcis deponere cannae,[1]
Flaventesque dein segetes prosternere falce
Instrue; et aurato spumantia dolia melle
Candida coctilibus metis in sacchara verte.
[*ll. 8-14*]

Melligenis postquam calamis legit arva serendis,
Aut nemus exurit flamma crepitante colonus,
Continuo fortes, lectique ad aratra juvenci
Proscindunt altis felicia jugera sulcis
Et patulos volvunt repetito vomere campos.
Omnis hiat sulcus fossamque ostentat apertam
Usque pedes binos; ubi tres, aut quinque recumbant
Saccharei nodi, si campi gleba maligna
Germina rara ferat, cultumque ingrata recuset.
Nam quo terra magis succo languescit inerti,
Hoc mage mellita repletur arundine sulcus,
Quin densis vestita comis canneta recondat,
Prolixaeque premant nascentia germina frondes.
[*ll. 15-27*]

Elicibus crebro sudore, atque arte reclusis,
Africa turba cutem ferventi Sole perusta,
Viribus insignis, duroque infracta labore,
Torrida quam nobis mittit Nasamonia tellus[2]
Melligeros rastris culturam jugiter agros,
Ilicet ac luces aequabit Libra tenebris,
Maturis cultro cannis extrema recidit,
Queis foliata parat fessis alimenta juvencis.
Inde aliud truncat geminato vulnere fragmen,
Absconditque solo, ceu quondam semen, aperto;
Non rectos, ut saepe recens defigitur hortis
Talea; sed tensos calamos per rura serendo.[3]
Hinc tria (vel quatuor) cannae fragmenta recisae

SUGAR

The treasures hidden in the bowels of the rich earth may be the delight of the crowd. My delight is found in condensing sweet honey in earthen molds, not what the Sicilian bee gathers in the fields and industriously stores in the hollow trunks of trees, but what the Mexican planter, having pressed in the mill and condensed in copper kettles over the fire, takes as white sugar from cone-shaped molds of clay.

Come, O boy, skilled master of the bent plow, who train the sturdy oxen to perform their rural tasks, and when the ground has been broken and the soil prepared, show me how to lay in furrows the seeds of sugar cane,[1] then to cut the golden harvest with the sickle, and turn the foaming jars of golden honey into pure white sugar in the earthen molds.

After the farmer has selected the fields in which he wishes to plant the sweet stalks of cane, or has cleared with a crackling fire his wooded land, at once the sturdy oxen, chosen for the plow, cleave the fertile acres with deep furrows and with the plowshare continue to turn over the surface of the broad fields. Each furrow lies open forming a trench about two feet wide in which three or even five joints of sugar cane may lie, if the soil, being poor, should yield few shoots or be loath to respond to cultivation. For the weaker the soil through lack of vital juices, the more do they fill the furrow with the honeysweet stalks of cane, without, however, burying the field under a thick covering of stalks or letting their rank foliage smother the newborn sprouts.

Irrigation canals are skillfully opened with great toil; and Africans, with skin scorched by the blazing sun, noted for their strength and undaunted by hard work, whom the torrid land of Libya[2] sends to us to work unceasingly on the sugar plantations, as soon as Libra makes equal the days and nights,[2a] cut off with knives the leafy tops of the ripened cane to feed their weary oxen. Then again, they cut off another section which they bury in the furrowed earth as formerly they did the seed, planting the stalks throughout the fields, not uprightly as a young plant is usually set in the garden, but horizontally.[3] Hence they throw along the ground three or four cuttings of cane, spacing them alternately

Saccharum

Sternit humi, ac fossis altis sejuncta vicissim
Componit, ternoque simul locat ordine dextra.
Mox alias aliis directo limite cannas,
Extremis extrema addens, ac frustula frustis,
Adjungit. Quales pugnae discrimine adactus
nstruit aeratas mira Dux arte phalanges,
Partiturque sagax, ac terno milite densat.
Jt vero dulci complevit germine sulcos
Turba, supinatas fossam devolvit in altam
Jlebas, obducitque omnem velamine terrae;
Quin tamen obductas glebarum pondere plantas
Opprimat, atque adeo messes incauta retardet.
Jnde manu terram sensim componit avara
Absconditque levi diffusas cespite avenas.

[ll. 28-54]

Postera cum tenebras reparato lumine pellit
Jlara dies, formamque orbi cum Sole reducit,
Continuo rivi propter canneta fluentis
Jursum promptus agit celerem super arva colonus,
Astutusque vetat proprio ruere impete limphas,
Viscera ne campi rapiant, ac semina nudent;
Sed tenui rorat praegnantes murmure glebas
Consulto patiens, unda stagnante, liquorem
Pingui tranquillum longum tellure morari,
Arva quoad fusum rivum madefacta recusent.
Quod si terra vagis obsistat prava fluentis
Ac riguum sorbere amnem durata negarit,
Saepius arentes rorabit flumine campos,
Jermina dum videat ventrem abrumpere terrae,
Jugeraque umbrosa late pubescere fronde.

[ll. 55-69]

Roscida sed tandem, ter quinis lucibus actis,
Juxurie canneta videns velata comanti,
Ac totum teneris vestitum frondibus agrum,
Protinus Afra manus propriis accingitur armis,
Et curva runcare parat sata laeta securi,
Rustica ne faetus accrescens herba novellos
(Ut solet interdum furiis agitata noverca)
Suffocet, nocuosque tegat longo agmine mures.
Hinc terram videas totam nigrescere turba,
Inque atrum subito viridem mutare colorem.
Torrida namque amplum pubes diffusa per agrum
Runcat inexhaustis canneta virentia curis
Atque imis nocuam vellit radicibus herbam,
Luxuriare sinens nascentia germina plantae.
Mox iterum recreat ductis per jugera rivis,

in the deep furrows and carefully arranging them at the same time in rows of three. Then they join these stalks to one another in a straight line putting them end to end, and section to section, as a general, forced by the peril of battle, draws up with remarkable skill his heavily-armed lines, wisely dividing them and assembling them in triple line of battle. And when they have filled the furrows with the sweet seed, they roll the soil back into the deep trench, completely covering the plants with a mantle of earth; yet not to crush them by the weight of the soil and thus heedlessly delay the harvest. Hence, gently and with a sparing hand they arrange the soil over the scattered cuttings and bury them under a light coat of earth.

When the following day, aglow with renewed light, is dispelling the darkness and restoring to the earth its beauty and sunlight, straightway the farmer quickly diverts to his cane fields the current of a nearby stream, yet wisely preventing the waters from rushing along by their own force, lest they disembowel the field and lay bare the seeds. But with a gently murmuring stream he waters the fertile soil, purposely allowing the calm waters to linger for a long time in pools over the rich land until the soaked earth refuses the flow of water. But should the perverse earth withstand the wandering rivulets and stubbornly refuse to absorb the moisture, he will more often soak the dry fields until he sees the seeds bursting through the belly of the earth and his acres covered everywhere with shady leaves.

But when at last, after a fortnight, the Africans see a profusion of blades bedecking the moist field and covering it with new leaves, they straightway provide themselves with their own special implement, the curved hoe, and set themselves to the task of weeding the growing plants, lest weeds spring up and choke the tender young (as a stepmother sometimes does when driven by the furies), and shelter whole armies of destructive mice. Hence you will see the whole landscape darkened by the multitude, and the green field suddenly changing to black. Indeed, these sunburned people, scattered over the wide field, weed the green cane with infinite care, pulling out injurious plants by the roots and allowing the young sprouts to grow profusely. Then they again release refreshing streams of water over the ground, and again they remove the tares springing up from the

189

Et rursus lolium faecunda ex matre renascens
Arripit, alternoque diu colit arva labore,
Luteolis donec sylvescat campus avenis.
Tunc longis horrere hastis mirabere sulcos
Ruraque duratis circum frondere sagittis.
Ceu quondam natae serpentis dente cohortes
Prosiluere, satis abruptis cuspide terris,
Torquentes manibus primum lucentia teli
Spicula: tum pinus ferrum deduxit in auras,
Gramine dum medio tandem consurgeret hasta,
Horrentemque daret segetem, sylvamque minantem:
Haud aliter dulces pubescunt aequore messes
Inque hastas abeunt longas, dum Luna per orbem
Ardua protendit bis nono cornua motu.[4]

[*ll. 70-98*]

Post, ubi luteolis messis maturuit hastis,
Ambrosioque tubos succo replevit arista,
Impigra frondosum rursus dispersa per arvum
Armatos pubes invadit falce maniplos
Ac totam moesto populatur funere terram.
Pars densum caedit geminatis ictibus agmen,
Pars caeso currus onerat, pars urget onustos,
Pallida arundineo rorantes sanguine rura,
Indulgentque omnes, vel coelo ardente, labori.
Africa sed pubes Phoebo vexata furenti
Illudit dulci Solaria tela liquore,
Quem morsu compressa dedit sylvestris arundo.
Dente potens calamos ingrato cortice nudat,
Et niveam retegens, ceu cultro armata, medullam
Robore sub nigro contritam ruminat ore,
Expressoque levans arentes flumine fauces
Lethiferum pellit tetro de corpore Phoebum.
Tu tamen aestivo Titanis torridus aestu
Nectareo siquando velis te pascere succo,
Flaventes potius solers tibi delige cannas:
Ac primum nudare stude candentia cultro
Viscera, corticibus crudis, foliisque recisis:
Mox in frusta seca, crebrisque a fuste remotis
Articulis, dulces placido trahe dente liquores,
Et flammis combusta feris praecordia leni.

[*ll. 99-123*]

Haec animo secum reputans incautus ephebus
Praesentis vana deceptus imagine lucri

teeming mother-earth, and for a long time the
tend the fields, alternating their work until th
ground is thickly covered with golden can
Then you will marvel at the furrows bristlin
with long spears and the countryside yieldin
stiff arrows on every side. As once a company o
armed men, born from the teeth of a serpen
sprang out of the earth, having broken throug
with the point of their spears, and brandishe
in their hands first the gleaming tips, the
lifted into the air the steel shafts until at las
spears were rising up all over the middle of th
greensward, yielding a terrifying crop and
menacing forest of weapons, in like manner, a
the harvests of sugar cane mature in the fiel
they produce long spears until the time whe
the moon is extending its horns far up in th
sky for the eighteenth time.[4]

Afterwards, when the yellow stems are read
for harvest and loaded with ambrosial juic
the workmen again quickly deploy over th
thick-leafed field, assail with sickles these arme
divisions, and devastate all the land wit
grievous destruction. Some with repeated blow
cut down thick clumps of cane, others lift the
into the wagons, while others drive the loade
wagons away; and the blood of the cane mean
while drips on the pale earth. Everyone applie
himself to the work, though the weather be ho
But the Africans, when plagued by the ragin
heat of Phoebus, mock the sun's rays by th
sweet liquor which the cane gives up whe
crushed by the teeth. With a powerful grip c
the teeth they strip the bitter bark from th
cane, laying bare the gleaming white marrow a
if with a knife. In their powerful black cheek
they chew it, thus relieving the dryness in the
throats by the extraction of the juice and pr
tecting their sweating bodies from the dead
rays of the sun. And you too, if ever you shoul
be parched by the heat of the summer sun an
should desire to feast upon the nectarean juic
carefully select for yourself the yellow cane
First take pains to lay bare the white center b
peeling off the coarse rind with a knife an
stripping off the leaves. Then, having cut it in
small pieces and removed from the stem i
numerous nodes, gently extract the sweet liqu
with your teeth and refresh your body consume
by the terrific heat.

Heedless young men, considering these ma
ters and deceived by the false appearance c
immediate profit, have their men despoil th

Saccharum

Melligero spoliare jubet canneta decore
Juncta simul, nodosque omnes submittere praelo;
Quin tantam possit deinceps reparare ruinam,
Divitias quamvis breviori tempore multas
Cogat. Nam siccum corrumpunt otia praelum,
Totaque tranquillo torpet languore juventus.
Quare usu doctus longo sua praela colonus
Cautus arundineo durat sudantia melle,
Alternisque jubet ferro exercere novales:
Ut cum flava seges agris'percussa recumbat,
Altera luxurians una se tollat in auras,
Tertiaque effuso sensim de semine surgat;
Ut densata cadis exsudent mella quotannis
[ll. 124-138]

5Sed prius aurato roret quam dulcis arundo
Nectare, tecta subit magno latissima gyro,
Fortis ubi grandi consurgit machina mole
Fixa solo penitus, ternisque extructa cylindris (a)
Aere coronatis, solidoque ex robore sectis.
Quisque petit coelum verso in sublimia collo (d),
Arrectusque terit proprio revolubilis axe
Subjectum pontem (b) robusta ex arbore scissum,6
Cui grandis tumulata solo submittitur arca, (c)
Hospitio dulces large exceptura liquores.
Sed tenues adeo sylvestria tigna trapetum
Recludunt aditus, ut tergis terga propinquis
Immineant, digitumque queant urgere rotata.
Tum vero medius, surgit qui ponte, cylinder
Dentibus infractis horret, quibus ipse volutus
Admordet reliquos, unaque intorquet in orbem.
Nam quamvis alii vix collo (d) tigna (e) superna
(Machina queis acri firmatur concita motu)
Vincant, ast proprium medius (f) protendit in altum,
Rumpereque axe domus prolixo tecta minatur.
Inde trabes (g) binae compactae mordicus axi
In terras obliqua fluunt, terraeque propinquant,
Ut circum flexae praecinctis pectora (h) mulis
Immensos glomerent gyros, secumque revolvant
Aeriis spiris axem, mediumque cylindrum;
Qui reliquos juxta mordaci dente premendo
Inflectat, magnoque omnes stridore rotentur.
[ll. 139-165]

7Si tamen ipse velis robustis parcere mulis
Atque minore graves sumptu versare trapetes,
Flumina convolvant gravido labentia casu,

cane fields of their melliferous glory all at the same time and put all the cane through the press without being able afterwards to repair such a ruinous loss, although they may accumulate great riches in a shorter time. For idleness dries out and ruins the press, and all the boys become demoralized by continued inactivity. Therefore the wise planter,schooled by long experience, keeps his presses wet with the honey which oozes from the cane, and orders his men to plow the land at alternate times in order that when a yellow harvest is cut and lies on the fields another lush crop may at the same time be lifting itself high into the air, and a third may be slowly coming up from the scattered seed, so that every year the condensed syrup may distil from the tanks.

5But before the sweet cane gives up its golden nectar, it is brought under a large circular shed, where stands a large and very heavy machine firmly fastened to the ground and provided with three rollers (a) hewed out of solid oak and incased in metal. Each one stands in an upright position with a high upturned neck (d) and revolves vertically on its own axis which rests on a bridge (b) below, cut from sturdy timber.6 Underneath is placed a large tank (c) buried in the ground to receive freely the sweet liquors. Now the wooden rollers of the mill are so close together that each is joined back to back to the one next to it, and rotating, they can crush a finger. Moreover, the middle roller which extends from the bridge bristles with stout teeth with which, when rotated, it clutches the others and turns them around along with it. For although the necks (d) of the other two barely extend higher than the top beam (e) by which the machine is held secure when in rapid motion, the middle one (f), on the other hand, extends very high, almost bursting through the roof with its long shaft. From this two poles (g), securely fastened to the shaft, fall in an oblique direction almost to the ground, so that when fastened to the breasts of mules (h) and turned around, they describe immense circles, and as they revolve at the top they cause the axle and the middle roller to rotate along with them. This middle roller sets in motion the other adjacent to it by sinking its sharp teeth into them, and they rotate with a loud creaking sound.

7But if you should wish to spare the sturdy mules and run the heavy presses with less expense, let streams of water turn the rollers with the full weight of their fall. Having entirely

191

Trapetum commune.

L.C.f.

Fig. 1.   Mule-drawn sugar mill

Et trabibus prorsus frendenti ab mole remotis,
Orbita (*a*) tunc axem (*b*) tignis compacta profusum
Ambiat, aeriumque adeo diffusa per orbem
Dentibus in terram versis volet aspera circum
Aere renidenti, ferratisque orbibus arcta,
Ac totum vacuo praelum librata coronet.
Sed simul ingentem praeli extra tecta repostam
Ingenio compone rotam (*c*), quam plurima parvis
Capsula (*d*) distinguat circum penetralibus auctam,
Excipiatque ruens constanti flumen (*e*) hiatu.
Hanc vero mediam transfigat fervidus axis (*f*)
Aere laboratus, studioque politus ad unguem,
Quique rotam duplici sublatam cardine verset,
Ac longo mucrone domus penetralia lustret.
Inde axis longa producti cuspide cinge
Extremum breviore rota (*g*), quae dentibus usque
Duratis ferro dentes admordeat orbis
Aere librati medio, qui praela coronat.
Ocyus ipse undis objecta repagula tolle,
Libera ut ingenti volvantur flumina casu,
Quae magnam violenta rotam, laevemque volutent
Axem: et continuo miraberis axe rotato
Et minimum sinuari orbem glomeramine lento,
Et morsu torquere rotam per inane volantem,
Murmure quam magno confestim praela sequuntur.

[*ll. 166-193*]

Interea vectas utraque ex parte juventus
Irrequieta gravi praelo submittit avenas,
Incumbitque vigil noctesque diesque labori.
Hic cannas rimis flaventes ingerit arctis,
Ille studet pressis iterum complere meatus,
Et fractos calamos prorsus siccare premendo,
Frustula dum rigidi reddant exsucta trapetes,
Exuviasque rogis exhausto humore pararint.
Sacchareum rorat subjectam flumen (*i*) in arcam (*h*),
Ac totum limphis circum spumantibus undat.
Vae tamen huic, digitos cui moles forte momordit!
Quippe manus digitos sequitur, sequiturque lacertus,
Integrumque dein abducunt brachia corpus.
Tunc opus est retro mulas agitare per orbem,
Aut labentis aquae subito compescere pondus,
Seu potius ferro cubitum rescindere pressum,
Ne fera dente terat crudeli machina corpus.
Ah! quoties fato truncati membra maligno
Indolui sortem transfixus saeva dolore!
Hinc decet alternis nocturnum fallere somnum
Vocibus, aut vigiles noctes aequare canendo.

[*ll. 194-214*]

removed the poles from the creaking structure, let a wheel (*a*), supported by braces, encircle the long axle (*b*), and as it reaches far around in the air, rough with teeth pointing to the ground and incased in a metal rim, let it rotate and, as it hangs suspended in mid air, let it crown the entire press. And, at the same time, skillfully mount a large wheel (*c*) outside the building, providing it all the way around with many small cups (*d*) to receive constantly the flow of water (*e*) as it falls into their wide-open mouths. Through the center of this wheel let there be transfixed a strong axle (*f*), made of brass and polished to perfection, and such that it will cause the elevated wheel to rotate on its two pivots as it extends far into the building. And then install on the end of this long shaft a smaller wheel (*g*), provided with metal teeth interlocking with those on the wheel which hangs in the air to crown the press. Quickly lift the retaining gates to permit the streams to flow freely down with a heavy fall and cause the large wheel with its smooth axle to rotate; and immediately you will be amazed to see, as the axle rotates, the small wheel also slowly turning and engaging the wheel suspended in the air, which in turn is immediately followed by the rumbling presses.

In the meantime boys stand on either side and keep feeding the cane into the heavy presses, diligently devoting themselves to the work day and night. One pushes the yellow stalks of cane through the narrow opening, another promptly feeds them back into the mill, and by pressing the crushed cane they extract all the juice until bagasse is discharged from the relentless machine which, when thoroughly dried, provides fuel for the fire. The sweet juice (*i*) flows into the receiving pan (*h*) below and is entirely covered with foam. But woe to that one whose fingers are accidentally caught in the mill! For indeed the hand follows the fingers, and then the arm, and finally the whole body is dragged in by the arm. It is necessary in such a case to reverse the direction of the mules, or suddenly to stop the fall of water, or rather to amputate the crushed member, lest the cruel machine grind the body between its fierce teeth. Ah! how many times have I been stricken with grief and bitterly mourned the misfortune of one who suffered the loss of his limbs. It is important, therefore, for them to avoid falling asleep at night by carrying on conversations, or to keep awake through the night by singing.

Trapetum aquarium.

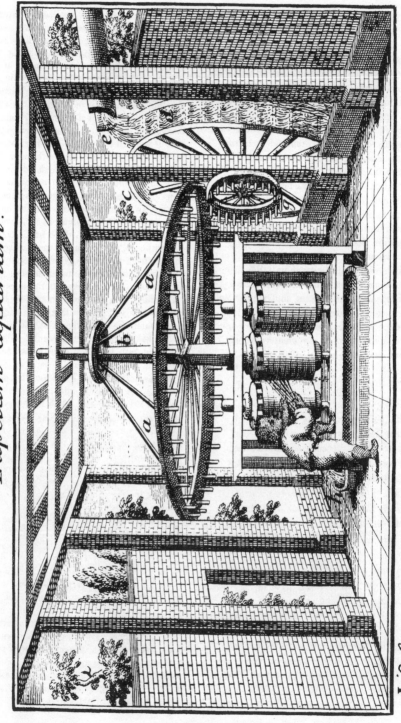

L.C.f.

Fig. 2.   Water-run sugar mill

Haec ubi sacchareo sudarunt praela liquore,
Iactraque spumosis exundat lignea labris,
nde per oblongum dulcis deducta canalem
Jnda fluit, praecepsque petit, ceu rivus, ahenum
'ornice suspensum, flammaeque ardore perustum,
ngenti quod mole domus vicina recepit.
Iontinuo succus magno exultare furore
Iorrida concutiens undanti littora fluctu,
'erventesque diu faeces innare per undas.
'rovidus ast totam cribro capulator amuream
Igerit, ac versans turpatum flumen ab imo
nnanti rursum detergit dolia sorde.
Illa dein gremio latices vicina resumit
Ardentemque iterum Vulcano exasperat iram;
Iedula queis pubes toties lixivia miscet,
nfectis quoties sordes innaverit undis.
Iunc magnis videas bullis canescere mella
Iaecibus immixtis, queis nuper flamma pepercit.
Namque furens subito purgant lixivia flumen,
Et minimas etiam sordes super aequora jactant.
Non tamen has opifex longum sinit ire per aequor:
Quin potius creber fluitantes egerit alto,
Pura quoad rutilans aurato limpha nitore
Inde alium subeat, cyathis capulata, lebetem.
Sed cave, ne calido largus lixivia melli
Plus aequo infundas: aspris onerata fluentis
Mordicus obscurum retinebunt mella colorem,
Quem nunquam mollis potis est abstergere creta.
[*ll. 215-242*]

Ut vero purum cannarum tertia succum
Excipit olla sinu, subjectis frondibus ignem
Integrat ingentem pubes, purgataque nuper
Addensare studet renovatis mella caminis.
Quare opifex magnum promptus cochleare recludit
Longo munitum capulo, quod dextra juventus
Versat utraque manu, laticesque attenta revolvit,
Nunc calidum summo confundens aequor ab imo,
Nunc superas tollens, fumo volitante, per auras.
Tum gyros nectit, cyathumque evolvit in orbem,
Et rursus coelo limpham jacit illa volutam.
Scilicet impulsu dextrae jactata frequenti
Densantur citius, coeuntque fluentia mella.
[*ll. 243-255*]

Post, ubi limpha cado sistit densata sub alto
Inque atros ex parte abiit tenuata vapores,
Protinus in gelidum rursus capulatur ahenum
Totque cremata rogis tandem refrigerat aestum.
Ut solet aestivo Titane viator adustus

When the presses have distilled the saccharine liquor, and foam is pouring over the sides of the wooden receiver, then the sweet fluid is made to flow through a long pipe and quickly empty into a large boiler suspended from the archway of a large house nearby, and heated over a hot fire. At once the juice dances with great agitation, shaking the walls of the hot vessel with its surging billows, and hot scum floats for a long time on the waves. An attendant, however, carefully strains all this off, and having stirred the murky liquid from the bottom, he again clears off the floating scum. A kettle standing nearby then receives the liquid into its bosom, which again provokes the fierce wrath of Vulcan. Into this the boys carefully mix lye as often as scum floats on the discolored fluid. Then you can see the syrup forming large white bubbles combining with the impurities which shortly before escaped the fire. For the lye immediately clears the raging liquid and brings even the slightest impurities to the surface. But the men do not allow these to remain long on the surface, but keep drawing off the floating matter from the surface until the pure liquid, sparkling with a golden splendor, is transferred by ladles into another vessel. But be careful not to pour lye into the hot syrup more generously than is proper, for if the caustic solution is added in excess, it will retain a dark color which soft clay can never remove.

Now when a third vessel has received into its bosom the clear sweet juice of the cane, the men bring sticks and build another hot fire, and then they diligently undertake to condense the sweet liquor, which was just purified, by reheating. For this purpose the manager promptly provides a large spoon with a long handle, which a skillful young man turns with both his hands as he carefully stirs the liquid, now mixing the hot substance from the bottom to the top, now lifting it high into the air amidst wreaths of steam. Then turning the ladle in a circular motion he weaves circles and flings the whirling liquid up again, for the sweet liquor condenses and thickens more quickly by repeated stirring and beating.

When the water has finally thickened and settled in the deep vessel, and the volatile matter has in part disappeared into black vapor, they immediately pour it again into a cold kettle and allow it at last to become cool, having been heated so many times over the fire. As a sun-

Algentes intrare umbras, aestumque levare:
Haud aliter rigido mellita excepta lebetp
Juscula ferventem ponunt tepefacta calorem,
Incipiuntque gelu sensim concrescere cupri,
Ac gluten densata dein, viscumque referre.

[*ll. 256-265*]

Interea pubes magnum glomerabit acervum
Fictilibus structum formis, ardente recoctis
Vulcano, quarum reserata foramine cuspis
Sidat humi, coelumque basis satis ampla requirat.
Hinc primum creta praecludit dextra foramen,
Asseribusque locat bifidis recto ordine formas,
Cuspide ut inde fluant stillantia mella reclusa.
Tum densum formis condit cochleare liquorem
Sepositumque sinit contracto frigore cogi.
Haec ubi coctilibus conis compacta residunt
Sacchara, nec cyathis latices undare videntur,
Continuo metae, conversa cuspide sursum,
Obstrusi primum parvi reserantur hiatus,
Sacchareumque uterum ferro terebrare laborat
Palmari pubes, non dum coeunte repurget
Ut formas humore omnem fluitante per alvum.
Hac siquidem proprio devexus pondere rorat,
Exceptusque cadis alios servatur in usus.

[*ll. 266-283*]

Non tamen albescent fulgenti pura nitore
Sacchara, ni creta conum velaveris atra.
Idcirco argilla, vitreo jam fonte liquata,
Tinge superficiem metae, crustaque madenti
Saepius ora basis nuper densata reconde.
Omnia creta subit dulcis penetralia coni,
Visceraque interius mundat, mellisque fluentis
Reliquias toto demum de corpore pellit,
Candida vicenis exactis lucibus ora
Recludens, niveoque ferens ornata colore.
Quis tamen haec, Musae, nobis arcana retexit?
Unde homines traxere artis primordia tantae?
Fertur in aurato cono lutulenta columba
Turpatos fixisse pedes, rostroque frequenti
Tenuia frusta dein mellis praedata coacti:
Mox vero furto volucris, dapibusque potita
Aethera supremum pennis petiisse fugata
Sordida luteolo linquens vestigia cono;
Quae sensim Phoebi radiis exsucta furentis
Induerant niveum, dudum fuscata, colorem.
Scilicet arcano detecto furta rependit
Dulcis avis, docuitque luto canescere formas.

burned traveler is wont to go into the cool shade
and find relief from the heat, in the same manner the honey-sweet juices that have been heated, when received into the cold vessel, become cool and gradually begin to condense in the chilly environment of the copper, and con densed, they resemble glue or birdlime.

In the meantime, the men assemble a large pile of fire-baked clay molds, the pointed ends of which, being open, rest on the ground, while the wide base extends upward. Then, first of all they carefully seal the holes with clay and place the molds in a straight row along a split log in order that, when the sharp end is again opened up, the honeysweet liquor may drip through Then with a spoon they dip the thick substance into the molds, and putting it aside, allow it in cooling to coagulate. When thick sugar settles in the earthen cones, and no longer any liquid is seen oozing out, at once the ends of the cones are turned up, the little openings, which at first were sealed, are opened, and the men proceed to bore into the center of the sugar a few inches to remove from the molds any fluid matter not yet crystallized, for it then flows out carried by its own weight. This is received into vessels and kept for other uses.

But not yet will the sugar be clear and shine with a white luster unless you cover the cone with dark clay. For this reason moisten the surface of the cone with a layer of clay soaked in clear water, and when this has hardened, add other layers. The clay penetrates the whole interior of the sweet cone, purifies the contents, and finally drives from the entire mass the rest of the sweet water, revealing after twenty days a bright and snowy white surface. But who, O Muses, revealed to us these secrets? From what source have men derived the knowledge of such an art? It is said that a dove, bedaubed with mud, planted her dirty feet on a golden cone, and then, by pecking and pecking, pilfered tiny bits of the crystallized sweets. Whereupon the bird, having finished her stolen meal, soared high into the air in flight, leaving behind dirty tracks on the yellow cone. When these had slowly dried under the fierce rays of the sun, though they had been dark before, they had assumed a snow-white color. Indeed the kindly bird repaid her theft by revealing the secret, and she showed how to bleach the molds of sugar with mud. So

Non secus atque olim rigido Conchylia morsu
Forte premens catulus perfudit murice rictum,
Purpureoque dedit vestes fucare veneno.

[*ll. 284-308*]

Post, ubi canescunt repetito sacchara limo
albaque nigrantes posuerunt ventre liquores,
Fulgenti sub Sole locat tabulata juventus,
Atque relegatis luteis in limina metis,
Desuper imponit candentes sedula conos
Marmora pyramidum simulantes alta Canopi.
Tota repercussis radiis argentea massa
Clara micat, circumque almo vestita nitore
Errantes fulgore oculos perstringit acuto.
Sol teneras penetrat sensim fervore medullas
Ac pulso penitus candenti ab mole madore,
Quem reliquum limus conclusa fecerat alvo,
Indurat prorsus, conosque in marmora vertit.

[*ll. 309-321*]

Ut tamen incertos flectat solertia casus,
Et nocui possint detrudi finibus hostes,
Dives inaccessis praecingitur area muris
Mobilibus velata super sine pondere tectis.
Exiguis instructa rotis vaga tecta per amplos
Discurrunt muros; longoque agitata rudenti
Nunc Austrum motu tepidum veloce sequuntur,
Nunc gelidum repetunt Septem-regressa-trionem.
Hisce locat pubes tectis tabulata sub altis,
Quae duro tolerent urgentia sacchara tergo.
Cum vero Phoebus, nimbis ardore fugatis,
Extollit claro fulgentem lampada coelo,
Ilicet illa trahit tereti laquearia fune,
Albentesque nivis conos candore revelat.
Si tamen e nigris impendat nubibus imber,
Tecta trahens retro, fune in contraria ducto,
Marmora densatis obducit cana tenebris.
Ast, ubi fumantem repetito Sole madorem
Expulit, et coni tenues trusere vapores,
Confestim niveas in cellam turba reponit
Pyramides, concisa legit fragmenta, domumque
Divitiis replet magno sudore paratis,
Ampla quibus faustae tollit commercia terrae,
Lucraque dives herus, pretium sudoris, adeptus
Delicias largus mensis Regalibus offert.

[*ll. 322-346*]

it was that once upon a time a pup, accidentally clutching with his tenacious teeth a purple shellfish, smeared his jaws with purple juice and showed how to color clothes with purple dye.[8]

When by repeated applications of clay the sugar has turned white, having given up its black liquors, the boys then erect platforms under the bright sun; on these, after removing the clay forms to the inside of the house, they carefully place the cones glistening like the mighty marble pyramids of Egypt. The entire silvery mass reflects the rays of the sun and shines brightly, enveloped in a glorious sheen which by its intense brightness dazzles the eyes which glance in its direction. The warmth of the sun gradually penetrates the soft inner part, driving out all the moisture which the clay had allowed to remain in its innermost bosom and turning the cones throughout into marble-like hardness.

Now that ingenuity may avert the uncertainties of fortune and dangerous enemies be kept from the country, the rich area is surrounded by impenetrable walls and covered overhead with a light movable roof. This adjustable roof, provided with small rollers and propelled by a long rope, runs back and forth along the great walls, swiftly following at one time the warm south wind, at another time going in reverse direction toward the cold north. Under this high roof the men place the platforms which support the heavy sugar on their strong backs. Now when Phoebus has chased away the clouds with his warmth and is lifting his glowing torch into the bright sky, then with the stout rope they draw back the canopy and uncover the cones becoming white as snow. But if from out the black clouds rain should threaten, they pull the rope in the opposite direction and draw the roof back again, enveloping the white marble in dense darkness. When, however, the sunshine has returned again and driven out the steaming moisture, and the cones have thrust off the light vapors, at once the company of workers put the snow-white pyramids back into the storeroom, they gather up the broken fragments, and with great effort fill the house with riches by which they lavishly extend the commerce of the prosperous land. The wealthy lord, having made profitable gains in return for his toils, generously provides delicacies for the tables of kings.

Sed prius umbrosam penetrent quam sacchara
   cellam,
Saepe vorax sylva lapsus latrunculus atra
Invadit Turdus candentia frustula rostro.
At miranda tibi solertia rara volucris.
Ille rapit furtim mellis fragmenta coacti:
Ne tamen haec tenues corrodant aspera fauces,
Sed delapsa fluant guttur resoluta per altum,
Saepe sagax ales undis intingere visus.
Ore tenens furtum nunc purum mergit in amnem,
Nunc rectus sorbet manantes inde liquores:
Mox iterum tingit limphis, iterumque liquatum
Ebibit humorem sublato ad sydera rostro.

[*ll. 347-358*]

Nec contenta satis niveo candore volucris
Excipit insidiis etiam flaventia frusta
Exiguis formis, limoque coacta remoto.
Cannarum siquidem cultis ignobile vulgus
Consurgit persaepe agris, quibus aurea condi
Mella decet, flavisque cados implere placentis.
Quare altas postquam praelo contorsit avenas,
Ac flammis solers purgavit mella juventus,
Ante furens quam plus aequo densaverit ignis.
In gelidum capulat cochleari abstersa lebetem,
Jusculaque oblongis miscens ferventia contis
Addensat, paulumque cado subsidere donat.
Tum formis brevibus nuper densata recondit,
Quae durata ferunt calido sub Sole placentas.
Ore subobscuram, ceramque referre recentem
Advertas massam: mirum at, quam laeta coemptis
Exiguo pretio vilis plebecula plaudat.
His onerat dapibus mensas, epulasque coronat;
His quoque probrosa validos trahit arte liquores,
Ebria queis planta graditur titubante per urbes.
Hinc facile exilio non nulli candida pellunt
Sacchara, et obscuras gaudent densare placentas:
Scilicet ut pretio merces breviore parandae
Allicerent plebem, nummosque augeret avarus.

[*ll. 359-382*]

FINIS LIBRI NONI

But before the sugar finds its way into the dark storehouse, the thrush, a ravenous sneak thief, often slips through the black forest and devours the white grains. Yet you must admire the unusual cleverness of this bird. He stealthily seizes the bits of hard sugar, and that the rough pieces not scratch his tender throat but, melted, flow smoothly down his deep gullet, the ingenious bird has often been seen to dip them in water. Holding in his mouth the stolen food, he now dives into a clear stream, and then standing erect drinks the dripping juice. Soon he dips it into the waters again, and again he swallows the melted drops, lifting his beak toward the heavens.

Not entirely satisfied with the white sugar, the crafty bird also takes the yellow pieces condensed in small molds without the use of clay. For many inferior canes often grow in the cultivated fields from which one may produce a golden honey and fill jars with yellow cakes. When, therefore, the young men have turned the long stalks of cane through the press and carefully purified the sweet water over fire, before the intense heat has condensed it too much, they transfer it with a spoon to a cold container, and stirring the hot juice with long poles, they condense it and let it settle slowly in the vessel. As soon as it has become thick, they put it in small molds. When this is placed under the hot sun, it forms hard cakes. You will notice that the substance is rather dark in appearance and resembles fresh wax, yet it is remarkable how pleased the poor are to buy it for a paltry sum. With this delicacy they load their tables and crown their banquets; with it they also extract, with ignominious dexterity, strong liquors, from which they become intoxicated and walk through the cities with unsteady step. From it some readily isolate white sugar and joyously thicken their dark cakes, apparently in order that their wares, purchasable at a lower price, may attract the people, and the avaricious dealer increase his profits.

X

ARMENTA

Pinguia vernantes late diffusa per agros
Angustis armenta juvat concludere septis.
Nunc opus infracto, natoque ad dura bubulco,
Agmina qui pecudum cogat palantia campis,
Montanosque bobes regnis detrudat avitis.

[*ll.1-5*]

Vos campos, Nymphae, vos saltus cingite, Divae,
Et cursu celeres damas captare suetae
Arva per, et sylvas pecudes agitate fugaces;
Et quas Pegaseo nobis contingere cursu
Instabilis Fortuna negat, vos claudite vallo;
Fundere ni telo placeat stridente rebelles:
Et juvenum primis fidus comes additus ipse
Vobis sacra jugo Parnassi templa locabo.

[*ll. 6-13*]

Praedia Mexiceis late florentia terris,
Divitias quae larga sinu telluris opimo
Hactenus agricolis magnas, populoque pararunt,
Non parvos arctis concludunt sepibus agros;
Plurima sed partes circum diffusa per omnes[1]
Ter denis leucis volvuntur jugera in orbem
Aurea nunc plantis, nunc densis abdita sylvis,
Nunc aprica solo, vitreis nunc uda fluentis.
Pinguia nervosus ferro movet arva colonus,
Et gramen pecori, sylvasque, amnesque relinquit.
Hinc passim videas nullo rectore per arva
Progenie sociata nova pecuaria ferri.

[*ll 14-25*]

Haec inter facile tumidus praecordia fastu
Praestat equus niveus cauda spectabilis atra.
Ille per auratos, herbosa sedilia, campos
Impexis per colla jubis, per terga, per aures,
Arrectaque simul cauda, colloque retorto,
Quadrupedante ferox sensim quatit aequora passu,
Poneque densatum candenti corpore equarum[2]
Agmen agit, campoque vigil spatiatur amoeno.
Quod si lenta sequi quaedam contemnat euntem,
Ocyus hinnitu sonipes urgebit acuto,
Cunctantemque dolens iterumque iterumque vocabit.
Femina si vero parere immota recuset,
Saepius ille petet furiali dente morantem

HORSES AND CATTLE

It is pleasing to bring within the confines of the corrals the fat herds that roam far out over the green countryside. There is need now of a herdsman, strong and naturally fitted for a strenuous life, to bring together the cattle which range over the fields and to dislodge the mountain cattle from their ancestral realms.

Do you, O nymphs divine, surround the fields and woods, and accustomed to chasing swift-footed deer, drive the swift cattle across the fields and through the forests; and those which fickle fortune does not permit us to catch, though we equal the speed of Pegasus, do you encircle in a valley, unless it please you to bring down the rebellious animals with a twanging dart; and as for myself, as a loyal comrade of noble youth, I will erect for you on the crest of mount Parnassus a sacred temple.

The estates, which flourish far and wide throughout the land of Mexico and have till now lavishly provided people with great wealth from the rich bosom of the earth, are not narrowly confined to small farms, but extend in every direction over many acres embracing areas thirty leagues[1] in circumference, now covered with golden harvests, now hidden by thick forests, sometimes bathed in sunshine, sometimes watered by sparkling streams. The sturdy farmer turns the rich soil with his plow, yet he leaves the meadow, and the woods, and the streams for his herd. Hence you may see unattended herds moving about in various places through the fields, accompanied by their young.

Among these animals the white horse, swelling with pride and flaunting a beautiful black tail, is easily preeminent. Over the golden plains, cushioned with grass, the fiery animal gently shakes the ground as he gallops along, his tail raised high and neck arched, while at the same time the mane falls loosely over his neck and back and ears. As he roams over the delightful field, he attentively brings along in the rear a closely united column of white mares.[2] But if some mare, being slow, should disdain to follow him as he goes along, he will urge her on with a loud neigh, and if she lags, he will plaintively call to her again and again. If, however, the mare should remain unmoved and refuse to obey, he will often fly at the loitering animal

Inque agmen subito pressam terrore reducet.
Nec tamen usque gregi poenas intentat acerbas:
Quin etiam vigili rediviva ad pascua cura
Ille movet secum teneris cum foetibus agmen
Femineum, ducitque sitim sedare fluentis:
Dumque redux turbam foecunda ad prata revexit,
Allicit annosis umbram captare sub Ornis.
Inde tot ardentes generoso sanguine creti
Quadrupedes, Solis rapidas augere quadrigas
Promeriti, passimque agris sine lege vagantes,
Dum senos Phoebi currus compleverit orbes.
Quippe virescentis frondoso gramine campi
Nec premit arva gelu, nec frondes bruma nivalis
Concremat, aut duro concrescunt frigore rivi,
Sed coelo semper rident arbusta benigno.

[*ll, 26-53*]

Si vero alipedem rigidis cicurare lupatis
Ardeat insignis nota virtute buculcus,
Continuo e gregibus delectum pluribus unum
Chortibus elatis propter penetralia tecti
Sedulus includit, socium adspirante caterva.
Tum laqueo persaepe manu super alta rotato
Prendit equum, totoque adnixus corpore firmat,
Dum loris aliis pubes sociata revincat
Torva reluctantem, rictuque, et calce petentem,
Circumdetque agilis nodosis ora capistris.
Mox dorsum, phaleris quod turba instruxit obesum,
Scandit eques, missumque dein e chortibus imis
Barbarus alipedem patulos agit ille per agros.
Ast equus insanus dorsum in sublime retorquet,
Et nunc arrectus manibus, nunc cernuus auras
Calce ferit tergoque ardet vibrare sedentem.
Poplite sed bino domitor spumantia stringit
Terga feri, manibusque regit sublimis habenas;
Queis modo fraenat equum, modo longum flectit in
    orbem,
Calce citat crebro, mediaque coercet in herba,
Quadrupedem donec repetito examine fractum
Composito doceat metiri gramina passu.

[*ll. 54-75*]

Plurima cum vero cogunt armenta bubulci
Matribus immixtis arcta intra septa morari,
Zelotypi subito rabie succensus amoris
Calcibus et rictu tegit emissarius agmen

with savage teeth and quickly bring her, terribly frightened, back again into the ranks. But not always does he assail the herd with severe punishment, but with watchful care he also escorts the females together with their tender young to fresh pastures, and leads them to streams where they may quench their thirst. And when he has brought them back to the fertile meadows, he encourages them to seek shade under an old mountain ash. So many then are the fiery steeds, born of noble blood and worthy of a place beside the swift coursers of the sun, that roam at large over the fields until the car of Phoebus has traversed the orbits of six signs of the zodiac. Indeed frost does not touch the grass-covered fields of the green plain, nor does winter's cold freeze its foliage, neither do the rivers congeal by dint of freezing temperatures, but all vegetation is ever smiling under a kindly sky.

But if a cowboy, known for his daring spirit, should wish to tame a winged steed with a hard toothed bit, at once he selects one from the several herds, and assisted by a crowd of companions, carefully shuts him within a high corral near the farm buildings. Then with his hand repeatedly swinging a lasso high into the air, he catches the horse, and straining every muscle he holds him until his young associates fasten the animal with other ropes as he violently struggles and attacks with mouth and heel, and quickly put a knotted halter around his nose. Soon the horseman is mounting the plump back on which the boys have fastened a saddle, and then as it is released from the corral he drives the horse madly over the wide fields. But the horse violently circles his back, now he stands erect, and now he stoops down and beats the air with his heels, determined to shake the rider from his back. The breaker of horses, however, tightly grips the foaming back of the infuriated animal with both his knees, and sitting erect manages the reins. With them he now checks the horse and now turns him in a long circle. He frequently applies the spur and keeps the animal in the middle of the turf until, after repeated trials, he has broken him and taught him to travel across the meadow with an even gait.

Now when the cowboys compel the vast herds of horses to remain with the mares inside the narrow inclosures, each leader, suddenly fired by the passion of jealous love, protects his own herd with his heels and teeth. He is consumed

Quisque suum, flagratque ira, pugnamque lacessit.
Dentibus exsertis vigilem petit arduus hostem
Intrepidusque ciet mediis fera praelia claustris.
Concurrunt rabidi, pedibusque arrectus uterque
Alter in alterius desudat torva ruinam,
Pectora nunc lanians manibus, nunc dentibus aures,
Nunc reliquos densis discerpens calcibus artus.
Tum prona cervice minax hinnitibus instat,
Et rursum plantis, rictuque insurgit in hostem,
Dente quoad rabido sudantia colla premendo
Hostem fundat humi, victumque extendat arena.
Inde pedem retro, parto contentus honore,
Victor agit, latosque coma volitante per armos
Protinus armentum repetit, matresque revisit.
Non secus ac claro generatus sanguine miles
Irrequietus amat turmam superare minantem,
Cedere sed gaudet votis, ac parcere victis.

[*ll.* 76-96]

Sed jam pressa diu septis armenta reclusis
Vernantem custos rursus sinit ire per agrum.
Aspice, ut immixtis agmen procedat equabus,
Angustisque petat turmatim gramina valvis:
Sed quam sollicito proprium emissarius aestu
Agmen ab agminibus, matresque a matribus arcens
Providus in campos, ac pascua nota reducat.
Vae tamen huic pecudi, sociis quae rure relictis
Alterius commixta gregis se matribus addit,
Clamorique sui renuit parere mariti.
Praepes enim pedibus Zephyri superantibus alas
Fertur equus, strictoque petens pecuaria dente
Omnia confundit, limphatusque omnia turbat,
Dum sociam media commixtam plebe repertam
In proprium revehat repetitis morsibus agmen.

[*ll.* 97-111]

Saepe etiam gregibus, Sileni pignus, asellus
Terribilis rictu, patulaque inglorius aure
Praeficitur. Sed, quem genus alto a sanguine Regum
Nobilitat, regioque frequens Madurensis honorat,[3]
Non nisi ferventes nobis, ceu fulmina, mulas
Procreat insignes pedibus, gressuque quieto;
Queis longum metimur iter, perque aspra viarum
Vincimus aerios superantes nubila montes;
Et quibus aurati magno splendore per urbes
Difficilesque vias currus, et plaustra feruntur.

with anger and provokes a fight. With the show
of his teeth he descends upon his waiting foe
and fearlessly arouses him to fierce combat in
the middle of the corral. Furiously they clash,
and rearing up they both struggle desperately to
bring about the ruin of the other, at one time
cutting the breasts of one another with their
forefeet, now biting ears, and now slashing the
other members of the body with thickly flying
heels. Then bending down his neck and neighing
threateningly he presses on and again with feet
and teeth he rises against his adversary, pressing
his sharp teeth into his sweating neck until he
brings him to the ground and stretches him out
in defeat upon the sand. Then the victor, satisfied with the glory he has achieved, steps back
and with mane flying over his broad shoulders
returns at once to his herd and to the mother
horses. So also the soldier, descended from noble
blood and with restless spirit, likes to overcome
a threatening squadron, yet gladly yields to en-
treaties and spares the conquered.

But the keeper opens the gates and permits
the herds which had been long confined to go
again over the green fields. See how they march
along, accompanied by the mares, and in companies seek pasture beyond the narrow gates,
and observe also with what anxious concern the
intelligent leader keeps his own group from the
others, and one group of mares from another,
as he conducts them back into the fields and to
their familiar grazing grounds! But woe to
that mare which forsakes her companions in the
field and associates with the mares of another
herd, refusing to heed the call of her own mate;
for the horse bears himself along on feet swifter
than the wings of the west wind, he assails the
whole herd with clenched teeth, throwing it into
a state of great disorder, and in his anger gives
the herd no rest until he has found his mate in
the midst of the others and brings her back into
his own herd, biting her again and again.

Often too an ass, the favorite of Silenus, is
placed over the herds. He has a frightful mouth
and long ungainly ears. Yet honored by his
descent from the noble blood of kings and frequently celebrated by the people of Madura,[3] he
sires for us only mules, impetuous as bolts of
lightning and famous for their lightness of step.
With them we make long journeys and over
rugged paths we scale lofty mountains that soar
above the clouds, and with them we draw through
cities and over different roads chariots, brilliant-

201

Haec quoque ponderibus proles assueta biformis
Assiduo peragrat campos, montesque labore
Proscinditque gravi duratas vomere glebas.
[*ll. 112-124*]

Dum vero campis armento mixta vagatur,
Dux gregis insomni sobolem cum matre tuetur
Cura, ac torvus equos propriis a pastibus arcet.
Quod si luxuriantis equi, aspernata maritum,
Femina blanditias, vocemque incauta sequatur,
Dentibus armatus, rabieque accensus asellus
Bella movet, rictuque procum petit efferus aspro,
Effunditque solo miseranda voce gementem,
Et crebro fusum morsu, manibusque fatigat.
Ut solet abjecta maculatus origine puber,
Egregium postquam superavit viribus hostem,
Exultare ferox, teloque extinguere victum.
[*ll. 125-136*]

Nec tamen ille gregis curis exhaustus amaris
Immensum Solis cursum metitur in agris;
Quin etiam jussus pingue ad praesepe morari
Venturum pastu vires restaurat in annum
Frumento nutritus edax, lactisque liquore,
Distinguat dum prata novum ver roscida gemmis.
Ut tamen arva toris rident herbosa novellis,
Densatos asinus renes detonsus et armos
Saepe madet Syrio succo fragrantis olivae,
Et prisco pecudum rursum perculsus amore
Armentum repetit vesano fervidus aestu.
[*ll. 137-147*]

Haud secus ardentes, natique ad fortia tauri,
Ruricolaeque boves, docilisque juvenca vagantur,
Errantesque diu saltus et rura frequentant,
Quin noctis redeant nigras ad septa sub umbras,
Aut molles tectis unquam stabulentur opimis.
Cum vero mediis enixa puerpera campis
Pone trahit vitulum, sylvisque obducta recondit,
Continuo captum, multum lugente juvenca,
Sollicitus condit parva intra claustra bubulcus,
Ingentemque domi vitulorum cogit acervum,[4]
Ubera ne siccent avidi turgentia matrum,
Utque parens sobolis nativo absentis amore
In mulctram veniat, seseque in tecta remittat.
Quod si vacca suum contemnens perfida natum
Frondosis lateat nemorum defensa tenebris,
Inque aedes remeare neget lactare tenellum,

ly adorned with gold, and wagons. These animals, accustomed to a double pack, also travel laboriously over the fields and the mountains, and they cleave the tough sod with heavy plows.

While the leader roams over the plains, associated with the herd, he protects the young and the mother with watchful care and savagely wards off the horses from his own grazing grounds. But if a mare should thoughtlessly spurn her own mate and follow the wooing and the call of a passionate horse, the ass, angrily displaying his teeth, provokes battle, and with his savage mouth furiously assails the suitor and brings him piteously groaning to the ground. He then torments his prostrate foe biting him and pawing him again and again. Thus a young man, disgraced by lowly birth, having vanquished by force a distinguished foe, usually insolently exults and dispatches his victim with a sword.

But the ass does not, when exhausted by the arduous cares of the herd, continue in the fields during the sun's long journey, but he is required to remain at a full manger, restoring his strength for the coming year on fodder and greedily feeding on corn and milk until early spring adorns the dewy meadows with buds. And when the fields smile again with beds of grass, the shaggy loins and shoulders of the ass are clipped, he is often bathed with the fragrant juice of the Syrian olive and, moved again by his former devotion to the herd, he turns again to them, fired with an ungovernable passion.

In like manner the bulls, fiery-spirited and naturally suited to strenuous tasks, and the oxen of the field, and the docile heifers, roam about in long wanderings through the woods and fields, but return to the corrals as the dark shades of night draw near, or are gently cared for in the ever bountiful stables. But whenever a calf is born in the middle of the fields, and the mother takes it away and hides it under cover of the forest, at once the anxious herdsman catches it, and though the young mother grievously laments, he puts it into a little corral. Thus he assembles at home a large number of calves[4] lest they greedily drain the swollen udders of their mothers, and that the latter, led by an innate longing for their absent young, return to the barn to be milked. But if an unfaithful mother should disregard her young and conceal herself deep in the darkly wooded

Rustica tunc pubes conscendit terga citorum
Quadrupedum, quos non flagrans praecederet
Aethon,
Quaesitamque diu nemoris per frondea vaccam
Acris agit cursu, ramisque excedere cogit.
Hinc equitum numerosa cohors avulsa cubili
Protinus ac coelo tenebras Aurora repellit,
Et nemus, et pratum, fontesque attenta revisit
Quotidie, pecudesque movens de rure rebelles
Sepibus excelsis, sobolis prope tecta, coercet.
[*ll. 148-172*]

Tum vitulum gemitus amissa matre cientem
Confectumque fame reserato carcere tollit.
Ilicet assiduus questu vocat ille parentem,
Et nutrix prolem tenero clamore salutat.
Vix tamen aure sonum clamantis buculus hausit,
Cum subito cursu confusa per agmina matrem
Vestigat, donec geminata voce vocantis
Ubera festivus matris lactantia sugat.
Sed diram vitulo rabiem compescere ventris
Armatus prohibet crudeli fune bubulcus.
Nam simul ac natus distentis labra papillis
Admovet, ac niveum coepit gustare liquorem,
Ille renitentem materno ex ubere raptum
Fune tenet subito, matrisque ad crura revincit.
(Bucula quippe negat celatos arte maligna
Nectareos fontes absente recludere nato).
Inde cadum profert annosa ex arbore sectum,
Uberaque alternis pressans turgentia palmis
Arboreum cyathum candenti nectare replet,
Fluminaque exundant plenis spumantia labris:
Unde fluit pleno butyri copia cornu,
Totque orbes lactis praelo stridente coacti.
Sed prudens uni parcit tamen ille papillae,
Quae vitulum lactet vinclis mox plena solutum.
Post aliam atque aliam munctas de more juvencas
In campos tandem claustris effundit apertis
Carpere gramen agris, aestumque expellere rivis.
Providus ast vitulos, puero custode, tenellos
Sepositis mittit campum tondere sub Alnis,
Maternoque vetat sitientes lacte levari.
[*ll. 173-202*]

Ast ubi majores vitulus se tollit in artus
Infensisque tegit porrectas cornibus aures,

forest, and refuse to return home to nurse her
little one, then the boys of the ranch mount
their swift steeds, unsurpassed by fiery-spirited
Aethon, and having found the cow after a long
search through the underbrush, they swiftly
press upon her and compel her to come forth
from the forest. For this purpose a large company of cowboys are routed from their beds as
soon as Aurora is dispelling the darkness from
the sky, and daily they diligently visit the woods
and meadows and streams to bring the unruly
cows from the fields and to shut them inside the
high inclosures next to the calves.

Then opening the prison door, they bring out
the half-starved calf bemoaning the loss of its
mother. At once it plaintively cries for its
mother, and she greets her young with a tender
lowing. Scarcely, however, has the calf heard the
sound of her voice, when suddenly it runs
through the disorderly ranks in search of her,
and guided by her repeated calls gleefully
suckles at last the mother's full udder. But the
cowherd, provided with a rope, cruelly prevents
the calf from satisfying the dreadful pangs of
its stomach; for as soon as it brings its lips to
the distended teats and begins to taste the white
liquid, the cowherd pulls it away from its
mother and fastens it to her legs with a rope
(this is done because the young cow, when her
calf is away, refuses to give up her streams of
nectar, spitefully holding them back). Then he
brings a bucket, made of seasoned wood, and
pressing the swollen teats now with one hand and
then with the other, he fills the wooden vessel
with the white nectar; and streams of foam pour
over the sides as it is filled. From this there
comes a great abundance of butter and many
rolls of cheese condensed in the creaking press.
But the wise cowherd spares one teat in order
that it may yield plenty of milk for the calf
when freed a little later. When the heifers have
thus been milked, one after another, he finally
opens the gates and drives them out into the
fields to pasture and to refresh themselves in
the brooks. But the little calves are placed by the
skilled herdsman in the keeping of a boy who
sends them out to crop the grass underneath
some secluded alders, and forbids them, when
thirsty, to refresh themselves on their mothers'
milk.

Now when the calves have developed larger
limbs, and threatening horns are covering their
long ears, the herdsman quickly confines within

Ocyus angusta concludit chorte bubulcus
Natorum ingentem turmam jam rure vagantem,
Mollia designet flammato ut tergora ferro.
Ille bobis laqueis obstringit crura novelli,
Obstantemque diu facili protendit arena.
Tum proprio fundi, flammasque imitante sigillo
Terga renitentis signat combusta juvenci.
Bellua crudeli ferri commota rigore
Aestuat impatiens spumantis fluctibus irae,
Invaditque ferox, nodoso fune soluta,
Collectam juvenum media intra septa cohortem.
Sed saevis gaudet pubes illudere plagis,
Et saltu vires crebro lassare petentis.

[*ll. 203-217*]

Interdum rabidos etiam mirabere tauros
Submitti, facilesque globum concurrere in unum.
Vix etenim lucem reddit mortalibus almam
Phosphorus eois surgens redivivus ab undis,
Alitibus cum fortis equis advecta juventus
Obscuras penetrat sylvas, camposque peragrat,
Dispersumque pecus repetitis cursibus urget.
Pars cogit tetro tauros discedere luco,
Pars agit in pratum celso de monte ruentes,
Et pars invigilat medio jam rure coactis,
Immensum donec taurorum congerat agmen.
Quod si aliquis celerare fugam, turmamque paravit
Linquere, continuo laxatis puber habenis
Calce fatigat equum crebro, sequiturque volantem,
Dum longo fessum cursu, caudaque prehensum
Flectat in adversum, taurumque effundat in agro;
Unde gravis monitum poena ad pecuaria ducat.
Mox pingues pubes, seponit cauta macello,
Et fortes, queis colla toris robusta pilosis,
Provida vertendis agris ad aratra reservat,
Ac reliquum medio dimittit gramine vulgus.

[*ll. 218-238*]

Ut vero subigat lectos ad rura juvencos,
Castratos primum sociali foedere bobus
Admiscet, nexosque aliis jam forte subactis
Ire jubet, rabiem donec, moresque ferinos
Exuerint, et colla jugo demittere norint.
Idcirco bobus binis adjungit arator
Indocilem, ternosque jugo supponit eidem:
Ut cum taurus agrum rabie commotus avita

a corral this large herd of young cattle that now roams the countryside in order that he may brand their soft backs with the hot iron. He tightly binds the legs of a young bull with ropes and throws him on the soft sand, though he stubbornly resists. Then with the red-hot branding iron belonging to the ranch, he marks the back of the struggling animal. Stung by the relentless iron, the beast raves with ungovernable fury and foams and, when loosed from the knotted rope, charges fiercely upon the crowd of young men gathered inside the corral. But the lads make sport of him by inflicting cruel blows and wear out his resistence by constantly jumping away as he attacks.

You will also marvel at times to see the furious bulls subdued and willingly gathered into one herd. Scarcely indeed does the morning star, as he rises anew from the eastern waves, bring glorious light of day to mortals, when valiant young men, mounted on winged steeds, penetrate the deep forests, scour the fields, and with repeated sallies gather the scattered herd. Some force the bulls to withdraw from the dark woods, others bring them swiftly down from the high mountain into the meadows, while still others watch over those that have already been assembled in the middle of the plain until they have brought together an immense number of bulls. But if one of these has decided to make a speedy escape and to abandon the herd, at once a man relaxes the reins, plies his horse with the spur, and takes after the fugitive bull until, wearied by the long chase, he is caught by the tail, whirled around, and forced to the ground. He is then brought back to the herd, having been taught a bitter lesson. Then the men carefully separate the fat ones for the market and properly reserve for the plow the strong ones whose stout shoulders are thickly covered with hair; and the rest of them, the common run of the herd, they send away into the pasture lands.

Now in order that the plowman may tame the young bulls that have been selected for work in the fields, he first castrates them, and then closely associates them with oxen, forcing them to walk along attached to the others which happen to be already broken, until they have given up their fierceness and wild disposition and have learned to submit their necks to the yoke. For this purpose the plowman places an untrained animal between two oxen and brings the three under the same yoke in order that when the bull,

Ardeat insanus celeri percurrere planta,
Vomeribus pridem sueti, qui hinc inde laborant,
Indomitum froenent, aequalique aequora passu
Metiri sensim doceant, flectantque furentem.
Ast ubi composito glebas proscindere gressu
Edoctus taurus violentum corde furorem
Expulit, et doctis novit parere magistris,
Tertius actutum duro temone juvencus
Pellitur; et longo detentum cornua fune,
Quem retro solers capulo connectit arator,
Lenta movet taurum conantem plurima frustra,
Dum magnis operis, duroque assuetus aratro
Noverit incessu glebas renovare quieto.

[*ll. 239-259*]

Ast solet interdum taurorum turma rebellis
Usque tenebrosis nemorum se condere ramis,
Quos gramen campi, Solemque, auramque perosos
Non nisi tonsa nigris viridis juvat herba sub Ornis.
Nec potis est ullus turbam detrudere luco,
Ni sitis arentem compellat noctis in umbris
Quaerere tranquillos aprico gramine fontes.
Sed pubes noctu tauros operosa fugaces
Invadit cursu, fessosque in gramine caedit.
Insignes siquidem planta pernice juventus
Aptat equos, propriisque audax accingitur armis;
Hic rapit aerata munitam cuspide pinum,
Ille renidenti lunam quatit aere bicornem,
Cetera dum pubes caudis adstringit equorum
Taurina pridem tortos e pelle rudentes.[5]
Ut vero de more cohors sua tela paravit
Se campo fundit patulo, sub nocte silenti,
Tempore quo Luna replet fulgentior orbem,
Et taciturna locis passu cunctante propinquat,
Unde feros novit prodire ad flumina tauros.
Tunc manus umbrosas nemoris distracta per oras
Frondentem vigili lucum statione coronat,
Exspectata petat fontes dum praeda quietos.
Ast ubi nigrantes saltusque, umbrasque relinquit
Incessuque gravi latum bos prodit in agrum,
Prompta cohors equitum ferrato calce citatos
Quadrupedes urget, sequiturque fluenta petentem.
Hic prior armata taurum prosternere pinu,
Ille pedes certat curvata scindere luna,

prompted by his innate fierceness, has a mad impulse to rush across the field with swiftness of foot, those that work on either side, long accustomed to the plow, may hold in check the unbroken one and gradually train him to make his way over the plain at an even pace, having subdued his impetuous spirit. And when the ox has driven the violent passion from his heart, has learned to cleave the soil at a moderate gait, and knows how to obey his experienced teachers, he is immediately removed from the stout pole by the skilled plowman and tied behind to the plow handle by a long rope fastened around his stout horns. The ox is moved along, struggling violently, though without avail, until he has become accustomed to heavy tasks and to the hard plow and has learned to turn the sod with a gentle gait.

Sometimes, however, a rebellious company of bulls is wont to hide under the branches of the black forest, loathing the grass of the field, the sunlight, and the open air, and delighting only in browsing on the green vegetation that grows underneath the dark mountain ashes. And no one can dislodge them from the forest unless extreme thirst should compel them under cover of night to seek the quiet springs in the open meadow. But the industrious men make a raid by night upon these wild oxen and after wearing them out slay them on the meadow. The young men, accordingly, provide themselves with horses famous for their swiftness, and daringly equip themselves with appropriate weapons. This one seizes a bronze-tipped sword, another brandishes a crescent-shaped weapon made of glittering bronze, while others tie twisted cowhide ropes to the tails of their horses.[5] When the men have duly prepared their weapons, they deploy over the broad plain in the silence of night, at the time when the moon is filling the earth with its brightest light, and they quietly and cautiously approach the places from which they know the wild bulls come forth to the streams. Then the company, drawing apart along the shady edges of the forest, surround the thick woods with alert sentries until their awaited prey seeks the quiet springs. And when the cattle leave the dark shadows of the forest and with heavy footstep come forth into the open field, the ready horsemen spur on their swift steeds and pursue the bulls as they go in search of the streams. One man with his spear strives to be the first to lay low a bull, another to hamstring one with his

Ni prius alter agat celsa inter cornua funem,
Adnexumque bobem cauda refraenet equina.
Bellua terribili subito correpta furore
Alipedem curva celerem petit ardua fronte:
Sed consultus eques cursu declinat anhelo
Cominus urgentem lethumque, ictumque, minantem,
Dum socii ferro bacchantis crura recidant,
Aut propiora volans ipse intra septa reponat.
Continuo pubes, circum diffusa, juvenci
Lymphati loris taurinis crura revincit,
Eripit ense cutem, costasque, et pectora nudat;
Unde domum vectat, flammisque trementia torret.

[*ll. 260-300*]

FINIS LIBRI DECIMI

curved knife, or still another may be the first to throw a rope around the bull's uplifted horns and hold him fast to the tail of his horse. The beast at once becomes infuriated and assails the swift-footed steed, rising up against him with his arched forehead. But the skilled horseman in breathless haste swerves away from the animal as he crowds closely upon him and threatens him with a deadly blow until his comrades hamstring the crazed beast with a knife or the driver himself in great haste brings him into the nearest corral. At once the men gather around and bind the legs of the crazed bull with cowhide thongs, they tear off the skin with a knife, laying bare the ribs and the breast, and then they carry home the flesh, still quivering, to roast it over a fire.

XI

GREGES

Armentis sociare greges per rura vagantes,
Lanigerumque pecus, caprasque, haedosque petulcos,
Atque saginatos aurato germine porcos,
Musa jubet. Procul hinc, Nymphae, procul este,
   Napaeae:
Nil mihi vulnificis ferro lucente sagittis,
Nec visco, aut laqueis fallaci gramine tectis
Est opus. Expertis tantum pastoribus utar,
Errantesque agro pecudes in septa molossis
Ducam, torva quibus discedat bellua campis.
                             [*ll. 1-9*]

Tu, qui Maenalia, Capripes, modulatus avena
Et campo, et nigra ducis pecuaria sylva,
Pastorumque frequens demulces pectora cantu,
Protinus ante oculos resonis pecus omne cicutis
Accerse, et blanda pastores voce vocatos
Naturam pecorum variam compelle docere:
Et tibi septenos avulsos ubere natos
Ocyus ipse tuis libabo cernuus aris.
                            [*ll. 10-17*]

Non omnes armenta juvant, strepitusque bubul-
   cum:
Alter enim placidas ardet tondere bidentes:
Alter amat celsis errantes collibus haedos
Tergore nudatos fusis condire salinis,
Ac vario mollire hirtam medicamine pellem;
Dum porcos alius curat pinguescere fundo
Et largus genti convivia lauta parare.
                            [*ll. 18-24*]

Praedia, quae pecori pascendo addicit ovillo
Dives herus, patuli circumdant undique campi
Pastibus obducti teneris, et gramine multo,
Flumina quos passim vitreis undantia limphis
Irrorant, gelidosque ferunt sitientibus haustus.
His tamen alternas agris interserit umbras
Densatum quandoque nemus, quandoque comanti
Luxurie in medio surgentes aequore quercus.
Nam quamvis nullas norint pecuaria caulas,
Libera sed campis semper spatientur apertis,
Ast cautus pecudes, fido aspirante molossum
Agmine, pastor agit nigrae sub robora sylvae,
Seu flammas Phoebus coelo jaculetur in orbem,
Seu denso terras quatiat Saturnius imbre.

SHEEP, GOATS, AND SWINE

To the herds of horses and cattle the Muse
bids me add the herds of smaller animals that
roam over the fields—the fleecy sheep, the goats,
the frisky kids, and the swine, fattened on gold-
en grain. Far hence, far hence, O nymphs of
the wooded dell; no need have I for wound-
inflicting arrows of shining steel, or for lime, or
treacherous nets hidden in the grass. I shall
need only skilled herdsmen, and I shall bring
the herds that wander over the field into the
fold with the help of dogs which drive wild
beasts from the fields.

Do you, O goat-footed Pan, who play on the
Arcadian pipe, who lead the herds through field
and dark forest and often console the hearts of
the shepherds with your song, promptly summon
all the herd into my presence with your resounding flute and, having called the shepherds with
your seductive voice, have them teach me the
manifold nature of the animals; and to you
seven kids weaned from the breast I, with
bowed head, shall promptly sacrifice on your
altar.

Not all take delight in the herds of larger
animals and in the yelling of the cowboys; for
one man likes to shear his gentle ewes, another
finds pleasure in stripping the hides from his
goats which wander over the hill tops, in salting
away their meat, and in softening with various
chemicals the shaggy pelts, while still another
concerns himself with fattening swine on his
estate and generously providing people with
elegant feasts.

The estates which the wealthy lord devotes to
the grazing of sheep are surrounded on every
side by open plains covered with lush pastures
and watered by rivers which send their crystal
streams here and there affording a cool drink
for the thirsty animals. In these fields, moreover, alternating shade is provided—sometimes
a thick grove appears, sometimes oaks with luxuriant foliage stand in the middle of the plain.
And although the flocks have no knowledge of
folds, but always roam at large over the open
plains, yet the watchful shepherd, assisted by
a pack of faithful dogs, drives his flocks under
the oaks of the dark forest whether Phoebus is
hurling his fiery rays from the heavens against
the earth, or Saturn's sun is striking the land

Pastor enim ternis sociis comitatus adhaeret
Erranti pecori, noctesque diesque per arva
Fidus oves, vigilesque canes moderatur eundo.¹
[ll. 25-41]

Vix etenim pecudum nudatis vellera costis
Sollicitus ferro tondet candentia pastor,
Cum subito abducit reclusis agmina caulis
In campum, cautusque pigro per gramina passu
Carpit iter longum,² calidis quo pinguia terris
Rura vocant, oditque algentes frigore tractus.
Agmina procedunt campis, quin patribus agni,
Aut mollis possit misceri sponsa marito.
Hic agit ante alios tonsas per prata bidentes;
Ille patres ducit, qua Sol festinat in undas;
Alter amat terris verveces ducere eois;
Atque agnos alter subeuntes pone per aequor.
Hinc fusis videas gregibus canescere campum
Implerique vagis tremulas balatibus auras.
Haec ubi corripuere viam, pecorumque caterva
Procedunt agro, pastorum turba morantem
Persequitur baculo pecudem, poenasque minatur,
Gramina ut herboso detondens aequore, coeptum
Pergat iter, gressuque pari comitetur euntes.
Ni prudens magno Solis ferventis in aestu
Cautus agat nemoris densas pecus omne sub umbras.
Quod si nulla toros ardentes fraxinus umbret,
Optatae jussus grex indulgere quieti
Sistitur, inque globum dispersum cogitur agmen:
Utque pecus Solis flagrantia spicula vitet,
Mutua quaeque sagax sibi certa levamina curat;
Ac prona cervice caput sub ventre recondens
Alterius, dorsum telis incauta recludit.
[ll. 42-69]

Ast vero tacitae celsis ut montibus umbrae
Praecipitant, orbemque tegit nox atra tenebris,
Villicus actutum, latis qui praesidet arvis,
Ulterius pecudes prohibet per rura vagari,
Palantesque greges medio consistere campo
Imperat, ac fessos placido dare membra sopori.
Tunc tacet omne pecus, catuli, pecorumque magistri,
Herbosisque toris turba inclinata recumbit,

with heavy rain. The shepherd, accompanied by three companions, stays close to his wandering herd, and traveling across the country day and night, he faithfully guides his sheep and watchful dogs.¹

Scarcely indeed has the diligent shepherd shorn the white fleeces, laying bare the ribs, when suddenly he opens the folds and leads his flocks away into the plains. Slowly and cautiously he pursues his long journey² over the prairies to a place where the rich country invites him with its warm fields, for he dislikes a cold climate. The herds file across the fields, but the lambs are not able to accompany their sires, nor the gentle ewe her mate. One man, going ahead, drives the shorn ewes across the prairie, another guides the rams toward the place where the sun makes haste to descend into the waves, another is wont to guide the wethers through the country toward the east, and a fourth man leads the lambs over the plain, and they follow close behind him. And so you may see the country turning white with the scattered flocks and hear tremulous bleatings carried by the shifting winds. When the sheep, having begun their journey, are proceeding across the field, the shepherds, carrying their staffs, follow them and threaten with punishment those that loiter, so that, as the herds browse over the grass-covered plain, they may pursue the journey they have begun, and travel at the same speed as their comrades. Yet the wise shepherd, when the sun is very hot, will cautiously drive all his flock under the deep shade of a grove. But if there should be no tree to shade the hot land, the flock is made to stop and take a welcome rest, and those that had been scattered gather in a close circle; and in order that they may avoid the hot rays of the sun, they cleverly provide for themselves some mutual relief. One with bended neck buries her head under the belly of another, though heedlessly exposing her back to the rays of the sun.

But when the shadows are silently descending from the high mountains and black night is mantling the earth in darkness, at once the superintendent who presides over the vast estate keeps the herds from wandering farther through the country. He has them stop in the middle of the field and give peaceful rest to their weary limbs. Then the whole herd becomes quiet, the dogs, too, and the masters of the herds; and they all lie stretched out on beds of

Dum somno pressam Phoebi lux alma revisat.
Sed prius infirmos quam pastor providus artus
Fronde super viridi, nigraque sub ilice ponat,
Mollia carnivoris partitur frusta molossis,
Ardoremque famis, rabiemque extinguit edenti.
Fida canum subito plebes diffusa per herbam
Intrepidisque armata minis pecuaria cingit
Prompta fero quoscumque hostes invadere rictu.
Aequore tunc medio cameram sibi pastor adornat
Curvatis fictam storeis, et gramine fusus
Tranquillum proflat rauco de pectore somnum.

[*ll. 70-88*]

Quod si forte greges invadat latro sub umbras,
Aut lupus e sylva nuper digressus ab alta
Iratus cladem jejuno ventre minetur,
Protinus insomnis latratu turba molossum
Bella parat, percorumque duces in tela vocabit.
Collecti e somno, raptisque ex aequore membris
Vulgus in arma ruit, circumque armenta peragrans,
Nunc virgulta movet, nunc nigri montis ad oras
Accelerat gressum, qua fervet vividus Umber,
Nunc ipsas pecudes fumanti lampade lustrat,
Toto quoad saevum pulsarit rure latronem.

[*ll. 89-99*]

Interea calidis tangit pecuaria telis
Blanda Venus, levibusque urgens praecordia flammis
In furias, ignemque patres, matresque procaces
Praecipitat, magno campos turbante tumultu.
Tunc subito accitos semoto ex agmine patres,
Procerae queis molis honos, viridisque juventa,
Matribus admiscet pubes studiosa petulcis
Admixtamque regit deinceps per prata catervam,
Pinguia dum tenero turgescant viscera foetu.

[*ll. 100-108*]

Ut vero toto palantes aequore finem
Imposuere viae pecudes, calidoque sub axe
Pervenere locos, vernant ubi pascua Sole,
Crebraque nigranti se tollunt robora fronde,
Assiduo tondent viridantia pabula dente
Ac totum crassa velant pinguedine corpus.

[*ll. 109-114*]

Nectare mox niveo distentis femina mammis
Quaeque suos gremio faetus educit in auras,
Pignora cara gregis, notum quae sanguine nomen
Lanigeraeque decus tollant per saecula gentis.
Haec ubi dissecto florentia gramina ventre

grass until the refreshing light of Phoebus comes to find them sunk in sleep. But before the wise shepherd rests his weary limbs on the grass beneath a black holm oak, he distributes bits of meat to his dogs, satisfying their consuming hunger and ravenous appetites. The faithful dogs spread out at once on the grass, and, fearlessly barking, surround the sheep, ready to attack any enemy whatsoever. Then the shepherd provides for himself on the open plain a hut made of arched mats and stretches himself out upon the grass where he snores in calm repose.

But if it happen that a robber assail the flocks in the darkness of night, or a hungry wolf having just emerged from the deep forest savagely threaten disaster, quickly the lightly-sleeping dogs prepare for battle and with barking call the shepherds to arms. Aroused from sleep and hurriedly arising from the ground the shepherds rush to arms, and as they make the rounds of the flocks, now they beat the bushes, now they hurry to the edge of the black mountain where a hound rages furiously, and now with smoking torch they search among the flocks themselves until they have routed the fierce enemy from the country.

In the meantime Venus, the seducer, touches the flocks with her fiery darts and kindles in their hearts the gentle flames of love, driving the wanton males and females into a hot passion and creating widespread turmoil over the plains. Then the attentive shepherds immediately bring forth from their separate company those males which are esteemed for their size and youthful vigor and join them to the frisky ewes, and they guide the flock, thus united, through the meadows until the wombs are swelling with tender young.

And when the flocks have traveled across the entire plain and have come to the end of their journey, having reached a country that lies beneath a warm sky where the grass flourishes in the sunshine and numerous thick-leafed oak trees grow, they feed uninterruptedly on the green pastures and cover their bodies all over with thick fat.

Presently udders are distended with white nectar, and each ewe brings forth into the light of day her young, the darlings of the flock, destined by their blood to extend throughout the ages the fame and glory of the wool-bearing race. When the lush meadows receive them from

Excipiunt, blandisque toris excepta reclinant,
Infaustam credas vitae praecurrere mortem,
Et matres utero natis finxisse sepulcrum.
Tantum sub tenero languescunt corpore vires!
Ast ubi membra parens abstergit mollia lingua,
Et blandis Zephyrus durat languentia flabris,
Agnus inexpertis plantis consistit in agro,
Continuoque petit nutanti corpore mammas
Nectareas, flexoque genu, caudaque frequenti
Lactea compressis placide trahit ubera labris.
Mox curvata movens sensim per gramina crura
Paulatim vires agnus confirmat eundo,
Ausit ut exiguo gramen submittere saltu,
Saepius et sociis laetus colludere campo.

[*ll. 115-133*]

Si tamen in mediis partus enixa tenellos,
Immensum dum pergit iter, profuderit agris
Mollis ovis, pastor robustis excipit ulnis
Invalidos, gremiove fovet pudibunda puella,
Aut pueri, aut conjux campis haerere marito
Sueta, quoad proles consistat fortis in arvo
Palantumque legat matrum vestigia gressu.

[*ll. 134-140*]

Cum vero violenta lues pecuaria vexat,
Aut premit infaustis morbus male saucia plagis,
Ilicet incolumi semotas agmine custos
Alter agit pecudes, febrique, aut vulnere laesis
Apta parat cautus magnis penetralia septis,
Quae teneri subeunt nullo discrimine nati
Et matres una, vervexque, ariesque petulcus.
Huic molli cingit nutantia crura Machaon
Fasciola; tenues olli de vulnere pellit
Vermiculos; herbisque sagax lenimen adaptat.
Quod si blanda parens morboso lacte tenellum
Nutriat, aut, prorsus siccatis aegra mamillis,
Pignoribus jucunda suis alimenta recuset,
Imbellem custos, matre intra claustra retenta,
Nutricis curae gnatum committit alendum.
Hinc illam firmat, mammisque extensa refertis
Labra simul figit multum sitientis alumni,
In natum donec nutrix adsciverit agnum,
Aut pastor reddat valido jam corpore matri.

[*ll. 141-159*]

Floribus interea ridens ver dulcia pingit
Arva novis; mollisque puer, castaeque puellae
Exultant pictis velati tempora gemmis.

the open womb and provide for them a resting place on the soft grass, you would believe that death was unhappily preceding life and that the mothers had made their wombs a sepulcher for their young. So weak is the vitality in their little bodies! But when the mother licks the limbs of her tender young, and the west wind strengthens the frail body with its gentle breezes, though the lamb's feet are untrained, it stands up and immediately seeks with its tottering body the nectar-filled breast of its mother; and as it flexes its knees and waggles its tail, it gently presses its lips about the teat and draws forth the milk. Presently the lamb moves its crooked legs slowly through the meadow and gradually gains strength as it goes, until it ventures to trip with short leaps across the grass and often frolics with its mates in the field.

But if a gentle ewe, during the long journey, should bring forth her young out in the middle of the fields, the shepherd takes up the feeble lambs in his strong arms, or his little daughter fondles them in her bosom, or his boys, or his wife, who usually accompanies her husband over the plains, until the young are strong enough to stand firmly on the ground and to follow the footsteps of their roving mothers.

When, moreover, a fierce pestilence assails the flocks, or infection unfortunately enters their deep wounds, at once another keeper segregates the sick from the well, wisely providing for those attacked by fever or for the wounded suitable quarters inside high fences, into which the newly born and the mothers, too, and the wethers and butting rams go without distinction. A doctor wraps a soft bandage around their shaking limbs, he cleans the tiny maggots out of the wounds, and wisely administers relief with herbs. And if the loving mother should be giving her little one diseased milk or, on account of her illness, have no milk at all and thus deprive her lambs of their sweet nourishment, the shepherd keeps the mother in confinement and intrusts her helpless young to the care of a wet nurse. He then holds the nurse and at the same time brings the outstretched lips of the thirsty nursling to the full udder until the nurse accepts the lamb as her own, or until the shepherd returns it to its mother, now in full strength of body.

In the meantime smiling spring paints the sweet countryside once more with flowers; and the young men and demure young ladies, with their temples garlanded with bright flowers,

Florea tunc pastor rursus per jugera ducens
Pingue pecus, sensimque viam dimensus amoenam,
Consilio nectente moras, in tecta reducit,
Radere terga manu niveis rorantia lanis.

[*ll. 160-166*]

Sed prius impexum quam pubes tondeat agmen,
Lanigeras praedives herus numerare cohortes
Imperat, ac dena toto de prolis acervo
Sacratis aris confestim parte soluta,
Mox alios denos teneris a caetibus agnos
Invitos removere jubet; quos villicus agri
Pro digna tanti teneat mercede laboris.

[*ll. 167-173*]

Inde gregem jussus concludit pastor in arctis
Quisque suum caulis, tecti prope limina ductis;
Et subito juvenum ferro praecincta caterva
Fune ligat, funditque solo de more bidentes,
Vellera divellit costis, ac tergora nudat.
Vellera quaeque globum pubes convolvit in unum
Asservatque sagax, ut cum persolvere pensum
Cogat herus, nummos totidem, quot vellera, pendat.

[*ll. 174-181*]

Haec vero assiduo peragit dum turba labore,
Arma movet, gaudetque aries concurrere cornu.
Quisque suum telis armatus provocat hostem,
Ac totis urget septis, lassumque fatigat.
Fortis enim gressus retro gladiator uterque
Alter ab alterius simulans se proripit armis:
Sed subito rabie succensus quisque maligna
Invisum, ceu tela volant, volat acer in hostem,
Ac duras duris frontes cum frontibus urget.
Mox iterum retro porrecta gressus arena
Rursus in arma ruit, rursusque insurgit in acrem
Hostem. Sylva fremit tanto vicina tumultu,
Et tremulus reboat duratis ictibus aer.
Sed, cito pastores compescunt praelia ferro,
Lymphatamque domant rigida sub forfice plebem.

[*ll. 182-196*]

Post, ubi clamosum radit pecuaria vulgus,
Continuo magnum, semotis patribus, agmen
Addensat maribus, prudens quos pastor in escam
Olim castrarat juvenes, pinguesque macello
Inde relegat, iter docta monstrante capella.

[*ll. 197-201*]

make merry. Then the shepherd again guides his rich flock across the flower-clad fields and having slowly wended his way along the lovely road, brings them after ingenious delays to the fold to shear the snow-white wool from their dewy backs.

But before the men shear the woolly flock, the rich lord bids them count all the sheep, and when a tithe of all the animals has been promptly set apart for the sacred altars, he then orders the men to separate another tenth of the lambs, though they are loath to be separated, for the manager of the ranch, as a fitting reward for his hard work.

Then each shepherd, as ordered, shuts his flock in narrow folds built near the house, and at once a company of young men provided with shears bind the sheep with a rope and throw them in the accustomed manner to the ground; they strip the fleeces from their sides and lay bare their backs. Each man rolls his fleeces into a bundle and keeps close guard over them in order that, when the master requires him to render an accounting of his day's work, he may pay him an amount of money commensurate with the number of fleeces.

While the men are assiduously engaged in this work, the rams stir up battles and take delight in clashing their horns together. Each one, fully armed, challenges his enemy, and pursuing him throughout the corral, wearies him to the point of exhaustion. Each valiant fighter draws back, the one pretending to escape the attack of the other, but suddenly, fired by a violent fury, he flies head-long into his hated foe like a flying dart, and thrusts his hard head against hard head. Then they step back again in the wide arena, and again they rush to arms, again they assail their hated enemy. The neighboring forest resounds with the mighty turmoil, and the air vibrates and re-echoes from the heavy blows. But quickly the shepherds with iron weapon break up the battle and tame the infuriated animals by placing them under the unyielding shears.

After the boisterous workmen have sheared the flocks, they immediately remove the rams and assemble a large company of young males, which the wise shepherd had previously castrated for his food-supply, and from which he sends to market the fat ones, guided by a trained she-goat.

Sed jam rus video niveis albescere capris
Barbigerumque pecus ramos tondere comantes.
Horret enim fundus maculosis agmina signis,
Quae vario natura linit foecunda colore:
Noctis enim dum grata quies animalia fessa
Occupat, et somnum tranquilla silentia suadent,
Tergora picta gregis, variisque coloribus aucta
Percutiunt magna pecudes formidine pressas,
Agminaque umbrosis fundunt palantia sylvis.
Quare omnes pastor maculas expellit ab agris
Lacteolumque gregem cygni candore micantem
Tutus agit, cogitque virens canescere gramen.
Ut solet interdum niveis albere pruinis,
Argentique diu lamnis effulgere pratum:
Haud aliter canis albescunt aequora capris.
[*ll. 202-216*]

Dum tamen halantes errat de more per herbas[3]
Improbaque herboso sedat jejunia campo
Irrequieta pecus, saltusque, agrosque peragrat,
Nunc frondes pedibus summis arrecta recidens,
Nunc saltu veteris conscendens brachia quercus,
Aut riguum quaerens etiam sitibunda fluentum.
Agmina sed fidis custos dispersa molossis
Cogit iter longum totis urgere diebus.
[*ll. 217-224*]

Ut tamen aurato curru lux alma recessit,
Noxque pecus celat densis obducta tenebris,
Villicus actutum gregibus consistere jussis,
E silicis venis excussum colligit ignem
Frondibus, ingentemque rogum mox suscitat arvis.
Tunc circum flammas effusum protinus agmen
Omne recumbit agris, positoque pavore quiescit.
[*ll. 225-231*]

Si tamen umbrosis jaculatus nubibus ignis
Aera perfundat telis, tonitruque resultent
Horrida montanis concussis collibus antra,
Ilicet hirsutae correptae horrore capellae
Aequore palantes toto, clademque timentes
Accelerant cursu densis se condere sylvis:
Nec potis est pastor, vigilans nec turba molossum
Praecipitem prohibere gradum. Replet arva
    tumultus,
Ductorisque graves agitant praecordia curae.
Ast, ubi restituit rebus lux alma colorem,
Ocyus ille vagum parvo ferit aethera cornu,[4]
Et campum, et sylvae frangit clangoribus oras,
Dum sonitu errantes capraeque hircique recepto

But now I see the countryside growing white as snow with goats and the bearded herd browsing on green twigs; for indeed the ranch has an aversion to spotted animals richly tinted by nature in various colors; for when in the night sweet repose overtakes the tired animals, and a deep silence invites slumber, the bodies of those animals that are spotted and designed in various colors confuse the herds, filling them with great panic and sending them wandering through the shadows of the forest. Therefore the goatherd expels all the spotted animals from the fields and thus safely drives along his milk-white flock which shines with the brilliance of a swan and causes the green pastures to turn white. As the meadow often turns white as snow with frost and glistens for a long time with a silvery sheet, so the plains become white with goats.

Now as the restless flock wanders, as is its custom, over the sweet-scented grass[3] and relieves its insatiate appetite in the green field, it roams through woodland and field, now rising on tiptoe to break off sprouts, now leaping onto the limbs of an oak, or again, if thirsty, seeking a fresh stream. But the keeper assisted by his faithful dogs requires the scattered herds to continue each day their long journey.

And when the glorious light of day has departed in its chariot of gold, and night is hiding the flock, surrounding it with complete darkness, the manager immediately orders the flocks to be stopped, and striking a spark from a piece of flint, ignites some leaves, and soon has a large fire burning on the plain. Then the whole flock at once gathers around the fire, reclines on the ground, and rests, free from alarm.

If, however, lightning should flash across the black clouds, filling the heavens with its bolts, and the mountain ranges should shake with peals of thunder and their terrible caverns reverberate, then the shaggy goats are seized with terror, in fear of destruction they scatter over/the whole plain and run at full speed into the thick woods to hide, and neither the goatherd nor the alert dogs can check their headlong flight. Confusion fills the plains and grave anxiety rends the heart of the leader. But when the glorious light has restored color to objects, he quickly blasts the shifting winds with his little horn,[4] and the sound breaks over the fields and along the borders of the forest until the wandering goats, both male and female, hear the sound

Gramina nota petant, totumque coiverit agmen.
Non secus ac pavidas lituis in castra vocaret
Dux acies, hostis quas dudum fuderat armis.
[*ll. 232-247*]

Tot perfuncta cohors pastorum sedula curis
Urget iter coeptum; Venerisque ardore crematis
Armentis armenta jubet, caprosque capellis
Misceri, unde genus referat barbata propago.
Dum tamen halanti custodes rure vagantur
Quisque virescenti concisis arbore Palmis
Innumeros torquet, sudanti cortice, funes,
Mollia vincturus pariturae pignora turbae.
[*ll. 248-255*]

Vix etenim partus pendenti ventre propinquat,
Cum pastor promptus concludit gramina septis
Dumosis; intusque sudes affigit in orbem.
Post, ubi turpe pecus foetus emisit in auras,
Funiculis ad tigna capram cum prole revincit,
Dum mater sobolem noscat, sobolesque parentem,
Ac plenis suescant lactentia labra papillis.
Cum vero blandis vinclis utrumque ligavit
Pectus amor, matremque urget jam cura tenelli,
Capreolo semper larga intra septa retento,
Incomitata parens aprico rure pererrat,
Bisque venit foetum materno pascere lacte.
Ut tamen a pastu reducem sub claustra capellam
Pastor agit, matri plaudit balatibus haedus,
Emicat in campo creber, luditque per herbam.
Quod si pastor amet, curae pertaesus iniquae,
Enixam cum prole recens educere campo,
Immemor ingeniti prorsus plebs vilis amoris
Nec mater gremio vecors demulcet alumnum,
Nec proles confecta fame petit ubera matris.
[*ll. 256-275*]

Haec ubi difficili complevit turba labore,
Continuo bimo turbantes agmina cornu
Incumbit castrare capros; patresque resignat,
Parva quibus nondum velarunt cornua frontem.
Tunc totam subito videas pinguescere gentem
Semimaresque capros, haedosque, hirtasque capellas,
Et magnum turpi lanio portendere quaestum.
[*ll. 276-282*]

and return to their familiar pastures, and the entire flock is united. In like manner a general might take his bugle and call into camp his frightened lines, recently routed in battle by the enemy.

The diligent herdsmen, after suffering so many worries, resume their journey; and when the herds are inflamed with the passion of love, they are united, the he-goats with the she-goats, in order that a bearded offspring may come forth to carry on the race. And as the keepers roam through the scented fields, each one cuts off palms from a green tree and twists them while damp into many ropes with which to tie the tender offspring of those about to bear young.

As soon as their bellies are swelling and the time for bringing forth young is near, the shepherd promptly puts a fence of thorn-bushes around the pasture and drives stakes all around on the inside. Afterwards, when the ill-smelling herd has brought forth its young into the light of day, the herdsman takes ropes and ties the mother along with her kid to the stakes until she has learned to recognize her young, and the young its mother, and until the suckling lips become used to the full teats. When, however, sweet bonds of affection have united the hearts of both, and the mother is now filled with concern for her little one, although the kid is always kept inside the large inclosure, the mother roams alone through the open country and comes twice a day to feed it her milk. Moreover, when the she-goat has returned from grazing and has been driven by the herdsman into the pen, the kid bleats its delight, darts over the ground, and frolics on the grass. But if the goatherd, tired of exerting so much care, should decide to put the mother out into the field along with her newly-born, since this is a mean tribe and utterly unmindful of innate love, the senseless mother does not lovingly care for her nursling, nor does the newly-born seek its mother's udder, though weakened by hunger.

When the herdsmen have completed these difficult tasks, at once they hasten to castrate the troublesome two-year old males. Those, however, whose horns are small and do not as yet cover the forehead, they disregard. Then suddenly you may see the whole family getting fat, the castrated goats, the kids, and the shaggy she-goats, promising a rich reward for the merciless butcher.

Interea niveis vernantia prata ligustris,
Frugibus et variis hortos Pomona decorat.
Vix tamen arva novo florent ridentia vere,
Ignitis cum tota movens pecuaria terris
Rursus iter peragit, rursusque invictus obesa
Rure trahit lente, ducitque in praedia pastor,
Magnus ubi populus tota regione coactus
Infenso mucrone greges laniare paratur.[5]

[*ll. 283-290*]

Villicus hinc primum binas praecingere caulas
Sepibus excelsis, arctisque ad limina valvis
Praecipit et proprium partitur cuique laborem.
Hunc jugulare jubet pecudes, hunc tergore costas
Exuere, atque artus illum condire salinis.
Haec ubi praeses agri consulta mente paravit,
Semimares pubes raptatos pastibus hircos
Includit caulis, ac prima in septa remittit.
Ostia tunc pleni praevertunt arcta caprilis
'Hinc atque hinc bini juvenes, mucrone recluso:
Alter obest, ne uno plures se limine fundant;
Fusum alter cornu prendit; promptusque prehensi
Ense ferit jugulum, laesumque in claustra relegat
Alterius caulae rorantem sanguine multo.
Mox alium atque alium nullo discrimine dextra
Verberat, et ferro candentia colla resolvit.
Barbiger interea crudeli saucius ictu
Tollitur in coelum gemitu, saltuque fugaci
Interdum sepes altas transcendere visus,
Purpureumque vomens lethali e vulnere flumen
Transmittit flavam cursu bacchatus arenam
Infelix, dum tota fluit cum sanguine vita.
Protinus, exanimis secto plebecula ventre,
Exuit hirsuto fumantia tergore membra,
Discerpitque artus, adipis velamine primum
Nudatos ferro; partemque a parte remotam
Excipiunt prompti juvenes ad munia lecti
Quisque suum munus jamjam complere parati.
Pars sale concisos aspergit corporis artus,
Pars vario macerat rigidas medicamine pelles,
Et pars incumbit sevum compingere pilis:
Omnia quae praeses legat mox inde sub urbem.

[*ll. 291-322*]

Nunc agite, et vires quando, mentemque secundam
Sufficit alma Pales; pingui ditissima porco

In the meantime, Pomona adorns the verdant meadows with snow-white ligustrum and arrays the gardens with her various fruits. Yet scarcely are the smiling fields blossoming with the return of spring, when the undaunted herdsman again makes a journey, moving his entire herds out of the hot country, and again he brings them, fattened, slowly back from the plains to the ranch, where a large number of people gather from all the region and prepare to slaughter the animals with the cruel knife.[5]

The manager then orders his men to prepare two folds with high fences and with narrow gates at the entrances and assigns to each man his task. He directs one to slaughter the animals, another to strip the skin from their sides, and a third to cure their legs in brine. When the manager of the ranch has carefully completed these preparations, his men take the castrated goats from the pasture and shut them in the folds, consigning them to the first one. Two young men with ready knives then stand on either side of the narrow gate leading from the crowded fold. The one blocks the exit so that no more than one can leap through; the other catches the goat by the horns as it is making its way out, and holding it quickly stabs its throat with his knife and lets it pass thus wounded and bleeding profusely into the adjoining yard. He then indiscriminately strikes one after another and causes their white necks to droop beneath the iron. For a moment the bearded animal, wounded by the cruel blow, rears toward the sky with a groan and seems at times to be scaling the high fences as he swiftly leaps about; and a scarlet stream flows from his deadly wound. The hapless creature runs frantically across the yellow sand until his entire life ebbs away along with his blood. Straightway they slash the belly of the lifeless animal, they strip the shaggy pelt from the steaming body and cut off the legs, having first stripped them of their coat of fat. The men selected for the task promptly take the separate parts, each one now ready to carry out his own duties. Some sprinkle salt over the pieces which have been cut off, others tan the stiff hides with various chemicals, while still others busy themselves with processing the fat. All of these articles the overseer soon sends away to the city.

Come now, and since bountiful Pales gives me strength and fertility of mind, I shall start from the beginning to tell of the ranches richly stock-

Greges

Praedia, setigerosque greges ab origine dicam.[6]
Principio consultus herus prope tecta domorum
Includit celsis apricum moenibus agrum,
Et binas sumptu fingit praedivite chortes
Aequore diffusas, vitreoque liquore paratas.
(Nam, nisi pura pecus recrearit fluminis unda
Setigerum, nunquam dorso pinguescit obeso,
Hordea saepe vorax quamvis flaventia pascat).
Altera chors, foetis colitur quae matribus, aequor
Undique praecinctum contractis aedibus offert.
Altera, quam vulgus rediens ex rure frequentat
Femineum, immensis constratis pulvere tectis
Cingitur, et turbae jucunda cubilia praebet.
Inde etiam maribus, disjuncta in prata remotis,
Intus haris totidem, limphisque, ac divite chorte
Instructas videas immensis sumptibus aedes,
Unde agros abeant turmae tondere recentes.

[*ll. 323-341*]

Sed prius ardenti rodant quam mollia rictu
Arva sues; dum mane novum, dum Lucifer undis
Exoritur, camposque redux Aurora revisit,
Munera sollicitus larga Cerealia dextra
Disseminat custos, flaventiaque hordea fundit,
Agmina queis avidi solvant jejunia ventris.
Mox satiata petunt, pueris, rectoribus, agrum
In plures distracta greges, effusaque campis
Nunc tranquilla metunt sinuato pascua dente,
Nunc laetis lusura toris dispersa feruntur:
Nec potis est gentem custos cohibere fugacem,
Pinguia ni rigido proscindat terga flagello.
Ast ubi diffusum campis pecus omne coegit,
Et medio Phoebus properat sublimis Olympo,
Ocyus instructo rursus longo agmine turmam
Circumstante manu socium, sub tecta reducit.
Illa renidentis Titanis torrida flammis
Chorte recepta sua vitreos petit anxia fontes,
Et gelidis aestum gaudet relevare fluentis:
Ceu quondam cervus cursu vexatus anhelo,
Vulnere quem laesum longae sitis ardor adurit,
Exhaurit promptis undantia flumina labris.
Mox terris pastor nitratis aequora chortis
Perfundit, cogitque pecus, saturatque salinis,
Ac tectis umbram mittit captare sub altis,

ed with fat swine, and of their bristly herds.[6]
The skilled owner first of all surrounds an open
field near the farm buildings with high walls
and constructs at great expense two inclosed
fields which extend out over the plain and are
provided with crystal clear water; for unless
there is a clear stream of water to refresh the
coarse-haired animals, they never acquire sleek
fat backs, no matter how often or how greedily
they feed upon the yellow barley. The one inclosure, which is occupied by the farrowing
sows, provides a level space surrounded on every
side by small houses. The other, to which the
rest of the sows come when they return from
the field, is provided with large houses having
dirt floors and affording pleasant sleeping
quarters for them. And then you may also see
houses built at great cost for the boars which
are consigned to separate feeding grounds. These
have inside them the same number of sties,
running water, and a richly provided yard out
of which they may go in great numbers to graze
in the fresh fields.

But in the early morning, before the swine
gluttonously feed upon the grassy fields, while
Lucifer is rising out of the waters and Aurora
is revisiting the fields, the attentive keeper of
the swine scatters the gifts of Ceres with lavish
hand and pours out the yellow barley with which
the greedy animals drive hunger from their
stomachs. When satisfied they soon make their
way to the field guided by the boys. Divided
into several droves they spread out over the
fields, and now they peacefully mow the grass
with their curved teeth, now they scatter about
on the delightful turf to play; and the keeper
cannot keep the herd from running away unless he lashes their fat backs with a hard whip.
Now when he has assembled all the herd which
had been scattered over the fields, and Phoebus
is hastening through the middle of the heavens,
he again promptly forms a long column, and
accompanied by his assistants, brings the herd
back to the quarters. Having become hot from
the bright rays of the sun, they eagerly repair
to the crystal waters as soon as they have come
inside their quarters and joyfully cool themselves in the cold stream, as sometimes a panting deer wearied by running and wounded,
when parched by long thirst, drinks with eager
lips from the full streams. Presently the swine-
herd spreads earth mixed with soda over the
floor of the pen, assembles the herds, provides

215

Dum vires Phoebus curru impendente remittat.
Tunc armenta movet, mollique abrepta cubili
Vernantes iterum pastus jubet ire sub agri,
Et gramen tondere novum; spumantia donec
Mergat equos fessos praeceps in caerula Titan.
Ilicet ille greges opulenta ad tecta retorquet
Largaque per chortem reclusis hordea saccis
Objicit, ac multo solatur viscera pastu.
Vix tamen haec avido consumit pabula dente
Cum subito plebes obducti claustra suilis
Pulverulenta petit, tritaque volutat arena
Artus, prolixamque capit per membra quietem.

[*ll. 342-378*]

Saepe etiam fortes experta Cupidinis arcus
Agmina sollicitat flammis Vulcania conjux;
Ferventesque mares sejuncto e rure vocatos
Femineo pecori permiscet villicus agris.
Non tamen ille diu confusam gramine turbam
Imprudens patitur, mixtamque in chorte morari:
Quin etiam patribus lectis ex agmine denas
Praefigit luces; queis magno examine prolem
Suscipiant, repleantque nova penetralia gente.

[*ll. 379-387*]

Post, ubi porca tumens ingenti mole gravatum
Aegre uterum gestat, porrectisque arva papillis[7]
Verrere visa, statim communi chorte remota
Hospitio paritura brevi concluditur arcta,
Grandis ubi pridem gentem manet area foetam,
Infelixque latet diuturno carcere porca.
Hinc aliam atque aliam foecundo pondere pressas
Angustis concludit haris studiosa juventus,
Enixisque replet contracta suilia turmis.
Interdum nec prata Sui vernantia foetae,
Nec propriam quandoque licet percurrere chortem.
Farra tamen videas totis fusa aurea cellis
Et vitreo puros undantes fonte canales,
Languida queis mater, prolisque caterva recentis
Torquentem placare famem, dirumque bibendi
Ardorem possit nitidis extinguere limphis.

[*ll. 388-403*]

Mox, ubi progeniem repetitis nixibus edit
Turba suam, cautis oculis examina lustrat
Villicus; et quos tenues, aut mole minores
Reperit, immeritos subito dat prodiga pullos
Dextra neci, quinis tantum, ternisve relictis,
Quos plenis foecunda parens alat usque mamillis.

[*ll. 404-409*]

them with salt, and permits them to enjoy shade underneath the high roofs until Phoebus in his descending car is diminishing his strength. Then he arouses the pigs from their soft beds and again has them go into the green pastures of the field and graze on the fresh grass until the sun plunges his wearied steeds down into the foaming sea. He then turns the herds back to their well-provided quarters and from open bags throws generous quantities of barley about the pen, amply satisfying their appetites. As soon as they have greedily finished their meal, they at once go inside their dusty sties to wallow in the fine sand and relax their bodies with a long rest.

Often, too, the herds are hit by the arrows from Cupid's stout bow and stirred by the flames of Venus, Vulcan's wife. The manager has the impetuous boars brought from their separate field and united with the sows. But he is not so foolish as to permit them to stay together in the pasture or remain united in the pens for a great length of time, but he allows just ten days for the boars chosen from the herd to beget a prolific offspring and to fill their sties with a new family.

Later on, when the sow has become heavy with young and is scarcely able to carry her burden, and her protruding teats are seen to be brushing the ground,[7] at once she is removed from the common quarters and confined to a small pen in a large area, which had been reserved long before for the farrowing sows, in order that she may there shortly bear her litter. Unhappily she lies in her long confinement. The busy young men shut the sows in the narrow sties, one after another, until the little houses are full of them. A farrowing sow is not permitted in the meantime to travel across the green meadows, nor at times her own inclosure. You will see, however golden grain scattered through all the pens and clean troughs filled with clear water by which the weak mother and her young litter can satisfy their pangs of hunger and quench their thirst.

As soon as the sows, after repeated labor, have brought forth their young, the manager of the ranch examines the litters carefully, and those pigs which he finds weak or too small he wantonly puts to death without delay, undeserving though they be of such treatment, and he leaves only five, or even three, to each mother to suckle from a full udder.

Parva tamen legio claustris jucunda reclusis
Effundit sese, bis denis lucibus actis,
Et teneros lusura ciens per clausa sodales
Atria, praecipiti gaudet concurrere planta.
Inde volutabro juvenilia membra revolvit,
Et lutulenta petit detentam carcere matrem,
Uberaque exhaurit labris conferta tenellis.
Aequora tum chortis repetit, tum limina matris,
Itque reditque viam totis festiva diebus.
[ll. 410-418]

Quatuor ut vero numeravit cornua Lunae
Chortibus excedit subito numerosa juventus
In plures distincta greges, latosque per agros
Improvisa ruit pastus tonsura virentes.
Mascula sed pubes, nunquam visura sorores,
Acta loco longe, campis, ubi turma parentum,
Pellitur, et tectis haeres succedit avitis,
Femineis pullis muliebri in chorte relictis.
[ll. 419-426]

Villicus hic castrare jubet matresque, patresque,
Atque saginandas aurato semine turbas
Providus obsignat, patresque in rure futuros,
Quos postrema dedit porcos faetura novellos.
[ll. 427-430]

Cum vero castrata fabis armenta saginat,
Nec pecus, ut quondam, laetis spatiatur in arvis,
Gramina nec deinceps campi florentia mandit;
Chorte sed ignavum noctesque diesque moratur
Dente fabam crebro, flaventiaque hordea pastum,
Tertia decrescens acuat dum cornua Phoebe.
Tunc artus magna circum pinguedine tectos
Lenta trahunt pecudes. Sed largus villicus instat
Indica densatae frumenta obtrudere genti,
Dum quaesita prius moveat fastidia mensa
Luminaque assiduo succumbant victa sopori.
[ll. 431-441]

Haud mora: continuo ferro praecincta juventus
Agmina crassa movet, raptisque ex agmine porcis
Hic jugulum duro tenerum mucrone resolvit,
Ille adipem solers subjectis purgat ahenis,
Artubus aut pistis farcit de more sagimen,
Cetera dum condit densatum turba cruorem.
Fervet opus, mensasque parat laniena superbas,
Queis opulentus herus repetat cum foenore sumptus.
[ll. 442-449]

FINIS LIBRI UNDECIMI

Now when twenty days have passed, the pens are opened, and the little company happily pours out. They urge their young mates to play throughout the pens and take delight in running swiftly about. Then they wallow in the mud and come back all dirty to their mother still confined to her sty, and with their soft lips they drain her full supply of milk. After that they return to the corral lot and then home again to their mother; and thus they merrily come and go day after day.

When four crescent moons have been counted, numerous young, divided into several herds, immediately leave the corrals. At once they overrun the open fields to feed upon the green pastures. The young males, however, are destined never again to see their sisters, but driven far away to the country of their fathers, they fall heir to the ancestral abodes, while the young females are left in their mothers' quarters.

At this juncture, the manager has both males and females sterilized, wisely marking the females that are to fatten on rich grain, and those young males, born in the last farrowing, that are to become the fathers on the estate.

But when the barrows are being fattened, no longer do they roam over the glad fields as once they did, nor do they continue to graze on rich pastures, but they idly linger day and night in their pens, constantly feeding on beans and yellow barley until waning Phoebe is drawing her horns to a point for the third time. Then the animals slowly draw themselves along, so completely enveloped are they in thick fat. But the generous feeder continues to throw out maize to the heavy swine until the feed, which they formerly craved, is loathed, and their eyes, becoming heavy, frequently succumb to sleep.

Without delay the men, provided with knives, move the fatted herds, and as soon as the animals are caught, one man cuts their tender throats with his cruel knife, another skillfully renders lard in a kettle placed nearby, or, according to custom grinds meat and makes sausage, while the rest of them save the clotted blood. They apply themselves diligently to the work; and the butcher's stall provides sumptuous tables by which the wealthy lord may more than compensate himself for his expenses.

XII

FONTES

Non mihi praecipites violentis fluctibus amnes
Pinguia maturis populantes messibus arva
Cura sequi. Blando vitrei me murmure raptant
Usque redundantes niveo de pumice fontes,
Tuta queis Nymphae captant ad littora somnum.

[*ll. 1-5*]

Numina, quae tacitas ripas habitare sueta
Fronde sub umbrosa frigus captatis opacum,
Lacteaque alternis recreatis membra fluentis,
Dicite, quo duras proscindant impete cautes,
Ac rupto saliant resonantes marmore rivi;
Munere si vestro manant e rupibus undae.

[*ll. 6-11*]

Aethereas qua sacra domus se tollit in auras
Turribus insignis, vastisque augusta columnis,
Religione virum multis cumulata talentis;
Cujus inauratis nitidas fulgoribus aedes
Ornatas gemmis, argento, auroque recocto
Coelicolum Regina tenet Guadalupia Virgo,
Plurima quae larga partitur munera dextra;
Hac rivus mediis ebullit salsus arenis
Impuris limi commiscens faecibus undas,
Quae fauces alveo sitientes turpiter arcent.
Scilicet infectis tetra salsugine campis
Ebibit ingratos labris fons ille liquores.

[*ll. 12-23*]

Ast si lenta tibi febris praecordia rodat,
Divinosque velis pulsare Machaonas omnes
Ipse tui factus languoris doctus Apollo,
Arripe turpatum commixtis sordibus amnem
Despectoque gravi limique, salisque sapore,
Ebibe coenoso certam cum fonte salutem.

[*ll. 24-29*]

Hinc etiam medio putei miraberis alveo
Impete sic magno luteas erumpere limphas,
Ut plenum credas amnem fluere inde per aequor.
Vix tamen alveolo discedit sordibus humor,
Cum subtilis aquae reptat per gramina vena.
Quippe undas furialis agit vesania venti
Carcere conclusi tetro, rabieque maligna
Per rimas agri coelum quaerentis apertum.

[*ll. 30-37*]

SPRINGS

I care not to follow streams that rush along
with impetuous waves and devastate rich lands
along with the ripened harvests. I am attracted
by the clear springs which softly flow in a continuous stream from snow-clad rocks, and on
whose sheltered banks the nymphs doze.

O nymphs, who are wont to inhabit the peaceful banks and enjoy cool shade under the thick
bushes, refreshing your milk-white bodies in one
stream after another, tell me by what force
rivers cut through the hard rocks and leap with
a resounding roar over the precipice, if it be by
your gift that waters issue from the rocks.

There is a place where a sacred house rises
heavenward, famous for its stately towers and
magnificent columns. It was erected at great cost
through the religious zeal of men. Its inner
sanctuary shines with golden splendor, adorned
with precious stones, pure silver, and gold. It
is the shrine of the Virgin of Guadalupe, Queen
of Heaven, who distributes her countless gifts
with a lavish hand. Near this place a salty
stream comes bubbling out of the middle of the
sands, joining its waters to foul and dirty sediment which repels thirsty lips by its unpleasant
taste; for since the fields are soaked with bitter
brine, that spring absorbs within its borders the
disagreeable waters.

But if a persistent fever should be consuming
your vitality, and you should wish to dismiss all
your skilled physicians and become a learned
Apollo for your own malady, take up the waters
sullied by their admixture with sediment, and
disregarding the distasteful mud and salt, drink
them to your certain health.

Then, too, you will be surprised to see how
the muddy stream bursts forth from the middle
of the spring's bed with such violence that you
might suppose a full-sized river to be flowing
out across the plain. Yet the muddy waters
scarcely leave the pit except to seep through the
grass in a tiny rivulet. For it is the fury of a
raging wind, confined within the dark prison
and trying with a desperate madness to find the
open air through crevices in the earth, that
forces the water out.

Nil autem nomen peperit praestantius undis,
Quam facto miranda novo sublimis origo.
Ioannem-postquam-Didacum Vadalupia Virgo
Mexiceasque palam clemens inviserat arces,
Insolitis Indus[1] mentem turbatus et ora
Prodigiis, amissa negat se signa locorum,
Quos plantis Regina suis sacraverat ante,
Posse sequi; mediisque haeret suspensus in arvis
Incertam ducens socium per devia turbam.
Cum subito ruptis salsi compagibus agri
Terra salutiferos (dictu mirabile!) rivos
Ructat, certa loci quondam monumenta futuros,
Virgineos cui Diva pedes insculpserat olim.[2]
Ut solet interdum Princeps, cum sedibus hospes
Succedit, cumulare amplis penetralia donis,
Hospitibusque suum testari gratus amorem:
Haud secus hospitio Virgo suscepta benigno,
Prata salutigeri decoravit munere fontis,
Aeternumque urbi pignus concessit amoris.

[*ll. 38-56*]

Hocce quidem patiens laudis viduatur honore
Dulcis aquae rivus vicina ad tecta redundans
Exigui pagi, Tzapopan nomine dicti.
Sed quae rara polus fonti portenta negavit
Donorum faecunda parens natura rependit.
Funditur immensus siccata per aequora campus,
Nullus ubi effusis humectat rivulus undis
Jugera pressa siti, quam non compesceret Ister.
Totaque flammatis Solis fervoribus usta.
Non ibi cultus ager flaventia semina reddit,
Nec natis arbor curvatur frondea pomis:
Ac nisi cauta solum velaret gramine tellus
Horrida vel pecudes siccis arceret ab arvis.

[*ll. 57-69*]

Qua vero exigui surgunt magalia pagi
Tzapopae, binas in partes scinditur aequor,
Imbreque manantem largo recludit hiatum.
Intus enim gremio fossae penetrabilis alto,
Egregios artis longe superante labores
Natura, recta tectum se fundit in auras
Pumice connexum nullo, totumque pusillis
Undique compactum globulis subtilis arenae,
Abruptamque offert secta compage cavernam,

Nothing, however, has given these waters a higher reputation than their sublime origin, remarkable because of its unusual character. After the Virgin of Guadalupe had shown Juan Diego and the city of Mexico an open manifestation of her mercy, the Indian,[1] mentally disturbed and showing perplexity on his countenance because of the miraculous event, said that he was unable to trace the places which the Queen had made sacred with her footsteps because he had lost the trail; and he stood bewildered out in the middle of the plains as he was guiding his hesitant crowd of companions over the byways, when suddenly the surface of the salty field burst open and the earth—strange to say— belched forth streams of salty water, destined one day to be an everlasting memorial to the spot on which the divine lady had once imprinted her virgin feet.[2] As a prince, when he comes as a guest to a home, often enriches that home with magnificent gifts, bearing grateful testimony of appreciation to his hosts, so the Virgin, having been received with gracious hospitality, adorned the meadow with the gift of a health-bringing fountain and granted to the city an everlasting pledge of her devotion.

Deprived of the glory of such praise, though indeed with resignation, is the stream of fresh water that flows near a small village known by the name of Tzapopan. Yet whatever remarkable portents heaven has denied to this spring, nature, the bountiful mother of gifts, has made a recompense. An immense area extends across the dry plains, which not a rivulet moistens with its flowing waters, for it is parched with a thirst which the Danube might not satisfy and completely scorched by the fiery rays of the sun. There the fields, though cultivated, yield no yellow harvests, nor is there a green tree bending under the weight of new fruit; and if the ground were not by good fortune covered with sod, it would be forbidding and would even keep the flocks away from its dry tracts.

Now where the huts of the little village of Tzapopan appear, the plain is split apart and reveals an abyss out of which there issues an abundance of water. Within the deep bosom of the pit, which is accessible, nature far surpasses the splendid works of art, for a roof extends straight up into the air, not bound together by stone, but entirely constructed of small grains of sand. It presents in its open chamber a deep cavern, not hidden from the

Non clausam Phoebo, tenebrisque nigrantibus atram,
Sed quae avido bibit ore diem, noctemque repellit.
[*ll. 70-80*]

Non tamen undantem quisquam penetrare reces-
sum
Ausit, ni magno coeli fervore coactus
Amne velit gelido totum perfundere corpus.
Tot siquidem dulces protenso e fornice guttae
Crystallo similes, antri per inane ruentes
Praecipitant, ruptos ut credas aethere nimbos
Subjectum rorare solum pluvialibus undis;³
Quin tamen imber humum simili diverberet ictu:
Dextra namque specus magnas fastigia guttas
Disseminant; quales pluvia impendente feruntur
In terram, subitumque cient per tecta fragorem.
Pensilis at vero camerae de parte sinistra
Deucalionaeos tectum se fundit in imbres.
Ut solet irriguos, liquefactis nubibus, agros
Illuvies Australis aquae replere fluentis
Ardua concutiens pluviali tecta tumultu,
Tempore quo terras urit Leo fervidus aestu:
Haud aliter limphis sudant laquearia fossae.
Occupat hinc lustri medium densissimus imber:
Sed blandus, sed lenis aquae, sed murmure lento
Fornicis undantis sensim delapsus ab alto:
Qualis ubi inflexa nimbosus Aquarius urna
Distrahit in tenues coeli per inania guttas
Flumina tranquillo segetes rorantia lapsu.
[*ll. 81-104*]

Inde super videas humentia strata recessus
Aequora diffundi tumidis undantia bullis,
Quae vitreum subito tacitae glomerantur in amnem
Et totam coeco percurrunt impete fossam.
[*ll. 105-108*]

Has tamen ingenti pluvias discrimine lustrum
Distinguit, varioque sagax insignit honore.
Nam, quae saeva lacum fusis quatit imbribus, unda
Opprimit insolito turgentem pondere ventrem.
Quae vero e summo guttatim volvitur arcu
Impendentis aquae simulans alterna fragorem,
Non ita difficili vexat praecordia mole.
At quae tranquillo, tenuique adlabitur imbre,
Nata levare sitim, Phoebique arcere calorem,
Nec plenis epota cadis levis unda nocebit.⁴
[*ll. 109-118*]

Quam vero praestant riguae spiracula limphae,
Flumine quae vitreo, solidoque e marmore tracto
Uruapam circum facilis recurrit amoenam.

sun nor obscured by intense darkness, but on which drinks in the daylight through its wid mouth and repels the night.

No one, however, would venture to enter th moist recess unless, compelled by an extremel hot day, he should wish to bathe his entir body in the cool water; for so many are th sweet crystal-like drops that fall from the high vaulted ceiling and descend through the inter spaces of the cave, that you might think cloud were opening up in the sky and soaking the eartl with rain,³ except that raindrops strike th earth uniformly. On the right, the roof of th cavern lets fall large scattered drops such a fall to earth when a shower is near and a clat tering is suddenly heard on the housetops; or the left side of the high archway, however, ther pours forth from the roof of the cave rain suc as fell in the time of Deucalion. Just as when fiery Leo is parching the earth with heat, a squall arises from the south, and the clouds dis solve in rain, filling the dampened fields with streams of water and causing high buildings to totter in the tempest, so the ceiling of the abyss exudes its waters. The center of the cave, how ever, has a heavy rainfall, though it is a soft and gentle one which slowly falls from the top of the dripping grotto with a soft rippling sound, just as rainy Aquarius, having overturned his pitch er, breaks into little drops his waters in the sky and sprinkles the crops with a gentle shower.

Then you may see a surge of water pouring over the damp floor of the recess, suddenly formed from large bubbles into a crystal stream which by a force unseen, quietly spreads over the entire abyss.

Now the grotto draws a sharp distinction be tween these waters, wisely giving to them dif ferent virtues. For the stream that wildly stirs the lake with heavy rains rests unusually heavy on a full stomach, but the one which comes roll ing down drop by drop from the top of the archway, like the pitter-patter of first raindrops, does not distress the system with such heaviness. Moreover, that which descends in a calm and gentle rain is just right for allaying thirst and for warding off the heat of Phoebus, and since it is light, will do no harm even though drunk from full cups.⁴

But how much better is the spring of cool waters whose stream proceeds crystal-clear from the solid marble and gently flows around beau-

lla urbem propter, montis radice sub alti,
¡axea telluris violento viscera rumpit
mpete, et horrentes linquens fugitiva cavernas
nde per ora novem ternis hiscentia palmis,
¡ec vasto spatio multum distracta vicissim,
¡rumpit convexa tumens argentea limpha,
Aspergitque omnes bullis turgentibus alveos.
Quisque fuga deinceps labris se subtrahit arctis
'ons, vastumque petens, ripa crepitante, canalem
Undantem replet geminatis fluctibus amnem.
Reptat humi rivus cursu per opaca sonoro,
Abluit Uruapam, campoque eductus aperto
¡axa per, et glebas barathrum declivis in altum
Accelerat gressum; praeceps ubi fossa profundam
Vallem aperit duris horrentem cautibus, atque
Virgultis densam rimosa ex rupe renatis,
Quae pennata cohors volucrum festiva frequentat.

[*ll. 119-138*]

Hanc vero in vallem praeceps instante ruina
Volvitur amnis aqua coelum volitante per omne.
Nec tamen aequali claustrum transcendere saltu
Correnti natura dedit; pars quippe supremas
Conscendit rupes, horrentia labra, canalis;
Indeque praecipiti saltu petit ima per auras,
Dum reliquum lato, limphae stagnantis ad instar,
Alveo subsidit flumen, simulatque quietem.
Nam cum dura silex hinc inde repagula tollens
Innumeris circum rimis incisa fatiscat,
Ceu magnum densa terebratum cuspide cribrum,[5]
Praebet iter tectum clauso ingeniosa liquori.
Hinc cautes summo compressos impete fontes
In jactus totidem, quot rimis dura dehiscunt
Maenia, divisos ludens jaculatur in auras.
Ceu tenso quondam nervo contorta sagitta
Impete lapsa fero vacuum proscindit inane
Effugiens arcum magno conamine flexum:
Haud secus unda fluens cursu fugit alite saxa.
Aspera quae superat violento maenia saltu
Unda tenet medium: cribroque elisa frequenti
Hac illac fluvio salienti e rupibus astat,
Raraque divinae referat miracula dextrae.
Inde lacum quatiunt lapso jam fonte coactum,
Vitreus unde fluens sinuosis flexibus amnis
Algenti recreat pecudes, agrosque liquore.

[*ll. 139-164*]

Non ita rivus aquis unquam refrigerat arva,
Quem tetra clivus revomit Chucandirus alvo.

tiful Uruapan. Near the city and at the foot of a high mountain it bursts with great force from the earth's rocky bosom, and escaping from the horrible caverns through nine mouths, three palms wide and not very far from one another, the swelling stream of silver bursts from the vaulted chamber and fills all its channels with its bubbling waters. Each spring then withdraws in haste from the narrow openings and babbling along inside its banks comes to a large canal, and joining with it, forms a full surging stream. The stream creeps along the ground through shady grove, babbling as it goes. It bathes Uruapan, and moving out through the open country increases its speed over the rocks and through the fields and falls into an abyss lying far below. There its deep channel reveals a vast ravine bristling with rocks, thickly covered with bushes growing in the cracks of the rocks and inhabited by happy throngs of birds.

Now down into this ravine the stream instantly goes tumbling, and its spray flies all through the air. Yet nature has not allowed the torrent to leap uniformly across the barrier, for one part rises over the highest rocks which form the rough brim of the channel and then with a downward bound falls through the air to the bottom, while the rest of the stream settles over the wide bed just like a pool of still water and pretends to be calm. Since the solid rock removes its barriers here and there by opening up innumerable cracks all around like a huge thickly perforated sieve,[5] it ingeniously provides a secret outlet for the water. Hence the rough rock divides and playfully tosses the stream, which had been held back, with the greatest violence into the air from as many places as there are holes through the rocky wall. As an arrow once shot from a tightly drawn bow flies away with terrific force, cleaving the interspaces of the sky, so the stream flies along on its winged course from the rocks. The water which leaps madly over the rocky wall occupies the center, and constantly buffeted on this side and that by the streams which leap through the rocky sieve, it reveals the wonders of the divine hand. These waters strike the pool formed by the water already fallen, and there flows out in a winding course a crystal stream which refreshes the herds and the fields with its cool waters.

Not in such a way does the stream which the hill of Chucándiro ejects from its dark bosom

Ille per auriferae silicis praecordia cursu
Praecipiti fertur caecum terebrasse canalem,
Magnanimoque ausu pinguem penetrare fodinam.
Ut vero torvi Plutonis regna revisit,
Volvitur in praeceps patulo fons aureus ore,
Non gelidum rigidis eructans faucibus amnem
Fertilibus campi recreandis faetibus aptum;
Sed ferventis aquae glebas rigat ille fluentis,
Ut limphis mollire dapes, carnemque domare,
Ac tauri possis costis avellere tergus.

[*ll. 165-176*]

Si tamen aeger ames quemvis expellere morbum,
Tu solers propter fumantia flumina thermas
Extrue: dumque ignem furialis limpha remittit,
Membra tepescentes demergas creber in undas,
Tota quoad fracto discedat corpore pestis:
Tabida ni febris lento fervore medullas
Rodat, languentesque diu tenuaverit artus.
Scilicet in certam pellit fons ille ruinam
Tabe laborantes, lethoque immergit acerbo.

[*ll. 177-185*]

Insolitis etiam fervescunt aestibus undae
Grata salutifero rorantes flumine rura,
Vilia quae tenuis cingunt magalia pagi,
Nomine quem proprio effert Bartholomaeus in astra.
Dives erat propter spectandus gramine multo
Campus, ubi parvo curvantur jugera dorso,
Tectaque visceribus latitat Vulcania pestis
Undique flagrantes dorsi radice liquores
Eructans, multoque immiscens aequora fumo.
Parvus enim puteus subjectis ignibus ustus
Tam violenta tumens incendia concipit aestu,
Moenibus ut propriis, nigrisque iratus arenis
Bulliat insanus, coelique ad culmina nubem
Fumantem tollat, Solemque umbrare minetur.
Ast mirum, quantum parvo digressus ab alveo
Et laetas faciat segetes, et largus aristis
Foenore multiplici Cerealia munera donet.
Non campus gravidis fusos de nubibus imbres,
Nec limosa sitit turgentis flumina Nili;
Ductilibus roret puteus dum prata fluentis.

[*ll. 186-205*]

Nemo tamen fontis calidas sitit amplius undas,
Quam duri gravibus morbi cruciatibus ustus.
Nullus enim tanto vexabit membra dolore,
Nec putridis adeo depascet febribus artus
Morbus, quem calido non pellant balnea fonte.

ever refresh the fields. With its swift current i
is said to have formed an underground passage
way through the heart of gold-producing rock
and to have penetrated a rich mine with high
handed boldness. And when it has visited gri
Pluto's realm, the fountain of gold comes flow
ing swiftly out through a wide opening, emit
ting no cool stream from its rocky outlet fit fo
refreshing the bountiful crops of the field, bu
soaking the land with streams of water so ho
that you can cook food in it, boil meat, and eve
take the skin from the sides of a bull with it.

If, then, when sick, you should desire to ri
yourself of the malady, whatever it be, carefull
construct a bath near the steaming waters, an
while the turbulent water is cooling, kee
bathing your limbs in it until the illness leave
your frail body, unless a persistent fever i
wasting away your strength and has emaciate
your weakened body, for this spring causes cer
tain destruction to those afflicted with tubercu
losis and plunges them into a painful death.

With extraordinary heat, also, do the water
boil which pour their salutary streams over th
delightful country surrounding the lowly cot
tages of a little village which Bartholomew
exalts with his own name. A rich field lies near
by, remarkable for its thick grass, on which
there rises a gently sloping hill, in the inner
most part of which the destructive force o
Vulcan lies concealed, exhaling boiling liquid
all around from the foot of the hill and filling
the plain with thick vapor. Indeed, the little
spring, heated by the fires below, boils and be
comes so hot that it angrily swells up and madly
bubbles inside its own walls of black sand. It
throws a cloud of smoke to the pinnacle of
heaven and all but darkens the sun. Yet it is
remarkable how, when it has left its little basin,
it gladdens the crops and generously bestows
to the heads of wheat the gifts of Ceres with
manifold increase. The field does not thirst for
showers of rain from heavy clouds, nor for the
muddy floods of a swollen Nile so long as the
spring irrigates the meadows with its waters.

No one, however, thirsts for the warm waters
of the spring as much as one who is suffering
severely from a dread disease. For no disease
tortures the body with such intense pain or
wastes away the limbs with such devastating
fever that hot baths in the spring will not drive

Non febris, non plaga putris, non gallica pestis,
Nec quae perpetuis constringit corpora vinclis
Prava lues, unquam limphis immota resistet.
[*ll.-206-213*]

Praeterea crebro terebrata foramine tellus
Ardentem circum puteum, nunc ignea limphas
Ferventes revomit, coeco nunc impete fumum
Projicit, et totum coelumque, agrumque vapore
Umbrat. Quaeque tamen pretioso provida limo
Large spumanti, ac tergendis vestibus apto,
Rima verecundis semper succurrit egenis.⁶
Indica ceu vestes Aloe,⁷ potumque, cibosque,
Tectaque Mexiceis constanti munere donat:
Haud secus accensus rapido fons limpidus aestu
Smegma tibi, limphasque dabit, certamque medelam.
[*ll. 214-224*]

Nil tamen occiduos exornat gratius agros
Quam largis rivus limphis insignis et ortu,
Priscus Aticpacus quem coelo laudibus aequat.
Subter enim vicum tellus saxosa dehiscens
Aspera sublimis recludit viscera montis,
Ingentemque aperit nivea inter marmora fossam
Collibus hinc atque hinc septam, scopulisque rigen-
tem.
Quae cyathum tereti referens curvata figura
Volvitur in gyrum, muscosoque hispida mento
Saxa tegit vasis, quod non alata sagitta
Trajiciat, nec Cola queat superare natatu.
[*ll. 225-235*]

Imminet huic cyatho praecelso vertice conus,
Arbore densus apex, frondisque obscurus ab umbra,
Et qui sublimi superante cacumine nubes
Solus opem posset turbae praestare gigantum,
Si celsum rursus vellet conscendere coelum.
Inde per abruptas resonanti gurgite rimas
Praecipites rorant niveis de rupibus amnes
Immensam claro qui totam flumine fossam
Replent, et grato pulsant cava saxa tumultu.
Ast adeo purus manat pellucidus humor,
Ut pisces valeas facile numerare natantes,
Calculus et fundo pateat numerabilis omnis.
Cum vero vitreis muscosas abluit undis
Cautes, turgenti decurrens gurgite latus
Amnis iter praebet ratibus venientibus alto,
Inceditque gravis per amoenos frondibus agros,
Nunc lucos rorans dextra, nunc prata sinistra,
Tergemino donec contingat vortice pontum.
[*ll. 236-253*]

it out. Neither fever, nor putrefying plague, nor social diseases, nor the dreadful malady which keeps the body continually paralyzed, will ever stand unshaken by these waters.

Besides, the earth, being perforated with numerous holes around the hot spring, is very hot, and now vomits forth a stream of boiling waters, and now by an unseen force shoots out steam overshadowing all the sky and land. Moreover, each opening always yields a precious clay which foams freely and which, because it is good for cleaning clothes, is an aid to the needy.⁶ As the Indian aloe⁷ provides the Mexicans with a constant supply of drink and food and shelter, so the crystal-clear spring, heated to a high temperature, will provide you with a cleaning substance, with water, and with a sure remedy.

Nothing, however, more pleasingly adorns the country of the west than the river, famous for its source and its plentiful waters, which the people of old Aticpac praise to the sky. For just below the village the stony ground opens up, revealing the rough interior of the high mountain and disclosing between white marble walls a large ravine bordered on either side by hills and rocky ledges. It assumes the uniform roundness of a bowl, and conceals its jagged rocks by a moss-covered brim. It is so wide that a winged arrow could not traverse it nor a Colaⁿ swim across it.

Overhanging this bowl is a lofty mountain peak, its summit thickly covered with trees and hidden under the shade of foliage, and which, since it towers above the clouds, could by itself lend aid to the host of giants, if again they should essay to scale the heights of heaven. Through the rocky crevices of this mountain and over its white cliffs streams go thundering down filling all the immense ravine with clear water and splashing against the hollowed rocks with a pleasing sound. Indeed, so clear and pure is the water that you can easily count the fishes as they swim about, and every pebble that lies on the bottom can be numbered. And when these crystal waters have bathed the moss-covered cliffs, they then flow out in a full stream, providing a wide passageway for those who come on ships from the sea. The river travels along majestically through the beautiful green fields, at one time moistening the groves on the right, and now the meadows on the left until, divided into three streams, its rolling waters reach the sea.

Dulcior at nobis largo fons vitreus amne,
Mollis ubi populus languentia corpora thermis
Recreat, et nocuum gaudet lenire calorem.
Non formosus aquas viridanti culmine clivus,
Aut vomit abscisso scabrosus marmore collis,
Sed medio paulum subsidens aequore fossa
Exsecta in lunam, vicenisque amplior ulnis,
Arida quam circum muris argilla coronat.
Inde potens agri gremio natura recluso
Per bis ter sectos nullo sudore canales
Ingentem populo cumulum permittit aquarum.
Ut tamen accepto misceret seria ludo,
Alternis fontem solers insigniit undis.
Haec siquidem calido desudat flumine rima;
Illa tepescentem facili vomit ore liquorem;
Frigida queis alio ructata foramine limpha
Succedit, variisque replent humoribus alveum
Mobilibus stratum globulis candentis arenae.
His opulentus aquis medio fons semper adornat
Balnea rure, gelu mixto jucunda calori;
Quae neque marmoreis alibi fulgentia labris,
Vana nec argento quondam radiantia puro
Ductilibus potuere unquam superare fluentis.

[*ll. 254-276*]

Ah! Quoties olim tepidis demersus in undis,
Ebria cum tumidis undat vindemia botris,
Fracta salutiferis recreabam corpora thermis:
O! utinam fesso rursum mihi prisca licerent
Balnea, crystalloque pares invisere fontes,
Et coelo, terraque iterum gaudere benignis!

[*ll. 277-282*]

Sed quoniam truculenta negat Fortuna levamen
Omne mihi, facili modulatus carmina plectro
Dulcia rura sequar, doctasque Heliconis ad undas
Turbida sylvestri solabor taedia cantu.
Vos rupes, Nymphae, vos vestros pandite fontes,
Et patrii miranda soli reserare professi
Mexiceae majora Deae portenta canamus.

[*ll. 283-289*]

Pagus erat latis Istlanus nobilis agris
Et riguis opulentus aquis, ac divite gleba,
Quam partim cupidus rastris domat usque colonus,
Armentis partim largus concedit alendis.
Hinc laetas videas messes flavescere terra,
Ac passim tondere altos pecuaria pastus.
Divitias agri mediis effusus arenis
Illimi fons auget aqua, quae jugera circum

But sweeter to me is the large crystal-clear spring in which the sick restore their failing strength by hot baths and joyfully relieve their feverish heat. No lovely green-crested hill, nor mountain ridged with jutting marble ejects streams of water, but a crescent-shaped ravine lying rather low in the middle of the plain, more than twenty cubits wide and surrounded with walls of dry clay. Here mighty nature without any effort opens up the bosom of the earth and through two or three openings supplies the people with an abundance of water. But to add a lighter vein to the serious, the spring is remarkable for the ingenious way in which it varies its waters, for one opening gives out warm water, a second one freely emits a stream of tepid water, followed in turn by cold water gushing from another opening. With their respective waters they fill the channel, the bottom of which is covered with white grains of shifting sands. Abundantly fed by these waters, the fountain always provides baths out in the open country with cold water agreeably mixed with hot, baths which could never be excelled elsewhere at any time, though their waters be poured into tubs of gleaming marble or vainly shine in those of sterling silver.

Ah! how often in time past have I dived into those warm waters, at the time when juicy grapes were waving in heavy clusters on the vine, and refreshed my weary body with a healing bath! Oh that I might be permitted again, when wearied, to enjoy those baths of old, to visit those waters crystal-clear, and to enjoy once more the pleasant sky and land!

But since cruel fortune denies me every relief, I shall repair to the fields singing sweet melodies to the accompaniment of the lyre, and beside the learned waters of Helicon I shall alleviate my depressing weariness with a song of the country. Open, O nymphs, your rocks and springs, and since I have promised to reveal the marvels of my native land, allow me to sing of the greater wonders of the goddess of Mexico.

There is a place known as Ixtlán, famous for its wide fields, rich supply of water, and fertile soil, one portion of which the ambitious farmer tills with hoe, another he generously turns over to his herds for grazing. You may, therefore, see across the land abundant harvests turning yellow and scattered herds browsing in the deep pastures. The bounty of the field is increased by a spring of unsullied water which is-

'unditur, egregiumque sibi per saecula nomen
'ecit. Namque per abruptum fons missus hiatum
Jum vagas effusos campos riget amne perenni,
Attamen alveolo quisquam si forte propinquet
Obtutu lustrare vigil miranda fluenti,
'rotinus unda pedem, veluti suffusa rubore,
Jauta refert retro, gressumque exterrita torquet;[8]
Moxque iterum latici vitreas producit habenas.
Jt solet herba toro surgens Pudibunda virenti
ngenti bifidas luxu depromere frondes;
5i tamen ipse comas unquam temerarius ausis
ncauta tractare manu, tunc ilicet omnes
Herba plicat frondes, roseo correpta pudore:[9]
Non secus unda pudens oculos fontana refugit.
Juod si tantillum rivi digressus ab alveo
Ingeniosus ames passus iterare relictos,
Cunctantemque prius repetito examine fontem
Aspicias, fluitans non amplius unda moratur,
Sed cursu reptat celeri fugitiva per agrum.

[*ll. 290-316*]

His autem majora tibi portenta recludit
Crebra jugis, Phoeboque flagrans Guasteca furenti.
Non pavidas undas, nec stagna fluentia vitro
Jactat; sed limpham, promptas quae vocibus aures
Porrigit, ingratoque furit commota fragore.
Tollitur e calidae gremio telluris amoeno
Tranquilla fons mitis aqua, tenuique susurro,
Culmine quem clivus ructat Tamapachius alto,
Tergaque delapsis rorat vernantia limphis.
Ast placidi fontis cornu si forte sonoro,
Incautusve agites raucis clamoribus amnem,
Unda furens subito magnas exardet in iras.
Saevit inops animi, circumque insana per alveum
Ducitur, et jactis putei quatit aspera limphis
Moenia: quoque magis litui clangoribus aether
Personat, aut alto montes clamore tremiscunt,
Hoc magis, amenti similis, furit undique rivus.
Ut vero posito tranquilla silentia cornu
Succedunt, aut ora sonum, vocemque coercent,
Fons rabiem ponit, nec rursus commovet undas.[10]

[*ll. 317-336*]

Non· ita, flagranti vesanis fluctibus irae
Teguacanus aqua laetos fons irrigat agros;[11]
Sed foliis leviora parit per saxa fluenta,
Semina queis reddit pinguis flaventia gleba.
Amnis enim gremio missus telluris ab imo

sues forth from the midst of the sand and flows over acres of territory, and which through the years has made for itself a great name. Although the spring rises abruptly from its source and flows forever in a winding stream across the broad fields, yet if anyone chance to come near its mouth to examine closely the strange nature of its flow, at once its waters cautiously recede, as if blushing and turning away in fright,[8] but a little later again unloose the reins of their crystal stream. As the sensitive plant growing in a green bed is wont with much pomp to put forth its bifid leaves, yet if ever you should be rash enough to stretch a heedless hand to its foliage, with a flush of modesty it immediately folds its leaves,[9] so the fountain in modesty shrinks from sight. But if, carefully retracing your steps, you should withdraw just a little distance from its source and re-examine the spring that before lingered, you will see that the stream no longer delays its flow, but swiftly creeps away through the field.

But greater wonders than these are revealed to you by Guasteca, covered by mountain ridges and heated by a fierce sun. It throws out no timid waters, neither does it have pools of crystal clearness, but it has waters which stretch eager ears for voices and become infuriated when disturbed by an unpleasant noise. There rises out of the warm bosom of the fair land a gentle stream of quiet and softly rippling water which Mount Temapache sends forth from its high summit, and with which it moistens its green slopes. But if by chance you should heedlessly disturb the quiet spring with the sound of a horn or by loud shouting, the water suddenly goes into a rage, it burns with great anger, and bereft of mind it raves and moves madly around in its channel shaking the rocky walls of the pit with its heaving waters. And the more the air rings with the blast of the horn, or the mountains vibrate from the loud noise, the more the stream rages on every side like a madman. When, however, the horn has been put aside and a peaceful silence follows, or when the sound of voices has ceased, the spring abates its fury, nor again agitates its waters.[10]

Not with such angry waves of surging waters does the spring of Teguacán irrigate the fertile fields,[11] but through the rocks it brings forth streams lighter than leaves and causes the fertile soil to produce its golden seeds. For the stream comes from the deep bosom of the earth and does

Aequora nequaquam perfundit fonte perenni;
Alternis sed enim manat mutabilis horis,
Nunc grato virides irrorans flumine campos,
Nunc, inter montis cursu spelaea retento,
Destituens parcus sitientes prorsus arenas.
Nec compressa siti rursus fluit unda per arva
Quin prius e sectis horrentia flamina rimis
Praemittat, trepidoque sonent cava lustra boatu.¹²
Ut solet instabili rivus Lavyelius amne
Nunc instare labris, nunc furto abducere limphas,
Nunc superare moras, nunc inter saxa morari.¹³

[*ll. 337-352*]

Nec tamen hos tractus adeo faecunda decorat
Prodigiis natura suis, ut caetera fastu
Aequora despiciens, ipsis portenta negarit:
Quin etiam diris Nexapa obnoxia morbis
Fontanos docuit latices manare vicissim.
Surgit enim celsum media regione cacumen
Suprema Phoebo minitans cervice ruinam,
Cujus per latum, scissa radice, foramen
Purior argento, vitroque simillimus amnis
Manat, qui luces cursu metitur et umbras
Alterno, Solemque fugit, Lunamque requirit:
Vix siquidem flavas Solaris lampas arenas
Lumine perfundit, Phoeboque effulgere fluctus
Incipiunt, cum limpha gradum taciturna retorquens,
Ceu Solis radios odio nascentis haberet,
Continuo nigro se claudit montis in antro.
Ast ubi Phoebus equos Neptuni mergit in undas.
Humida nox instat, Phoebeque incerta propinquat,
Ocyus instabilis repetit sua flumina cursu
Fons celeri, camposque irrorat noctis in umbris.

[*ll. 353-372*]

Larga tamen nusquam plures natura coegit
Prodigio similes fontes, quam montis in alvo
Lenibus undanti labris, lustrisque frequenti,
Quem populi prisca Quincum de voce vocarunt.
Nunc siquidem videas fluitantes amne cavernas
Dulci; nunc liquido sudantes sulphure; fontes
Nunc etiam salsos nitrato flumine, cujus
Candenti spuma fastigia dura renident.
Haec gelida rorat celso de culmine fossa;
Illa per occultos calido fluit amne canales;
Ni mordax revomat per rimas cautis alumen.
Undique limpha fluit vario medicamine mixta,
Congrua deliciis, et morbis nata mederi.

[*ll. 373-385*]

FINIS LIBRI DUODECIMI

not spread across the plains with perennial flow, but changes its course with the alternating hours, at one time watering the green fields with a pleasant river, now holding its course inside the caves of the mountain, entirely forsaking the thirsty sands. Nor does the water flow again over the dry fields without first sending forth frightening blasts through the cracks and causing the cavernous places to resound with a dreadful sound.¹² Thus the fickle waters of the Lavyelio river are wont to stay inside their borders at one time, to withdraw stealthily at another time, now they overcome their inertia, again they linger among the rocks.¹³

Yet bountiful nature does not glorify these regions with her marvels to such a degree that, in high disdain of all other lands, she has denied to them wonders. On the contrary, Nexapa, subject to dreadful diseases, has produced fountains which flow intermittently. A tall mountain peak, whose summit threatens the sun with ruin, rises in the middle of the country, and through a wide aperture at its foot flows a stream purer than silver and very glassy which measures the light of day and the shadows of night with its alternating course, for it avoids the sun, yet seeks the moon. Indeed, no sooner is the light of the sun bathing the yellow sands with light and sending its beams across the billows when the waters quietly turn back, as if to loath the rays of the rising sun, and immediately confine themselves to the dark cave of the mountain. But when Phoebus is plunging his horses down into Neptune's waves, as moist night presses on and Phoebe is dimly appearing, the changing fountain suddenly reverses its course and with a swift current waters the fields during the shades of night.

Moreover, generous nature has nowhere assembled more miraculous springs than those which gently flow from the bosom of a thickly wooded mountain, called in early times Quinceo. You may see grottoes from which flow streams of fresh water, at one time distilling sulphur, and again fountains of tangy natron whose salty surface glistens with bright foam. One stream flows from the lofty summit through a cool ravine, another, having hot water, flows through an underground channel or disgorges its acrid salts through clefts in the rocks. On every side the streams are combined with various minerals, pleasing to the taste and designed to heal the sick.

XIII

AVES

Indigenas cano ruris aves,[1] quas praedia lucis
Usque renascentes donant obsonia mensis;
Et quas umbroso ramorum nigra recessu
Sylva tegit pictas vario splendore colorum,
Et blandas resono modulantes gutture voces;
Ac demum quas arma juvant, et vivere rapto.
[*ll. 1-6*]

Magna quidem aggredior. Vestras reserate,
    Napaeae,
Vallis opes, totoque omnes accersite luco
Ante oculos volucres, moresque, habitusque benignae
Dicite, et alternos nemoris per frondea cantus.
[*ll. 7-10*]

Innumeras quondam sylvis America volantes
Condidit insignes nitido velamine plumae,
Egregiasque adeo dulcis modulamine linguae.
Inde etiam patrias cicuratas chorte volucres
Nutrierat, multosque sinu complexa feraci
Ediderat teneros pipienti examine pullos,
Cum generosa dedit nobis Hispania dono
Gallinas, charaeque tulit convivia genti.
Ut vero Hispanus vectas super alta carinis
Chortibus has junxit, praestantia dona, volucres,
Gallinis resonant passim glocientibus urbes,
Praediaque, et pagi, et miserae magalia plebis.
Quis tamen has memoret, postquam Vanierius omnes
Providus implevit pretioso munere chortes,
Aoniamque tulit, Phoebo plaudente, coronam?
[*ll. 11-25*]

Chortibus hinc tutis, et chortis gente relicta,
In nigras sylvae tacitus decedo latebras
Fallere sylvestres laqueo, viscoque volantes.
[*ll. 26-28*]

Jamque Indum longe nemora inter frondea Pavum
Agmine densato sobolis, turbaque sororum
Stipatum cerno gramen tondere sub umbra.
Nam modo qui longo chortes examine replet,
Continuisque agitat nostras clamoribus aures,
Incoluit memorum, nullo moderante, recessus,
Principiumque trahens silvestri a sanguine patrum
Immortale genus frondoso in monte reliquit.
[*ll. 29-36*]

BIRDS

I sing of the country's native birds[1] which
ever flourish in the woodlands and provide the
estates with delicacies for the table, of those
brilliantly arrayed in many colors which the
black forest hides in the shady recesses of its
branches, of those that lift their rich voices in
sweet song, and finally of those that enjoy war-
fare and like to feast on their prey.

A great theme indeed it is that I undertake.
Reveal, O nymphs of the wood, the riches of your
valley and bring before my eyes all the birds
from every forest and kindly tell me of their
habits, their character, and of their songs which
reverberate among the branches of the woodland.

America once concealed in her forests innumerable birds, exquisitely cloaked in bright plumage and excelling in sweetness of song. Then,
too, she had raised at home her own domesticated
fowl and had produced in her fertile bosom
many chirping pullets when Spain generously
sent us as a gift the chicken to provide feasts
for the dear people. And now that Spain has
brought these fowl in ships across the sea to
become a splendid addition to our poultry-
yards, clucking hens are heard everywhere in
the cities, on the ranches, in the hamlets, and
about the huts of the poor. But who is to tell of
these, since eloquent Vaniere[1a] has filled the
poultry-yards with his precious gift of song, and
borne away an Aonian crown with the applause
of Phoebus?

I shall therefore leave the sheltered poultry-
yard with its flocks and go quietly into the dark
recesses of the forest to trap the wild birds with
snare or lime.

And now I see the native peacock far away
among the underbrush with a large number of
young ones and a company of hens picking the
thick grass beneath the shade. Indeed, the peafowl that in large numbers now fills the yards
and assails the ears with its constant outcries
once freely inhabited the recesses of the forest
and has left behind in the thickly wooded mountain an immortal race from whose wild blood
it traces its origin.

227

Segnis ad effusum volucris montana volatum
Praevalet ardenti prolixa per aequora cursu.
Illa sagax nidos subter virgulta tenellos
Constituit, gaudetque umbris obducere prolem,
Et totam socium, Phoebo flagrante catervam.
Ut vero auratum Titan caput extulit umbris,
Ilicet in campum turbam mas ducit amoenum,
Alternisque orbes innectens orbibus unus
Accensum sociis intus testatur amorem.
Turgidus ingluviem, colloque in terga retorto
Erigit hirsutas magno conamine plumas;
Radit humum pennis, velatque proboscide rostrum,
Expansoque altae sinuoso sirmate caudae
Flexilis in gyrum toto devolvitur agro,
Et circum denso cingit glomeramine Pavas.
Utque omnes petulans turbae persolvit honores,
Fonte levare sitim vicina in flumina ducit
Inde reducturus nota ad virgulta sodales.

[*ll. 37-54*]

Tu tamen ut captis agites convivia Pavis
(Quippe cohors avium, nescit quae septa domorum,
Obtegit aurata totum pinguedine corpus)
Sollicitus dextra teretes tibi sume bacillos,
Et dum turba levis sub frondis pipilat umbra,
Pelle loco denso, productumque ejice in aequor.
Illa catervatim cursu se proripit acri,
Praecipitique fuga patulum se fundit in agrum.
Ocyus ipse tuis jactis in crura bacillis
Obtruncare pedes, lucoque arcere labora.
Illa pedes subito binos truncata quiescit,
Et gemebunda sedet frondentis gramine campi.

[*ll. 55-66*]

Ast solet interdum noctis pennata sub umbras
Turba virescentes alis conscendere truncos
Arboribusque latens placido indulgere sopori.
Ipse tuos solers laqueis tunc cinge bacillos,
Et socium magna munitum lampade tecum
Educ, qui flammis Pavorum lumina pascat.
Ut vero tacita laxarit membra quiete
Alituum sociata cohors, rumore profundum
Rumpe gravi somnum, flammatamque objice taedam
Turbae commotae, subitoque fragore timenti.
Illa coruscanti subjectam lampada luce
Luminibus lustrat fixis, porrectaque colla
Obtutu mirata jubar defigit in uno,
Rustica ceu quondam, campisque assueta juventus,
Oppida quae nunquam, nec magnas viderat urbes,

This mountain bird, too slow for prolonged flight, excels in speed of foot as it runs across the wide plains. The mother bird wisely builds her soft nest under bushes and joyously covers her little ones and the whole flock of companions with shade when Phoebus is ablaze. When, however, the Titan has thrust his golden head from the shades of night, then the cock leads his company into the lovely plain, and turning himself around in one circle after another he alone bears testimony to his mates of the love that burns within him. With swollen crop and arched neck he slowly lifts his ruffled plumage and scrapes the ground with his wings. His crest falls across his beak, and his long tail spreads out like a trailing robe as he circles about over all the field and walks around the closely gathered peahens. And when with an important air he has paid full respects to the flock, he leads it to a neighboring stream to quench its thirst, and then back again to the familiar bushes.

Now that you may capture peafowls and have the pleasure of eating them, seeing that these birds, strangers to the restraints of domestication, have their entire bodies covered with yellow fat, diligently take in your hand a round stick, and while the company is gently chirping beneath the shade of the bushes, drive it forth from the thicket and chase it out into the open plain. The fowl rush swiftly out in flocks and pour into the open field in headlong flight. Quickly throw the stick at their legs in an effort to cut off their feet and keep them from the woods. When both their feet have been cut off, at once they stop and lie moaning on the grassy field.

Sometimes, however, the feathered company is wont at nightfall to rise on wing into dense trees and enjoy peaceful slumber, hidden among the branches. In that case, carefully fix a noose to your sticks and take along with you a helper provided with a large torch with which to blind the eyes of the peafowls. Now when the birds are huddled together relaxed in sleep, stir them from their deep slumber with a loud noise, and when they are awake and frightened by the sudden disturbance, flash the lighted torch on them. They gaze down upon the torch fastening their eyes on the dazzling light, and in rapt amazement they stretch out their necks to stare at its brightness, as sometimes country boys, accustomed to the fields and never having seen large towns or cities, if ever they are permitted

Si quando auratos liceat spectare penates,
Inscia turba silet, mentemque per omnia volvens
Circumfert oculos, laribusque abscedere nescit.
Interea quercum sensim conscende comantem
Armatus baculis, cautusque silentia serva.
Tunc Pavi collum laqueo connecte retortum,
Innexumque statim sublimi dejice trunco,
Quem socii ramis delapsum dextra prehendat.
Mox alium atque alium laqueatis prende bacillis,
Dum totam Pavis quercum nudaveris altam.

[*ll. 67-91*]

Mole refert Pavum cristatus Phasidis ales
Seu fulvus fuerit, nigrave rubigine tinctus:
At molem facile praestanti corpore vincit.
Erigit ille brevi sublimem vertice cristam
Mollibus effictam plumis, cultuque decoram;
Ac Cyprium flava penna referente metallum,
Aut potius nigra pulchrum superante Gagatem
Obtegit egregios artus; croceoque veneno
Crura nitent, rostrumque audent aequare colore.
Non celeri volucris praestat festina volatu,
Nec celsas audet pennis conscendere pinus:
Sed superat crebro nemorum sublimia saltu
Arduaque impavidum gaudet captare soporem.
Tarda tamen pennis, plantis producta citatis
Aequora metitur; camposque emensa patentes
Eludit celeres subeuntes pone molossos.
Hinc opus est laqueis rapidam captare volantem,
Laedere vel jacto lethalis fulmine plumbi,
Regia si cupias obsonia ponere mensis;
Quippe avibus praestat reliquis jucunda sapore,
Lautaque magnifico decorat convivia luxu.
Et si mactandis desint aconita molossis,
Ipsa tibi dirum praestabunt ossa venenum.
Si vero Scythica chortes augere volucri
Pronus ames, laribus volucris cicurata benignis
Atria tota domus pipienti prole replebit.

[*ll. 92-117*]

Interdum binis avibus, quae cursibus auras
Praevertunt, socium gallus se Phasidis addit.
Altera, quae plumbi simulat pennata colorem,
Garrulitate potens, Chachalacaque nomine dicta,
Robustas nunquam gallinas artubus aequat.
Altera, quae pluma sordet velata nigranti,
Pava peregrino de nomine dicta colonis,
Corporea superat gallinas mole minores.

to see palaces of gold, stand in dumb silence, casting their eyes around and looking intently at everything until they are unable to find their way out of the mansion. In the meantime, gently climb the thick-leafed tree holding the stick in your hand and maintaining a discreet silence. Then throw the noose about the peacock's outstretched neck, and when he is tightly fastened, bring him down at once from his high perch so that your companion can take him as he is lowered from the branch. Then catch them one after another with your looped stick until you have stripped the tall tree of all its peafowl.

Equal to the peacock in size is the crested pheasant, whether he be of golden hue or of a dull rust color. But he is more remarkable for the beauty of his body than for his size. There rises on his little head a high crest composed of soft dainty feathers, his pretty body is covered with yellowish copper-colored plumage or sometimes with black plumage glossier than beautiful jet. His legs shine with a saffron hue and dare to rival the color of his beak. The bird does not excel in swiftness of flight, nor does he venture to rise on wing into a lofty pine, but by repeated leaping he climbs to the top of trees and there delights to catch undisturbed sleep. Though he is slow of wing, yet his swift feet carry him swiftly over the wide plains, and as he crosses the open fields he keeps himself beyond the reach of the swift dogs which come close behind. It is necessary, therefore, to catch the swift bird in snares or to wound it with deadly missiles of lead if you wish to serve a kingly dish; for its delicious flavor excels that of all other birds, and it graces elegant banquets with magnificent splendor. And if there should be lacking poisons for killing dogs, their bones will provide you with a dreadful poison. If, moreover, you should be inclined to add this Scythian bird to your poultry-yard, it will fill the entire space with peeping chicks when once it has become domesticated in the friendly environment of the home.

Sometimes the pheasant associates with two birds which outstrip the speed of the winds. The one, known by the name of *chachalaca*, has feathers of leaden color, is extremely garrulous, and never reaches the size of a large hen. The other, attractive in its dark plumage, is given by farmers the foreign name, *pava*, and has a body larger than that of pullets. The first one immediately betrays itself in the lovely grove by

229

Garrula prima statim luco se prodit amoeno,
Insidiisque virum nigros indagine saltus
Lustrantum capitur crocitantis murmure linguae;
Dum ramis tacito nigrantibus ore quieta
Pascitur interea maturos altera fructus.
Neutra tamen mensis praebebit pinguibus escam,
Ni simul ac fato volucris concedit acerbo,
Venator plumis promptus nudaverit artus,
Nudaque paulatim frigescant aere membra.
Viscera si vero ferventi traxeris alvo,
Nulla satis fuerit duratum flectere pectus
Flamma, furetque datis frustra Vulcanus habenis.

[*ll. 118-137*]

Eminet ast sylvis, Latonae sacra volucris,
Perdix, insigni semper quaesita sapore;
Quam laetis comitatur agris peregrina Coturnix,
Solemnesque dapes mensis regalibus offert.
Utraque sublimes impos conscendere frondes
Propter humum celeri scindit suspensa volatu
Aera densatum, vilesque abjecta penates
Incolit, et nidos subter virgulta locatos
Pullorum foecunda parens examine replet.
Pinguibus his avibus solers hic retia tende;
Aut sensim tacitis figens vestigia campis
Nocte quiescentes, pressasque invade sopore,
Si quandoque velis regali accumbere mensae.

[*ll. 138-150*]

His sociatus edax frondosis agmina campis
Turdus agit, nigrosque metu correpta Palumbes
Montes innumeris avibus stipata frequentat,
Apta quibus licuit venatu lina parare.

[*ll. 151-154*]

Has tamen alter amet mensas, praedamque recentem
Undique collatis apponat festus amicis.
Me juvat alituum cantus haurire sonoros
Auribus, atque oculos vario recreare colore.

[*ll. 155-158*]

Ac primos dulcis tollat Julqueus honores,
Egregium cui penna tegit totum aurea corpus
Eximia forma praestans, ac Passere majus.
Guttura nigranti fulgent distincta colore,
Et cauda, longisque una nigrantibus alis
Miscentur pennae pennis albentibus atrae.
Illa cito volucris nostris cicuratur in aulis,
Inque humeros veniens saltu festiva frequenti
Ore legit Cererem, cantuque arguta salutat,
Et dominum variis oblectat candida ludis.

[*ll. 159-168*]

its garrulity, and when its croaking tongue cries out, it is surrounded in the dark ravines by hunters and caught in their snares. The other one, however, quietly sitting among the dark branches, holds her peace and feeds meanwhile on ripe berries. But neither will provide choice food for the table unless, just as soon as the bird yields to its bitter fate, the hunter promptly plucks the feathers from its body, and allows the body thus stripped to cool slowly in the open air. But if you should draw the fowl while it is still warm, no amount of roasting will be sufficient to make tender the hardened breast, and in vain will Vulcan give free reins to his fury.

Conspicuous in the forest, moreover, is the sacred bird of Latona, the partridge, always highly desired for its excellent flavor. It is accompanied through the fertile fields by an alien bird, the quail, which provides the customary dish served at royal banquets. Neither bird can mount high branches, but close to the ground they cleave the heavy air, suspending themselves on swiftly moving wings; and they humbly dwell in unpretentious places. The prolific mother arranges her nest underneath bushes and fills it with a flock of young. Here skillfully stretch your nets for these fat birds, or slowly make your way through the quiet fields and attack them by night while they are sound asleep if ever you should wish to dine at a table fit for a king.

Associated with these is the greedy thrush that leads his flocks over the green fields, and the timid dove which in company with countless birds frequents the dark mountains. In order to hunt these it is necessary to provide appropriate nets.

But let another have the pleasure of these tables and entertain gatherings of friends with fresh game. As for myself, I find pleasure in listening to the sweet songs of birds and in refreshing my eyes by the sight of their many colors.

First honors belong to the charming *yulqueo* whose lovely body is entirely covered with golden plumage. It is of surpassing beauty and greater in size than the sparrow. Its throat is brightly adorned with black, and its tail and long dark wings are interspersed with black and white feathers. This bird is quickly tamed in our houses. It leaps upon the shoulders, in glee it pecks at grain, it gives a clear greeting in song, and cheerfully entertains its master with its many capers.

Non sic alternis variatur nobilis ales
Passeribus longe major, sed munere formae
Insignis, tyrio velat cui tincta veneno
Membra chlamys fluitans, totumque a vertice fusa
Egregium roseo decorat velamine corpus.
Ille quatit recta cristam cervice rubentem
Plumis effictam levibus, oculisque serenis
Educit suaves resonanti e gutture voces.
[*ll. 169-176*]

Sed praestat dulci famosa Acredula cantu
Praestanti forma, ternisque coloribus aucta.
Luteolis mixtas maculis cineraceus ales
Ostentat niveo plumas candore micantes
Molliaque argutis oculis spectacula praebens,
Concentus, Philomela, tuos imitatur acutos.
[*ll. 177-182*]

Nulla tamen Pito volucris certare canendo
Aut aequare potest dulcis modulamine vocis.
Olli turpe caput, breve rostrum, ac plumbea vestis,
Et moestum gracili prae se fert pectore luctum.
Ut vero modulis mordaces fallere curas
Incipit, et vocem suavissima colla canoram
Flectunt, sollicitum presso de corde dolorem
Projicit, insolitaque aures dulcedine mulcet.
[*ll. 183-190*]

Hanc habitu simulat volucris, pennisque referret,
Quae valles habitat pronas, saltusque frequentat,
Ni longas fuco flaventi immergeret alas.
Illa tenebrosis sylvarum condita ramis
Cymbala concentu visa est pulsare sonoro.
Principio volucris tinnitu murmurat alto,
Effusis exinde aliis lusura camoenis,
Dulcia dum simili tinnitu guttura claudat.
[*ll. 191-198*]

Non ita festivo resonat tristissimus ales
Cantu, Centzontlus fucato nomine dictus,[2]
Omnia consimilis Merulae formamque, coloremque;
At minor est cantu, gratis et vocibus impar.
Dulce canit volucris, sed moesto pectora luctu,
Tristitiaeque lares densatis nubibus umbrat.
[*ll. 199-204*]

Sed quae crudeli compressit corda dolore
Ille, levat dulci parvus modulamine Risis
Caeruleo totum velatus tegmine corpus.
Usque ciet modulos cavea festivus in arcta;
Et si luce nigras noctis pulsaveris umbras,
Ille tibi blandis mulcebit lusibus aures.
[*ll. 205-210*]

Not thus adorned by varied colors is the famous bird, much larger than the sparrow but known for its gifted beauty, over whose body flows a robe dyed in Tyrian scarlet extending over all the body from the head and decking it in a rose-colored dress. With neck erect he shakes the dainty feathers of his ruddy crest and with clear eyes pours forth sweet songs from his melodious throat.

But the famous *calandria*, of matchless beauty and adorned in triple colors, excels in the sweetness of its song. This ashen-colored bird displays plumage white as snow interspersed with dashes of yellow, and its sharp eyes present a pleasing sight, as it imitates your treble notes, O Philomela.

Yet no bird can rival in song the *pito-real* or match it in sweetness of voice. It has an unattractive head, a blunt beak, leaden plumage, and carries on its lean neck the sign of mourning. But when it begins to beguile its gnawing pangs of care with strains of music, and keys its sweet-voiced throat to a melodious pitch, it thrusts off distressing grief from its heavy heart and soothes the ears with the extraordinary sweetness of its song.

Like this bird in shape, and in color, too, if its wings were not tinged with yellow, is a bird which dwells in deep ravines and frequents the woodlands. Hidden among the branches of the dark forest it seems to be beating cymbals in a sweet symphony. At first the bird gives out a shrill ringing sound, followed immediately by an outpouring of other strains, and then closes its sweet mouth with the same ringing sound.

In no such gay song does the saddest of birds, improperly called *centzontle*,[2] sing, in every respect like the blackbird both in shape and color, but inferior in song and unequal in the quality of its voice. The bird sings a sweet song, but it saddens hearts with its lamentations and darkens homes with thick clouds of gloom.

But the hearts which that bird has made heavy with depressing sorrow are lightened by the sweet strains of the little *rise* whose whole body is clad in blue. Unceasingly does he sing his cheerful songs in his little cage; and if with a lamp you should remove the dark shades of night, he will soothe your ears with his soft ditties.

Mole coloratus vario medicamine passer
Et gratis etiam Risem concentibus aequat.
Ast quantum rutilis praestat fulgoribus ales!
Sydonio totam fucatam murice plumam
Ostentat violisque caput, fucoque nitentes
Caeruleo pennas mixtas fulgente smaragdo.

[*ll. 211-216*]

Nil tamen exiguo novit praestantius orbis
Colibrio dulcis spoliato murmure vocis,[3]
Sed claro tenues penna radiante per artus.
Exiguum corpus, forsan non pollice majus,
(Quod rostro natura parens munivit acuto
Atque artus ferme totos aequante volucris)
Induit aurato viridantes lumine plumas
Et varios miscet tractos de Sole colores.
Ille volat rapidum Zephyrum superante volatu,
Et raucum penna tollit stridente susurrum.
Roscida si vero fragranti educere flore
Mella velit rostro, viresque reducere membris,
(Quippe alia quacumque negat se pascere mensa)
Sistitur in medio concussis aere pennis,
Nectareum donec tereti trahat ore liquorem.
Ast adeo prompte subtiles concutit alas,
Ut vigiles fugiant oculos, ludantque citatae;
Suspensamque putes volucrem super aethera filo.
Sin autem sylvis borealis bruma propinquet,
Plusque vagus solito frigescat Jupiter imbre,
Frigida praecipiti linquit Colibrius arva
Nostra fuga, linquitque levi viridaria penna,
Et longum montis nigris absconditus umbris
Indulget placido, ceu Progne arguta, sopori,
Dum luces Aries stellatis noctibus aequet,
Verque novum pratis antiquum reddat honorem.

[*ll. 217-242*]

Quos vero resono superare Canarius ore,
Florida quem misit nobis Hispania, certat.
Ille ciet varios crepitanti gutture cantus,
Dulciaque argutus sectatur plectra vicissim
Instabilis saltu metitus claustra frequenti.
Quod si animum ludis fessum recreare jocosis
Pronus ames, caveam digito continge canentis:
Ocyus ille modis, dapibus, limphisque relictis,
Advolat urbanus digito colludere tenso
Oblatosque cibos compresso ex ore revellit;
Inque caput volitans rostro discriminat alas,
Ordine disponit plumas, et pectora comit.
Cum vero pullis nidos aptare tenellis
Ardet avis, facili consternit brachia pinus

The highly colored sparrow equals the *rise* both in size and in the cheerfulness of his song. And how this glorious bird excels in brilliance! It has feathers completely tinted in Tyrian purple, a head of violet, and wings brightly interspersed with dark blue and glittering emerald.

But the world knows nothing more remarkable than the tiny humming bird, bereft of the gift of sweet song,[3] but renowned for the brilliant plumage which covers its small frame. Its body is diminutive, perhaps no larger than the thumb, but protected by mother nature with a beak, sharp and almost as long as the bird's entire body. It has green plumage of golden brightness interspersed with the various colors of the sun. It surpasses in flight the speed of the west wind and creates a dull humming sound with its whirring wings. Moreover, if it should wish to draw dewy nectar from a fragrant flower to nourish its body, for it refuses to feed on any other food, on fluttering wings it holds itself suspended in midair while it draws out the nectarine liquor through its slender mouth. So fast, indeed, does it beat its delicate wings that they elude the watchful eye by their rapid motion, and you might suppose the bird to be suspended in the air by a thread. Now if winter should descend upon the forest from the north, and the shifting winds become colder with the coming of the rainy season, on light wing the humming bird swiftly abandons our chilly country and flower gardens, and hiding away for a long time in the dark shadows of the mountain like cunning Procne, indulges in peaceful slumber until Aries makes the days equal to the starlit nights, and the return of spring restores to the meadows their former glory.

But the canary which Spain, a country of flowers, has sent us rivals all these birds with its melodious song. With its resounding throat it produces various melodies and skillfully accompanies the sweet strains of the lyre, nervously dancing about in its cage. Now if you should be inclined to refresh your weary spirits with light diversion, place your finger near the songster's cage. Quickly it forsakes its singing, food, and drink, and amiably flies up to play with your outstretched finger and pulls the food offered it through the narrow opening. And flying above, it parts its wings with its beak, preens its feathers, and tidies its breast. Now when this bird desires to build a nest for its little ones, it overlays twigs with soft cotton and modestly pre-

Gossipio, mollesque parat pudibunda penates.
Sin autem matri quaesitis vellera nidis
Desint, cauta patri densato e pectore plumas
Avellit, duroque pater dat corda dolori.
Tantus amor volucri, et generandae gloria prolis!
[ll. 243-261]

Dum moror, et vigili contemplor lumine nidos
Obscuris crocitat lucis en regius ales
Carnoso pulchram vinctus diademate frontem,
Collaque purpurea praecinctus candida torque.
Mole refert Aquilam, sed picto ornatus amictu
Alituum praestat Reginae munere formae.
Incolit audaci Sylvarum devia fastu,
Nigrantique gregi, sceptro, regnoque potitus
Sylvestri, prudens tacitis dominatur in agris.
Hinc sociata cohors, Zopiloti nomine dicti,
Siquando tauri retegit sub monte cadaver,
Ante suum vitat Regem contingere praedam,
Reliquias exinde vorax haustura cruentas.
[ll. 262-274]

Non sua regali distinguit membra nitore,
Nec felix ullo decoratur Tzacua sceptro;
Induit at varias, ceu dulcis Acredula, vestes,
Et socialis amat propriae succurrere genti.
Seligit umbroso sublimem vertice truncum,
Pensilibusque comas exornans provida nidis
Tota virescenti latitat respublica fronde.
Hinc prudens sobolis custodem deligit unam,
Quae subito Cerasi ramis elata supernis
Insidias hostis vigili statione revelat;
Quaeque renascentes invisens sedula nidos
Ore ciet cantus, frondisque reversa cacumen
Externas rostro volucres, alisque repellit.
Sin Cerasis homines, gens olli inimica, propinquent,
Protinus incautos hortatur voce sodales,
Ut penna nidos celeri, truncumque relinquant:
Ut solet interdum demersus flumine Castor
Subjectas agitare undas, sociosque monere.
[ll. 275-292]

Sed jam desertis humanae vocis imago
Saepius in sylvis resonat, meque ipsa vocavit.
Quas ego dum reputo voces, et lumina circum
Volvo, garrit honos nemoris resupinus in alno
Psittacus, obductus viridanti membra colore,
Luteolisque notis cervicem pictus honestam,
Atque etiam nitidam media inter tempora frontem.
Ingeniosa domi volucris cicurata magistro

pares a pleasant home. And if the mother bird should lack sufficient down for the nest, she carefully plucks feathers from the thickly covered breast of the male, and he submits to the sharp pain. So great is the bird's love and the glory of producing young!

As I linger and with a keen eye observe a nest, behold a kingly bird raises a loud raucous sound in the deep forest. His pretty forehead is encircled with a fleshy diadem and his white neck has a scarlet collar around it. In size he resembles the eagle, but his ornate cloak causes him to excel the queen of birds in natural beauty. With high disdain he inhabits the unfrequented places of the forest. He holds sway over the black flock in his kingdom in the forest. He is their wise master in the silent fields. And, therefore, whenever the assembled birds, called *zopilotes*, have found at the foot of a mountain the carcass of a bull, they refuse to touch the booty before their king, but after him will greedily devour the bloody remains.

The *tzacua* is not distinguished by the royal splendor of its body, nor does it successfully hold any sceptered power, but like the charming *calandria* it is covered with variegated plumage, and since it is a gregarious bird, it is wont to look out for its own family. These birds select a tall shady-topped tree and skillfully bedeck the branches with pensile nests, while the entire community hides among the green leaves. Then they wisely select a sentinel for their young, and she quickly flies to the topmost branches of a tree and from this outlook detects any treachery on the part of an enemy. As she busily visits the nests that are hatching, she pours forth in song, and returning to the tree top drives away strange birds with beak and wings. But if men, a race unfriendly to her, should approach the tree, with a cry she immediately urges her unwary companions to leave their nests and the tree in swift flight, just as sometimes Castor underneath a river troubles the waters below to warn his comrades.

Moreover, the likeness of the human voice is often heard in the lonely forest, and it has called to me. And while I consider the sound and look about, the glory of the forest, the parrot, sits idly chattering in an alder. His body is clothed in green, and his glorious neck and the center of his sleek forehead between the temples are marked with yellow. This intelligent bird, when tamed at home, talks to its master and imitates

Verba facit, risumque refert, cantusque movebit,
Et lacerum morsu digitum scelerata cachinnis
Irridet, gaudetque domos. evertere rostro.⁴
[ll. 293-303]

Cum vero garrit, plauditque sibi ipsa volucris,
Arripit incautam, plumasque et viscera vellit
Praepetibus pennis, armatusque unguibus ales.
[ll.304-306]

Subter enim frondes habitu formosa superbo
Alituum Regina ferox, et gloria sylvae
Regnat avis, pedibus, rostroque insignis adunco.
Illa nigro totum corpus fucata colore,
Intextis variat plumis candentibus alas,
Quas pandit volitans bis senas lata per ulnas,
Et curvis digitos, ac longis unguibus armat.⁵
Incolit obscuro nigrantes robore lucos
Sepositosque agros, avibus praedaque frequentes.
Ut tamen hostili ventrem saturare rapina
Ardet avis, castrisque suis optata propinquat
Praeda, nemus subito linquit Jovis armiger atrum
Erectisque ferum summo de vertice plumis,
Fulmineo praedam raptat per inane volatu,
Impatiensque famis pedibus exenterat uncis,
Seu volucris fuerit, vitulus seu raptus ab agris.
[ll. 307-322]

Ast Aquilae praestat celeri super aethera lapsu
Crudelis fulvo vestitus tegmine Falco,
Et pulchrum rubro maculatus murice collum.
Mole quidem Gallum simulat, sed praepete penna
Exsuperat volucres obductas monte rapaces.
Vix etenim penna mollis petit alta Palumbes,
Cum subito celsas replicatis orbibus auras
Conscendit Falco rapidis velocior Euris,
Vincat avem donec, levibusque supervolet alis.
Tunc praedo, gravido ceu nimbo jacta sagitta,
Irruit in volucrem, sparsisque per aera plumis,
Ungue premit tepido rorantia membra cruore,
Absconditque vorax media inter robora sylvae.
[ll. 323-335]

Non ita praecipiti penna secat aera Nisus
Et forma, et fusco volucris turpata colore;
Sed pullis nido saepe insidiatur iniqua,
Audacique rapit furto scelerata parentes.
Praedonem circum glomeratur turba volantum,
Infixisque diu plagis avellere praedam
Tentat, sed pinguem constringit praedo rapinam,
Dum tectus silva proscindat viscera rostro.
[ll. 336-343]

laughter, and will sing songs. The rascal will laugh derisively as it bites your finger, and it delights in disarranging the house with its beak.⁴

But while the parrot is talking and pleased with itself, a bird provided with swift wings and talons swoops down upon the unsuspecting creature, tears out its feathers, and eviscerates it.

For, indeed, underneath the trees, elegant in her grand attire, the fierce queen of birds and the glory of the forest reigns, a bird famous for her claws and curved beak. Her entire body is black; her wings, which extend six cubits wide when she flies, are interlaced with white feathers; and her toes are provided with long curved claws.⁵ She dwells in forests darkly shaded with thick oaks and in far away fields frequented by birds and other prey. And when this bird, the armorbearer of Jove, desires to glut her stomach on the fruit of her wanton robbery, and when suitable prey comes near her stronghold, she suddenly leaves the black forest, and lifting the feathers on the crown of her head, she fiercely swoops through the air like a flash of lightning upon her prey and with insufferable hunger disembowels it with her curved claws, whether it be a bird or a calf that she has carried away from the fields.

But the eagle is exceeded in swiftness of flight through the air by the fierce falcon. Its body is covered with a coat of yellow, and its handsome neck is speckled with deep purple. It approximates the size of a cock, but in swiftness of wing surpasses all the birds of prey that lurk in the mountains. Scarcely does a gentle dove rise on wing into the air, when swifter than the wind the falcon circles high into the air until it overtakes the bird and is flying swiftly above. Then the plunderer, like a bolt hurled from a heavy raincloud, rushes upon the bird, scatters its feathers through the air, and clutches between its talons the body, dripping with warm drops of blood, and gluttonously hides it among the trees of the forest.

On wing less swift the sparrow hawk cleaves the air, unattractive both because of its shape and its drab color; but the wicked bird often lies in wait at the nest for fledglings and with fearless robbery villainously catches the mother birds. A host of birds encircle the plunderer and, by inflicting many wounds, try to snatch away his booty, but he clings to his fat prize until under cover of the forest he rends its vitals with his beak.

Huic similis forma, fuscoque indutus amictu,
Mole minor chortes pravus subvertere Cenchris
Nititur. Hinc tensis liquidum super aethera pennis
Consistit firmus, placidas neque commovet alas.
Ut vero pullos subjecta in chorte vagantes
Aut colubrum campis cernit fera colla tumentem,
Ilicet infestis pipientes unguibus ales
Arripit, et raptos superas extollit in oras,
Dilaniatque ferox artus, et viscera pascit.
Sin vero pedibus serpentem sustulit uncis,
Unguibus, et rostro discerpit corda furentis,
Dum rabiem vita ponat, fugiatque sub umbras.

[*ll. 344-355*]

Nunc vero postquam sylvae spectacula nostrae
Grata dedi, subito volucrum mirabile monstrum
Saltibus abducam densis, circumque per orbem
Ipse feram, morbis laturum forte medelam.
Abdita desertis nemoris frondentis in umbris
Degit avis, gracili subtilis mole, sed atrae
Obducit tanto corpus velamine pennae,
Ut tenui simulet mediocrem corpore molem.
Olli cauda brevis, crus longum, binaque plumis
Sculpta nota, alterno volucrem medicamine pingens;
Altera, quae minio dorsum fulgente decorat,
Altera, qua pectus niveos excedit olores:
Utraque magna tamen, latumque effusa per orbem:
Sed quas omnino turpat spectabile rostrum
Assimulans concham variisque coloribus auctum;
At gravius volucri; siquidem prope pollice latum,
Corpore quin etiam plumoso longius ipso.
Perfectam vero tactu suavissima plumam
Lingua refert, cordis languoribus apta mederi.
Aeger enim sylva tractam nigrantis ab alta
Includit cavea, vinclisve tenere volucrem
Invigilat: dumque ipsa sitim sedavit in amne,
Abstersitque frequens pennatam flumine linguam,
Excipit ille undas sitienti saepius ore,
Et dirum fracto pellit de pectore morbum.[6]

[*ll. 356-380*]

FINIS LIBRI DECIMI-TERTII

Like this bird in appearance and also clad in dark plumage but smaller in size is the wicked hawk that strives to ravish the poultry-yards. With outstretched pinions he holds himself steady in the upper air without moving his gentle wings. When, however, he sees young chickens strolling about in the yard below, or a serpent puffing up its fierce neck in the field, at once he pounces upon the chirping fowl with his deadly talons and carries his prey high into the air. He savagely tears its body to pieces and feeds upon its vitals. If, however, it is a snake he has carried away in his claws, with talons and beak he plucks the heart out of the frantic creature until it puts aside its fury along with its life and flees to the shades of death.

Now that I have presented the delightful aspects of our woods, I shall bring forth from the dense forest a remarkably freakish bird and shall carry it about through the world that I may perhaps bring healing to the sick. The bird dwells far away in the deep shadows of the thick forest. It is small of size and slender, but such a thick coat of black feathers covers its body that, though slight of body, it appears of medium size. Its tail is short, its legs long, and two markings on the plumage give the bird alternating colors; the one which graces its back is bright vermillion, the other makes its breast exceed the whiteness of the swan. Both marks, however, are large and cover a large area. But these are marred by a conspicuous beak which resembles a shellfish and is composed of various colors. This is heavier than the bird, nearly as wide as the thumb, and longer even than the feathered body itself. But the tongue, very soft to the touch, is like delicate down, suitable for healing diseases of the heart; indeed the sick person brings the bird from the depths of the dark forest and shuts it in a cage, or sees that it is fettered, and when it has slaked its thirst in water and has again and again bathed its downy tongue in it, he repeatedly drinks of the water and thus drives the dreadful disease from his afflicted heart.[6]

XIV

FERAE

Nunc mihi lustra diu fidis agitanda molossis,
Quae sylvis obducta nigris numerosa ferarum
Turba colit. Pavido, Nymphae, succurrite vati
Monticolae, lucos solitae miscere silentes,
Et mores, habitumque trucem, rabiemque ferinam,
Infandamque agri cladem reserate benignae;
Et quas Odrysio damas captavero plectro,
Hisce memor donis vestras operabor ad aras.

[*ll. 1-8*]

Sylva fuit late quercu nemorosa frequenti
Arboreis obducta comis, atque obsita dumis,
Umbrosos cujus pressus formidine Phoebus
Horret inauratis saltus lustrare quadrigis.
Ast circum dives patulos se fundit in agros
Rivis perfusos vitreis, et graminis herba.

[*ll. 9-14*]

Hoc nemus, has undas, haec gramina torvus amavit
Impexis per terga comis Bos saepe jubatus[1]
Dictus, et antiquo forma spectabilis orbi.
Ille quidem vasta simularet mole juvencum,
Ni majora gravi turpis curvamine terga
Flecteret, et magno sinuaret gibbere dorsum.
Fortia quin etiam tensis per membra capillis
Obtegit Attalico nervosum vellere corpus,
Et caput inflexis, ceu Taurus, cornibus armat.
Crinibus exutam prorsus sine nomine caudam,
Caeruleisque notis oculos, duo lumina frontis,
Ostentat, patulisque exspirans naribus ignem
Omne decus profert, majestatemque leonis.
Membra venenatis fixus villosa sagittis
Suscitat ardenti vesanum corde furorem,
Invaditque atrox duratis cornibus hostem,
Mollia qui rigido violavit tergora ferro.
Ast postquam flava rabidus prostravit arena,
Obtinuitque acri pulchram certamine palmam ,
Prostratum pedibus longum proculcat acerbis,
Artubus infelix maneat dum vita cruentis.

[*ll. 15-35*]

Hinc armatus eques prolixo robore dextram,
Ferrea quod cingunt lucentis cornua lunae,
Impetit insignem spatiosa per aequora praedam:
Dumque levis campos pedibus secat illa citatis,
Avolat ille levis, celeri pernicior aura,

WILD BEASTS

Now with my ever faithful hounds I must disturb the dens in which great multitudes of wild beasts dwell under cover of the black forests. O nymphs of the mountain, who often arouse the silent forest to action, assist the timid bard and kindly reveal the habits, the grim appearance, and the fierceness of the beasts, and their unspeakable destruction of the land; and the deer which I attract with the lyre of Orpheus I shall, in remembrance of your favors, sacrifice on your altars.

There is a large densely wooded forest, thickly covered with heavy oaks and overgrown with bushes, the dark recesses of which Phoebus shrinks from penetrating with his golden chariot. Around it stretch large fertile fields washed by clear streams and covered with deep grass.

This forest, these waters, and this grass were the delight of the wild ox, often called the maned ox because of the shaggy hair over his back,[1] and having an appearance which amazes the people of the Old World. Indeed, because of his great size, he would resemble a young bull if his broad back were not disproportionately rounded into a large arch to form a huge hump. Besides, hair extends over his sturdy limbs and a thick fleecelike covering over his sinewy body. His head, like a bull's, is provided with curving horns. He has a nondescript tail totally devoid of hair and a pair of bluish eyes serving as lamps for his forehead. As he breathes out fire from his wide nostrils, he presents all the glory and majesty of the lion. When his shaggy body has been pierced by deadly arrows, a mad fury is awakened in his impetuous heart, and with his stout horns he fiercely assails the enemy who has wounded his soft back with the hard steel. And when the enraged animal has brought him down upon the yellow sand and has won a glorious victory in the fierce struggle, he continues to trample his prostrate victim with sharp hoofs as long as the unlucky life remains in the bloodstained body.

At this juncture a horseman grasps in his hand a long wooden rod to which is attached a crescent-shaped hook of iron and pursues this remarkable animal over the wide plains. While the beast lightly crosses the fields with great swiftness of foot, the hunter lightly flies in pur-

Ferae

Insequiturque feram cursu, promptusque jubati
Bina bovis luna fugientis crura recidit.
Si tamen hic rapido teli male saucius ictu
Irruat in fortem cornuta fronte latronem,
Seu ferro confisus eques, seu corpore duro,
Aggreditur magno saevam discrimine pugnam.
Ille petit cornu, rabie commotus amara;
Hic collum dexter lunata vulnerat hasta;
Admiscentque diu propriis fera praelia telis,
Exsanguis donec fuso ruat ille cruore.

[*ll. 36-50*]

Non ita limphatus furiali accenditur ira,
Nec latis regnat facilis Tapyrus in agris.[2]
Olli densa parat tranquillos sylva penates,
Quae placidos aditus vitreae vicina paludi
Exhibeat, tectamque viam, tutamque periclis
Monstret inoffensa per devia rura quiete.
Gaudet enim tacitis corpus recreare fluentis,
Et magnos celeri fluvios tranare natatu
Bellua, porcinam membris imitata figuram.
Illa capillato sinuosum pondere dorsum,
Arrectasque aures, turpique proboscide nares
Exhibet, et fusco velatum tegmine corpus,
Quod modico sublime gerit, ceu bucula, crure,
Saepeque lugubres educit pectore questus.

[*ll. 51-64*]

Quod si villosam costis avellere pellem
Pastor ames, corioque ferae, spoliisque potiri,
(Fertur enim pellis docto macerata labore
Deridere minas, saevisque obsistere telis).
Limosam propter laqueos compone paludem
Abdita nodatos vicino ad littora trunco.
Bellua nodoso collum conclusa rudenti
Conatur funem repetito frangere nisu;
Dumque reluctanti trunco gemebunda recedit,
Gutture compresso vitam sub robore ponit.

[*ll. 65-74*]

Sed prope rugitu lucus reboare Leonis[3]
Auditur, pavidasque sonus pervenit ad aures.
Vasta mole Leo fulvo velamine tectus,
Armatusque pedes duratis unguibus, alta
Extollit cervice caput, caudaque trementem
Verrit agrum, torvusque feras dominatur in omnes.
Accensus rabie terret camposque, nemusque,
Impastusque diu numerosa armenta feroci
Voce quatit, tenerosque ovium de pectore foetus,
Aut vitulum, aut etiam praestanti mole juvencum
Ore rapit, laniatque cruentis unguibus artus.

[*ll. 75-85*]

suit, swifter than the speed of the wind and with his curved weapon he quickly cuts both hocks of the fleeing ox. Now if the ox should be insufficiently wounded by the hurried stroke of the spear and direct his horns against the valiant hunter, the horseman, depending either upon steel or strength of body, begins a fierce and perilous battle. The animal, driven into a furious passion, attacks with his horns. The hunter skillfully deals a blow to the neck with his crescent-shaped spear; and for a long time they fight a fierce battle, each using his own weapons until the animal pours out his life-blood and falls.

With no such fierce anger is the gentle tapir maddened and infuriated, nor does he rule over the wide fields.[2] For him a peaceful home is provided in the dense forest affording him a safe approach to an adjoining pool of clear water and providing a pathway, protected and safe from danger, that leads through untrodden places of uninterrupted quiet. For this animal, similar in appearance to the hog, is fond of refreshing his body in quiet waters and swimming swiftly across wide rivers. He has an arched back thickly covered with bristles, upright ears, and ugly snout, and a body covered with dark skin and supported by short legs like those of a heifer. Frequently he utters a plaintive cry.

Now if you were a shepherd and wished to tear the shaggy pelt from the animal's sides and to acquire his skin as your spoils (for it is said that the hide when skillfully tanned defies and resists the threat of fierce weapons), fasten a noose to a tree near the edge of a secluded marsh. The beast, caught in the loop by the neck, tries with repeated effort to break the rope, and when with a groan he draws back from the unyielding trunk, he strangles himself and gives up his life underneath the tree.

But not far away the forest is heard to resound with the roaring of a lion,[3] and the sound reaches the ears of the frightened. The huge lion, covered with a tawny skin, and with feet protected by hard claws, lifts high his head and sweeps the quaking earth with his tail, grimly lording it over all the wild beasts. When he is fired with anger, he terrorizes the fields and the woods; when hungry, he harasses for a long time the numerous herds and in his mouth carries young lambs away from their mothers, or a calf, or even a young bull of considerable size, and tears their bodies to pieces in his bloody claws.

Saepe etiam fulvo comitem dumosa Leoni
Sylva dedit Tigrim; qua non audacior ulla
Bellua spumantis semper sitibunda cruoris,
Et quae constanti nunquam cicurata magistro
Ardentem crudelis alit sub corde furorem.
Pelle tegit corpus, maculis quam desuper atris
Ornat inaurato distinctus lumine fucus,
Et rictum validis accingit dentibus atrum,
Prolixaque furens animis quatit aequora cauda.
Lustra colit, campisque audax spatiatur apertis
Hircani superans cladem furibunda Leonis.

[*ll. 86-96*]

Sed caecam pubes rabiem domat ignea telis.
Vix etenim latis resonat palantis in arvis
Pernicies horrenda gregis, fumatque recenti
Sanguine tinctus ager, subito cum fida molossum
Agmina limphati ducunt in bella bubulci.
Praecedit pedibus velox, et naribus acer,
Dilaniare feras, et vestigare suetus,
Caetera quem certat plebes aequare sequendo.
Ut vero lacerum concreto sanguine taurum
Invenere viri, cinctique ad bella molossi,
Nare sagax subito delibat membra cruenta,
Caecaque praedonis quaerens vestigia rostro
Innumeros circum ducit per gramina gyros,
Signa pedum donec captarit fervidus Umber.
Mox rapido cursu, pronoque per aequora rostro
Reliquias furis dispersas cespite cogens
Arva petit, sylvasque diu, fontesque revisit,
Ingenti socium propter subeunte caterva,
Dum tectum luco praedonem detegat alto.
Frondea tunc omnes latratu regna feroci
Complent, et praedam circum clamoribus urgent.
Bellua terribili trepidat compressa corona,
Maturatque citis robur conscendere plantis.
Sed truncum rursus praecingit murmure turba
Fida canum, densoque instat furibunda latratu.
Interea resono moniti clamore bubulci
Nigrantem penetrant sylvam, rabieque frementes
Arma parant, canibusque citi, truncoque
    propinquant.
Ille feram jacto media inter tempora plumbo
Transadigit, ramisque ictu detrudit ab altis:
Ille laborantem, nigroque cruore fluentem

Often, too, the jungle has given as a companion to the tawny lion the tiger, excelled in boldness by no other beast. Always thirsty for foaming blood he is never tamed by a patient trainer, but savagely nourishes in his heart a violent passion. His body is clad in a skin adorned with bright gold and decorated over the top with black spots. His black jaws are encircled with mighty teeth, and when angry he whips the plain with its long tail. He dwells in the forest and boldly roams over the open fields, and, in a fit of madness, exceeds the destruction of the Hyrcanian lion.

But fiery-spirited young men tame his reckless fury with their weapons. Scarcely indeed do they hear the dreadful destruction of the herd which roams over the wide fields, and scarcely is the earth soaked and steaming with fresh blood, when suddenly the angry herdsmen lead their faithful packs of dogs to war. A dog, swift of foot, keen-scented, and trained in tracking wild animals and tearing them to pieces, goes ahead, while the rest strive to keep pace with it in the chase. And when the men and their dogs, girded for war, have found a bull torn and covered with clotted blood, at once the keen-scented dog quickly sniffs the bloody body and traces out with his nose the unseen footsteps of the marauder, circling about many times over the grass until he has discovered its trail. Then he hastens away keeping his nose to the ground and picking up scraps left strewn over the grass by the thief. For a long time he searches through the fields and woods and visits the springs, closely followed by his many companions until he finds the ravisher hidden in the depths of the forest. Then all the dogs fill the wooded realms with ferocious barking and crowd around their prey in wild confusion. The beast, held at bay by the frightening circle, shrinks back and makes haste to scamper up a tree. But again the faithful dogs gather about the tree, growling and furiously threatening by continuous barking. Meanwhile the herdsmen, guided by the resounding noise, penetrate the black forest. Grumbling with anger they get ready their weapons and hasten to the tree where the dogs are barking. One man shoots the beast between the temples with lead, and the blow dislodges him from the high limb. Another quickly rushes with a naked sword upon the animal while he

Irruit in praedam velox mucrone recluso,
Obtruncatque caput rursum fera fata minantis,
Membraque partitur fessis alimenta molossis.
[ll. 97-130]

His etiam quandoque Ursus miscetur avarus
Hispida nigranti contectus corpora seta,
Ungueque deformes plantas armatus acuto,
Ac totum valido munitus robore corpus.
Saepius ille pecus sectatus dente voraci
Pinguia lanigero spoliat pecuaria foetu:
Et, si tranquillum telis, aut voce lacessant,
Pastores audet ferventi invadere rictu.
Inde etiam fructus curvantes pondere ramos,
Seminaque auratos passim dispersa per agros
Arripit ingluvie nunquam saturatus iniqua,
Divitiasque agri rabie consumit edendi.
Quin etiam pravo messis correptus amore
Quae nequit oppletus patulam demittere in alvum,
Haec mutata manu curva sub rupe reponit.
[ll. 131-145]

Crimina sed pubes justis ulciscitur armis.
Ne tamen ille furens robustis viribus usus
Opprimat innexis venantis terga lacertis,
Hic invectus equo, pinuque armatus acuta
Impetit a tergo gemmata in prata ruentem,
Et plagis rabidum vexat lethalibus Ursum.
Bellua robustis ardet constringere nervis,
Ac dentes, interque manus laniare latronem.
Sed dum lenta movet sensim vestigia retro,
Flectit equum, praedamque iterum diverberat hasta
Venator rigida, secto dum viscera ventre
Fundat humi, venisque fluat cum sanguine vita.
[ll. 146-157]

Hos inter gracilis rictu Pantera feroci
Occupat obscura densatos arbore lucos,
Quin campis exosa diem spatietur apricis.
Olli frontis honos, brevis alvus, pictaque terga,
Caudaque versicolor ternas producta per ulnas.
Prolixis obducta pilis, fuscoque veneno
Tincta tegit pellis praestantia membra decore,
Quam circum maculae sinuatis orbibus atrae
Distinguunt, superantque decus nigrore Gagatis.
Hoc fera terribili circum vestita nitore
Pantheram magnam praeclaris dotibus aequat.
[ll. 158-168]

struggles and pours out his black blood, and if he again threatens a dire fate, the herdsman cuts off his head and distributes the parts of his body among the weary hounds for food.

Sometimes the greedy bear joins these animals. His shaggy body is covered with black bristles, his clumsy feet are provided with sharp claws, and his entire body is fortified by mighty strength. Often, when driven by a ravenous appetite, he pursues the herd and robs the fat flocks of their fleecy lambs; and if the shepherds, either by weapons or by sound of voice, disturb his peace, he boldly attacks them with his fierce teeth. Then, too, he seizes branches when they are bending with heavy fruit, and gathers up the seeds that are scattered here and there through the golden fields, without ever satisfying his prodigious gluttony, and he consumes the riches of the land by reason of his insatiate appetite. When, moreover, he is seized by an evil desire for the harvest, whatever he is unable to crowd into his spacious stomach he carries away in his paws and hides in a cave.

But the men avenge his crimes with proper weapons. Lest, however, he become infuriated and employ his mighty strength to clutch in his forearms the back of the hunter, the latter, mounted on a horse and provided with a sharp spear, attacks the enraged bear from behind and tortures him with deadly blows as he rushes across the blossoming meadows. The beast is eager to clutch his assailant with mighty force and to tear him apart with his teeth and claws, but while he slowly turns around, the hunter deflects his horse and again strikes his prey with the stiff spear until his stomach, having been torn open, discharges the entrails upon the ground, and life ebbs away as the blood flows from the veins.

Among these animals the gaunt fierce-toothed jaguar occupies the depths of the dark forest. It does not range over the sunny fields, for it loathes the light of day. It has a graceful forehead, a short belly, a spotted back, and a vari-colored tail three cubits long. Its skin, thickly covered with long tawny hair, adds a glory to its beautiful body. It is completely adorned with black spots which form intricate circles and surpass in blackness the splendor of jet. Invested with this awesome glory the animal is equal to the mighty panther in its amazing gifts.

Tu tamen hanc crebra turbans indagine praedam
Aut caput, aut pectus certis configere plagis
Nitere: quippe solet rigido male saucia telo
Extemplo totas irae permittere habenas,
Invadensque ferox vibrantem cominus ictus
Dente terit corpus, seponitque artubus artus,
Crudelisque omnes latis disseminat arvis.

[ll. 169-175]

Non ita limphatus caeca lupus aestuat ira;
Sed magnam pecori portendit saepe ruinam.
Ille palam pecudes agris abducit apricis,
Seu crudelis amet raptos e matribus agnos,
Seu vexante fame pullos suspiret equinos.
Averso pastore Lupus, canibusque sopore
Devictis, plenum solers invadit ovile.
Cum vero in foetus audax irrumpit equorum
Subdolus infestis se totum fraudibus armat.
Principio gregibus passu cunctante propinquat,
Et tacitum replet magnis ululatibus agrum.
Continuo pullos cogunt armenta tenellos
Et pavidos forti praecinctos orbe recondunt,
Quem patrum, matrumque una densata caterva
Calcibus in furem versis miro ordine fingunt.
Ast longo praedo pecudes educere circo
Aggressus rabie, nunc hos, nunc impetit illos:
Sed rabidum coetus repetitis calcibus urget.
Ille fremens ira sinuatum circumit orbem,
Abrupto donec circo, nexuque soluto,
Territa diffundat patulas armenta per herbas.
Tunc praepes cursu pullum properante fatigat
Interea lanians iteratis morsibus alvum,
Dum laxata fluant utero praecordia rupto.
Ut vero scissa ventrem compage recludit
Praedo, gradum sistit constringens viscera rictu,
Totaque dissecto ducit fumantia ventre.
Ut solet interdum vallatam Martius heros
Explorare urbem, densisque invadere telis,
Nunc dextros tentans aditus, nunc ille sinistros,
Alta quoad rigido proscindat moenia ferro:
Mox aliquot letho saevus demittere cives
Constituit, dirumque extinguit morte furorem.

[ll. 176-208]

Hanc tamen ipse velis campis si avertere pestem,
Retibus obductis pravum conclude latronem,
Aut citius confige acto per tempora telo.

[ll. 209-211]

But be sure, when you rout this animal by closely encircling it, to pierce it through the head or heart with an unerring aim, for, when slightly wounded with the unyielding dart, it is wont immediately to give full vent to its fury and to attack you as you deal blows at close range. It tears the body with its teeth, pulls limb from limb, and savagely scatters them over the wide fields.

Not with such blind fury does the wolf rage, yet he often threatens the herd with destruction. He openly carries away animals from the sunny fields, or he may wantonly choose to steal lambs from their mothers, or when assailed by hunger, sigh for a young colt. When the shepherd has gone away and the dogs have fallen asleep, the wolf slyly attacks the crowded sheepfold. When, however, he boldly bursts upon young colts, he subtly puts on the full armor of trickery and wicked deceit. At first he approaches the herd with lingering step and fills the silent field with loud howling. At once the frightened young animals are assembled and surrounded by a close circle of many horses, both male and female, which curiously turn their heels in the direction of the plunderer. But he, attempting to force the animals out of the large circle, attacks now these and now those, but they beat off the savage beast by a barrage of heels. Growling with anger he circles about until, having broken the chain and burst through, he scatters the frightened animals over the open meadow. Increasing his speed, he then swiftly chases a colt and meanwhile with repeated efforts tears its belly open until the entrails are loosed and pouring out. When, moreover, the thief has torn open the body and laid bare the stomach, he arrests his step to grasp the steaming viscera in his mouth and to draw them completely out of the lacerated belly. Thus a brave warrior is sometimes wont to investigate a walled city and to assail it by a barrage of darts, attempting now an approach on the right and now on the left until he has made a breach in the wall with the hard steel; and then he decides to inflict ruthless death upon some of the citizens and satisfies his dreadful fury by murder.

Now if you should desire to rid the fields of this plague, catch the wicked thief with concealed nets or quickly shoot him through the temples with a well-aimed dart.

Pinguibus hanc vero felix si ejeceris agris
Cladem, projicienda etiam tibi jure Lycisca,
Cujus forma Lupum simulat, simulatque molossum,
Et quae vulpino pellem depicta colore
Vulpinos etiam sectatur callida mores.
Haec semper tenero vigil insidiatur ovili,
Ac plenos avibus nudat chortalibus agros.
Non vaga turba canum, pecorum non ense magister
Fraudibus armatam clausis ab ovilibus arcent.
Lenta gradu, sylvaeque nigris obducta sub umbris,
Chortibus, aut plenis propior fit sedula caulis;
Dumque agnum stabulis, aut pullum surripit arvis,
Protinus illa nemus repetens festina profundum
Discerpit praedam, rictu spumante, tenellam.
Siquando ventrem rabies affligit edendi,
Disparibus complet totas ululatibus auras,
Ut magnam campis credas ululare catervam.

[*ll. 212-228*]

Hanc vigil ipse tuis cura depellere terris
Compressam laqueis, aut certa cuspide caesam,
Ni cupias saeva vastari praedia clade.

[*ll. 229-231*]

Hic admixtus Aper nemorum per devia densum
Agmen agit, camposque vorax populatur opimos.
Membra tegit nigris, duratisque hispida setis,
Quas horrens armat candenti cuspide telum.
Dentibus immanis rictus spumantibus horret;
Et magnam dorso tollens redolente crumenam
Semper odorifera plenam pinguedine,[4] praeceps
Caetera coenosos imitatur bellua porcos.
Sed magnas ira visa est portendere clades
Morsibus insanis agitans hominesque, canesque,
Fusaque discerpens crudeli corpora rictu.
Scilicet ut Phoebus medio vicinior orbi
Aurata flagrans accendit lampade terras,
Turba venenatis dentes cum dentibus urgens
Verberat horrisono lucos rumore silentes,
Inque orbem subito totum devolvitur agmen.
Tunc siquem longe campis aspexerit hostem,
Advolat, ut tenso nervo lethalis arundo,
Adversumque petens cursu fera turba rapaci
Horrentes irae limphata effundit habenas.
Ac, nisi ferrata munitus cuspide fluctus
Compescas irae, aut jacto praecordia plumbo
Ventre trahas rupto, repetitis morsibus atram
Effundes vitam, fatumque subibis acerbum.

[*ll. 232-255*]

And if you are fortunate enough to drive this scourge from the fertile fields, you are also obliged to expel the coyote, which bears a close resemblance both to the wolf and the dog and which by the color of its hair and by reason of its sly habits resembles the fox. It always lurks near the young sheepfold and robs the well-stocked poultry fields. Neither the roving dogs, nor the shepherd with his spear keeps this crafty animal away from the closed folds. Concealed by the dark shadows of the forest, it slowly and cautiously approaches the full poultry-yards or cotes, and having stolen a lamb from the fold or a young fowl from the fields, it immediately hurries back to the deep forest and in its foaming mouth tears to pieces its tender prey. If ever ravenous hunger be gnawing at its stomach, it fills all the air with such fitful barking that you might believe a large pack was howling in the fields.

Give diligent heed that you banish this animal from your lands either by catching it in traps or by killing it with an unerring dart, unless you wish your estates ravished by this terrible pest.

In addition to these there is the wild boar that leads his large herd through the secluded regions of the forest and ravenously devastates the rich fields. His shaggy body is covered with stiff black bristles which, when standing upright, reveal a white tip on the end. Foam-covered tusks jut out of his enormous mouth, and a large sac appears on the back always filled with a scented fat.[4] In all other respects this violent beast resembles the swine of the wallow, but it has been seen, when angry, to betoken vast destruction with its deadly tusks by pursuing men and dogs and tearing to pieces their prostrate bodies in its savage maw. Indeed, when bright Phoebus is drawing near the middle of the heavens and lighting the world with his golden lamp, the animals, gnashing their venomous teeth and blasting the still forest with a frightful sound, all suddenly gather in a circle. Then, if they catch sight of an enemy far away in the fields, they fly toward him in hot haste like a deadly arrow shot from a tightly drawn bow, and in their wild state of frenzy give free rein to their dreadful anger. And, unless you are protected by a sharp-pointed spear and stay their surge of wrath or tear open their bellies with a shot of lead and bring out their vitals, you will pour out your unfortunate life and meet a bitter death from their repeated bites.

241

Non ita terribilis luco sua jura tuetur,
Nec fera venantes laniabit dentibus Histrix,
Quam natura novis armavit provida telis.
Olli sylva minax dumoso e vertice surgit,
Telorumque seges reliquos diffusa per artus;
Altera, quae brevior pellem tegit horrida dumis,
Altera, quae hamatis se tollit longior hastis,
Et quam saepe Histrix magno correpta furore
Excutit, et magno dirum jacit impete in hostem.
Ore refert porcos, oculisque ardentibus ignem,
Calce tamen catulum, dumoso et corpore sylvam.
[*ll. 256-266*]

Sed flammas oculis, sylvamque e pelle recides,
Horrida si crudo contundas ora bacillo:
Ilicet illa minas, vitamque in gramine ponet.
Quippe acres cursu declinat vafra molossos
Pinguia latrantum jactis in terga sagittis.
[*ll. 267-271*]

Sed jam laeta vocat rursum me Cervus ad arva,
Cervus ab umbrosis veniens ad flumina sylvis
Cornigeram secum ducens per devia turbam.
En tibi septenos praestanti corpore Cervos,
Ingentem superant qui vasta mole juvencum[5]
Arboreisque caput distinguunt cornibus altum,
Queis caudam radunt, contorto vertice retro.
Infando pridem Veneris succensa furore
Turba volat, sequiturque levis per gramina Cervam,
Anxia quae sylvis foetus enixa gemellos
Educat insignes maculis candentibus ambo.
Hanc natura parens infestis exuit armis
Turbam, non duris praecingens dentibus ora,
Unguibus aut calces, violento aut impete cornu;
Sed ventos studiosa dedit praevertere plantis,
Et pernice fuga tristes evadere casus.
[*ll. 272-287*]

Hinc totam telis optes si sternere turbam,
Tu clamore avidos prohibe, cursuque molossos,
Ne nigris densum diffundant saltibus agmen,
Maturentque omnes patulis excedere campis.
Sed ferro Cervam vita spoliare labora,
Et totam figes repetita cuspide plebem.
Quippe mares, cerva telis super aequora lapsa,
Ulterius prohibere gradus, ac sistere visi,
Quin dare terga velint, aut campis linquere victam.

The porcupine, an animal which is not so dreadful, protects its rights in the forest, yet will not fiercely tear hunters to pieces with its teeth, for a wise nature has equipped it with different weapons. A threatening forest of spines rises on its head; and a great number of quills extends over the rest of the body. Some, being shorter, form a rough covering over the skin, others, of greater length and barbed, are often shaken loose and hurled with mighty force against a fierce enemy whenever the porcupine is very angry. Its snout resembles that of a pig and its eyes are bright as fire, but its feet resemble those of a whelp, and its thorny back a forest.

But you will take the fire out of its eyes and the forest off its hide if you bruise its rough head with a stout club. It will immediately put aside its threats and give up its life on the grass. Indeed it craftily turns back the fiercely barking dogs by throwing its quills into their plump backs.

But now the stag calls me again to the fertile fields, the stag that comes from the shady woods to the rivers, leading with him over obscure paths his antlered band, Behold, will you, seven stags of surpassing beauty, exceeding the size of a young bull.[5] Their uplifted heads are adorned with branching horns which brush their tails as they bend their necks. When once inflamed with the passion of love, the herd lightly speeds across the meadows in pursuit of a doe; and she, giving birth to twins beautifully spotted with white, anxiously cares for them in the forest. Mother nature has deprived this animal of fierce weapons by failing to gird its mouth with hard teeth or its feet with claws or to provide its horns with fierce might, but she has kindly allowed it to outstrip the winds in swiftness of foot and to escape dread disaster by hasty flight.

If you should, therefore, desire to slay the entire herd with darts, keep your eager hounds from barking and running lest they scatter the thick company through the black forest, and all of them, hurry from the open fields in flight. But try with a dart to take the life of a doe, and you will strike all the herd by repeated shots. For, when a doe shot by a dart has fallen on the plains, the bucks are seen to slow down and to cease their desire for flight or for leav-

Tunc alium atque alium certis confige sagittis,
Coritumque prius vacuabit arundine dextra,
Quam Cervam mittat confossam robore turma.

[*ll. 288-299*]

Si vero Cervum per aperti jugera campi
Videris errantem, canibus, cursuque fatiga.
Ille potens pedibus fulmen praevertit et auras,
Aequora metitur plantis, arbustaque saltu
Praeterit, eluditque fuga pernice sequentes
Pone canes. Nacti vero manifesta latrantes
Signa pedum, cursu certant agitare fugacem.
Jamque propinquantis resono clamore catervae,
Et prope crura ferae rictu praecelsa tenentis
Illa levis saltu subito se subtrahit ore
Omnia deludens fidae conamina turbae.
Turba tamen patulos iterum diffusa per agros
Insistit cursu Cervum turbare volantem,
Dente quoad rigido, fugientis crure retento,
Saeva feram vincat, cursusque abrumpat anhelos.
Ceu quondam frondente Jovi sacer ales ab orno
Irruit in pavidam magno stridore columbam;
Mollis avis pavitans liquidum quatit aera pennis,
Itque, reditque levis, crebro glomeramine gyros
Innectens, tutumque dolens exposcit asylum:
Ast volucrem rapidis urget Jovis armiger alis,
Innocuamque neci demittit promptus acerbae:
Haud secus imbellem sequitur fera turba molossum,
Ore tenet, violatque immani vulnere Cervum.
Ocyus infaustum venator liberat ensem
Vagina, mollique ferae sub pectore condit.

[*ll. 300-325*]

Acrius at campis turbam vexabit anhelam
Eludetque Lepus cursu bene notus, et astu.
Vallis erat latos circum diffusa per agros⁶
Usque virescentes ridenti gramine, et amne
Perfusos vitreo, florumque decore nitentes:
Sed qui perpetuo ventorum flamine membra
Inflectunt pecori, torrentque armenta calore:
Tot vero auriti Lepores haec rura frequentant,
Ut vallem Dictinna putet stabula alta ferarum.
Non tamen optatam Lepori captare quietem
Turma sinit celerum rabido clamore molossum.
Agmen enim certat vestigia cogere gressus,
Insequiturque feram ventis pernicius ipsis,

ing her that was slain on the field. Then with your unfailing arrows shoot them one after another, and you will empty your quiver of arrows before the herd forsakes the wounded doe.

But if you should see a stag wandering over the wide open spaces, chase him with your dogs and wear him out. Being swift of foot, he outstrips the speed of lightning and of the winds, he overruns the plains, he leaps over bushes, and by swift flight escapes from the dogs that follow behind. But the barking dogs, having found clear signs of his tracks, vie in chasing the fleeing animal. And now as the sound of the approaching dogs is heard, they are nearly grasping in their open mouths the outstretched legs of the wild beast, with a sudden lunge he quickly makes his escape, frustrating every effort of the faithful pack. But they again scatter out over the wide fields and continue to weary the fleeing stag by their pursuit until, grasping hold of his legs with their tenacious teeth, they savagely overpower him and cause his panting career to cease. As the bird, sacred to Jupiter, sometimes swoops down with a great whirring of wings from a thick-leafed mountain-ash upon an affrighted dove, and the gentle bird, quaking with fear, beats the clear air with her wings, darts this way and that, and weaves countless circles in her yearning to find a safe retreat, yet Jove's armor-bearer presses upon the bird with his swift wings and soon brings bitter death to the innocent creature, in like manner the fierce dogs pursue the peace-loving stag, they hold him with their teeth, and inflict deep wounds. The hunter quickly unsheaths his deadly knife and buries it in the animal's soft breast.

But the hare, well known for its agility and tricky ways, will more subtly worry and baffle the panting dogs. There is a valley⁶ which stretches around through the wide fields, always green with pleasant pastures, bathed by a crystal stream, and bright with beautiful flowers, but which from the constant blowing of the winds withers the bodies of the herds and burns them with the heat. Yet so many long-eared hare inhabit this region that Diana regards the valley as a deep haven for her wild animals. But the swift dogs, by their savage barking, do not allow the hare to get its required rest, for they try to scent its tracks and they pursue the wild creature more swiftly than the winds themselves until they tear the hated animal to pieces with their teeth. Scarcely, however, do they

Invisam donec liceat discerpere morsu.
Vix tamen audaci gaudet contingere rictu,
Cum Lepus ingenti jacto in contraria saltu
Inde alios celerat cursus, luditque latrantes.
Saltibus hinc crebris iterumque iterumque sequentes
Exagitat, rabiemque fugax, ac vota lacessit,
Languida dum tetro cedit data praeda furori.

[*ll. 326-345*]

Quae tamen ardenti Cervusque, Lepusque pericla
Effugiunt planta, versuto callidus astu
Declinat, proprioque illudit saepius hosti
Cercopithecus, honor campi, pars maxima sylvae,
Ingenioque vafro decus immortale ferarum.[7]
Saepe nigro totum circumdat corpus amictu
Omnia contectus neglectis membra capillis:
Non venter, non crura vacant, non brachia villo,
Aut caput, aut renes, aut ora, manusque nigranti.
Si vero Nicaragua tibi det prodiga dono,
Quem praecincta lacu nutrit gratissima tellus,[8]
Ille alvum certe, pectusque albescet, et ora.
Haec vero humanam simularet bellua formam,
Ni magno contorta sinu, contorta deorsum,
Cauda ferae reliquos turparet corporis artus.
Mole tamen plures adeo se attollere visi,
Aethiopem ut primo credas spectare decennem;
Viribus at cinctum validis, hominisque vigore,
Raptandis, ut saepe solent, uxoribus apto.[9]

[*ll. 346-364*]

Sed quem parca quidem privavit munere formae
Ingenio prudens tanto natura decorat,
Ut Fibro possit facile praestare sagaci,
Et reliquum salibus nemorum deludere vulgus.
Hinc cauda quandoque Alno suspenditur alta,
Indus ubi Solem fluvii Crocodilus ad oras
Captat, et ingluviem gaudet ridere ferinam.
Vix etenim fallax frondosae Simius Alni
Consulto ramos coepit versare sonantes,
Cum fera clamoso ventris commota furore
Dentibus exsertis, oris recludit hiatum
Ingentem, mimique ardet celerare ruinam.
At vafer, infausto simulans procumbere casu,
Volvitur in praeceps, ceu jam lapsurus in ora;
Quae fera confestim, praedam quasi dente teneret,

succeed in touching the hare with their fierce mouths, when it makes a long jump in the opposite direction and then hastens along on another course, deceiving the barking dogs. And so the fleeing animal by repeatedly leaping about continues to baffle the dogs that chase it and creates in them a ravenous desire until it grows weak and falls an easy prey to their dreadful fury.

Now the dangers from which the deer and the hare escape by swiftness of foot, the clever monkey avoids by craftiness and deceit, and he often makes sport of his enemy though at close range. The monkey is the pride of the field, the principal inhabitant of the forest, and by reason of his subtle nature, the everlasting glory of wild animals.[7] His entire body is clothed in a shaggy mantle of black hair. Neither his belly, legs, or arms are without black hair, nor his head and loins, neither his face and hands. If, however, Nicaragua should generously present to you the monkey which the pleasant country surrounded by the lake produces,[8] it will be found to have a white belly, breast, and face. This animal, moreover, would resemble a human being in appearance if it did not have a long winding tail that hangs down to mar the appearance of the rest of the body. Some have been seen to stand so high that you would at first suppose that you were looking at a ten year old Ethiopian, but they are endowed with great strength and with the capacities of a man sufficient for violating women, as they often are accustomed to do.[9]

But the animal which wise nature has deprived of the gift of beauty is endowed with so much ingenuity that it can readily surpass the cunning beaver and outwit the other denizens of the forest by its cleverness. Hence it sometimes dangles by its long tail from an alder under which a native crocodile is sunning himself along the edge of a stream, and it takes delight in teasing the gluttonous beast. Scarcely, indeed, does the sly monkey decide to rustle the branches of the thick-leafed alder, when the savage monster, prompted by the fierce clamoring of his stomach, opens wide his mouth and spreads apart his teeth eagerly desiring to hasten the destruction of the actor. But the prankster, pretending to stage an accidental fall, tumbles headlong as if to fall right into his mouth; and the fierce creature quickly closes his mouth as if to grasp the prey in his teeth, while the

Claudit; dum cauda trunci suspensus ab alto
Simius irridet dentes, atque ora prementem.
Mox rursus lapsum simulat, rursusque minantem
Deludit rabiem; fluvii dum bellua mimum
Aspernata vafrum notas se condit in undas.

[ll. 365-384]

Quare opus insidiis semper fallacibus uti,
Si quandoque velis solers illudere capto.
Arboreis siquidem protectus Simius umbris,
Pendulus et cauda truncos se jactat in omnes,
Ac totum saltu percurrens praepete lucum
Astutus telum, plagasque evitat acerbas.
Bina tamen poterit vacuata cucurbita ventre
Insidias praebere tibi, fraudemque jocosam.
Sole prius siccas, parvoque foramine sectas
Desuper, umbrosi deferto montis ad oras,
Majus ubi nugax mimorum cogitur agmen,
Non nullis intro granis per labra remissis
Frumenti patrii, aut lectis ex amne lapillis,
Qui sicco reddant concussi ventre fragorem.
Simius (explorare juvat quem cuncta), relictis
Frondibus, apricum praepes delapsus in agrum
Nunc istam lustrat cupidus, nunc concutit illam,
Arrectaque sonum frumenti suscipit aure.
Mox resonum manibus ventrem penetrare laborat,
Principiumque dati simul observare susurri.
Extensis intus vasis per inane lacertis
Grana manu prendit subito, valideque prehensa
Saepius ex alvo conatur tollere frustra:
Scilicet abreptis globulis manus aucta recusat
Ferre gradum retro, parvaque abscedere rima.
Ast licet ore premat jam prima cucurbita dextram,
Ille tamen laeva rimatur promptus alius
Viscera; grana premit rursum; rursumque retardant
Callida labra manum; cubitumque adnexus
        utrumque
Vertere terga fugax vano conamine tentat;
Quin compressa semel deponat Simius unquam,
Insidiis quamquam miserum data praeda dolosis.
Tantus amor furti, furtumque notare libido!

[ll.385-417]

Tunc captum promptus venator suscipit ulnis,
Ilia fune ambit, caveamque includit in arctam
Insidias fremitu, claustrumque, astumque gementem.
Sed cavet astutus, longae glomeramine caudae

monkey, hanging by his tail from a limb, laughs at him as he closes tightly his teeth and jaws. Presently he again feigns a fall and again makes sport of the threatening fury of the beast until the latter turns away from the cunning actor and hides himself in the waters of his own familiar stream.

It is always necessary, therefore, to employ strategy if at any time you should wish to trick a monkey into being captured. For the monkey, protected by the shadows of the forest, jumps into all the trees, hangs by his tail, and by nimbly leaping along throughout the entire forest cunningly avoids the painful wounds of the arrow. But a pair of hollow gourds can afford you a trap and an amusing lure. After first drying them in the sun, cut a small hole through the top of each and take them to the edge of a shady mountain where a large crowd of silly monkeys is gathered, having deposited inside them a few grains of corn or pebbles from the brook to provide a rattling sound in the dry interior. The monkey, fond of investigating everything, abandons the branches and hurriedly slips down into the open field and now eagerly examines the one and now shakes the other, listening intently to the rattling of the grain. Then he tries to thrust his hands into the resounding cavity and to discover at the same time the cause of the noise. Extending his arm inside he suddenly seizes the grains in his hand and holding on tightly to them tries again and again, though in vain, to bring them out. Obviously, the hand, made larger by grasping the grains, refuses to come out through the small opening. Now although the first gourd already holds the right hand in its mouth, nevertheless he immediately investigates the inside of the other one with his left hand. Again he grasps the grains, and again the ingenious opening holds fast his hand, and with both arms thus held fast, the animal quickly puts forth an idle effort to extricate himself, though never willing to put aside that which he has once taken, even if it be his misfortune to fall prey to guile and treachery. So great is the animal's delight in stealing and its desire to behold what it has stolen!

Then the hunter promptly takes the prisoner in his arms, places a rope around its body, and confines it to a narrow cage, while with a loud outcry it bewails the treachery, the imprisonment, and the deceit. But he cautiously watches the monkey fearing that it become inflamed

Ne sibi colla liget violenta Simius ira
Flagrans: quippe adeo crudeli guttura nodo
Illigat, ut vitae facile spiracula rumpat.

[*ll. 418-424*]

Quod si lactantes cupiat deludere matres,
Et pullos juxta gremio raptare tenellos,
Ligna parat, multaque rogum mox excitat Alno,
Cujus inaccessum flammato turbine centrum
Occupat infracto, plenoque cucurbita ventre.
Simius assiduo vexatus frigore flammas
Promptus adit, circumque atrum diffunditur ignem
Turba patrum, matresque una, juvenesque, senesque,
Et quos cauta parens humeris gestabat alumnos,
Gaudentes frigus tandem depellere membris.
Vix tamen optato gens indulgere calori
Incipit, et nocuum detrudere corpore frigus,
Cum subito secto tumefacta cucurbita ventre
Insonat horrendo, ceu nubes rupta, fragore.
Tunc gelido correpta cohors nemorosa timore
Arva per, et frondes celeri petit avia cursu,
Attonitis medio pullis in rure relictis;
Quos pavidos prompte densis egressus ab umbris
Colligit, et moesto venator carcere condit.

[*ll. 425-443*]

FINIS LIBRI DECIMI-QUARTI

with a violent passion and entwine its long tail about his neck, for so tight is the knot it ties around the throat that it easily cuts off the breath of life.

But if the hunter should want to deceive the nursing mothers by taking their tender babes out of their arms, he gets a large amount of alder wood and immediately starts a fire. In the center of the fire, inaccessible on account of the swirling flames, is placed a gourd with unbroken rind and a solid interior. The monkey, distressed by continuous cold, promptly comes to the fire, and a crowd of males gather around the hot flames together with the mother monkeys, the young and old, and the infants carried on the shoulder of their attentive mothers, for they are happy at last to drive the chill from their bodies. But no sooner does the family begin to enjoy the pleasant warmth and to be driving the severe cold from the body, when suddenly the gourd, having become swollen, bursts open with a terrific blast as if a cloud were bursting apart. Then these dwellers of the forest, seized with fear, scamper away over the ground and through the trees into hiding places, leaving behind in the middle of the field their terror-stricken young, which the hunter, immediately appearing from the thick bushes, gathers up and consigns to a dingy prison.

XV

LUDI

SPORTS

Lustra venenatis postquam montana sagittis
Horrentesque canum turbavi murmure saltus,
Fert animus pravum ludis miscere laborem,[1]
Et vires blanda fractas revocare quiete.
Tyndaridae juvenes, tenui quos ludere disco
Saepe juvat, durasque animo depellere curas,
Dicite, quae festis praestet spectacula ludis
Occiduis emissa plagis animosa juventus:
Et vidistis enim pueri, et reserate potestis.

[*ll. 1-9*]

Now that I have disquieted the mountain
retreats with deadly weapons and troubled the
dreadful forests with barking dogs, I am inclined to add amusements to wearisome toil[1] and
to repair broken strength with gentle relaxation.
O sons of Tyndarus, whose delight it is to play
often with the thin discus and to dispel heavy
cares from the mind, tell me what spectacles
are produced in the western world and presented
at the festivals by gallant youth, for you boys
have seen them and can tell about them.

Protinus armatos generosa in praelia Gallos
Ipse sequar. Nec enim fas est obducere pugnas,
Quae nova limphati recludunt monstra furoris.
Vix cervice minax, fastuque elata superbo,
Incessuque ferox graditur cristata volucris
Assiduo gaudens socias invadere bello,
Cum ludi vesanus amor, cum saeva voluptas
Chortibus abreptam parva concludit in aula,
Fune pedem retinet, solersque ad praelia servat.
Moeret avis primum, longisque insana querelis
Corpus inexpertis conatur solvere vinclis.
Mox vero dapibus, laribusque assueta benignis,
Majestate gravis toto spatiatur in antro,
Saepius et Phoebem cantu, Phoebumque salutat.
Olli flavus apex cristato vertice surgit,
Barba rubet, rorantque jubae per colla fluentes,
Caudaque flexibilis crispatis crinibus aucta
In caput erigitur flexu sinuata decoro,
Corneaque armati retegit calcaria Galli.
Arma tamen, cristamque truces, barbamque recidunt,
Effera qui gaudent volucres in bella ciere,
Exigua laevi calcaris parte retenta,
Lusor ubi parvum, tenuemque accommodat ensem
Funiculo pressum tereti, crurique revinctum.
Utque optata dies pugnis praefixa redivit,
Quisque suum rutilo pugilem mucrone frementem
Jactantemque minas saeva in certamine ducit.

[*ll. 10-36*]

Straightway shall I myself turn to the cocks
ready for gallant battles, nor is it right that I
should fail to disclose fights which reveal an
unheard-of form of wild insanity. Scarcely is
the crested fowl strutting fiercely along with
arched neck, maintaining an air of haughty disdain and eager to assail his mates with unceas-
ing battles, when an insane passion for sport and
a barbarous desire for pleasure causes him to
be taken from the poultry-yard and placed in
a small cage. His foot is tied fast with a rope
and he is carefully kept for fights. The bird at
first frets and makes long laments, frantically
trying to free himself from his new fetters.
Soon, however, he becomes accustomed to his
food and pleasant surroundings and struts
majestically around in the coop, frequently
saluting in song both the moon and the sun.
A reddish comb rises on his crested head, his
wattles too are red, and a tuft of feathers
streams over his neck. His waving tail spreads
out in ruffled plumage, gracefully arching his
head and leaving uncovered the hornlike spurs
by which he defends himself. But the unscrupulous men who delight in driving these fierce birds
into bitter conflict cut off their weapons and
their comb and wattles, leaving only a small
portion of the left spur, to which the gamester
attaches a tiny little blade, fastening it tightly
to the leg with a small cord. And when the
eagerly awaited day appointed for the fights
arrives, each man brings into the bloody fray
his brightly armed gamecock growling and
flinging out threats.

Exstat enim semper plano brevis area dorso
Sanquineis aspersa notis, lethoque recenti,
Ac diro Martis pridem sacrata furori,

There is always a small area of level ground,
previously dedicated to the dreadful fury of
Mars, splotched with the blood of recent slaugh-

Plurima quae circum tabulata sedilia turbae
Offert plaudenti magno clamore triumphis,
Atque inter sese certanti pignore multo.
[*ll.-37-42*]

Haec ubi clamosum replet subsellia vulgus,
Continuo media binos deponit arena
Dextra manus pugiles lethali cuspide cinctos.
Tunc subita accensae rabie fera corda volucres
Ore rubent, oculisque flagrant, et crinibus hirtis
In pugnam celeres prona cervice feruntur.
Non tamen ancipiti praeceps se credere bello,
Aut conferre manus, hostemque lacessere pugna
Audeat, hostiles ni primum lumine motus
Atque omnes aditus exploret Martius ales.
Inde repentino missus super aera saltu
Surgit in adversum quatiens cum pectore pectus,
Ferratisque ferox urget calcaribus hostem
Immiscens pedibusque pedes, atque ensibus enses,
Quin unquam rabido ponat de corde furorem,
Ense quoad victum flava prosternat arena.
Pluma volat, scissoque fluunt praecordia ventre,
Et latum tepido perfundens flumine campum
Occumbit pugnax fato gladiator acerbo.
Victor ovat, magna circum plaudente corona,
Pictaque concutiens auratis pectora pennis
Concinit egregium sublimi voce triumphum.
Ceu quondam toto bacchantes aequore tauri
Cornibus innexis crebro se vulnere caedunt,
Ingeminantque ictus armis, hostemque fatigant,
Ardua quoad rigido cedat victoria cornu:
Haud secus armatus fulgenti cuspide Gallus
Infesto certat palmam certamine ferre.
Si vero ignavus, letho dum volvitur hostis,
Expaveat victor, tenuesque e fronte capillos
Extollat, vertatque dato vestigia tergo,
Continuo lauri, victricis praemia frontis,
Infami, segnique procul victore relicto,
Exanimem potius certant ornare corona.
[*ll. 43-76*]

Mox aliam atque aliam summo discrimine pugnam
Instituit vulgus, medium dum Phoebus Olympum
Contingat, nigrisque polum nox occulat umbris.
[*ll. 77-79*]

Prompta tamen pugnas fastidit turba volucrum,
Si quando stadium levium certamen equorum
Offert, collatisque licet contendere nummis.

ter and surrounded with many wooden benches
which provide seats for the spectators as they
loudly cheer the victors and vie with one another in heavy betting.

When the bustling crowd has filled these
benches, at once a pair of fighters, equipped with
deadly spurs, is set down in the middle of the
arena. The ferocious hearts of the cocks are
immediately fired with anger, their cheeks turn
red, fire comes into their eyes, and with ruffled
feathers and necks bent low they advance swiftly to battle. Yet not too fast may the bird of
Mars dare to commit himself to the perils of
war or to challenge his foe to armed conflict,
but first he must watch the movements of his
enemy and explore every avenue of approach.
Then with a sudden leap he flings himself into
the air toward his opponent, beating breast
with breast, and with iron-tipped spur he fiercely thrusts him back, interlocking foot with foot
and spur with spur, nor does he ever dismiss the
violent passion from his heart until he has his
victim lying prostrate on the yellow sand.
Feathers fly and entrails flow from the lacerated
stomach; and the brave warrior pours out a
warm stream of blood upon the wide field as he
succumbs to an evil fate. The winner exults
amid the cheers of the large gathering, he shakes
his golden breast, and lustily sings of his glorious triumph. As bulls that wildly run over all
the plain sometimes interlock horns and slash
one another with many a wound and continue
to deal blow after blow and to weary the foe
until a hard won victory comes to the one with
invincible horns, so the cock, protected by his
shining spur, struggles desperately to win the
victory. If, however, the dastardly winner should
become frightened while his foe is writhing in
the agony of death and raising his fluffy feathers from off his forehead turn away in flight, at
once the infamous and cowardly victor is deserted, and the laurels, the victor's prize, are
placed instead upon the brow of the dead.

Then the people stage one deadly fight after
another until Phoebus touches the middle of the
heavens and night veils the sky in dark shadows.

But the crowds soon tire of cockfighting when
ever the turf affords horse racing and they may
compete for the stakes. The skilled horsemen
choose for the uncertain contests horses con

Deligit illa sagax dubia in certamina binos
Quadrupedes, forma insignes, animisque superbos,
Ilia queis arctat gracilis subtilia venter,
Quos caput argutum, patulisque e naribus ignis,
Lataque distinguunt prolixo pectora crure.
Impigra ferratis soleis vestigia nudant
Certantes, ipsoque jubent considere tergo
Imberbes pueros, contorto vimine cinctos.
Emicat exultans solis contenta lupatis
Laetitiaque fremit gaudens equitare juventus.

[*ll. 80-92*]

Mox ubi composito dimensi jugera gressu
Pervenere locum fixum certantibus, unde
Tentat Olympiacum cursu traducere campum
Quisque prior, pedibus quadrupes arrectus uterque
Irrequietus amat celeri praecurrere planta.
Sed pueris latos dextra palpantibus armos,
Et pexas cervice comas hinc inde fluentes,
Quadrupedes aestum calido sub pectore laxant,
Et manibusque manus, et frontes frontibus aequant.

[*ll. 93-101*]

Ast ambo clamore tubae, signoque recepto,
Ocyus imperio parent, fugiuntque per aequor.
Evolat hic praepes, ceu jactum fulmen ab aethra;
Avolat ille levis Zephyri velocior alis;
Contenduntque acres pedibus praestare citatis,
Et cursu fixam citius contingere metam.
Cumque leves summo pervadunt aequora nisu,
Arvaque confuso reboant aprica fragore,
Alter abit primus, mox primum praeterit alter,
Mox simul accelerant aequatis frontibus ambo,
Incertisque diu volitat victoria pennis.
Interea pueri cursores calce fatigant,
Et densis urgent virgis per colla, per armos,
Victori donec victum praevertere cursu
Sorte datur, cinguntque decorae tempora lauri.
Clamore excipiunt puerum, plausuque salutant
Et nova festivi geminant certamina cives.

[*ll. 102-118*]

Nil tamen occiduis pubes ardentius oris
Optat, quam circo tauros agitare feroces.
Area lata patet duro circumdata vallo,
Plurima quae fusae praebet subsellia turbae
Pulchra coloratis, variisque ornata tapetis,
Et quam solus adit ludo indulgere suetus,
Sive pedes norit tauros illudere saltu,
Seu flagrantis equi duris regat ora capistris.

[*ll. 119-126*]

spicuous for their beauty, high-spirited, having slender bellies and gaunt flanks, heads graceful in motion, wide nostrils that breathe forth fire, broad breasts and long legs. The contenders strip the iron shoes from the agile feet of their horses and order beardless boys, provided with whips of twisted osier, to mount their backs. The young men gladly come forth with joyful shouts, happy to ride horses provided only with bridles.

Then when they have traversed the course with an even gait and reached the place set for the contenders, from which each one tries to be the first to start across the field, each horse, with head erect, is nervous and eager to be the first to be off. But as the boys stroke their broad shoulders and well groomed manes which flow along their necks on either side, the steeds suppress the fiery spirit that burns within their breasts and stand side by side, hoof to hoof, and shoulder to shoulder.

But when the blast of the trumpet sounds, both quickly heed the command and fly across the plain. The one darts forth like a bolt of lightning from the sky; the other speeds away faster than the wings of the light west wind; and each eagerly strives to excel by swiftness of foot and to be the first in the race to reach the goal. And when with straining effort they are speeding across the field, and the open plain resounds with a deafening din, the one gets ahead, and soon the other is leading the way, and now they both are speeding along together breast to breast, and for a long time victory flits about on uncertain wings. In the meantime, the boys plague the racers with their spurs and urge them on by repeatedly lashing their necks and shoulders until fate allows the one to triumph in the race over the other and to have his temples wreathed with comely laurel. The lighthearted citizens welcome the boy with shouts, they cheer him, and continue with new races.

But the youth of the western world love nothing better than to torment the fierce bulls in the ring. There is a wide open area, surrounded by a solid wall which provides a great many seats for the thronging crowd and is beautifully decked with many-colored awnings. Into this there comes alone a man trained in the sport, skilled in deceiving bulls, either by maneuvering on foot or by riding a fiery-spirited horse guided by a stout bridle.

His ita longaevo gentis de more paratis
Protinus agrestis procera mole juvencus
Elata cervice minax, oculisque furore
Accensis, iramque trucem sub corde volutans
Prosilit, et rabiem sitiens relevare cruore
Tota ferox agitat circum subsellia cursu,
Alba quoad lusor depromat lintea dextra,
Collectamque ex longo irritet cominus iram.
Ille, velut forti nervo contorta sagitta,
Fertur in adversum certus transfigere cornu
Lusorem, fixumque leves extollere ad auras.
Lintea tunc lusor duratis ictibus offert,
Corripit e spatio corpus, promptusque recedens
Evadit celeri lethalia vulnera saltu.
Ille venenato rursus ferventior aestu
Connixus toto lusorem corpore contra
Aggreditur, spumatque ira, mortemque minatur.
Ast lusor parva munitus arundine dextram
Lintea dum prona versat cervice juvencus,
Ipse toris velox figit penetrabile ferrum.
Tollitur in coelum telo transfixus acuto
Et totum taurus Circum mugitibus implet.

[*ll. 127-148*]

Cum vero confixa toris divellere tela
Et cursu rabidum tentat lenire dolorem,
Robustis parvum torquens hastile lacertis
Lusor equum toto spirantem corpore flammas
Objicit adverso, pugnamque ardore lacessit.
Corniger interea ferratae vulnera pinus
Expertus, longum solers hinc inde fatigat
Quadrupedem, pedibusque attritam spargit arenam,
Diversos quaerens aditus. Stat fervidus Aethon
Auribus arrectis intentus fallere plagam,
Dum lusor nocuos hostis considerat astus.
Tum fera praecipiti plantas velocior aura
Motat, quadrupedemque petit, ferrumque, virumque.
Sed subito flexis solers moderator habenis
Cornipedis patulos urget calcaribus armos,
Aerataque ferae compescens cuspide collum
Sedulus interea diro se submovet ictu.

[*ll. 149-165*]

Sin autem morti repetito vulnere fractum
Demitti jubeat summo certamine praeses,
Fulmineo mucrone potens athleta periclum,
Aut eques hastili pariter munitus acuto
Intrepidi subeunt, cornuta fronte minacem
Hortantes clamore bovem, ferroque petentes.

When these arrangements have been made according to the ancient custom of the country, straightway a young wild bull rushes in. He is large, has a high arched neck, his eyes are inflamed with madness, and he harbors bitter anger in his heart. Thirsty for blood by which to allay his fury, he runs wildly around the seats until the bullfighter brings out a white cloth and at close range aggravates the bull's slowly mounting fury. The bull, like an arrow shot from a tightly drawn bow, rushes against his foe, determined to pierce him with his horns and to toss him into the air. Then the matador holds the cloth before the animal's hard thrusts and swerving quickly away escapes the deadly wounds with a leap. The bull is then fired with a more furious passion, and foaming with anger and bearing a threat of death, summons all his strength and attacks the actor. But the fighter, protected by a small spear, swiftly drives the sharp steel into the bull's body as he is turning aside the cloth with his lowered head. Pierced by the sharp weapon the bull rears into the air and fills all the arena with bellowing.

But when the animal attempts to draw from his back the transfixed dart and to lighten the agonizing pain by running, the toreador, brandishing in his strong arms a small spear, throws his horse, which exhales a fiery spirit from his whole body, against his opponent and eagerly challenges him to battle. The bull, in the meantime, suffering from the blow of the steel dart, skillfully harasses the horse for a considerable time on this side and that and tramples over the whole arena searching out different avenues of approach. The spirited Aethon stands with ears erect, ready to evade the blow, while the toreador carefully watches the enemy's vicious stratagem. Then more swiftly than the rushing wind the beast sets his feet into motion and advances upon the armed horseman. But suddenly the rider deftly turns the reins, puts the spurs to the broad shoulders of his steed, and by quickly pushing the wild beast's neck away with the end of his spear escapes in the meantime a dreadful blow.

Now if at the end of the contest the referee should rule that the bull, weakened by repeated wounds, be put to death, a mighty athlete, armed with a deadly sword, or a horseman, likewise defended by a keen-edged spear, fearlessly risks danger by urging the threatening bull on with a loud shout and by pricking him with the sword.

Hic subito totam rumore exasperat iram
Invaditque virum telis, ac voce vocantem.
Tunc athleta toris capulo tenus occulit ensem,
Aut eques aerata venientem verberat hasta,
Et medium telo gemina inter cornua collum
Vulnerat, exanimisque genu convolvit humi bos.
Insequitur plaususque virum, clamorque triumphi,
Contenduntque omnes palmam celebrare latronis.
[*ll. 166-179*]

Non nunquam, gladio nimium dum fidit acuto,
Tollitur in coelum confossus viscera cornu
Conceditque acer fatis gladiator iniquis.
Ille cruentata corpus pervolvit arena;
Horrescit visu populus, sociique periclo.
Hinc aliis aliae succedunt ordine pugnae,
Dum juvat alternis ludos confundere ludis.
[*ll. 180-186*]

Nam solet interdum praestanti corpore taurum
Viribus insignem, clademque ardore minantem
Armento tractum pubes aptare sedendo.
Villoso juvenis constringit ephippia dorso
Instar equi, et tereti circumdat colla rudenti,
Quo mox impavidus pro latis usus habenis
Torva reluctantis conscendit terga juvenci
Calcibus armatus rigidis, et robore fisus.
Ille fremens rabie partes se jactat in omnes,
Et praeceps equitem conatur pellere tergo;
Nunc superas flexis invadens cornibus auras
Tollit se arrectum; nunc aethram calcibus urgens
Fertur in adversos cursu furibundus anhelo:
Dumque cavum tentat saltu conscendere Circum
Omnia permiscet trepidae subsellia turbae.
Ceu quondam Lybicus rigido Leo saucius ictu
Dente minax, oculisque ferox fremit ore cruento,
Exsertisque petit versutos unguibus hostes,
Et nunc praecipiti jacitur per inania saltu,
Nunc velox cursu turbam pernice fatigat:
Haud secus indignans insueto pondere taurus
Permiscens Circum nunc hos, nunc impetit illos.
Ast puer immoto taurinum corpore dorsum
Usque tenet, crebrisque fodit calcaribus armos.
[*ll. 187-210*]

Quin etiam valida tauro puer arduus alto
Prolixum dextra vibrans hastile, reclusis

The bull's full anger is suddenly provoked by the shouting and he rushes toward the man who thus challenges him with weapons and shouts. The athlete thereupon buries the sword in the flesh clear to the hilt, or the horseman strikes him with the spear as he advances, wounding him in the neck midway between the horns; and the bull sinks lifeless to the ground. Cheers from the people and a shout of triumph follow, for all are eager to celebrate the victory of the matador.

Sometimes the brave fighter, trusting too much his keen sword, is tossed into the air, pierced through his vitals by a horn, and succumbs to a bitter fate. His body rolls across the blood-stained arena. The people and the man's companions shudder at the dangerous spectacle. Fights then continue in due order, one after another, until it pleases them to vary the contests.

Oftentimes, indeed, the men bring forth from the herd a bull to ride, one of remarkable beauty and strength of body and having a spirit that threatens ruin. A young man fastens a saddle on his shaggy back just as on a horse, he puts around his neck a stout rope which he soon fearlessly uses in place of wide reins, and, provided with sharp spurs and relying on his strength, he mounts the back of the unruly young bull. The bull bellows loudly and jumps about in every direction in an attempt to throw the rider headlong from his back. Now he stands erect, tossing his curved horns high into the air, now he beats the air with his heels and with breathless haste runs toward those who block his way, and he throws the frightened spectators into great consternation in his effort to jump out of the ring. As a Lybian lion, when once wounded by a hard blow, threateningly shows his teeth, glares ferociously, and gives forth loud roars from his bloody mouth, then rushes with outstretched claws at his wily foe, at one time springing suddenly through the air, at another alarming the crowd by his quick movements, so the bull, angered by the unusual burden, throws the circus into an uproar and rushes now toward these and now toward those. But the boy, unshaken, continues to cling to the back of the bull and to put the spur to his sides again and again.

In addition, the boy, mounted aloft on the back of the bull and holding in his strong hand a long pointed rod, has another bull brought

Cornigerum septis alium deducier imis
Imperat, et toto gaudens agit aequore plagis.
Ille nova primum stupefactus imagine friget,
Et socium cursu phaleratum praepete vitat.
Sed longum dira stimulatus arundine tergum
Aestuat accensus rabie, cornuque sequentem
Invadit, miscentque ambo fera praelia cornu.
Ast robustus eques dirimit certamina telo
Continuatque ardens tauros agitare per aequor,
Quoad ponant sudore minas, fractique quiescant.
[*ll. 211-222*]

Tum pubes tauris cursus admiscet equorum,
Certa queis juvenis firmat vestigia dorso
Calce premens dextro dextrum, laevumque sinistro,
Arrectusque supra binos compescit habenis.
Ilicet alipedes in cursum concitat acres
Firmus eques, durisque tenens devincta capistris
Ora, citum solers gressum moderatur equorum,
Quadrupedesque pari transcendunt aequora cursu.
Inde alios flexus ducens, aliosque reflexus
Cursores magnum volucres inflectit in orbem,
Quin plantas unquam dorsis amoverit altis.
[*ll. 223-233*]

Non nunquam populus rejectis aequore tauris
Gaudet inexpertos homines celebrare volantes.
Ardua truncatur sudanti cortice pinus,[2]
Quae impexa feriat lucentia sydera fronte.
Umbrosis deinceps tonsis de more capillis
Arbor (*a*) Olympiaco medio Cybeleia circo
Erigitur, circumque obsepta ex fune (*b*) catena
Exhibet illa gradus fastigia summa petenti.
Inde coronatur porrecto ex Ilice (*c*) Quadro
Innumeros apto sinuare per aethera gyros;
E cujus possit medio se attollere centro
Visceribus vacuata sudes (*d*), ac secta bicorni
Vertice (*e*); quae quadrum motu festina sequatur
Opposito, secumque sedentem culmine volvat.
Huic siquidem puber (*f*) tigno femur aptat utrumque
Poplite terga premens et toto pectore supra est.
Sedula mox pubes replicato fune (*g*) bifurcum
Includit lignum, (fidens ubi sidit ephebus)
Et totam loris circum stringentibus ambit,
Quae circi verrant proprio glomeramine campum
Explicito, vacuumque ferant per inane volantes.
Ut solet interdum cingi versatile buxum
Funibus in gyrum ductis, arcteque rotatis;

out of the stables which he drives all over the field at the point of the goad. This bull is at first bewildered by the strange sight and with great speed seeks to escape from his caparisoned companion. But when his back has been pricked a great many times by the sharp rod, he becomes infuriated and turns his horns against his pursuer. The two interlock horns in a desperate battle, but the gallant rider breaks up the struggle by the use of his goad and continues to drive the bulls wildly over the field until, overcome with weariness, they put aside their threats and become gentle.

Then the people add to the bullfights horseback riding in which a young man firmly sets his feet on the backs of two horses in such a way that his right foot rests upon the back of the one on the right and his left foot on the back of the one on his left, and standing erect he directs the team with the reins. At once the balanced equestrian causes the spirited steeds to run, and by keeping their mouths subject to the hard bit he skillfully controls their speed; and they cross the field with an even gait. Then after making several turns and counter turns, he drives his winged steeds in a large circle, never once removing his feet from their high backs.

Sometimes the people, turning away from the bullfights in the field, find pleasure in going to witness amateur fliers. A tall pine[2] which strikes the shining stars with its bushy top is stripped of its resinous bark. The shady foliage is then duly shorn off and the tree (*a*), sacred to Cybele, is erected in the middle of the circus, having a chain of rope (*b*) wrapped about it to afford a ladder for one seeking to reach the top. Then it is crowned with a large wooden square frame (*c*) free to revolve around and around through the air and such that from its center a pole (*d*) that has been hollowed out and has a crescent-shaped top (*e*) will rapidly accompany the motion of the frame in a reverse direction and will carry around with it the person who sits on its top, for, indeed, a young boy (*f*) sits astride the top of the pole with both his legs around it and with his entire breast exposed above. Then the young men carefully wrap with coiling ropes (*g*) the crescent-shaped pole on which the boy sits and install around the entire device leather girdles which sweep across the field of the circus carrying the fliers through empty space as the coil to which each one is fastened unwinds. As a

Fig. 3 — Voladores

Dum vero curvo per terram volvitur orbe,
Explicat actutum sinuata volumina motu,
Vinclaque versatus rumpit servilia turbo:
Haud aliter loris arctatum mobile tignum
Flectitur in gyrum praeceps, nexusque remittit.
[*ll. 234-261*]

Tum quatuor lecti vernanti e flore juventae
Omnes larvati, fulgentes vestibus omnes
Conscendunt Quadrum planta veloce supernum,
Considuntque aliis alii e regione remoti,
Nectantur donec sinuatis ilia loris.
Restibus ut vero novit se quisque revinctum,
Praecipites saltu terram volvuntur in imam
Ilia suspensi (*h*) juvenes: mox machina gyro
Flectitur, et bifido evolvens revoluta cylindro
Lora, urget subito producto fune volantes
Ducere lunatos circum per inania flexus,
Nectereque immensis immensos orbibus orbes.
Tunc quatiunt coelum pedibus, manibusque sonora
Sistra movent, magnoque replent subsellia plausu,
Impetus in terram laxis dum prorsus habenis
Ceu Baccho victos, nutanti poplite, fundat.
[*ll. 262-277*]

Huic aliud populus sublimi vertice tignum
Substituit, fusisque ardet celebrare cachinnis.
Scilicet ut ferro pinum raditque, politque,
Utque faber totam solers aequavit ad unguem,
Imbuit aequatum crassa pinguedine lignum,
Tota quoad pinus circum perfusa nitescat.
Tunc medio laevis lucenti cortice truncus
Erigitur circo, dives cui summa coronat
Aere laborato plenus fastigia crater.
Non tamen argentum studiosum vulgus habebit,
Ni prius ingenti pinum sudore malignam
Conscendat, fixumque manu cratera revellat.
[*ll. 278-289*]

Hinc plures vario tignum conamine tentant
Exspoliare bonis, astuque, et viribus usi.
Funibus hic tortis nutantia crura revincit,
Certa queis fuso figat vestigia tigno.
Ille manus ambas clavis accingit acutis,
Cuspideque infixo constringens terga peruncti
Attollit magno labentia membra labore.
Vix tamen annosae trepidanti poplite pinus
Exiguum emensi spatium ducuntur inani
Spe, subito praeceps cum trunco lapsus ab alto
Corruit in terram votis frustratus uterque.

spinning top often has a string wound tightly about it, and while it spins over the floor in an even circle constantly unwinds the string and by its turning loosens its servile bonds, so the revolving pole, inclosed in ropes, loosens its bonds as it swiftly turns around.

Then four young men, selected from the flower of youth, all of them wearing masks, all of them gaudily attired, swiftly climb to the top of the platform and sit down opposite one another until they are fastened around the waist by the leather girdles. When each one finds that he has been fastened to the ropes, the youths all plunge toward the ground below, suspended (*h*) by their waists. Soon the machine begins to revolve and as the ropes around the crescent-shaped cylinder unwind, at once the fliers on the ends of the ropes are forced to swing round and round through the air like madmen and to interweave many large circles. Then as they kick the air with their feet and shake loud sistrums in their hands they fill the bleachers with loud applause until the ropes are completely unwound and the force of gravity brings the boys to the ground, where they reel about as if under the influence of Bacchus.

In place of this pole the people set up another tall one and enjoy a contest amid shouts of laughter. A workman skillfully scrapes and polishes a pine log with his steel tools, smoothing it off to perfection, and then smears its slippery surface with a thick layer of grease until it is entirely covered and glistening. This sleek and shining pole is then made to stand upright in the middle of the ring, having on its top a bowl generously filled with coins. But no one from the eager crowd will possess the money unless first by a strenuous effort he scales the pole and grasps in his hand the bowl that is fixed on top.

Several, then, by various means of exertion attempt to despoil the pole of its treasures, employing both skill and strength. One man binds twisted ropes around his faltering limbs by which to hold firmly his position on the greased pole. Another provides both hands with sharp spikes and by fixing the sharp ends firmly into the surface of the pole lifts his slipping body with great exertion. But scarcely has each, led by idle hope, climbed with quivering knees a short distance up the old pine when suddenly he comes sliding down the tall trunk to the earth, and his hopes are frustrated. The surrounding

Laetitia, fusisque fremit vaga turba cachinnis,
Hortaturque viam rursus tentare molestam
Defessos, lucri probroso ingentis amore.
Acrius incumbunt illi molimine summo
Plura volutantes animo, casumque verentes.
Sed lapsi in terram miseranda saepe ruina
Desistunt ambo coeptis, nec munera curant.
Ast quandoque puer tanto conamine ludum
Aggreditur, tignumque adeo premit ille lacertis,
Ut dextra pateram supremo e vertice tollat.
Omnia tunc forti manibus subsellia plaudunt
Victori, nomenque canunt, et laudibus ornant.

[*ll. 290-312*]

Nil vero miranda magis spectacula praebet
Quam numerosa vacans Indorum copia ludo.
Illa prius densum sudanti ex arbore gummi[3]
Cogit (cui virtus donavit elastica nomen),
Atque pilam vario magnam glomeramine format,
Quae tenues superet geminatis saltibus auras.
Tunc manus ingentem fingit sinuata coronam,
Primus ubi grandem sursum jacit impetus orbem,
Quin ulli manibus liceat contingere jactum;
Sed potius femore, aut cubitis, humerisque, genuque.
Inde, globus medium simul ac vibratur in aequor,
Tota manus crebro fervet super aequora saltu.
Hic illum cubito pellit; femore ille repellit;
Hic caput objectat labenti desuper orbi;
Ille genu promptus rursum super astra remittit,
Aut ferit alterna volitans coxendice gummi.
Si vero quandoque pilam lata area tergo
Excipiat; cubito, aut genibus revocare cadentem
Est opus, inque auras aequato attollere campo.
Hic toto videas Indos tunc rure rotari,
Dum rursum tollant ulnis, aut poplite lapsam.
Quod si aliquis manibus sphaeram pulsare volantem
Ausit, et incautus legem violare severam,
Ille, notam passus, patitur dispendia ludi.[4]

[*ll. 313-336*]

FINIS LIBRI DECIMI-QUINTI

crowd is amused and roars with shouts of laughter. It urges them, though exhausted, to try again the difficult feat, attracted, as it is, by an inordinate desire for great gain. More keenly they apply themselves, engrossed in the supreme effort yet fearing a fall. But if at each attempt they unfortunately slip and fall to the ground, they give up and disregard the reward. Sometimes, however, a boy enters the contest with so great an effort and grasps the pole in his arms in such a way that he succeeds in lifting in his hand the bowl from the top of the pole. All the spectators applaud the gallant victor with the clapping of hands, they sing his name, and heap praises upon him.

Nothing, however, provides a more amazing spectacle than a large company of Indians given to play. They first gather a thick gum,[3] discharged by a tree, which gets its name from its elastic properties, and by rolling it together form a large ball which freely bounces high into the air. The crowd then forms a large circle into which the large ball is first tossed, and it is not permitted for anyone to touch it with his hands when once it has been thrown, but rather he must hit it with his hips, or elbows, or with his shoulders, or knees. Then as soon as the ball is tossed into the middle of the field, the whole crowd excitedly bounds over the plain darting this way and that. One hits the rubber ball with his elbow, another drives it back with his hip, one thrusts his head in its way as it comes down, another with his knee quickly sends it back again into the sky or darting back and forth strikes it with one hip and then with the other. But if at any time the ball should alight on the broad surface of the ground, the grounded ball must be retrieved with the elbow or the knees and lifted from the level plain into the air. For this reason you will see the Indians at this point of the game rolling all over the ground until they have raised the fallen ball with their elbows or knees. But if someone should venture to strike the ball with his hands while it is in the air and carelessly disregard the strict rule, he is reprimanded and suffers the loss of the game.[4]

255

APPENDIX

CRUX TEPICENSIS

Hactenus in medio florentes aequore campos;
Mulciberisque iras; undasque e collibus actas;
Atque imbuta dedi vario velamina fuco;
Liminaque alta Fibri; clivoque avulsa metalla.
Cogere mella dein; pecudumque agnoscere mores;
Et fontes juxta, volucresque, ferasque secutus,
Festivis animi curas compescere ludis
Edocui. His autem, mutata mente, remotis,
Nunc tibi sacra cano mundi monumenta redempti,
Quae nostris natura sagax excudit in agris.

[*ll. 1-10*]

Ne tamen ulla meam turpet contagio mentem,
Aut violare queat cantus sacrata profanus,
Protinus Aoniae gressus removete sorores;
Castaliasque undas, citharamque, carmina vates
Delphicus amoveat praestare silentia jussus.
Tu sola Omnipotens summi Sapientia Patris,
Provida quae toto terrarum ludis in orbe
Cuncta regens uno mundi confinia nutu,
Dextra fave, dum plectra manu percussa trementi
Certa tui celebrant clari monumenta triumphi.

[*ll. 11-20*]

Immensas America potens diffusa per oras,
Qua late gelidam terras extendit in Arcton
Pluribus alta jugis, aut campo acclivis aperto,
Eduxit geminos gremio connixa tumenti
Verticis aerii montes, qui nubila collo
Exsuperant, altoque ferunt fastigia coelo.
Hos inter vallis multum porrecta profundo
Aequore plana jacet, rigidis nunc horrida brumis,
Nunc herbis frondosa novis, Calthisque renatis,
Limina cum vernum pandit coelestia signum:
Hanc rigat illimis lapsu per saxa sonoro
Amnis humum, mediamque citis intersecat undis.

[*ll. 21-32*]

Sed campo, et fluvio, et clivis dominatur in altis
Valle situs media Tepicus, nomen adeptus
Egregium, quod fama volans extollit in astra.
Non tectis floret sublimi mole superbis,
Marmore nec Pario subsectas arte columnas
Enumerat, nec templa manu fabricata vetusta,
Aut auro, aut rutilis circum lucentia gemmis:

THE CROSS OF TEPIC

Thus far I have been telling of the flower gardens which grow in the middle of the lakes, of Vulcan's wrath, of waters streaming from the hills, of cloth steeped in various dyes, of the deep haunts of the beaver, and of metals torn from the mountain. I have then explained how to refine sugar, how to learn the ways of the herds and flocks, and, after telling of the fountains, I have described the birds and beasts and shown how to relieve the worries of the mind with merriment and sport. And now that these subjects have been put aside, I change my purpose and now sing to you of the sacred memorial of the redeemed world which nature in her wisdom has forged in our fields.

But in order that no corruption may defile my mind or worldly song be able to profane that which is sacred, begone, O Aonian sisters, and let the Delphian bard be constrained to hold his silence and to put aside his Castalian waters, cithara, and songs. Do Thou alone, Almighty Wisdom of the Supreme Father, who in thy providence dost play in all the world, controlling all the limits of the universe by a single nod, be gracious unto me as with trembling hand I play the lyre in celebration of the unfailing memorial of thy glorious triumph.

Mighty America, which spreads across an immense area, travailed and brought forth two high mountains whose summits rise above the clouds and soar heavenward in the land which stretches far toward the cold Arctic, arising in countless peaks or ascending from the open plains. Between these lies a level valley extending far across the vast plain, at one time stiff with icy winter, and now green with fresh grass and young marigolds as springtime opens up its glorious portals. This valley is intersected through the center by a clear stream of swiftly moving waters which babble over the rocks.

But Tepic, located in the middle of the valley, is mistress of the field, the stream, and the high mountains, having acquired a distinguished name which winged rumor has exalted to the stars. It is famous not for its proud mansions, nor does it boast of columns skillfully hewn from Parian marble or of temples built long ago and shining on every side with gold or bright

256

Tecta tamen populus cultu laudanda modesto,
Templaque perpetuis votis ornata frequentat.
Ast gemmas, aurumque fugax, fastumque domorum
Prodigio natura novo generosa rependit.

[*ll. 33-43*]

Propter enim, pagi virides felicis ad oras,
Gramen ubi campo ridens pubescit aperto,
Terra solum supra reliquum se tollere visa
Semi excelsa pedem, pratoque elata patenti
Extendi longo duodenas circiter ulnas
Cespite; quem plusquam terno solertia novit
Pollice latum, altaque simul transversa resectum
Gleba, quae trunco lethalia brachia fingit,
Expromitque crucem, divini pignus amoris.
Ceu quondam celso sublata cacumine montis
Arbore laeta viret, lucoque obscura nigranti
Tot tibi densa cruces offert, quot robora, sylva.[1]
Ridenti contecta viret crux gramine campi,
Arida quin unquam languescat frigore brumae,
Aut saltem rigidis expalleat usta pruinis:
Quin potius glacie pagi languentibus agris,
Sola toros proprio laetos alit usque virore.
Si vero largis frondescant imbribus arva,
Luxurieque nova progignant florida gemmas,
Ilicet herba crucis macie tabescere fertur
Infesta, tristique diu pallore teneri,
Caetera dum rursus deformet jugera tabes.
Ut solet umbrosas hiberno tempore frondes
Pandere laeta salix, folioque induta comanti
Brachia per vacuum fastosa extendere coelum;
Cumque agri denso vernantes gramine rident,
Lurida combustis tabescere tota capillis:[2]
Haud aliter densata comis crucis herba praeustis
Visa virescenti reliquo marcescere campo,
Et florere iterum camporum fronde peresa.

[*ll. 44-73*]

Nec minus insuetum certe mirabere monstrum,
Quo, clavis veluti stipes transfixus acutis,
Ternas usque, loco clavorum, emittit avenas,
Gramine majores reliquo, juxtaque virentes.
Quin etiam perfossa latus crux mira foramen
Ostentat, plagaeque locum (qua corda reclusit
Lancea dira) rubro rorantis flumine signat.
Inde olim vitreum fama est manasse liquorem,
Arida quo febris, virusque, et lurida tabes,
Grassantesque lues, et quovis languida morbo

gems; but its people dwell in houses praised for their modest style and they throng the temples permanently adorned with votive offerings. And in place of gems, perishable gold, and palaces, nature has lavishly provided an unparalleled miracle.

Near the edge of this happy village, in the open fields where grass grows in profusion, a mound of earth is seen to rise a half foot above the rest of the ground and form an oblong turf about a dozen cubits long. It is known to be over three palms wide and to be, at the same time, intersected by another mound of earth which with the main body forms the deadly arms of a cross, the symbol of divine love. So it is that sometimes far up on the lofty summit of a mountain a forest, heavy with trees and darkened with shady branches, presents to you as many crosses as there are trees.[1] The cross of the field is covered with a lovely coat of green grass, nor does it ever become dry and withered by winter's cold, nor does it even turn pale when nipped by hard frosts, but when the fields of the land are frozen and dying, it alone continues to sustain the lovely bed of grass with its own vitality. If, on the other hand, an abundance of rain should refresh the fields and cause a profusion of flowers to blossom again, then the cross of grass is said to undergo a deadly blight and to maintain for a long time a ghastly pallor until the rest of the fields are again withering. As the luxuriant willow often puts forth its shady leaves in the winter, stretching through the air its proud branches clothed in dense foliage, but when the fields are growing green and smiling with thick grass, all its foliage turns yellow and withers in the heat,[2] likewise the thick blades of grass on the cross are seen to burn and wither while the rest of the field is turning green, but to come to life again when the foliage of the field is dying.

And you will certainly marvel no less at the phenomenal manner in which the cross, as if pierced by the sharp nails, sends forth in place of the nails three blades, higher than the surrounding grass but growing alongside it. Besides, this wondrous cross has a hole pierced in its side from which there issues a red stream revealing the spot where the cruel sword exposed the heart. There is a tradition that a stream of clear water once flowed from this, affording a ready cure for burning fever, poisons, consumption, infectious diseases, and every dis-

257

Corpora praesentem crebro traxere medelam,
Ultricesque Deas properantes fata fugarunt.
Ast aegri quondam manibus correpta salubris
Unda luem fertur pepulisse, aegrumque catenis
Exemisse quidem; sed secum condita terrae
Contumulasse sinu, populo lugente, salutem.

[*ll. 74-89*]

His excita diu celebris vicinia pagi
Religiosa crucem, collatis undique nummis,
Praecinxit muro semotam rure profano,
Atque frequens votis, multaque observat acerra.³

[*ll. 90-93*]

En tibi, primaevo florens ardore juventus,
Cui coelo natura dedit gaudere benigno,
Atque auras mulcere avibus, pictisque tueri
Libratas pennis coeli per inania turbas,
Cuique herbosus ager late viridantia praebet
Gramina odorifero semper fulgentia flore;
En tibi, queis tetras, violenti ad littora Reni,
Fallere conabar curas, atque otia, cantus.
Disce tuas magni felices pendere terras,
Divitiasque agri, praestantia munera coeli,
Explorare animo, ac longum indagare tuendo.
Alter inauratos Phoebeo lumine campos
Incautis oculis, brutorum more, sequatur,
Omniaque ignavus consumat tempora ludis.
Tu tamen interea, magnum cui mentis acumen,
Antiquos exuta, novos nunc indue sensus,
Et reserare sagax naturae arcana professa
Ingenii totas vestigans exere vires,
Thesaurosque tuos grato reclude labore.

[*ll. 94-112*]

FINIS

order whatsoever that affects the body, and that
it repelled the avenging goddesses which hasten
death. But once, when this healing water was
taken into the hands of a sick man, it is said to
have driven out the disease and to have released
its hold on him, but, to the regret of the people,
having hidden itself in the bosom of the earth,
it buried its healing power with it.

The religious people of this famous community remained for a long time stirred by these
events, and when they had collected money from
the surrounding country, they erected a wall
around the cross, separating it from the unhal-
lowed ground, and they frequently honor it
with votive offerings and the burning of much
incense.³

Behold, O youth, glorying in the enthusiasm
of your early years, whom nature has permitted
to enjoy the kindly sky, to listen to the sweet
songs of birds, and to watch them flying through
the air poised on wings of many colors, for whom
the field provides on every hand green meadows
always bright with sweet-scented flowers, behold, to you is my song directed in which I have
tried to beguile my grievous cares and my leisure
hours spent near the banks of the turbulent
Reno. Learn to esteem highly your fertile lands,
to search out and determine with care the riches
of the field and the matchless blessings of heaven.
Let another, like the beasts, go with unseeing
eyes through the fields gilded by the golden
sunlight, and let him indolently waste his time
in play. But you, on the contrary, who have
great keenness of mind, abandon old ideas and
adopt the new, and with a high resolve to uncover the mysteries of nature, bring into the
search the full vigor of your mind, and with
joyful work uncover your treasures.

Notes on the Funeral Declamation and Marian Poems

Funebris Declamatio:
The Funeral Declamation for Figueredo

1. Popayán, one of the oldest cities in Colombia, was founded in 1538 by Sebastián de Belalcázar. Situated south of Cartagena on the route to Quito and Lima, Popayán had an important role in the colonial period.

2. Libitina, the Roman goddess of corpses and funerals (which were registered in her temple on the Esquiline) often signifies death itself in classical Latin literature: Horace, *Odes* 3.30.7, *Satires* 2.6.19; Juvenal, *Satires* 12.122; Phaedrus, *Fabulae* 4.18.

3. The Latin diction in Landívar's parenthesis – *absit verbo invidia* – recalls Livy, *Ab urbe condita* 9.19: *absit iniuria verbo* ('may there be no offence at this being said').

4. Dauphin Louis, son of Louis XV, was a defender of the Jesuits, although the Society was expelled from France in 1764 as a result of opposition led by the *Parlement* of Paris. The Dauphin died in 1765, the same year as Figueredo: Martin (1988).

5. This 'oracle' may have its actual source in Plato, *Laws* 717b quoted later in §9 (n. 15 below).

6. Lattimore (1961), 135-41 and Toynbee (1971) treat flowers in Greco-Roman burial ritual. Anchises' well known exclamation on the premature death of Marcellus in Virgil, *Aeneid* 6.883-6 (*manibus date lilia plenis* 'Give me lilies in armfuls') and Valerius Flaccus, *Argonautica* 6.492-4 both seem to associate lilies with premature death.

7. A comparable repetition of verbs ending a sentence in Cicero, *Catiline* 2.1: *abiit, excessit, evasit, erupit*. On the importance of that particular Ciceronian speech, see p. 85 n. 39 above.

8. Ignatius of Loyola (1491-1556) who founded the Jesuits was canonised in 1622: Cross and Livingstone (1997), 818-19.

9. This oath is idiomatic in classical Latin. It is especially common in Cicero's speeches and dialogues, and in the comedies of Plautus and Terence. Invocation of Hercules is clearly anomalous in this ecclesiastical context: compare n. 14 below.

10. Charles of Lorraine (1590-1631) was consecrated Bishop of Verdun at the age of 24. At first his behaviour appeared to contravene his pledge to respect the obligations of the high office he had accepted, but he subsequently avoided the temptations of secular life and petitioned to renounce the bishopric and become a Jesuit. He joined the Society in 1619, with opposition from his family and those loyal to the diocese who attributed Charles' decision to the machinations of the Jesuits. After a novitiate in Rome, he earned a reputation for his charity in times of hunger and plague as governor of the Society's houses in Bordeaux and Toulouse.

11. For the Latin expression here (*quae cum ita sint*), compare Cicero, *Catiline* 1.10, 4.18, and n. 7 above.

12. Literally 'God immortal!'. Compare e.g. Cicero, *Catiline* 4.1: *per deos immortales!*

13. According to Livy, 40.34, the temple to *Pietas* was dedicated in 181 BC. Versions of the story told here are given by Valerius Maximus (5.4.7) and Pliny, *Natural History* 7.121. Landívar draws details and expressions from both of these accounts. Compare Festus (228, ed. Lindsay). According to Hyginus, *Fabulae* 254, Xanthippe saves her father Mycon in the same way.

14. The metonymic use of *Phoebus*, the appellation of Apollo, for 'sun' is common in classical Latin poetry and occurs over 20 times in the *Rusticatio Mexicana*. The deployment here is decorative, but its juxtaposition with the Christian God (*Deus*) in the sentence immediately following is still striking.

15. Plato, *Laws* 717b. The importance of hero-worship, relevant to section 11 below, is also emphasised in this passage of Plato's dialogue.

16. Table 10, fr. 1 in Crawford (1996), 40: *hominem mortuum in urbe ne sepelito neve urito* ('let no one bury or cremate a dead man in the city').

17. Prudentius, *Contra Orationem Symmachi* ('A Reply to the Address of Symmachus') 1.190-2. The verses are not quoted precisely: pp. 38-9 above.

18. According to Lactantius, *De mortibus persecutorum* ('The Deaths of Persecutors') 39, Valeria, the widow of the Emperor Maximianus Galerius, refused a proposal of marriage from her husband's nephew, Maximinus, which he made while she was still in mourning. Her refusal is not directly quoted by Lactantius.

19. The expression 'grief is so firmly lodged in your heart' seems to echo Virgil, *Aeneid* 4.4: *haerent infixi pectore*.

20. The words *Ad Majorem Dei Gloriam* or their initials *AMDG* ('To the greater glory of God') constitute a common hallmark of Jesuit texts. The inscription of this expression is still visible over the entrance of the seminary Landívar attended in Tepotzotlán.

The Marian Poems: A Horatian Ode and a Castilian Sonnet

1. The work commended is the biography of the Virgin Mary by José Ignacio Vallejo: *Vida de la Madre de Dios y siempre Virgen María*. These poems prefaced the book which was published in Cesena, Italy in 1779. The word 'sang' (*canebat*) is appropriate because the composition to follow is an ode, a lyric poem in alcaic strophes.

2. This opening structure resembles Horace, *Ode* 1.9.1 (*Vides ut*), a poem in the same alcaic metre.

3. The oxymoron (*probrosa ... generosa*) conveys the humiliation and victory at once involved in Christ's passion: similar verbal effects are a feature of Horace's lyric poetry: compare e.g. *Odes* 1.6.9: *tenues grandia* ('too weak for lofty themes') and also *sordibus insigne opus* ('with dark grime your glorious creation') in this poem at lines 21-2 below.

4. Significantly, *Christiades*, the rare word for 'Christian' used here and in *RM* 1.129, is found in the medieval hymn *Te Joseph*: Blaise (1954), sv. *Christias*. The form *Christiadum* also appears in the opening stanza of an anonymous seventeenth-century Latin ode in the Third Asclepiad metre, again addressed to Joseph: *Te, Joseph, celebrent agmina coelitum, / Te cuncti resonent Christiadum chori, / Qui clarus meritis, junctus es inclytæ / Casto foedere Virgini.* A text of the *Te Joseph* is in Britt (1922). As a hymn from the Catholic Breviary, it was probably known to Landívar, and to Vallejo, who is addressed as *Joseph* in lines 17 and 27 of this ode.

5. The name of Clio, the Muse associated with history, suggests the celebration of heroic glory (*kleos* in Greek): compare Horace, *Odes* 1.12.2.

6. The idea of a literary reputation reaching the stars recalls Horace, *Odes* 1.1.36 ('I will strike the stars with my exalted head': *sublimi feriam sidera vertice*), and Ovid, *Metamorphoses* 15.875-6 ('I shall be borne immortal above the high stars': *super alta perennis / astra ferar*). The phrase *sic itur ad astra* ('This is the way to the stars'), spoken by Apollo as he promises immortality to Iulus and his descendants in Virgil, *Aeneid* 9.641 may well be pertinent too: Sigüenza y Góngora, the author of some important Marian poems (see pp. 16-17 above), frequently used that phrase as a motto to convey his sense of pride in New Spain and of the ambition New Spaniards had for their country.

7. Commemoration in marble and stone can also be emblematic of literary immortality: Propertius, *Elegies* 3.3.11-26; Horace, *Odes* 3.30.1-5, picking up *Ode* 1.1 cited in the previous note; and again Ovid, *Metamorphoses* 15.871-9, as well as 15.807-15. Fowler (2000), 193-234 is an illuminating discussion of this topos in classical Latin literature.

8. The rhyme scheme followed in the sonnet is Petrarchan: ABBA ABBA in the octave, and BCB CBC in the sestet. Ciplijauskaité (1985), 19-23 describes Góngora's use and development of the sonnet form in Spanish.

9. Horace, *Epistles* 2.1.238; Propertius, *Elegies* 1.2.22, 3.9.11; Pliny, *Natural History* 35.79-104 and Quintilian, *Institutio oratoria* 12.10.6 are among the classical sources which secured the reputation of the painters Apelles and Protogenes for posterity.

10. The Eagle is the symbol of Saint John the Evangelist, who was exiled to Patmos (Revelation 1:9). A Mexican tradition had long identified the Virgin of the Apocalypse in Revelation 12:1 with the Virgin of Guadalupe: Poole (1995), 106-7. In his poem *De Deo* 42.627-9, Landívar's exiled compatriot, Diego José Abad, claimed that the vision of Mary seen by John in Patmos had taken the form of the Guadalupan Virgin, and – in an earlier 1775 version of that poem – Abad had also said that the Virgin on the Indian's cloak 'could scarcely have been painted by Apelles' (*Palliolo est qualem vix fingere posset Apelles* 38.620). The equivalent verse in the later Bologna edition of the *De Deo* (1780) reads: 'On the cloak was an Image of the Mother of God' (*Palliolo est quam pulchra Dei Genetricis Imago* 42.621). Abad made the alteration, presumably, to avoid any implication that the achievement of the mythological painter Apelles could be compared with that of God himself. As the earlier versions of the *De Deo* were still current in 1779 when Landívar's sonnet was published, Abad's original references to Apelles and to John in Patmos may possibly have something to do with the conjunction of the two subjects in this sonnet. However, topoi involving Apelles and Protogenes were not uncommon: both are connected to the image of the Virgin of Guadalupe in Villerías y Roelas' *Guadalupe* 4.101-2, quoted on p. 41 above.

11. As in the fifth and the last stanza of the Latin ode, the word 'Joseph' emphasises *José* Vallejo's nominal connection with the saint.

12. Compare Horace, *Odes* 2.20.11-12 and Góngora, *Para la cuarta parte de la 'Pontifical' del Doctor Babia*: sonnet 26 in Ciplijauskaité (1985), 83-4 (see pp. 41-2 above).

Landívar's Notes to the *Rusticatio Mexicana* with additional commentary

Rafael Landívar's Latin prose annotations to his poem are reproduced and translated below. The poet's quotations of French, Italian, and Spanish sources have also been rendered into English. Although the conventions of typography and spelling in the Bologna original have been largely retained, one or two obvious printing errors in that 1782 edition have been corrected.

My own additional comments, indented and marked with a bullet point (•), will provide details of classical or later sources, relevant historical or geographical information, recent bibliography, or fuller references to the works mentioned by Landívar – when they can be given. Regenos' brief remarks on passages in Books 1, 6, 9 and 13 are incorporated as well, and indicated by the initials 'G.W.R.'. A couple of those observations by Regenos are again supplemented by my own commentary.

Landívar's annotations originally appeared not as endnotes, but as footnotes which ran below the text of the poem, and a mixture of asterisks, letters, and numbers were employed as footnote markers. Regenos re-numbered the Notes in Books 1, 3, 4, 9, 11 and 14, where the original numbering was either inconsistent or misleading. That practice has been adopted here: wherever the footnote markers deviate from those of the 1782 edition, the original ('orig.') digit or asterisk will appear in curved brackets, after the *functioning* number of the Note, which is in bold type. And in all cases, a lemma and a verse number from the passage of the *Rusticatio Mexicana* in question have been added in square brackets, for convenient reference, as follows:

10 (orig. 9) [**Zapata** 1.287]

The words in the lemmata may not always bear directly on the subject of the Notes that succeed them: Landívar often uses his annotations to illuminate an entire passage or topic, and not only to clarify particular terms or expressions.

Book 1: *LACUS MEXICANI*
'The Lakes of Mexico'

1 [**percurrere cymba** 1.10]
Horti enim Mexicani lacui innatant.
'Mexican gardens float on the lake.'

2 [**Regi** 1.145]
Rex Axcapusalci.
'King of Atzcapotzalco.'
  • Landívar's contemporary Clavigero (see pp. 25-6 above) also mentions this tradition about the king of Atzcapotzalco in his *Ancient History of Mexico,*

first published in Italian: Clavigero (2003), 107-9. The conquistador Bernal Díaz del Castillo describes how the Spaniards, on their arrival in Mexico, discovered a city divided by waterways. The source for the story Landívar recounts is provided by José de Acosta, *Historia natural y moral de las Indias* (1590), book 7, ch. 9: Acosta (2003), 434-6. Landívar will specifically refer to this passage in the next Note.

3 [Veneri quondam sacrata profanae 1.190]

Hortos hosce testis oculatus P. Acosta Hispanus describit, laudatque; cujus haec sunt concepta verba: Los que no han visto las sementeras, que se hacen en la laguna de Mexico, en medio de la misma agua, terran por patraña lo que aqui se cuenta, o quando mucho creeran, que era encantamiento del demonio, a quien esta gente adoraba. Mas en realidad de verdad es cosa muy hacedera, y se ha hecho muchas veces hacer sementera movediza en el agua, porque sobre juncia, y espandaña se hecha tierra, y alli se siembra, y cultiva, y crece, y se lleva de una parte a otra. *Lib. 7 histor. natur. & mor. totius Americ. c. 5.*

Gemelli testis etiam oculatus haec ait: In fatti l'anno seguente portarono a quel Re un orto natante di diversi legumi: e fine al dì d'oggi coltivasi sì fatto terreno mobile nella lacuna.

Pongono essi sopra l'acqua giunchi, e gramigna intessuti con terreno sopra, che resista all'acqua e poscia conducono facilmente, dove meglio vogliono, il natante giardino. *Tom. 6. lib. 1. c. 4.*

'An eyewitness, a Spaniard, Father Acosta, describes and praises gardens like this. These are his words as he put them: "Those who have not seen the seed beds that are customary in the Lake of Mexico, in the midst of the water itself, are frightened – by the yarn that is told here, or when they are just too credulous – that this was the enchantment of the devil that this people used to worship. But in actual fact, putting a mobile seedbed in the water is something very practical, and it has been done many times: because it is over sedge, it expands and becomes like land, and from there it is sown, cultivated, and grown, and it can be moved from one place to another." Book 7 *Natural History and customs of all America*, ch. 5.

Gemelli, another eyewitness, says this: "The following year they brought to the King a floating garden of various vegetables: right up to the present day they cultivate land which can be made to move on the lake. They place sedge over the water, and woven with grass with earth on top, it is waterproof. Then they can easily direct the floating garden where they most want it." Vol. 6, book 1, ch. 4.'

- José de Acosta (1540-1600), a Jesuit born in Medina del Campo in Spain, travelled to Peru. His numerous works include *De procuranda indorum salute* ('On securing the health of Indians') published in 1577, and a Spanish translation of Xenophon's *Cyropaedia* (1592). Acosta returned to Spain and died in Salamanca. His *Historia Natural y Moral de las Indias* (1590) was translated into Latin, Italian, French, English, German, and Dutch. Landívar misquotes the title of the work and cites the wrong chapter: the quotation above is actually from Book 7, chapter 9: Acosta (2003), 435.
- The Italian naturalist Gemelli Careri travelled to Mexico and other parts of the world from 1693-8; Landívar here cites his *Giro del mondo del dottor Giovanni Francesco Gemelli Careri* (Venice 1719, reprinted Naples 1721); see comment on Book 14, Note 3 below.

4 [Dulce canit Passer 1.216]
Il Gorrion, massimamente il maschìo, canta molto soavemente, ed è grande quanto un paßero. Gemelli lib. 2. c. 9.
'The Gorrion, predominantly the male, sings very sweetly, and is as big as a sparrow. Gemelli, book 2, ch. 9.'

5 [Centzontlus 1.220]
Centzontle *vox corrupta est ab antiqua* Centzontlatolis, *quae* innumeras voces *indicat. De hac avi Franciscus Hernandes Hispanus haec habet: In caveis, in quibus detinetur, suavissime cantat, nec est avis ulla, animalve, cujus vocem non reddat luculentissime, & exquisitissime aemuletur. Quid? Philomelam ipsam longo superat intervallo.* Histor. avium novae Hispan. c. 30.
Tum Bomare verb. Poliglotte. *C'est l'oiseau, que les Mexicains nomment* Centzotlatolis, *c'est à dire, qui a quarante langues ...On pretend, que son chant est si doux, & si melodieux, qu'il surpasse en agrement celui de quelche autre oiseau, que ce soit. On assure même, qu'il contrefait la voix des autres oiseaux &c.*
Mr. Barrington Vice-President de la Societé Royale de Londres aßure avoir vu cet oiseau contrefaire dans l'espace d'un minute le chant de l'alouette des bois, du pinçon, du merle, de la grive, & du moineau.
'*Centzontle* is a word corrupted from the ancient *Centzontlatolis,* which means "countless voices". On this bird, the Spaniard Francisco Hernández says the following: "In the hollows in which it is trapped it sings very sweetly, and there is not any bird, or animal, whose sound it cannot render most brilliantly and imitate most exquisitely. Indeed it beats Philomela by a long way." *History of Birds of New Spain,* ch. 30.
Then Bomare under the word *Poliglotte* says: "There is a bird, that the Mexicans name *Centzotlatolis,* that is to say, 'having forty tongues' ... It is supposed that its song is so soft and so melodious that it surpasses in pleasantness that of any bird there might be. It is even maintained that it can fake the voices of other birds etc."
Mr Barrington, Vice-President of the Royal Society of London, professes to have seen this bird imitating, within the space of a minute, the song of the wood lark, chaffinch, blackbird, thrush, and sparrow.'
- See Burke (1976) and p. 88 n. 41 above, on Valmont de Bomare. The natural historian Francisco Hernández (1517-78) also wrote an account of pre-Hispanic civilisation in Mexico: Somolinos Dardois (1960). Corona Martínez (2002) surveys the early study of birds in colonial New Spain.

6 (orig. *) [Qui voces hominum simulat 1.221]
Voces hominum saepe imitatur haec avis, non articulando ut Psittacus, sed sibilando.
'This bird often imitates human voices, not by using articulation like the parrot, but by whistling.'

7 (orig. 6) [Carnerus 1.278]
P. Jo. Carnero Angelopolitanus Passionem Domini versu hispano vulgavit.
'Father Juan Carnero, of Puebla de los Angeles published *Passion of the Lord* in Spanish verse.'
- Carnero, now an obscure figure, was the subject of a biography by J.A. Villalobos, printed in Puebla in 1723.

8 (orig. 7) [**succensus Abadius** 1.281]
Didacus Josephus Abad Michoacanensis Heroica de Deo Carmina in lucem edidit.
'Diego José Abad of Michoacán brought to life his *Heroic Poem on God*.'
- See pp. 26-7 above for a brief account of Abad and his work.

9 (orig. 8) [**cantaret Alegrius** 1.285]
Franciscus Xaverius Alegre Veracrucensis Homeri Iliadem e graeco in latinum vertit carmine elegantissimo; cui Alexandriadem adjunxit.
'Francisco Xavier Alegre of Veracruz turned Homer's *Iliad* from Greek into Latin in the most elegant verse; he added to it the *Alexandriad*.'
- See pp. 27-9 above on Alegre.

10 (orig. 9) [**Zapata** 1.287]
Zapata Mexicanus, poeta lyricus.
'Zapata from Mexico, a lyric poet.'
- The reference is probably to Luis Sandoval y Zapata who wrote in the 1600s.

11 (orig. 10) [**Reyna** 1.287]
Reyna Michoacanensis D. Joannis Nepomuceni vitam hispano carmine edidit.
'Reyna from Michoacán published a life of Saint John Nepomucene in Spanish verse.'
- Miguel de Reina Ceballos was a lawyer for Royal Audience of Spain in the early 1700s. According to Menéndez y Pelayo (1958), 60, Reina's hagiographical poem was entitled *La elocuencia del silencio*.

12 (orig. 11) [**socco celebratus Alarco** 1.287]
Alarcón Mexicanus, poeta comicus celeberrimus. Alios bene multos, quos numerare poßem, poetas Mexicanos missos facio, ne taedio sim, ut Cardenas, Munnoz, Fuentes, Arriola, Leon, &c. &c.
'Alarcón from Mexico, a very famous comic poet. A good many others, from the Mexican poets I could list, I am leaving out, so as not to be tedious – like Cardénas, Muñoz, Fuentes, Arriola, León etc. etc.'
- Juan Ruíz de Alarcón, who was born in Mexico City *c.* 1580 and died in Madrid in 1639, is now well known as a dramatist of the Castilian Golden Age. His comedies include *Las paredes oyen* ('Walls Have Ears'), and *La verdad sospechosa* ('Truth Suspected'); the latter provided the model for Corneille's *Le Menteur*.

13 (orig. 12) [**occinuit modulis Joanna canoris** 1.289]
Joanna Agnes a Cruce, Virgo ad D. Hieronymi Deo sacra, omnigena eruditione exornata, & ob elegantissima carmina trib. voluminib. in lucem edita inter Musas merito computanda.
'Juana Inés de la Cruz, a nun in the Order of St Jerome, distinguished by her learning of every kind and for her three published volumes of very graceful poems, is rightly to be counted among the Muses.'
- This note, though marked at 1.289 actually seems to support the assertion made next in 292-4. On Sor Juana, see pp. 19 and 65-7 above.

14 (orig. 13) [**fallit maris unda phasellos** 1.319]
Mais aucun lac n'est aussi singulier, que celui du Mexique; une partie des eaux de ce lac est douce, et stagnante; l'autre est salée, & a un flux & reflux; mais qui n'étant

pas assujeti à des heures fixes, paroit occasioné par le souffle de vents, qui rendent quelque fois le lac aussi orageux, que la mer même. Bomar. verb. lac.
' "No lake is quite like that of Mexico: one part of the waters of that lake is calm and stagnant, the other is briny and has a high and low tide, but since this is not subject to certain hours, it would seem to be prompted by the gusts of wind that sometimes make the lake as stormy as the sea itself." Bomare, under the word *"lac".'*

15 (orig. 14) [**quin flumen ab oris/ Exeat, aut aliis ineat commercia pontis** 1.341-2]
Ne ullam hac super re opinionem amplecti cogar, placuit rem, ut oculis substat, exponere.
'So that I am not forced to hold to an opinion on this matter, I have preferred to present it as it appears to the eyes.'

Book 2: *XORULUS*
'Jorullo'

* The volcano of Jorullo, in the south of the Mexican state of Michoacán, erupted on 29 September 1759: as Landívar explains (2.19-28), sugar was refined in the surrounding regions.

1 [**Nunc quoque Xoruli** 2.1]
Mons ignivomus Provincia Michoacanensis.
'A volcanic mountain in the province of Michoacán.'
   * There is no single Latin word for 'volcano'.

2 [**Purpureaque urbes implerent luce remotas** 2.188]
Urbs Pastquaro 40 *milliaria a* Xorulo *dissita ejus flammis tota illuminabatur.*
'The city of Patzcuaro, situated 40 miles from Jorullo, was completely illuminated by its flames.'

3 [**Disjunctos populos** 2.190]
In urbe Queretaro *centum quinquaginta milliaria a* Xorulo *remota cineres quotidie in chortibus colligebant cives.*
'In the city of Querétaro, 150 miles away from Jorullo, residents were sweeping up ash from their patios every day.'

4 [**Ingentem mediis montem** 2.194]
Congesta saxa montem in medio vallis efformant altitudinis ad milliaria tria.
'The rocks are piled up in the middle of a valley to form a mountain nearly three miles high.'

5 [**sic prava Lycisca** 2.225]
Fera haec ab Indis Coyote *appellatur.*
'This wild animal is called a *coyote* by the Indians.'

6 [**rutilo Solis fervore rigere** 2.285]
On dit, que la Cyrenaique en a une fontaine qui est froide le jour, & chaude la nuit, Cette fontaine me fait souvenir de celle de Jupiter Ammon. Selon Lucrèce elle était froide le jour, & chaude la nuit. Regnauld tom. 2. Entretien 12.

' "It is said that there is a fountain in Cyrenaica which is cold in the daytime and hot at night. This fountain reminds me of that of Jupiter Ammon. According to Lucretius it was cold during the day and hot at night." Regnauld, vol. 2, Excursus 12.'
- Lucretius' account of the spring by the shrine of Ammon is in *De rerum natura* 6.848-78. Herodotus 4.181 describes the same phenomenon.

7 [Infensus populis, flammisque Colima 2.330]

Colima *mons etiam ignivomus septuaginta circiter milliaria a* Xorulo *dissitus ignes suos extinxisse dicitur, simul atque ille flammas evomere coepit.*
'Colima, another volcanic mountain about 70 miles from Jorullo is said to have extinguished its own fires as soon as Jorullo began to erupt.'

Book 3: *CATARACTAE GUATIMALENSES*
'The Waterfalls of Guatemala'

1 [gentisque lares absorpsit, et urbem 3.28]

Die 10. *Septemb. Ann.* 1541.
'On 10 September 1541.'
- The city was destroyed on that date by a current of water and mud which flowed down from a volcanic mountain.

2 [terrae concussa tremore 3.48]

Die 29. Julii. Anno 1773.
'On 29 July, 1773.'
- On the consequences of this earthquake for Landívar, see p. 33 above, p. 49 (on the dedicatory poem), and p. 60 on its association with the earthquake in Bologna.

3 (orig. *) [multasque extensa per ulnas 3.149]

Quotiescumque ulnarum *mensura utor,* ulnas *pro* cubitis *usurpo. Vide, sis, Facciolatum.*
'Every time I measure in ells, I use "ells" in place of "cubits". See Facciolati.'
- *Ulna* ('ell') is prevalent as unit of measurement in classical Latin poetry (e.g. Virgil, *Eclogues* 3.105; Horace, *Epode* 4.8; Ovid, *Met.* 8.748; the *cubitum* was far more common in prose. Landívar is explaining his usage probably in order to emphasise that scientific precision is not being sacrificed for poetic effect: see his *Monitum* p. 122, and pp. 52-3 above.
- Iacopo Facciolati (1682-1769) was a logician and prolific lexicographer. His *Totius Latinitatis lexicon*, published in Padua in 1771, laid particular emphasis on distinctions between classical words.

4 (orig. 3) [Pica 3.177 (incorrectly numbered as 3.182 in the 1782 edition)]

Picam appello avem Guacamaya *dictam (Ital* Rara.) *Psittaco majorem, cauda oblonga, miraque colorum varietate distinctam, quod* Picae *figuram aliquomodo referat. Neque enim aliud lingua latina verbum suppeditat.*
'The bird called *guacamaya* (or *rara* in Italian) is bigger than the parrot, with a long tail and it is distinguished by its amazing variety of colours. I call it a "magpie" (*pica*) because it resembles the magpie in a certain way. No other word in Latin is adequate.'

Book 4: *COCCUM, ET PURPURA*
'Cochineal and Purple'

1 [Vallis Oaxacae 4.15]
Proprium civitatis nomen Anticaria (Antequera). Vulgo tamen a vallis nomine
Oaxaca *appellatur.*
'The actual name of the province is Anticaria (*Antequera* in Spanish). However it
is commonly called "Oaxaca", after the valley.'
- The 'Lydian girl' (*Lydam ... puellam* 4.7) is Arachne, whose story is told in
  Ovid *Metamorphoses* 6.5-145. Valdés (1965), 116 suggests that 'Lyda' here
  might also be connected to the Lyda in Acts of the Apostles 16:4.

2 [Ac multas arbor sinuetur crassa per ulnas 4.27]
Inter alias bene multas vidi egomet in hac valle, ad Pagum S. Mariae de Tule,
arborem amplius 40. ulnas in orbem latam.
'Among a good many others trees in this valley, near the district of Santa María
de Tule, I myself saw a tree more than 40 cubits in circumference.'

3 [Nopalis vivida frondes 4.32]
Frondes *dico, satius ramos dicturus: sed usui ut inserviam, receptoque loquendi*
modo, frondes *appellare ausus sum* Nopalis *ramos.*
'I say "leaves" but it would be more adequate to say "branches", but in order to
conform to usage and the accepted way of speaking, I presumed to call the Nopal's
branches "leaves".'

4 (orig. 3) **[At micat occiduo jam dudum pulchrior orbe** 4.210]
On a parlé dans le Journal de Trevoux (Octob. 1712) d'un petit limaçon des Indes,
qu'on trouve au Sud de Guatimala, où l'Amerique Septentrionale confine avec
l'isthme de Darien. Ce petit animal, dit Lemery, parait être le Murex de[s] anciens:
il est de la grosseur d'une Abeille. Sa conquille est mince, & peu dure: on le remasse
à mesure qu'on en trouve, & on le conserve dans un pot plein d'eau. Mais comme il
est rare d'en trouver beaucoup à la fois, les Indiens font long temps à en ramaßer la
quantité necessaire pour teindre un morceau d'etoffe d'une certaine grandeur. Bom.
v. Murex.
'There has been mention in the *Journal de Trevoux* (October 1712) of a small snail
from the Indies, that is to be found in the south of Guatemala where northern
America borders on the isthmus of Darién. This little animal, says Lemery,
appears to be the *murex* of the ancients: it is the size of a bee. Its shell is thin and
a little hard: it is gathered whenever one is found and kept in a pot of water. But
as it is rare to find many of them at once, the Indians spend a long time on
gathering the quantity necessary to dye a piece of fabric of a particular size.
Bomare, under *Murex*.'
- For Valmont de Bomare, see p. 88 n. 41 above.

5 (orig. 4) **[cum crescens extollit cornua Luna** 4.236]
Juxta Horatianum illud: Lubrica nascentes implent Conchylia lunae.
'Very much as Horace says: "New moons swell the slippery shellfish".'
- The quotation is from Horace, *Satires* 2.4.30.

6 (orig. 5) **[Extrahit e cyatho conchas, frangitque sub ictu** 4.249]
Enfin on les ecrase avec une pierre bien polie, & on mouille aussi tout le fil de coton,

ou l'etoffe dans la liqueur rouge: il s'y fait une teinture de pourpre la plus riche, que se puisse voir. Ce qu'il y a s'avantageux, est, que plus on lave l'etoffe, qui en est teinte, plus la couleur en devient belle, & éclatantes: elle ne s'altere point par la vieillesse. Bomare vb. sup.

' "Finally they are crushed with a well polished rock, and the entire length of cotton or the fabric is moistened in the red liquid, making the richest hue of purple ever seen. The advantage of it is that the more one washes the fabric that is dyed, the more beautiful and brilliant its colour becomes: it is scarcely changed by age". Bomare on the word above [*murex*].'

Book 5: *INDICUM*
'Indigo'

1 [Indica prima sequor 5.3]

Indicum hocce Guatimalense dictum, (Hisp. Añil., Ital. Indaco; Gall. Indigo) quòd in Regni Guatimalensis provinciis colligatur, omni alio superius habetur. Lege, sîs, Bomare verb. Indigo, & Robertson tom. 4. Hist. Americ. lib. 8.

'This indigo is called *Guatimalan* (Spanish *añil*, Italian *indacco*; French *indigo*) because it is gathered in the provinces of the kingdom of Guatemala – it is considered superior to all others. Read Bomare s.v. *Indigo*, and Robertson *History of America*, vol. 4, book 8.'

- The Scottish historian, William Robertson, a clergyman and principal of Edinburgh University, became the king's historiographer in 1764. As well as his *History of America* (1777) and a study entitled *The Knowledge which the Ancients had of India* (1791), Robertson wrote a popular *History of Scotland 1542-1603* (1759) and a *History of Charles V* (1769) which was praised by Voltaire and Gibbon. (For Valmont de Bomare, see p. 88 n. 41 above.)

2 [Tunc senis tollunt segetes caput altius ulnis 5.73]

Herba isthaec, cujus succo Indicum conficitur, Giquilite appellatur.

'This herb, from the juice of which indigo is made, is called *giquilite*.'

3 [Inde coloratum fulgenti vase liquorem 5.157]

Huic experimento vas argenteum aptari solet; sed certe fictile apprime tersum satis est.

'A silver container is usually prepared for this endeavour, but one of clay is good enough if it is cleaned first.'

4 [Indica vulgato patriae de nomine dicta 5.201]

Indici triplex est genus, supremum, medium, & infimum. Nullus autem, ne peritissimus quidem, unquam novit, cujus generis Indicum confecturus sit. Eâdem quippe herbâ, iisdem laboratâ curis, nunc supremum, nunc medium, nunc etiam infimum extrahitur.

'There are three kinds of indigo: high, medium, and low grade. No one, not even the most experienced worker, knows what kind of indigo he is about to prepare. For from the same plant, treated with the same care, at one time high grade indigo is extracted, at another it is a medium yield, and, at another again, it is low grade.'

Book 6: *FIBRI*
'Beavers'

1 [Fibros 6.1]
Castores.
'Beavers.'

1a [Dictynna potens 6.5]
An epithet of the huntress goddess, Diana. [G.W.R.].

2 [Quas inter cautum, praestantique indole Fibrum 6.14]
*On trouve des Castors en Amerique depuis le trentieme degrè de latitude nord jusq'
au soixantieme, et au delà. Bomare. v.* Castor.
*Exploratum etiam est mihi, in novo Mexici regno fibros inventos, paucisque ab hinc
annis in Septentrionali Californiae parte aliquot fustibus occisos.*
' "Beavers can be found in America from the 30th degree of northern latitude to the
60th and below." (Bomare s.v. *Castor*).
I have also discovered that beavers have been found in the realm of New Mexico,
and a few years ago some were beaten to death in northern California.'

3 [Machaon 6.37]
Son of Aesculapius, the Greek god of medicine. [G.W.R.]

4 [Sydera Cancri 6.60]
The summer solstice when the sun reaches the northern limit of its course. [G.W.R.]

5 [Ni Libram solito Titan fervore revisat 6.268]
The time of the autumnal equinox. [G.W.R.]

Book 7: *FODINAE ARGENTI ATQUE AURI*
'The Mining of Silver and Gold'

1 [Ocyus immensis undabunt oppida gazis 7.60]
*Debueram venarum signa in medium adducere. Sed cum ab optimis quibusque
metallariis ea omnino incerta esse noverim, unoque experimento dignosci, ab iis
abstinere consultius habui.*
'I ought to have gone into the signs for the veins, but as I realised they are utterly
unknown to some of the best metallurgists and can be recognised by experience
alone, I considered it better to keep away from them.'

Book 8: *ARGENTI, ATQUE AURI OPIFICIUM*
'Processing of Silver and Gold'

1 [pestis febrilis adurat 8.62]
Hac eadem metaphora tamquam artis propria metallarii utuntur.
'Metallurgists use this same metaphor in their art.'

2 [Limbum mox pollice calcat 8.112]
Calcat, *inquam* pollice *manûs.*
'By saying *calcat* ("he stamps down"), I mean with the thumb.'

Book 9: *SACCHARUM*
'Sugar'

1 [Semina nectareae sulcis deponere cannae 9.11]
Canna saccharifera arundinibus notis valde similis brevioribus tubis, crebrioribusque articulis distinguitur. Candida illi medulla, ac succo plena dulcissimo, tenuis cortex, sed durus. In quolibet articulo germen habet ciceri non dissimile magnitudine, sed oblongum, unde frutices postea pullulant.
'The sugar cane, very similar to familiar reeds, is distinguished by its shorter stem and more frequent joints. Its core is white, and full of the sweetest juice; its casing is thin, but hard. In each joint there is a seed, similar in size to a chickpea but oblong in shape, from which shoots spring out later.'

2 [Torrida quam nobis mittit Nasamonia tellus 9.31]
In Angola, Guinea, & Congo Aethiopes innumeros emunt Angli, quos deinde in America vendunt magno pretio. Iis & cannarum cultus, & sacchari opificium saepissime injungitur.
'In Angola, Guinea, and the Congo, the English buy countless Africans, whom they then sell in America at a costly price. The cultivation of the cane is imposed on them, and very often the refinement of the sugar as well.'

2a [luces aequabit Libra tenebris 9.33]
The autumnal equinox. [G.W.R.]

3 [sed tensos calamos per rura serendo 9.39]
Pro regionum varietate aliter & aliter seruntur cannae, ac saccharum conficitur. Eam ego secutus sum methodum, quam in America septentrionali in more positam novi; praeterquam in insulis, ubi aliam serendi rationem sequi solent incolae.
'Cane is planted and sugar is refined in different ways in different regions. I myself have followed the method in the manner that I know is applied in northern America – except on the islands, where the inhabitants usually have a different system of planting.'

4 [orig. 1] [bis nono cornua motu 9.98]
Pro regionis temperie tardius, aut citius cannae maturescunt. In regionibus calidis post menses duodeviginti messis colligitur: in temperatis vero ad viginti quatuor differri solet.
'Cane matures more quickly or more slowly according to the regional climate. In warm regions, the harvest is after eighteen months; in temperate climates it is often delayed until after twenty four months.'
- Landívar's simile in 9.90-8 recalls Ovid's version of the Argonautic myth in *Metamorphoses* 7.120-33.

5 [orig. *] [Sed prius aurato roret quam dulcis arundo 9.139]
Prae oculis habe trapeti communis typum obsignatum litteris respondentibus iis, quibus ejus partes in descriptione notantur.
'Look at this illustration of the common mill, marked with letters corresponding to those with which the parts of it are annotated in the text.'

6 [orig. 5] [Subjectum pontem robusta ex arbore scissum 9.146]
Tabulata, quibus cylindri innituntur, pontis nomine appellari solent.

'Illustrated: the parts that the cylinders rest on are customarily called the "bridges".'

7 [orig. *] [**Si tamen ipse velis robustis parcere mulis** 9.166]
Prae oculis habe trapetum aquarium variis etiam literis signatum.
'Look at the water mill, again marked with different letters.'

8 [**Purpureoque dedit vestes fucare veneno** 9.308]
Cf. Book 4.261 ff. [G.W.R.]

Book 10: *ARMENTA*

'Horses/Cattle'

1 [**Plurima sed partes circùm diffusa per omnes/ Ter denis leucis volvuntur jugera in orbem** 10.18-19]
Hac mensura plurima praedia metiri quisque potest: quam tamen etsi multa non attingant, innumera excedunt.
'By this measurement [i.e. 'thirty leagues in circumference' 10.19] one can measure very many estates: although many do not reach that size, countless others exceed it.'

2 [**densatum candenti corpore equarum/Agmen** 10.32-3]
Equorum armenta equabus constant viginti quatuor, quibus preest emissarius. Haec armenta pro magnitudine praediorum, ac divitiarum ad quadraginta, vel octoginta eße solent. Sunt tamen aliqui, quos maximopere juvat equas cujuslibet armenti ejusdem eße coloris cum emissario.
'The herds of horses are composed of 24 mares, over which a stallion is put in charge. These herds, depending on the size of the ranches or their wealth, can have forty or eighty horses. There are indeed some who take great pleasure in the mares of a particular herd being of the same colour as the leader.'

3 [**regioque frequens Madurensis honorat** 10.115]
Madurenses magno honore asinos prosequuntur, quòd Reges suos ab asino quodam oriundos autument, inque asinos nobilium animas transmigrare.
'The people of Madaura bestow much honour on asses, because they think that their kings are descended from a certain ass and that the souls of their nobility transmigrate into asses.'

- This remark appears to have some connection to Apuleius' *Metamorphoses* (or *Golden Ass*), *c.* 150 AD. Apuleius' narrator, Lucius of Madaurus, was transformed into an ass, but very much against his will. Landívar could be alluding to Augustine's garbled version of the story (*City of God* 18.18). This hints at transmigration and could have been taken to imply that the transformation into an ass – credited to Apuleius himself – was voluntary: *accepto veneno humano animo asinus fieret* ('after taking the poison he became an ass with a human mind'). The same version of events is given by the character Pármeno, at the end of the eighth act of Fernando de Rojas' *La Celestina* (1499) – the first vernacular Spanish text to mention Apuleius. However in the 1600s, Apuleius' description of Isis, mediated by Athanasius Kircher's *Oedipus Aegyptiacus*, appealed to Mexican authors interested in hermeticism, including Sor Juana and Sigüenza y Góngora: Leonard (1983), 210, Paz (1988), 164, 175-6. The Isaic procession in Apuleius *Met.* 11.11 (cf. *Met.*

272

10.30-2, 11.3) could also have influenced the *máscara* for the Virgin of Guadalupe described in Sigüenza y Góngora's *Glorias de Querétaro* (1680). The 'Egyptomania' of Baroque Mexico may have a bearing on the comparisons between Guatemala and Egypt in *RM* 3.165-70, 3.200-8 and 3.288-95 (see pp. 63-4 above). Osorio Romero (1980), 63 makes reference to the circulation of Apuleius in Mexico.

- Ovid's association of Silenus with an ass (*Fasti* 1.399-440), perhaps recalled in 10.112 above (*Sileni pignus, asellus*), was a frequent subject of representation in visual art.

4 [Ingentemque domi vitulorum cogit acervum 10.157]
Cogi solent in septis vituli centum, & amplius pro praedii magnitudine.
'A hundred calves are normally forced into pens, or more, depending on the size of the ranch.'

5 [Taurina pridem tortos e pelle rudentes 10.274]
Bubulcis Regni Guathimalensis mos est ligato ad equi caudam taurino fune tauros illaqueare, & quocumque volunt illaqueatos ducere. Alii aliter tauros innectunt.
'It is the custom for herdsmen in the kingdom of Guatemala to lasso bulls with a bullhide rope to a horse's tail, and to lead them, thus entrapped, wherever they want. Others secure the bulls in other ways.'

Book 11: *GREGES*

'Herds/Flocks'

1 [vigilesque canes moderatur eundo 11.41]
Praedia educandis ovibus destinata viginti quinque ut minimum gregibus instructa esse debent. Omnis autem grex ovibus, aut arietibus bis millibus constat. Aliter fundus praedii nomine indignus censetur.
'Ranches for raising sheep should be designed for 25 flocks at the very least. Every flock should then comprise two thousand ewes or rams. Otherwise the piece of land is not considered worthy of the name "farm".'

2 [Carpit iter longum 11.46]
Iter hocce ad milliaria 200, aut etiam 300 extendi solet, quo greges a frigida in regionem calidam, autumnali tempore traducuntur, ibique hibernant.
'This journey can be extended to 200, or even 300 miles. In autumn, the flocks are led from a cold region to a warmer one, where they winter.'

3 [orig. 5] [Dum tamen halantes errat de more per herbas 11.217]
Caprarum greges idem, quod oves, iter conficiunt, eademque ratione gubernantur, iis exceptis quae singillatim addimus.
'The herds of goats make the same journey as the sheep, and are guided in the same way, with the exceptions that we append here one by one.'

4 [orig. 6] [Ocyus ille vagum parvo ferit aethera cornu 11.242]
Cornu istud (Gamitadera dictum) è ligno constructum solido, pollices non amplius quatuor longum est, foramine tantum recto perfossum, sonumque reddit stridentem, & acutum. Eo in primis venatores utuntur ad cervos, aliasque feras ad se vocandas.
'This horn (called a *gamitadera*), made out of solid wood, is no longer than four

273

thumbs in length, but pierced through cleanly, it gives out a sharp, shrieking sound. Hunters principally use it to call deer and other wild animals towards them.'

5 [orig. 7] [**greges laniare paratur** 11.290]
Greges caprini totidem esse solent in praediis, quot ovilli, totidem capris, quot ovibus greges constant.
'There are usually as many herds of goats on the ranches as of sheep, and there are as many goats in each herd as there are sheep.'

6 [orig. 8] [**Praedia, setigerosque greges ab origine dicam** 11.325]
Praedia porcis educandis destinata ad 10 *vel* 12 *millia porcorum educere solent.*
'The ranches devoted to raising pigs generally produce ten or twelve thousand of them.'

7 [orig. 9] [**porrectisque arva papillis** 11.389 (11.388 in 1782 edition)]
Papillae supra modum porrectae porcam indicant illa die parituram.
'Unduly distended teats show that the sow will give birth on that day.'

Book 12: *FONTES*

'Springs'

1 [**Insolitis Indus mentem turbatus** 12.42]
Indo Mexicano, cui Guadalupana *Virgo apparuit, Io. Didacus nomen erat.*
'The name of the Mexican Indian to whom the Virgin of Guadalupe appeared was Juan Diego.'
- On the Virgin of Guadalupe, see pp. 17-18 above. Brading (2001) offers a contemporary assessment of Juan Diego's varied names and status. Even though this individual may not have actually existed, he was canonised as 'Juan Diego Cuauhtlatoatzin' by Pope John Paul II on 31 July 2002 in the Basilica of Our Lady of Guadalupe in Mexico City.

2 [**Virgineos cui Diva pedes insculpserat olim** 12.50]
Vide sis, Zodiacum Marian. P. Oviedo, pars. 2. cap. 1. § 7.
'See the *Zodiaco Mariano* by Father Oviedo, part 2, chapter 1, §7.'
- The Jesuit Juan Antonio de Oviedo (1670-1757), though he came from Bogotá, lived for many years in Guatemala, where he received a doctorate in theology and held a chair in philosophy. Oviedo, who would thus have been personally known to Landívar, edited the *Zodiaco Mariano* (1755). The original manuscript of this general history of the images of the Virgin venerated in northern Spanish America was by another Jesuit: Francisco de Florencia (1620-95), a native of Florida who eventually became Rector of the Colegio Máximo in Mexico. Oviedo corrected Florencia's manuscript, eliminated digressions, and added accounts of images omitted in the earlier version. The passage to which Landívar refers is entitled 'In which notice is given of the places in which Our Lady appeared to Juan Diego and of their present situation': Florencia and Oviedo (1995), 104-7. The account explains (106) that Juan Diego had prayed to the Virgin to indicate where she had appeared to him: a spring appeared to mark the place, 'as if its waters were saying: *hic est locus ubi steterunt pedes ejus.*' See further Brading (2001),

139-41. The church known as El Pocito ('The Little Well') stands on the site of the spring, to the east of the original Basilica of Guadalupe.

• Recollection of *candida diva pede* from Catullus 68.70 (where the tread of the adulterous Lesbia is likened to that of a goddess) in Landívar's *Diva pedes* would appear unwarranted – were it not for the fact that this evocation is supported by the imagery of water and springs which runs through Catullus' poem.

3 [ruptos ut credas aethere nimbos/ Subjectum rorare solum pluvialibus undis 12.86-7]

Descriptio adeo fictione vacat, ut fons iste non alio quam pluviae nomine cognoscatur.

'The description is so devoid of fiction that this spring is called by no other name than "the rain spring".'

• Zapopan, where Landívar locates this spring (12.59), is in the Mexican state of Jalisco.

4 [Nec plenis epota cadis levis unda nocebit 12.118]

Mihi persuasum habeo, aquas omnes dulces ejusdem esse ponderis. Sed cum aliae citiùs, aliae tardius viscera penetrent, idque vulgò earum levitati, aut gravitati tribuatur, placuit Pithagoricae sententiae in descriptione indulgere.

'I myself hold the view that all fresh waters are of the same mass. But as some reach the bowels more quickly, and others more slowly – something commonly attributed to their relative lightness or heaviness – it seemed preferable to give way to the Pythagorean notion in this description.'

5 [Ceu magnum densa terebratum cuspide cribrum 12.149]

Huic fonti Tzararaqua nomen est, quod in lingua Tarascensi, Provinciae Michoacanensis propria, cribrum denotat.

'The name of this spring is *Tzararaqua*, which in the Tarascan language of the province of Michoacán, means "sieve".'

• This waterfall, now known as Tzaráracua, and Chucándiro (12.166 below) are both in the state of Michoacán.

6 [Rima verecundis semper succurrit egenis 12.220]

Pauperes vestibus suis tergendis hoc limo pro sapone interdum utuntur.

'Poor people often use this clay to clean their clothes instead of soap.'

7 [Aloe 12.221]

Planta isthaec Maguei appellata quoddam vini genus Pulque dictum suppeditat largissime. Folia pro tegulis aptant Indi, iisdemque assis pro cibo utuntur; ni ex eorum fibris fila ducant, telasque conficiant.

'This plant called the *maguey* supplies in very generous measure a kind of wine called *pulque*. The Indians fashion its leaves into roofs; they cook and use the same leaves as food – if they do not draw out their fibres to make yarns.'

7a [nec Cola queat superare natatu 12.235]

Pece Nicolao was a famous swimmer of Catania, who lived about the end of the fifteenth century. He is mentioned in *Don Quixote*. See *Edición y Notas de Francisco Rodríguez Marín*, Madrid, La Lectura, 1912. *Clásicos Castellanos*, V, XVIII, p. 330 [G.W.R.].

- Valdés (1965), 288 notes that the Benedictine polymath and critic Benito Jéronimo Feijoo had recorded details of the life of Pece Nicolao, and cites two passages from his *Teatro crítico universal*: vol. 5 (1733), *Discurso* 6, n. 7 and vol. 6 (1734), *Discurso* 8, n. 19. For a selection of Feijoo's work with bibliography, including excerpts from the *Teatro*, see Feijoo (1990).
- On the location of the ravine in Aticpac (12.227), Valdés (1965), 288 notes: 'There are three places with that name – perhaps the reference is to the town of Zongolica, Veracruz.'

8 [**Cauta refert retro, gressumque exterrita torquet** 12.304]
Hic aquarum regressus, quolibet ad fontem accedente, adeo notum est in omni provincia Michoacanensi, ut nullus sit, qui dubitet.
'This retreat of the current from anyone who approaches the spring is so well known throughout the province of Michoacán that there is no one in doubt of it.'
- Valdés (1965), 292 quotes García Cubas (1896) on the location of this spring in Ixtlán [*Istlanus* 12.290] in Michoacán: 'there are sixty-six streams of thermal and medicinal water of a very high temperature that contain sodium, calcium, magnesium and a large quantity of sulphur.'

9 [**Herba plicat frondes, roseo correpta pudore** 12.310]
Herba Pudibunda, seu verecunda dicta, lippis ac tonsoribus nota est in omni America septentrionali; de eaque disserte agit Polignac.
'The "modest" or "bashful" plant, as it is called, is well known for its uses to the bleary-eyed and to barbers in all of northern America: Polignac offers a methodical treatment of it.'
- The *mimosa pudica*, appropriately named the 'sensitive plant' in Australia, is indeed native to southern Mexico and Central America and has small bipennate leaves. Landívar's claim that the shrub modestly retreats from a sudden approach by folding its leaves is derived from the *Anti-Lucretius* (6.409-28), the highly influential didactic poem by Melchior de Polignac, to which the above Note refers. Cardinal de Polignac described the attributes of the *herba fugiens* which 'simulates flight and timid modesty' (6.428) in his dismissal of the proposition that plants have souls. The *Anti-Lucretius* published in 1742, some time after de Polignac's death, was a major influence on the *De Deo* by Landívar's contemporary Diego José Abad.

10 [**Fons rabiem ponit, nec rursus commovet undas** 12.336]
En la Guasteca ... en la cumbre de Tamapachi esta una fuente, que con las voces, o con ruido de trompetas, o clarines se inquieta, y sale con grande fuerza; y si multiplican las voces, multiplica su furia, y en callando sosiega. Vetancurt Theatro Mexic. p. I t. 2. c. 6.
' "In Guasteca ... on the ridge of Temapache there is a spring that becomes worked up at the sound of voices, or at the sound of trumpets and bugles. If the sounds multiply, its frenzy multiplies accordingly, but as they go quiet, it calms down." Vetancourt, *Teatro Mexicano* part I, vol. 2, ch. 6.'
- In this part of the *Rusticatio Mexicana* Landívar has more or less versified the passage he quotes here from Augustín de Vetancourt's compendious anecdotal history, originally published in 1698: Vetancourt (1971).

11 [**Teguacanus** 12.338]
Proprius urbis nomen Tehuacan; vulgo tamen Teguacan.

'The name of the city is more properly *Tehuacán,* but it is commonly called *Teguacán.*'

12 [trepidoque sonent cava lustra boatu 12.349]

Entre los quales un riachuelo, que nace en Tehuacan ... *el qual no corre de ordinario, sino a horas: porque se ve, que una hora corre ... y por otra se suspende... Y es de manera este prodigio, que todas las veces que el agua asoma por esta boca, viene bufando, y embiando por delante cantidad de ayre, que hace espantoso ruido. Torquemada t. 2. lib. 14. cap. 30.*

' "Among them there is a rivulet which has its source in Tehuacán ... this does not run in an ordinary manner, but at certain hours: for it is apparent that at one hour it is flowing, and at another it stops ... And this marvel is such that every time the water accumulates around the mouth of the stream, it proceeds to gurgle and expel a quantity of air, which makes a horrible noise." Torquemada, vol. 2, book 14, ch. 30.'

- The citation here is from the *Monarquía indiana,* the sixteenth century chronicle by the Franciscan Juan de Torquemada: Torquemada (1969).

13 [Nunc superare moras, nunc inter saxa morari 12.352]

Vide Bomare verb. fontaine.
'See Bomare s.v. *fontaine.*'

- On 12.376: *Quincum* is known generally as 'Cointzio' or 'Coincho'. Valdés (1965), 298 quotes García Cubas (1896): 'Very pleasant baths three and a half leagues south of Morelia. The streams are abundant with a water temperature of 29° and contain a large quantity of barium sulphate.'

Book 13: *AVES*

'Birds'

1 [Indigenas cano ruris aves 13.1]

De avibus in hoc libro, deque feris ac ludis in continentibus duobus dicturus monere operae pretium duco, nequaquam mihi proposuisse omnes omnino in medium adducere; quod profecto carminis hujus angustias praetergrederetur; sed nobiliores tantum, atque insigniores.
'As I am about to address birds in this book, and animals and games in the two books to follow, I consider it worth giving the proviso that I had not resolved to devote attention to all of them by any means – to do so would be beyond the scope of this poem – but only to the more pre-eminent and famous ones.'

1a [Vanierius 13.23]

Jacques Vanière, a Jesuit priest, born at Causses in 1664, died at Toulouse in 1739. He wrote several pastoral poems in Latin, the most important of which was entitled *Praedium Rusticum,* which appeared in 1707. [G.W.R.].

- For a brief account of Vanière and his influence on Landívar, see pp. 47-8 above.

2 [Centzontlus fucato nomine dictus 13.200]

De vero Centzontlo *plura dixi lib. I, a v. 216, sicut etiam de Paβere Mexicano ibid. a v. 214.*
'Concerning the *centzontle* I have said more in Book 1, 216ff., just as I also have in

regard to the Mexican sparrow in the same book, 214ff.' [The references should rather be 218 ff. and 216 ff. respectively. G.W.R.]

3 [Colibrio dulcis spoliato murmure vocis 13.218]
Avicula haec Colibri *in America Meridionali; in Septentrionali vero* Chupa-mirto *dicitur.*
'This little bird is called *colibrí* in South America; in North America the word is actually *chupa-mirto.*'

4 [Irridet gaudetque domos evertere rostro 13.303]
De Pica Guacamaya *dicta egi lib. 3 a v. 182.*
'I have said something about the *guacamaya* magpie in Book 3, verse 182ff.'
 • Landívar explains his use of the word *pica* in his Note to the verse more correctly numbered 3.177 in Regenos' text: see Note 4 to Book 3 above.

5 [Et curvis digitos, ac longis unguibus armat 13.313]
Inter plures Aquilas, quae Americam incolunt, praestantiorem elegi, Aquilam regiam vulgo dictam.
'Among several eagles which inhabit America, I have chosen the more conspicuous one, the eagle commonly called "royal".'
 • The *aquila adalberti* is the species commonly known as the Spanish 'Royal' or 'Imperial' eagle. Landívar's comment may also point to an allegorical significance for his description of this bird: p. 71 above.

6 [Et dirum fracto pellit de pectore morbum 13.380]
Avem istam, qualem vidi, describo; quamvis alias ejusdem generis esse non ignorem diversis coloribus depictas.
'I describe this bird as I saw it, although I am well aware that there are others of the same species which are differently coloured.'

Book 14: *FERAE*

'Wild Beasts'

1 [Bos saepe jubatus 14.16]
Fera haec a Mexicanis Cibolus *appellatur. Lege sis Bomare verb.* Bison.
'This wild animal is what Mexicans call the *cibolo*. Read Bomare on the word *Bison.*'

2 [Tapyrus 14.52]
Fera haec in America Septentrionali Danta *appellatur.*
'This wild animal is called the *danta* in North America.'

3 [rugitu lucus reboare Leonis 14.75]
Nonnulli Americam Leonibus destitutam contendunt, quod ferae illae Leones dictae jubis careant. Sed praeterquam quod Plinius expresse asserit Leones alios esse jubatos, alios non jubatos, vidi egomet Florentiae apud magnum Hetruriae Ducem Leones binos, & quidem non jubatos, nostrisque omnino similes; quos veros esse Leones nullus in dubium revocaverat. Haec pro Leonib. Americae Septentrionalis; quidquid sit de Leone illo Meridionali Puma *dicto.*
'Several people maintain that America is deprived of lions, because the wild animals there called lions do not have manes. But over and above the fact that

Pliny plainly asserts that "some lions have manes and others do not", I myself have seen a pair of lions at the court of the Grand Duke of Etruria which did not actually have manes, and they were like our own lions in every respect: no one had doubted that these were real lions. So it is for the lions of northern America; whatever may be said about the southern American lion which is known as the *puma*.'

- Landívar's source in Pliny appears to be *Natural History* 8.17, where it is claimed that lions without manes are those fathered by leopards.
- Gemelli Careri vol. 6, 123 (the same volume cited by Landívar in Note 3 to Book 1 above) remarks that there are 'lions' in America which are 'not so fierce as in Africa – for when chased by dogs they flee into the woods'.

4 (orig. *) [**odoriferâ plenam pinguedine** 14.238]
Haec Apri pinguedo muscum odore refert.
'This wild boar fat smells of musk.'

5 (orig. 4) [**Cervos,/ ingentem superant qui vastâ mole juvencum** 14.275-6]
Inter omnes Mexicanos Cervos praestantiores elegi; è quibus duo ad Regem Catholicum delati sunt anno circiter 1755.
'Out of all the deer from Mexico I have chosen the ones that are more distinguished: two of them were sent to the Catholic King around the year 1755.'

6 (orig. 5) [**Vallis erat latos circum diffusa per agros** 14.328]
Huic valli Chicapa *nomen est.*
'The name of this valley is *Chicapa*.'
- The valley is east of Oaxaca.

7 (orig. 6) [**Ingenioque vafro decus immortale ferarum** 14.350]
Simios nostros, quod omnes caudati sint, Cercopithecos *appello.*
'I call our monkeys *cercopitheci* because they all have tails.'
- Ovid, *Metamorphoses* 14.90-100 describes how Jupiter turned the people of the island of Pithecusa, the Cercopes, into monkeys as a punishment for their deceitfulness and mendacity.

8 (orig. 7) [**praecincta lacu nutrit gratissima tellus** 14.356]
In lacu Nicaraguensi, 224 milliaria extenso, parva attollitur insula arboribus frequens, omnique amoenitate gratissima, ac parvis Cercopithecis referta.
'In the lake of Nicaragua, which is 224 miles long, there is a small, densely wooded island. It is delightful in every respect, and heavily populated by small monkeys.'

9 (orig. 8) [**Raptandis, ut saepe solent, uxoribus apto** 14.364]
Feminas ab hujusmodi Cercopithecis furto in Africa abduci fertur. Apud nos autem nunquam contigisse arbitror.
'It is said that women are abducted by monkeys of this sort in Africa. But I do not believe this has ever happened to our people.'

Book 15: *LUDI*

'Sports'

1 [**ludis miscere laborem** 15.3]
Equidem scio ludos hosce saepius in urbibus celebrari, sed multoties etiam in praediis.

'I know that games like these are quite often held in cities, but very often they take place on farms as well.'

2 [Ardua truncatur sudanti cortice pinus 15.236 (15.235 in 1782 edition)]
Prae oculos habe hujus spectaculi typum. Illud autem, pro ut vidi, describo; non pro ut quondam a Mexicanis fieri solebat.
'Keep before you the illustration of this spectacle. I am describing it as I saw it, not as it was was once played by Mexicans in the past.'

3 [sudanti ex arbore gummi 15.315 (15.314 in 1782 edition)]
Gummi istud Ule *dictum mirâ elasticitate praeditum est.*
'This gum, called *ule*, has remarkable elasticity.'

4 [patitur dispendia ludi 15.336 (15.335 in 1782 edition)]
Hic ludus tantum apud Nayaritas, Taraumaros, aliasque nationes septentrionales in usu est hodie.
'This game is only customary today among the Nayarits, Tarahumaras, and some other northern peoples.'

APPENDIX: *CRUX TEPICENSIS*
'The Cross of Tepic'

1 [Tot tibi densa cruces offert, quot robora sylva 55]
Montem istum vidi egomet arboribus densum, quorum vel minimi rami in crucis formam conficti sunt.
'I myself have seen this very mountain thick with trees, whose branches, even the smallest, were arranged in the form of a cross.'

- A similar phenomenon can still be seen in a courtyard of the Convento de la Santa Cruz in the city of Querétaro: the trees (a type of mimosa, known simply as *Arbol de la Cruz*) grow thorns in the shape of crosses. Attempts to plant seedlings elsewhere have failed.

2 [tabescere tota capillis 70]
In regno Guatimalensi notum est, salices hiberno tempore frondescere; aestivo autem (quo pluviae ingruunt) macie confici.
'In the kingdom of Guatemala it is well known that willows put forth leaves in winter time, but in summer (when the rains fall) they wither away.'

3 [Atque frequens votis, multaque observat acerra 93]
Qui hujusmodi crucis descriptioni non acquieverit, historiam adeat, ab Illustrissimo Texada Episcopo Guadualaxarensi in lucem editam.
'Anyone who might be uncomfortable with the description of a cross like this, may turn to the history published by the most Eminent Tejada, Bishop of Guadalajara.'

- Tepic is capital of the state of Nayarit on the Pacific coast of Mexico. On sources for the miracle, see Noriega Robles (1972): according to tradition the cross first appeared in 1540, but testimonies of it only go back to the seventeenth century. I have not been able to locate the study by Texada which Landívar cites here. Compare Gil Alonso (1947), 60, citing Mota Padilla (1742): 'As I could not get hold of the *History* of Texada cited by Landívar ... I will cite another testimony, that of Don Martín de la Mota Padilla, referred to and summarised in the *Diccionario de Curiosidades Históricas de la*

República de México by Don Félix Ramos Y Duarte: "Since the conquest of Tepic, a large cross made of earth and straw has been venerated. It is in the sanctuary of the Holy Cross. The cross, including its base and sign, measures five and a half yards. The chapel of the sanctuary was built by Don Alonso Hernández Alatorre, then lord of the *hacienda* of De Guimarais and of those of Papalote and Castilla". Vol. 1, chapter 36, p. 390. And in the work of Mota Padilla there is reference to the miraculous phenomenon: "it keeps the plants green all year round, so that the severity of the month of May does not dry them out, which is what usually happens". *Historia de Nueva Galicia*, vol. 1, pp. 388-389.'

Record of Baptism and *Acta Defunctionis* for Rafael Landívar

(i) *Acta de Bautismo* from the Parish Church of San Sebastián, Santiago de los Caballeros

En el año del Sr. de mill setesientos y treinta y uno en veinte y sinco de Noviembre de lizentia *et presentia Parochi*: yo el R. P. Prior, que fui en mi Conbento de Predicadores fr. Juan Chrisostomo Ruiz de Aguilera, hize los Exorsismos puse oleo y chrísma, a un Infante que nació el Veinte y siete de Octubre, hijo legítimo del Capn. don Pedro de Landibar y Cavallero, Alcalde Ordinario actual, por su Majestad, y de Da. Juana Ruiz de Bustamante, aviendolo Baptisado en ese sidad el Br. D. Luis de Bolaños, alqual puso por nombre Raphael, fué su Padrino el Capn. Dn. Miguel de Vivas, casado con Dña Catharina Batres y lo firmé.

Dn. Bernadino de
Sarazua.

[In the year of the Lord, one thousand seven hundred and thirty one, on the twenty-fifth of November, with the licence and in the presence of the Parish Priest, I, the Reverend Father Prior, as I was in my Convent of Preachers Brother Juan Chrisostomo Ruiz de Aguilera, performed the Exorcisms, applied oil and chrism to an infant born on the twenty-seventh of October, legitimate son of Captain Don Pedro de Landibar y Cavallero, now Civic Mayor for His Majesty, and of Doña Juana Ruiz de Bustamante, the Venerable Don Luis de Bolaños having baptised him in this city, to which infant he has given the name Raphael. His Godfather was Captain Don Miguel de Vivas, married to Doña Catharina Batres, and I signed it.

Don Bernadino de Sarazua].

A facsimile of this baptismal notice is in Arriola (1950), 79. It is also transcribed in Chamorro (1987), xv.

(ii) *Acta Defunctionis* from the Parish Church of Santa Maria delle Muratelle, Bologna

Anno 1793 die 27 Septembris.
    Raphael Landivar, Civitatis Guatemala, Regni Mexicani,
Sacerdos ex-Jesuita, clarus sanguinis nobilitate, ingenio
doctrina, Religione in Deum, in homines pietate obque morum
ejus integritatem, gravitatem, suavitatemque omnibus maxi-
me acceptus, quo anno inter hujus Paroeciae officiales Rectoris
munere adeo pie sancteque fungebatur, ut dum aliis cum
dignitate et verbis, et exemplo praeerat, magis in dies illorum
animos sibi devinxerit, molesto, diuturnoque morbo affectus,
perpetua ejus confratrum adsistentia recreatus, divinis Sacra-
mentis Eucharistiae et extremae Unctionis singulari religionis
affectu susceptis, die 27 sept. h. 13 in domo Marchionis Ugonis
Albergati in via *Saragozza*, et novo Parrocho, et caeteris huius
Paroeciae, omnibusque, qui eum noverant, maerentibus, in osculo
Jesu, quem in prosperis aeque, ac adversis ab ineunte usque
aetate in corde, et in ore semper habuit, quemque partem ejus
et hereditatem sibi optime elegerat, annos natus 63, supremum diem obiit, ejusque corpus in hac ecclesia decenti
funeri expositum, hic tumulatum fuit beatam resurrec-
tionem expectans.
        Cajetanus Tomba Parrochus.

[In the year 1793 on the 27th day of September: Rafael Landívar, of the City of
Guatemala, of the Kingdom of Mexico, a former Jesuit Priest, renowned for his
noble blood, his talent, his learning, his observance to God, his piety to men, and
on account of the integrity of his conduct, his seriousness and his gentleness, was
very greatly welcomed by all in the year in which, among the officials of this
Parish, he performed the duty of Rector with such piety and holiness, while he led
others by his dignity – in his words as in his example – so that day by day he
increasingly bound their feelings to himself. He was afflicted by a troublesome,
chronic infirmity and relieved by the constant assistance of his fellow brothers.
After taking the divine Sacraments of the Eucharist and of the last Unction with
his singular religious devotion, on the 27th September at 13.00 hours in the house
of the Marchese Ugo Albergati in Via Saragozza – mourned both by the new parish
priest and by those remaining in this Parish Church and by all who had known
him – in the kiss of Jesus, whom right from his infancy in favourable and adverse
conditions alike he had in his heart and on his lips, and whose cause and
inheritance he had very well chosen for himself, he died on his last day after living
for 63 years. His body was displayed in this church with an honourable funeral and
buried here, awaiting his happy resurrection.
        Caietano Tomba Parish Priest.]

Suárez (1996a) has a facsimile, transcription, and full discussion of the rhetorical
and historical significance of this Latin sentence.

Bibliography

Studies specifically devoted to Landívar are marked with an asterisk (*).
'México' indicates Mexico City as place of publication.

Abbott, D.P. (1987), 'The ancient word: rhetoric in Aztec culture', *Rhetorica* 5: 251-64.
────── (1996), *Rhetoric in the New World: rhetorical theory and practice in colonial Spanish America* (Columbia: University of South Carolina Press).
*Accomazzi, G. (1961), *Pensamiento Clásico Landivariano* (Guatemala: Universidad de San Carlos).
Acosta, J. de (2003), *Historia Natural y Moral de las Indias* (ed. J. Alcina Franch; orig. 1590) (Madrid: Dastin).
Acuña, R. (1988), *Vasco de Quiroga, De debellandis indis: un tratado desconocido* (México: UNAM).
*Albizúrez Palma, F. (1985), *Landívar, Virgilio y la Religión* (Guatemala: Universidad Editorial).
*Arriola Ligorría, J.L. (1950), 'Los restos de Landívar', *Revista Universidad de San Carlos* 21.
Ashfield, A. and Bolla, P. de, eds (1996), *The Sublime: a reader in British eighteenth-century aesthetic theory* (Cambridge: CUP).
Bailey, C. (1947) *Titi Lucreti Cari De Rerum Natura libri sex, with prolegomena, critical apparatus, translation, and commentary*, 3 vols (Oxford: Clarendon Press).
Balbuena, B. de (2001), *La Grandeza Mexicana y Compendio Apologético en Alabanza de la Poesía* (ed. L. Adolfo Domínguez) (México: Porrúa).
Barrow, R.H. (1973), *Prefect and Emperor: the Relationes of Symmachus, AD 384* (Oxford: OUP).
Batllori, M. (1953), *El Abate Viscardo. Historia y mito de la intervención de los Jesuítas en la independencia de Hispanoamérica* (Caracas: Instituto Panamericano de Geografía e Historia).
────── (1966), *La Cultura Hispano-Italiana de los Jesuitas Expulsos; Españoles, Hispano-Americanos, Filipinos, 1767-1814* (Madrid: Gredos).
*Batres Jáuregui, A. (1957), 'Landívar e Irisarri', *Literatos Guatamaltecos* 16, 2nd edn, 23-9 (orig. 1896).
Bausi, F. (1996), *Silvae. Angelo Poliziano: studi e testi* (Florence: Istituto Nazionale di Studi sul Renascimento 39).
Beltrán, E. (1975), 'Sigüenza y Góngora', *Dictionary of Scientific Biography*, vol. 12 (New York: Scribner's), 431.
Bergman, J. (1926), *Aurelii Prudentii Clementis Carmina: Corpus Scriptorum Ecclesiasticorum Latinorum*, vol. 61 (Vienna: Hoelder-Pichler-Tempsky).
Beristáin de Souza, J.M. (1980-1), *Biblioteca Hispanoamericana Septentrional* (México: UNAM; orig. México: A. Valdés, 1816-21).
Bertoni, G. (1937), 'Tiraboschi, Gerolamo', *Enciclopedia Italiana* 23, 908 (Rome: Istituto della Enciclopedia Italiana; repr. 1949).
Beuchot, M. (1998), *The History of Philosophy in Colonial Mexico* (Washington DC: Catholic University of America Press).
──────, ed. (2001), *Diccionario de Humanistas Clásicos de México* (México: UNAM).
Blaise, A. (1954), *Dictionnaire latin-français des auteurs chrétiens* (Turnhout: Brepols).
Bolaños A.F. (2002), 'On the issues of academic colonization and responsibility when reading and writing about colonial Latin America today' in Bolaños and Verdesio (2002), 19-49.

Bibliography

—— and Verdesio G., eds (2002), *Colonialism Past and Present: reading and writing about colonial Latin America today* (Albany: State University of New York).

Bosworth, A.B. (2000), 'A Tale of Two Empires: Hernán Cortés and Alexander the Great', in A.B. Bosworth and E.J. Baynham, eds, *Alexander the Great in Fact and Fiction* (Oxford: OUP), 23-50.

Boys-Stones, G., ed. (2003), *Metaphor, Allegory and the Classical Tradition* (Oxford: OUP).

Brading, D.A. (1971), *Miners and Merchants in Bourbon Mexico 1763-1810* (Cambridge: CUP).

—— (1991), *The First America: the Spanish monarchy, Creole patriots, and the liberal state 1492-1867* (Cambridge: CUP).

—— (2001), *Mexican Phoenix: Our Lady of Guadalupe: image and tradition across five centuries* (Cambridge: CUP).

Brito Mariano, A. de (forthcoming) 'New World "Ethiopians": visions of slavery and mining in early modern Brazil', in Y. Haskell, ed., *Latinity and Alterity in the Early Modern Period* (Ithaca: Renaissance Society of America).

Britt, M. (1922), *The Hymns of the Breviary and Missal: edited with introduction and notes* (London and Manchester: Burns, Oates and Washbourne).

Brody, J. (1958) *Boileau and Longinus* (Geneva, Droz).

*Browning, J. (1985), 'Rafael Landívar's *Rusticatio Mexicana* and political subversion', *Ideologies and Literature* 1.3: 9-30.

Buelna Serrano, M.E. (1994), *La Alexandriada o la Toma de Tiro por Alejandro de Macedonia de Francisco Xavier Alegre* (México: UNAM).

Burke, E. (1987), *A Philosophical Enquiry into the Origin of our Ideas of the Sublime and Beautiful* (ed. J.T. Boulton) (Oxford: Blackwell; orig. 1759).

Burke, J.G. (1976), 'Valmont de Bomare, Jacques-Christophe', *Dictionary of Scientific Biography*, vol. 13 (New York: Scribner's), 565-6.

Bush Malabehar, E. (2002), *La Batrachomyomachia de Francisco Alegre* (México: thesis for Licenciado en Letras Clásicas, Universidad Nacional Autónoma de México).

Cabrera, F.J. (2004), *Tres Ciudades: Tres Cantos Neolatinos* (with introduction, Spanish verse translation and notes by T. Herrera Zapién) (México: UNAM).

Cañizares-Esguerra, J. (2001), *How to Write the History of the New World: histories, epistemologies, and identities in the eighteenth century Atlantic world* (Stanford: Stanford University Press).

*Carboni, A. (1951), 'Landívar durante su exilio en Bolonia' (tr. E. Solares and J.-L. Arriola), *Estudios Landivarianos* 2: 83-111.

Castro Pallares, A. (1979), *La Californiada. José Mariano de Iturriaga: transcripción paleográfica, introducción, versión y notas* (México: UNAM; Cuadernos del Centro de Estudios Clásicos 7).

*Chamorro, F. (1987), *Rafael Landívar, Rusticatio Mexicana: introducción, texto crítico, y traducción rítmica al español* (Costa Rica: Libro Libre).

Cheney, P. (2002), 'Introduction' to P. Cheney and F.A. de Armas, eds, *European Literary Careers: the author from antiquity to the Renaissance* (Toronto: University of Toronto), 3-24.

Ciplijauskaité, B. (1985), *Luis de Góngora: Sonetos Completos* (Madrid: Castalia).

Claassen, J.-M. (1999), *Displaced Persons: the literature of exile from Cicero to Boethius* (London: Duckworth).

Clavigero, F.J. [Clavijero] (1973), *Rules of the Aztec Language* (tr. A.J.O. Anderson, with modifications, of Francis Xavier Clavigero's *Reglas de la Lengua Mexicana*) (Salt Lake City: University of Utah).

—— (1974), *Reglas de la Lengua Mexicana con un Vocabulario: edición, introducción, paleografía y notas* (ed. A.J.O. Anderson; preface by M. León-Portilla) (México: UNAM).

—— (2003), *Historia Antigua de México* (ed. M. Cuevas) (México: Porrúa; Italian orig. Bologna, 1780).

Coroleu, A. (1999), 'Some teachers on a poet: the uses of Poliziano's Latin poetry in the sixteenth-century curriculum', in Haskell and Hardie (1999), 167-81.

—— (2001), 'Poliziano in print: editions and commentaries from a pedagogical perspective, 1500-1560', *Les Cahiers de l'Humanisme* 2: 191-222.

Bibliography

Corona Martínez, E. (2002), *Las Aves en la Historia Natural Novohispana* (México: Instituto de Antropología e Historia).

Courtney, E. (1996), 'Cornelius Gallus, Gaius' in N. Hornblower and A.J. Spawforth, eds, *Oxford Classical Dictionary*, 3rd edn (Oxford: OUP), 395.

Couttolenc Cortés, G. (1973), *Federico Escobedo. Traductor de Landívar* (México: Jus).

Crawford, M.H. (1996), *Roman Statutes*, 2 vols (London: Institute of Classical Studies).

Crosby, H. (1994), *Antigua California: mission and colony on the peninsular frontier, 1697-1768* (Albuquerque: University of New Mexico).

Cross, F.L. and Livingstone, E.A., eds (1997), *The Oxford Dictionary of the Christian Church*, 3rd edn (Oxford: OUP).

Cruz, M. de la (1991), *Libellus de Medicinalibus Indorum Herbis: manuscrito azteca de 1552 según traducción latina de Juan Badiano* (México: Fondo de Cultura Económica).

Cuevas, M. (1944), *Tesoros Documentales de México, Siglo XVIII: Priego, Zelis, Clavijero* (México: Ediciones Galatea).

Daly, L.W. (1961), 'Hesiod's fable', *Transactions of the American Philological Association* 92: 45-51.

Davis, P.J. (2002), 'The colonial subject in Ovid's exile poetry', *American Journal of Philology* 123: 257-73.

Deck, A.F. (1976), *Francisco Javier Alegre: a study in Mexican literary criticism* (*Sources and Studies for the History of the Americas*, vol. 13) (Rome and Tucson, Arizona: Jesuit Historical Institute).

Decorme, G. (1941), *La Obra de los Jesuítas Mexicanos durante la Época Colonial, 1572-1767*, vol. 1: *Fundaciones y Obras*; vol. 2: *Misiones* (México: Porrúa).

Eatough, G. (1984), *Fracastoro's Syphilis: introduction, text, translations, and notes* (Liverpool: Francis Cairns).

——— (1998), *Selections from Peter Martyr: De Orbe Novo* (Turnhout: Brepols).

——— (1999a), 'Peter Martyr's account of the first contacts with Mexico', *Viator* 30: 397-421.

——— (1999b), 'Fracastoro's beautiful idea' in Haskell and Hardie (1999), 105-24.

Enzinger, C. (1998), *LEO's Palindrome Collection: Latin palindromes* (Internet: http://www.cosy.sbg.ac.at/~leo/palindrome/latin/htm.)

Escobedo, F. (1969), *Geórgicas Mexicanas: traducción en verso castellano del poema latino del R.P. Rafael Landívar*, Rusticatio Mexicana (Puebla: Cajica; orig. 1924).

Fantazzi, C., ed. (2004), *Angelo Poliziano, Silvae* (Cambridge, Mass.: Harvard University Press).

Feeney, D.S. (1991), *The Gods in Epic* (Oxford: Clarendon Press).

Feijoo, B.J. (1990), *Obras Escogidas* (ed. A. Souto Alabarce) (México: Porrúa).

Fernández Valenzuela, B. (1974), *Diego José Abad, Poema Heroico: introducción, versión y aparato crítico.* (México: UNAM).

Ferrer Benimeli, J.A. (1994), *Córcega y los Jesuitas Españoles Expulsos, 1767-1768* (San Cristóbal: Universidad Católica del Táchira).

Florencia, F. de and Oviedo, J.A. de (1995), *Zodiaco Mariano* (ed. A. Rubial García) (México: Consejo Nacional para la Cultura y las Artes; orig. 1755).

Fowler, D. (2000), *Roman Constructions: readings in postmodern Latin* (Oxford: OUP).

Fuente, A.D. de la (1971), *Poema Guadalupano 1773: edición facsimilar y versiones castellanas* (México: Basílica de Guadalupe).

Gale, M.R., ed. (2004), *Latin Epic and Didactic Poetry* (Swansea: Classical Press of Wales).

Gallego Morell, A. (1990) 'El error político de decir "latinoamérica" ', *Abc*, 15 May (Madrid), 52.

García, G. (1980), *Origen de los Indios de el Nuevo Mundo e Indios Occidentales* (México: Fondo de Cultura Económica; facsimile of Spanish orig., 1729).

García Cubas, A. (1896), *Diccionario Geográfico, Histórico y Biográfico de los Estados Unidos de México*, vols 1-5 (México; orig. 1888-91).

García Icazbalceta, J.G. (1889), *Opúsculos Inéditos Latinos y Castellanos del P. Francisco Javier Alegre* (México: Imprenta de Francisco Díaz de León).

Garin, E., ed. (1952), *Prosatori Latini del Quattrocento* (Milan: Ricciardi).

George, E. (1998), 'Latin and Spanish: Roman culture and Hispanic America' in R.A.

Bibliography

LaFleur, ed., *Latin for the 21st Century: from concept to classroom* (Reading, MA: Scott Foresman – Addison Wesley), 227-36.

Giard, L. (1995), *Les Jésuites à la Renaissance: système educatif et production du savoir* (Paris: Presses Universitaires de France).

*Gil Alonso, I. (1947), *La 'Rusticatio Mexicana' de Rafael Landívar: Ensayo de interpretación humanística* (México: thesis for Maestro en Letras Clásicas, Universidad Nacional Autónoma de México).

Gómez, F. (2001), *Good Places and Non-places in Colonial Mexico: the figure of Vasco de Quiroga (1470-1565)* (Lanham, Maryland: University Press of America).

Gómez Álvarez, C. and Téllez Guerrero, F. (1997), *Una Biblioteca Obispal: Antonio Bergosa y Jordán* (Puebla: Benemérita Universidad Autónoma de Puebla).

Grafton, A., Shelford, A., and Siraisi, N. (1992), *New Worlds, Ancient Texts: the power of tradition and the shock of discovery* (Cambridge Mass.: Belknap).

Gray, E.G. and Fiering, N. (2000), *The Language Encounter in the Americas 1492-1800* (New York: Berghahn Books).

Greenblatt, S. (1991), *Marvelous Possessions: the wonder of the New World* (Chicago: University of Chicago).

——, ed. (1993), *New World Encounters* (Berkeley: University of California Press).

Griffin, C. (1991), *Los Cromberger: la historia de una imprenta del Siglo XVI en Sevilla y Méjico* (Madrid: Ediciones de Cultural Hispánica).

Gruzinski, S. (2002), *The Mestizo Mind: the intellectual dynamics of colonization and globalization* (tr. D. Dusinberre) (London and New York: Routledge).

Guedea, V. (2000), 'The Old Colonialism ends, the New Colonialism begins' in M.C. Meyer and W.H. Beezley, eds, *The Oxford History of Mexico* (Oxford: OUP), 277-99.

Guzmán, E. (1964), *Manuscritos sobre México en Archivos de Italia* (México: Sociedad Mexicana de Geografía y Estadística).

Haase, W. and Reinhold, M., eds (1994), *The Classical Tradition and the Americas* 1.1 (Berlin and New York: W. de Gruyter).

Habinek, T. (1998) *The Politics of Latin Literature: writing, identity, and empire in ancient Rome* (Princeton, NJ: Princeton University Press).

—— (2002) 'Ovid and empire' in Hardie (2002b), 46-61.

Handy, J. (1996), *Gift of the Devil: a history of Guatemala* (Boston: South End Press).

Hardie, P.R. (1986) *Virgil's Aeneid: cosmos and imperium* (Oxford: OUP).

—— (2002a), *Ovid's Poetics of Illusion* (Cambridge: CUP).

——, ed. (2002b) *The Cambridge Companion to Ovid* (Cambridge: CUP).

—— (2004), 'Virgilian Imperialism, Original Sin, and Fracastoro's *Syphilis*' in Gale (2004), 223-34.

——, ed. (forthcoming), *The Cambridge Companion to Lucretius* (Cambridge: CUP).

Harrison, S.J. (1991): *Vergil Aeneid 10* (Oxford: OUP).

Haskell, Y.A. (1999), 'Between fact and fiction: the Renaissance didactic poetry of Fracastoro, Palingenio and Valvasone' in Haskell and Hardie (1999), 77-103.

—— (2003), *Loyola's Bees: ideology and industry in Jesuit Latin didactic poetry* (Oxford: OUP).

—— and Hardie, P.R., eds (1999), *Poets and Teachers: Latin didactic poetry and the didactic authority of the Latin poet from the Renaissance to the present* (Bari: Levante).

Henríquez Ureña, P. (1945), *Literary Currents in Hispanic America* (Cambridge, Mass.: Harvard University Press).

Heredia Correa, R. (2000a), *Fray Alonso de la Vera Cruz, De dominio infidelium et iusto bello I-II: texto bilingüe, introducción, traducción y notas* (México: UNAM).

—— (2000b), *Dissertatio – Diego José Abad* (Aguascalientes, Mexico: Universidad de Aguascalientes).

Hernández, F. (2003), *Antigüedades de la Nueva España* (ed. A. Hernández) (Madrid: Gastin; 16th c. orig.).

Herrejón Peredo, C., ed. (1984), *Humanismo y Ciencia en la Formación de México* (Michoacán: Conacyt).

Herrera Zapién, T. (1991), *México Exalta y Censura a Horacio: ensayos en el segundo milenio de su muerte e inmortalidad* (México: UNAM).

Bibliography

—— (2000), *Historia del Humanismo Mexicano: sus textos y contextos neolatinos en cinco siglos* (México: UNAM).

*Higgins, A. (2000), *Constructing the Criollo Archive: subjects of knowledge in the Bibliotheca Mexicana and the Rusticatio Mexicana* (West Lafayette: Purdue University Press).

*—— (2002), '(Post-)colonial sublime: order and indeterminacy in eighteenth-century Spanish American poetics and aesthetics' in Bolaños and Verdesio (2002), 119-49.

Hofmann, H. (1994), '*Adveniat tandem Typhis qui detegat orbes*. COLUMBUS in neo-Latin epic poetry (16th-18th centuries)' in Haase and Reinhold (1994), 420-656.

Humboldt, A. von (1811), *Political Essay on the Kingdom of New Spain*, vol. 2 (London); ed. M. Dunn (University of Oklahoma, 1988).

Irigoyen Troconis, M.P., ed. (2003), *La Universidad Novohispana* (México: UNAM).

Israel, J.I. (1975), *Race, Class and Politics in Colonial Mexico 1610-1670* (Oxford: OUP).

Juarros, D. (1936), *Compendio de la Historia de la Ciudad de Guatemala*, vol. 1 (Guatemala: Tipografía Nacional).

Kagan, R.L. (2000), *Urban Images of the Hispanic World 1493-1793* (New Haven and London: Yale University Press).

Kaimowitz, J.H. (1990), 'Translation of the Apologetical Essay appended to the *Alexandriad* of Francisco Javier Alegre', *Dieciocho* 13.1-2: 135-48.

Kallendorf, C. (2003), 'Representing the Other: Ercilla's *La Araucana*, Virgil's *Aeneid*, and the New World encounter', *Comparative Literature Studies*, 40.4: 394-414.

Kant, I. (1963), *On History* (ed. L. White Beck) (Indianapolis: Bobbs-Merrill).

—— (1987), *The Critique of Judgment* (tr. W.S. Pluhar) (Indianapolis: Hackett; orig. 1790).

*Kerson, A.L. (1976), 'El concepto de Utopía de Rafael Landívar en la *Rusticatio Mexicana*', *Revista Iberoamericana* 96-7: 363-79.

—— (1981), 'Francisco Javier Alegre's translation of Boileau's *Art poétique*', *Modern Language Quarterly* 41.2: 153-65.

—— (1988), 'Enlightened thought in Diego José Abad's *De Deo, Deoque Homine Heroica*', *Acta Conventus Neo-Latini Guelpherbytani: Proceedings of the Sixth International Congress of Neo-Latin Studies* (Binghamton, New York), 617-23.

*—— (1990), 'The Heroic Mode in Rafael Landívar's *Rusticatio Mexicana*', *Dieciocho* 13.1-2: 149-64.

—— (1991), 'Diego José Abad, *Dissertatio Ludicro-Seria*: edition, translation and notes', *Humanistica Lovaniensia* 40: 357-422.

Knight, A. (2002), *Mexico: the colonial era* (Cambridge: CUP).

*Lafragua, J.-M. (undated), Untitled anthology of funeral speeches (including Landívar's *Declamatio Funebris*) compiled in the 19th century (Biblioteca Nacional de México classification: 1358 LAF).

Laird, A. (2002), 'Juan Luis de la Cerda and the predicament of commentary' in C. Kraus and R. Gibson, eds, *The Classical Commentary* (Leiden: Brill), 171-204.

—— (2003), 'La *Alexandriada* de Francisco Xavier Alegre: *arcanis sua sensa figuris*', *Nova Tellus* 21.2: 165-76.

—— (2003b) Review of Herrera Zapién (2000) and Higgins (2000), *Journal of Roman Studies* 93: 345-7.

—— (2004a), 'Selenopolitanus: Diego José Abad, Latin, and Mexican identity', *Studi Umanistici Piceni: Atti dei Congressi* 24: 231-7.

—— (2004b), 'Politian's *Ambra* and reading epic didactically' in Gale (2004), 27-47.

——, ed. (2006), *Ancient Literary Criticism* (Oxford: OUP).

—— (forthcoming), 'The Virgin of Guadalupe and the birth of Mexican epic: Bernardo Ceinos de Riofrío's *Centonicum Virgilianum Monimentum*' in J. Andrews and A. Coroleu, eds, *Mexico 1680: cultural and intellectual life at the apogee of the Barroco Indias* (Bristol: HiPLAM).

*Landívar, R. (1781), *Rusticatio Mexicana, seu rariora quaedam ex agris mexicanis decerpta, atque in libros decem distributa a Raphaele Landívar* (Modena).

*—— (1782), *Rusticatio Mexicana. Editio altera auctior et emendatior* (Bologna: Typographia S. Thomae Aquinatis).

Lanning, J.T. (1956), *The Eighteenth-Century Enlightenment in the University of San Carlos de Guatemala* (Ithaca, NY: Cornell University Press).

Bibliography

Las Casas, B. de (1967), *Apologética Historia Summaria*, 2 vols (ed. E. O'Gorman) (México: Serie de historiadores y cronistas de Indias 1).

Lattimore, R. (1961), *Themes in Greek and Latin Epitaphs* (Urbana: University of Illinois).

Lavarenne, M., ed. (1948), *Prudence*. Tome III: *Psychomachie*. *Contre Symmaque* (Paris: Les Belles Lettres).

Leeber, V.F. (1965), *El Padre Diego José Abad, S.J., y su Obra Poética* (Madrid: J. Porrúa Turanzas).

León Portilla, M. (2001), *México en 1554: trés diálogos latinos de Francisco Cervantes de Salazar* (México: UNAM).

—— (2002), *Bernardino de Sahagún: first anthropologist* (University of Oklahoma Press).

Leonard, I.A. (1929), *Don Carlos de Sigüenza y Góngora, a Mexican savant of the seventeenth century* (Berkeley: University of California).

—— (1983), *Baroque Times in Old Mexico* (Ann Arbor: University of Michigan; orig. 1959).

—— (1992), *Books of the Brave: being an account of books and of men in the Spanish conquest and settlement of the sixteenth-century New World* (Berkeley and Los Angeles: University of California; orig. Harvard, 1949).

Logan, G., Adams, R., Miller, C. (1995), *Thomas More, Utopia: Latin text and English translation* (Cambridge: CUP).

*Loureda, I. (1924), *Rusticación Méjicana de Rafael Landívar. Traducción literal y directa de la segunda edición de Bolonia, 1782* (México: Sociedad de Edición y Librería Franco Americana).

Lupher, D. (2003), *Romans in a New World: classical models in sixteenth-century Spanish America* (Ann Arbor: University of Michigan Press).

Macc. Armstrong, A. (1953), 'The Conquistadores and the Classics', *Greece and Rome* 23.65: 88-9.

MacCormack, S. (1975), 'Latin Prose Panegyrics' in T.A. Dorey, ed., *Empire and Aftermath. Silver Latin II* (London and Boston: Routledge and Kegan Paul), 143-205.

—— (1991), *Religion in the Andes: vision and imagination in Early Colonial Peru* (Princeton, NJ: Princeton University Press).

—— (1998), 'The Incas and Rome' in J. Anadón, ed., *Garcilaso Inca de la Vega: an American Humanist* (Notre Dame: University of Notre Dame Press), 8-31.

Mack, P. (2005), 'Vives's *De ratione dicendi*: structure, innovations, problems', *Rhetorica* 23.1: 65-92.

Maneiro, J.L. (1988), *Vidas de Algunos Mexicanos Ilustres*, vol. 1 (tr. A. Valenzuela Rodarte, introduction by I. Osorio Romero) (México: UNAM).

Marrone, D. (2000), '*L'Apologeticon* di Battista Spagnoli', *Atti e Memorie. Nuova serie* (Mantova: Accademia Nazionale Virgiliana di Scienze, Lettere e Arti 68), 19-155.

Martin, A.L. (1988), *The Jesuit Mind: the mentality of an elite in Early Modern France* (Ithaca and London: Cornell University Press).

Mason, P. (1994), 'Classical ethnography and its influence on the European perception of the peoples of the New World', in Haase and Reinhold (1994), 135-72.

*Mata Gavidia, J. (1950), *Rafael Landívar: Rusticatio Mexicana* (facsimile of the Bologna 1782 edition, with an introduction) (Guatemala: Editorial Universitaria).

Matthews, J.F. (1996), 'Symmachus (2)' in *Oxford Classical Dictionary*, 3rd edn, 1460.

Maury, J.M. (1806), *La Agresión Británica. Poema* (Madrid: Imprenta Real).

Mayer, A., ed. (2000-2), *Carlos de Sigüenza y Góngora: Homenaje 1700-2000*, 2 vols (México: UNAM).

McDonald, I.T. (1932), *Renati Rapini (1621-1687) Hortorum Libri IV* (with an English translation by J. Gardiner) (Worcester, Mass.: Holy Cross Press).

McLaughlin, M.L. (1995), *Literary Imitation in the Italian Renaissance* (Oxford: Clarendon Press).

Méndez Plancarte, A., ed. (1994), *Obras Completas de Sor Juana Inés de la Cruz: edición, prólogo y notas*, 4 vols (México: Fondo de Cultura Económica; 3rd edn, orig. 1951-7).

Méndez Plancarte, G. (1937), *Horacio en México* (México: UNAM).

—— (1941), *Humanistas del Siglo XVIII* (México: UNAM; repr. 1991).

—— (1944), *Índice del Humanismo Mexicano* (México: Ábside).

Bibliography

—— (1948), 'Don Guillén de Lámport y su Regio Salterio, Manuscrito de 1655: estudios, selección, versión y notas', *Ábside* 12.2-3.

—— (1994), *Humanistas Mexicanos del Siglo XVI: introducción, selección y versiones* (México: UNAM; orig. 1944).

*Menéndez y Pelayo, M. (1958), *Historia de la Poesía Hispano-Americana* (ed. E. Sánchez Reyes) (Santander: Aldus, S.A. de Artes Gráficas; orig. 1893).

Micheli, A. de (1976-7), 'Corrientes de cultura entre Italia y la Nueva España', *Revista de la Universidad de México* 314-15, December-January: 89-93.

Mignolo, W. (1993), 'Colonial and postcolonial discourse: cultural critique or academic colonialism?', *Latin American Research Review* 28.3: 120-34.

—— (1995), *The Dark Side of the Renaissance: literacy, territoriality and colonization* (Ann Arbor: University of Michigan).

Millares Carlo, A. (1986), *Cuatro Estudios Bibliográficos Mexicanos* (México: Fondo de Cultura Económica).

—— (1996), *Dr. D. Juan José de Eguiara y Eguren: prólogos a la Bibliotheca Mexicana* (México: Fondo de Cultura Económica).

Miranda Cancela, E. (2003), *La Tradición Helénica en Cuba* (Havana: Editorial Arte y Literatura).

*Molina, F. (1766), *El llanto de los ojos ...* (Puebla de los Angeles).

Monk, S.H. (1960), *The Sublime* (Ann Arbor: University of Michigan Press).

Morreale, M. (2002), 'El Nuevo Mundo en las "Notaciones" de Juan de Guzmán a su versión de las *Geórgicas* (1586)', *Bulletin Hispanique* 2 (décembre): 577-626.

Moses, B. (1919), *Spain's Declining Power in South America, 1730-1806* (Berkeley: University of California).

Mota Padilla, M. de la (1743), *Historia de Nueva Galicia* (Guadalajara).

'Motolinía': Fray Toribio de Benavente (2001), *Historia de los Indios de la Nueva España* (ed. E. O'Gorman) (México: Porrúa; orig. México, 1858).

Mynors, R.A.B. (1990), *Virgil, Georgics* (Oxford: OUP).

Navarro, B. (1983), *Cultura Mexicana Moderna en el Siglo XVIII* (México: UNAM).

—— (1989), *Juan Luis Maneiro, Manuel Fabri: Vidas de mexicanos ilustres del siglo XVIII*, vol. 1 (Spanish tr. A.V. Rodarte) (México: UNAM; Latin orig.).

*Nemes, G. (1971), 'Rafael Landívar and poetic echoes of the Enlightenment' in Owen Aldridge (1971), 298-306.

Newton, F., ed. (1973), 'Laurentius Monachus Casinensis Archiepiscopus Amalfitanus – Opera', *Monumenta Germaniae Historica* 7: 81-3.

Noriega Robles, E. (1972), 'Los Jesuitas y la Cruz de Tepic' in Pérez Alonso (1972), 327-34.

Ordoñez Mazariegos, C.S. (2003), 'Vida y Obra de Jorge Luis Arriola Ligorría (1906-1995)' in J.E.R. Ordoñez Cifuentes, ed., *El Derecho a la Lengua de los Pueblos Indígenas* (Mexico: UNAM), 99-109.

Osorio Romero, I. (1976), *Tópicos sobre Cicerón en México* (México: UNAM).

—— (1980), *Floresta de Gramática, Poética y Retórica en Nueva España (1521-1767)* (México: UNAM).

—— (1989), *Conquistar el Eco: la paradoja de la conciencia criolla* (México: UNAM).

—— (1990), *La Enseñanza de Latín a los Indios* (México: UNAM).

—— (1991a), 'Latín y Neolatín en México' in I. Osorio Romero, T. Herrera Zapién, M. Beuchot, S. Díaz Cíntora and R. Heredia Correa, eds, *La Tradición Clásica en México* (México: UNAM), 1-76.

—— (1991b), *El Sueño Criollo: José Antonio de Villerías y Roelas* (México: UNAM).

—— (1993), *La Luz Imaginaria. Epistolario de Atanasio Kircher con los novohispanos* (México: UNAM).

Owen Aldridge, A., ed. (1971), *The Ibero-American Enlightenment* (Urbana, Chicago, London: University of Illinois).

Pareja, F. (1883), *Crónica de la Provincia de la Visitación de Nuestra Señora de la Merced, para la Redención de los Cautivos de la Nueva España* (México).

Paz, O. (1988), *Sor Juana: her life and her world* (tr. M. Sayers Peden) (London: Faber; Spanish orig. *Sor Juana Inés de la Cruz, o Las Trampas de la Fe*).

Bibliography

—— (2001), 'In search of the present' in P. Lange-Churión and P. Mendieta, eds, *Latin America and Postmodernity* (Amherst, New York: Humanities Books), 59-71.

Peconi, A. (1978), 'Libri e stampatori italiani nella Nuova Spagna nel secolo XVI', *Quaderni iberoamericani* 751-2 (June/December): 164-70.

*Peñalosa, J.A. (1985), *Rafael Landívar, Orador y Prosista Latino* (México: Jus).

—— (1987), *Flor y Canto de la Poesía Guadalupana: Siglo XVII* (México: Jus).

*—— (1998), 'Las Obras Menores de Rafael Landívar', *Novahispania* 3 (México: UNAM), 261-303.

*Pérez Alonso, M.I. (1950), 'El Padre Rafael Landívar, SJ', *Estudios Centro Americanos* (Mayo) 5.40: 24-32.

——, ed. (1972), *La Compañía de Jesús en México* (México: Jus).

Perry, B.E. (1952), *Aesopica* (Urbana: University of Illinois Press).

Piastra, C.M. (1994), *La Poesia Mariologica dell'Umanesimo Latino: Repertorio e incipitario* (Spoleto: Centro italiano di studi sull'alto Medioevo).

Pimentel Álvarez, J. (1990), *Francisco Javier Alegre y Diego José Abad, Humanistas Gemelos: prólogo, selección, traducción, edición y notas* (México: UNAM).

Poole, S. (1995), *Our Lady of Guadalupe: the origins and sources of a Mexican national symbol* (Tucson: University of Arizona Press).

Preminger, A., ed. (1965), *Princeton Encyclopedia of Poetry and Poetics* (Princeton, NJ: Princeton University Press).

Pym, A. (2000), *Negotiating the Frontier: translators and intercultures in Hispanic history* (Manchester: St. Jerome Publishing).

Quint, D. (1993), *Epic and Empire: politics and generic form from Virgil to Milton* (Princeton, NJ: Princeton University Press).

Raaflaub, K. and Samons, L.J. (1990), 'Opposition to Augustus' in K. Raaflaub and M. Toher, eds, *Between Republic and Empire: interpretations of Augustus and his principate* (Berkeley: University of California), 417-54.

Rama, A. (1996), *The Lettered City* (ed./tr. J.C. Chasteen) (Durham, NC and London: Duke University Press).

Ramírez Cabañas, J., ed. (1944), *Bernal Díaz del Castillo, Historia Verdadera de la Conquista de la Nueva España* (México: Pedro Robredo).

Redmond, W. and Beuchot, M. (1987), *Pensamiento y Realidad en Fray Alonso de la Vera Cruz* (México: UNAM).

*Regenos, G.W. (1948), 'Rafael Landívar's *Rusticatio Mexicana* [Mexican Country Scenes]. The Latin Text, with an introduction and an English prose translation', *Middle American Research Institute Philological and Documentary Studies*, vol. 1.5: 155-314.

Revelli, P. (1926), *Terre d'America e Archivi d'Italia* (Milan: Treves).

Rivas Sacconi, J.M. (1993), *El Latín en Colombia: Bosquejo histórico del humanismo colombiano* (Bogotá: Instituto Caro y Cuervo; orig. 1949).

Roger, J. (1970), 'Buffon-Leclerc, George-Louis', *Dictionary of Scientific Biography*, vol. 2 (New York: Scribner's), 576-82.

Ronan, C.E. (1977), *Francisco Javier Clavigero, S.J. (1731-1787), Figure of the Mexican Enlightenment: his life and works* (Chicago: Loyola University Press).

Rubio, D. (1934), *Classical Scholarship in Spain* (Washington DC: Mimeoform Press).

Russell, D.A. (1964), *'Longinus', On the Sublime, edited with Introduction and Commentary* (Oxford: OUP).

—— and Winterbottom, M. (1972), *Ancient Literary Criticism: the principal texts in new translations* (Oxford: OUP).

Sahagún, B. de (1981), *Historia General de las Cosas de la Nueva España, escrita por Bernardino de Sahagún y fundada en la lengua mexicana recogida por los mismos naturales*, 4 vols, ed. A. María Garibay (México: Porrúa).

Said, E. (2000), *Reflections on Exile and Other Essays* (Cambridge, Mass.: Harvard University Press).

Sarolli, G. (1971), *Prolegomena alla 'Divina Comedia'* (Florence: Olschki).

Sayers Peden, M., ed./tr. (1997), *Sor Juana Inés de la Cruz: poems, protest, and a dream* (Harmondsworth: Penguin).

Bibliography

*Scheifler, R. (1950a), 'Rafael Landívar y su "Rusticatio Mexicana"': I. Su Vida', *Estudios Centro Americanos*, 5.41 (Junio): 32-7.

*———— (1950b), 'Rafael Landívar y su "Rusticatio Mexicana"': II. Rusticatio Mexicana', *Estudios Centro Americanos*, 5.42 (Julio): 4-10.

Sepúlveda, J.G. (1951), *Democrates Segundo, o de las justas causas de la guerra contra los Indios* (ed./tr. A. Losada) (Madrid: Consejo Superior de Investigaciones Científicas).

Sigurdsson, H. (1999), *Melting the Earth: the history of ideas on volcanic eruptions* (New York: OUP).

Sommervogel, C. (1890-1909), *Bibliothèque de la Compagnie de Jésus* (Brussels: Schepens; Paris: Picard).

Somolinos Dardois, G. (1960), 'Vida y Obra de Francisco Hernández' in Francisco Hernández, *Obras completas*, vol. 1 (México: UNAM).

*Suárez, M.A (1994), 'Asimilación y recreación del *adynaton* y la *similitudo* en el libro II del la *Rusticatio Mexicana*', *Nova Tellus* 12: 227-38.

*———— (1995), 'Los discursos del poder en la *Rusticatio Mexicana*', *Nova Tellus* 13: 107-15.

*———— (1996a), 'Análisis del acta de defunción del P. Rafael Landívar', *Faventia* 18.2: 99-107.

*———— (1996b) 'Ecos virgilianos en la *Rusticatio Mexicana*: la alusión y la inclusión', *Praesentia – Revista Venezolana de Estudios Clásicos* 1.1: 349-58.

*———— (1997), 'La Cruz del Chalco: lo local y lo universal en la *Rusticatio Mexicana*', *Nova Tellus* 15: 167-74.

*———— (2002), '*Lector benevole, te monitum velim* [...]: claves ideológicas y estéticas de la *Rusticatio Mexicana*', *Stylos* 11 (11): 125-39.

*———— (2004), 'Mitología y memoria poética en la *Rusticatio Mexicana*' *Nova Tellus* 22.2: 99-120.

Taylor, B. and Coroleu, A., eds (1999), *Latin and Vernacular in Renaissance Spain* (Manchester: Cañada Blanch Monographs 3).

Téllez, H. (2003), 'Un documento de tradición nebrisense: el vocabulario trilingüe en español, latín, y náhuatl', *Chicomóztoc: Boletín del Seminario de Estudios para la Descolonización de México* 7: 97-107.

Todorov, T. (1984), *The Conquest of America: the question of the other* (New York: Harper and Row).

Torquemada, J. de (1969), *Monarquía Indiana* (facsimile of 1723 ed. M. León Portilla) (México: Porrúa).

Torre Villar, E. de la (1973), 'El Libro Belga en México', *Boletín del Instituto de Investigaciones Bibliográficas* 10 (July/December): 9-15.

———— (1980), *Testimonios Históricos Mexicanos en los Repositorios Europeos: Guía para su estudio* (México: Instituto de Estudios y Documentos Históricos).

Toynbee, J. (1971), *Death and Burial in the Roman World* (London: Thames and Hudson).

Troncarelli, F. (2001), 'The man behind the mask of Zorro: William Lamport of Wexford', *History Ireland* 9.3 Autumn: 22-5.

Vaillant, G.C. (1965), *Aztecs of Mexico* (Harmondsworth: Penguin).

*Valdés, O. (1965), *Rafael Landívar, Rusticatio Mexicana: Por los Campos de México. Prólogo, versión y notas* (México: Jus; orig. 1942).

Van der Poel, M. (1990), 'Teaching Latin in eighteenth-century Mexico: the *Prolusio Grammatica De Syntaxi* by Francisco Javier Alegre', *Dieciocho* 13.1-2: 119-34.

Vanière/Vanierius, J. (1746), *Praedium Rusticum* (Paris: apud Marcum Bordelet; orig. 1707).

Vargas Alquicira, S. (1987), *Diálogo de Abril: Introducción, traducción y notas* (México: UNAM).

Venegas, M. (1929), *Juan María de Salvatierra of the Company of Jesus: Missionary in the province of New Spain, and apostolic conqueror of the Californias*, ed./tr. M.E. Wilbur (Cleveland: Arthur H. Clark; Mexican 18th c. orig.).

Verdesio, G. (2002), 'Colonialism now and then: colonial Latin American studies in the light of the predicament of Latin Americanism' in Bolaños and Verdesio (2002), 1-17.

Vetancourt, A. de (1971), *Teatro Mexicano: descripción breve de los sucesos ejemplares históricos y religiosos del nuevo mundo de las Indias* (México: Porrúa; orig. 1698).

Bibliography

*Villacorta, J.A. (1931), *Estudios Bio-bibliográficos sobre Rafael Landívar* (Guatemala CA: Tipografía Nacional).

Viscardo y Guzmán, J.P. (2002), *Letter to the Spanish Americans: a facsimile of the second English edition (London, 1810)* (Providence, RI: John Carter Brown; orig. London, 1810).

Waquet, F. (2001), *Latin or the Empire of a Sign* (London and New York: Verso).

Ward, P., ed. (1978), *Oxford Companion to Spanish Literature* (Oxford: OUP).

Weinberg, B. (1950) 'Translations and commentaries of Longinus up to 1600: a bibliography', *Modern Philology* 47 (February): 145-51.

West, M.L. (1978), *Hesiod, Works and Days. Edited with Prolegomena and Commentary* (Oxford: OUP).

Zambrano, F. (1965), *Diccionario Bio-bibliográfico de la Compañía de Jesús en México*, vol. 5: 1600-1699 (México: Jus).

—— and Gutiérrez Casillas, J. (1977), *Diccionario Bio-bibliográfico de la Compañía de Jesús en México*, vol. 16: Siglo XVIII (México: Tradición), 32.

Zavala, S. (1955), *Sir Thomas More in New Spain: a Utopian adventure of the Renaissance* (London: Hispanic and Luso-Brazilian Councils).

—— (1965), *Recuerdo de Vasco de Quiroga* (México: Porrúa).

Index of Passages Cited

This Index mainly lists passages from European and Mexican texts in Latin. More works and authors are given in the General Index. References to the page and note numbers of this book are given in **bold**.

General Index

This Index serves the essay studies and notes in Part I of this volume as well as the texts, translations and notes in Part II. References to the *Funebris Declamatio* (*FD*) and to the *Rusticatio Mexicana* (*RM*) are given in brackets after the relevant page numbers.

General Index